PATTERN RECOGNITION BY
SELF-ORGANIZING NEURAL NETWORKS

PATTERN RECOGNITION BY
SELF-ORGANIZING NEURAL NETWORKS

edited by

Gail A. Carpenter and Stephen Grossberg

A Bradford Book
The MIT Press
Cambridge, Massachusetts
London, England

This book was printed and bound in the United States of America.

Library of Congress Cataloging-in-Publication Data

Pattern recognition by self-organizing neural networks / edited by Gail A. Carpenter and
    Stephen Grossberg.
        p.   cm.
     "A Bradford Book."
     Includes bibliographical references and indexes.
     ISBN 0-262-03176-0
     1. Pattern recognition systems. 2. Neural networks (Computer science) I. Carpenter,
    Gail A. II. Grossberg, Stephen, 1939–
    TK7882.P3P394 1991
    006.4—dc20   90–29071
                                                                                    CIP

DEDICATION

For Deborah,

Our favorite self-organizer,

With love.

TABLE OF CONTENTS

PART III: ADAPTIVE RESONANCE THEORY

PART IV: SPECIALIZED ARCHITECTURES
AND BIOLOGICAL CONNECTIONS

LIST OF AUTHORS

Dr. Jean-Paul Banquet
Hôpital de la Salpêtrière
Laboratoire d'Electrophysiologie
47 boulevard de l'Hôpital
75651 Paris FRANCE

Professor Gail Carpenter
Boston University
Center for Adaptive Systems
111 Cummington Street
Boston, Massachusetts 02215

Professor Michael Cohen
Boston University
Center for Adaptive Systems
111 Cummington Street
Boston, Massachusetts 02215

Professor Stephen Grossberg
Boston University
Center for Adaptive Systems
111 Cummington Street
Boston, Massachusetts 02215

Dr. Robert Hecht-Nielsen
Hecht-Nielsen Neurocomputer Corp.
5501 Oberlin Drive
San Diego, California 92121

Professor Teuvo Kohonen
Helsinki University of Technology
Department of Technical Physics
Rakentajanaukio 2C
SF-02150 Espoo 15
FINLAND

Professor Bart Kosko
University of Southern California
Department of Electrical Engineering
Los Angeles, California 90089

Professor Christoph von der Malsburg
Ruhr Universität Bochum
Institut für Neuroinformatik
D-4630 Bochum 1
FEDERAL REPUBLIC OF GERMANY

Mr. John H. Reynolds
Boston University
Cognitive & Neural Systems Program
111 Cummington Street
Boston, Massachusetts 02215

Dr. T.W. Ryan
Science Applications International Corp.
5151 E. Broadway
Suite 1100
Tucson, Arizona 85710

Professor Nestor Schmajuk
Northwestern University
Department of Psychology
Evanston, Illinois 60201

Prof. Dr. Med. Wolf Singer
Max-Planck-Institut für Hirnforschung
Deutschordenstrasse 46
6000 Frankfurt/M. 71
FEDERAL REPUBLIC OF GERMANY

Professor David Stork
Stanford University
Departments of Psychology and
   Electrical Engineering
Jordan Hall
Stanford, California 94305

Dr. C.L. Winter
Science Applications International Corp.
5151 E. Broadway
Suite 1100
Tuscon, Arizona 85710

EDITORIAL PREFACE

This book provides a resource for teaching and research in the vitally important area of pattern recognition by self-organizing neural networks. Pattern recognition is a core competence that is as important for understanding biological intelligence as it is for inventing new types of intelligent machines. The flexible and autonomous behavior of humans and other animals is founded on an ability to self-organize adaptive responses to rapidly changing environments in real time. Flexible autonomy is also a design goal towards which many modern technologies aspire. The present book describes both classical and recent contributions towards understanding autonomous pattern recognition and related processes.

To this end, the book brings together neural network models that have typically been derived from analyses of biological intelligence or from heuristics suggested by observing properties of intelligent organisms. In many cases, these models were first used to explain and predict behavioral and neural data. They were further developed through mathematical and computational analyses aimed at sharply articulating their organizational principles and computational properties, including their strengths and weaknesses. Such analyses clarify how a model can be varied without disturbing its main computational properties. A model can then undergo technology transfer in applications whose practitioners need the model's computational properties, but who may not know or care about the biological data that suggested the models. Once a mathematical understanding is available, people interested in technological applications can often tailor a model to best match their own needs.

Due to the fundamental importance of pattern recognition and the interdisciplinary nature of the book's material, the book should be of interest to cognitive scientists and neuroscientists on the one hand, and computer scientists, engineers, mathematicians, and physicists on the other. Although pattern recognition forms the core that unites the book's results, its various chapters include contributions to understanding vision, speech and language, cognitive information processing, recognition learning, reinforcement learning, associative mapping, adaptive timing, adaptive sensory-motor control, and the self-organization of temporally organized plans. These results contribute to a better understanding of mind and brain on several levels, from functional analyses of macroscopic brain regions such as visual cortex and hippocampus, to functional analyses of chemical transmitters and other microscopic synaptic processes. The book also includes examples of neural network predictions that have subsequently been supported by behavioral and neural experiments. As of this writing, there are many such examples across the field.

In addition to these biological analyses, the book includes chapters whose primary focus is on technological applications. The book has been organized to illustrate the synergetic interactions that exists between these two types of scientific activity. Due to the way in which such interactions have evolved through time, it seemed natural to organize the book to reflect both historical and conceptual linkages. Such a hybrid approach is also intended to help new investigators in the field to more efficiently grasp the significance and direction of current research by seeing where it came from and how it has evolved.

Part I of the book contains two survey chapters that develop an historical and conceptual framework for understanding many neural network models in the pattern recognition area and in neural networks generally. Part II includes key articles that formed the foundation for contemporary research on competitive learning, self-organizing feature maps, and learned vector quantization, leading to recent articles by Kohonen on the neural phonetic typewriter and by Hecht-Nielsen on associative maps and adaptive look-up tables.

Part III includes several of the main articles that developed Adaptive Resonance Theory, or ART, including the primary ART 1, ART 2, ART 3, and ARTMAP articles. ART networks are capable of self-organizing stable pattern recognition codes in real time in response to arbitrary sequences of input patterns. Their ability to stably function in real time in response to arbitrary event sequences provides one of the few examples known today of a rigorously demonstrated autonomous learning capability. Within the ART context, pattern recognition is part of the larger theme of cognitive information processing, including hypothesis testing, knowledge discovery, selective attention, attentive priming, and the learning of expectations about the world. Such properties suggest that variants of ART networks will give rise to new types of self-organizing expert systems in technological applications. The supervised, but self-organizing, ARTMAP model is an example of this sort of development. Other technological variations of ART networks herein include the results of Ryan and Winter on a variant of ART 1, and the description by Kosko of an adaptive bidirectional associative memory, or BAM.

Part IV embeds ART modules into larger architectures for vision, speech, word recognition, reinforcement learning, and adaptive behavioral timing. These articles include some of the varied experimental evidence from neurophysiology, event-related potentials, and psychology that ART mechanisms exist in the brain.

This book is appearing at a time of unprecedented interest in neural network research. The scale and speed of renewed interest may be viewed as a major paradigm shift in contemporary science. Such paradigm shifts are often driven by internal pressures within one or more scientific mainstreams. In the case of neural networks, internal transformations in several fields all converged at around the same time. In the late 1970's, the Cognitive Science Society was born. One of its major roles was to reaffirm the importance of theoretical models in psychology. At the outset, this was expressed through a temporary marriage between psychological experimentalists and the von Neumann computer. "Temporary" because the brain is not that type of architecture. At first, the notion of a cognitive "computer model" derived as much from the fact that psychologists were using computers in the lab as from any strong conviction that the brain is itself a von Neumann computer. Once theory became respectable again, however, the von Neumann metaphor was gradually replaced by a more eclectic approach, including a rebirth of Connectionism.

At about the same time, the Society for Neuroscience was established to effect a radical restructuring of experimental neuroscience departments. Gradually the new emphasis on interdisciplinary experimental approaches, and the realization that even a huge bottom-up data base could not, in itself, explain brain function, led to the Computational Neuroscience movement.

In Artificial Intelligence, billions of dollars of funding led to a final product: the expert system. Many problems could not be accommodated in this framework, and even expert systems needed faster computers on which to run. The need for faster computer architectures, notably parallel architectures, became urgently felt in AI as well as throughout the computer industry. Once the monopoly of the von Neumann architecture was broken, and parallel architectures, particularly parallel architectures to support intelligent computation, were sought, the research goals thereby defined naturally included neural networks as one particularly promising type of parallel architecture.

In physics, the interest in nonlinear collective phenomena, including global equilibrium behaviors, phase transitions, nonlinear oscillations, and chaos, naturally drew interest to neural networks. In mathematics, a burgeoning community studying complex phenomena of nonlinear dynamical systems was attracted. In engineering, new approaches were sought to deal with nonparametric problems in noisy, nonstationary environments where an increasing degree of autonomous control was required. It became clear that new models, particularly learning models, were needed to tackle unsolved problems in image processing, speech understanding, pattern recognition, adaptive control, and robotics.

These mainstreams were thus driven by deep-seated intellectual and social requirements. Various individuals naturally became identified as the chief spokesmen of the new movements within their respective mainstreams. Typically, these individuals did not invent the ideas that they popularized, if only because the main ideas had already been discovered outside the mainstreams before the mainstreams were ready to assimilate them. That is perhaps the main reason that neural networks have taken hold so quickly once this massive cross-disciplinary paradigm shift began. One did not have to invent a whole new field. By and large, known results were, at first, packaged or applied in a way that met the communication needs of the new mainstream audience. The same ideas were hereby "rediscovered" in several fields almost simultaneously.

Much excellent new work has been done in the past decade. But many of the foundations of the field—such as the additive model, shunting model, symmetric autoassociator, global content addressable memory, instar, outstar, avalanche, 3-level universal associative map, cooperative-competitive feedback network, competitive learning network, self-organizing feature map, adaptive resonance system, and gated dipole field—that are described and further developed in this book, came out of an interdisciplinary synthesis that emerged before 1980.

The story of how this foundation was built provides a fascinating lesson in scientific history. Here is a case where major ideas and models that were vigorously published in mainstream journals for two decades were not widely assimilated by these mainstreams until a massive paradigm shift was ready to take place. Now that such a shift is well underway, interdisciplinary books such as the present one, which provide both historical and scientific accounts of theory development, may make these theories easier to follow.

Each chapter of the book is preceded by a preface that links the chapters together both historically and scientifically, highlights some of its major contributions, and comments upon future directions for research. The majority of the chapters have been published by our own group at the Center for Adaptive Systems and the graduate program in Cognitive and Neural Systems of Boston University. The work reported within these articles has been supported over the years by the Air Force Office of Scientific Research, the Advanced Research Projects Agency, the Alfred P. Sloan Foundation, the Army Research Office, the National Science Foundation, and the Office of Naval Research. We are grateful to these agencies for making our work possible.

We wish to thank the authors and publishers for their permission to reprint the articles in this volume. We are also grateful to Cynthia Bradford, known to many Center readers over the years by her maiden name of Suchta, for once again doing a marvelously competent job of preparing the text.

Gail A. Carpenter
Stephen Grossberg
Boston, Massachusetts
November, 1990

PATTERN RECOGNITION BY
SELF-ORGANIZING NEURAL NETWORKS

CHAPTER 1

NEURAL NETWORK MODELS FOR PATTERN RECOGNITION AND ASSOCIATIVE MEMORY
by
Gail A. Carpenter

Preface

This 1989 article grew out of a tutorial lecture that was given in 1988 at the First Annual Meeting of the International Neural Network Society. The goal of the chapter is to provide a compact introduction to some of the basic neural network modules for associative memory, pattern recognition, and category learning. Many systems developed and applied in recent years are variations on one or more of these modular themes. A unified adaptive filter formalism is used to clarify formal linkages between several different approaches to building supervised and unsupervised systems. The chapter traces the historical trend from algebraically defined models that can operate in an off-line mode under external supervision towards dynamically defined models that can operate in an on-line, or real-time, mode without external supervision.

Neural Networks
1989, **2**, 243–257
©1989 Pergamon Press, Inc.

NEURAL NETWORK MODELS
FOR PATTERN RECOGNITION AND ASSOCIATIVE MEMORY

Gail A. Carpenter†

Abstract

This review outlines some fundamental neural network modules for associative memory, pattern recognition, and category learning. Included are discussions of the McCulloch-Pitts neuron, perceptrons, adaline and madaline, back propagation, the learning matrix, linear associative memory, embedding fields, instars and outstars, the avalanche, shunting competitive networks, competitive learning, computational mapping by instar/outstar families, adaptive resonance theory, the cognitron and neocognitron, and simulated annealing. Adaptive filter formalism provides a unified notation. Activation laws include additive and shunting equations. Learning laws include back-coupled error correction, Hebbian learning, and gated instar and outstar equations. Also included are discussions of real-time and off-line modeling, stable and unstable coding, supervised and unsupervised learning, and self-organization.

1. Introduction

Neural network analysis exists on many different levels. At the highest level (Figure 1) we study theories, architectures, hierarchies for big problems such as early vision, speech, arm movement, reinforcement, cognition. Each architecture is typically constructed from pieces, or *modules*, designed to solve parts of a bigger problem. These pieces might be used, for example, to associate pairs of patterns with one another or to sort a class of patterns into various categories. In turn, for every such module there is a bewildering variety of examples, equations, simulations, theorems,

† Acknowledgements: This article is based upon a tutorial lecture given on September 6, 1988 at the First Annual Meeting of the International Neural Network Society in Boston, Massachusetts. The author's research is supported in part by grants from the Air Force Office of Scientific Research (AFOSR F49620-86-C-0037 and AFOSR F49620-87-C-0018) and the National Science Foundation (NSF DMS-86-11959). I wish to thank these agencies for their long-term support of neural network research, and also to thank my colleagues at the Boston University Center for Adaptive Systems for their generous ongoing contributions of knowledge, skills, and friendship.

implementations, studied under various conditions such as fast or slow input presentation rates, supervised or unsupervised learning, real-time or off-line dynamics. These variations and their applications are now the subject of hundreds of talks and papers each year. In this review I will focus on the middle level, on some of the fundamental neural network modules that carry out associative memory, pattern recognition, and category learning.

Even then this is a big subject. To help organize it further I will trace the historical development of the main ideas, grouped by theme rather than by strict chronological order. But keep in mind that there is a much more complex history, and many more contributors, than you will read about here. I refer you to the Bibliography, in particular to the recent collection of articles in the book **Neurocomputing: Foundations of Research**, edited by James A. Anderson and Edward Rosenfeld (1988).

2. The McCulloch-Pitts Neuron

We would probably all agree to begin with the McCulloch-Pitts neuron (Figure 2a). The McCulloch-Pitts model describes a neuron whose activity x_j is the sum of inputs that arrive via weighted pathways. The input from a particular pathway is an incoming signal S_i multiplied by the weight w_{ij} of that pathway. These weighted inputs are summed independently. The outgoing signal $S_j = f(x_j)$ is typically a nonlinear function—binary, sigmoid, threshold-linear—of the activity x_j in that cell. The McCulloch-Pitts neuron can also have a bias term θ_j, which is formally equivalent to the negative of a threshold of the outgoing signal function.

3. Adaptive Filter Formalism

There is a very convienient notation for describing the McCulloch-Pitts neuron, called the *adaptive filter*. It is this notation that I will here use to translate models into a common language so that we can compare and contrast them. The elementary adaptive filter depicted in Figure 2b has:

(1) a level F_1 that registers an input pattern vector;

(2) signals S_i that pass through weighted pathways; and

(3) a second level F_2 whose activity pattern is here computed by the McCulloch-Pitts function:

$$x_j = \sum_i S_i w_{ij} + \theta_j. \tag{1}$$

The reason that this formalism has proved so extraordinarily useful is that the F_2 level of the adaptive filter computes a pattern match, as in equation (2):

$$\sum_i S_i w_{ij} = \mathbf{S} \cdot \mathbf{w}_j = \|\mathbf{S}\|\|\mathbf{w}_j\| \cos(\mathbf{S}, \mathbf{w}_j). \tag{2}$$

The independent sum of the weighted pathways in (2) equals the dot product of the signal vector S times the weight vector w_j. This term can be factored into the "energy," the product of the lengths of S and w_j; times a dimensionless measure of "pattern match," the cosine of the angle between the two vectors. Suppose that the weight vectors w_j are normalized and the bias terms θ_j are all equal. Then the

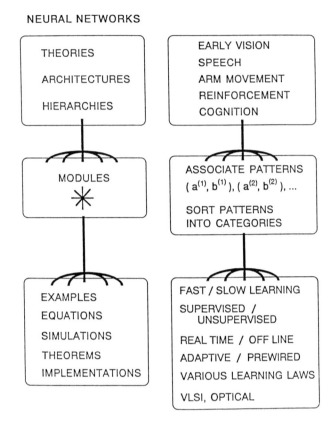

Figure 1. Levels of neural network analysis.

activity vector x across the second level describes the degree of match between the signal vector S and the various weighted pathway vectors w_j: the F_2 node with the greatest activity indicates the weight vector that forms the best match.

4. Logical Calculus and Invariant Patterns

The paper that first describes the McCulloch-Pitts model is entitled "A logical calculus of the ideas immanent in nervous activity" (McCulloch and Pitts, 1943). In that paper, McCulloch and Pitts analyze the adaptive filter without adaptation. In their models, the weights are constant. There is no learning. The 1943 paper shows that given the linear filter with an absolute inhibition term:

$$x_j = \sum_i S_i w_{ij} + \theta_j - [\text{inhibition}] \tag{3}$$

and binary output signals, these networks can be configured to perform arbitrary logical functions. And if you are looking for applications of neural network research you need only read the memoires of John von Neumann (1958) to see how heavily the McCulloch-Pitts formalism influenced the development of present-day computer architectures.

In a sense this was looking backwards, to the early 20th century mathematics of **Principia Mathematica** (Russell and Whitehead, 1910, 1912, 1913). A glance

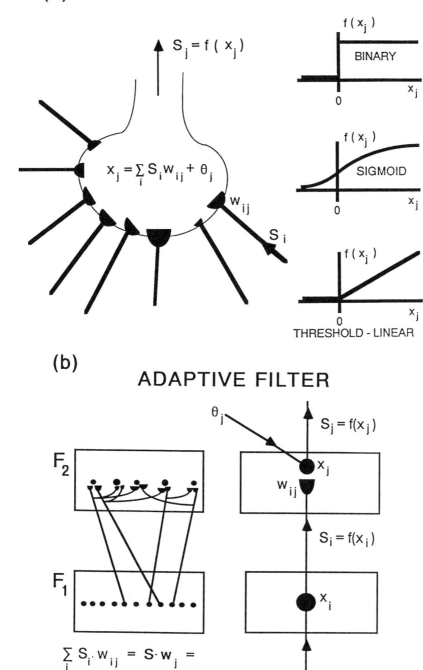

Figure 2. The McCulloch-Pitts model (a) as a neuron, with typical nonlinear signal functions; (b) as an adaptive filter.

ROSENBLATT PERCEPTRON

McCULLOCH-PITTS + LEARNING

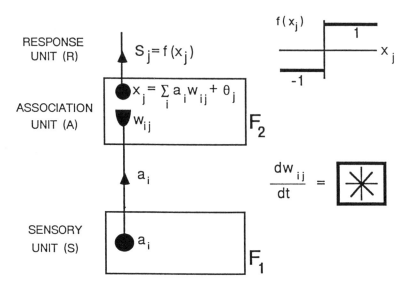

Figure 3. Principal elements of a Rosenblatt perceptron: sensory unit (S), association unit (A), and response unit (R).

at the 1943 McCulloch-Pitts paper shows that it is written in notation with which few of us are now familiar. (This is a good example of revolutionary ideas being expressed in the language of a previous era. As the revolution comes about a new language evolves, making the seminal papers "hard to read.") McCulloch and Pitts also clearly looked forward toward present day neural network research. For example, a later paper is entitled "How we know universals: the perception of auditory and visual forms" (Pitts and McCulloch, 1947). There they examine ideas in pattern recognition and the computation of invariants. They thus took their research program into a domain distinctly different from the earlier analysis of formal network groupings and computation. Still they considered only models without learning.

5. Perceptrons and Back-Coupled Error Correction

The McCulloch-Pitts papers were extraordinarily influential, and it was not long before the next generation of researchers added learning and adaptation. One great figure of the next decade was Frank Rosenblatt, whose name is tied with the perceptron model (Rosenblatt, 1958). Actually, "perceptron" refers to a large class of neural models. The models that Rosenblatt himself developed and studied are numerous and varied; see, for example, his book, **Principles of Neurodynamics** (1962).

The core idea of the perceptron is the incorporation of learning into the McCulloch-Pitts neuron model. Figure 3 illustrates the main elements of the perceptron, including, in Rosenblatt's terminology, the sensory unit (S); the association unit (A), where the learning takes place; and the response unit (R).

One of the many perceptrons that Rosenblatt studied, one that remains important to the present day, is the *back-coupled perceptron* (Rosenblatt, 1962, Section IV).

Figure 4a illustrates a simple version of the back-coupled perceptron model, with a feedforward adaptive filter and binary output signal. Weights w_{ij} are adapted according to whether the actual output S_j matches a target output b_j imposed on the system. The actual output vector is subtracted from the target output vector; their difference is defined as the error; and that difference is then fed back to adjust the weights, according to some probabilistic law. Rosenblatt called this process *back-coupled error correction*. It was well known at the time that these two-level perceptrons could sort linearly separable inputs, which can be separated by a hyperplane in vector space, into two classes. Figure 4b shows back- coupled error correction in more detail. In particular the error δ_j is fed back to every one of the weights converging on the jth node.

6. Adaline and Madaline

Researchers in the 1960's did not stop with these two-level perceptrons, and continued on to multiple-level perceptrons, as indicated below. But first let us consider another development that took place shortly after Rosenblatt's perceptron formulations. This is the set of models used by Bernard Widrow and his colleagues, especially the *adaline* and *madaline* perceptrons. The adaline model has just one neuron in the F_2 level in Figure 5; the madaline, or many-adaline, model has any number of neurons in that level. Figure 5 highlights the principal difference between the adaline/madaline and Rosenblatt's two-level feedforward perceptron: an adaline/madaline model compares the *analog* output x_j with the target output b_j. This comparison provides a more subtle index of error than a law that compares the *binary* output with the target output. The error $b_j - x_j = \delta_j$ is fed back to adjust weights using a Rosenblatt back-coupled error correction rule:

$$\frac{dw_{ij}}{dt} = \alpha \delta_j \frac{a_i}{|a|^2}. \tag{4}$$

This rule minimizes the mean squared error:

$$\sum_j \delta_j^2 \tag{5}$$

averaged over all inputs (Widrow and Hoff, 1960). It is therefore known as the *least mean squared* error correction rule, or LMS.

Once again, adaline and madaline provide many examples of the technological spinoffs already generated by neural network research. Some of these are summarized in a recent article (Widrow and Winter, 1988) in a *Computer* special issue on artificial neural systems. There the authors describe adaptive equalizers and adaptive echo cancellation in modems, antennae, and other engineering applications, all directly traceable to early neural network designs.

7. Multi-Level Perceptrons: Early Back Propagation

We have so far been talking only about two-level perceptrons. Rosenblatt, not content with these, also studied multi-level perceptrons, as described **Principles of Neurodynamics**. One particularly interesting section in that book is entitled "Back-Propagating Error Correction Procedures." The back propagation model described

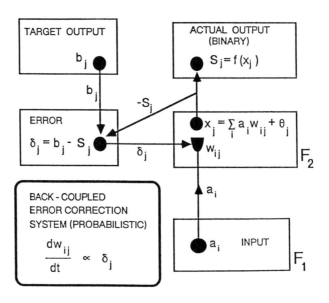

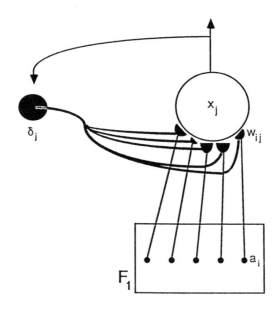

Figure 4. Back-coupled error correction. (a) The difference between the target output and the actual output is fed back to adjust weights when an error occurs. (b) All weights w_{ij} fanning in to the jth node are adjusted in proportion to the error d_j at that node.

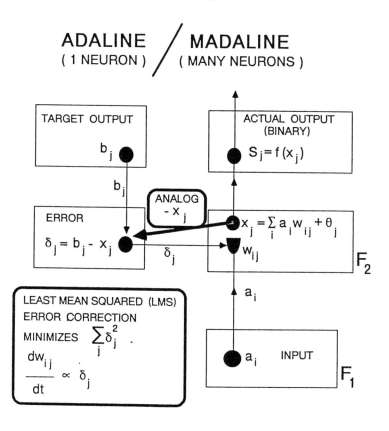

ADALINE / MADALINE
(1 NEURON) / (MANY NEURONS)

Figure 5. The adaline and madaline perceptrons use the analog output x_j, rather than the binary output S_j, in the back-coupled error correction procedure.

in that section anticipates the currently used back propagation model, which is also a multi-level perceptron. In Chapter 13, Rosenblatt defines a back propagation algorithm that has, like most of his algorithms, a probabilistic learning law; he proves a theorem about this system; and he carries out simulations. His chapter, "Summary of Three-Layer Series-Coupled Systems: Capabilities and Deficiencies," is equally revealing. This chapter includes a hard look at what is lacking as well as what is good in Rosenblatt's back propagation algorithm, and it puts the lie to the myth that all of these systems were looked at only through rose-colored glasses.

8. Later Back Propagation

Let us now move on to what has become one of the most useful and well-studied neural network algorithms, the model we now call back propagation. This system was first developed by Paul Werbos (1974), as part of his Ph.D thesis "Beyond regression: New tools for prediction and analysis in the behavioral sciences;" and independently discovered by David Parker (1982). (See Werbos (1988) for a review of the history of the development of back propagation.)

The most popular back propagation examples carry out associative learning: during training, a vector pattern **a** is associated with a vector pattern **b**; and subsequently **b** is recalled upon presentation of **a** (Rumelhart, Hinton, and Williams, 1986). The back propagation system is trained under conditions of *slow learning*, with each pattern pair $(\mathbf{a},\mathbf{b})$ presented repeatedly during training. The basic elements of a typical back propagation system are the McCulloch-Pitts linear filter with a sigmoid output signal function and Rosenblatt back-coupled error correction. Figure 6 shows a block diagram of a back propagation system that is a three-level perceptron. The input signal vector converges on the "hidden unit" F_2 level after passing through the first set of weighted pathways w_{ij}. Signals S_j then fan out to the F_3 level, which generates the actual output of this feedforward system. A back-coupled error correction system then compares the actual output S_k with a target output b_k and feeds back their difference to all the weights w_{jk} converging on the kth node. In this process the difference $b_k - S_k$ is also multiplied by another term, $f'(x_k)$, computed in a "differentiator" step. One function of this step is to ensure that the weights remain in a bounded range: the shape of the sigmoid signal function implies that weights w_{jk} will stop growing if the magnitude of the activity x_k becomes too large, since then the derivative term $f'(x_k)$ goes to zero. Then there is a second way in which the error correction is fed back to the lower level. This is where the term "back propagation" enters: the weights w_{jk} in the feedforward pathways from F_2 to F_3 are now used in a second place, to filter error information. This process is called *weight transport*. In particular, all the weights w_{jk} in pathways fanning *out* from the jth F_2 node are transported for multiplication by the corresponding error terms δ_k; and the sum of all these products, times the bounding derivative term $f'(x_k)$, is back-coupled to adjust all the weights w_{ij} in pathways fanning *in* to the jth F_2 node.

9. Hebbian Learning

This brings us close to the present in this particular line of perceptron research. I am now going to step back and trace another major neural network theme that goes under the name *Hebbian learning*. One sentence in a 1949 book, **The Organization of Behavior**, by Donald Hebb is responsible for the phrase Hebbian learning:

> "When an axon of cell A is near enough to excite a cell B and repeatedly or persistently takes place in firing it, some growth process or metabolic change takes place in one or both cells such that A's efficiency, as one of the cells firing B, is increased." (Hebb, 1949)

Actually, "Hebbian learning" was not a new idea in 1949: it can be traced back to Pavlov and earlier. But in the decade of McCulloch and Pitts, the formulation of the idea in the above sentence crystallized the notion in such a way that it became widely influential in the emerging neural network field. Translated into a differential equation (Figure 7), the Hebbian rule computes a correlation between the presynaptic signal S_i and the postsynaptic activity x_j, with positive values of the correlation term $S_i x_j$ leading to increases in the weight w_{ij}.

The Hebbian learning theme has since evolved in a number of directions. One important development entailed simply adding a passive decay term to the the Hebbian correlation term:

$$\frac{dw_{ij}}{dt} = \alpha S_i x_j - w_{ij} \tag{6}$$

(Grossberg, 1968). Other developments are described below. In all these rules,

BACK PROPAGATION ALGORITHM

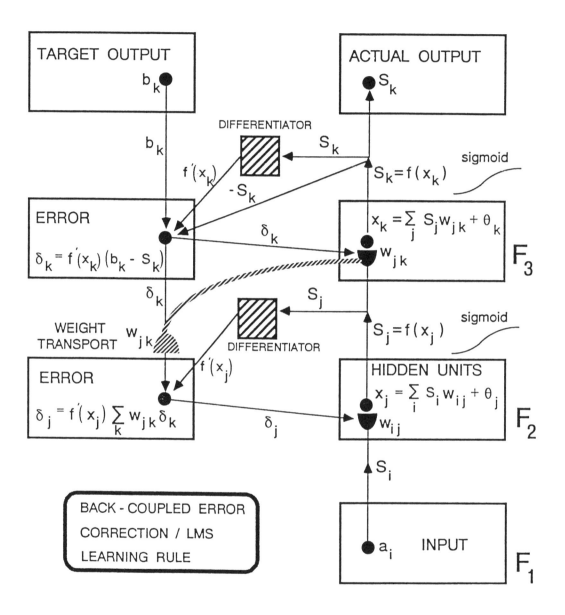

Figure 6. Block diagram of a back propagation algorithm for associative memory. Weights in the three-level feedforward perceptron are adjusted according to back-coupled error correction rules. Weight transport propagates error information in F_2-to-F_3 pathways back to weights in F_1-to-F_2 pathways.

HEBBIAN LEARNING

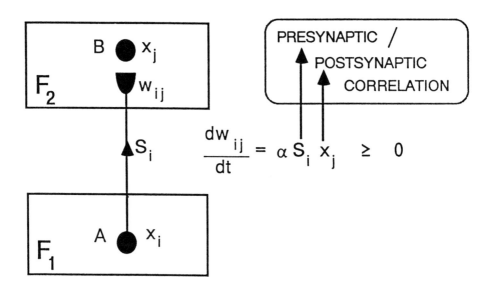

Figure 7. Donald Hebb (1949) provided a qualitative description of increases in path strength that occur when cell A helps to fire cell B. In the adaptive filter formalism, this hypothesis is often interpreted as a weight change that occurs when a presynaptic signal S_i is correlated with a postsynaptic activity x_j.

changes in the weight w_{ij} depend upon a simple function of the presynaptic signal S_i, the postsynaptic activity x_j, and the weight itself, as in (6). In contrast, back-coupled error correction requires a term that must be computed away from the target node and then transmitted back to adjust the weight.

10. The Learning Matrix

Many of the models that followed the perceptron in the 1950's and 60's can be phrased in Hebbian (plus McCulloch-Pitts) language. One of the earliest and most important is the learning matrix (Figure 8) developed by K. Steinbuch (1961). The function of the learning matrix is to sort, or partition, a set of vector patterns into categories. In the simple learning matrix illustrated in Figure 8a, an input pattern **a** is represented in the vertical wires. During learning a category for **a** is represented in the horizontal wires of the crossbar: **a** is placed in category J when the Jth component of the output vector **b** is set equal to 1. During such an input presentation the weight w_{iJ} is adjusted upward by a fixed amount if $a_i = 1$ and downward by the same amount if $a_i = 0$. Then during performance the weights w_{ij} are held constant; and an input **a** is deemed to be in category J if the weight vector $\mathbf{w}_J = (w_{1J}, \ldots w_{NJ})$ is closer than any other weight vector to **a**, according to some measure of distance.

Recasting the crossbar learning matrix in the adaptive filter format (Figure 8b) helps us to see that this simple model is the precursor of a fundamental module widely used in present day neural network modeling, namely *competitive learning*. In particular, activity at the top level of the learning matrix corresponds to a category

LEARNING MATRIX

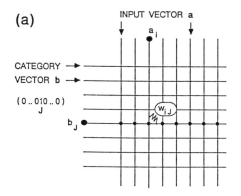

(a)

INPUT VECTOR **a**

a_i

CATEGORY →
VECTOR **b** →

$(0 .. 010 .. 0)$
J

b_J

w_{iJ}

LEARNING

$$b_J = 1 : \quad \Delta w_{iJ} = \begin{cases} \alpha & \text{if } a_i = 1 \\ -\alpha & \text{if } a_i = 0 \end{cases}$$

$$b_j = 0 \ (j \neq J) : \quad \Delta w_{ij} = 0$$

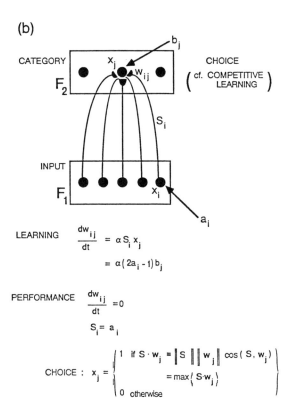

(b)

b_j

CATEGORY x_j CHOICE

F_2 w_{ij} $\left(\begin{array}{c} \text{cf. COMPETITIVE} \\ \text{LEARNING} \end{array} \right)$

S_i

INPUT

F_1 x_i

a_i

LEARNING $\dfrac{dw_{ij}}{dt} = \alpha S_i x_j$

$= \alpha (2a_i - 1) b_j$

PERFORMANCE $\dfrac{dw_{ij}}{dt} = 0$

$S_i = a_i$

CHOICE : $x_j = \begin{cases} 1 & \text{if } S \cdot w_j = |S| \, \|w_j\| \cos(S, w_j) \\ & = \max\{ S \cdot w_j \} \\ 0 & \text{otherwise} \end{cases}$

Figure 8. The learning matrix, for category learning. (a) Cross-bar architecture for electronic implementation. (b) The learning matrix in adaptive filter notation. The learning matrix was a precursor of the competitive learning paradigm.

representation. Setting activity x_J equal to 1, while all other x_j's are set equal to 0, corresponds to the dynamics of a *choice*, or *winner-take-all*, neural network. Steinbuch's learning rule can also be translated into the Hebbian formalism, with weight adjustment during learning a joint function of a presynaptic signal $S_i = (2a_i - 1)$ and a postsynaptic signal $x_j = b_j$. (This rule is not strictly Hebbian since weights can decrease as well as increase.) Then during performance, weight changes are prevented; a new signal function $S_i = a_i$ is chosen; and an F_2 choice rule is imposed based, for example, on the dot product measure illustrated in Figure 9b.

A model comparative analysis of the learning matrix and the madaline models and their electronic implementations can be found in a paper by K. Steinbuch and B. Widrow (1965). This paper, entitled "A critical comparison of two kinds of adaptive classification networks," carries out a side-by-side analysis of the learning matrix and the madaline, tracing the two models' capabilities, similarities, and differences.

11. Linear Associative Memory (LAM)

We will now move to a different line of research, namely the linear associative memory (LAM) models. Pioneering work on these models was done by J. Anderson (1972), T. Kohonen (1972), and K. Nakano (1972). Subsequently, many other linear associative memory models were developed and analyzed, for example by Kohonen and his collaborators, who studied LAM's with iteratively computed weights that converge to the Moore-Penrose pseudoinverse (Kohonen and Ruohonen, 1973). This latter system is optimal with respect to the LMS error (5), and so is known as the optimal linear associative memory (OLAM) model. Variations included networks with partial connectivity, probabilistic learning laws, and nonlinear perturbations.

At the heart of all these variations is a very simple idea, namely that a set of pattern pairs $(\mathbf{a}^{(p)}, \mathbf{b}^{(p)})$ can be stored as a correlation weight matrix:

$$w_{ij} = \sum_{p \text{ (all patterns)}} a_i^{(p)} b_j^{(p)}. \tag{7}$$

The LAM's have been an enduringly useful class of models because, in addition to their great simplicity, they embody a sort of perfection. Namely, perfect recall is achieved, provided the input vectors $\mathbf{a}^{(p)}$ are mutually orthogonal. In this case, during performance, presentation of the pattern $\mathbf{a}^{(p)}$ yields an output vector $\mathbf{x}$ proportional to $\mathbf{b}^{(p)}$, as follows:

$$
\begin{aligned}
x_j \equiv \mathbf{a}^{(p)} \cdot \mathbf{w}_j &= \sum_i a_i^{(p)} w_{ij} = \sum_i a_i^{(p)} \left(\sum_q a_i^{(q)} b_j^{(q)} \right) \\
&= \sum_q \left(\sum_i a_i^{(p)} a_i^{(q)} \right) b_j^{(q)} = \sum_q (\mathbf{a}^{(p)} \cdot \mathbf{a}^{(q)}) b_j^{(q)}.
\end{aligned} \tag{8}
$$

If, then, the vectors $\mathbf{a}^{(p)}$ are mutually orthogonal, the last sum in (8) reduces to a single term, with

$$x_j = \|\mathbf{a}^{(p)}\|^2 b_j^{(p)}. \tag{9}$$

Thus the output vector $\mathbf{x}$ is directly proportional to the desired output vector, $\mathbf{b}^{(p)}$. Finally, if we once again cast the LAM in the adaptive filter framework, we see that

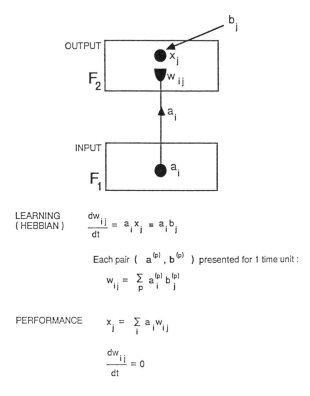

LINEAR ASSOCIATIVE MEMORY

Figure 9. A linear associative memory network, in adaptive filter/Hebbian learning format.

it is a Hebbian learning model (Figure 9).

12. Real-Time Models and Embedding Fields

Most of the models we have so far discussed require external control of system dynamics. In the back propagation model shown in Figure 6, for example, the initial feedforward activation of the three-level perceptron is followed by error correction steps that require either weight transport or reversing the direction of flow of activation. In the linear associative memory model in Figure 9, dynamics are altered as the system moves from its learning mode to its performance mode. During learning, activity x_j at the output level F_2 is set equal to the desired output b_j, while the input $S_i a_i w_{ij}$ coming to that level from F_1 through the adaptive filter is suppressed. During performance, in contrast, the dynamics are reversed: weight changes are supressed and the adaptive filter input determines x_j.

The phrase *real-time* describes neural network models that require no external control of system dynamics. (*Real-time* is alternatively used to describe any system that is able to process inputs as fast as they arrive.) Differential equations constitute the language of real-time models. A real-time model may or may not have an external teaching input, like the vector **b** of the LAM model; and learning may or may not be shut down after a finite time interval. A typical real-time model is illustrated in Figure

TYPICAL REAL-TIME MODEL

ACTIVATION EQUATION   (ADDITIVE MODEL)

$$\frac{dx_j}{dt} = -x_j + \sum \begin{bmatrix} \text{excitatory} \\ \text{inputs} \end{bmatrix} - \sum \begin{bmatrix} \text{inhibitory} \\ \text{inputs} \end{bmatrix}$$

LEARNING EQUATION

$$\frac{dw_{ij}}{dt} = \epsilon(t) \; F(S_i, x_j, w_{ij})$$

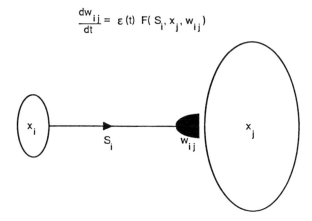

Figure 10. Elements of a typical real-time model, with additive activation equations.

10. There, excitatory and inhibitory inputs could be either internal or external to the model, but, if present, the influence of a signal is not selectively ignored. Moreover the learning rate $\epsilon(t)$ might, say, be constant or decay to 0 through time, but does not require algorithmic control. The dynamics of performance are described by the same set of equations as the dynamics of learning.

Real-time modeling has characterized the work of Stephen Grossberg over the past thirty years, work that in its early stages was called a theory of *embedding fields* (Grossberg, 1964). These early real-time models, as well as the more recent systems developed by Grossberg and his colleagues at the Boston University Center for Adaptive Systems, portray the inextricable linking of fast nodal activation and slow weight adaptation. There is no externally imposed distinction between a learning mode and a performance mode.

13. Instars and Outstars

Two key components of embedding field systems are the *instar* (Grossberg, 1972b, 1976b; von der Malsburg, 1973) and the *outstar* (Grossberg, 1968). Figure 11 illustrates the fan-in geometry of the instar and the fan-out geometry of the outstar.

Instars often appear in systems designed to carry out adaptive coding, or content-addressable memory (CAM) (Kohonen, 1980). For example, suppose that the incoming weight vector $(w_{1J}, \ldots, w_{NJ})$ approaches the incoming signal vector $(S_1, \ldots, S_N)$ while an input vector **a** is present at F_1; and that the weight and signal vectors are normalized. Then equation (2) implies that the filtered input $\sum_i S_i w_{iJ}$ to the Jth F_2

node approaches its maximum value during learning. Subsequent presentation of the same F_1 input pattern **a** maximally activates the Jth F_2 node; that is, the "content addresses the memory," all other things being equal.

The outstar, which is dual to the instar, carries out spatial pattern learning. For example, suppose that the outgoing weight vector $(w_{J1}, \ldots, w_{JN})$ approaches the F_1 spatial activity pattern $(x_1, \ldots, x_N)$ while an input vector **a** is present. Then subsequent activation of the Jth F_2 node transmits to F_1 the signal pattern $(S_J w_{J1}, \ldots, S_J w_{JN}) = S_J(w_{J1}, \ldots, w_{JN})$, which is directly proportional to the prior F_1 spatial activity pattern $(x_1, \ldots, x_N)$, even though the input vector is now absent; that is, the "memory addresses the content."

The upper instar and outstar in Figure 11 are examples of *heteroassociative* memories, where the field F_1 of nodes indexed by i is disjoint from the field F_2 of nodes indexed by j. In general, these fields can overlap. The important special case in which the two fields coincide is called *autoassociative* memory, also shown in Figure 11. Powerful computational properties arise when neural network architectures are constructed from a combination of instars and outstars. We will later see some of these designs.

14. Additive and Shunting Activation Equations

The outstar and the instar have been studied in great detail and with various combinations of activation, or short-term memory, equations and learning, or long-term memory, equations. One activation equation, the *additive model*, is illustrated in Figure 10. There, activity at a node is proportional to the difference between the net excitatory input and the net inhibitory input. Most of the models discussed so far employ a version of the additive activation model. For example, the McCulloch-Pitts activation equation (3) is the steady-state of the additive equation (10):

$$\frac{dx_j}{dt} = -x_j + \left[\sum_i S_i w_{ij} + \theta_j\right] - [\text{inhibition}]. \tag{10}$$

Grossberg (1988) reviews a number of neural models that are versions of the additive equation.

An important generalization of the additive model is the *shunting model*. In a shunting network, excitatory inputs drive activity toward a finite maximum, while inhibitory inputs drive activity toward a finite minimum, as in equation (11):

$$\frac{dx_i}{dt} = -x_i + (A - x_i)\sum\left[\text{excitatory inputs}\right] - (B + x_i)\sum\left[\text{inhibitory inputs}\right]. \tag{11}$$

In (11), activity x_i remains in the bounded range $(-B, A)$, and decays to the resting level 0 in the absence of all inputs. In addition, shunting equations display other crucial properties such as normalization and automatic gain control. Finally, shunting network equations mirror the underlying physiology of single nerve cell dynamics, as summarized by the Hodgkin-Huxley (1952) equations:

$$\frac{dV}{dt} = -V + (V_{Na} - V)\bar{g}_{Na} m^3 h - (V_K + V)\bar{g}_K n^4. \tag{12}$$

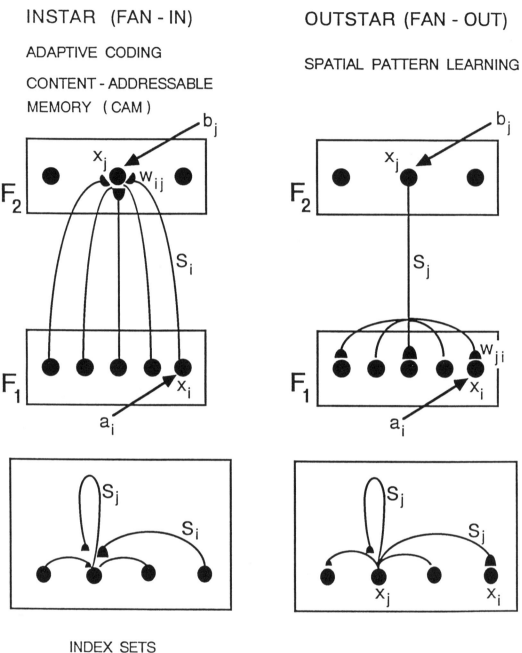

INDEX SETS

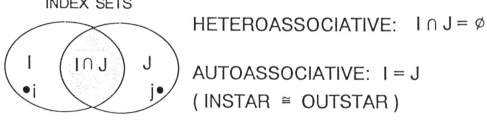

HETEROASSOCIATIVE: $I \cap J = \emptyset$

AUTOASSOCIATIVE: $I = J$
(INSTAR $\cong$ OUTSTAR)

Figure 11. Heteroassociative and autoassociative instars and outstars, for adaptive coding and spatial pattern learning.

In this single nerve cell model, during depolarization, sodium ions entering across the membrane drive the potential V toward the sodium equilibrium potential V_{Na}; during repolarizaion, exiting potassium ions drive the potential toward the potassium equlibrium potential $-V_K$; and in the balance the cell is restored to its resting potential, which is here set equal to 0. In 1963 A.L. Hodgkin and A.F. Huxley won the Nobel Prize for their development of this classic neural model.

15. Learning Equations

A wide variety of learning laws for instars and outstars have also been studied. One example is the Hebbian correlation + passive decay equation (6). There, the weight w_{ij} computes a long-term weighted average of the product of presynaptic activity S_i and postsynaptic activity x_j.

A typical learning law for instar coding is given by equation (13):

$$\frac{dw_{ij}}{dt} = \epsilon(t)[S_i - w_{ij}]x_j. \tag{13}$$

Suppose, for example, that the Jth F_2 node is to represent a given category. According to (13), the weight vector $(w_{1J}, \ldots, w_{NJ})$ converges to the signal vector $(S_1, \ldots, S_N)$ when the Jth node is active; but that weight vector remains unchanged when a different category representation is active. The term x_J thus buffers, or *gates*, the weights w_{iJ} against undesired changes, including memory loss due to passive decay. On the other hand, a typical learning law for outstar pattern learning is given by equation (14):

$$\frac{dw_{ji}}{dt} = \epsilon(t)[x_i - w_{ji}]S_j. \tag{14}$$

In (14), when the Jth F_2 node is active the weight vector $(w_{J1}, \ldots, w_{JN})$ converges to the F_1 activity pattern vector $(x_1, \ldots, x_N)$. Again, a gating term buffers weights against inappropriate changes. Note that the pair of learning laws described by (13) and (14) are non-Hebbian, and are also non-symmetric. That is, w_{ij} is generally not equal to w_{ji}, unless the F_1 and F_2 signal vectors S are identical to the corresponding activity vectors x.

A series of theorems encompassing neural network pattern learning by systems employing a large class of these and other activation and learning laws was proved by Grossberg in the late 1960s and early 1970s. One set of results falls under the heading *outstar learning theorems*. One of the most general of these theorems is contained in an article entitled "Pattern learning by functional-differential neural networks with arbitrary path weights" (Grossberg, 1972a). This is reprinted in **Studies of Mind and Brain** (Grossberg, 1982), which also contains articles that introduce and analyse additive and shunting equations (10) and (11); learning with passive and gated memory decay laws (6), (13), and (14); outstar and instar modules; and neural network architectures constructed from these elements.

16. Learning Space-Time Patterns: The Avalanche

While most of the neural network models discussed in this article are designed to learn spatial patterns, problems such as speech recognition and motor learning require

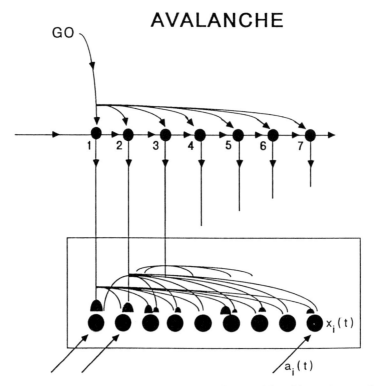

Figure 12. The avalanche: a neural network capable of learning and performing an arbitrary space-time pattern.

an understanding of space-time patterns as well. An early neural network model, called the *avalanche*, is capable of learning and performing an arbitrary space-time pattern (Grossberg, 1969). In essence, an avalanche is a series of outstars (Figure 12). During learning, the outstar active at time t learns the spatial pattern $\mathbf{x}(t)$ generated by the input pattern vector $\mathbf{a}(t)$. It is useful to think of $\mathbf{x}(t)$ as the pattern determining finger positions for a piano piece: the same field of cells is used over and over, and the sequence ABC is not the same as CBA. Following learning, when no input patterns are present, activation of the sequence of outstars reads-out, or "performs," the space-time pattern it had previously learned. In its minimal form, this network can be realized as a single cell with many branches. Learning and performance can also be supervised by a nonspecific GO signal. The GO signal may terminate an action sequence at any time and otherwise modulate the performance energy and velocity. In general, the order of activation of the outstars, as well as the spatial patterns themselves, need to be learned. This can be accomplished using autoassociative networks, as in the theory of serial learning (Grossberg and Pepe, 1970) or adaptive signal processing (Hecht-Nielsen, 1981).

17. Adaptive Coding and Category Formation

Let us now return to the theme of adaptive coding and category formation, introduced earlier in our discussion of Steinbuch's learning matrix. As shown in Figure 8b, the learning matrix can be recast in the adaptive filter formalism, with the dynamics of the F_2 level defined in such a way that only one node is active at a given time. The active node, or category representation, is selected by a "teacher" during learning. During performance the active node is selected according to which weight vector forms the best match with the input vector. Now compare the learning matrix in Figure 8b with the instar in Figure 11. The pictures, or network "anatomies," seem to indicate that the instar is identical to the learning matrix. The difference between the two models lies in the dynamics, or network "physiology." The fundamental characteristic of the instar that distinguishes it from the learning matrix and other early models is the constraint that instar dynamics occur in real time. In particular, the instar filtered input $\mathbf{S} \cdot \mathbf{w}_j$ influences x_j at all times, and is not artificially suppressed during learning. However, the desire to construct a category learning system that can operate in real time immediately leads to many questions. The most pressing one is: how can the categories be represented if the dynamics are not imposed by an external agent? For the choice case, for example, the *internal* system dynamics need to allow at most one F_2 node be be active, even though other nodes may continue to receive large inputs, either internally, via the filter, or externally, via the vector $\mathbf{b}$. Even when the category representation is a distributed patttern, this representation is generally a compressed, or contrast-enhanced, version of the highly distributed net pattern coming in to F_2 from all sources. This compression is, in fact, the step that carries out the process wherein some or many items are grouped into a new unit, or category.

18. Shunting Competitive Networks

Fortunately, there is a well-defined class of neural networks ideally suited to play the role of the category representation field. This is the class of on-center/off-surround shunting competitive networks. Figure 13 illustrates one such system. There, the input vector $\mathbf{I}$ can be the sum of inputs from one or more sources and is, in general, highly distributed. *On-center* here refers to the feedback process whereby a cell sends net excitatory signals to itself and to its immediate neighbors; *off-surround* refers to the complementary process whereby the same cell sends net inhibitory signals to its more distant neighbors. In a 1973 article entitled "Contour Enhancement, Short-Term Memory, and Constancies in Reverberating Neural Networks," Grossberg carried out a mathematical characterization of the dynamics of various classes of shunting competitive networks. In particular he classified the systems according to the shape of the signal function $f(x_j)$. Depending upon whether this signal function is linear, faster-than-linear, slower-than-linear, or sigmoid, the networks are shown to quench or enhance low-amplitude noise; and to contrast-enhance or flatten the input pattern $\mathbf{I}$ in varying degrees. In particular, a faster-than-linear signal function implements the choice network needed for many models of category learning. A sigmoid signal function, on the other hand, suppresses noise and contrast-enhances the input pattern, without necessarily going to the extreme of concentrating all activity in one node. Thus an on-center/off-surround shunting competitive network with a sigmoid signal function is shown to be an ideal design for a category learning system with distributed code representations. This parametric analysis thus provided the foundation for constructing larger network architectures that use a competitive network as a component with well-defined functional properties.

ON - CENTER / OFF - SURROUND

SHUNTING COMPETITIVE NETWORK

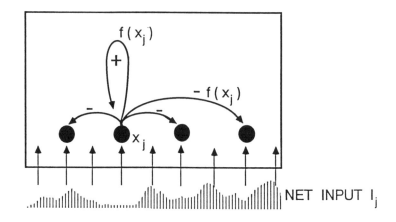

$$\frac{dx_j}{dt} = -x_j + (A-x_j)\left[I_j + f(x_j) \right] - x_j \sum_{k \neq j} f(x_k)$$

Figure 13. An on-center/off-surround shunting competitive network. Qualitative features of the signal function $f(x_j)$ determine the way in which the network transforms the input vector **I** into the state vector **x**.

19. Competitive Learning

A module of fundamental importance in recent neural network architectures is described by the phrase *competitive learning*. This module brings the properties of the learning matrix into the real-time setting. The basic competitive learning architecture consists of an instar filter, from a field F_1 to a field F_2, and a competitive neural network at F_2 (Figure 14). The competitive learning module can operate with or without an external teaching signal **b**; and learned changes in the adaptive filter can proceed indefinitely or cease after a finite time interval. If there is no teaching signal at a given time, then the net input vector to F_2 is the sum of signals arriving via the adaptive filter. Then if the category representation network is designed to make a choice, the node that automatically becomes active is the one whose weight vector best matches the signal vector, as in equation (2). If there is a teaching signal, the category representation decision still depends on past learning, but this is balanced against the external signal **b**, which may or may not overrule the past in the competition. In either case, an instar learning law such as equation (13) allows a chosen category to encode aspects of the new F_1 pattern in its learned representation.

20. Computational Maps

Investigators who have developed and analyzed the competitive learning paradigm over the years include K. Steinbuch (1961); S. Grossberg (1972b, 1976a, 1976b);

COMPETITIVE LEARNING

INSTAR + CONTRAST ENHANCEMENT

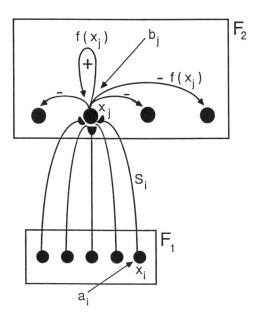

Figure 14. The basic competitive learning module combines the instar pattern coding system with a competitive network that contrast-enhances its filtered input.

C. von der Malsburg (1973); S.-I. Amari (1977); S.-I. Amari and A. Takeuchi (1978); E. Bienenstock, L. Cooper, and P. Munro (1982); D. Rumelhart and D. Zipser (1985); and many others. Moreover, these and other investigators proceeded to embed the competitive learning module in higher order neural network systems. In particular, systems were designed to learn computational maps, producing an output vector $\mathbf{b}$ in response to an input vector $\mathbf{a}$. The core of many of these computational map models is an instar-outstar system. Recognition of this common theme highlights the models' differences as well as their similarities. An early self-organizing three-level instar-outstar computational map model was described by Grossberg (1972b), who later replaced the instar portion of this model with a competitive learning module (Grossberg, 1976b). The self-organizing feature map (Kohonen, 1984) and the counter-propagation network (Hecht-Nielsen, 1987) are also examples of instar-outstar competitive learning models.

The basic instar-outstar computational map system is depicted in Figure 15. The first two levels, F_1 and F_2, form a competitive learning system. Included are the fan-in adaptive filter, contrast-enhancement at the "hidden" level F_2, and a learning law for instar coding of the input patterns $\mathbf{a}$. The top two levels then employ a fan-out adaptive filter for outstar pattern learning of the vector $\mathbf{b}$. This three-level architecture allows, for example, two very different input patterns to map to the same output pattern: each input pattern can activate its own compressed representation at F_2, while each of these F_2 representations can learn a common output vector. In the

COMPUTATIONAL MAPS

INSTAR / OUTSTAR FAMILIES

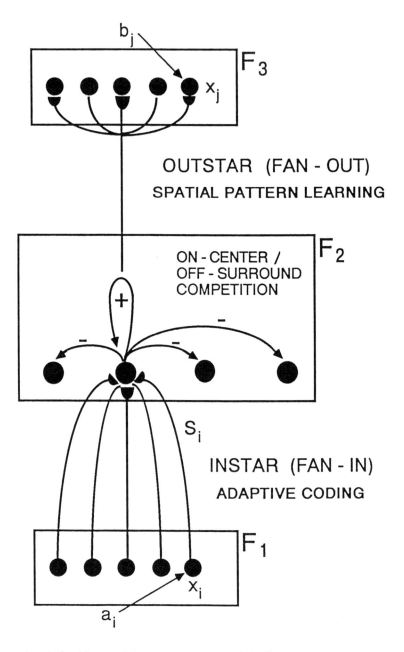

Figure 15. A three-level, feedforward instar-outstar module for computational mapping. The competitive learning module (F_1 and F_2) is joined with an outstar-type fan-out, for spatial pattern learning.

extreme case where each input vector a activates its own F_2 node the system learns any desired output. The generality of this extreme case, which implements an arbitrary mapping from $\mathbf{R}^m$ to $\mathbf{R}^n$, is offset by its lack of generalization, or continuity, as well as by the fact that each learned pair $(\mathbf{a},\mathbf{b})$ requires its own F_2 node. Distributed F_2 representations provide greater generalization and efficiency, at a cost in complete a priori generality of the mapping.

21. Instability of Computational Maps

The widespread use of instar-outstar families of computational maps attests to the power of this basic neural network architecture. This power is, however, diminished by the instability of feedforward systems: in general, recently learned patterns tend to erode past learning. This instability arises from two sources. First, even if a chosen category is the best match for a given input, that match may nevertheless be a poor one, chosen only because all the others are even worse. Established codes are thus vulnerable to recoding by "outliers." Second, learning laws such as equation (13) imply that a weight vector tends toward a new vector that encodes the presently active pattern, thereby weakening the trace of the past. Thus weight vectors can eventually drift far from their original patterns, even if learning is very slow and even if each individual input makes a good match with the past as recorded in the weights.

The many existing variations on the three-level instar-outstar theme illustrate some of the ways in which this family of models can be adapted to cope with the basic system's intrinsic instability. One stabilization technique causes learning to slow or cease after an initial finite interval; but then a subsequent unexpected pattern cannot be encoded, and instability could still creep in during the initial learning phase. Another approach is to restrict the class of input patterns to a stable set. This technique requires that the system can be sufficiently well analyzed to identify such a class, like the orthogonal inputs of the linear associative memory model (Figure 9); and that all inputs can be confined to this class. An often successful way to compensate for the instability of these systems is to slow the learning rate to such an extent that learned patterns are buffered against massive recoding by any single input. Of course, then, each pattern needs to be presented very many times for adequate learning to occur, a fact that was discussed, for example, by Rosenblatt in his critique of back propagation.

22. Adaptive Resonance Theory (ART)

It was analysis of the instability of feedforward instar-outstar systems that led to the introduction of adaptive resonance theory (ART) (Grossberg, 1976c) and to the development of the neural network systems ART 1 and ART 2 (Carpenter and Grossberg, 1987a, 1987b). ART networks are designed, in particular, to resolve the *stability-plasticity dilemma*: they are stable enough to preserve significant past learning, but nevertheless remain adaptible enough to incorporate new information whenever it might appear.

The key idea of adaptive resonance theory is that the stability-plasticity dilemma can be resolved by a system in which the three-level network of Figure 15 is folded back on itself, identifying the top level (F_3) with the bottom level (F_1) of the instar-outstar mapping system. Thus the minimal ART module includes a bottom-up competitive learning system combined with a top-down outstar pattern learning system. When an input **a** is presented to an ART network, system dynamics initially follow the course of competitive learning (Figure 14), with bottom-up activation leading to a contrast-enhanced category representation at F_2. In the absence of other inputs to F_2, the active category is determined by past learning as encoded in the adaptive weights in the bottom-up filter. But now, in contrast to feedforward systems, signals are sent from F_2 back down to F_1 via a top-down adaptive filter. This feedback process allows the ART module to overcome both of the sources of instability described in Section 21, as follows.

First, as in the competitive learning module, the category active at F_2 may poorly match the pattern active at F_1. The ART system is designed to carry out a matching process that asks the question: should this input really be in this category? If the answer is no, the selected category is quickly rendered inactive, before past learning is disrupted by the outlier, and a search process ensues. This search process employs an auxiliary *orienting subsystem* that is controlled by the dynamics of the ART system itself. The orienting subsystem incorporates a dimensionless *vigilance parameter* that establishes the criterion for deciding whether the match is a good enough one for the input to be accepted as an exemplar of the chosen category.

Second, once an input is accepted and learning proceeds, the top-down filter continues to play a different kind of stabilizing role. Namely, top-down signals that represent the past learning meet the original input signals at F_1. Thus the F_1 activity pattern is a function of the past as well as the present, and it is this blend of the two, rather than the present input alone, that is learned by the weights in both adaptive filters. This dynamic matching during learning leads to stable coding, even with fast learning.

An example of the ART 1 class of minimal modules is illustrated in Figure 16. In addition to the two adaptive filters and the orienting subsystem, Figure 16 depicts gain control processes that actively regulate learning. Theorems have been proved to characterize the response of an ART 1 module to an arbitrary sequence of binary input patterns (Carpenter and Grossberg, 1987a). ART 2 systems were developed to self-organize recognition categories for analog as well as binary input sequences. One principal difference between the ART 1 and the ART 2 modules is shown in Figure 17. In examples so far developed, the stability criterion for analog inputs has required a three-layer feedback system within the F_1 level: a bottom layer where input patterns are read in; a top layer where filtered inputs from F_2 are read in; and a middle layer where the top and bottom patterns are brought together to form a matched pattern that is then fed back to the top and bottom F_1 layers.

23. ART for Associative Memory

A minimal ART module is a category learning system that self-organizes a sequence of input patterns into various recognition categories. It is not an associative memory system. However, like the competitive learning module in the 1970's, a minimal ART module can be embedded in a larger system for associative memory. A system such as an instar-outstar module (Figure 15) or a back propagation algorithm (Figure 6) directly pairs sequences of individual *vectors* (**a**,**b**) during learning. If an ART system replaces levels F_1 and F_2 of the instar-outstar module, the associative learning system becomes self-stabilizing. ART systems can also be used to pair sequences of the *categories* self-organized by the input sequences (Figure 18). Moreover

ART 1

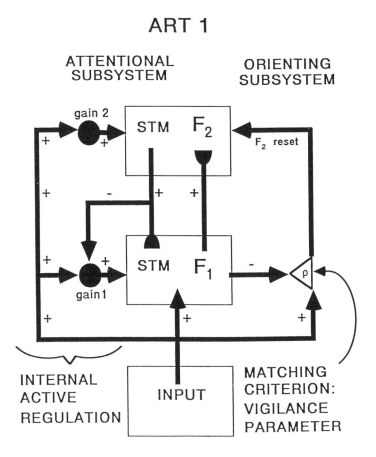

Figure 16. An ART 1 module for stable, self-organizing categorization of an arbitrary sequence of binary input patterns.

the symmetry of the architecture implies that pattern recall can occur in either direction during performance. This scheme brings to the associative memory paradigm the code compression capabilities of the ART system, as well as its stability properties.

24. Cognitron and Neocognitron

In conclusion, we will consider two sets of models that are variations on the themes previously described. The first class, developed by Kunihiko Fukushima, consists of the cognitron (Fukushima, 1975) and the larger-scale neocognitron (Fukushima, 1980, 1988). This class of neural models is distinguished by its capacity to carry out translation-invariant and size-invariant pattern recognition. This is accomplished by redundantly coding elementary features in various positions at one level; then cascading groups of features to the next level; then groups of these groups; and so on. Learning can proceed with or without a teacher. Locally the computations are a type of competitive learning that use combinations of additive and shunting dynamics.

ART 2

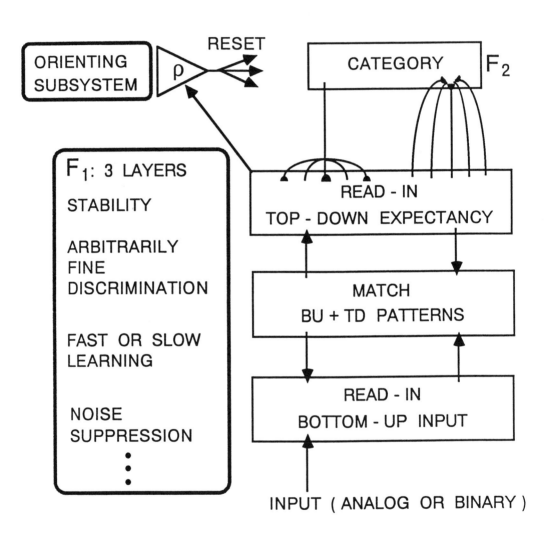

Figure 17. Principal elements of an ART 2 module for stable, self-organizing categorization of an arbitrary sequence of analog or binary input patterns. The F_1 level is a competitive network with three processing layers.

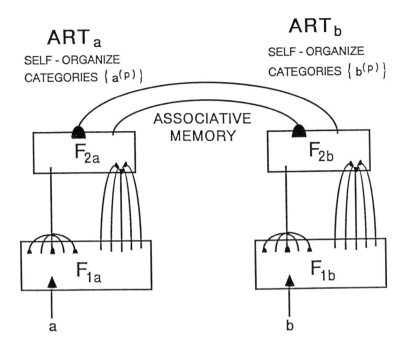

Figure 18. Two ART systems combined to form an associative memory architecture.

25. Simulated Annealing

Finally, in addition to the probabilistic weight change laws which were a prominent feature of, for example, the modeling efforts of pioneers such as Rosenblatt and Amari, another class of probabilistic weight change laws appears in more recent work under the name *simulated annealing*, introduced by S. Kirkpatrick, C.D. Gellatt, and H.P. Vecchi (1983). The main idea of simulated annealing is the transposition of a method from statistical mechanics, namely the Metropolis algorithm (Metropolis *et al.*, 1953), into the general context of large complex systems. The Metropolis algorithm provides an approximate description of a many-body system, namely a material that anneals into a solid as temperature is slowly decreased. Kirkpatrick *et al.* drew an analogy between this system and problems of combinatorial optimization, such as the traveling salesman problem, where the goal is to minimize a cost function. The methods and ideas, as well as the large scale nature of the problem, are so closely tied to those of neural networks that the two approaches are often linked. This link is perhaps closest in the Boltzmann machine (Ackley, Hinton, and Sejnowski, 1985), which uses a simulated annealing algorithm to update weights in a binary network similar to the additive model studied by Hopfield (1982).

26. Conclusion

We have seen how the adaptive filter formalism is general enough to describe a wide variety of neural network modules for associative memory, category learning, and pattern recognition. Many systems developed and applied in recent years are variations on one or more of these modular themes. This approach can thus provide a core vocabulary and grammar for further analysis of the rich and varied literature of the neural network field.

BIBLIOGRAPHY

Many of the articles cited above can be found in the collections listed below. In the References, the location of an article in one of these collections is indicated by the corresponding number in brackets.

A. Collections of Articles

[1] Amari, S.-I. and Arbib, M.A. (Eds.) (1982). **Competition and cooperation in neural nets.** Lecture Notes in Biomathematics, **45**, Berlin: Springer-Verlag.

[2] Anderson, J.A. and Rosenfeld, E. (Eds.) (1988). **Neurocomputing: Foundations of research.** Cambridge, MA: MIT Press.

[3] Carpenter, G.A. and Grossberg, S. (1987). *Applied Optics*, Special Issue on Neural Networks, **26**(23), December 1.

[4] Grossberg, S. (Ed.) (1981). **Mathematical psychology and psychophysiology.** Providence, RI: American Mathematical Society.

[5] Grossberg, S. (1982). **Studies of mind and brain: Neural principles of learning, perception, development, cognition, and motor control.** Boston: Reidel Press.

[6] Grossberg, S. (1988). **Neural networks and natural intelligence.** Cambridge, MA: MIT Press.

[7] McCulloch, W.S. (Ed.) (1965). **Embodiments of mind.** Cambridge, MA: MIT Press.

[8] Rumelhart, D., McClelland, J., and the PDP Research Group (1986). **Parallel distributed processing.** Cambridge, MA: MIT Press.

[9] Sanders, A.C. and Zeevi, Y.Y. (Eds.) (1983). *IEEE Transactions on Systems, Man, and Cybernetics*, Special Issue on Neural and Sensory Information Processing, **SMC-13(5)**, September/October.

[10] Shriver, B. (Ed.) (1988). *Computer*, Special Issue on Artificial Neural Systems, **21(3)**, March.

[11] Szu, H.H. (Ed.) (1987). **Optical and hybrid computing.** Bellingham, WA: The Society of Photo-Optical Instrumentation Engineers, SPIE–634.

B. Journals

[12] *Kybernetik* (1961–1974); *Biological Cybernetics* (1975–).

[13] *Neural Networks* (1988–).

C. Reviews

[14] Grossberg, S. (1988). Nonlinear neural networks: Principles, mechanisms, and architectures. *Neural Networks*, **1**, 17–61.

[15] Kohonen, T. (1987). Adaptive, associative, and self-organizing functions in neural computing. *Applied Optics*, **26**, 4910–4918. In [3].

[16] Levine, D. (1983). Neural population modeling and psychology: A review. *Mathematical Biosciences*, **66**, 1–86.

[17] Simpson, P.K. (1990). **Artificial neural systems: Foundations, paradigms, applications, and implementations.** Elmsford, NY: Pergamon Press.

REFERENCES

Ackley, D.H., Hinton, G.E., and Sejnowski, T.J. (1985). A learning algorithm for Boltzmann machines. *Cognitive Science*, **9**, 147–169. Reprinted in [2].

Amari, S.-I. (1972). Learning patterns and pattern sequences by self-organizing nets of threshold elements. *IEEE Transactions on Computers*, **C-21**, 1197–1206.

Amari, S.-I. (1977). Neural theory of association and concept-formation. *Biological Cybernetics*, **26**, 175–185.

Amari, S.-I. and Takeuchi, A. (1978). Mathematical theory on formation of category detecting nerve cells. *Biological Cybernetics*, **29**, 127–136.

Anderson, J.A. (1972). A simple neural network generating an interactive memory. *Mathematical Biosciences*, **14**, 197–220. Reprinted in [2].

Bienenstock, E., Cooper, L.N., and Munro, P.W. (1982). A theory for the development of neuron selectivity: Orientation specificity and binocular interaction in the visual cortex. *Journal of Neuroscience*, **2**, 32–48. Reprinted in [2].

Carpenter, G.A. and Grossberg, S. (1987a). A massively parallel architecure for a self-organizing neural pattern recognition machine. *Computer Vision, Graphics, and Image Processing*, **37**, 54–115. Reprinted in [6].

Carpenter, G.A. and Grossberg, S. (1987b). ART 2: Self-organization of stable category recognition codes for analog input patterns. *Applied Optics*, **26**, 4919–4930. In [3].

Fukushima, K. (1975). Cognitron: A self-organizing multilayered neural network. *Biological Cybernetics*, **20**, 121–136.

Fukushima, K. (1980). Neocognitron: A self-organizing neural network model for a mechanism of pattern recognition unaffected by shift in position. *Biological Cybernetics*, **36**, 193–202.

Fukushima, K. (1988). Neocognitron: A hierarchical neural network capable of visual pattern recognition. *Neural Networks*, **1**, 119–130.

Grossberg, S. (1964). **The theory of embedding fields with applications to psychology and neurophysiology**. New York: Rockefeller Institute for Medical Research.

Grossberg, S. (1968). Some nonlinear networks capable of learning a spatial pattern of arbitrary complexity. *Proceedings of the National Academy of Sciences USA*, **59**, 368–372.

Grossberg, S. (1969). Some networks that can learn, remember, and reproduce any number of complicated space-time patterns I. *Journal of Mathematics and Mechanics*, **19**, 53–91.

Grossberg, S. (1972a). Pattern learning by functional-differential neural networks with arbitrary path weights. In K. Schmitt (Ed.), **Delay and functional differential equations and their applications** (pp. 121–160). New York: Academic Press. Reprinted in [5].

Grossberg, S. (1972b). Neural expectation: Cerebellar and retinal analogs of cells fired by learnable or unlearned pattern classes. *Kybernetik*, **10**, 49–57. Reprinted in [5].

Grossberg, S. (1973). Contour enhancement, short-term memory, and constancies in reverberating neural networks. *Studies in Applied Mathematics*, **52**, 217–257. Reprinted in [5].

Grossberg, S. (1976a). On the development of feature detectors in the visual cortex with applications to learning and reaction-diffusion systems. *Biological Cybernetics*, **21**, 145–159.

Grossberg, S. (1976b). Adaptive pattern classification and universal recoding, I: Parallel development and coding of neural feature detectors. *Biological Cybernetics*, **23**, 121–134. Reprinted in [2] and [5].

Grossberg, S. (1976c). Adaptive pattern classification and universal recoding, II: Feedback, expectation, olfaction, and illusions. *Biological Cybernetics*, **23**, 187–202.

Grossberg, S. and Pepe, J. (1970). Schizophrenia: Possible dependence of associational span, bowing, and primacy vs. recency on spiking threshold. *Behavioral Science*, **15**, 359–362.

Hebb, D.O. (1949). **The organization of behavior**. New York: Wiley. Reprinted, in part, in [2].

Hecht-Nielsen, R. (1981). Neural analog information processing. *Proceedings of the Society of Photo-Optical Instrumentation Engineers*, **298**, 138–141.

Hecht-Nielsen, R. (1987). Counterpropagation networks. *Applied Optics*, **26**, 4979–4984. In [3].

Hodgkin, A.L. and Huxley, A.F. (1952). A quantitative description of membrane current and its application to conduction and excitation in nerve. *Journal of Physiology*, **117**, 500–544.

Hopfield, J.J. (1982). Neural networks and physical systems with emergent collective computational abilities. *Proceedings of the National Academy of Sciences USA*, **79**, 2554–2558.

Kirkpatrick, S., Gelatt, C.D. Jr., and Vecchi, M.P. (1983). Optimization by simulated annealing. *Science*, **220**, 671–680. Reprinted in [2].

Kohonen, T. (1972). Correlation matrix memories. *IEEE Transactions on Computers*, **C-21**, 353–359. Reprinted in [2].

Kohonen, T. (1980). **Content-addressable memories**. Berlin: Springer-Verlag.

Kohonen, T. (1984). **Self-organization and associative memory**. Berlin: Springer-Verlag.

Kohonen, T. and Ruohonen, M. (1973). Representation of associated data by matrix operators. *IEEE Transactions on Computers*, **C-22**, 701–702.

Metropolis, N., Rosenbluth, A.W., Rosenbluth, M.N., Teller, A.H. and Teller, E. (1953). Equations of state calculations by fast computing machines. *Journal of Chemical Physics*, **21**, 1087–1091.

McCulloch, W.S. and Pitts, W. (1943). A logical calculus of the ideas immanent in nervous activity. *Bulletin of Mathematical Biophysics*, **9**, 127–147. Reprinted in [2] and [7].

Nakano, N. (1972). Associatron: A model of associative memory. *IEEE Transactions on Systems, Man, and Cybernetics*, **SMC-2**, 381–388.

Parker, D. (1982). Learning logic. Invention report, S81-64, File 1, Office of Technology Licensing, Stanford University.

Pitts, W. and McCulloch, W.S. (1947). How we know universals: The perception of auditory and visual forms. *Bulletin of Mathematical Biophysics*, **9**, 127–147. Reprinted in [2] and [7].

Rosenblatt, F. (1958). The perceptron: A probabilistic model for information storage and organization in the brain. *Psychological Review*, **65**, 386–408. Reprinted in [2].

Rosenblatt, R. (1962). **Principles of neurodynamics**. Washington, DC: Spartan Books.

Rumelhart, D.E., Hinton, G.E., and Williams, R.J. (1986). Learning internal representations by error propagation. In D.E. Rumelhart and J.L. McClelland (Eds.), **Parallel distributed processing: Explorations in the microstructures of cognitions, I** (pp. 318–362). Cambridge, MA: MIT Press. In [8]. Reprinted in [2].

Rumelhart, D.E. and Zipser, D. (1985). Feature discovery by competitive learning. *Cognitive Science*, **9**, 75–112.

Russell, B. and Whitehead, A.N. (1910/1912/1913). **Principia mathematica I–III**. Cambridge: Cambridge University Press.

Steinbuch, K. (1961). Die Lernmatrix. *Kybernetik*, **1**, 36–45.

Steinbuch, K. and Widrow, B. (1965). A critical comparison of two kinds of adaptive classification networks. *IEEE Transactions on Electronic Computers*, **EC-14**, 737–740.

von der Malsburg, C. (1973). Self-organization of orientation sensitive cells in the striate cortex. *Kybernetik*, **14**, 85–100. Reprinted in [2].

von Neumann, J. (1958). **The computer and the brain**. New Haven: Yale University Press. Reprinted, in part, in [2].

Werbos, P.J. (1974). Beyond regression: New tools for prediction and analysis in the behavioral sciences. Ph.D. Thesis, Harvard University.

Werbos, P.J. (1988). Generalization of backpropagation with application to a recurrent gas market model. *Neural Networks*, **1**, 339–356.

Widrow, B. and Hoff, M.E. (1960). Adaptive switching circuits. 1960 IRE WESCON Convention Record, part 4, 96–104. Reprinted in [2].

Widrow, B. and Winter, R. (1988). Neural nets for adaptive filtering and adaptive pattern recognition. *Computer*, **21**, 25–39. In [10].

CHAPTER 2

NONLINEAR NEURAL NETWORKS:
PRINCIPLES, MECHANISMS, AND ARCHITECTURES
by
Stephen Grossberg

Preface

This 1988 article grew out of a tutorial lecture that was given in 1986 at an NSF-sponsored meeting on Neural Networks and Neuromorphic Systems. The chapter traces historical and conceptual linkages between neural network models of current interest. It begins with an historical analysis of how the nonlinear, nonstationary, and nonlocal nature of behavioral and brain data have helped to spawn many of the intellectual controversies over the past century that have been characteristic of experimental and theoretical approaches to understanding mind and brain. These controversies have continued to the present day as scientists from many different disciplines begin to use and further develop neural network models with many different goals in mind.

The article then provides a classification of several basic models of short term memory (STM) and long term memory (LTM), such as additive and shunting STM models and non-Hebbian LTM models. Models of global content-addressable memory, or CAM, are next classified as special cases of the Cohen-Grossberg model, which arose from a series of mathematical and computational analyses of additive and shunting models over a period of two decades. Key results that classify properties of nonlinear competitive feedback networks are then described and used to introduce models of competitive learning and self-organizing feature maps. Adaptive Resonance Theory, or ART, models for self-organization of pattern recognition codes are then compared and contrasted with supervised learning models such as the Boltzmann machine and back propagation.

Self-organizing models of adaptive sensory-motor control are next reviewed. Based on these results, recent research on designing self-organizing sensory-motor controllers has led to the discovery of a Vector Associative Map, or VAM, by Gaudiano and Grossberg (1991). The VAM is a class of models for unsupervised real-time error-based learning. As noted in this chapter, ART learning occurs in an *approximate match* mode. In contrast, VAM learning occurs in a *mismatch* mode. Many contemporary models that learn in a mismatch mode, such as those reviewed herein, need to do so in an off-line setting. This is not true of VAM models. Taken together, ART and VAM models provide a framework for designing stable real-time fast-learning systems that exploit both approximate-match learning and mismatch learning.

Reference

Gaudiano, P. and Grossberg, S. (1991). Vector associative maps: Unsupervised real-time error-based learning and control of movement trajectories. *Neural Networks*, in press.

Neural Networks
1988, **1**, 17–61
©1988 Pergamon Press, Inc.

"The foundations of science as a whole, and of physics in particular, await their next great elucidations from the side of biology, and especially from the analysis of the sensations ... psychological observation on the one side and physical observation on the other may make such progress that they will ultimately come into contact, and that in this way new facts may be brought to light. The result of this investigation will not be a dualism but rather a science which, embracing both the organic and the inorganic, shall interpret the facts that are common to the two departments." (Mach, 1914)

NONLINEAR NEURAL NETWORKS:
PRINCIPLES, MECHANISMS, AND ARCHITECTURES

Stephen Grossberg†

Abstract

An historical discussion is provided of the intellectual trends that caused 19th century interdisciplinary studies of physics and psychobiology by leading scientists such as Helmholtz, Maxwell, and Mach to splinter into separate 20th century scientific movements. The nonlinear, nonstationary, and nonlocal nature of behavioral and brain data are emphasized. Three sources of contemporary neural network research— the binary, linear, and continuous-nonlinear models—are noted. The remainder of the article describes results about continuous-nonlinear models: Many models of content-addressable memory are shown to be special cases of the Cohen-Grossberg model and global Liapunov function, including the additive, brain-state-in-a-box, McCulloch-Pitts, Boltzmann machine, Hartline-Ratliff-Miller, shunting, masking field, bidirectional associative memory, Volterra-Lotka, Gilpin-Ayala, and Eigen-Schuster models. A Liapunov functional method is described for proving global limit or oscillation theorems for nonlinear competitive systems when their decision schemes are globally consistent or inconsistent, respectively. The former case is illustrated by a model of

† Based upon a lecture given on October 7, 1986 at the NSF meeting on Neural Networks and Neuromorphic Systems, Woburn, Massachusetts. This work was supported in part by the Air Force Office of Scientific Research (AFOSR F49620-86-C-0037 and AFOSR F49620-87-C-0018) and the National Science Foundation (NSF IRI-84-17756). Thanks to Cynthia Suchta and Carol Yanakakis for their valuable assistance in the preparation of the manuscript and illustrations.

a globally stable economic market, and the latter case is illustrated by a model of the voting paradox. Key properties of shunting competitive feedback networks are summarized, including the role of sigmoid signalling, automatic gain control, competitive choice and quantization, tunable filtering, total activity normalization, and noise suppression in pattern transformation and memory storage applications. Connections to models of competitive learning, vector quantization, and categorical perception are noted. Adaptive resonance theory (ART) models for self-stabilizing adaptive pattern recognition in response to complex real-time nonstationary input environments are compared with off-line models such as autoassociators, the Boltzmann machine, and back propagation. Special attention is paid to the stability and capacity of these models, and to the role of top-down expectations and attentional processing in the active regulation of both learning and fast information processing. Models whose performance and learning are regulated by internal gating and matching signals, or by external environmentally generated error signals, are contrasted with models whose learning is regulated by external teacher signals that have no analog in natural real-time environments. Examples from sensory-motor control of adaptive vector encoders, adaptive coordinate transformations, adaptive gain control by visual error signals, and automatic generation of synchronous multijoint movement trajectories illustrate the former model types. Internal matching processes are shown capable of discovering several different types of invariant environmental properties. These include ART mechanisms which discover recognition invariants, adaptive vector encoder mechanisms which discover movement invariants, and autoreceptive associative mechanisms which discover invariants of self-regulating target position maps.

1. Introduction

The physical and mathematical theory of neural networks has been developing rapidly during the past twenty-five years. It is a theory whose diversity and complexity reflect the multifaceted organization of the brain processes that it sets out to explain. In this article, I will summarize some of the unifying principles, mechanisms, and mathematical methods that arise in this theory, as well as some of the specialized neural architectures which are important both in physical analyses of behavioral and brain data and in the development of novel technologies.

I will begin this article with some historical remarks that may clarify the complex and often confusing sociological milieu in which these exciting intellectual developments have been taking place.

2. Interdisciplinary Studies during the Nineteenth Century: Helmholtz, Maxwell, and Mach

Interdisciplinary studies flourished during the nineteenth century. In addition to pursuing their great work in physics, scientists such as Helmholtz, Maxwell, and Mach also made seminal contributions to psychology and neurobiology (Boring, 1950; Campbell and Garnett, 1882; Glazebrook, 1905; Koenigsberger, 1906; Ratliff, 1965). Their interests in the structure of physical space-time were balanced by a fascination with psychological space-time. Thus their contributions to understanding the observed world developed side-by-side their analysis of the observer.

For example, every physicist knows about the Mach numbers and about the influence of Mach's ideas upon Einstein's thinking during the development of relativity theory. Mach is also famous, however, for his investigations of the Mach bands in vision. Surprisingly few scientists have studied both types of contributions in school. In a similar way, every physicist knows about Maxwell's fundamental contributions to electromagnetic theory and to the molecular theory of gases. Maxwell is equally well known, however, for his work on developing trichromatic color theory.

Helmholtz's life is an inspiration to us all. Trained as an M.D., his experiments on the velocity of electrical signals in nerve axons led him to help discover the principle of conservation of energy, which is one of the cornerstones of nineteenth century physics. He made fundamental contributions to optics, which served as a foundation for his classical contributions to vision. His work in acoustics likewise supported his major contributions to hearing.

Thus during the last half of the nineteenth century, a number of great scientists functioned successfully in an interdisciplinary research mode and made lasting contributions to both the physical and psychobiological sciences.

3. The Schism between Physics and Psychology

It is often accepted as a truism that success breeds success, just as money makes money. Likewise, the great interdisciplinary successes of Helmholtz, Maxwell, and Mach might have been expected to breed droves of dedicated interdisciplinary disciples. This did not, however, occur. In the next generation of physicists, Einstein himself, in a letter to his friend Queen Elizabeth of Belgium in 1933, wrote: "Most of us prefer to look outside rather than inside ourselves; for in the latter case we see but a dark hole, which means: nothing at all" (Nathan and Norden, 1960, p. 567).

Thus a schism of major scientific importance occurred towards the end of the nineteenth century. Scientists whose work was previously greatly energized by interdisciplinary investigations of physics and psychology were rapidly replaced by scientists who rarely had even a rudimentary knowledge of the other field. Although the explosion of scientific knowledge during the twentieth century, with its attendant requirement to specialize, surely contributed to this schism, deeper intellectual factors exacerbated this schism. An understanding of these factors is useful for appreciating the scientific climate in which neural network research has been carried out during the past few decades.

4. The Nonlinear, Nonlocal, and Nonstationary Phenomena of Mind and Brain

Basic causes of this schism emerged from the scientific work of the very pioneers, such as Helmholtz, Maxwell, and Mach, whose interdisciplinary careers we have been considering. Two examples from Helmholtz's work on visual perception are illustrative.

A. Color Theory

In the classical Newtonian approach to color theory, white light is defined by an energy spectrum that is locally measurable at each point in space. In contrast, Helmholtz realized that, during visual perception, the average color of a whole scene tends to look white (Beck, 1972; Helmholtz, 1866/1962). Thus, instead of being reduceable to local measurements at each location, the analysis of how humans perceive white light at each location necessitates an investigation of long-range (or *nonlocal*) interactions across a network of locations. Such investigations disclosed the role of these interactions in "discounting the illuminant," or enabling humans and other species to detect the actual reflectances of visible surfaces under a wide variety of illumination conditions. In addition to being nonlocal, the network interactions which discount the illuminant, being sensitive to image reflectances, are also *nonlinear*. The neural processes whereby illuminants are discounted are still the subject of intensive experimental and theoretical investigation (Arend, Buehler, and Lockhead, 1971; Cornsweet, 1970; Hurvich, 1981; Land, 1977; Mollon and Sharpe, 1983) and only recently have a large number of paradoxical brightness and color phenomena been analysed in a unified way using a real-time neural network model (Cohen and Grossberg, 1984; Grossberg, 1987a, 1987b; Grossberg and Mingolla, 1985a, 1985b; Grossberg and Todorović, 1987).

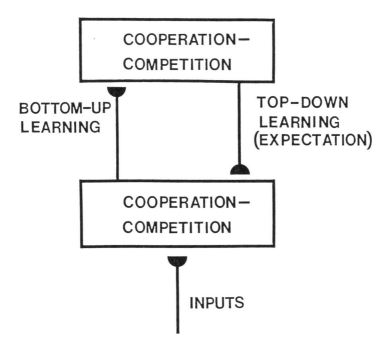

Figure 1. Bottom-up inputs and learned top-down expectations interact via a cooperative-competitive matching process until they generate an emergent consensus which represents the final, or resonant, percept.

B. Top-Down Learning, Expectation, and Matching

Helmholtz faced another barrier when he attempted to conceptualize the process of visual perception itself. His conception is known as the doctrine of *unconscious inference* (Boring, 1950). This doctrine held that a raw sensory datum, or perzeption, is modified by previous experience via a learned imaginal increment, or vorstellung, before it becomes a true perception, or anschauung. Thus Helmholtz realized that we perceive, in part, what we *expect* to perceive based upon past *learning*.

Helmholtz's doctrine can be recast in more modern terminology as follows (Figure 1). Bottom-up environmentally-activated input signals trigger the read-out of learned top-down expectations. These bottom-up and top-down data cooperate and compete through a matching process until they generate an emergent consensus which is the final percept. Such a cooperative-competitive network interaction also requires nonlinear and nonlocal interactions. In addition, the learning of top-down expectations requires a *nonstationary* process. Thus Helmholtz's experimental discoveries about visual perception led to the realization that theoretical understanding of these phenomena would require the discovery of appropriate nonlinear, nonlocal, and nonstationary mathematics, which are now being developed on multiple fronts.

In contrast, much of the mathematics available for physical theorizing during the nineteenth century was linear, local, and stationary mathematics. Thus the experimental discoveries about mind and brain by workers like Helmholtz, Maxwell, and Mach clarified that the available mathematics were not sufficient for supporting a sustained theoretical penetration of mind and brain mechanisms. Since theoretical scientists rely upon appropriate mathematical bread-and-butter techniques to express and develop their deepest intuitive ideas, the mismatch between psychological phenomena and nineteenth century mathematics created an intellectual crisis for all theorists who might have wished to study mind and brain.

This schism was exacerbated by the fact that the major revolutions of twentieth century physics could be supported by nineteenth century mathematics. For example, when Einstein finally realized that he needed a certain type of mathematics to express general relativity theory, his burden was significantly lightened by the fact that nineteenth century Riemannian geometry provided a perfect tool. As the early quantum mechanicians struggled towards expressing their intuitive insights using matrix theory and linear operator theory, they too were greatly aided by strong nineteenth century mathematical traditions.

A major approach-avoidance paradigm was hereby established in the practice of theoretical science. Theoretical physicists abandoned psychology and neurobiology to rapidly fashion theories about the external world that could be quantitatively supported by available mathematical concepts and methods. Psychologists and neurobiologists returned the favor by abandoning physical concepts and mathematics that seemed irrelevant to their data and, over time, by also eschewing and even denigrating theoretical and mathematical training in general. This bifurcation was already apparent during the unfolding of Helmholtz's scientific life. Beginning his career as an M.D., he ended it as the first President of the new Physico-technical Institute in Berlin (Koenigsberger, 1906).

5. The Nature of an Enduring Synthesis

Left without an appropriate framework of concepts and mathematical techniques for interpreting and unifying their experiments, psychologists and neurobiologists nonetheless went about accumulating one of the largest and most sophisticated sets of data bases in the history of science. Remarkably, they accomplished this feat during a century of controversy that was spawned by the unavailability of a unifying theoretical and mathematical framework for explaining their data. As Hilgard and Bower (1975) have noted in their important textbook about theories of learning "Psychology seems to be constantly in a state of ferment and change, if not of turmoil and revolution."

While most mind and brain experimentalists ignored theory and most theorists looked for more hospitable frontiers, there arose the widespread tendency to interpret brain function in terms of whatever technological development happened to be current. The ever-expanding list of technological metaphors to which the brain has been compared includes telegraph circuits, hydraulic systems, information processing channels, digital computers, linear control systems, catastrophies, holograms, and spin glasses. All of these metaphors have been unable to explain a substantial data base about brain and behavior, as well they might, since none of them arose from a sustained analysis of behavioral or brain data.

The schism between physics and psychology encouraged theorists trained in the physics tradition to believe that no theories of behavior and brain exist. An inquiry about available theories by an interested physicist more often than not would confirm this impression, because the schism has prevented most psychologists and neurobiologists from getting the training necessary to understand the theories that have begun to cope with the nonlinear, nonlocal, and nonstationary nature of behavioral and brain data. Thus the theories which hold the greatest promise have been the ones that have been most difficult to evaluate in the social climate spawned by the great schism.

We can recognize in this sociological milieu touches of irony when we acknowledge that a key scientific issue in understanding behavior and brain is to explain how humans rapidly and spontaneously adapt to noisy and complex environments whose rules may change unexpectedly, or in William James' engaging phrase: How do we cope with the "blooming buzzing confusion" of every day? It remains to be seen how the several scientific communities now converging with enthusiasm but vastly different training and goals upon the interdisciplinary study of mind and brain will assimilate the noisy and unexpected constraints imposed by each other's existence, notably by the fact that, despite the extra burden of difficult sociological conditions, relevant theories of mind and brain have been developing rapidly during the past few decades.

6. Sources of Neural Network Research: Binary, Linear, Continuous-Nonlinear

A. Binary

At least three sources of neural network research can be identified which have had a substantial influence on contemporary research. The streams of research generated by the sources have intersected in complex ways through the years and have tended to converge during the past several years. The present brief review merely sets the stage for the article's later discussions. Due to the sheer size and complexity of the neural network literature, this review must necessarily be selective. Other recent collections of classical and current neural network results include both articles (Carpenter and Grossberg, 1985; Grossberg, 1987e; Hecht-Nielsen, 1986; Hestenes, 1987; Levine, 1983; Szu, 1986) and books (Amari and Arbib, 1982; Denker, 1986; Grossberg, 1982a, 1987c, 1987d, 1988; Grossberg and Kuperstein, 1986; Hinton and Anderson, 1981; Kohonen, 1977, 1984; McClelland and Rumelhart, 1986; Rumelhart and McClelland, 1986).

Table 1 indicates several of the contributions that initiated or illustrate significant research developments. The stream of *binary* neural networks was initiated by the classical article of McCulloch and Pitts (1943). This article investigated threshold logic systems of the form

$$x_i(t+1) = \text{sgn}[\sum_j A_{ij} x_j(t) - B_j], \tag{1}$$

where $\text{sgn}(w) = +1$ if $w > 0$, 0 if $w = 0$, and -1 if $w < 0$. Such binary systems were inspired in part by neurophysiological observations showing that neural signals between many cells are carried by all-or-none spikes. The variables x_i in (1) are often called short term memory (STM) traces, or activations. Caianiello (1961) used a binary STM equation of the form

$$x_i(t+\tau) = 1[\sum_{j=1}^{n} \sum_{k=0}^{l(m)} A_{ij}^{(k)} x_j(t - k\tau) - B_i] \tag{2}$$

where $1(w) = 1$ if $w > 0$ and 0 if $w \leq 0$. Rosenblatt (1962) used an STM equation of the form

$$\frac{d}{dt} x_i = -A x_i + \sum_{j=1}^{n} \phi(B_j + x_j) C_{ij} \tag{3}$$

where $\phi(w) = 1$ if $w \geq \theta$ and 0 if $w < \theta$. Mueller, Martin, and Putzrath (1962) designed circuits which used the McCulloch-Pitts logical operations and also extended their analysis to analog circuits for applications to acoustic pattern recognition.

The binary, discrete-time approach to neural modelling was encouraged by the technical liberation which the use of oscilloscopes brought to neurophysiology. After years of heroic efforts to measure the tiny electrical signals in nerves, each spike could at last be easily amplified until it filled the whole oscilloscope screen. The all-or-none property of the individual spike was celebrated by making each spike much bigger than life. Although the oscilloscope provided a way for people to look at spikes, this representation did not necessarily correspond to what the cells which received the spikes were measuring. Cell body potentials may vary slowly and continuously

TABLE 1

Binary	Linear
McCulloch-Pitts (1943)	Anderson (1968)
Caianiello (1961)	Widrow (1962)
Rosenblatt (1962)	Kohonen (1971)

Continuous and Nonlinear

Ratliff-Hartline-Miller (1963)
Grossberg (1967, 1968)
Sperling-Sondhi (1968)
Wilson-Cowan (1972)

relative to the time scale of a single spike. Thus neurons may process the frequencies or other statistical properties of spike sequences through time. If, for example, the spiking activity of a visual cortical feature detector is amplified by a microphone instead of by an oscilloscope, and if an object to which the detector is sensitive is brought in and out of its receptive field, one hears a continuous waxing and waning of the sound of the cell's spike discharges through time. If the potentials of the cells receiving these spike sequences fluctuate slowly enough to average across clusters of spikes, then such cells will be better modelled by continuous than binary dynamics.

Both Caianiello (1961) and Rosenblatt (1962) also introduced equations to change the weights $A_{ij}^{(k)}$ in (2) and C_{ij} in (3) through learning. Such adaptive weights are often called long term memory (LTM) traces. Both workers decoupled the interactions between STM traces and LTM traces in order to partially analyse their nonlinear equations. These LTM equations also had a digital aspect. The equations of Caianiello (1961) increased or decreased at constant rates until they hit finite upper or lower bounds. Those of Rosenblatt (1962) were used to classify patterns into two distinct classes, as in the Perceptron Learning Theorem.

The historical importance of the binary McCulloch-Pitts (1943) model cannot be overestimated. For example, in addition to its seminal influence on neural modelling *per se*, it also was very much in the thoughts of von Neumann as he developed his ideas for the modern digital computer. In fact, a number of brain-inspired developments have found spin-offs over the years into other technologies.

B. Linear

Concepts from linear system theory have provided a classical source of models for representing some of the continuous aspects of neural dynamics. Solutions of simultaneous linear equations $Y = AX$ using matrix theory and concepts about cross-correlation have been among the useful tools.

Inspired by an interest in brain modelling, Widrow (1962) developed his classical gradient descent *Adaline* adaptive pattern recognition machine before using this background to make his major contributions to the theory of adaptive antennas. Anderson (1968) initially described his intuitions about neural pattern recognition using the spatial cross-correlation function

$$\phi_{12}(x,y) = \sum_{i=1}^{n} \sum_{j=1}^{n} f_1(i,j) f_2(i+x, j+y). \tag{4}$$

Kohonen (1971) made his transition from linear algebra concepts such as the Moore-Penrose pseudoinverse to more biologically motivated studies which he has summarized in his influential books (Kohonen, 1977, 1984). These workers thus began to develop their intuitions within a mathematically familiar engineering framework which was progressively developed to include more biologically motivated nonlinear interactions.

C. Continuous-Nonlinear

Continuous-nonlinear network laws typically arose from a direct analysis of behavioral or neural data. One distinguished modelling tradition can be traced directly to the influence of Mach (Ratliff, 1965). This tradition set out to model data taken from the lateral eye of the *Limulus*, or horseshoe crab, and led to the award of a Nobel prize to H.K. Hartline.

The basic model from this tradition is the steady state Hartline-Ratliff model

$$r_i = e_i - \sum_{j=1}^{n} k_{ij}[r_j - r_{ij}]^+ \tag{5}$$

where $[w]^+ = \max(w, 0)$. This model describes how cellular excitations e_i are transformed into net responses r_i due to inhibitory feedback interactions governed by threshold-linear signals $-k_{ij}[r_j - r_{ij}]^+$. Thus the Hartline-Ratliff model is a type of continuous threshold-logic system. Ratliff, Hartline, and Miller (1963) extended this steady-state model to a dynamical model of the form

$$r_i(t) = e_i(t) - \sum_{j=1}^{n} k_{ij} \left[\frac{1}{\tau} \int_0^t e^{-\frac{(t-s)}{\tau}} r_j(s) ds - r_{ij} \right]^+, \tag{6}$$

which also behaves linearly in the suprathreshold range. This model is a precursor of the additive model that is described below.

Another classical tradition arose from the analysis of how the excitable membrane of a single neuron can generate electrical spikes capable of rapidly and nondecrementally traversing the axon, or pathway, of the cell. The original experimental and modelling work on the squid giant axon by Hodgkin and Huxley (1952) also led to the award of a Nobel prize. Since this work focussed on individual cells rather than networks of cells, it will not be further discussed herein except to note that it provides the foundation for the shunting model that is described below. The Hodgkin-Huxley model and some of its variations are reviewed elsewhere (Carpenter, 1981; Hodgkin, 1964; Hodgson, 1983; Katz, 1966; Plonsey and Fleming, 1969; Ricciardi and Scott, 1982; Scott, 1977).

Another source of continuous-nonlinear network models arose through a study of adaptive behavior, rather than of neural mechanisms *per se*, in Grossberg (1964, 1967, 1968a, 1968b). Its primary concern was to understand how the behavior of individuals adapts stably in real-time to complex and changing environmental contingencies. In order to analyse adaptive behavior, it is necessary to characterize the functional level on which a system's behavioral success is defined and achieved, as well as the computational units that are manipulated by this level. This behavioral analysis led to the derivation of continuous neural networks defined by nonlinearly coupled STM and LTM traces, and to the mathematical proof that the computational units of these networks are not individual STM and LTM variables, but are rather distributed spatial patterns of STM and LTM variables (Grossberg, 1968b, 1969a, 1969b, 1970a). Thus neural networks describe a proper level for an analysis of adaptive behavior because the functional units which govern behavioral success are emergent properties due to interactions on the network level.

As in the tradition of binary models, this continuous-nonlinear approach defined laws for STM traces and LTM traces (Figure 2). The two primary versions of the STM equation which were introduced through this approach in the 1960's have been used in many subsequent applications and have received increasing experimental support.

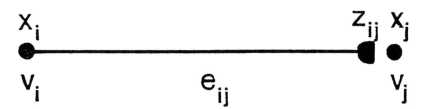

Figure 2. Short-term memory traces (or potentials) x_i at cell populations v_i emit signals along the directed pathways (or axons) e_{ij} which are gated by long-term memory traces z_{ij} before they can perturb their target cells v_j. (Reprinted with permission from Grossberg, 1987c.)

Additive STM Equation

$$\frac{d}{dt}x_i = -A_i x_i + \sum_{j=1}^{n} f_j(x_j)B_{ji}z_{ji}^{(+)} - \sum_{j=1}^{n} g_j(x_j)C_{ji}z_{ji}^{(-)} + I_i. \tag{7}$$

Equation (7) includes a term for passive decay $(-A_i x_i)$, positive feedback $(\sum_{j=1}^{n} f_j(x_j)B_{ji}z_{ji}^{(+)})$, negative feedback $(-\sum_{j=1}^{n} g_j(x_j)C_{ji}z_{ji}^{(-)})$, and input (I_i). Each feedback term includes a state-dependent nonlinear signal $(f_j(x_j), g_j(x_j))$, a connection, or path, strength (B_{ji}, C_{ji}), and an LTM trace $(z_{ji}^{(+)}, z_{ji}^{(-)})$. If the positive and negative feedback terms are lumped together and the connection strengths are lumped with the LTM traces, then the additive model may be written in the simpler form

$$\frac{d}{dt}x_i = -A_i x_i + \sum_{j=1}^{n} f_j(x_j)z_{ji} + I_i. \tag{8}$$

Early applications of the additive model included computational analyses in vision, associative pattern learning, pattern recognition, classical and instrumental conditioning, and the learning of temporal order in applications to speech and language behavior and to planned sensory-motor control (Grossberg, 1969a, 1969b, 1969c, 1970a, 1970b, 1971a, 1972a, 1972b, 1974; Grossberg and Pepe, 1971). The additive model has continued to be a cornerstone of neural network research to the present day; see, for example, Amari and Arbib (1982) and Grossberg (1982a). Some physicists unfamiliar with the classical status of the additive model in neural network theory erroneously called it the Hopfield model after they became acquainted with Hopfield's first application of the additive model in Hopfield (1984); see Section 9A. The classical McCulloch-Pitts (1943) model in equation (1) has also erroneously been called the Hopfield model by some physicists who became acquainted with the McCulloch-Pitts model in Hopfield (1982). These historical errors can ultimately be traced to the schism between physics and psychology that was described in Section 3. As new practitioners of neural networks have learned the well-documented history of the field, these errors have gradually been corrected.

A related behaviorally derived STM equation (Grossberg, 1968a) more adequately incorporates the shunting dynamics of individual neurons into a neural network formalism (Hodgkin, 1964; Kandel and Schwartz, 1981; Katz, 1966; Plonsey and Fleming, 1969). In such a shunting equation, each STM trace is restricted to a bounded interval $[-D_i, B_i]$ and automatic gain control, instantiated by multiplicative shunting terms, interacts with balanced positive and negative feedback signals and inputs to maintain the sensitivity of each STM trace within its interval (see Section 15).

Shunting STM Equation

$$\frac{d}{dt}x_i = -A_i x_i + (B_i - x_i)[\sum_{j=1}^{n} f_j(x_j)C_{ji}z_{ji}^{(+)} + I_i]$$
$$- (x_i + D_i)[\sum_{j=1}^{n} g_j(x_j)E_{ji}z_{ji}^{(-)} + J_i]. \tag{9}$$

Several LTM equations have been useful in applications. Two particularly useful variations have been:

Passive Decay LTM Equation

$$\frac{d}{dt}z_{ij} = -F_{ij}z_{ij} + G_{ij}f_i(x_i)h_j(x_j) \tag{10}$$

and

Gated Decay LTM Equation

$$\frac{d}{dt}z_{ij} = h_j(x_j)[-F_{ij}z_{ij} + G_{ij}f_i(x_i)]. \tag{11}$$

In both equations, a nonlinear learning term $f_i(x_i)h_j(x_j)$, often called a Hebbian term after Hebb (1949), is balanced by a memory decay term. In (10), memory decays passively at a constant rate $-F_{ij}$. In (11), memory decay is gated on and off by one of the nonlinear signals. A key property of both equations is that the size of an LTM trace z_{ij} can either increase or decrease due to learning. Neurophysiological support for an LTM equation of the form (11) has recently been reported (Levy, 1985; Levy, Brassel, and Moore, 1983; Levy and Desmond, 1985; Rauschecker and Singer, 1979; Singer, 1983). Extensive computational analyses of these STM and LTM equations in a number of specialized circuits led gradually to the identification of a general class of networks for which one could prove invariant properties of associative spatio-temporal pattern learning and recognition (Grossberg, 1969a, 1971b, 1972c, 1982).

Sperling and Sondhi (1968) utilized a shunting STM equation in an important contribution to visual psychophysics. Wilson and Cowan (1972) introduced a modified shunting STM equation of the form

$$\frac{d}{dt}x_i = -A_i x_i + (B_i - x_i)f_i(\sum_{j=1}^{n} x_j C_{ji}) \tag{12}$$

which replaces the sum $\sum_{j=1}^{n} f_j(x_j)C_{ji}z_{ji}^{(+)}$ of nonlinear signals in (9) with a nonlinear function of the sum. Equation (12) possesses one automatic gain control term $(B_i - x_i)$, whereas (9) possesses two. Consequently the dynamics of (12) saturate in many situations where the dynamics of (9) remain sensitive to input fluctuations (see Section 15).

7. Nonlinear Feedback between Fast Distributed STM Processing and Slow Associative LTM Processing

These dynamical equations incorporate two general types of nonlinear processes which explicate some of the themes that were already touched upon in Helmholtz's work. On the one hand, there are the cooperative-competitive nonlinear feedback processes which operate on a relatively fast time scale. These processes instantiate the distributed information processing and STM storage capabilities of the network. They can, for example, carry out matching of bottom-up data with top-down expectations (Figure 1) to generate the perceptual consensus discussed by Helmholtz.

Interacting with these fast STM interactions via nonlinear feedback are the more slowly varying LTM processes which instantiate associative learning. Such a learning process can, for example, adaptively tune the bottom-up filters and encode the learned top-down expectations (Figure 1) that were adumbrated in Helmholtz's concept of unconscious inference.

8. Principles, Mechanisms, and Architectures

Such STM and LTM equations were discovered through the analysis of two mutually supportive, but complementary, types of results.

On the one hand, a small number of general design principles and their mechanistic instantiations were discovered through a comparative analysis of several interdisciplinary data bases. For example, the functional importance of the shunting STM equation (9) became clear through analyses of data about perception, conditioning, and cognitive information processing. Such analyses led to the realization that a single type of network was needed that was capable of ratio processing, conservation or normalization of total activation (limited capacity), Weber law modulation, adaptation level processing, noise suppression, contrast enhancement, short term memory storage, energetic amplification of matched input patterns, and energetic suppression of mismatched input patterns. The discovery that these multiple constraints are all satisfied by a ubiquitous type of on-center off-surround network of cells which obey the membrane equations of neurophysiology created an irresistable intellectual pressure to study them exhaustively (see Sections 9F and 13–15).

In addition to such general laws, a growing number of specialized architectures have also been developed. Each architecture is a synthesis of several types of design principles and mechanisms in a carefully crafted circuit. The organization of the brain into functionally distinctive regions—such as cerebellum, hippocampus, retina, visual cortex, parietal cortex, frontal cortex, hypothalamus, septum, amygdala, and reticular formation—illustrates why a considerable number of specialized architectures need to be developed.

Due to the highly interactive nature of brain dynamics, the development of general organizational principles, mechanisms, and specialized architectures have proceeded hand-in-hand, each bootstrapping the scientific understanding of the others. Here is a research area where it is essential to keep the forest, the trees, and the individual branches simultaneously in view. In the remainder of the article, I will summarize several of the principles, mechanisms, and architectures whose further development is still engaging the efforts of many scientists.

9. Content-Addressable Memory Storage: A General STM Model and Liapunov Method

From a mathematical perspective, the question of content-addressable memory (CAM) in a neural network can be formulated as follows: Under what conditions does a neural network always approach an equilibrium point in response to an arbitrary, but sustained, input pattern? The equilibrium point represents the stored pattern in response to the input pattern. In a satisfactory analysis of this problem, the behavior of the network in response to arbitrary initial data, an arbitrary sustained input pattern, and an arbitrary choice of network parameters is provided. Also an account of how many equilibrium points exist and of how they are approached through time is desirable. Such a mathematical analysis is called a global analysis, to distinguish it from a local stability analysis around individual equilibrium points.

Amari and Arbib (1982) and Levine (1983) include a number of contributions to the local analysis of neural networks. Our concern herein is with global methods. A global analysis of equilibrium behavior is of importance for an understanding both of CAM and of the types of nonequilibrium behavior—such as travelling waves, bursts, standing waves, and chaos—which can be obtained by perturbing off systems which always approach equilibrium (Carpenter, 1977a, 1977b, 1979, 1981; Cohen and Grossberg, 1983; Ellias and Grossberg, 1975; Ermentrout and Cowan, 1979, 1980; Hastings, 1976, 1982; Hodgson, 1983; Kaczmarek and Babloyantz, 1977). A global mathematical analysis of nonlinear associative learning networks was begun in Grossberg (1967, 1968b). A global mathematical analysis of nonlinear shunting cooperative-competitive feedback networks was begun in Grossberg (1973). Some of the main articles in these series are brought together in Grossberg (1982a).

One approach to the global approach to equilibrium which has attracted widespread interest is the use of global Liapunov, or energy, methods. Such global methods were introduced for the analysis of neural networks in the 1970's (see Section 11). First I summarize a general model of a nonlinear cooperative-competitive neural network for which a global Liapunov function has been explicitly constructed. I then show that a number of popular models are special cases of the general model, and thus are capable of CAM. This general model was first announced in Grossberg (1982b, Section 18; reprinted in Grossberg, 1987c, Chapter 9), where its development to include the additive and shunting models summarized below was noted. The model was systematically analysed in Cohen and Grossberg (1983).

Cohen and Grossberg (1983) described a general principle for designing CAM networks by proving that models that can be written in the form

$$\frac{d}{dt}x_i = a_i(x_i)[b_i(x_i) - \sum_{j=1}^{n} c_{ij}d_j(x_j)] \tag{13}$$

admit the global Liapunov function

$$V = -\sum_{i=1}^{n} \int^{x_i} b_i(\xi_i)d_i'(\xi_i)d\xi_i + \frac{1}{2}\sum_{j,k=1}^{n} c_{jk}d_j(x_j)d_k(x_k) \tag{14}$$

if the coefficient matrix $C = \| c_{ij} \|$ and the functions a_i, b_i, and d_j obey mild technical conditions, including

Symmetry:
$$c_{ij} = c_{ji}, \tag{15}$$

Positivity:
$$a_i(x_i) \geq 0 \tag{16}$$

Monotonicity:
$$d_j'(x_j) \geq 0. \tag{17}$$

Integrating V along trajectories implies that

$$\frac{d}{dt}V = -\sum_{i=1}^{n} a_i d_i'[b_i - \sum_{j=1}^{n} c_{ij}d_j]^2. \tag{18}$$

If (16) and (17) hold, then $\frac{d}{dt}V \leq 0$ along trajectories. Once this basic property of a Liapunov function is in place, it is a technical matter to rigorously prove that every trajectory approaches one of a possibly large number of equilibrium points.

For expository vividness, the functions in the Cohen-Grossberg model (13) are called the *amplification* function a_i, the *self-signal* function b_i, and the *other-signal* functions d_j. Specialized models are characterized by particular choices of these functions.

A. Additive STM Equation

Cohen and Grossberg (1983, p.819) noted that "the simpler additive neural networks ... are also included in our analysis". The additive equation (8) can be written using the coefficients of the standard electrical circuit interpretation (Plonsey and Fleming, 1969) as

$$C_i \frac{dx_i}{dt} = -\frac{1}{R_i}x_i + \sum_{j=1}^{n} f_j(x_j)z_{ji} + I_i. \tag{19}$$

Substitution into (13) shows that

$$a_i(x_i) = \frac{1}{C_i} \quad \text{(constant!)} \tag{20}$$

$$b_i(x_i) = \frac{1}{R_i}x_i + I_i \quad \text{(linear!)} \tag{21}$$

$$c_{ij} = -T_{ij} \tag{22}$$

and

$$d_j(x_j) = f_j(x_j). \tag{23}$$

Thus in the additive case, the amplification function (20) is a positive constant, hence satisfies (16), and the self-signal term (21) is linear. Substitution of (20)–(23) into (14) leads directly to the equation

$$V = \sum_{i=1}^{n} \frac{1}{R_i} \int^{x_i} \xi_i f_i'(\xi_i)d\xi_i - \sum_{i=1}^{n} I_i f_i(x_i) - \frac{1}{2} \sum_{j,k=1}^{n} T_{jk} f_j(x_j)f_k(x_k). \tag{24}$$

This Liapunov function for the additive model was later published by Hopfield (1984). In Hopfield's treatment, ξ_i is written as an inverse $f_i^{-1}(V_i)$. Cohen and Grossberg (1983) showed, however, that although $f_i(x_i)$ must be nondecreasing, as in (17), it need not have an inverse in order for (24) to be valid.

B. Brain-State-in-a-Box Model: $S\sum$ Exchange

The BSB model was introduced in Anderson, Silverstein, Ritz, and Jones (1977). It is often described in discrete time by the equation

$$x_i(t+1) = S(x_i(t) + \alpha \sum_{j=1}^{n} A_{ij}x_j(t)) \tag{25}$$

using symmetric coefficients

$$A_{ij} = A_{ji} \tag{26}$$

and a special type of nonlinear signal function $S(w)$ that characterizes the model. The signal function is a symmetric ramp function:

$$S(w) = \begin{cases} F & \text{if } w \geq F \\ w & \text{if } -F < w < F \\ -F & \text{if } w \leq -F \end{cases} \tag{27}$$

Thus each STM trace x_i obeys a *linear* equation until its argument reaches the *hard saturation* limit F.

The BSB model has been used to discuss categorical perception in terms of its formal contrast enhancement property that each x_i tends to approach a limiting value $\pm F$, and thus that the vector $(x_1, x_2, \ldots, x_n)$ tends to approach a corner of the box $(\pm F, \pm F, \ldots, \pm F)$ as time goes on. An alternative explanation of contrast enhancement by a nonlinear feedback network was provided in Grossberg (1973) using a sigmoid signal function, rather than a function linear near zero, coupled to the soft saturation dynamics of a shunting network, rather than the hard saturation of a symmetric ramp (see Section 15). This is still a topic undergoing theoretical discussion (Anderson, Silverstein, Ritz, and Jones, 1977; Grossberg, 1978b, 1987d).

The BSB model can be rewritten as an additive model with no input and a special signal function that satisfies (17). Hence it is a special case of model (13). To see this, rewrite (25) in the form

$$x_i(t+1) = S(\sum_{j=1}^{n} B_{ij} x_j(t)) \tag{28}$$

using the coefficient

$$B_{ij} = \delta_{ij} + \alpha A_{ij} \tag{29}$$

where $\delta_{ij} = 1$ if $i = j$ and 0 if $i \neq j$. By (26), it follows that

$$B_{ij} = B_{ji}. \tag{30}$$

Although (28) is written in discrete time for computational convenience, it needs to be expressed in continuous time in order to represent a physical model, as in

$$\frac{d}{dt} x_i = -x_i + S(\sum_{j=1}^{n} B_{ij} x_j). \tag{31}$$

Define the new variables y_i by

$$y_i = \sum_{j=1}^{n} B_{ij} x_j. \tag{32}$$

Then

$$\frac{d}{dt} y_i = -y_i + \sum_{j=1}^{n} B_{ij} S(y_j). \tag{33}$$

Comparison of (33) with (19) shows that the BSB model is an additive model such that each $I_i = 0$. Because this simple change of coordinates is so important in neural modelling, I give it a name: $S \sum$ *Exchange*.

The observation that, via $S \sum$ Exchange, a nonlinear signal of a sum, as in (31), can be rewritten as a sum of nonlinear signals, as in (33), shows that a number of models which have been treated as distinct are, in reality, mathematically identical. In contrast, this type of transformation cannot be carried out on shunting models such as (9) and (12).

The Liapunov function for (33) is found by directly substituting into model (13) expressed in terms of the variables y_i:

$$\frac{d}{dt} y_i = a_i(y_i)[b_i(y_i) - \sum_{j=1}^{n} c_{ij} d_j(y_j)]. \tag{34}$$

Since $a_i(y_i) = 1$, $b_i(y_i) = -y_i$, $c_{ij} = -B_{ij}$, and $d_j(y_j) = S(y_j)$, substitution into (14) yields

$$V = \sum_{i=1}^{n} \int^{y_i} \xi_i S'(\xi_i) d\xi_i - \frac{1}{2} \sum_{k=1}^{n} B_{jk} S(y_j) S(y_k). \qquad (35)$$

Using the definitions in (27), (29), and (32), (35) can be rewritten in terms of the original variables x_i as follows:

$$V = -\frac{\alpha}{2} \sum_{j,k=1}^{n} A_{jk} x_j x_k. \qquad (36)$$

Golden (1986) has derived (36) from a direct analysis of the BSB model.

C. The McCulloch-Pitts Model

This classical model takes the form

$$x_i(t+1) = \text{sgn}(\sum_{j=1}^{n} A_{ij} x_j(t) - B_i). \qquad (1)$$

Letting

$$M(w) = \text{sgn}(w - B_i), \qquad (37)$$

(1) can be rewritten as

$$x_i(t+1) = M(\sum_{j=1}^{n} A_{ij} x_j(t)). \qquad (38)$$

As in the analysis of (31), (38) can be rewritten in continuous time in terms of the variables y_i via $S\sum$ Exchange:

$$\frac{d}{dt} y_i = -y_i + \sum_{j=1}^{n} A_{ij} M(y_j) \qquad (39)$$

and is thus also a symmetric additive model with zero inputs. In addition, its signal function $M(y_j)$ has a zero derivative $(M'(y_j) = 0)$ except at $y_j = 0$. Substitution of this additional property into (35) shows that the Liapunov function for the continuous time McCulloch-Pitts model is

$$V = -\frac{1}{2} \sum_{j,k=1}^{n} A_{jk} M(y_j) M(y_k), \qquad (40)$$

which is the continuous time version of the discrete time Liapunov function described by Hopfield (1982).

D. The Boltzmann Machine

The STM equation of the Boltzmann machine (Ackley, Hinton, and Sejnowski, 1985) has the same form as (31) and (38), and is thus also an additive equation with symmetric coefficients. Its signal function is the sigmoid logistic function

$$f(w) = \frac{1}{1 + e^{-w}}, \qquad (41)$$

which satisfies (17) and is thus a special case of model (13). Thus the Boltzmann machine is a specialized additive model regulated by simulated annealing as developed by Geman (1983, 1984), Geman and Geman (1984), and Kirkpatrick, Gelatt, and Vecchi (1982, 1983).

E. The Hartline-Ratliff-Miller Model

The $S \sum$ Exchange is not the only change of variables whereby CAM models can be transformed into an additive model format. For example, the STM equation (6) of the classical Hartline-Ratliff-Miller model is transformed into an additive model under an exponential change of variables

$$x_i(t) = \int_0^t e^{-\frac{(t-s)}{\tau}} r_j(s) ds. \tag{42}$$

Then (6) becomes

$$\frac{d}{dt} x_i = -\frac{1}{\tau} x_i - \sum_{j=1}^n [\frac{1}{\tau} x_j - r_{ij}]^+ k_{ij} + e_i. \tag{43}$$

F. Shunting Cooperative-Competitive Feedback Network

All additive models lead to constant amplification functions $a_i(x_i)$ and linear self-feedback functions $b_i(x_i)$. The need for the more general model (13) becomes apparent when the shunting STM equation (9) is analysed. Consider, for example, a class of shunting models in which each node can receive excitatory and inhibitory inputs I_i and J_i, respectively, and each node can excite itself and can inhibit other nodes via nonlinear feedback. Such networks model on-center off-surround interactions among cells which obey membrane equations (Grossberg, 1973; Hodgkin, 1964; Kandel and Schwartz, 1981; Katz, 1966; Plonsey and Fleming, 1969). In particular, let

$$\frac{d}{dt} x_i = -A_i x_i + (B_i - x_i)[I_i + f_i(x_i)] - (x_i + C_i)[J_i + \sum_{j=1}^n D_{ij} g_j(x_j)]. \tag{44}$$

In (44), each x_i can fluctuate within the finite interval $[-C_i, B_i]$ in response to the constant inputs I_i and J_i, the state-dependent positive feedback signal $f_i(x_i)$, and the negative feedback signals $D_{ij} g_j(x_j)$. It is assumed that

$$D_{ij} = D_{ji} \geq 0 \tag{45}$$

and that

$$g_j'(x_j) \geq 0. \tag{46}$$

In order to write (41) in Cohen-Grossberg form, it is convenient to introduce the variables

$$y_i = x_i + C_i. \tag{47}$$

In applications, C_i is typically nonnegative. Since x_i can vary within the interval $[-C_i, B_i]$, y_i can vary within the interval $[0, B_i + C_i]$ of nonnegative numbers. In terms of these variables, (44) can be written in the form

$$\frac{d}{dt} y_i = a_i(y_i)[b_i(y_i) - \sum_{j=1}^n C_{ij} d_j(y_j)] \tag{34}$$

where

$$a_i(y_i) = y_i \quad \text{(nonconstant!)}, \tag{48}$$

$$b_i(y_i) = \frac{1}{x_i}[A_i C_i - (A_i + J_i) x_i + (B_i + C_i - x_i)(I_i + f_i(x_i - C_i))] \quad \text{(nonlinear!)}, \tag{49}$$

$$C_{ij} = D_{ij}, \tag{50}$$

and

$$d_j(y_j) = g_j(y_j - C_j) \quad \text{(noninvertible!)}. \tag{51}$$

Unlike the additive model, the amplification function $a_i(y_i)$ in (48) is not a constant. In addition, the self-signal function $b_i(y_i)$ in (49) is not necessarily linear, notably because the feedback signal $f_i(x_i - C_i)$ is often nonlinear in applications of the shunting model; in particular it is often a sigmoid or multiple sigmoid signal function (Ellias and Grossberg, 1975; Grossberg, 1973, 1977, 1978c; Grossberg and Levine, 1975; Sperling, 1981). Sigmoid signal functions, and approximations thereto, also appear in applications of the additive model and its variants (Ackney, Hinton, and Sejnowski, 1985; Amari and Arbib, 1982; Freeman, 1975, 1979; Grossberg, 1969a, 1982a; Grossberg and Kuperstein, 1986; Hinton and Anderson, 1981; Hopfield, 1984; Rumelhart and McClelland, 1986). Such applications do not require the full generality of the Liapunov function (13) because the nonlinear signal function can then be absorbed into the terms $d_j(x_j)$.

Property (16) follows from the fact that $a_i(y_i) = y_i \geq 0$. Property (17) follows from the assumption that the negative feedback signal function g_j is monotone nondecreasing. Cohen and Grossberg (1983) proved that g_j need not be invertible. A signal threshold may exist below which $g_j = 0$ and above which g_j may grow in a nonlinear way. The inclusion of nonlinear signals with thresholds better enables the model to deal with fluctuations due to subthreshold noise. On the other hand, thresholds are not the only mechanisms which can suppress noise in a cooperative-competitive feedback network. (See Section 15D.)

G. Masking Field Model

In many applications of the shunting and additive models, the coefficients c_{ij} in (13) may be asymmetric, thereby rendering the Liapunov function (14) inapplicable. Asymmetric coefficients typically occur in problems relating to the learning and recognition of temporal order in behavior. Consequently, a number of mathematical methods were developed from the earliest days of the continuous-nonlinear approach to analyse models with asymmetric interaction coefficients.

On the other hand, certain network models may have asymmetric interaction coefficients, yet be reduceable to the form (13) with symmetric interaction coefficients through a suitable change of variables. The masking field model is a shunting network of this type. The masking field model was introduced in Grossberg (1978a; reprinted in Grossberg, 1982a) to explain data about speech learning, word recognition, and the learning of adaptive sensory-motor plans. It has been further developed through computer simulations in Cohen and Grossberg (1986, 1987). A masking field is a multiple-scale, self-similar, automatically gain controlled, cooperative-competitive nonlinear feedback network (Figure 3) which can generate a compressed but distributed STM representation of an input pattern as a whole, of its most salient parts, and of predictive codes which represent larger input patterns of which it forms a part. The masking field model is thus a specialized type of vector quantization scheme (Gray, 1984). Its multiple-scale self-similar properties imply its asymmetric interaction coefficients.

The STM equation of a typical masking field is defined by

$$\frac{d}{dt} x_i^{(J)} = -A x_i^{(J)} + (B - x_i^{(J)})[\sum_{j \in J} E_j p_{ji}^{(J)} + D \mid J \mid f(x_i^{(J)})]$$

$$- (x_i^{(J)} + C) \frac{\sum_{m,K} g(x_m^{(K)}) \mid K \mid (1 + \mid K \cap J \mid)}{\sum_{m,K} \mid K \mid (1 + \mid K \cap J \mid)}. \tag{52}$$

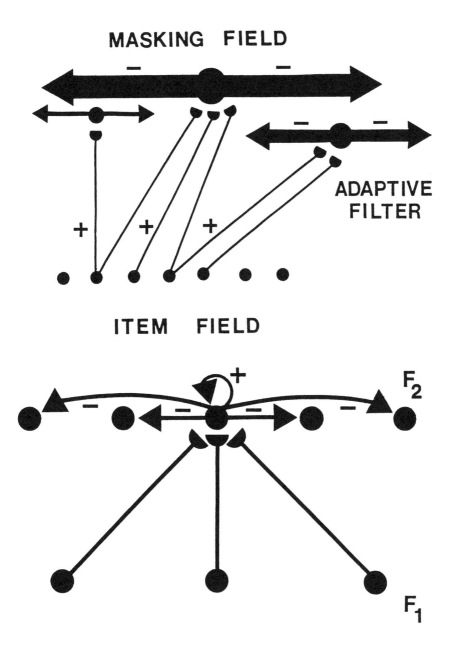

Figure 3. Masking field interactions: (a) Cells from an item field F_1 grow randomly to a masking field F_2 along positionally sensitive gradients. The nodes in the masking field grow so that larger item groupings, up to some optimal size, can activate nodes with broader and stronger inhibitory interactions. Thus the $F_1 \to F_2$ connections and the $F_2 \leftrightarrow F_2$ interactions exhibit properties of self-similarity. (b) The interactions within a masking field F_2 include positive feedback from a node to itself and negative feedback from a node to its neighbors. Long term memory (LTM) traces at the ends of $F_1 \to F_2$ pathways (designated by hemidisks) adaptively tune the filter defined by these pathways to amplify the F_2 reaction to item groupings which have previously succeeded in activating their target F_2 nodes. (Reprinted with permission from Cohen and Grossberg, 1987.)

In (52), $x_i^{(J)}$ is the STM trace of the ith masking field node that receives excitatory input $\sum_{j \in J} E_j p_{ji}^{(J)}$ from the unordered set J of input items. Notation $|J|$ counts the number of items in set J and thereby keeps track of the number of spatial scales that go into each version of the model.

The inhibitory interaction coefficient

$$\frac{|K|(1+|K \cap J|)}{\sum_{m,K} |K|(1+|K \cap J|)} \tag{53}$$

in (52) is an asymmetric function of J and K. Despite this fact, (52) can be written in Cohen-Grossberg form as

$$\frac{d}{dt} y_i^{(J)} = a_i^{(J)}(y_i^{(J)})[b_i^{(J)}(y_i^{(J)}) - \sum_{m,K} c_{JK} d^{(K)}(y_m^{(K)})] \tag{54}$$

with symmetric coefficients

$$c_{JK} = c_{KJ} = 1 + |K \cap J| \tag{55}$$

in terms of the variables

$$y_i^{(J)} = F_{|J|}^{-1}(x_i^{(J)} + C) \tag{56}$$

where

$$F_{|J|} = \sum_{m,K} |K|(1+|K \cap J|). \tag{57}$$

This is seen as follows. Since $F_{|J|}$ is the denominator of (53), it can be used to divide term $x_i^{(J)} + C$ in (52). Then the asymmetric term $|K|$ in the numerator of (53) can be absorbed into the definition of g in (54). Then by redefining and rearranging terms as in (47)–(51), equation (54) holds with

$$a_i^{(J)}(y_i^{(J)}) = F_{|J|}^{-1} y_i^{(J)} \tag{58}$$

$$b_i^{(J)}(y_i^{(J)}) = \frac{1}{y_i^{(J)}} [AC - AF_{|J|} y_i^{(J)} + \left(\frac{B+C}{F_{|J|}} - y_i^{(J)}\right)$$
$$(I_i^{(J)} + D|J|F^{|J|} f(F^{|J|} y_i^{(J)} - C))] \tag{59}$$

where

$$I_i^{(J)} = F^{|J|} \sum_{j \in J} E_j p_{ji}^{(J)}, \tag{60}$$

and

$$d^{(K)}(y_m^{(K)}) = |K| g(F^{|K|} y_m^{(K)} - C). \tag{61}$$

Thus the masking field model is a specialized Cohen-Grossberg model.

H. Bidirectional Associative Memories: Symmetrizing an Asymmetric Interaction Matrix

Other procedures have also been devised for dealing with systems having asymmetric coefficients. For example, given an arbitrary $n \times m$ coefficient matrix $Z = \|z_{ij}\|$ from a network level F_1 to a network level F_2 with STM traces x_i and y_j, respectively.

Kosko and Guest (1987) and Kosko (1987) have shown that (13) and (14) can be used to construct feedback pathways from F_2 to F_1 so that the two-level feedback network $F_1 \leftrightarrow F_2$ has convergent trajectories.

For example, if the bottom-up interaction $F_1 \rightarrow F_2$ obeys an additive equation

$$\frac{d}{dt}y_j = -A_j y_j + \sum_k f_k(x_k) z_{kj} + I_j, \tag{62}$$

then the top-down interaction $F_2 \rightarrow F_1$ is defined to obey an additive equation

$$\frac{d}{dt}x_i = -B_i x_i + \sum_l g_l(y_l) z_{il} + J_i, \tag{63}$$

where I_j and J_i are input terms. This definition creates a symmetric interaction matrix by closing the top-down feedback loop, since if $f_i(x_i)$ influences y_j with coefficient z_{ij} in (62), then $g_j(y_j)$ influences x_i with the same coefficient z_{ij}. Thus by defining an augmented vector $(x_1, x_2, \ldots, x_n, y_1, y_2, \ldots, y_m)$ of STM activities, system (62)–(63) as a whole defines an additive model (19) with an $(n+m) \times (n+m)$ symmetric coefficient matrix.

The same procedure can be used to symmetrize many other neural network models. Kosko and Guest (1987) have described optical implementations for this procedure, and Kosko (1987) has used the symmetrized additive model to discuss minimization of fuzzy entropy.

I. Volterra-Lotka, Gilpin-Ayala, and Eigen-Schuster Models

The Cohen-Grossberg model was designed to also include models which arose in other areas of biology than neural network theory. For example, it includes the classical

Volterra-Lotka Model

$$\frac{d}{dt}x_i = A_i x_i (1 - \sum_{j=1}^{n} B_{ij} x_j) \tag{64}$$

of population biology (Lotka, 1956), the

Gilpin-Ayala Model

$$\frac{d}{dt}x_i = A_i x_i \left[1 - \left(\frac{x_i}{B_i}\right)^{\theta_i} - \sum_{j=1}^{n} C_{ij} \left(\frac{x_j}{B_j}\right) \right], \tag{65}$$

also from population biology (Gilpin and Ayala, 1973), and the

Eigen-Schuster Model

$$\frac{d}{dt}x_i = x_i (A_i x_i^{p-1} - q \sum_{j=1}^{n} A_j x_j^p) \tag{66}$$

from the theory of macromolecular evolution (Eigen and Schuster, 1978). In all of these models, either the amplification function $a_i(x_i)$ is non-constant, or the self-signal function $b_i(x_i)$ is nonlinear, or both.

The specialized models summaried in Sections 9A–9I illustrate that model (13) and Liapunov function (14) embody a general principle for designing CAM devices

TABLE 2

$$
\text{CG (1983)} \left\{
\begin{array}{l}
\text{ADDITIVE (1967)} \left\{
\begin{array}{l}
\text{MP (1943)} \\
\text{BSB (1977)} \\
\text{BM (1985)} \\
\text{BAM (1987)}
\end{array}
\right. \\[2ex]
\text{SHUNTING (1973)} \quad \text{MF (1978, 1986)}
\end{array}
\right.
$$

Organization in terms of decreasing generality of the models described in Section 9. Abbreviations: CG = Cohen-Grossberg; MP = McCulloch-Pitts; BSB = Brain-State-in-a-Box; BM = Boltzmann Machine; BAM = Bidirectional Associative Memory; MF = Masking Field.

from cooperative-competitive feedback models. These models are said to be *absolutely stable* because the CAM property is not destroyed by changing the parameters, inputs, or initial values of the model. The persistence of the CAM property under arbitrary parameter changes enables learning to change system parameters in response to unpredictable input environments without destroying CAM. The STM transformation executed by a network with adaptively altered parameters can differ significantly from its original STM transformation. A finer analysis is needed to choose models, as in Sections 9A-9I, which are optimally designed to carry out specialized processing tasks.

The Cohen-Grossberg analysis emphasizes the critical role of mathematical analysis in classifying and understanding very large systems of nonlinear neural networks (VLSN). Without such an integrative approach, it is difficult to tell whether or not a model is really new computationally, or whether it is a special case of a known model in slightly different coordinates or notation. For example, many scientists have not realized that models (31) and (33) are mathematically equivalent. Table 2 describes the relationships between models disclosed by such an analysis. Thus the BSB model enjoys a CAM property for the same reason that any additive or CG model does. On the other hand, the BSB model may have special properties that may make it ideal for certain tasks, or it may be too specialized to accomplish certain tasks which are better dealt with using a shunting model.

10. Other Liapunov Methods

A considerable amount of work was done on finding Liapunov functions for special cases of (13) before the appearance of Cohen and Grossberg (1983). A global Liapunov method was also developed which is in some respects more general than that of Cohen and Grossberg (1983).

In the former category, MacArthur (1970) described a quadratic Liapunov function for proving local asymptotic stability of isolated equilibrium points of Volterra-Lotka systems with symmetric coefficients. Goh and Agnew (1977) described a global Liapunov function for Volterra-Lotka and Gilpin-Ayala systems in cases where only one equilibrium point exists. Liapunov functions were also described for Volterra-Lotka systems whose off-diagonal terms are relatively small (Kilmer, 1972; Takeuchi, Adachi, and Tokumaru, 1978). Such constraints are, however, too limiting for the design of CAM systems aimed at transforming and storing a large variety of patterns.

11. Testing the Global Consistency of Decisions in Competitive Systems

An alternative approach began with the global analysis in Grossberg (1973) of the nonlinear dynamics of shunting cooperative-competitive feedback networks. The goal of this analysis was to design CAM networks capable of transforming and stably storing in STM large numbers of patterns. (See Section 15.) The first analyses carried out direct proofs of the STM transformation and storage properties for small classes of shunting networks which arose in specialized applications. Later articles (Ellias and Grossberg, 1975; Grossberg and Levine, 1975; Levine, 1979; Levine and Grossberg, 1976) classified the global CAM behavior of increasingly large sets of networks.

These results led to the progressive development in Grossberg (1977, 1978c, 1978d, 1980) of a global Liapunov method for classifying the dynamical behaviors of a wider variety of competitive dynamical systems. A competitive dynamical system is, for present purposes, defined by a system of differential equations such that

$$\frac{d}{dt}x_i = f_i(x_1, x_2 \ldots, x_n) \tag{67}$$

where

$$\frac{\partial f_i}{\partial x_j} \leq 0, \quad i \neq j, \tag{68}$$

and the f_i are chosen to generate bounded trajectories. By (68), increasing the activity x_j of a given population can only decrease the growth rates $\frac{d}{dt}x_i$ of other populations, $i \neq j$, or may not influence them at all. No constraint is placed upon the sign of $\frac{\partial f_i}{\partial x_i}$. Typically, cooperative behavior occurs within a population and competitive behavior occurs between populations, as in the on-center off-surround networks (44). Since this Liapunov method led to results which are still of current interest and which seem amenable to further development, some of its most salient points will be summarized here.

The method makes mathematically precise the simple intuitive idea that a competitive system can be understood by keeping track of who is winning the competition. To do this, write (67) in the form

$$\frac{d}{dt}x_i = a_i(x_i)M_i(x) \quad x = (x_1, x_2, \ldots, x_n), \tag{69}$$

which factors out the amplification function $a_i(x_i) \geq 0$. Then define

$$M^+(x) = \max\{M_i(x) : i = 1, 2, \ldots, n\} \tag{70}$$

and

$$M^-(x) = \min\{M_i(x) : i = 1, 2, \ldots, n\}. \tag{71}$$

These variables track the largest and smallest rates of change, and are used to keep track of who is winning. Using these functions, it is easy to see that there exists a property of *ignition*: Once a trajectory enters the *positive ignition region*

$$R^+ = \{x : M^+(x) \geq 0\} \tag{72}$$

or the *negative ignition region*

$$R^- = \{x : M^-(x) \leq 0\}, \tag{73}$$

it can never leave it. If $x(t)$ never enters the set

$$R^* = R^+ \cap R^-, \tag{74}$$

then each variable $x_i(t)$ converges monotonically to a limit. The interesting behavior in a competitive system occurs in R^*. In particular, if $x(t)$ never enters R^+, each $x_i(t)$ decreases to a limit; then the competition never gets started. The set

$$S^+ = \{x : M^+(x) = 0\} \tag{75}$$

acts like a competition threshold, which is called the *positive ignition hypersurface*.

We therefore consider a trajectory after it has entered R^*. For simplicity, redefine the time scale so that the trajectory is in R^* at time $t = 0$. The Liapunov functional for any competitive system is then defined as

$$L(x_t) = \int_0^t M^+(x(v))dv. \tag{76}$$

The Liapunov property is a direct consequence of positive ignition:

$$\frac{d}{dt}L(x_t) = M^+(x(t)) \geq 0. \tag{77}$$

This functional provides the "energy" that forces trajectories through a series of competitive decisions, which are also called *jumps*. Jumps keep track of the state which is undergoing the *maximal* rate of change at any time ("who's winning"). If $M^+(x(t)) = M_i(x(t))$ for times $S \leq t < T$ but $M^+(x(t)) = M_j(x(t))$ for times $T \leq t < U$, then we say that the system *jumps* from node v_i to node v_j at time $t = T$. A jump from v_i to v_j can only occur on the *jump set*

$$J_{ij} = \{x \in R^* : M^+(x) = M_i(x) = M_j(x)\}. \tag{78}$$

The Liapunov functional $L(x_t)$ moves the system through these decision hypersurfaces through time. The geometry of S^+, S^-, and the jump sets J_{ij}, together with the energy defined by $L(x_t)$, can be used to globally analyse the dynamics of the system. In particular, due to the positive ignition property (77), the limit

$$\lim_{t \to \infty} L(x_t) = \int_0^\infty M^+(x(v))dv \tag{79}$$

always exists, and is possibly infinite.

The following results illustrate the use of these concepts (Grossberg, 1978d):

Theorem 1: Given any initial data $x(0)$, suppose that

$$\int_0^\infty M^+(x(v))dv < \infty. \tag{80}$$

Then the limit $x(\infty) = \lim_{t \to \infty} x(t)$ exists.

Corollary 1: If in response to initial data $x(0)$, all jumps cease after some time $T < \infty$, then $x(\infty)$ exists.

Speaking intuitively, this result means that after all local decisions, or jumps, have been made in response to an initial state $x(0)$, then the system can settle down to a global decision, or CAM $x(\infty)$. In particular, if $x(0)$ leads to only finitely many jumps because there exists a jump tree, or partial ordering of decisions, then $x(\infty)$ exists. This fact led to the analysis of circumstances under which no jump cycle, or repetitive series of jumps, occurs in response to $x(0)$, and hence that jump trees exist.

Further information follows readily from (80). Since $M^+(x(t)) \geq 0$ for all $t \geq 0$, it also follows that $\lim_{t \to \infty} M^+(x(t)) = 0$. This tells us to look for the equilibrium points $x(\infty)$ on the positive ignition hypersurface S^+ in (75):

Corollary 2: If $\int_0^\infty M^+(x(t))dt < \infty$, then $x(\infty) \in S^+$.

Thus the positive ignition surface is the place where the competition both ignites and is stored if no jump cycle exists. Using this result, an analysis was made of conditions under which no jump cycle exists in response to any initial vector $x(0)$, and hence all trajectories approach an equilibrium or CAM state.

The same method was also used to prove that a competitive system can generate sustained oscillations if it contains globally inconsistent decisions. These results are important for understanding the role of symmetric coefficients in the design of CAM systems. They identified circumstances under which, in response to initial data $x(0)$,

$$\int_0^\infty M^+(x(v))dv = \infty, \tag{81}$$

thus that infinitely many jumps occur, hence a jump cycle occurs, and finally that the trajectory undergoes undamped oscillations.

This method was used to provide a global analysis of the oscillations taking place in the May-Leonard (1975) model of the voting paradox. In this specialized Volterra-Lotka model,

$$\frac{d}{dt}x_1 = x_1(1 - x_1 - \alpha x_2 - \beta x_3)$$

$$\frac{d}{dt}x_2 = x_2(1 - \beta x_1 - x_2 - \alpha x_3) \tag{82}$$

$$\frac{d}{dt}x_3 = x_3(1 - \alpha x_1 - \beta x_2 - x_3)$$

and the parameters are chosen to satisfy $\beta > 1 > \alpha$ and $\alpha + \beta > 2$. System (82) represents the following intuitive situation. Three "candidates" are run against each other in pairwise elections. If v_1 wins over v_2, v_2 wins over v_3, and v_3 wins over v_1, what happens when all three candidates run against each other? If the winning relationship were transitive, then v_1 could win over himself! Thus the voting paradox illustrates how a globally inconsistent decision scheme can arise.

In (82) the relationship "v_i wins over v_j" is represented by "v_i inhibits v_j more than v_j inhibits v_i". In particular, $v_1 > v_2 > v_3 > v_1$. May and Leonard (1975) did computer simulations which showed that the trajectories of (82) oscillate. Grossberg (1978d) proved that the trajectories oscillate because system (82) generates a globally inconsistent decision scheme, characterized by a jump cycle $v_1 \to v_2 \to v_3 \to v_1$ with $L(x_\infty) = \infty$, for almost all trajectories.

The interaction matrix

$$\begin{pmatrix} 1 & \alpha & \beta \\ \beta & 1 & \alpha \\ \alpha & \beta & 1 \end{pmatrix} \tag{83}$$

of system (82) can be chosen arbitrarily close to a symmetric matrix by letting α and β approach 1 without violating the constraint $\beta > 1 > \alpha$ and $\alpha + \beta > 2$. Thus there exist competitive systems whose matrices are arbitrarily close to symmetric matrices almost all of whose trajectories oscillate, albeit slowly. There also exist competitive systems without jump cycles whose coefficients are not symmetric, yet approach equilibrium points, because they satisfy Theorem 1. Although symmetry may be sufficient to generate CAM, as in model (13), the concepts of jump cycle and jump tree illustrate that one needs to analyse more global geometrical concepts to understand the relationship between a system's symmetry and its emergent CAM properties.

The Liapunov functional method led to the Cohen and Grossberg (1983) analysis in the following way. The Liapunov functional method was used to prove a theorem about the global CAM behavior of the competitive *adaptation level systems*

$$\frac{d}{dt}x_i = a_i(x)[b_i(x_i) - c(x)] \tag{84}$$

which were identified through an analysis of many specialized networks. In system (84), each state-dependent amplification function $a_i(x)$ and self-signal function $b_i(x_i)$ can be chosen with great generality without destroying the system's ability to reach equilibrium because there exists a state-dependent *adaptation level* $c(x)$ against which each $b_i(x_i)$ is compared. Such an adaptation level $c(x)$ defines a strong type of long-range symmetry within the system.

The examples which motivated the analysis of (84) were additive networks

$$\frac{d}{dt}x_i = -A_i x_i + \sum_k f_k(x_k)B_{ki} + I_i \tag{85}$$

and shunting networks

$$\begin{aligned}\frac{d}{dt}x_i = &-A_i x_i + (B_i - x_i)[I_i + \sum_k f_k(x_k)C_{ki}]\\ &-(x_i + D_i)[J_i + \sum_k g_k(x_k)E_{ki}]\end{aligned} \tag{86}$$

in which the symmetric coefficients B_{ki}, C_{ki}, and E_{ki} took on different values when $k = i$ and when $k \neq i$. Examples in which the symmetric coefficients varied with $|k - i|$ in a graded fashion were also studied through computer simulations (Ellias and Grossberg, 1975; Levine and Grossberg, 1976), but an adequate global mathematical convergence proof was not available before Cohen and Grossberg (1983).

In the proof of the global convergence theorem (Grossberg, 1978c, 1980) for systems of the form (84), it was shown that each $x_i(t)$ gets trapped within a sequence of decision boundaries that get laid down through time at the abscissa values of the highest peaks in the graphs of the functions b_i. The size and location of these peaks reflect the statistical rules, which can be chosen extremely complex, that give rise to the output signals from the totality of cooperating subpopulations within each node v_i. In particular, a b_i with multiple peaks can be generated when a population's positive feedback signal function is a multiple-sigmoid function which adds up output signals from multiple randomly defined subpopulations within v_i.

After all the decision boundaries get laid down, each x_i is trapped within a single valley of its b_i graph. This valley acts, in some respects, like a classical potential. Correspondingly, it was proved that after all the x_i get trapped in such valleys, the function

$$B[x(t)] = \max\{b_i(x(t)) : i = 1, 2, \ldots, n\} \tag{87}$$

is a Liapunov function. This Liapunov property was used to complete the proof of the theorem.

The adaptation level model (84) is in some ways more general and in some ways less general than model (13). Cohen and I began our study of (13) with the hope that we could use the symmetric coefficients in (13) to prove that no jump cycles exist, and thus that all trajectories approach equilibrium as a consequence of the general Theorem 1. Such a proof is greatly to be desired because it would be part of a more general theory and, by using geometrical concepts such as jump set and ignition surface, it would clarify how to perturb off the symmetric case without generating oscillations such as the voting paradox (82). As it is, the Liapunov function (14) does not necessarily require that the system (13) be competitive because, by (16), $\frac{d}{dt}V_i \leq 0$ whether or not the coefficients c_{ij} are all nonnegative.

Hirsch (1982, 1985) has proved powerful global theorems about the class of cooperative systems

$$\frac{d}{dt}x_i = f_i(x_1, x_2, \ldots, x_n) \tag{88}$$

where

$$\frac{\partial f_i}{\partial x_j} \geq 0, \quad i \neq j. \tag{89}$$

One of the outstanding mathematical problems in neural network theory is to find more general methods than the Cohen and Grossberg, Grossberg, and Hirsch results for designing mixed cooperative-competitive feedback systems with desired global behavior.

12. Stable Production Strategies for a Competitive Market

The properties of adaptation level systems may prove useful in areas far removed from neural networks. To illustrate this possible range, consider the problem of how to design a competitive market such that every competing firm can choose one of infinitely many production strategies, each choice is unknown to the other competitors, yet the market generates a stable price and each firm balances its books.

Let x_i denote the amount produced by firm i of the commodity; $P(x)$ denote the market price per item of the commodity, where $x = (x_1, x_2, \ldots, x_n)$; $C_i(x_i)$ denote the cost per item of firm i; and $A_i(x)$ (≥ 0) denote a multiplier chosen by firm i. Let the firms agree to govern their individual production plans according to the adaptation level system

$$\frac{d}{dt}x_i = x_i A_i(x)[P(x) - C_i(x_i)]. \tag{90}$$

The competitive property of the market is expressed by the conditions

$$\frac{\partial P}{\partial x_i} < 0, \quad i = 1, 2, \ldots, n. \tag{91}$$

In order to play this market, each firm compares its private cost function with the publicly known market price. If $A_i(x)$ depends only on x_i, then this is all that the firm needs to know to determine its production rate $\frac{dx_i}{dt}$. If $A_i(x)$ depends on amount x_j produced by other firms, then each firm needs also to know how much the other firms are producing. In either case, no firm knows the internal strategies $A_i(x)$ and $C_i(x_i)$ of the other firms, which can be very complex. Nor does any firm need to know the function $P(x)$, which can also be very complex. All it needs to know are the values of $P(x(t))$ through time, which it can read in a trade newspaper.

By the adaptation level convergence theorem, limits $\lim_{t \to \infty} P(x(t))$ and $\lim_{t \to \infty} C_i(x_i(t))$ exist and are equal. Thus the market price is stable and every firm breaks even. If the definition of $C_i(x_i)$ also includes a savings factor, then the savings functions of all the firms would also be satisfied.

In this generality, the theorem does not say what firms will get rich. It only says that if firms are willing to play the game, then they can attain some much-valued properties of market stability and predictability. Just as the existence of stable CAM in neural networks must be supplemented by a mathematical classification theory which determines who, if anyone, will win a specially designed competition, the existence of a stable market must be supplemented by an analysis of how firms should choose their strategies to maximize their gains despite ignorance of their competitors' strategies.

Before turning to a discussion of some recent specialized architectures, I shall further discuss two issues that naturally arise from the preceding text:

1) Why bother studying shunting interactions? Why aren't the simpler additive interactions always sufficient?

2) Are symmetric coefficients necessary to achieve stable learning and memory storage? In Section 11, it was noted that the answer is "no" for CAM systems whose storage is in short term memory (STM). The answer is also well-known to be "no" for associative learning systems whose storage is in long term memory (LTM). This is true for networks designed to accomplish associative pattern learning as well as for networks designed for spatiotemporal pattern recognition and planned sensory-motor performance. Some asymmetric associative networks which arise in adaptive pattern recognition and adaptive sensory-motor control are discussed in Sections 16–20.

13. Sensitive Variable-Load Parallel Processing by Shunting Cooperative-Competitive Networks: Automatic Gain Control and Total Activity Normalization

The value of shunting networks is clarified by their ability to help overcome one of the problems which has confronted recent investigators who have been using additive networks. Amit, Gutfreund, and Sompolinsky (1987, p.2294) found spurious memory states in the additive model that they studied. Their analysis led them to conclude that "there must be some global control on the dynamics of the network, which prevents too high or too low activity." In other words, it is important to carefully regulate the network's total activation through time. The importance of this property, called *total activity normalization*, has been recognized in the neural network literature for the past two decades, and is one of the basic properties of shunting cooperative-competitive networks (Grossberg, 1970b, 1972a, 1973, 1982a).

More generally, shunting networks provide a design for sensitive variable-load parallel processors. Suppose that the STM traces or activations $x_1, x_2, \ldots, x_n$ at a network level fluctuate within fixed finite limits at their respective network nodes. Setting a bounded operating range for each x_i has the advantage that fixed decision criteria, such as output thresholds, can also be defined. On the other hand, if a large number of intermittent input sources converge on the nodes through time, then a serious design problem arises, due to the fact that the total input converging on each node can vary wildly through time. I have called this problem the *noise-saturation dilemma*: If the x_i are sensitive to large inputs, then why do not small inputs get lost in internal system noise? If the x_i are sensitive to small inputs, then why do they not all saturate at their maximum values in response to large inputs?

Shunting cooperative-competitive networks possess automatic gain control properties capable of generating an infinite dynamic range within which input patterns can be effectively processed, thereby solving the noise-saturation dilemma. Specialized shunting networks have been classified in terms of their specific pattern processing and memory storage properties, thereby providing a storehouse of networks which serves as a resource for solving particular computational problems. Since the design and properties both of feedforward and feedback shunting networks have been reviewed in a number of places (Grossberg, 1981, 1982a, 1987d), the present summary considers briefly only the simplest feedforward and feedback networks to convey some of the main ideas. First the simplest feedforward network will be described to illustrate how its solves the sensitivity problem raised by the noise-saturation dilemma.

Let a spatial pattern $I_i = \theta_i I$ of inputs be processed by the cells v_i, $i = 1, 2, \ldots, n$. Each θ_i is the constant relative size, or reflectance, of its input I_i and I is the variable total input size. In other words, $I = \sum_{k=1}^{n} I_k$, so that $\sum_{k=1}^{n} \theta_k = 1$. How can each cell

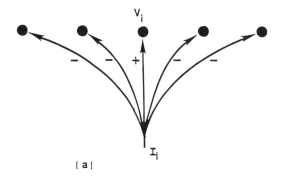

[a]

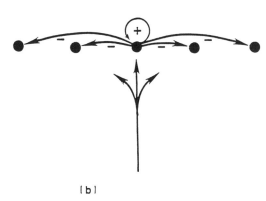

[b]

Figure 4. Two types of on-center off-surround networks: (a) A feedforward network in which the input pathways define the on-center off-surround interactions; (b) A feedback network in which interneurons define the on-center off-surround interactions. (Reprinted with permission from Grossberg and Kuperstein, 1986.)

v_i maintain its sensitivity to θ_i when I is parametrically increased? How is saturation avoided?

To compute $\theta_i = I_i(\sum_{k=1}^{n} I_k)^{-1}$, each cell v_i must have information about all the inputs I_k, $k = 1, 2, \ldots, n$. Moreover, since $\theta_i = I_i(I_i + \sum_{k \neq i} I_k)^{-1}$, increasing I_i increases θ_i whereas increasing any I_k, $k \neq i$, decreases θ_i. When this observation is translated into an anatomy for delivering feedforward inputs to the cells v_i, it suggests that I_i excites v_i and that all I_k, $k \neq i$, inhibit v_i. This rule represents the simplest feedforward on-center off-surround anatomy (Figure 4a).

How does the on-center off-surround anatomy activate and inhibit the cells v_i via mass action? Let each v_i possess B excitable sites of which $x_i(t)$ are excited and $B - x_i(t)$ are unexcited at each time t. Then at v_i, I_i excites $B - x_i$ unexcited sites by mass action, and the total inhibitory input $\sum_{k \neq i} I_k$ inhibits x_i excited sites by mass action. Moreover, excitation x_i can spontaneously decay at a fixed rate A, so that the cell can return to an equilibrium point (arbitrarily set equal to 0) after all inputs cease. These rules say that

$$\frac{d}{dt} x_i = -A x_i + (B - x_i) I_i - x_i \sum_{k \neq i} I_k. \qquad (92)$$

If a fixed spatial pattern $I_i = \theta_i I$ is presented and the background input I is held constant for awhile, each x_i approaches an equilibrium value. This value is easily found by setting $dx_i/dt = 0$ in (92). It is

$$x_i = \theta_i \frac{BI}{A+I}. \tag{93}$$

Note that the relative activitiy $X_i = x_i(\sum_{k=1}^n x_k)^{-1}$ equals θ_i no matter how large I is chosen; there is no saturation. This is due to automatic gain control by the inhibitory inputs. In other words, $\sum_{k\neq i} I_k$ multiplies x_i in (92). The total gain in (92) is found by writing

$$\frac{d}{dt}x_i = -(A+I)x_i + BI_i. \tag{94}$$

The gain is the coefficient of x_i, namely $-(A+I)$, since if $x_i(0) = 0$,

$$x_i(t) = \theta_i \frac{BI}{A+I}(1 - e^{-(A+I)t}). \tag{95}$$

Both the steady state and the gain of x_i depend on the input strengths. This is characteristic of mass action, or shunting, networks but not of additive networks. Many alternative models cannot retune themselves in response to parametric shifts in background intensity.

The simple law (93) combines two types of information: information about pattern θ_i, or "reflectances", and information about background activity, or "luminance". In visual psychophysics, the tendency towards reflectance processing helps to explain brightness constancy, and the rule $I(A+I)^{-1}$ helps to explain the Weber-Fechner law (Cornsweet, 1970).

Another property of (93) is that the total activity

$$x = \sum_{k=1}^n x_k = \frac{BI}{A+I} \tag{96}$$

is independent of the number of active cells. This *normalization* rule is a conservation law which says, for example, that a network that receives a fixed total luminance, making one part of the field brighter tends to make another part of the field darker. This property helps to explain brightness contrast (Cornsweet, 1970; Grossberg and Todorović, 1987). Brightness constancy and contrast are two sides of a coin: on one side is Weber-law modulated reflectance processing, as in (93), and on the other side is a normalization rule, as in (96).

Equation (93) can be written in another form that expresses a different physical intuition. If we plot the intensity of an on-center input in logarithmic coordinates K_i, then $K_i = ln(I_i)$ and $I_i = \exp(K_i)$. Also write the total off-surround input as $J_i = \sum_{k\neq i} I_k$. Then (93) can be written in logarithmic coordinates as

$$x_i(K_i, J_i) = \frac{Be^{K_i}}{A + e^{K_i} + J_i}. \tag{97}$$

How does the response x_i at v_i change if we parametrically change the off-surround input J_i? The answer is that x_i's entire response curve to K_i is shifted, and thus its dynamic range is not compressed. Such a shift occurs, for example, in bipolar cells of the Necturus retina (Werblin, 1971) and in a modified form in the psychoacoustic data of Iverson and Pavel (1981). The shift property says that

$$x_i(K_i + S, J_i^{(1)}) = x_i(K_i, J_i^{(2)}) \tag{98}$$

for all $K_i \geq 0$, where the amount of shift S caused by changing the total off-surround input from $J_i^{(1)}$ to $J_i^{(2)}$ is predicted to be

$$S = ln\left(\frac{A + J_i^{(1)}}{A + J_i^{(2)}}\right). \tag{99}$$

14. Physiological Interpretation of Shunting Mechanisms as a Membrane Equation

Equation (92) is a special case of a law that occurs *in vivo*; namely, the membrane equation on which cellular neurophysiology is based. The membrane equation is the voltage equation that appears in the Hodgkin-Huxley equations mentioned in Section 6C. This equation embodies the classical electrical circuit interpretation (Hodgkin, 1964; Katz, 1966; Plonsey and Fleming, 1969) which is used to physically interpret the additive and shunting neural networks.

The membrane equation describes the voltage $V(t)$ of a cell by the law

$$C\frac{\partial V}{\partial t} = (V^+ - V)g^+ + (V^- - V)g^- + (V^p - V)g^p. \tag{100}$$

In (100), C is a capacitance; V^+, V^-, and V^p are constant excitatory, inhibitory, and passive saturation points, respectively; and g^+, g^-, and g^p are excitatory, inhibitory, and passive conductances, respectively. We will scale V^+ and V^- so that $V^+ > V^-$. Then *in vivo* $V^+ \geq V(t) \geq V^-$ and $V^+ > V^p \geq V^-$. Often V^+ represents the saturation point of a Na^+ channel and V^- represents the saturation point of a K^+ channel. There is also symmetry-breaking in (100) because $V^+ - V^p$ is usually much larger than $V^p - V^-$. This symmetry-breaking operation, which is usually mentioned in the experimental literature without comment, achieves an important noise suppression property when it is coupled to an on-center off-surround anatomy.

To see why (92) is a special case of (100), suppose that (100) holds at each cell v_i. Then at v_i, $V = x_i$. Set $C = 1$ (rescale time), $V^+ = B$, $V^- = V^p = 0$, $g^+ = I_i$, $g^- = \sum_{k \neq i} I_k$, and $g^p = A$.

The reflectance processing and Weber law properties (93), the total activity normalization property (96), and the shift property (98) set the stage for the design and classification of more complex feedforward and feedback on-center off-surround shunting networks. Some results classifying feedforward on-center off-surround networks are reviewed in Grossberg (1981, 1987d).

15. Sigmoid Feedback, Contrast Enhancement, and Short Term Memory Storage by Shunting Feedback Networks

Feedback additive and shunting networks possess useful CAM properties that eventually led to the Cohen-Grossberg model reviewed in Section 6. During the last few years, many investigators have realized the importance of sigmoid feedback signals for generating effective pattern processing and CAM properties; [e.g., Ackley, Hinton, and Sejnowski (1985); Hopfield (1984); McClelland and Rumelhart (1986)]. The first complete global analysis which rigorously demonstrated these properties was provided in Grossberg (1973). There the importance of sigmoid feedback was clarified by classifying the manner in which different types of feedback signal functions—linear, slower-than-linear, faster-than-linear, and sigmoid—transform input patterns and store the transformed patterns in STM. The simplest shunting on-center off-surround feedback network was chosen for this demonstration because it possessed the key properties of: (1) solving the noise-saturation dilemma by using the interaction between automatic

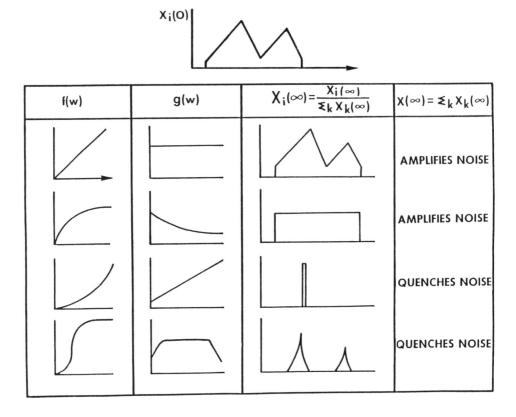

Table 3.

gain control and on-center off-surround interactions, (2) normalizing or conserving its total activity, and (3) being capable of absolutely stable STM.

This simplest such network is defined by the equations

$$\frac{d}{dt}x_i = -Ax_i + (B - x_i)[I_i + f(x_i)] - x_i[J_i + \sum_{k \neq i} f(x_k)], \qquad (101)$$

$i = 1, 2, \ldots, n$ (Figure 4b). Suppose that the inputs I_i and J_i acting before $t = 0$ establish an arbitrary initial activity pattern $(x_1(0), x_2(0), \ldots, x_n(0))$ before being shut off at $t = 0$. How does the choice of the feedback signal function $f(w)$ control the transformation of this pattern at $t \to \infty$? The answer is schematized in Table 3.

Table 3 displays choices of the feedback signal function $f(w)$ and the corresponding function $g(w) = w^{-1}f(w)$ which measures how much $f(w)$ deviates from linearity at prescribed activity levels w. The network's responses to these choices are summarized using the functions $X_i = x_i(\sum_{k=1}^{n} x_k)^{-1}$ and $x = \sum_{k=1}^{n} x_k$. The relative activity X_i of the ith node computes how the network transforms the input pattern through time. The functions X_i play the role for feedback networks that the reflectances θ_i in (93) play for feedforward networks. The total activity x measures how well the network normalizes the total network activity and whether the pattern is stored $(x(\infty) = \lim_{t \to \infty} x(t) > 0)$ or not $(x(\infty) = 0)$. Variable x plays the role of the total input I in (93).

Using these functions, (101) can be rewritten as the system

$$\frac{d}{dt} X_i = B X_i \sum_{k=1}^{n} X_k [g(X_i x) - g(X_k x)] \tag{102}$$

and

$$\frac{d}{dt} x = x[-A + (B - x) \sum_{k=1}^{n} X_k g(X_k x)]. \tag{103}$$

Using system (101)–(103), the following types of results were proved.

A. Linear Signal: Perfect Pattern Storage and Noise Amplification

If $f(w)$ is chosen linear, as in $f(w) = Cw$, then $g(w) = C = $ constant. Hence by (102), all $\frac{d}{dt} X_i = 0$, so that $X_i(t) = $ constant in response to an arbitrary initial pattern $x_i(0)$. This system thus possesses a continuum of nondistorting CAM states. Why, therefore, is not a linear feedback signal a perfect choice for sensory pattern processing?

The answer becomes clear through consideration of the total activity variable $x(t)$. In the linear case, (103) reduces to

$$\frac{d}{dt} x = x[-A + (B - x)C]. \tag{104}$$

Hence such a system either cannot store any pattern ($x(\infty) = 0$ if $B - AC^{-1} < 0$), or it amplifies noise as vigorously as it amplifies signals if it is capable of CAM ($x(\infty) = B - AC^{-1}$ if $B - AC^{-1} > 0$, no matter how small $x(0) > 0$ is chosen). This amplification property generalizes to other models, and challenges those models, such as the BSB model (Section 9B), whose feedback signals are linear at small activity values.

Equation (102) suggests how to define slower-than-linear, faster-than-linear, and sigmoid feedback signals for purposes of pattern processing. Just as a linear $f(w) = Cw$ generates a constant $g(w) = C$, a slower-than-linear $f(w)$, such as $Cw(D+w)^{-1}$, generates a decreasing $g(w)$, such as $C(D + w)^{-1}$; a faster-than-linear $f(w)$, such as Cw^n with $n > 1$, generates an increasing $g(w)$, such as Cw^{n-1}; and a sigmoid $f(w)$, such as $Cw^n(D^n + w^n)^{-1}$ with $n > 1$, generates a hill-shaped $g(w)$, such as $Cw^{n-1}(D^n + w^n)^{-1}$.

B. Slower-than-Linear Signal: Pattern Compression and Noise Amplification

Slower-than-linear signal functions $f(w)$ also amplify noise. Analysis of (102) and (103) shows that a slower-than-linear feedback signal exerts a compressive effect on the reverberating activity pattern which obliterates all differences between initially active nodes ($X_i(\infty) = \frac{1}{n}$) if the network is capable of CAM ($x(\infty) > 0$).

C. Faster-than-Linear Signal: Winner-Take-All, Noise Suppression, and Total Activity Quantization in an Emergent Finite State Machine

A faster-than-linear signal function can tell the difference between small and large initial values by amplifying and storing only sufficiently large activities. Analysis of (102) and (103) shows that a faster-than-linear signal function amplifies the largest initial activities so much more than smaller initial activities that it makes a *choice*: Only the node with the largest initial activity gets stored in STM. This is a remarkable property from several perspectives.

It shows how a very large network of nodes can quickly choose a winner in a single processing step without any search, simply by letting its nodes compete. Choice networks were originally designed for use in the many applications wherein the computational task is to choose a winner from noisy data. Feldman and Ballard (1982) have called this choice property winner-take-all. Platt and Hopfield (1986) have, for example, mentioned this property in their discussion of error-correcting codes.

A faster-than-linear signal function also generates remarkable normalization and quantization properties in the total activity domain. Combined with the winner-take-all property, the quantization property shows that a faster-than-linear signal function generates emergent properties of a finite-state machine, even though system (101) is defined by continuous laws. In particular, at large times, (103) is approximated by the equation

$$\frac{d}{dt}x \sim x[-A + (B - x)g(x)].$$ (105)

Thus the stored total activity $x(\infty)$ is a root of the equation

$$g(w) = \frac{A}{B - w},$$ (106)

where both $g(w)$ and $A(B - w)^{-1}$ are increasing functions of w. The stored total activity is normalized because the roots of (106) are independent of the number n of competing nodes.

Total activity quantization and noise suppression supplement the normalization property if the following hypotheses are satisfied. Suppose that $A > Bg(0)$ and that there are m roots $E_1 < E_2 < \ldots < E_m < B$ of equation (106). Then the roots $E_1, E_3, \ldots$ are unstable equilibrium points of $x(t)$, whereas the roots $E_2 < E_4 < \ldots$ are stable equilibrium points of $x(t)$. Root E_1 defines the level below which $x(t)$ is treated as noise and suppressed. Roots $E_2, E_4, \ldots$ are stable, quantized, normalized limit values of $x(\infty)$. Function $g(w)$ can also be chosen to equal $A(B - w)$ along an interval of values, thereby leading to a continuum of stable equilibium values. Thus one can use system (101) with a faster-than-linear feedback signal function to design infinitely many finite-state machines or continuous energy spectrum machines capable of rapidly making choices in noise and possessing as many normalized asymptotic activity levels as one pleases.

D. Sigmoid Signal: Tunable Filter, Quenching Threshold, Noise Suppression, and Normalization

Although a faster-than-linear signal function suppresses noise, it does so with such vigor that only the node with maximal initial activity survives in CAM. In many applications, one needs a spatially distributed CAM code, albeit one that contrast-enhances and thereby compresses an input pattern before the transformed pattern is stored in CAM. A sigmoid signal function generates these properties. Indeed, the classification of signal function properties in (A)–(C) shows that a signal function $f(w)$ which suppresses noise must be faster-than-linear at small activity values w. In addition, every physical signal function is bounded at large activity values w, thereby suggesting the use of a hybrid signal function which is faster-than-linear at small activities, slower-than-linear at large activities, and thus, by continuity, approximately linear in between; viz., a sigmoid signal function (Table 3).

Grossberg (1973) proved that a sigmoid signal function generates a *quenching threshold* (QT): Activities less than the QT are suppressed, whereas the pattern of activities that exceeds the QT is contrast-enhanced before being stored in STM. Speaking heuristically, the QT property is a consequence of pattern processing properties of faster-than-linear and linear signal functions combined with normalization properties in the total energy domain: The faster-than-linear property at small activity levels begins to contrast-enhance the input pattern as the total activity shifts due to normalization. As the partially contrast-enhanced activity pattern is normalized, it is influenced by the (approximately) linear range of the sigmoid signal function, which stores whatever pattern it detects (Table 3), including the partially contrast-enhanced pattern. Thus a sigmoid signal function can be used to design a noise-suppressing network with infinitely many stable equilibrium points, representing partially contrast-enhanced, or compressed, input patterns.

Any network that possesses a QT can be adaptively tuned. By increasing or decreasing the QT, the criterion of which activities represent functional signals—and hence should be processed and stored in STM—and of which activities represent functional noise—and hence should be suppressed—can be flexibly modified through time. An increase in the QT can cause all but the largest activities to be quenched. Then the network behaves like a choice machine. A sudden decrease in the QT can cause all recently presented input signals to be stored. If a novel or unexpected event suddenly decreases the QT, then all recently presented data can be stored in CAM until the cause of the unexpected event can be determined and learned. This property is important in actively regulating the focus of attention of a neural network sensory processor (Grossberg, 1982a).

It cannot be overemphasized that the existence of the QT and its desirable tuning and CAM properties follow from the use of a nonlinear sigmoid signal function. When these properties were first proved in the early 1970's, the popularity of linear control models and of digital serial models in applications to intelligent systems prevented their acceptance, or often even their toleration. The recent popularity of connectionist models and of Liapunov methods have turned the obscure into the obvious, which is a sure sign of major progress.

The QT has been explicitly computed in a special case (Grossberg, 1973, pp.355–359). In system (101) with $I_i = J_i = 0$, let

$$f(w) = Cwg(w) \tag{107}$$

where $C \geq 0$, $g(w)$ is increasing for $0 \leq w \leq x^{(1)}$, and $g(w) = 1$ for $x^{(1)} \leq w \leq B$. Then

$$QT = \frac{x^{(1)}}{B - AC^{-1}}. \tag{108}$$

Thus all the parameters of the network influence the QT. An important open problem is to compute the QT of more general cooperative-competitive networks that arise in computational applications.

In summary, several factors work together to generate desirable pattern transformation and STM-CAM properties: the dynamics of mass action, the geometry of competition, and the statistics of competitive feedback signals work together to define a unified network module whose several parts are designed in a coordinated fashion through development. How such a network module is self-organized *in vivo* is a profound open problem whose solution is worthy of a major scientific effort. A great deal more mathematical work will also be needed to fully understand even the properties of those shunting and additive networks which have already arisen in applications. For example, mixed cooperative-competitive nonlinear feedback networks have been designed to analyse and predict properties of emergent visual segmentation (Grossberg, 1987a, 1987b; Grossberg and Mingolla, 1985a, 1985b, 1987). Although the computer simulations of these networks were guided by previous theorems about competitive and cooperative nonlinear feedback networks, no global theorems have yet been proved about these mixed cooperative-competitive feedback networks. The additional insights that such theorems are bound to bring are much to be desired if only because of the great practical importance of emergent visual segmentation in a number of applications.

16. Competitive Learning Models

Another application of a choice network occurs in competitive learning models. In the simplest competitive learning model, normalized input patterns pass through an adaptive filter before the maximal filter output is chosen by a winner-take-all network. The winning population then triggers associative pattern learning within the vector of LTM traces which sent it inputs through the adaptive filter. Such a competitive learning model is a particular type of adaptive vector quantization scheme (Gray, 1984) which possesses Bayesian processing properties (Duda and Hart, 1973). In cognitive psychology, competitive learning properties are used to model categorical perception (Anderson, Silverstein, Ritz, and Jones, 1977; Elman, Diehl, and Buchwald, 1977; Hary and Massaro, 1982; Miller and Liberman, 1979; Pastore, 1981; Sawusch and Nusbaum, 1979; Sawusch, Nusbaum, and Schwab, 1980; Schwab, Sawusch, and Nusbaum, 1981; Studdert-Kennedy, 1980). During categorical perception, input patterns are classified into mutually exclusive recognition categories which are separated by sharp categorical boundaries. A sudden switch in pattern classification can occur if an input pattern is deformed so much that it crosses one of these boundaries.

The development of competitive learning models was achieved through an interaction between results of Grossberg (1970b, 1972b, 1973) and of Malsburg (1973), leading in Grossberg (1976a, 1976b) to the model in several forms which have subsequently been further analysed and applied by a number of authors; e.g., Amari and Takeuchi, 1978; Bienenstock, Cooper, and Munro, 1982; Carpenter and Grossberg, 1985, 1987a; Grossberg, 1982a, 1982b; Grossberg and Kuperstein, 1986; Rumelhart and Zipser, 1985). Kohonen (1984) has used competitive learning models in his work on self-organizing maps. His theorem on the statistical distribution of such maps applies in the stochastic case the Grossberg (1976a) theorem on the stability of map learning in response to sparsely distributed input patterns. Kohonen's analysis of the distribution properties of a self-organizing map in the stochastic case reflects the property in the deterministic case that LTM vectors in the adaptive filter are a time average of their learned input vectors, and thus track the distribution of these input vectors within their convex hull under suitable conditions. Such deterministic analyses include stochastic analyses in the sense that they predict the time course of learning in response to arbitrary sequences of input patterns, including stochastically controlled input patterns. A historical discussion of the development of competitive learning models is given in Grossberg (1987e).

Although competitive learning models are useful in many situations, their learning becomes unstable in response to a variety of input environments, as was first shown in Grossberg (1976a). An effort to understand how to design an adaptive pattern recognition and map learning system that could self-stabilize its learning in response to arbitrary input environments led to the introduction of adaptive resonance theory in Grossberg (1976b). In this theory, competitive learning mechanisms are embedded in a larger network which includes learned top-down expectations and other modulatory mechanisms that were identified through an analysis of data concerning perception, cognition, conditioning, attention, event-related potentials, and neurophysiology.

In addition to suggesting mechanistic explanations of many interdisciplinary data from these subjects, the theory also made a number of predictions which have since been partially supported by experiments. For example, Grossberg (1976b) predicted that both norepinephrine (NE) mechanisms and attentional mechanisms modulate the adaptive development of thalamocortical visual feature detectors. Kasamatsu and Pettigrew (1976) and Pettigrew and Kasamatsu (1978) described NE modulation of feature detector development and Singer (1982) reported attentional modulation. Grossberg (1978a) predicted a word length effect in word recognition paradigms. Samuel, van Santen, and Johnston (1982, 1983) reported a word length effect in word superiority experiments. Grossberg (1978a, 1980b) predicted a hippocampal generator of the P300 event-related potential. Halgren et al. (1980) reported the existence of a hippocampal P300 generator in humans. The existence and correlations between other event-related potentials, such as processing negativity (PN), early positive wave (P120), and N200 were also predicted in these theoretical articles. See Banquet and Grossberg (1987) for further discussion.

The next section describes a number of the key properties which emerged from such data analyses and subsequent mathematical developments and computational analyses of Carpenter and Grossberg (1985, 1987a).

17. Stable Self-Organization of Pattern Recognition Codes

A number of basic computational distinctions can be used to differentiate neural network architectures and to clarify the applications for which they are best suited. Since a given computational property may be advantageous for one application and disadvantageous for a different application, such a classification is well worth keeping in mind.

In this section, I compare and contrast properties of the adaptive resonance theory (ART) for the stable self-organization of pattern recognition codes with properties of alternative models for the learning of pattern recognition codes. Since ART was introduced in Grossberg (1976b), it has undergone substantial development and analysis. A number of articles which contributed to the theory are brought together in several books (Grossberg, 1982a, 1987c, 1987d, 1988). The discussion herein will be based upon properties of an ART architecture, called ART 1, whose key properties were developed, proved mathematically, and illustrated through extensive computer simulations in Carpenter and Grossberg (1987a). The architecture and processing cycle of ART 1 are summarized in Figures 5 and 6. The main computational distinctions to be discussed are outlined under separate headings:

A. Real-Time (On-Line) Learning versus Lab-Time (Off-Line) Learning

An ART architecture is designed to run in real-time, or on-line, when it is implemented in hardware. Various other architectures can only be run in lab-time, or off-line. This is perhaps the most important distinction that separates neural network architectures. Although some problems, such as the travelling salesman problem (Hopfield and Tank, 1985, 1986), can be run off-line, other problems, such as learning to recognize novel objects in a rapidly changing environment, must be solved online. Many of the computational properties which set apart ART architectures from other currently available learning algorithms are imposed to enable them to learn and recognize well in real-time.

B. Nonstationary Unexpected World versus Stationary Controlled World

Real-time environments are often nonstationary; their statistical properties can change unexpectedly through time. In addition, the world does not stop in a real-time environment. A ceaseless flow of input patterns of variable complexity can occur. ART architectures are designed to cope with nonstationary worlds of unlimited complexity. In contrast, many alternative learning and recognition schemes are off-line models that work well only in a stationary world whose inputs are carefully controlled both in number and statistical properties. The following discussion sharpens this basic difference.

C. Self-Organization versus Teacher as a Source of Expected Output

An ART architecture self-organizes its recognition code, without a teacher, through a direct interaction with its input environment. Self-organizing networks contrast sharply with learning networks which require an external teacher who presents an explicit correct answer, in the code of the network, for comparison with every output generated by the network, as in back propagation. Back propagation uses the Adeline learning rule of Widrow (1962). It is a steepest descent algorithm which was discovered by Werbos (1974), rediscovered and further developed by Parker (1982,

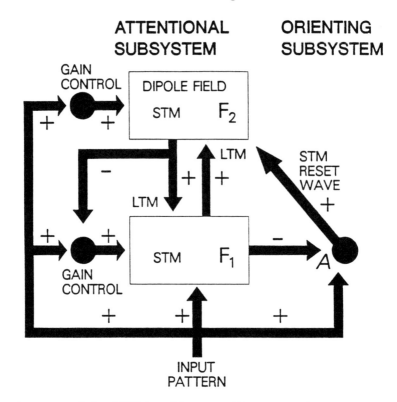

Figure 5. Anatomy of the ART 1 architecture: Two successive stages, F_1 and F_2, of the attentional subsystem encode patterns of activation in short term memory (STM). Bottom-up and top-down pathways between F_1 and F_2 contain adaptive long term memory (LTM) traces which multiply the signals in these pathways. The remainder of the circuit modulates these STM and LTM processes. Modulation by gain control enables F_1 to distinguish between bottom-up input patterns and top-down priming, or template, patterns, as well as to match these bottom-up and top-down patterns. Gain control signals also enable F_2 to react supraliminally to signals from F_1 while an input pattern is on. The orienting subsystem generates a reset wave to F_2 when mismatches between bottom-up and top-down patterns occur at F_1. This reset wave selectively and enduringly inhibits active F_2 cells until the input is shut off. (Reprinted with permission from Carpenter and Grossberg, 1987a, p. 56.)

1985, 1986) under the name learning-logic, and popularized and applied to cognitive science applications by Rumelhart, Hinton, and Williams (1986) under the name back propagation.

The off-line nature of back-propagation, at least as it is used in many applications, is illustrated by the fact that its teaching signals often have no analog with analogous learning experiences *in vivo*. For example, the popular NETtalk back-propagation simulation of Sejnowski and Rosenberg (1986) uses a phoneme-by-phoneme matching scheme that has no analog during human real-time learning to read. The use of such a pre-coded teacher also has major implications for the structure of the learned code—notably the invariants of this code (see items F and G below)—and the way in which matching occurs within the network (see item H below).

D. Self-Stabilization versus Capacity Catastrophe

An ART architecture can self-stabilize its learning in response to arbitrarily many inputs. New inputs may either refine the criteria for accessing already established

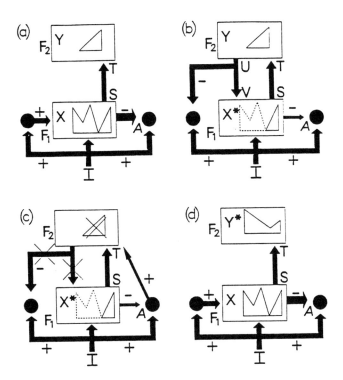

Figure 6. Search for a correct F_2 code: (a) The input pattern I generates the specific STM activity pattern X at F_1 as it nonspecifically activates A. Pattern X both inhibits A and generates the output signal pattern S. Signal pattern S is transformed into the input pattern T, which activates the STM pattern Y across F_2. (b) Pattern Y generates the top-down signal pattern U which is transformed into the template pattern V. If V mismatches I at F_1, then a new STM activity pattern X* is generated at F_1. The reduction in total STM activity which occurs when X is transformed into X* causes a decrease in the total inhibition from F_1 to A. (c) Then the input-driven activation of A can release a nonspecific arousal wave to F_2, which resets the STM pattern Y at F_2. (d) After Y is inhibited, its top-down template is eliminated, and X can be reinstated at F_1. Now X once again generates input pattern T to F_2, but since Y remains inhibited T can activate a different STM pattern Y* at F_2. If the top-down template due to Y* also mismatches I at F_1, then the rapid search for an appropriate F_2 code continues. (Reprinted with permission from Carpenter and Grossberg, 1987a, p. 61.)

recognition codes, or may initiate the learning of a new recognition code, until the full capacity of the architecture is utilized. Input patterns which cannot refine prior knowledge, or which are first experienced after full capacity is utilized, are rejected by the architecture's self-stabilizing mechanisms.

In architectures which cannot self-stabilize their learning, later input patterns can wash away the learning of prior input patterns, leading to an unstable cycle of learning and forgetting. These architectures include essentially all the classical versions of autoassociators, competitive learning mechanisms, and steepest descent algorithms such as back propagation.

Effective use of a non-self-stabilizing architecture depends upon results which estimate the architecture's capacity. The capacity estimates the maximum number of input patterns which the architecture can learn, recognize, or remember. Typically, an autoassociator's capacity is $\sim .15n$, where the autoassociator's memory is defined by an $n \times n$ matrix (Anderson, 1983; Hopfield, 1984; Kohonen, 1984; McEliece, Posner, Rodemich, and Venkatesh, 1980; Psaltis and Park, 1986; Venkatesh, 1986). Thus an autoassociator cannot effectively use its full capacity. Moreover, if the number of input patterns exceeds this capacity, a capacity catastrophe occurs which renders the architecture's output unreliable. Such non-self-stabilizing architectures are thus inherently off-line machines whose lab-time world of inputs is under strict control. In an ART architecture, estimates of capacity play a different role than in an autoassociator or steepest-descent algorithm, since no catastrophe occurs when the input world contains more patterns than the architecture can encode.

E. Maintain Plasticity in an Unexpected World versus Externally Shut Off Plasticity

An ART architecture retains its plasticity, or ability to learn, for all time; that is, the parameters which enable its adaptive weights, or long-term memory (LTM) traces, to learn are not switched off as time goes on. The self-stabilization property is due to a dynamic buffering scheme which protects these LTM traces from changing except during appropriate circumstances. Thus, if an unfamiliar event occurs at any time in the future, an ART architecture can learn about it, without destabilizing its prior knowledge, just so long as it has not already committed its full capacity to prior learning.

In contrast, if a non-self-stabilizing architecture is exposed to a never-ending time-series of input patterns, as *in vivo*, then it will experience a fatal capacity catastrophe unless its plasticity is shut off; that is, unless the parameters of its individual LTM traces are switched to a no-learning mode by an external or internalized teacher.

Such a switching-off of plasticity does not work well in nonstationary environments whose properties are not predictable in advance. If learning is switched off too soon, then important later events cannot be learned. If learning is switched off too late, then important earlier learning may be washed away due to a capacity catastrophe. An omniscient teacher is needed to switch off learning at just the right time in response to an arbitrary input environment. If an effective model of an omniscient teacher is available, however, then a potentially unstable learning device will not be needed.

F. Self-Scaling Computational Units

An ART architecture can learn to distinguish arbitrary pairs of binary input patterns. In contrast, many alternative recognition architectures depend upon orthogonality, linear predictability, or other statistical constraints on input patterns in order to function well. In order to achieve this property, an ART architecture self-scales the processing of its input patterns. Individual input features are automatically given less weight when they occur within more complex input patterns. A side benefit of this type of feature normalization is that sufficiently small noisy changes in a complex input pattern may not force recoding of the pattern.

As a result of the self-scaling property, an input feature may be encoded in LTM when it occurs within a simple input pattern, yet be rejected from LTM when it occurs within a complex input pattern. In the former case, the input feature becomes a critical feature by being learned by the LTM code that helps to recognize the pattern. In the latter case, the input feature becomes a noise element by being deleted from the LTM code that helps to recognize the pattern. This decision depends upon the entire history of learning that has preceded the presentation of an input pattern which contains the feature. Thus the concept of critical feature is an emergent property of the network rather than a property which can be defined solely by choice of an input filter.

G. Learn Internal Expectations versus Impose External Costs

An ART architecture learns its own top-down expectations as a function of the unique input environment to which it is exposed. These expectations are emergent internal representations which capture invariant statistical properties of the entire input environment. Such learned top-down expectations are a key ingredient of ART architectures. They function as prototypes for an entire recognition category, and abstractly encode the similarity properties which are shared by all exemplars of the category. On the other hand, the manner in which these expectations are learned and manipulated sets them apart from classical prototype ideas. They may also be interpreted as "costs" which the architecture learns for itself, such that different costs are learned in response to different input environments (Figure 7). In order to avoid misinterpretations of these expectations due to such analogies with previous ideas, Carpenter and Grossberg (1987a) have called them *critical feature patterns*.

In contrast, architectures which use an external teacher often represent this teacher as a set of target patterns, or externally imposed costs. In NETtalk, for example, the mismatch between a target phoneme output code and the actual phoneme output code is used to drive learning at all the model's stages, from the visual representation of input letters to the auditory representation of output phonemes. Thus an auditory mismatch is used to determine the learned properties of a visual code. *In vivo*, by contrast, many objects can be visually recognized based upon visual invariants, even if the objects have no names; e.g., the familiar face of a check-out person at the supermarket. The verbal phrase "check-out person" does not determine how we visually recognize such a person's face, any more than we would visually recognize the same face differently if the same job were renamed "cashier attendant."

In ART, self-organization of invariant critical feature patterns can occur within each modality before intermodality transformations between these invariants, such as between a visual representation of a face and an auditory representation of a name, are learned via associative mechanisms (Grossberg, 1978, 1982a).

H. Active Attentional Focussing and Priming versus Passive Weight Change

A top-down learned expectation in ART is actively matched against bottom-up information (Figure 6). This matching process takes place within a processing stage, or level, and can rapidly reorganize the activations, or short-term memory (STM) traces, that are computed at the nodes of this stage. In particular, a top-down critical feature pattern can prime a lower level to get ready for an exemplar from an expected class of input patterns. It can amplify and thereby speed up processing of an input pattern that belongs to an expected class, while it actively reorganizes the information processing of this input. A top-down expectation can also attenuate processing of unexpected inputs through a mismatch between the bottom-up input and the top-down expectation.

In this way, a top-down expectation enables an ART architecture to function like an intentional machine that generates an active focus of attention. In contrast, the top-down mechanisms of a teacher-driven architecture such as back propagation does not directly prime the system, or focus its attention, or reorganize its fast information processing. Instead back propagation merely causes slow changes in the bottom-up adaptive weights of the network (Figure 8).

I. Closing versus Opening the Fast-Slow Feedback Loop

The bottom-up and top-down interactions in an ART architecture close the feedback loop between fast activations at network levels and slower learned changes in the pathways between levels (Figure 5). This fundamental property is what enables the ART architecture to learn stably in real-time. In contrast, back propagation opens this feedback loop (Figure 8), which makes this network easier to understand but computationally less robust.

J. Expectant Priming versus Grinding All Memory Cycles

Due to the closed feedback cycle in ART, a top-down prime that is locked into STM by a large gain control signal can prevent any input that is not in the expected

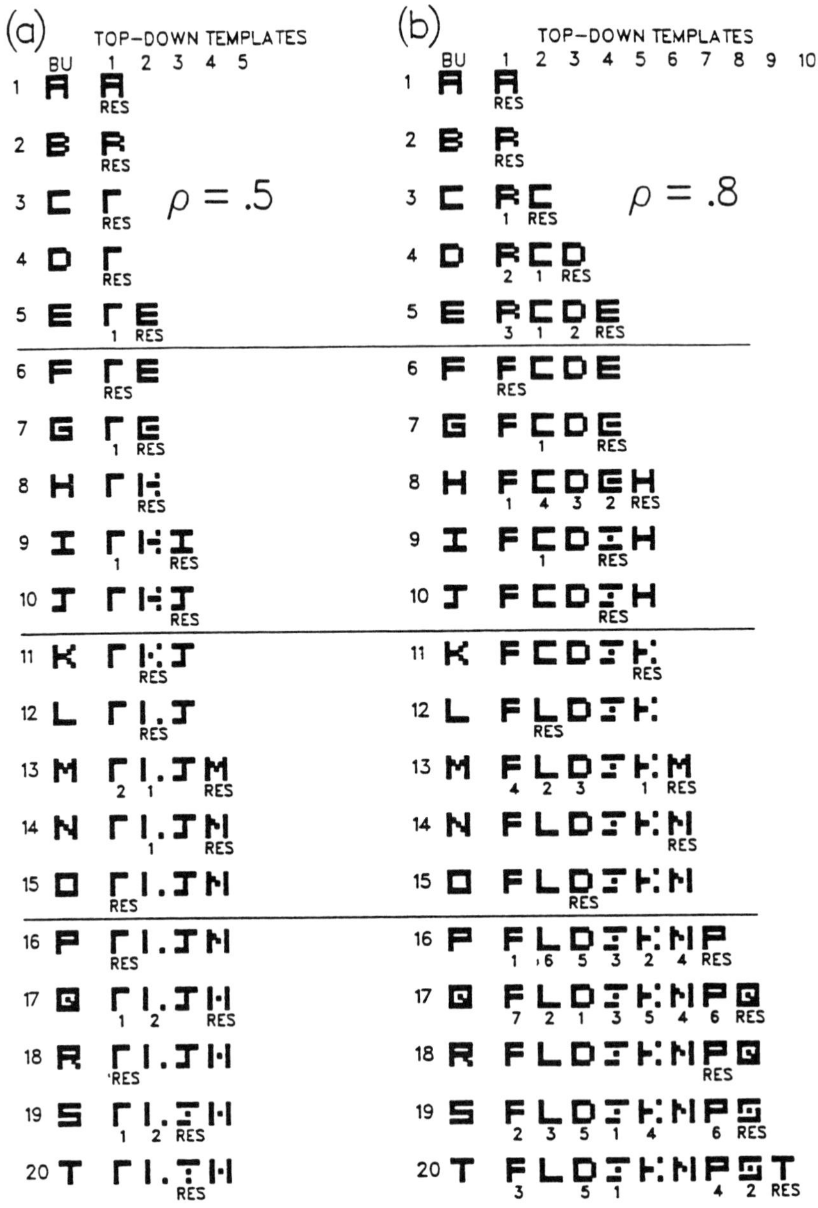
(a)
TOP-DOWN TEMPLATES
BU 1 2 3 4 5
ρ = .5
(b)
TOP-DOWN TEMPLATES
BU 1 2 3 4 5 6 7 8 9 10
ρ = .8
RES

Figure 7. Alphabet learning: Code learning in response to the first presentation of the first 20 letters of the alphabet is shown. Two different vigilance levels were used, $\rho = .5$ and $\rho = .8$. Each row represents the total code that is learned after the letter at the left-hand column of the row is presented at F_1. Each column represents the critical feature pattern that is learned through time by the F_2 node listed at the top of the column. The critical feature patterns do not, in general, equal the pattern exemplars which change them through learning. Instead, each critical feature pattern acts like a prototype for the entire set of these exemplars, as well as for unfamiliar exemplars which share invariant properties with familiar exemplars. The simulation illustrates the "fast learning" case, in which the altered LTM traces reach a new equilibrium in response to each new stimulus. Slow learning is more gradual than this. (Reprinted with permission from Carpenter and Grossberg, 1987a, p. 72.)

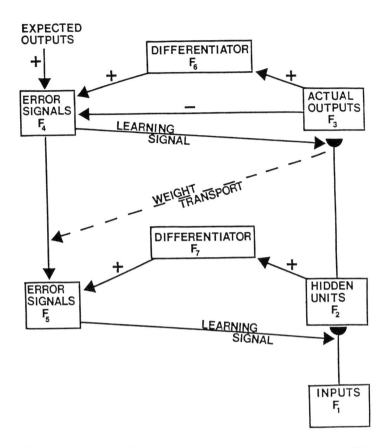

Figure 8. Circuit diagram of the back propagation model: In addition to the processing levels F_1, F_2, F_3, there are also levels F_4, F_5, F_6, and F_7 to carry out the computations which control the learning process. The transport of learned weights from the $F_2 \to F_3$ pathways to the $F_4 \to F_5$ pathways shows that this algorithm cannot represent a learning process in the brain. All feedback within the levels $F_1 \to F_2 \to F_3$ is expressed through learning signals which slowly change bottom-up adaptive weights but do not quickly reorganize the network's fast information processing.

recognition catgory from activating higher levels of the architecture, much as the verbal command to look for oranges enables one to avoid being too distracted by other objects.

In contrast, an architecture without a top-down expectation capable of actively suppressing mismatched exemplars will become fully engaged by any input patterns that may happen to occur. Its memory cycles may thus be so fully engaged by irrelevant inputs when a crucial event occurs that it cannot respond in time.

K. Learning in the Approximate Match Phase versus in the Mismatch Phase: Hypothesis Testing Avoids the Noise Catastrophe

Due to its possession of learned top-down expectations which actively suppress mismatched input patterns while prototypically deforming and amplifying matched input patterns, an ART architecture learns in the *approximate match* phase. In other words, if an input pattern causes the read-out of a learned top-down expectation which matches it well enough to prevent a reset event, then the matching process selects the information that is consistent between the input and the expectation. If these matched data include novel elements, they are used to refine the learned code of that recognition category. In other words, if the compressed recognition code, or hypothesis, generated by the input pattern does not cause reset due to read-out of its top-down expectation, then the architecture deems this input pattern to be consistent enough with that hypothesis to refine or update the hypothesis based upon any additional information that the pattern may contain. If reset does occur and leads to selection of an uncommitted code, then this code learns a complete representation of the input pattern, which is intuitively reasonable because the pattern could not be assimilated into any previously learned code.

Because an ART architecture learns in the approximate match stage, it is not degraded by noise fluctuating at its input level. If a noise pattern is very different from its learned codes, the architecture dynamically buffers these codes against relearning and selects an uncommitted code to learn the noise. If the noise does not repeat itself often enough and learning proceeds slowly, the noise will not cause significant learning within the uncommitted code. It will not, in any case, interfere with the codes of sufficiently different patterns even if learning proceeds quickly.

Architectures without a fast-slow feedback loop, such as back propagation, are designed so that learning occurs in the mismatch mode. Thus if noise can activate the teacher, or expected output stage, then all the LTM traces of the architecture can eventually be recoded. This noise catastrophe can be prevented only if the noise is infrequent and learning is slow. In ART, even frequent noise is simply treated as a new source of inputs that does not endanger the corpus of previously learned information.

Although learning in the mismatch phase can cause a noise catastrophe in an architecture which is designed to learn a recognition code in real-time, it is a useful type of learning in a number of alternative situations, notably during adaptive sensory-motor control (see Sections 18–21).

L. Fast or Slow Learning: The Oscillation Catastrophe

Another consequence of learning in the approximate match phase is that ART can learn at either a fast or slow rate. Fast learning occurs when each LTM trace can reach a new equilibrium value on a single learning trial. Successive learning trials may or may not cause the LTM trace to assume different equilibrium values. Slow learning may require many trials before the LTM traces reach any equilibrium point of the system.

When learning occurs in the mismatch phase, as in back propagation, fast learning can cause wild oscillations to occur in the network's LTM traces, since each mismatch can drag the LTM traces to a totally different region of phase space. Thus such architectures must learn slowly, which emphasizes their off-line character. Contrast the vivid recollection of an exciting movie after one-trial on-line learning *in vivo*.

M. Self-Adjusting Parallel Memory Search and Global Energy Landscape Upheaval versus Search Trees and Local Minima

Learning in the approximate match phase could be disastrous were it not for the existence in ART of a self-adjusting parallel memory search that maintains its efficiency as the learned code becomes more complex. When an input pattern causes read-out of a top-down expectation with which it cannot form an approximate match, the attenuation of activity due to the mismatch event resets the compressed code, or hypothesis, that caused the mismatch (Figure 6b). A parallel memory search is hereby triggered that rapidly tests a series of such hypotheses. This hypothesis testing scheme actively and globally reorganizes the energy landscape of the architecture. In this way, the architecture circumvents the problem of local minima that has plagued alternative architectures such as autoassociators, simulated annealing, and the Boltzmann machine.

The need to escape local minima has influenced the design of all content-addressable memory and learning architectures. Architectures which do not possess self-adjusting hypothesis testing schemes typically use two alternative approaches. In autoassociators, simulated annealing, and the Boltzmann machine, noise is used to help the classification to jump out of a local minimum. Such a scheme does not globally reorganize the energy landscape based upon the outcome of active information processing. Instead the nonspecific action of noise tries to exploit the fact that the local minima of a fixed energy landscape may be easier to escape than a global minimum, and that a nonspecific external temperature parameter may be used to control the rate of approach to equilibrium.

Steepest-descent methods, such as back propagation, use a mismatch to drag the system's LTM traces out of local minima, and do so slowly enough to reduce the potentially destabilizing effects of the oscillation catastrophe.

Traditional AI architectures often include search trees to escape erroneous classifications. Although a search tree may be efficient at one stage of learning, it cannot remain efficient at an arbitrary stage of learning unless it has a self-adjusting capability, as in ART.

N. Rapid Direct Access versus Increase of Recognition Time with Code Complexity

In ART, as learning self-stabilizes in response to a set of input patterns, the search mechanism is automatically disengaged. Thereafter rapid direct access to the recognition code occurs in response to familiar input exemplars as well as to novel exemplars that share invariant properties with familiar input exemplars. Direct access occurs because read-out of the top-down expectation of a familiar input pattern always leads to an approximate match (Carpenter and Grossberg, 1987a). Then the initial bottom-up event that led to top-down readout (Figure 6) can generate a resonant recognition event without causing reset. Thus an ART architecture reconciles the ostensibly conflicting demands of direct access and search. It uses reset and self-regulating search to build globally self-consistent recognition codes which avoid local minima in response to arbitrarily complex time-series of input patterns. It uses direct access to recognize familiar events with a speed as fast as one's hardware can run.

In contrast, an AI architecture with a search tree takes longer and longer to recognize an event as it needs to search more and more codes. If this were the case *in vivo*, it could take orders of magnitude more time to recognize our parents when we were 30 years old than it did when we were 5 years old. Fortunately, this is false.

O. Asynchronous or Synchronous Learning?

In ART 1, each LTM trace oscillates at most once through time in response to an arbitrary time-series of binary input patterns (Carpenter and Grossberg, 1987a). Were it not for the architecture's active reorganization of the energy landscape through hypothesis testing, this remarkable monotonicity property could easily cause the architecture to learn a local minimum. As it is, learning is allowed to occur only when the energy landscape reaches a configuration that leads to an approximate match. Due to these properties, an ART 1 architecture can learn asynchronously or synchronously: If input patterns come in too quickly to generate an approximate match or to terminate a search, then no learning occurs. If the input pattern stays on long enough for some learning to occur, then it does not matter too much how long it stays on because, due to the monotonicity property, the LTM traces will tend to change in the same direction no matter how long it stays on.

In contrast, if mismatch drives learning in such a way that each LTM trace can oscillate persistently as it approaches equilibrium, then variable durations of the input patterns may destabilize the learning process. The limiting case of this property is the oscillation catastrophe, which occurs if sufficiently many input patterns stay on long enough for LTM traces to reach equilibrium on each such learning trial.

P. Discriminative Tuning via Attentional Vigilance

Although an ART architecture self-organizes its learning, it can be tuned by environmental feedback to learn coarser or finer discriminations; that is, it can learn to categorize the same set of input patterns into larger or smaller groupings depending upon how strictly the performance demands of the external environment are imposed.

Such environmental feedback acts to change a single parameter of the network that is called the vigilance parameter (Carpenter and Grossberg, 1987a). This parameter determines how fine the mismatch between bottom-up input and top-down expectation must be in order to reset the code which read-out the expectation. A large vigilance parameter demands a high degree of match to prevent reset, hence finely categorizes the input patterns. A small vigilance parameter tolerates larger mismatches before forcing reset, hence more coarsely categorizes the input patterns.

This tuning parameter depends for its existence upon the fact that bottom-up and top-down matches occur as part of the real-time feedback cycle that determines the classification of input patterns. In particular, it can change dramatically the global reorganization of the energy landscape that regulates self-regulating search and learning by modifying the overall attentiveness, or sensitivity, of the circuit.

Q. Towards a General-Purpose Machine for Cognitive Hypothesis Testing, Data Search, and Classification

In ART, adaptive pattern recognition is a form of hypothesis discovery, testing, learning, and recognition in response to a nonstationary input environment. This property would seem to be essential for any cognitive theory which hopes to understand how ever-more-complex knowledge invariants are discovered, tested, and recognized, at any level of abstraction.

In particular, future ART machines may be designed to learn, search, and classify complex hierarchically organized data files. The properties of automatic self-stabilization and self-scaling will be essential for such an architecture to work reliably and quickly on enormous data bases. The advantages of such a self-organizing system become greater as the data sets are chosen larger, because the decision task for hand-sorting so much data or the discovery of rules for automatically sorting all the data, especially when new data are added later on, rapidly become unmanageably difficult as a function of scale.

The postulates of ART thus define a class of models for a broad range of cognitive science applications, which include examples that may or may not even possess an orienting subsystem and search mechanism (Figure 5), as discussed by Carpenter and Grossberg (1987c). McClelland (1987) has proposed that models of this class be renamed the "interactive activation framework" after the interactive activation model that was introduced by McClelland and Rumelhart (1981) and Rumelhart and McClelland (1982). The postulates of the interactive activation model are, however, inconsistent with those of an ART model. The postulates of the interactive activation model have been abandoned in favor of ART postulates because they are inconsistent with key cognitive data and possess some undesirable computational properties, as noted in Grossberg (1984, 1986, 1987e). Since ART was an established cognitive theory (Grossberg, 1978a, 1980b) before the interactive activation model was published, it seems historically and scientifically justified to retain the name Adaptive Resonance Theory for such models.

18. Internally Regulated Learning and Performance in Neural Models of Sensory-Motor Control: Adaptive Vector Encoders and Coordinate Transformations

In many real-time nonlinear neural network architectures other than ART architectures, learning is regulated by pattern matches and mismatches. For example, learning of intermodality associative maps between the target position commands of different sensory-motor systems (Figure 9a) is gated on and off by intramodality pattern matches and mismatches, respectively. These same matching processes transform automatically such a target position command into a synchronous multi-joint trajectory which automatically compensates for variable initial positions in a manner that quantitatively explains a large body of data about human and monkey arm movements (Bullock and Grossberg, 1987a). Thus just as in an ART model, model neural architectures which have been identified for the learning and performance of arm movements use internal matching processes to regulate both the fast information processing and the slower learning of the system.

The circuit depicted in Figure 9 schematizes key processing stages in a Vector Integration to Endpoint, or VITE, circuit. In its simplest form, the VITE circuit obeys the equations:

Difference Vector

$$\frac{d}{dt}V_i = \alpha(-V_i + T_i - P_i) \tag{109}$$

and

Present Position Command

$$\frac{d}{dt}P_i = G[V_i]^+, \tag{110}$$

where $[V_i]^+ = \max(V_i, 0)$. Equations (109) and (110) describe a generic component of a target position command $(T_1, T_2, \ldots, T_n)$, a difference vector $(V_1, V_2, \ldots, V_n)$, and a present position command $(P_1, P_2, \ldots, P_n)$ in response to a time-varying velocity command, or GO signal $G(t)$; see Figure 9b. The difference vector computes a mismatch between target position and present position, and is used to update present position at a variable rate determined by $G(t)$ until the present position matches the target position.

Such a scheme permits multiple muscles, or other motor effectors, to contract synchronously even though the total amount of contraction, scaled by $T_i(0) - P_i(0)$, may be different for each effector (Figure 10). Unlike many alternative schemes for motor control, present position in (110) is not computed using inflow signals from the muscles. Rather, it is determined by nonlinear integration of vectors computed by matching an outflowing target position command with feedback from outflowing present position signals.

The VITE circuit is not sufficient in itself to accomplish all the tasks required of a variable-speed variable-load arm movement system. In concert with several parallel circuits, however, it can generate flexible and adaptive trajectories without suffering from the combinatorial explosions and rigid performance of control systems which preplan an entire trajectory. Herein I outline some of the adaptive control issues which arise in the design of such neural architectures for movement control and mention where internal matching processes regulate their processes of learning and performance. Quantitative neural network solutions to such problems are suggested by Bullock and Grossberg (1987a, 1987b) and Grossberg and Kuperstein (1986).

The computation of a hand or arm's present position illustrates the complexity of the problem. As mentioned above, two general types of present position signals have been identified in discussions of motor control: *outflow* signals and *inflow* signals. Figure 11 schematizes the difference between these signal sources. An outflow signal carries a movement command from the brain to a muscle (Figure 11a). Signals that branch off from the efferent brain-to-muscle pathway in order to register present position signals are called *corollary discharges* (Helmholtz, 1866; von Holst and Mittelstaedt, 1950). An *inflow* signal carries present position information from a muscle to the brain (Figure 11b). A primary difference between outflow and inflow is that a change in outflow signals is triggered only when an observer's brain generates a new movement command. A new inflow signal can, in contrast, be generated by passive movements of the limb. Both outflow and inflow signals are used in multiple

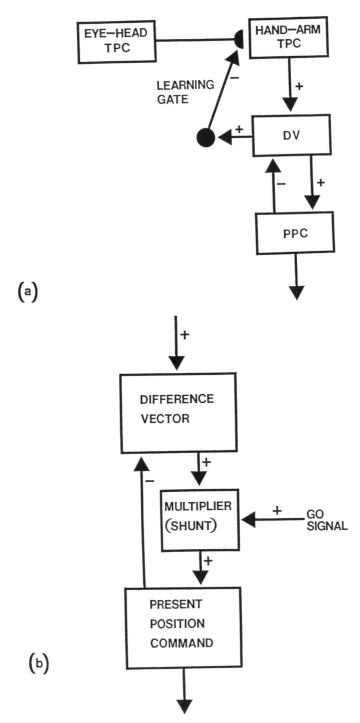

Figure 9. (a) Learning in sensory-motor pathways is gated by a difference vector (DV) process which matches target position command (TPC) with present position command (PPC) to prevent incorrect associations from forming between eye-head TPC's and hand-arm TPC's. (b) A GO signal gates execution of a primed movement vector and regulates the rate at which the movement vector updates the present position command. (Reprinted with permission from Bullock and Grossberg, 1987b.)

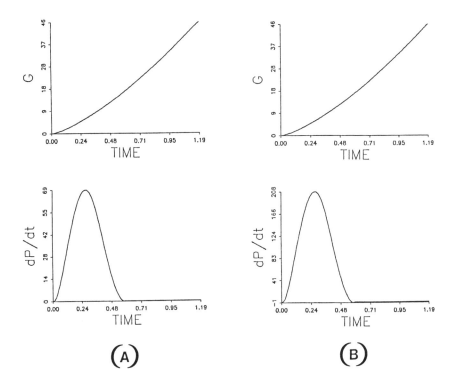

Figure 10. With equal GO signals, movements of different size have equal durations and perfectly superimposable velocity profiles after velocity axis rescaling. (A,B): GO signals and velocity profiles for 20 and 60 unit movements lasting 560 msec. (Reprinted with permission from Bullock and Grossberg, 1987b.)

ways to provide different types of information about present position. The following summary itemizes some of the ways in which these signals are used in our theory.

Although one role of an outflow signal is to move a limb by contracting its target muscles, or motor plant, the operating characteristics of the motor plant are not known *a priori* to the outflow source. It is not known *a priori* either how much the muscle will actually contract in response to an outflow signal of prescribed size, or how much the limb will move in response to a prescribed muscle contraction. In addition, even if the outflow system somehow possessed this information at one time, it might turn out to be the wrong information at a later time, because muscle plant characteristics can change through time due to development, aging, exercise, changes in blood supply, or minor tears. (State-dependent and history-dependent plant changes may occur on the factory assembly line or in a freely-moving robot, no less than in a living muscle.) Thus the relationship between the size of an outflow movement command and the amount of muscle contraction is, in principle, undeterminable without additional information which characterizes the muscle plant's actual response to outflow signals.

To establish a satisfactory correspondence between outflow movement signals and actual muscle contractions, the motor system needs to compute reliable present position signals which represent where the outflow command tells the muscle to move, as well as reliable present position signals which represent the state of contraction of the muscle. Corollary discharges and inflow signals can provide these different types of information. Grossberg and Kuperstein (1986) have shown how a match between corollary discharges and inflow signals can be used to modify, through an automatic

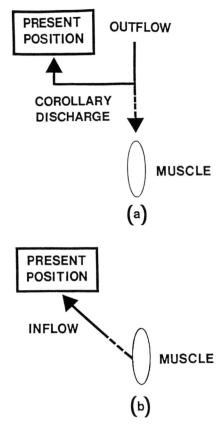

Figure 11. Both outflow and inflow signals contribute to the brain's estimate of the limb's present position, but in different ways.

learning process, the total outflow movement signal to the muscle in a way that effectively compensates for changes in the muscle plant (Figure 12). Mismatches act as error signals which change the gain of the total outflow movement signal. This automatic gain control process generates adaptively a linear correspondence between an outflow movement command and the amount of muscle contraction even if the muscle plant is nonlinear. The process which matches outflow and inflow signals to linearize the muscle plant response through learning is called *adaptive linearization* of the muscle plant.

The cerebellum is implicated by both the theoretically derived circuit and experimental evidence as the site of learning. Early cerebellar learning models were proposed by Albus (1971), Brindley (1964), Grossberg (1964, 1969d, 1972b), and Marr (1969). Later models and experimental support were provided by Fujita (1982a, 1982b), Ito (1974, 1982, 1984), McCormick and Thompson (1984), Optican and Robinson (1980), Ron and Robinson (1973), Vilis and Hore (1986), and Vilis, Snow, and Hore (1983). The present model introduces new features which are critical to its success in correcting behaviorally well-characterized types of movements errors.

For example, an adaptive gain (AG) stage in our theory—which is interpreted as a model cerebellum—is used by multiple circuits that contribute to both eye movement and arm movement accuracy and postural stability. Each of these circuits involves different—and specific—input, output, and error signal pathways, but all of these pathways are mediated by the same internal AG stage architecture. These AG stage results significantly extend recent data and models concerning the cerebellum's role

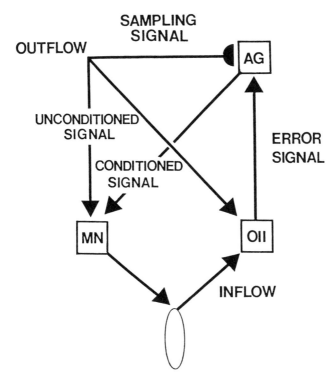

Figure 12. Some main features of the muscle linearization network, or MLN: The outflow-inflow interface (OII) registers matches and mismatches between outflow signals and inflow signals. Mismatches generate error signals to the adaptive gain (AG) stage. These error signals change the gain of the conditioned movement signal to the motoneurons (MN). Such an MLN adaptively linearizes the responses of a nonlinear muscle plant to outflow signals. The outflow signals can therefore also be used as a source of accurate corollary discharges of present eye position. (Reprinted with permission from Grossberg and Kuperstein, 1986, p. 136.)

in the conditioning of movements (Fujita, 1982a, 1982b; Ito, 1984; McCormick and Thompson, 1984; Optican and Robinson, 1980). For example, push-pull opponent processing of the error signals which govern adaptive gain changes at the AG stage is a novel, and computationally critical, part of this model. Such an arrangement enables the AG stage to correct undershoot, overshoot, or directionally skewed eye movement errors, as well as errors due to sustained wearing of curvature-distorting contact lens.

Although adaptive linearization is, like back-propagation, a form of error-driven learning in the mismatch mode, it is not susceptible to the instabilities of back-propagation because it merely changes the gains of internal command pathways via internal mismatches. It does not put at risk the spatial encoding of the commands that activate the pathways and is not subjected to noise fluctuations from the external environment.

Given that corollary discharges are matched with inflow signals to linearize the relationship between muscle plant contraction and outflow signal size, outflow signals can also be used in other ways to provide important information about present position. As Figure 9 illustrates, outflow present position signals can then be matched with target position commands to generate a trajectory with synchronous properties. Thus outflow signals are used in at least three ways, and all of these ways are automatically registered: They send movement signals to target muscles; they generate corollary discharges which are matched with inflow signals to guarantee linear muscle contractions even if the muscle plant is nonlinear; and they generate corollary discharges which are matched with target position signals to generate synchronous trajectories.

Inflow signals are also used in several ways. One way has already been itemized. A second use of inflow signals is suggested by the following gedanken example. When you are sitting in an armchair, let your hands drop passively towards your sides. Depending upon a multitude of accidental factors, your hands and arms can end up in any of infinitely many final positions. If you are then called upon to make a precise movement with your arm-hand system, this can be done with great accuracy. Thus the fact that your hands and arms start out this movement from an initial position which was not reached under active control by an outflow signal does not impair the accuracy of the movement.

Much evidence suggests, however, that comparison between target position and present position information is used to move the arms and that, as in Figure 9, this present position information is computed from outflow signals. In contrast, during the passive fall of an arm under the influence of gravity, changes in outflow signal commands are not responsible for the changes in position of the limb. Since the final position of a passively falling limb cannot be predicted in advance, it is clear that inflow signals must be used to update present position when an arm is moved passively by an external force, even though outflow signals are used to update present position when the arm moves actively under neural control.

This conclusion calls attention to a closely related issue that must be dealt with to understand the neural bases of skilled movement: How does the motor system know that the arm is being moved passively due to an external force, and not actively due to a changing outflow command? Such a distinction is needed to prevent inflow information from contaminating outflow commands when the arm is being actively moved. The motor system uses internally generated signals to make the distinction between active movement and passive movement, or postural, conditions. Computational gates are opened and shut based upon whether these internally generated signals are on or off.

Bullock and Grossberg (1987a) have suggested that the GO signal schematized in Figure 9b helps to computationally define the postural state. Offset of the GO signal is hypothesized to open a learning gate which enables inflow signals to be adaptively recalibrated until they are computed in the same measurement scale as outflow signals (Figure 13). This type of learning occurs in the mismatch mode, rather than the approximate match mode, using the mismatch between the coordinate systems as an error signal to drive the learning process. Offset of the GO signal is also hypothesized to open a gate which enables an outflow-inflow mismatch due to a passive movement to update the outflow present position command (Figure 13).

The circuit which accomplishes both of these learning and update functions is called the Passive Update of Position, or PUP, circuit. The equations of a typical PUP circuit are:

Present Position Command

$$\frac{d}{dt} P_i = G[V_i]^+ + G_p[M_i]^+ \tag{111}$$

Outflow-Inflow Match

$$\frac{d}{dt} M_i = -\beta M_i + \gamma I_i - z_i P_i \tag{112}$$

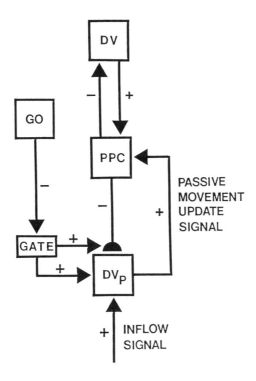

Figure 13. A passive update of position (PUP) circuit. An adaptive pathway $PPC \to DV_P$ calibrates PPC-outflow signals in the same scale as inflow signals during intervals of posture. During passive movements, output from DV equals zero. Hence the passive difference vector DV_P updates the PPC until it equals the new position caused by any passive movements that may occur due to the application of external forces.

Adaptive Gain Control

$$\frac{d}{dt}z_i = \delta G_p(-\epsilon z_i + [M_i]^+). \tag{113}$$

Equation (111) supplements equation (110) with an update signal $G_p[M_i]^+$ that is turned on only when the passive gating function, or "pauser" signal, G_p becomes positive in the passive, or postural, state. Function z_i in (113) is an LTM trace, or associative weight, which adaptively recalibrates the gain of outflow signals P_i until they are in the same scale as outflow signals γI_i in (112).

In summary, offset of the GO signal within the VITE circuit enables a pauser signal within the PUP circuit to drive its learning and reset functions. Such pauser-modulated learning of mismatches seems to occur in several adaptive sensory-motor control circuits. For example, Grossberg and Kuperstein (1986) have suggested that a pauser signal which defines the postural state of the ballistic eye movement system enables a mismatch signal analogous to M_i in (112) to adaptively recode the representation of a light-activated target position command into motor coordinates. This adaptive recoding scheme, which is called the Head-Muscle Interface, or HMI, permits the recoded target position to be matched against the present position of the eye, which is also coded in motor coordinates. Such a matching process generates a movement command in the form of a difference vector which measures the mismatch between target position and present position, much as in the VITE circuit of Figure 9.

Typical equations for an HMI circuit are:

Head-Muscle Match

$$\frac{d}{dt}x_i = -Ax_i + G(\sum_{j=1}^{n} S_j)(-\sum_{j=1}^{n} S_j z_{ji} + I_i), \tag{114}$$

Adaptive Gain Control

$$\frac{d}{dt}z_{ji} = P\{-Bz_{ji} + S_j[x_i]^+\}, \tag{115}$$

and

Vector
$$V = ([x_1]^+, [x_2]^+, \ldots, [x_n]^+) \tag{116}$$

where

Match Gate

$$G(\sum_{j=1}^{n} S_j) = \begin{cases} 1 & \text{if } \sum_{j=1}^{n} S_j > 0 \\ 0 & \text{if } \sum_{j=1}^{n} S_j = 0 \end{cases} \tag{117}$$

and $[x_j]^+ = \max(x_j, 0)$. In (114), I_i is the corollary discharge signal that represents the position of the ith muscle, S_j is the light-activated representation of the jth target position, z_{ji} is the LTM trace that adaptively adjusts the gain between S_j and I_i, P is a gating signal that switches on in the postural mode, and V is the output vector. Variable x_i in (114) plays the role of variable M_i in (112).

Due to the general importance of schemes such as the PUP circuit of (111)–(113) and the HMI circuit of (114)–(117) for adaptively recalibrating coordinate systems using vector computations, I have called all schemes of this type Adaptive Vector Encoders.

A third role for inflow signals is needed due to the fact that arms can move at variable velocities while carrying variable loads. Because an arm is a mechanical system embedded in a Newtonian world, an arm can generate unexpected amounts of inertia and acceleration when it tries to move novel loads at novel velocities. During such a novel motion, the commanded outflow position of the arm and its actual position may significantly diverge. Inflow signals are needed to compute mismatches leading to partial compensation for this uncontrolled component of the movement.

Such novel movements are quite different from our movements when we pick up a familiar fountain pen or briefcase. When the object is familiar, we can predictively adjust the gain of the movement to compensate for the expected mass of the object. This type of automatic gain control can, moreover, be flexibly switched on and off using signal pathways that can be activated by visual recognition of a familiar object. Inflow signals are used in the learning process which enables such automatic gain control signals to be activated in an anticipatory fashion in response to familiar objects (Bullock and Grossberg, 1987b).

19. External Error Signals for Learning Adaptive Movement Gains: Push-Pull Opponent Processing

The previous discussion outlined several of the types of learning whereby *internal* mismatches generate error signals capable of adaptively recalibrating a coordinate system or adaptively changing the gain of a movement command. *External* error

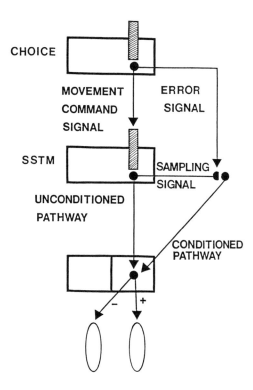

Figure 14. The representation of the chosen first light gives rise to an unconditioned movement signal and a conditioned movement signal. The unconditioned signal causes movements that are corrected by the conditioned movement signal via learning. The conditioned pathway carries sampling signals whose strength can be altered by second-light mediated error signals. These sampling signals give rise to the conditioned movement signal. The representation of the first light must be stored until after the end of the saccade, so that the second-light mediated error signal can act. (Reprinted with permission from Grossberg and Kuperstein, 1986, p. 38.)

signals are also used to alter the gain of a movement command. Such error signals function like an external "teacher." Unlike the hypothetical teachers employed in many examples of back-propagation, these error signals correspond to events which actually occur in the external environment during real-time learning.

Grossberg and Kuperstein (1986) have, for example, demonstrated how the accuracy of eye movements which do not successfully foveate a light can be improved by using the position of the light on the retina after the movement terminates as an error signal (Figure 14). Such an error signal adaptively changes the gain of the movement command. Mathematical and computer analyses demonstrate how to design such a system so that external error signals due to nonfoveated lights cooperate with internal error signals due to outflow-inflow mismatches to generate movements capable of adaptively maintaining their accuracy without the intervention of a human teacher (Figure 15).

The success of this learning model depends critically upon the hypothesis that errors are corrected in a push-pull, or opponent, fashion (Figure 16). The eye muscles, or other effectors, are assumed to be organized in reciprocal push-pull pairs, such as a pair for pulling to the right (R) and the left (L). Typical learning rules for such pairs are (expressed for convenience in discrete time n):

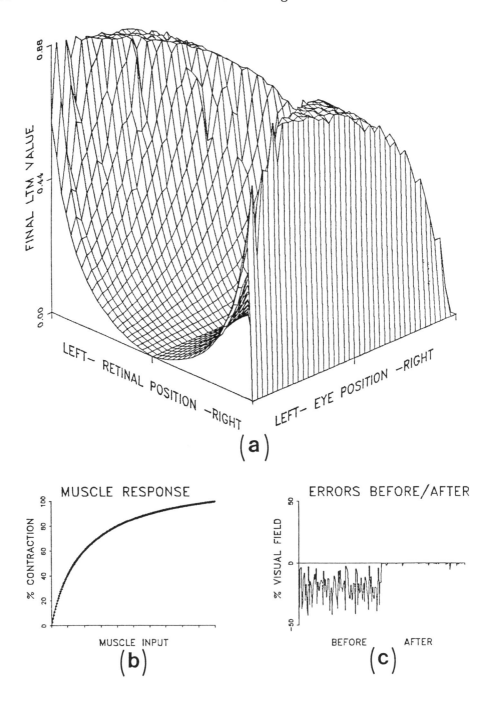

(a)

(b)

(c)

Figure 15. Computer simulation of saccadic error correction model with sampling from a non-invariant target position map using a slower-than-linear muscle function and a linear learning function. (a) Topographic distribution of LTM trace values after learning. (b) Muscle response function used in the simulation. (c) Errors in 100 trials before learning begins and 100 trials after learning ends. Negative values correspond to undershoots and positive values correspond to overshoots. (Reprinted with permission from Grossberg and Kuperstein, 1986, p. 89.)

Hemifield Gradient Learning Rule

$$z_{Ri}(n+1) = \delta z_{Ri}(n) + [L(E_n)]^+ \tag{118}$$

$$z_{Li}(n+1) = \delta z_{Li}(n) + [-L(E_n)]^+ \tag{119}$$

and the

Fractured Somatotopy Learning Rule

$$z_{Ri}(n+1) = [\delta z_{Ri}(n) + L(E_n)]^+ \tag{120}$$

$$z_{Li}(n+1) = [\delta z_{Li}(n) - L(E_n)]^+ \tag{121}$$

where in both cases E_n represents the position of the light error on the nth trial, and $L(E_n)$ is the error signal by which it drives the learning of adaptive gains. Function $L(w)$ is assumed to be an increasing function of $w \geq 0$, and to be an odd function of w; i.e., $L(w) = -L(^-w)$. Variables z_{Ri} and z_{Li} are the LTM traces controlled by the ith command source to the right and left motor effectors.

Due to the push-pull organization of the learning process, the output signal $O_R(n)$ to the right muscle depends upon the differences $z_{Ri}(n) - z_{Li}(n)$ of these LTM traces, whereas the output signal $O_L(n)$ to the left muscle depends upon the differences $z_{Li}(n) - z_{Ri}(n)$. Such push-pull terms suggest a physical way to instantiate the types of formal comparisons between increments and baseline terms that have been hypothesized in a number of learning models (Rescorla and Wagner, 1972; Sutton and Barto, 1981). Opponent processing has also been assumed to regulate learning in real-time neural network models of classical and instrumental conditioning (Grossberg, 1972a; Grossberg and Schmajuk, 1987).

20. Match-Invariants: Internally Regulated Learning of an Invariant Self-Regulating Target Position Map

Among the most important types of problems in neural network theory are those which concern the adaptive emergence of recognition invariants. Many different type of invariants can be identified; for example, the emergent invariants encoded by the critical feature patterns in an ART architecture enable the architecture to group all exemplars that share certain similarity properties into a single recognition category. As in ART, a number of other types of invariants are learned through a match-regulated process which gates on and off the learning mechanisms that enable individual events to be grouped together adaptively. I call such invariants *match invariants* to distinguish them from invariants that arise (say) due to a passive filtering process, such as Fourier-Mellin filtering.

Another model of a match invariant process was developed by Grossberg and Kuperstein (1986). This model shows how a matching process which defines the postural state can regulate the learning of an invariant self-regulating target position map in egocentric, or head-centered, coordinates. This problem arises when one considers how a visual signal to a moveable eye, or camera system, can be efficiently converted into an eye-tracking movement command.

To solve this problem, the positions of lights registered on the retina of an eye need to be converted into a head-coordinate frame so they can be compared with present eye positions which are also computed in a head-coordinate frame. In order to convert the position of a light on the retina into a target position in head coordinates, one needs to join together information about the light's retinal position with information about present position of the eye in the head (Figure 17). Kuperstein and I suggested that this type of transformation is learned. Otherwise, the retinal system and the eye position system—which are widely separated in the brain and

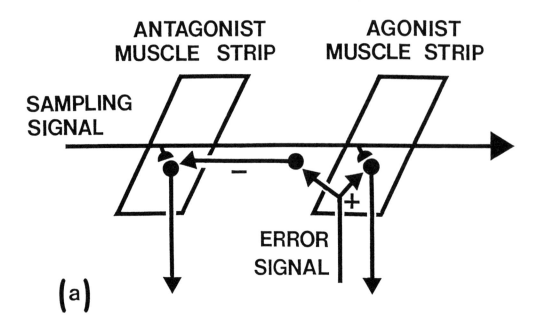

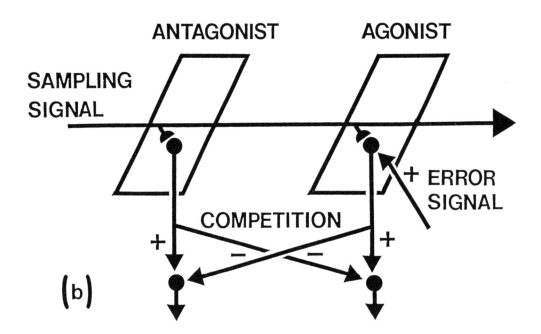

Figure 16. Two ways to achieve opponent conditioning of agonist-antagonist muscles: (a) An error signal increases the conditioned gain at the agonist muscle strip and decreases the conditioned gain at the antagonist muscle strip. (b) An error signal increases the conditioned gain at the agonist muscle strip. Competition between agonist and antagonist muscle strip outputs causes the decrease in the net antagonist output. (Reprinted with permission from Grossberg and Kuperstein, 1986, p. 70.)

designed according to different internal constraints—would have to be pre-wired with perfectly chosen parameters for their mutual interaction. We have shown how such a transformation can be learned even if parameters are coarsely chosen initially and if significant portions of either system are damaged or even destroyed. This type of learning exhibits properties which are of general interest in other biological movement systems, in cognitive psychology, and in the design of freely moving robots. I will therefore describe its major elements here.

The most important properties of this transformation are that it is many-to-one, invariant, and self-regulating. As Figure 17 illustrates, many combinations of retinal position and eye position correspond to a single target position with respect to the head. When a single target position representation is activated by all of these possible combinations, the transformation is said to be invariant (Figure 18a). The key difficulty in understanding how such an invariant transformation is learned arises from its many-to-one property. The many-to-one property implies that each retinal position and each eye position can activate many target positions in head coordinates (Figure 18b). Even after learning takes place, each pair of retinal and eye positions can activate many target positions in head coordinates, but only the correct target position should receive the maximal total activation.

What prevents learning due to one pair of retinal and eye positions from contradicting learning due to a different pair of positions? In particular, if pairing retinal position R_1 with eye position E_1 strengthens the pathways from these positions to target position T_1, then why does not future pairing of R_1 with a different eye position E_2 continue to maximally excite T_1 instead of the correct target position corresponding to R_1 and E_2? How is a globally consistent rule learned by a network, despite the fact that all computations in the network are local? How can a target position map be *implicitly* defined, such that each eye position and retinal position, taken separately, activates a large number of target positions, yet in combination always maximally activate the correct target position?

Finally, the property of self-regulation means that the map can correct itself even if a large fraction of the retinal positions and/or eye positions are destroyed, or if their parameters are otherwise altered through time. Destruction of a single retinal position eliminates all the combinations which that position made with all eye positions to activate target positions. In a similar fashion, destroying a single eye position can disrupt all target positions with which it was linked. A self-regulating map must thus be able to reorganize all of its learned changes to maintain its global self-consistency after removal of any of its components.

The self-regulation property is illustrated by the computer simulation from Grossberg and Kuperstein (1986) that is summarized in Figure 19. Each row in Figure 19 depicts learning of target positions corresponding to a different number of retinal and eye positions. More combinations of positions are represented in each successive row. The first column in each row depicts an intermediate learning stage, and the second column depicts a late learning stage. The abscissa plots topographic positions across the retinal and eye positions maps, whereas the ordinate plots the sizes of the adaptive path strengths, or learned long term memory (LTM) traces, in the pathways from these maps to the target position map. Such a scheme clarifies how the eye-head target position map that is schematized in Figure 9 may self-organize.

The LTM traces in Figure 19 were randomly chosen before learning began. A comparison of panels (b), (d), and (f) shows that the LTM traces can reorganize themselves when more combinations of positions are associated in such a way as to (approximately) preserve that part of the map which was learned when fewer combinations of positions were associated. This self-regulation property also holds when more combinations are replaced by fewer combinations, or if the initial LTM traces are not randomly chosen (Figure 20).

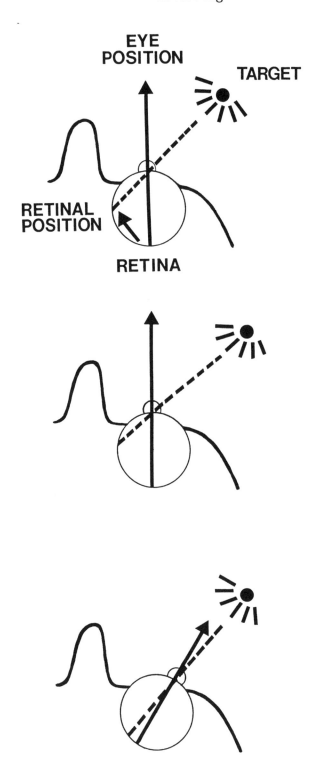

Figure 17. Many combinations of retinal position and eye position can encode the same target position.

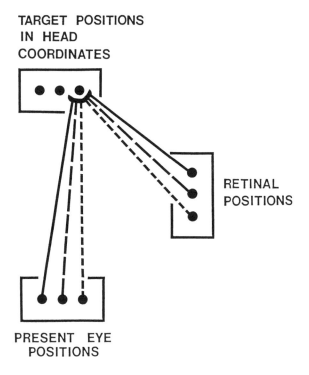

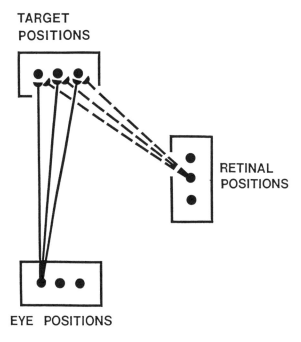

Figure 18. (a) When the many combinations of retinal position and eye position that correspond to each fixed target position all activate the same internal representation of that target position in head coordinates, the ensemble of such head coordinate representations is said to form an invariant map. (b) Every eye position and retinal position can send signals to many target position representations.

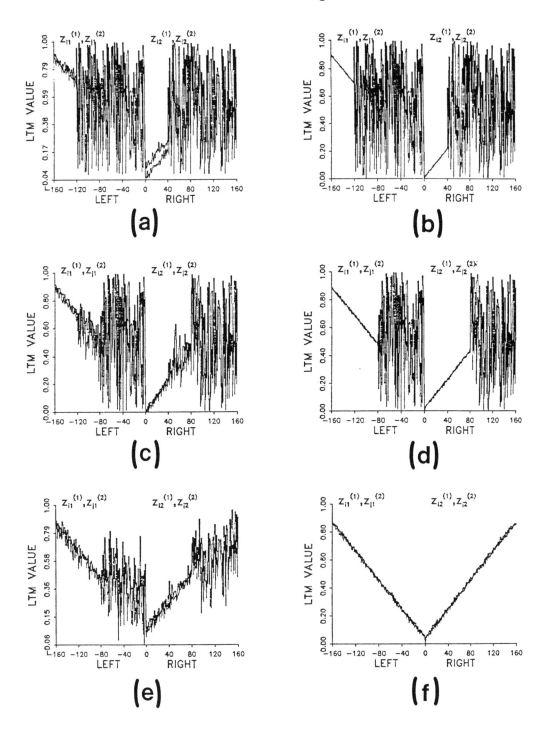

Figure 19. Expansion of LTM spatial maps due to increase of the number of light positions and eye positions being correlated. The learned LTM values in corresponding positions agree, thereby illustrating map self-regulation. Initial values of LTM traces were randomly chosen. (Reprinted with permission from Grossberg and Kuperstein, 1986, p. 246.)

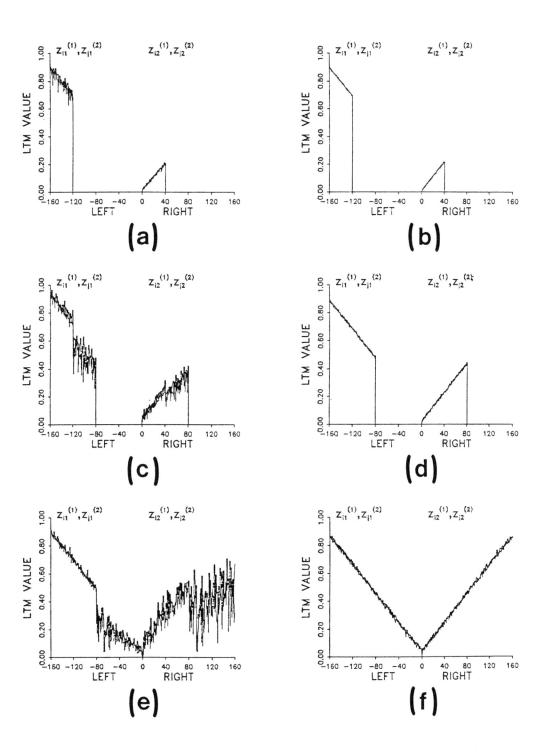

Figure 20. Same as in Figure 19, except initial values of LTM traces were chosen equal to zero. Note that learned spatial maps in Figures 19 and 20 agree, thereby illustrating the ability of map learning to overcome noise. (Reprinted with permission from Grossberg and Kuperstein, 1986, p. 239.)

21. Presynaptic Competition for Long Term Memory: Self-Regulating Competitive Learning

A complete model of how an invariant self-regulating target position map can be learned, as well as variants of this model, are described in Grossberg and Kuperstein (1986). Herein I emphasize one key point about the model.

The invariance and self-regulation properties of the TPM are due to the fact that all the LTM traces whose pathways project to a single TPM cell readjust themselves in a compensatory fashion when any one of these LTM traces changes due to learning (Figure 18). We suggested that the synaptic endings in which these LTM traces are computed contain autoreceptors (Cubeddu, Hoffmann, and James, 1983; Dubocovich and Weiner, 1982; Groves and Tepper, 1983; Groves, Fenster, Tepper, Nakamura, and Young, 1981; Niedzwiecki, Mailman, and Cubeddu, 1984; Siever and Sulser, 1984; Tepper, Young, and Groves, 1984). In a network whose cells contain autoreceptive synapses, when transmitter is released by one synaptic ending, a portion of it can undergo reuptake via the autoreceptors of other active and nearby synaptic endings. Reuptake has an inhibitory effect on the LTM trace of each active synaptic ending. Thus autoreceptors realize a type of presynaptic competition among all the LTM traces whose pathways converge upon the same cell within the TPM. Autoreceptors hereby mediate a novel type of self-regulating competitive learning.

Such an LTM trace obeys an equation of the form:

Autoreceptive Associator

$$\frac{d}{dt}z_{ij} = \epsilon S_i\left[-Fz_{ij} + Gx_j - H\sum_{k=1}^{n} S_k z_{kj}\right]. \tag{122}$$

In (122), z_{ij} is the LTM trace in the pathway from the ith cell in the retinotopic map or eye position map to the jth cell in the TPM; S_i is the signal emitted by the ith cell into this pathway; and x_j is the activity of the jth TPM cell. The terms ϵ, F, G, and H are constants. Equation (122) says that reuptake via autoreceptors of a fraction of released transmitter, as in term $-H\sum_{k=1}^{n} S_k z_{kj}$, inhibits the growth of the corresponding LTM trace.

Match-regulated learning processes also occur in applications to such spatio-temporal learning problems as speech and language learning, and planned sensory-motor control (Grossberg, 1982a, 1987b; Grossberg and Kuperstein, 1986). The totality of such known examples illustrate how combinations of internal matching processes and external error signals derived from natural real-time environments can regulate stable self-organized learning, recognition, and action in response to noisy and unpredictable environments.

REFERENCES

Ackley, D.H., Hinton, G.E., and Sejnowski, T.J. (1985). A learning algorithm for Boltzmann machines. *Cognitive Science*, **9**, 147–169.

Albus, J.S. (1971). A theory of cerebellar function. *Mathematical Biosciences*, **10**, 25–61.

Amari, S. and Arbib, M.A. (Eds.) (1982). **Competition and cooperation in neural networks**. New York: Springer-Verlag.

Amari, S. and Takeuchi, A. (1978). Mathematical theory on formation of category detecting nerve cells. *Biological Cybernetics*, **29**, 127–136.

Amit, D.J., Gutfreund, H., and Sompolinsky, H. (1987). Information storage in neural networks with low levels of activity. *Physical Review A*, **35**, 2293–2303.

Anderson, J.A. (1968). A memory model utilizing spatial correlation functions. *Kybernetik*, **5**, 113–119.

Anderson, J.A. (1983). Cognitive and psychological computation with neural models. *IEEE Transactions SMC-13*, **5**, 799–815.

Anderson, J.A., Silverstein, J.W., Ritz, S.R., and Jones, R.S. (1977). Distinctive features, categorical perception, and probability learning: Some applications of a neural model. *Psychological Review*, **84**, 413–451.

Arend, L.E., Buehler, J.N., and Lockhead, G.R. (1971). Difference information in brightness perception. *Perception and Psychophysics*, **9**, 367–370.

Banquet, J.-P. and Grossberg, S. (1987). Probing cognitive processes through the structure of event-related potentials during learning: An experimental and theoretical analysis. *Applied Optics*, **26**, 4931–4946.

Beck, J. (1972). **Surface color perception**. Ithaca, NY: Cornell University Press.

Bienenstock, E.L., Cooper, L.N., and Munro, P.W. (1982). Theory for the development of neuron selectivity: Orientation specificity and binocular interaction in visual cortex. *Journal of Neuroscience*, **2**, 32–48.

Boring, E.G. (1950). **A history of experimental psychology** (second edition). New York: Appleton-Century-Crofts.

Brindley, G.S. (1964). The use made by the cerebellum of the information that it receives from sense organs. *International Brain Research Organization Bulletin*, **3**, 80.

Bullock, D. and Grossberg, S. (1987a). Neural dynamics of planned arm movements: Emergent invariants and speed-accuracy properties during trajectory formation. *Psychological Review*, in press.

Bullock, D. and Grossberg, S. (1987b). Neuromuscular realization of planned trajectories: Adaptive and automatic mechanisms. In preparation.

Caianiello, E.R. (1961). Outline of a theory of thought and thinking machines. *Journal of Theoretical Biology*, **1**, 204–235.

Campbell, L. and Garnett, W. (1882). **The life of James Clerk Maxwell**. London: Macmillan.

Carpenter, G.A. (1977a). A geometric approach to singular perturbation problems with applications to nerve impulse equations. *Journal of Differential Equations*, **23**, 335–367.

Carpenter, G.A. (1977b). Periodic solutions of nerve impulse equations. *Journal of Mathematical Analysis and Applications*, **58**, 152–173.

Carpenter, G.A. (1979). Bursting phenomena in excitable membranes. *SIAM Journal on Applied Mathematics*, **36**, 334–372.

Carpenter, G.A. (1981). Normal and abnormal signal patterns in nerve cells. In S. Grossberg (Ed.), **Mathematical psychology and psychophysiology**. Providence, RI: American Mathematical Society, 49–90.

Carpenter, G.A. and Grossberg, S. (1985). Category learning and adaptive pattern recognition: A neural network model. *Proceedings of the Third Army Conference on Applied Mathematics and Computing*, **ARO-86-1**, 37–56.

Carpenter, G.A. and Grossberg, S. (1987a). A massively parallel architecture for a self-organizing neural pattern recognition machine. *Computer Vision, Graphics, and Image Processing*, **37**, 54–115.

Carpenter, G.A. and Grossberg, S. (1987b). Associative learning, adaptive pattern recognition, and cooperative-competitive decision making by neural networks. In H. Szu (Ed.), **Optical and hybrid computing**. Bellingham, WA: SPIE.

Carpenter, G.A. and Grossberg, S. (1987c). ART 2: Self-organization of stable category recognition codes for analog input patterns. *Applied Optics*, **26**, 4919–4930.

Cohen, M.A. and Grossberg, S. (1983). Absolute stability of global pattern formation and parallel memory storage by competitive neural networks. *Transactions IEEE*, **SMC-13**, 815–826.

Cohen, M.A. and Grossberg, S. (1984). Neural dynamics of brightness perception: Features, boundaries, diffusion, and resonance. *Perception and Psychophysics*, **36**, 428–456.

Cohen, M. and Grossberg, S. (1986). Neural dynamics of speech and language coding: Developmental programs, perceptual grouping, and competition for short term memory. *Human Neurobiology*, **5**, 1–22.

Cohen, M. and Grossberg, S. (1987). Masking fields: A massively parallel neural architecture for learning, recognizing, and predicting multiple groupings of patterned data. *Applied Optics*, **26**, 1866–1891.

Cornsweet, T.N. (1970). **Visual perception**. New York: Academic Press.

Cubeddu, L.X., Hoffmann, I.S., and James, M.K. (1983). Frequency-dependent effects of neuronal uptake inhibitors on the autoreceptor-mediated modulation of dopamine and acetylcholine release from the rabbit striatum. *Journal of Pharmacology and Experimental Therapeutics*, **226**, 88–94.

Denker, J.S. (Ed.) (1986). **Neural networks for computing**. New York: American Institute of Physics.

Dubocovich, M.L. and Weiner, N. (1982). Modulation of the stimulation-evoked release of 3H-dopamine through activation of dopamine autoreceptors of the D-2 subtype in the isolated rabbit retina. In M. Kohsaka *et al.* (Eds.), **Advances in the biosciences, Vol. 37: Advances in dopamine research**. New York: Pergamon Press.

Duda, R.O. and Hart, P.E. (1973). **Pattern classification and scene analysis**. New York: Wiley.

Eigen, M. and Schuster, P. (1978). The hypercycle: A principle of natural self-organization, B: The abstract hypercycle. *Naturwissenschaften*, **65**, 7–41.

Ellias, S.A. and Grossberg, S. (1975). Pattern formation, contrast control, and oscillations in the short term memory of shunting on-center off-surround networks. *Biological Cybernetics*, **20**, 69–98.

Elman, J.H., Diehl, R.L., and Buchwald, S.E. (1977). Perceptual switching in bilinguals. *Journal of the Acoustical Society of America*, **62**, 971–974.

Ermentrout, G.B. and Cowan, J.D. (1979). Temporal oscillations in neuronal nets. *Journal of Mathematical Biology*, **7**, 265–286.

Ermentrout, G.B. and Cowan, J.D. (1980). Large scale spatially organized activity in neural nets. *SIAM Journal on Applied Mathematics*, **38**, 1–21.

Feldman, J.A. and Ballard, D.H. (1982). Connectionist models and their properties. *Cognitive Science*, **6**, 205–254.

Freeman, W.J. (1975). **Mass action in the nervous system**. New York: Academic Press.

Freeman, W.J. (1979). EEG analysis gives model of neuronal template-matching mechanism for sensory search with olfactory bulb. *Biological Cybernetics*, **35**, 221–234.

Fujita, M. (1982a). Simulation of adaptive modification of the vestibulo-ocular reflex with an adaptive filter model of the cerebellum. *Biological Cybernetics*, **45**, 207–214.

Fujita, M. (1982b). Adaptive filter model of the cerebellum. *Biological Cybernetics*, **45**, 195–206.

Geman, S. (1983). Stochastic relaxation methods for image restoration and expert systems. **Proceedings of ARO workshop on unsupervised image analysis, Brown University, April.**

Geman, S. (1984). Stochastic relaxation methods for image restoration and expert systems. In D.B. Cooper, R.L. Launer, and D.E. McClure (Eds.), **Automated image analysis: Theory and experiments**. New York: Academic Press.

Geman, S. and Geman, D. (1984). Stochastic relaxation, Gibbs distributions, and the Bayesian restoration of images. *IEEE Transactions on Pattern Analysis and Machine Intelligence*, **6**, 721–741.

Gilpin, M.E. and Ayala, F.J. (1973). Global models of growth and competition. *Proceedings of the National Academy of Sciences*, **70**, 3590–3593.

Glazebrook, R.T. (1905). **James Clerk Maxwell and modern physics**. New York: Macmillan.

Goh, B.S. and Agnew, T.T. (1977). Stability in Gilpin and Ayala's models of competition. *Journal of Mathematical Biology*, **4**, 275–279.

Golden, R.M. (1986). The "Brain-state-in-a-box" neural model is a gradient descent algorithm. *Journal of Mathematical Psychology*, **30**, 73–80.

Gray, R.M. (1984). Vector quantization. *IEEE ASSP Magazine*, April, 4–29.

Grossberg, S. (1964). **The theory of embedding fields with applications to psychology and neurophysiology**. New York: Rockefeller Institute for Medical Research.

Grossberg, S. (1967). Nonlinear difference-differential equations in prediction and learning theory. *Proceedings of the National Academy of Sciences*, **58**, 1329–1334.

Grossberg, S. (1968a). Some physiological and biochemical consequences of psychological postulates. *Proceedings of the National Academy of Sciences*, **60**, 758–765.

Grossberg, S. (1968b). Some nonlinear networks capable of learning a spatial pattern of arbitrary complexity. *Proceedings of the National Academy of Sciences*, **59**, 368–372.

Grossberg, S. (1969a). On learning and energy-entropy dependence in recurrent and nonrecurrent signed networks. *Journal of Statistical Physics*, **1**, 319–350.

Grossberg, S. (1969b). Some networks that can learn, remember, and reproduce any number of complicated space-time patterns, I. *Journal of Mathematics and Mechanics*, **19**, 53–91.

Grossberg, S. (1969c). On the serial learning of lists. *Mathematical Biosciences*, **4**, 201–253.

Grossberg, S. (1969d). On learning of spatiotemporal patterns by networks with ordered sensory and motor components, I: Excitatory components of the cerebellum. *Studies in Applied Mathematics*, **48**, 105–132.

Grossberg, S. (1970a). Some networks that can learn, remember, and reproduce any number of complicated space-time patterns, II. *Studies in Applied Mathematics*, **49**, 135–166.

Grossberg, S. (1970b). Neural pattern discrimination. *Journal of Theoretical Biology*, **27**, 291–337.

Grossberg, S. (1971a). On the dynamics of operant conditioning. *Journal of Theoretical Biology*, **33**, 225–255.

Grossberg, S. (1971b). Pavlovian pattern learning by nonlinear neural networks. *Proceedings of the National Academy of Sciences*, **68**, 828–831.

Grossberg, S. (1972a). A neural theory of punishment and avoidance, II: Quantitative theory. *Mathematical Biosciences*, **15**, 253–285.

Grossberg, S. (1972b). Neural expectation: Cerebellar and retinal analogs of cells fired by learnable or unlearned pattern classes. *Kybernetik*, **10**, 49–57.

Grossberg, S. (1972c). Pattern learning by functional-differential neural networks with arbitrary path weights. In K. Schmitt (Ed.), **Delay and functional-differential equations and their applications**. New York: Academic Press.

Grossberg, S. (1973). Contour enhancement, short term memory, and constancies in reverberating neural networks. *Studies in Applied Mathematics*, **52**, 217–257.

Grossberg, S. (1974). Classical and instrumental learning by neural networks. In R. Rosen and F. Snell (Eds.), **Progress in theoretical biology**. New York: Academic Press.

Grossberg, S. (1976a). Adaptive pattern classification and universal recoding, I: Parallel development and coding of neural feature detectors. *Biological Cybernetics*, **23**, 121–134.

Grossberg, S. (1976b). Adaptive pattern classification and universal recoding, II: Feedback, expectation, olfaction, and illusions. *Biological Cybernetics*, **23**, 187–202.

Grossberg, S. (1977). Pattern formation by the global limits of a nonlinear competitive interaction in n dimensions. *Journal of Mathematical Biology*, **4**, 237–256.

Grossberg, S. (1978a). A theory of human memory: Self-organization and performance of sensory-motor codes, maps, and plans. In R. Rosen and F. Snell (Eds.), **Progress in theoretical biology**, Vol. 5. New York: Academic Press.

Grossberg, S. (1978b). Do all neural models really look alike? *Psychological Review*, **85**, 592–596.

Grossberg, S. (1978c). Competition, decision, and consensus. *Journal of Mathematical Analysis and Applications*, **66**, 470–493.

Grossberg, S. (1978d). Decisions, patterns, and oscillations in nonlinear competitive systems with applications to Volterra-Lotka systems. *Journal of Theoretical Biology*, **73**, 101–130.

Grossberg, S. (1980a). Biological competition: Decision rules, pattern formation, and oscillations. *Proceedings of the National Academy of Sciences*, **77**, 2338–2342.

Grossberg, S. (1980b). How does a brain build a cognitive code? *Psychological Review*, **87**, 1–51.

Grossberg, S., (Ed.) (1981). Adaptive resonance in development, perception, and cognition. In **Mathematical psychology and psychophysiology**. Providence, RI: American Mathematical Society.

Grossberg, S. (1982a). **Studies of mind and brain: Neural principles of learning, perception, development, cognition, and motor control.** Boston: Reidel Press.

Grossberg, S. (1982b). Associative and competitive principles of learning and development: The temporal unfolding and stability of STM and LTM patterns. In S.I. Amari and M.A. Arbib (Eds.), **Competition and cooperation in neural networks.** New York: Springer-Verlag.

Grossberg, S. (1984). Unitization, automaticity, temporal order, and word recognition. *Cognition and Brain Theory, 7,* 263–283.

Grossberg, S. (1986). The adaptive self-organization of serial order in behavior: Speech, language, and motor control. In E.C. Schwab and H.C. Nusbaum (Eds.), **Pattern recognition by humans and machines, Vol. 1: Speech perception.** New York: Academic Press, 187–294.

Grossberg, S. (1987a). Cortical dynamics of three-dimensional form, color, and brightness perception: I: Monocular theory. *Perception and Psychophysics, 41,* 87–116.

Grossberg, S. (1987b). Cortical dynamics of three-dimensional form, color, and brightness perception, II: Binocular theory. *Perception and Psychophysics, 41,* 117–158.

Grossberg, S. (Ed.) (1987c). **The adaptive brain, I: Cognition, learning, reinforcement, and rhythm.** Amsterdam: Elsevier/North-Holland.

Grossberg, S. (Ed.) (1987d). **The adaptive brain, II: Vision, speech, language, and motor control.** Amsterdam: Elsevier/North-Holland.

Grossberg, S. (1987e). Competitive learning: From interactive activation to adaptive resonance. *Cognitive Science, 11,* 23–63.

Grossberg, S. (Ed.) (1988). **Neural networks and natural intelligence.** Cambridge, MA: MIT Press.

Grossberg, S. and Kuperstein, M. (1986). **Neural dynamics of adaptive sensory-motor control: Ballistic eye movements.** Amsterdam: Elsevier/North-Holland.

Grossberg, S. and Levine, D. (1975). Some developmental and attentional biases in the contrast enhancement and short term memory of recurrent neural networks. *Journal of Theoretical Biology, 53,* 341–380.

Grossberg, S. and Mingolla, E. (1985a). Neural dynamics of form perception: Boundary completion, illusory figures, and neon color spreading. *Psychological Review, 92,* 173–211.

Grossberg, S. and Mingolla, E. (1985b). Neural dynamics of perceptual grouping: Textures, boundaries, and emergent segmentations. *Perception and Psychophysics, 38,* 141–171.

Grossberg, S. and Mingolla, E. (1987). Neural dynamics of surface perception: Boundary webs, illuminants, and shape-from-shading. *Computer Vision, Graphics, and Image Processing, 37,* 116–165.

Grossberg, S. and Pepe, J. (1971). Spiking threshold and overarousal effects in serial learning *Journal of Statistical Physics, 3,* 95–125.

Grossberg, S. and Schmajuk, N.A. (1987). Neural dynamics of Pavlovian conditioning: Conditioned reinforcement, habituation, and opponent processing. *Psychobiology, 15,* 195–240.

Grossberg, S. and Todorović, D. (1987). Neural dynamics of 1-D and 2-D brightness perception: A unified model of classical and recent phenomena. *Perception and Psychophysics,* in press.

Groves, P.M., Fenster, G.A., Tepper, J.M., Nakamura, S., and Young, S.J. (1981). Changes in dopaminergic terminal excitability induced by amphetamine and haloperidol. *Brain Research*, **221**, 425–431.

Groves, P.M. and Tepper, J.M. (1983). Neuronal mechanisms of action of amphetamine. In I. Creese (Ed.), **Stimulants: Neurochemical, behavioral and clinical perspectives**. New York: Raven Press, 81–129.

Halgren, E., Squires, N.K., Wilson, C.L., Rohrbaugh, J.W., Babb, T.L., and Crandall, P.H. (1980). Endogenous potentials generated in the human hippocampal formation and amygdala by infrequent events. *Science*, **210**, 803–805.

Hary, J.M. and Massaro, D.W. (1982). Categorical results do not imply categorical perception. *Perception and Psychophysics*, **32**, 409–418.

Hastings, S.P. (1976). The existence of periodic solutions to Nagumo's equation. *Quarterly Journal of Mathematics*, **27**, 123–134.

Hastings, S.P. (1982). Single and multiple pulse waves for the FitzHugh-Nagumo equations. *SIAM Journal of Applied Mathematics*, **42**, 247–260.

Hebb, D.O. (1949). **The organization of behavior**. New York: Wiley.

Hecht-Nielsen, R. (1986). Performance limits of optical, electro-optical, and electronic neurocomputers. In H. Szu (Ed.), **Hybrid and optical computing**. Bellingham, WA: SPIE.

Helmholtz, H. von (1866/1962). **Treatise on physiological optics**, J.P.C. Southall (Trans.). New York: Dover.

Hestenes, D. (1987). In C.R. Smith (Ed.), **Maximum entropy in Bayesian spectral analysis and estimation problems**. Boston: Reidel Press.

Hilgard, E.R. and Bower, G.H. (1975). **Theories of learning** (fourth edition). Englewood Cliffs, NJ: Prentice-Hall.

Hinton, G.E. and Anderson, J.A. (Eds.) (1981). **Parallel models of associative memory**. Hillsdale, NJ: Erlbaum.

Hirsch, M.W. (1982). Systems of differential equations that are competitive or cooperative, I: Limit sets. *SIAM Journal of Mathematical Analysis*, **13**, 167–179.

Hirsch, M.W. (1985). Systems of differential equations that are competitive or cooperative, II: Convergence almost everywhere. *SIAM Journal of Mathematical Analysis*, **16**, 423–439.

Hodgkin, A.L. (1964). **The conduction of the nervous impulse**. Liverpool: Liverpool University.

Hodgkin, A.L. and Huxley, A.F. (1952). A quantitative description of membrane current and its application to conduction and excitation in nerve. *Journal of Physiology*, **117**, 500–544.

Hodgson, J.E.P. (Ed.) (1983). **Oscillations in mathematical biology**. New York: Springer-Verlag.

Holst, E. von and Mittelstaedt, H. (1950). The reafference principle: Interaction between the central nervous system and the periphery. *Naturwissenschaften*, **37**, 464–476.

Hopfield, J.J. (1982). Neuronal networks and physical systems with emergent collective computational abilities. *Proceedings of the National Academy of Sciences*, **79**, 2554–2558.

Hopfield, J.J. (1984). Neurons with graded response have collective computational properties like those of two-state neurons. *Proceedings of the National Academy of Sciences*, **81**, 3058–3092.

Hopfield, J.J. and Tank, D.W. (1985). "Neural" computation of decisions in optimization problems. *Biological Cybernetics*, **52**, 141–152.

Hopfield, J.J. and Tank, D.W. (1986). Computing with neural circuits: A model. *Science*, **233**, 625–633.

Hurvich, L.M. (1981). **Colour vision**. Sunderland, MA: Sinauer Associates.

Ito, M. (1974). The control mechanisms of cerebellar motor systems. In F.O. Schmitt and F.G. Worden (Eds.), **The neurosciences third study program**. Cambridge, MA: MIT Press, 293–303.

Ito, M. (1982). Cerebellar control of the vestibulo-ocular reflex—around the flocculus hypothesis. *Annual Review of Neuroscience*, **5**, 275–296.

Ito, M. (1984). **The cerebellum and neural control**. New York: Raven Press.

Iverson, G.J. and Pavel, M. (1981). Invariant properties of masking phenomena in psychoacoustics and their theoretical consequences. In S. Grossberg (Ed.), **Mathematical psychology and psychophysiology**. Providence, RI: American Mathematical Society.

Kaczmarek, L.K. and Babloyantz, A. (1977). Spatiotemporal patterns in epileptic seizures. *Biological Cybernetics*, **26**, 199–208.

Kandel, E.R. and Schwartz, J.H. (1981). **Principles of neural science**. New York: Elsevier/North-Holland.

Kandel, E.R. and Schwartz, J.H. (1982). Molecular biology of learning: Modulation of transmitter release. *Science*, **218**, 433–443.

Kasamatsu, T. and Pettigrew, J.D. (1976). Depletion of brain catecholamines: Failure of ocular dominance shift after monocular occlusion in kittens. *Science*, **194**, 206–209.

Katz, B. (1966). **Nerve, muscle, and synapse**. New York: McGraw Hill.

Kilmer, W.L. (1972). On some realistic constraints in prey-predator mathematics. *Journal of Theoretical Biology*, **36**, 9–22.

Kirkpatrick, S., Gelatt, C.D., and Vecchi, M.P. (1982). Optimization by simulated annealing. IBM Thomas J. Watson Research Center, Yorktown Heights, New York.

Kirkpatrick, S., Gelatt, D.D., and Vecchi, M.P. (1983). Optimization by simulated annealing. *Science*, **220**, 671–680.

Koenigsberger, L. (1906). **Hermann von Helmholtz** (F.A. Welby, Translator). Oxford: Clarendon Press.

Kohonen, T. (1971). A class of randomly organized associative memories. *Acta Polytechnica Scandinavica*, El. 25.

Kohonen, T. (1977). **Associative memory—A system-theoretical approach**. New York: Springer-Verlag.

Kohonen, T. (1984). **Self-organization and associative memory**. New York: Springer-Verlag.

Kosko, B. (1987). Bidirectional associative memories. Submitted for publication.

Kosko, B. and Guest, C. (1987). Optical bidirectional associative memories. *Society for Photo-optical and Instrumentation Engineering (SPIE) Proceedings: Image Understanding*, **758**, in press.

Land, E.H. (1977). The retinex theory of color vision. *Scientific American*, **237**, 108–128.

Levine, D.S. (1979). Existence of a limiting pattern for a system of nonlinear equations describing inter-population competition. *Bulletin of Mathematical Biology*, **41**, 617–628.

Levine, D.S. (1983). Neural population modeling and psychology: A review. *Mathematical Biosciences*, **66**, 1–86.

Levine, D.S. and Grossberg, S. (1976). Visual illusions in neural networks: Line neutralization, tilt aftereffects, and angle expansion. *Journal of Theoretical Biology*, **61**, 477–504.

Levy, W.B. (1985). Associative changes at the synapse: LTP in the hippocampus. In W.B. Levy, J. Anderson, and S. Lehmkuhle (Eds.), **Synaptic modification, neuron selectivity, and nervous system organization**. Hillsdale, NJ: Erlbaum, 5–33.

Levy, W.B., Brassel, S.E., and Moore, S.D. (1983). Partial quantification of the associative symaptic learning rule of the dentate gyrus. *Neuroscience*, **8**, 799–808.

Levy, W.B. and Desmond, N.L. (1985). The rules of elemental synaptic plasticity. In W.B. Levy, J. Anderson, and S. Lehmkuhle (Eds.), **Synaptic modification, neuron selectivity, and nervous system organization**. Hillsdale, NJ: Erlbaum, 105–121.

Lotka, A.J. (1956). **Elements of mathematical biology**. New York: Dover.

MacArthur, R.H. (1970). Species packing and competitive equilibrium for many species. *Theoretical Population Biology*, **1**, 1–11.

Mach, E. (1914). **The analysis of sensation and the relation of the physical to the psychical**, C.M. Williams (Trans.), revised by S. Waterlow. London: Open Court Publishing.

Malsburg, C. von der (1973). Self-organization of orientation sensitive cells in the striate cortex. *Kybernetik*, **14**, 85–100.

Marr, D. (1969). A theory of cerebellar cortex. *Journal of Physiology (London)*, **202**, 437–470.

May, R.M. and Leonard, W.J. (1975). Nonlinear aspects of competition between three species. *SIAM Journal on Applied Mathematics*, **29**, 243–253.

McClelland, J.L. (1987). The case for interactionism in language processing. Preprint.

McClelland, J.L. and Rumelhart, D.E. (1981). An interactive activation model of context effects in letter perception, Part I: An account of basic findings. *Psychological Review*, **88**, 375–407.

McClelland, J.L. and Rumelhart, D.E. (Eds.) (1986). **Parallel distributed processing**, Vol. II. Cambridge, MA: MIT Press.

McCormick, D.A. and Thompson, R.F. (1984). Cerebellum: Essential involvement in the classically conditioned eyelid response. *Science*, **223**, 296–299.

McCulloch, W.S. and Pitts, W. (1943). A logical calculus of the ideas immanent in nervous activity. *Bulletin of Mathematical Biophysics*, **5**, 115–133.

McEliece, R.J., Posner, E.C., Rodemich, E.R., and Venkatesh, S.S. (1986). The capacity of the Hopfield associative memory. *IEEE Transactions in Information Theory*.

Miller, J.L. and Liberman, A.M. (1979). Some effects of later-occurring information on the perception of stop consonant and semivowel. *Perception and Psychophysics*, **25**, 457–465.

Mollon, J.D. and Sharpe, L.T. (Eds.) (1983). **Colour vision**. New York: Academic Press.

Mueller, P., Martin, T., and Putzrath, F. (1962). General principles of operations in neuron nets with application to acoustical pattern recognition. In E.E. Bernard and M.R. Kare (Eds.), **Biological prototypes and synthetic systems**, Vol. 1. New York: Plenum Press, 192–212.

Nathan, O. and Norden, H. (Eds.) (1960). **Einstein on peace**. New York: Schocken Books.

Niedzwiecki, D.M., Mailman, R.B., and Cubeddu, L.X. (1984). Greater potency of mesoridazine and sulforidazine compared with the parent compound, thioridazine, on striatal dopamine autoreceptors. *Journal of Pharmacology and Experimenal Therapeutics*, **228**, 636–639.

Optican, L.M. and Robinson, D.A. (1980). Cerebellar-dependent adaptive control of primate saccadic system. *Journal of Neurophysiology*, **44**, 1058–1076.

Parker, D.B. (1982). Learning-logic. Invention Report 581-64, File 1, Office of Technology Licensing, Stanford University, October.

Parker, D.B. (1985). Learning-Logic, TR-47, Center for Computational Research in Economics and Management Science, MIT, April.

Parker, D.B. (1986). A comparison of algorithms for neuron-like cells. In J.S. Denker (Ed.), **Neural networks for computing**. New York: American Institute of Physics.

Pastore, R.E. (1981). Possible psychoacoustic factors in speech perception. In P.D. Eimas and J.L. Miller (Eds.), **Perspectives in the study of speech**. Hillsdale, NJ: Erlbaum.

Pettigrew, J.D. and Kasamatsu, T. (1978). Local perfusion of noradrenaline maintains visual cortical plasticity. *Nature*, **271**, 761–763.

Platt, J.C. and Hopfield, J.J. (1986). Analog decoding using neural networks. In J.S. Denker (Ed.), **Neural networks for computing**. New York: American Institute of Physics.

Plonsey, R. and Fleming, D.G. (1969). **Bioelectric phenomena**. New York: McGraw-Hill.

Poggio, T. and Koch, C. (1987). Synapses that compute motion. *Scientific American*, **256**, 46–52.

Psaltis, D. and Park, C.H. (1986). Nonlinear discriminative functions and associative memories. In J.S. Denker (Ed.), **Neural networks for computing**. New York: American Institute of Physics.

Ratliff, F. (1965). **Mach bands: Quantitative studies on neural networks in the retina**. New York: Holden-Day.

Ratliff, F., Hartline, H.K., and Miller, W.H. (1963). Spatial and temporal aspects of retinal inhibitory interactions. *Journal of the Optical Society of America*, **53**, 110–120.

Rauschecker, J.P. and Singer, W. (1979). Changes in the circuitry of the kitten's visual cortex are gated by postsynaptic activity. *Nature*, **280**, 58–60.

Rescorla, R.A. and Wagner, A.R. (1972). A theory of Pavlovian conditioning: Variations in the effectiveness of reinforcement and nonreinforcement. In A.H. Black and W.F. Prokasy (Eds.), **Classical conditioning, II: Current research and theory**. New York: Appleton-Century-Crofts.

Ricciardi, L. and Scott, A. (Eds.) (1982). **Biomathematics in 1980**. Amsterdam: North-Holland.

Ron, S. and Robinson, D.A. (1973). Eye movements evoked by cerebellar stimulation in the alert monkey. *Journal of Neurophysiology*, **36**, 1004–1021.

Rosenblatt, F. (1962). **Principles of neurodynamics**. Washington, DC: Spartan Books.

Rumelhart, D.E., Hinton, G.E., and Williams, R.J. (1986). Learning internal representations by error propagation. In D.E. Rumelhart and J.L. McClelland (Eds.), **Parallel distributed processing**. Cambridge, MA: MIT Press.

Rumelhart, D.E. and McClelland, J.L. (1982). An interactive activation model of context effects in letter perception, Part 2: The contextual enhancement effect and some tests and extensions of the model. *Psychological Review*, **89**, 60–94.

Rumelhart, D.E. and McClelland, J.L. (Eds.) (1986). **Parallel distributed processing**, Vol. I. Cambridge, MA: MIT Press.

Rumelhart, D.E. and Zipser, D. (1985). Feature discovery by competitive learning. *Cognitive Science*, **9**, 75–112.

Samuel, A.G., van Santen, J.P.H., and Johnston, J.C. (1982). Length effects in word perception: We is better than I but worse than you or them. *Journal of Experimental Psychology: Human Perception and Performance*, **8**, 91–105.

Samuel, A.G., van Santen, J.P.H., and Johnston, J.C. (1983). Reply to Matthei: We really is worse than you or them, and so are ma and pa. *Journal of Experimental Psychology: Human Perception and Performance*, **9**, 321–322.

Sawusch, J.R. and Nusbaum, H.C. (1979). Contextual effects in vowel perception, I: Anchor-induced contrast effects. *Perception and Psychophysics*, **25**, 292–302.

Sawusch, J.R., Nusbaum, H.C., and Schwab, E.C. (1980). Contextual effects in vowel perception, II: Evidence for two processing mechanisms. *Perception and Psychophysics*, **27**, 421–434.

Schwab, E.C., Sawusch, J.R., and Nusbaum, H.C. (1981). The role of second formant transitions in the stop-semivowel distinction. *Perception and Psychophysics*, **29**, 121–128.

Scott, A.C. (1977). **Neurophysics**. New York: Wiley-Interscience.

Sejnowski, T.J. and Rosenberg, C.R. (1986). NETtalk: A parallel network that learns to read aloud. Johns Hopkins University, January.

Siever, L. and Sulser, F. (1984). Regulations of amine neurotransmitter systems: Implication for the major psychiatric syndromes and their treatment. *Psychopharmacology Bulletin*, **20**, 500–504.

Singer, W. (1982). The role of attention in developmental plasticity. *Human Neurobiology*, **1**, 41–43.

Singer, W. (1983). Neuronal activity as a shaping factor in the self-organization of neuron assemblies. In E. Basar, H. Flohr, H. Haken, and A.J. Mandell (Eds.), **Synergetics of the brain**. New York: Springer-Verlag.

Sperling, G. (1981). Mathematical models of binocular vision. In S. Grossberg (Ed.), **Mathematical psychology and psychophysiology**. Providence, RI: American Mathematical Society.

Sperling, G. and Sondhi, M.M. (1968). Model for visual luminance discrimination and flicker detection. *Journal of the Optical Society of America*, **58**, 1133–1145.

Studdert-Kennedy, M. (1980). Speech perception. *Language and Speech*, **23**, 45–66.

Sutton, R.S. and Barto, A.G. (1981). Toward a modern theory of adaptive networks: Expectation and prediction. *Psychological Review*, **88**, 135–170.

Szu, H. (1986). Three layers of vector outer product neural networks for optical pattern recognition. In H. Szu (Ed.), **Optical and hybrid computing**. Bellingham, WA: SPIE.

Takeuchi, Y., Adachi, N., and Tokumaru, H. (1978). The stability of generalized Volterra equations. *Journal of Mathematical Analysis and Applications*, **62**, 453–473.

Tepper, J.M., Young, S.J., and Groves, P.M. (1984). Autoreceptor-mediated changes in dopaminergic terminal excitability: Effects of increases in impulse flow. *Brain Research*, **309**, 309–316.

Venkatesh, S.S. (1986). Epsilon capacity of neural networks. In J.S. Denker (Ed.), **Neural networks for computing**. New York: American Institute of Physics.

Vilis, T. and Hore, J. (1986). A comparison of disorders in saccades and in fast and accurate elbow flexions during cerebellar dysfunction. In H.J. Freund, U. Büttner,

B. Cohen, and J. Noth (Eds.), **The oculomotor and skeletal motor systems: Differences and similarities**. New York: Elsevier.

Vilis, T., Snow, R., and Hore, J. (1983). Cerebellar saccadic dysmetria is not equal in the two eyes. *Experimental Brain Research*, **51**, 343–350.

Werblin, F.S. (1971). Adaptation in a vertebrate retina: Intracellular recordings in Necturus. *Journal of Neurophysiology*, **34**, 228–241.

Werbos, P. (1974). Beyond regression: New tools for prediction and analysis in the behavioral sciences. Ph.D. Thesis, Harvard University, Cambridge, Massachusetts.

Werbos, P. (1982). Applications of advances in nonlinear sensitivity analysis. In A.V. Balakrishnan, M. Thoma, R.F. Drenick, and F. Kozin (Eds.), **Lecture notes in control and information sciences, Vol. 38: System modeling and optimization**. Proceedings of the 10th IFIP conference. New York: Springer-Verlag.

Widrow, B. (1962). Generalization and information storage in networks of Adaline neurons. In M.C. Yovits, G.T. Jacobi, and G.D. Goldstein (Eds.), **Self-organizing systems**. Washington, DC: Spartan Books.

Wilson, H.R. and Cowan, J.D. (1972). Excitatory and inhibitory interactions in localized populations of model neurons. *Biophysical Journal*, **12**, 1–24.

CHAPTER 3

NEURAL PATTERN DISCRIMINATION
by
Stephen Grossberg

Preface

This 1970 article began to construct and classify neural networks for specialized pattern recognition tasks. Most of the networks are built up from cells that obey the additive equation (see Chapters 1 and 2). Some networks are built up from cells that obey the shunting equation. The content of the article is to show that suitable parameter choices within this unified computational framework can create pattern discriminators capable of a wide range of useful behaviors. These specialized additive and shunting networks and their descendents form the foundation for many recent pattern recognition models.

The article was motivated in part by the fact that neurobiological data concerning the existence of neurons with selective response profiles were proliferating even in the 1960's. A rational basis for analysing and classifying these cell properties was urgently needed. These neural data were then, however, inadequate as a reliable guide to theory construction. Fortunately, previously derived theoretical results uncovered a clearly focussed set of design problems and their most likely mechanistic realizations.

In particular, associative outstars and outstar avalanches had recently been discovered and mathematically analysed. A *spatial pattern* of activation across a network was shown in these studies to be the computational unit of associative learning. It was also shown that a *stimulus sampling* operation exists whereby associative learning could be gated on or off. These properties naturally led to the question of how selective filters of sensory data could be designed to turn outstars and outstar avalanches on and off at appropriate times. This question is equivalent to asking how a multi-level network could be designed to carry out a mapping between two arbitrary sets of input and output vectors.

The present article accomplished this task by constructing the first neural network *instars* and *instar avalanches*. The output node of such an instar is activated only by a prescribed set of input patterns. Explicit parameters in the network determine which input set is effective. The output node can then be used to activate an outstar or outstar avalanche which can be used to learn an arbitrary spatial pattern or space-time pattern. Subsequent presentation of the prescribed input patterns to the instar could then generate performance of the learned spatial pattern or space-time pattern by the outstars.

The design of the instar was motivated by a Principle of Equal Tuning; namely, given that the computational unit of associative learning is a spatial pattern, then the computational unit of pattern recognition should also be a spatial pattern. Mechanisms that discriminate novel patterns which could not be learned would presumably atrophy due to disuse, since they could not support any evolutionary advantage. This Equal Tuning constraint led to the discovery that at least two successive levels of inhibitory interaction, or equivalent operations, are needed to design a selective filter of input patterns. The first level normalizes the input pattern, and the second level completes the selection, or compression, of the instar's output code. This result was later incorporated into all competitive learning models and ART models.

In the course of this analysis, it was noted that a shunting on-center off-surround network could normalize an input pattern as it computed a Weber-law modulated ratio scale (also see Chapter 2). This observation has been successfully used to design a network capable of compensating for variable illumination in subsequent vision models (Cohen and Grossberg, 1984; Grossberg and Todorović, 1988). It also motivated the subsequent design and mathematical analysis of shunting feedback networks in terms of their ratio processing and normalization properties (Chapter 2).

The article also describes how to design an additive winner-take-all feedforward competitive network. This result motivated the subsequent analysis of how to design a winner-take-all feedback competitive network (Chapter 2).

The article noted how to perform motor synergies, and temporal sequences of such synergies, at speeds other than the ones at which they were learned. This property emphasized the need to *factorize* Target Position Commands from the speed-controlling GO signals that activate them. This factorization principle helped to motivate the subsequent discovery of the Vector Integration to Endpoint model (Chapter 2), which shows how a factorized Target Position Command and GO signal can control a variable-speed synchronous trajectory within a multi-joint motor synergy.

The article also showed how a feedforward inhibitory interneuron could be used to create a transient On and Off detector, whereas feedback inhibitory interneurons could not. Such an interneuron can selectively trigger learning in an outstar or outstar avalanche at the onset of an input pattern. More generally, it can be tuned to respond to only a prescribed range of changes in a fluctuating input stream. This result helped to motivate the discovery of the MOC Filter for preprocessing moving images in a recent theory of motion perception by visual cortex (Grossberg and Rudd, 1989).

References

Cohen, M.A. and Grossberg, S. (1984). Neural dynamics of brightness perception: Features, boundaries, diffusion, and resonance. *Perception and Psychophysics*, **36**, 428–456.

Grossberg, S. and Rudd, M.E. (1989). A neural architecture for visual motion perception. *Neural Networks*, **2**, 421–450.

Grossberg, S. and Todorović, D. (1988). Neural dynamics of 1-D and 2-D brightness perception: A unified model of classical and recent phenomena. *Perception and Psychophysics*, **43**, 241–277.

Journal of Theoretical Biology
1970, **27**, 291–337
©1970 Academic Press Inc.

NEURAL PATTERN DISCRIMINATION

Stephen Grossberg†

Abstract

Some possible neural mechanisms of pattern discrimination are discussed, leading to neural networks which can discriminate any number of essentially arbitrarily complicated space-time patterns and activate cells which can then learn and perform any number of essentially arbitrarily complicated space-time patterns in response to the proper input pattern. Among the topics that arise in this discussion are: use of non-recurrent inhibitory interneurons for temporal or spatial discrimination tasks which recurrent inhibitory interneurons cannot carry out; mechanisms of temporal generalization whereby the same cells control performance of a given act at variable speeds; a tendency for cells furthest from the sensory periphery to have the most specific response modes and the least ability to follow sensory intensities (e.g., on-off and bimodal responses are common); uses of non-recurrent on-off fields whose signals arrive in waves forming "interference patterns", with the net effect of rapidly choosing at most one behavioral mode from any number of competitive modes, or of non-specifically arousing or suppressing cells which can sample and learn ongoing internal patterns; uses of specific versus non-specific inhibitory interneurons, axon hillock inhibition, presynaptic inhibition, equal smoothing of excitatory and inhibitory signals, possible production of both excitatory and inhibitory transmitter in a single synaptic knob, blockade of postsynaptic potential response, logarithmic transduction of inputs to spiking frequencies, or saturation of cell body response in non-recurrent on-off fields for purposes of pattern discrimination.

---

† Supported in part by the National Science Foundation (NSF GP 9003), the Office of Naval Research (ONR N00014-67-A-0204-0016), and the A.P. Sloan Foundation.

1. Introduction

Recent electrophysiological experiments, such as those of Hubel and Wiesel (1965), Lettvin, Maturana, McCulloch, and Pitts (1960), and Sterling and Wickelgren (1969) have demonstrated the existence of nerve cells whose maximal output is triggered by complex input patterns; for example, by a line of light of fixed length moving across a cat's retina with a fixed orientation and a fixed velocity. Many different cellular preferences have already been described, and more are bound to be discovered in the future. The problem of classifying possible common mechanisms underlying these diverse preferences is therefore an urgent one. Still more important, perhaps, is the problem of discussing how complex cellular pattern discriminations are integrated into the ongoing learning behavior of the animal being discussed.

These problems cannot be separated from the following question, which is suggested by electrophysiological experiments on many sensory modalities. How do cells near the sensory periphery, which individually respond to many different input patterns, nonetheless act together to dscriminate one pattern from another with high precision? That is, how does "local non-specificity" co-exist with "global specificity" of cellular response?

This paper discusses some mathematical mechanisms of pattern discrimination that are built up from such familiar neurophysiological ideas as: existence of an axonal spiking threshold, dependence of spiking frequency on cell body membrane potential, additive combination of excitatory and inhibitory inputs at the cell body, exponential averaging of inputs through time by the cell body membrane potential, positive time lags for flow of spikes in axons, and—in some cases—saturation of cell response at finite values. We will find that these simple ideas can be used to create a substantial variety of pattern discriminators if they are arranged in suitable networks, or "anatomies".

It is, of course, very difficult, if not impossible, for a physiological experimentalist to simultaneously record from the millions of nerves that might be used to perform a given pattern discrimination task of even routine behavioral complexity. This limitation will not hamper our mathematical analysis, which is in principle as easily carried out for two as for 10^{10} cells. The independence of our results from considerations of cell population size has the empirical interpretation that *any* pattern resolution can be achieved by repeating the same mechanisms in more cells. It will also appear that knowing the anatomy of a given collection of cells does not characterize the capabilities of this colletion as an input filter. One must also know several physiological parameters of the network, such as the relative strengths and onset times of excitatory and inhibitory signals at a given cell, the relative speeds of exponential averaging at different cells, the spatial distribution of spiking threshold values at all cells, the relative specificity of excitatory and inhibitory synaptic fields, etc. These parameters are also difficult, if not impossible, to measure at millions of cells, but again a mathematical analysis will show that certain combinations of these parameters at individual cells are compatible with prescribed tasks carried out by millions of cells of the same type, whereas other parameter combinations are not. Our results therefore begin a catalog of the mathematical possibilities that can achieve prescribed behavioral discrimination tasks. Armed with such a catalog, the experimentalist can presumably better interpret the behavioral implications of data collected separately from small numbers of cells.

2. Connection with Learning Theory

The results to be described are part of a rigorous theory of learning that has a suggestive psychological, neurophysiological, anatomical, and in some cases biochemical interpretation. The networks of the theory are called *embedding fields* (Grossberg, 1969a–d). All results herein were motivated and derived to satisfy formal requirements that make efficient learning of complicated skills possible in embedding fields. In this sense, the learning mechanism provides a unifying teleology for constructing pattern discriminators. Some previous papers (Grossberg, 1969e, 1969f, 1970) consider this mechanism in detail. Our first results on pattern discrimination will discuss networks in which no learning occurs. If such a network can discriminate a given pattern at one time, it can discriminate the same pattern at future times. These networks will then be connected to networks which can learn. Together the entire network can learn to perform any finite number of output patterns of essentially arbitrary complexity selectively in respose to any finite number of input patterns of essentially arbitrary complexity. Once these results are before us, various advantages and disadvantages of including learning, e.g. transmitter potentiation, in the filtering cells themselves can readily be noted.

We will work primarily with networks of the form

$$\dot{x}_i(t) = -\alpha_i x_i(t) + \sum_{k=1}^{n} [x_k(t - \tau_{ki}) - \Gamma_{ki}]^+ \beta_{ki}$$
$$- \sum_{k=1}^{n} [x_k(t - \sigma_{ki}) - \Omega_{ki}]^+ \gamma_{ki} + I_i(t), \tag{1}$$

where $[w]^+ = \max(w, 0)$ for any real number w, all constant parameters are non-negative, all initial data and inputs are continuous, and $i = 1, 2, \ldots, n$ with n any fixed positive integer. Equation (1) has the following interpretation.

Let n cell bodies v_i be given with average potential $x_i(t), i = 1, 2, \ldots, n$. If $\beta_{ki} > 0 (\gamma_{ki} > 0)$, then an excitatory (inhibitory) axon $e_{ki}^+ (e_{ki}^-)$ leads from v_k to v_i. Denote the synaptic knob of $e_{ki}^+ (e_{ki}^-)$ by $N_{ki}^+ (N_{ki}^-)$. Let the spiking frequency which is released from v_k into $e_{ki}^+ (e_{ki}^-)$ in the time interval $[t, t + dt]$ be proportional to $[x_k(t) - \Gamma_{ki}]^+ \beta_{ki} ([x_k(t) - \Omega_{ki}]^+ \gamma_{ki})$. Let the time lag for the signal to flow from v_k to $N_{ki}^+ (N_{ki}^-)$ be $\tau_{ki}(\sigma_{ki})$, and let the spiking (or signal) threshold of $e_{ki}^+ (e_{ki}^-)$ be $\Gamma_{ki}(\Omega_{ki})$. Then by (1), in every time interval $[t, t + dt]$, a signal with size proportional to $[x_k(t) - \Gamma_{ki}]^+ \beta_{ki}$ enters e_{ki}^+ from v_k, travels to N_{ki}^+ at finite velocity, and creates a proportional signal at N_{ki}^+ that crosses the synapse to v_i at time $t + \tau_{ki}$, whence $\dot{x}_i (= dx_i/dt)$ increases proportionately. All excitatory signals from some v_k that reach v_i at time t have an additive effect on $\dot{x}_i$, as the term

$$\sum_{k=1}^{n} [x_k(t - \tau_{ki}) - \Gamma_{ki}]^+ \beta_{ki}$$

in (1) shows. A similar description holds for inhibitory signals in the axons e_{ki}^-. x_i also decays at the exponential rate α_i, and is perturbed by known inputs $I_i(t)$ that are under control of an experimentalist or independent cells. For my purposes, any synaptic mechanism—whether chemical or electrical—that obeys the above equations will suffice. Equations (1) are supported by substantial experimental evidence (Grossberg,

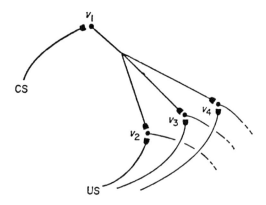

Figure 1.

1969b, Section 12). For example, they reduce in a special case to the Hartline-Ratliff equation and yield theoretical formulas for the empirical coefficients of that equation (Grossberg, 1969b, Section 13).

3. Local Temporal Discrimination

It is often necessary for the output of a given cell to have short duration even though its input has long duration. Consider Figure 1, for example. Figure 1 describes a respondent conditioning paradigm in a simple network. A conditioned stimulus (CS) activates the cell v_1, and an unconditioned stimulus (US) activates the cells $v_i, i \geq 2$. It has been shown (Grossberg, 1969e, 1970) that by pairing the CS and the US sufficiently often, then a future presentation of the CS alone can reproduce in the outputs of the cells $v_i, i \geq 2$, patterns previously elicited by the US. Grossberg (1969e) also shows that the duration of the signal from v_1 must be brief if the US fluctuates rapidly in time, or else the synaptic knobs of v_1 will learn only a coarse weighted average in time of all the patterns playing on the cells $v_i, i \geq 2$. On the other hand, the CS can have a long duration. For example, in Pavlov's famous experiments on dogs, the duration of the bell (CS) can in principle be very long. Thus we seek a mechanism that shuts off the output from v_1 shortly after it is created by the CS, no matter how prolonged the CS is. Shutting off the v_1 signal while the CS input is still large clearly requires an inhibitory input.

Two main ways exist whereby this inhibitory input might occur, and obvious modifications of them can be readily imagined (Figure 2). In Figure 2a, inhibition is *recurrent*: v_1 gives rise to an excitatory axon collateral which perturbs an inhibitory interneuron v_2 that thereupon inhibits v_1. In Figure 2b, inhibition is *non-recurrent*: the CS gives rise to an axon collateral which perturbs an inhibitory interneuron v_2 that thereupon inhibits v_1. Only the non-recurrent case has the desired effect, as we now prove.

The systems of Figure 2 satisfy the following equations.

Recurrent

$$\dot{x}_1(t) = -\alpha x_1(1) - \beta[x_2(t-\sigma) - \Omega]^+ + I_{CS}(t) \tag{2}$$

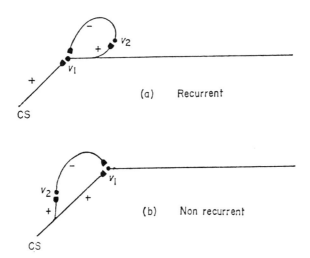

Figure 2.

and

$$\dot{x}_2(t) = -\gamma x_2(t) + \delta[x_1(t-\tau) - \Gamma]^+, \tag{3}$$

for suitable positive parameters and CS input $I_{CS}(t)$. Γ is the spiking threshold of the v_1 axon and Ω is the spiking threshold of the v_2 axon. Γ is also chosen as the spiking threshold of the axon collateral leading from the v_1 axon to v_2. A larger spiking threshold would only weaken the inhibition exerted by v_2 on v_1, and thereby make our ensuing conclusions easier to prove. A smaller spiking threshold is impossible unless v_1 sends out two independent axon collaterals, instead of one axon with an axon collateral.

A similar interpretation of Γ and Ω holds for the following system.

Non-Recurrent

$$\dot{x}_1(t) = -\alpha x_1(t) - \beta[x_2(t-\sigma) - \Omega]^+ + I_{CS}(t) \tag{4}$$

and

$$\dot{x}_2(t) = -\gamma x_2(t) + \delta I_{CS}(t-\tau). \tag{5}$$

To illustrate the essential differences between these networks when the CS is steadily applied for a long time, we consider the case in which the limit $I = \lim_{t\to\infty} I_{CS}(t)$ exists. We also suppose that the CS intensity is sufficiently great to create a signal from v_1 at large times; i.e., $I > \alpha\Gamma$. To avoid an unilluminating discussion of tedious cases, we start the system at equilibrium, i.e., $x_1(t) = 0, -\tau \le t \le 0$, and $x_2(t) = 0, -\sigma \le t \le 0$. (Any equilibrium levels P_i for x_i can be discussed in (1) by replacing $-\alpha_i x_i(t)$ by $-\alpha_i(x_i(t) - P_i)$.) [See Grossberg (1969b).]

Proposition 1 (recurrent). Under the above hypotheses, either the limits $x_i(\infty)$ $= \lim_{t=\infty} x_i(t)$ exist, $i = 1, 2$, with $x_1(\infty) > \Gamma$, or $x_1(t)$ oscillates above Γ infintely often and at arbitrarily large times.

In short, $x_1(t)$ cannot permanently be driven below threshold if the input is prolonged and sufficiently intense ever to drive $x_1(t)$ above threshold. The proof is given in Appendix A.

The non-recurrent case presents none of these difficulties. For definiteness, three classes of increasingly general inputs will be considered:

(I) *Steady state:* $I_{CS}(t) = I, t \geq 0$.

(II) *Monotonely concave:* $\dot{I}_{CS}(t) \geq 0$ and $\ddot{I}_{CS}(t) \leq 0, t \geq 0$ (one-sided derivatives are intended where two-sided derivatives do not exist).

(III) *Asymptotically steady state:* $I = \lim_{t \to \infty} I_{CS}(t)$ exists. The heuristic importance of (II) is the following. Let monotonely concave inputs perturb a finite number of cells $\mathcal{V}_1$ in equilibrium, and let these cells send excitatory signals to other cells $\mathcal{V}_2$ along axons having arbitrary time lags and thresholds. Let the cells $\mathcal{V}_2$ in turn send excitatory signals to cells $\mathcal{V}_3$, and so on. Then the potential of a cell body in some cell collection $\mathcal{V}_n$ will, except for unusually brief sigmoidal portions of its growth curve, be monotonely concave. Thus an essentially monotonely concave input to v_1 can represent the net effect of rather general excitatory preprocessing. This fact is summarized in the following simple lemmas.

Lemma 1. Let the non-negative functions $x_i(t)$ be monotonely concave, $i = 1, 2, \ldots, n$. Then the function

$$Y(t) = \sum_{i=1}^{n} [x_i(t - \tau_i) - \Gamma_i]^{+} \beta_i$$

is also monotonely concave if all parameters are non-negative.

Lemma 2. Define the sequence of functions $x_i(t)$ by

$$x_0(t) = \begin{cases} 0, & t < 0 \\ I, & t \geq 0 \end{cases}$$

and

$$\dot{x}_i(t) = -\alpha_i x_i(t) + \beta_i [x_{i-1}(t - \tau_i) - \Gamma_i]^{+}, \tag{6}$$

with $x_i(0) = 0$ and $i = 1, 2, \ldots, n$. Then $x_1(t)$ is monotonely concave, whereas each $x_i(t), i = 2, 3, \ldots, n$ is sigmoidal; i.e., $\dot{x}_i(t) \geq 0$ and $\ddot{x}_i(t)$ changes sign at most once from non-negative to non-positive.

The proof of Lemma 1 is obvious. The simple proof of Lemma 2 is given in Appendix B.

The following theorem shows that the non-recurrent network (4) to (5) can cut off the output produced by a prolonged input. This theorem also studies the number of oscillations in the output and the time needed to shut off the output given sufficiently simple test inputs. To simplify the equations, let $\tau = 0$, which synchronizes the CS onset at v_1 and v_2, and thereby causes the inhibitory signal from v_2 to v_1 to lag behind CS onset. In the steady-state case, for each I, $x_1(t)$ and $x_2(t)$ will henceforth be denoted by $x_1(t, I)$ and $x_2(t, I)$, respectively. The functions

$$S(I) = \min\{t : x_2(t - \sigma, I) = \Omega\}$$

and

$$T(I) = \max\{t : x_1(t, I) = \Gamma\}$$

will be used to denote the onset time of non-recurrent inhibition at v_1, and the time at which $x_1(t, I)$ is finally driven to subthreshold values by inhibition, whenever these times exist.

Theorem 1 (non-recurrent).† Let $\beta\delta > \gamma, \alpha\delta\Gamma > \gamma\Omega$ and $I > \alpha\Gamma$, and suppose $x_1(t)$ and $x_2(t)$ start out in equilibrium. If $I_{CS}(t)$ is asymptotically steady state, then $x_1(\infty) < \Gamma$. If $I_{CS}(t)$ is monotonely concave, then $\dot{x}_1(t)$ changes sign at most once from non-negative to non-positive. If $I_{CS}(t)$ is steady state, then $dS/dI < 0$ and the limit $T(\infty) = \lim_{I\to\infty} T(I)$ exists, is finite, and if $\alpha \neq \gamma$ satisfies the equation

$$\mu e^{-\gamma T} + \nu e^{-\alpha T} = \omega,$$

where

$$\mu = \gamma^{-1}(\alpha - \gamma)^{-1}\alpha\beta\delta e^{\gamma\sigma}, \quad \nu = (\gamma - \alpha)^{-1}e^{\alpha\sigma} - 1,$$

and

$$\omega = \gamma^{-1}\beta\delta - 1.$$

Also in the steady-state case, if $\alpha\Gamma \geq \beta\Omega$, then $dT/dI \geq 0$, whereas if $\alpha\Gamma < \beta\Omega$, then $(dT/dI)(I) \leq 0$ for $I \geq I_0$ if $(dT/dI)(I_0) \leq 0$. Moreover

$$(\alpha - \gamma)\frac{d}{dI}(T - S)(I) \leq 0 \quad \text{for } I \geq I_0$$

if

$$(\alpha - \gamma)\frac{d}{dI}(T - S)(I_0) \leq 0.$$

Remark. The intuitive meaning of the inequalities in the theorem is as follows. The inequality $\beta\delta > \gamma$ keeps $x_1(\infty, I)$ bounded from above as $I \to \infty$. The condition $\alpha\delta\Gamma > \gamma\Omega$ guarantees that inhibition sets in whenever v_1 can transmit a prolonged excitatory signal, and that ultimately the excitatory signal is inhibited away. If $I \leq \alpha\Gamma$, then no prolonged excitatory signal can occur, even without inhibition. Any monotonely concave input creates a single rise and fall in v_1's potential. The duration of suprathreshold response is essentially a monotonic function of input intensity: only one sign change in $T(I)$ can occur. A similar statement holds for $(T - S)^\bullet(I)$ with the following addition: If inhibition grows more rapidly than excitation ($\alpha < \gamma$), then $(T - S)^\bullet$ can change sign only towards the negative; i.e., then increasing input intensity tends to "contract" the time scale of suprathreshold response. This theorem guarantees than a non-recurrent inhibitory interneuron can limit the duration of the v_1 output even in response to an indefinitely prolonged CS input. As a result, the synaptic knobs of v_1 can learn the pattern weights at the cell bodies on which they impinge with arbitrarily good temporal discrimination.

The above conclusions are independent of how we interpret the CS. Suppose we could guarantee that only a prescribed space-time pattern at the sensory periphery ever creates a positive input at v_1. Then by Grossberg (1969e, 1970), we could also guarantee that any prescribed output pattern can be learned in response to the given one by letting v_1 be the source of an outstar avalanche. Moreover, if we were given n cells $v_i, i = 1, 2, \ldots, n$, rather than just v_1, and if each of these cells could respond

---

† This theorem is proved in Appendix C.

only to a prescribed space-time pattern $\mathcal{P}_i$, then we could guarantee that any output pattern can be learned in response to any of the n patterns $\mathcal{P}_i$ by letting each v_i be a source of an outstar avalanche. For example, such a network can in principle learn to play any sonata in response to any moving picture of external events.

The simplest networks of this kind will perform their discrimination and learning tasks in a wholly ritualistic way. Grossberg (1969e) indicates, however, that teleological factors such as "goals", "internal drive states", "paying attention", "novelty", and the like can be introduced into the network by suitably modifying its anatomy. A fuller discussion of such teleological factors will presumably be facilitated by a clear-cut description of the minimal mechanisms needed to discriminate and learn complicated tasks in a ritualistic way.

Non-recurrent inhibitory interneurons can be used as temporal discriminators in many anatomical situations. The following two examples illustrate some of the possibilities.

(A) Compatibility of Diffuse Arousal and Temporal Discrimination

Figure 1 can be augmented as in Figure 3, which is discussed in detail in Grossberg (1969e, 1970). In Figure 3, each US axon sends off an excitatory axon collateral to v_1. The inputs delivered to v_1 by these collaterals are called *diffuse arousal inputs* (DAI's), since they arrive at v_1 a fixed time η before the US is received by the cells $\mathcal{B}$, and at all other cells such as v_1 that send axon collaterals to $\mathcal{B}$. The DAI has the following function. Suppose that the US follows the CS by a time lag of T_i on the ith learning trial. If the CS alone can trigger a v_1 output, and if T_i is not independent of i, then a given synaptic knob of v_1 can learn different parts of the same pattern at $\mathcal{B}$ on different trials, and hence might learn no one pattern well as a result of repeated practice. To avoid this difficulty, require that the CS and the DAI be simultaneously active at v_1 before a signal from v_1 can be created. This is readily done by choosing a sufficiently large v_1 signal threshold once and for all. Then a signal from v_1 will occur approximately η time units before the US onset on all learning trials. Thus a given synaptic knob can practice the same part of the pattern on successive trials, thereby leading to perfect learning.

The inhibitory interneuron v_2 in Figure 3 furthermore guarantees that the v_1 signal will have a short duration, since by inhibiting the CS, the inhibitory signal also drives v_1 below its signal threshold, given the additivity of all inputs at v_1. Thus synchronizing v_1-US onset and achieving good local temporal discrimination can be simultaneously achieved. This example illustrates an important general theme: Spatio-temporally specific *and* diffuse interactions co-existing at the same cells can contribute to the overall well-being of the organism.

(B) Cerebellar Purkinje Cells as Non-Recurrent Temporal Discriminators

In Figure 4, the non-recurrent inhibitory interneuron is controlled by the US in a gridwork of interactions between perpendicular somatotopic representations of two cell collections having linearly ordered components. See Grossberg (1969g) for background details.

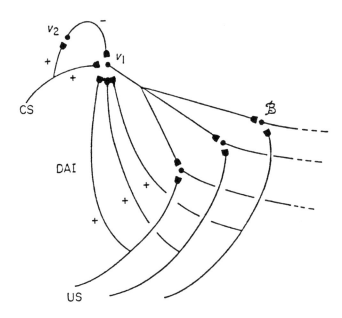

Figure 3.

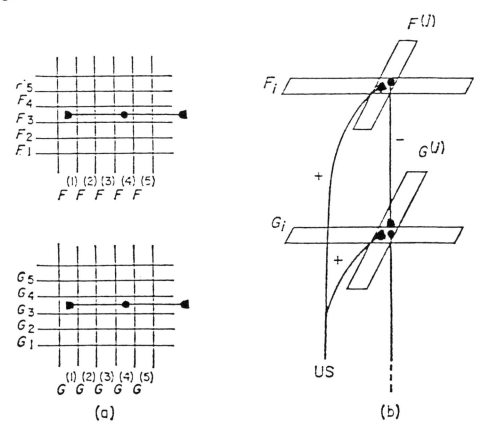

Figure 4.

Figure 4a shows a view from above of two pairs of perpendicular somatotopic representations: $F \equiv \{F_1, F_2, \ldots\}$ and $F^{\perp} \equiv \{F^{(1)}, F^{(2)}, \ldots\}$, and $G \equiv \{G_1, G_2, \ldots\}$ and $G^{\perp} \equiv \{G^{(1)}, G^{(2)}, \ldots\}$. The CS is delivered in duplicate to the F and G representations, and the US is delivered to the $F^{\perp}$ and $G^{\perp}$ representations. A CS to G_i (and thus to F_i) excites a strip of parallel fibers, as in Figure 4b, which carry their signals through the strip and thereupon excite its output cells at different times. The US excites a perpendicular strip $F^{(j)}$. In order to temporally tag the onset of the US, and thereby restrict the class of parallel fibers in G_j which form large cross-correlations with the output cells of $G^{(j)}$, a non-recurrent inhibitory interneuron in $F^{(j)}$ is also activated by the US and rapidly inhibits $G^{(j)}$. After learning occurs, the CS alone should produce an output from G. This output will also be rapidly inhibited due to parallel learning of which inhibitory interneurons in F should fire to G. Grossberg (1969g) points out a possible analogy between the system F and the cerebellar neo-cortex. In this analogy, the non-recurrent inhibitory interneurons from F to G are cerebellar Purkinje cells, whose role as temporal discriminators would be established were the analogy fully valid.

4. Choices between Incompatible Behaviors: "Majority Rule" in Non-Recurrent "Interference Patterns"

In many behavioral situations, a rapid choice between mutually incompatible behavioral modes is called for. Non-recurrent inhibitory interneurons can achieve such a choice between any finite number of behavioral alternatives in one processing step. In Figure 5a, the ith input sends an excitatory input to v_i and an equal inhibitory input to $v_k, k \neq i$. In Figure 5b, essentially the same process occurs but Dale's Principle is respected; i.e., the synaptic knobs of one cell are either all excitatory or all inhibitory. We will show that the total input of at most one cell v_i can ever be positive at any time, and thus that at most one $x_i(t)$ at a time can be driven up towards suprathreshold values.

The interpretation of the v_i outputs can be very varied. For example, a given v_i can serve as a diffuse arousal source for a large collection of cells V_i that are used to learn behavior sequences compatible with the ith behavioral mode; e.g., eating or sex. The cells V_i can be disjoint from all cells $V_j, j \neq i$, even if the cells V_i and V_j lie very close to one another. Keeping all cells V_i and V_j close might be necessary, for example, to give both behavioral modes equal access to the same motor pathways. On the other hand, cells which can be aroused by several modes can also be readily contemplated, but they would presumably control preparatory precursors of the overt behavioral modes that are mutually compatible.

Figure 5c illustrates a different possibility in the case of two cells v_1 and v_2. Here again only one cell output can be facilitated at any time. Whereas v_1 subliminally arouses a collection of cells, v_2 suppresses these cells. Suppose that exciting v_1 indicates the arrival of inputs $I_1(t)$ which portend good consequences for the organism, whereas exciting v_2 portends bad consequences; e.g., occurrence of food versus shock. If the instantaneous attraction of food, as manifested by the intensity of $I_1(t)$, is overwhelmed by the instantaneous repulsion of shock, as manifested by the intensity of $I_2(t)$, then the cells which would ordinarily be aroused by, and therefore learn from, the sequence of ongoing events can readily be suppressed by the diffuse v_2 output. The converse is also clearly true. The intensities of $I_1(t)$ and $I_2(t)$ in this case would

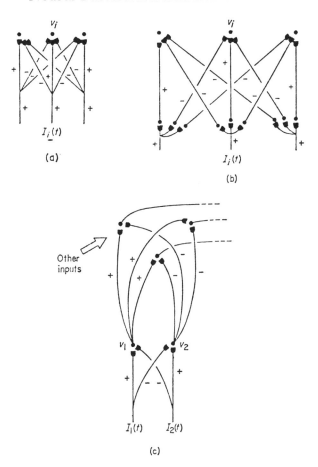

Figure 5.

presumably be partially determined by signals from internal homeostats.

The simplest equations of embedding field type that have these properties are given as follows.

$$\dot{x}_i(t) = -\alpha_i x_i(t) + I_i(t - \tau_i) - \sum_{k \neq i} I_k(t - \tau_k), \qquad (7)$$

where the output from v_i has the form

$$O_i(t) = \beta_i [x_i(t) - \Gamma_i]^+, \quad \Gamma_i > 0, \qquad (8)$$

$i = 1, 2, \ldots, n$. Note that the arrival time of all excitatory and inhibitory signals with the same source is the same, but that different sources can have different arrival times. In this sense, the individual input sources create incoming "waves", and the excitatory-inhibitory interaction between these waves creates "interference patterns" which give rise to unambiguous "choices". This restriction on arrival times can be guaranteed by choosing the signal velocity in axons proportional to axonal length; i.e., by spatiotemporal self-similarity (Grossberg, 1969g).

Analysis of (7) is readily accomplished by defining the functions

$$I(t) = \sum_{k=1}^{n} I_k(t - \tau_k)$$

and

$$\theta_i(t) = I_i(t - \tau_i)I^{-1}(t),$$

with the understanding that $\theta_i(t) = 0$ if $I(t) = 0$. Then (7) becomes

$$\dot{x}_i(t) = -\alpha_i x_i(t) + I(t)(\theta_i(t) - \sum_{k \neq i} \theta_k(t)),$$

and since $\sum_{k=1}^{n} \theta_k(t) = 1$ whenever $I(t) > 0$,

$$\dot{x}_i(t) = -\alpha_i x_i(t) + J_i(t), \tag{9}$$

where

$$J_i(t) = 2I(t)(\theta_i(t) - 1/2),$$

$i = 1, 2, \ldots, n$. Clearly at most one $J_i(t)$ is positive at any time t, namely the one for which $\theta_i(t) > 1/2$, since the $\theta_i(t)$'s form a probability distribution at any time t for which some $J_i(t) \neq 0$. Thus, by (9), at most some $x_i(t)$ at a time can be driven up by a positive input. This accomplishes our goal given *any* collection of non-negative and continuous inputs $I_i(t)$, no matter how oscillatory each input is.

In particular, if the $\theta_i(t)$ are constant in a sufficiently long time interval, then for any positive thresholds Γ_k, all outpus $O_k(t)$ will eventually be zero unless some $\theta_i > 1/2$; i.e., no mode is activated. In this latter case, only $O_i(t)$ can eventually be positive. The rate with which this asymptote is approached—indeed whether it ever is reached—depends on the intensity $I(t)$. For example, if $x_i(0) = 0$, then $x_i(t) = \Gamma_i$ at a time $t = T$ for which

$$(2\theta_i - 1) \int_0^T e^{-\alpha_i(T-v)} I(v) dv = \Gamma_i.$$

This shows, roughly speaking, that there is an inverse relationship between relative intensity and total intensity of inputs in determining the system's reaction time. The chance that all $\theta_i(t) \leq 1/2$ over long time intervals is reduced by assuming that the inputs to different modes build up according to different time scales.

Two interesting papers (Kilmer, 1969; Kilmer, Blum, and McCulloch, 1969) came to my attention after these facts were observed. These papers discuss competition of behavioral modes in the reticular formation using computer methods. Systems (7) and (8) represent a highly simplified case of an alternative attack on this phenomenon using embedding fields. Hierarchies of units such as those above can readily be constructed.

The equation (7) can be generalized as follows.

$$\dot{x}_i(t) = -\alpha_i x_i(t) + \beta_{ii} I_i(t - \tau_i) - \sum_{k \neq i} I_k(t - \tau_k)\beta_{ki}.$$

In this general setting, a wide variety of possibilities occurs in which the v_i are not totally incompatible. For example, in all cases, an input of sufficient intensity to a single cell v_i creates an output only from v_i. By choosing the β_{ki} sufficiently large, however, even an input for which $\theta_i(t) \cong 1-\epsilon$, with ϵ any prescribed small number, can be so strongly inhibited that v_i emits no signal. Alternatively, two cells v_i and v_j with $\theta_i(t) \cong \frac{1}{2} \cong \theta_j(t)$ can be so weakly coupled by mutual inhibition (i.e., $\beta_{ij} \cong 0 \cong \beta_{ji}$) that they can fire simultaneously.

The system

$$\dot{x}_i(t) = -\alpha_i x_i(t) + I_i(t - \tau_{ii}) - \sum_{k \neq i} I_k(t - \tau_{ki}) \tag{10}$$

can also yield mutually compatible outputs, even though all excitatory and inhibitory signals have equal strength. This is seen by defining

$$I^{(i)}(t) = \sum_{k=1}^{n} I_k(t - \tau_{ki})$$

and

$$\theta_{ki}(t) = I_k(t - \tau_{ki}) I^{(i)}(t),$$

and writing (10) as

$$\dot{x}_i(t) = -\alpha_i x_i(t) + 2 I^{(i)}(t)(\theta_{ii}(t) - 1/2).$$

One then checks that $\theta_{ii}(t) > 1/2$ does not imply $\theta_{jj}(t) \leq 1/2$ for all $j \neq i$, in general. Hence the restriction that the input sources create "waves" is of some importance, and more fundamentally, spatio-temporal self-similarity is called for.

5. Local Temporal Generalization: Variable Velocities of Motor Performance

Suppose that a given pattern of muscular motion can be reflexively produced at a fixed velocity. Can this pattern also be produced by the same nerve cells at other velocities? Suppose that the pattern is learned at a fixed velocity. Can the pattern be performed at several velocities? The answer to these questions in our network is "yes". It is also clearly "yes" in many instances chosen from real life: even complicated piano pieces, practiced at one speed, can be performed at several speeds.

First consider the simple case of reflexively performing a motor spatial pattern using the following network:

$$\dot{x}_i(t) = -\alpha_1 x_1(t) + I_1(t) \tag{11}$$

and

$$\dot{x}_i(t) = -\alpha x_i(t) + \beta[x_1(t - \tau_1) - \Gamma_1]^+ p_{1i} \tag{12}$$

$i = 2, 3, \ldots, n$, where the cell v_i sends an axon to an idealized muscle group $\mathcal{M}_i$ whose velocity of contraction at time t is $V_i(t) = \gamma x_i(t - \tau)$ (Figure 6). Suppose that the system starts out at equilibrium, and perturb the source v_1 with a positive input pulse $I_1(t)$. Then at any time $t \geq 0$, $x_i(t) = p_{1i} J(t)$, where

$$J(t) = \beta \int_0^t e^{-\alpha(t-v)} \left[\int_0^{v-\tau_1} e^{-\alpha_1(v-\tau_1-\xi)} I_1(\xi) d\xi - \Gamma_1 \right]^+ dv$$

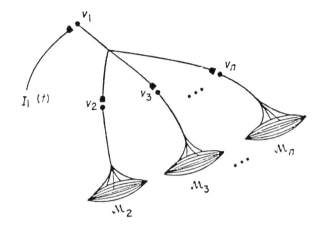

Figure 6.

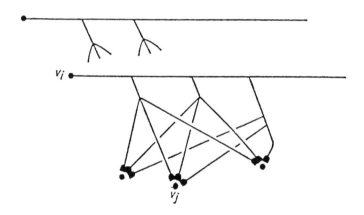

Figure 7.

for $t \geq 0$, and 0 otherwise. Thus $V_i(t) = p_{1i}K(t)$, where $K(t) = \gamma J(t - \tau)$. Either all $V_i(t) = 0$ due to an insufficiently intense input at v_1, or

$$\frac{V_i(t)}{V_j(t)} = \frac{p_{1i}}{p_{1j}},$$

and thus the muscle groups $\mathcal{M}_i$ each contract at fixed relative velocities p_{1i} which characterize the pattern. The absolute velocity of contraction is proportional to $K(t)$, which in turn depends only on the intensity of the input at the source. For example, if in addition to a specific input to v_1, v_1 also receives an arousal input due to some general threat to the organism, then the contraction of the muscles in their prescribed pattern will be speeded up.

This example can be generalized in many ways. Figure 7 provides a simple anatomy for controlling performance of any number of space-time patterns at variable velocities by the same idealized muscle groups. Figure 7 describes the system

$$\dot{x}_i(t) = -\alpha_i x_i(t) + I_i(t), \tag{13}$$

and

$$\dot{x}_j(t) = -\alpha x_j(t) + \sum_{i=1}^{n} \sum_{k=1}^{N} [x_i(t - \tau_i - k\xi_i) - \Gamma_i]^+ p_{ijk}, \tag{14}$$

where $i = 1, 2, \ldots, n$ and $j = n+1, n+2, \ldots, n+m$. Let the system start out at equilibrium and suppose that v_i alone is perturbed by a brief but intense input pulse, for some $i \leq n$. Then (14) becomes

$$\dot{x}_j(t) = -\alpha x_j(t) + \sum_{k=1}^{N} [x_i(t - \tau_i - k\xi_i) - \Gamma_i]^+ p_{ijk}.$$

In other words, v_j is perturbed every ξ_i time units by an input with relative weights p_{ijk}. Suppose that the duration of the signal $[x_i(t) - \Gamma_i]^+$ is less than ξ_i and that the decay rate α is large. Then $x_j(t)$ will substantially recover from the kth input burst before the $(k+1)$th burst begins. The response to the kth burst therefore satisfies

$$\frac{x_j(t)}{x_m(t)} \simeq \frac{p_{ijk}}{p_{imk}},$$

and thus the muscles can run through the space-time pattern with relative weights p_{ijk}. This is true for any i, so that any number of space-time patterns can be controlled in this way.

Concerning velocity of performance, we can again say that an increase in the absolute size of an axonal signal $[x_i(t) - \Gamma_i]^+$ will speed up performance due to proportionality of muscle contraction rate and $x_j(t-\tau)$ size. Another factor enters in the source signal $[x_i(t) - \Gamma_i]^+$ itself, since increase of $I_i(t)$ decreases the time it takes $x_i(t)$ to exceed Γ_i and to transmit a signal; i.e., decreases the source reaction time. On the other hand, a rate-limiting factor also enters, namely the time interval ξ_i between activation of successive clusters of axon collaterals. This time interval is independent of source energy, and thus pattern performance velocity has a finite upper bound.

All of the above remarks can be carried over to show that a task learned at one speed can be performed at several speeds by varying the source energy. One simply replaces system (13) and (14) by Γ-outstar avalanches, as in Grossberg (1969e, 1970). This more complex situation brings with it more interesting possibilities; e.g., a spontaneous speed-up of muscle contraction given a recall input to the source of fixed waveform after a moderate amount of practice (i.e., motor "reminiscence"), and motor manifestations of post-tetanic potentiation, listless response due to disuse, or perfect motor memory until "extinction" occurs on unrewarded trials (Grossberg, 1970).

Clearly Figures 6 and 7 do not describe "muscular" control *per se*, but merely illustrate one way of controlling variable performance rates in general without changing the controlling or learning cells and the pattern they have encoded. One can readily improve the description of the end-organ being controlled in specific cases without necessarily altering these conclusions. For example, in the case of muscular control, at least two improvements in the above discussion are easy to achieve. First, specification of $\mathcal{M}_i$'s contraction in terms of the velocity $V_i(t) = \gamma x_i(t-\tau)$ is insufficient, because when $x_i(t-\tau) = 0, V_i(t) = 0$ even if the muscle has not returned to its resting length. Second, some discussion of reciprocity between agonist and

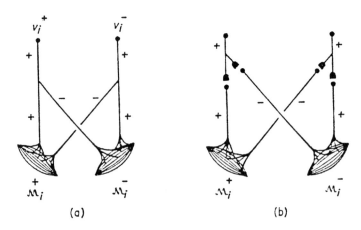

(a)   (b)

Figure 8.

antagonist muscles is needed. The following remarks briefly indicate that aspects of these phenomena can be built into the discussion in cases where muscles *per se* are the central concern. These remarks do not, however, pretend to exhaust even some simple macroscopic features of motor control. Our goal is merely to illustrate the flexibility of avalanche and related controllers.

Let $(\mathcal{M}_i^+, \mathcal{M}_i^-)$ be a pair of antagonistic muscles. Let the length of $\mathcal{M}_i^+(\mathcal{M}_i^-)$ at time t be $L_i^+(t)$ $(L_i^-(t))$, and (for simplicity) let the resting length of $\mathcal{M}_i^+$ and $\mathcal{M}_i^-$ be L_{i0}. Introduction of L_{i0} means, in particular, that we will here avoid a discussion of muscle spindles, Golgi tendon organs, and the structure of limb joints. Let a cell v_i^+ (v_i^-) send the excitatory input $\gamma x_i^+(t-\tau)$ $(\gamma x_i^-(t-\tau))$ to $\mathcal{M}_i^+$ $(\mathcal{M}_i^-)$. Then we replace the rule $V_i(t) = \gamma x_i(t-\tau)$ by the pair of equations

$$\dot{L}_i^+(t) = -\delta[L_i^+(t) - L_{i0}] + \gamma[x_i^+(t-\tau) - x_i^-(t-\tau)] \tag{15}$$

and

$$\dot{L}_i^-(t) = -\delta[L_i^-(t) - L_{i0}] + \gamma[x_i^-(t-\tau) - x_i^+(t-\tau)] \tag{16}$$

which describe the non-recurrent inhibitory interaction of Figure 8a. Figure 8b can also be used. These equations clearly generalize the rule for $V_i(t)$ while bringing the muscles back to a resting length in the absence of external forces, and accommodating agonist-antagonist reciprocity. In Figure 6 the cells v_i can now be replaced by the cell pairs (v_i^+, v_i^-) without changing our conclusions about variable performance velocity. Then we find equations of the form (11), (15), (16),

$$\dot{x}_i^+(t) = -\alpha x_i^+(t) + \beta[x_1(t-\tau_1) - \Gamma_1]^+ p_{1i}^+$$

and

$$\dot{x}_i^-(t) = -\alpha x_i^-(t) + \beta[x_1(t-\tau_1) - \Gamma_1]^+ p_{1i}^-,$$

$i = 2, 3, \ldots, n$. Figure 7 can be similarly generalized.

6. Why are Sensory Pathways in Different Modalities Anatomically Different if Universal Discriminators Exist?

The next section begins a study of the following question. Let n cells v_i, $i = 1, 2, \ldots, n$ be attached to independent peripheral receptors which create the input $I_i(t)$ at v_i. A peripheral environmental event creates a characteristic pattern of inputs $I_i(t)$ on the cells v_i. It is conceivable that events having very different behavioral significance for the organism all create large inputs to a fixed v_i. In spite of this "local non-specificity" of cellular response, the organism's response to the entire pattern of inputs can be quite specific. Is there a way to construct a cellular network which can discriminate any pattern playing on the cells v_i from any other pattern, to within a prescribed small error, in spite of local non-specificity?

The answer is "yes". Because of this fact, several implications immediately follow. First, the same construction will enable the cells to filter *any* pattern received from the receptors, be its interpretation auditory, tactile, olfactory, visual, etc.; i.e., the construction is "universal". It is also simple-minded and uses few cell bodies. Why then do not all the anatomies of sensory pathways in different modalities look alike? One answer seems to be that different modalities preserve different perceptual constancies or invariances, which improve the ability to make "operant" discriminations. For example, in hearing there is a pitch invariance, in vision a size invariance, etc. One can easily in principle imagine networks that include these invariances simply by joining all the input patterns that should create equivalent outputs by some type of "or" switch. Presumably Nature has chosen a more subtle path, if only because connecting up all the requisite "or" switches before they are needed would be very hard to do in a growing brain, and might create undesirable rigidity. Our present construction might therefore exist *in vivo* with the least modification in the most primitive discriminative systems, e.g., smell or taste (Frank and Pfaffmann, 1969). In any case, where anatomically more elaborate discriminators are found, it will henceforth be profitable to ask as a point of departure: why is the universal construction not adequate? Moreover, the same mechanisms are likely to reappear in some form within these more elaborate anatomies.

Second, the number n of receptive cells can be chosen arbitrarily large. Surely if n equals a small number, such as two, there might exist many different environmental events whose effect on two receptors will be the same. As n is taken to large values, however, even if individual receptors differ only slightly in their specificity of response, the chance that the inputs $I_i(t)$ really characterize the environmental event steadily improves. For any fixed choice of n, the network to be constructed can discriminate the pattern—as the organism perceives it—with arbitrarily good accuracy.

7. Unselective Filtering of Spatial Patterns by Excitatory Networks

Suppose that a given collection of n receptor cells v_i, $i = 1, 2, \ldots, n$ is presented with an arbitrary sequence of spatial patterns at widely separated onset times. What is the simplest embedding field network having m output cells that each respond to at most one spatial pattern, within some prescribed margin of error? Henceforth, we will set $m = 1$, since once the problem of filtering one pattern is overcome, any finite number of patterns can readily be filtered. Suppose for example that the given pattern is $I_i(t) = \theta_i I(t)$ with weights $\theta = (\theta_1, \theta_2, \ldots, \theta_n)$. We will construct a network such that the output cell fires only if the pattern weights $\tilde{\theta} = (\tilde{\theta}_1, \tilde{\theta}_2, \ldots, \tilde{\theta}_n)$ playing on the receptors satisfy the inequalities

$$\theta_i - \epsilon < \tilde{\theta}_i < \theta_i + \epsilon \tag{17}$$

$i = 1, 2, \ldots, n$ for some arbitrarily small $\epsilon > 0$, and if, moreover, the input pattern is presented with sufficient intensity over a sufficiently long time interval, where of course the minimum effective input intensity and duration will tend to vary inversely with respect to one another.

The simplest networks, conceptually speaking, contain only excitatory interactions. A routine example will show, however, that such a network cannot conveniently achieve the selectivity of response that we seek. A mixture of excitatory and inhibitory interactions will hereby be called for, and the deficiencies of the purely excitatory network will readily suggest procedures for connecting the excitatory and inhibitory components.

Let the cells v_i receive the spatial pattern $I_i(t) = \tilde{\theta}_i I(t), i = 1, 2, \ldots, n$. We suppose that all $\tilde{\theta}_i$ are positive without loss of generality, since otherwise we could simply delete the receptors receiving no input from our consideration. Denote the output cell which will be responsive to this pattern by v_{n+1}. v_{n+1} must be responsive to all weights $\tilde{\theta}_i$ of the pattern if ever it could succeed in discriminating this pattern from others. Signals from each v_i must therefore ultimately reach v_{n+1}. If we restrict ourselves to excitatory transmissions, then either an excitatory signal traverses an edge $e_{i,n+1}$ directly from v_i to v_{n+1}, or else several intermediate stages of excitatory processing will be juxtaposed between v_i and v_{n+1}. These intermediate stages can smooth the input, or sum it up, or truncate it using thresholds. We will suppose for simplicity that only direct interactions exist, since the deficiencies which arise in this case can only be made worse by intermediate processing. In the direct case, we find the equations

$$\dot{x}_i(t) = -\alpha_i x_i(t) + \tilde{\theta}_i I(t), \tag{18}$$

$$\dot{x}_{n+1}(t) = -\alpha_{n+1} x_{n+1}(t) + \sum_{k=1}^{n} [x_k(t - \tau_k) - \Gamma_k]^+ \beta_k, \tag{19}$$

where the output from v_{n+1} has the form

$$O_{n+1}(t) = [x_{n+1}(t) - \Gamma_{n+1}]^+ \beta_{n+1}. \tag{20}$$

Let the pattern play upon the receptors with a total intensity that eventually becomes steady state. Then $I = \lim_{t \to \infty} I(t) > 0$ exists, and by (18) and (19),

$$\lim_{t \to \infty} x_{n+1}(t) = \frac{1}{\alpha_{n+1}} \sum_{k=1}^{n} [\alpha_k^{-1} \tilde{\theta}_k I - \Gamma_k]^+ \beta_k. \tag{21}$$

By (20) and (21), an output will eventually arise from v_{n+1} if I is so large that

$$\sum_{k=1}^{n} [\alpha_k^{-1} \tilde{\theta}_k I - \Gamma_k]^+ \beta_k > \alpha_{n+1} \Gamma_{n+1}.$$

This shows, however, that a sufficiently large input intensity I can create an output from v_{n+1} for *any* choice of pattern weights $\tilde{\theta}_i$. Excitatory networks are therefore unselective if a wide range of total input intensities exists, a perhaps obvious conclusion, but one which when taken seriously has nontrivial consequences.

8. Two Stages of Non-Recurrent Inhibition for Pattern Discrimination

The difficulties encountered in the excitatory network are twofold, and can be overcome by two stages of non-recurrent inhibitory interaction.

(A) Pattern Normalization and Low-Band Filters

In the direct excitatory network, as the input intensity I increases, the asymptotic membrane potentials $x_i(\infty)$ increase linearly, and thus an output from v_{n+1} can be created by an ever less restrictive class of patterns. To avoid this, the potentials $x_i(t)$ must eventually approach a finite asymptote, even if $I \to \infty$. Moreover, the mechanism that creates the asymptote must not distort the recording of pattern weights $\tilde{\theta}_i$ in each $x_i(t)$. We will therefore seek a mechanism such that $x_i(t) \cong \tilde{\theta}_i \Omega$, for some finite constant Ω, and large times t, as $I \to \infty$. This phenomenon will be called *pattern normalization*.

Suppose that we have somehow achieved pattern normalization. This fact along with the existence of positive spiking thresholds now permits us to forbid an output from v_i unless the pattern weight $\tilde{\theta}_i$ satisfies $\tilde{\theta}_i > \theta_i - \epsilon$, for some $\epsilon > 0$. Simply choose the spiking threshold Γ_i of the axon emitted by v_i to equal

$$\Gamma_i = \Omega(\theta_i - \epsilon). \tag{22}$$

Since $x_i(t) \cong \tilde{\theta}_i \Omega(t)$ for some function $\Omega(t)$ which satisfies $\Omega(t) \leq \Omega$ for $t \geq 0$, clearly $x_i(t) \leq \Gamma_i$ unless $\tilde{\theta}_i > \theta_i - \epsilon$. One-half of the inequalities (17) can hereby be achieved.

(B) High-Band Filters

Now the temptation is great to try completing our construction of a selective spatial pattern by the following simple procedure. Let the outputs from each v_i converge on a cell v_{n+1}, and choose the spiking threshold Γ_{n+1} so high that v_{n+1} cannot emit a signal unless it receives a positive signal simultaneously from *all* cells v_i. Unfortunately, this device does not suffice. v_{n+1} will also be able to emit signals in response to patterns with weights very different from θ.

To see this, note the following facts. v_{n+1} must surely produce an output if the pattern weights satisfy $\tilde{\theta}_i = \theta_i, i = 1, 2, \ldots, n$. In this case, the total input to v_{n+1} is asymptotically approximately

$$\sum_{i=1}^{n} [\theta_i \Omega - \Gamma_i]^+ = n\epsilon\Omega, \tag{23}$$

by (19), where we have also let all $\beta_i = 1$ for simplicity. Suppose that $\theta_k = \min\{\theta_i : i = 1, 2, \ldots, n\}$ and present the pattern with weights

$$\tilde{\theta}_k = 1, \tilde{\theta}_i = 0, i \neq k. \tag{24}$$

The asymptotic input to v_{n+1} produced by this pattern is approximately

$$\sum_{i=1}^{n} [\tilde{\theta}_i \Omega - \Gamma_i]^+ = \tilde{\theta}_k \Omega - \Gamma_k$$

$$= \Omega(1 - \theta_k + \epsilon). \tag{25}$$

If the weights θ_i are not close to the weights in (24), then v_{n+1} should not respond. By (23) and (25), therefore, whenever the pattern θ is not concentrated at the one cell v_k,

$$n\epsilon\Omega \geq \Omega(1 - \theta_k + \epsilon),$$

or

$$\min\{\theta_i : 1 \leq i \leq n\} \geq 1 - \epsilon(n-1). \tag{26}$$

Fix n at any finite value. To achieve arbitrarily good pattern discrimination, an arbitrarily small choice of ϵ should be possible. But then (26) implies

$$\min\{\theta_i : 1 \leq i \leq n\} \cong 1,$$

which is clearly impossible unless $n = 1$, and if $n = 1$ no pattern discrimination whatsoever occurs.

A related deficiency of this approach is seen as follows. To achieve selective filtering of *any* pattern, the right-hand side of (26) must be non-positive. Then $\epsilon \geq 1/(n-1)$. But the total input (23) always satisfies

$$n\epsilon\Omega = \sum_{i=1}^{n}[\theta_i\Omega - \Gamma_i]^+$$

$$\leq \sum_{i=1}^{n}\theta_i\Omega = \Omega,$$

or $\epsilon \leq 1/n$. These two inequalities imply the contradiction $n - 1 \geq n$. Thus selective pattern filtering of all patterns is impossible for any n.

These facts show that an additional mechanism is needed to shut off outputs from v_{n+1} in response to patterns for which some $\tilde{\theta}_i > \theta_i + \epsilon$. In other words, if the signal from any v_i to v_{n+1} becomes too large, it must be shut off or competitively inhibited before $x_{n+1}(t)$ can exceed threshold. If this is achieved, then each v_i can transmit to v_{n+1} either no signal at all or a signal with a finite upper bound. Consequently, we can now choose the threshold Γ_{n+1} so that v_{n+1} transmits a signal only if it receives signals almost simultaneously from all v_i. Since $\Gamma_i = \Omega(\theta_i - \epsilon)$, the patterns transmitting these signals satisfy $\tilde{\theta}_i > \theta_i - \epsilon$. By shutting off the signal from v_i to v_{n+1} if it exceeds 2ϵ in size, these patterns also satisfy $\tilde{\theta}_i < \theta_i + \epsilon$.

The two stages of input processing—pattern normalization, which leads to low-band filtering, and high-band filtering—can both be accomplished by non-recurrent inhibition. An important heuristic lesson of this construction will be that the very same *local* inhibitory mechanisms acting at two different stages of input processing can have profoundly different effects on the *global* transformation of the input at each stage. Of course, only one stage of inhibition is needed to discriminate a pattern of *absolute* input intensities.

9. Specific versus Nonspecific Inhibitory Interneurons, Inhibition at the Axon Hillock, Presynaptic Inhibition, Equal Smoothing, and Dale's Principle

The title of this section lists some of the more detailed considerations that will arise while constructing our filter. They are listed here to avoid losing them later in technical details.

Pattern normalization can be accomplished by "non-specific", or "diffusely projecting", non-recurrent inhibitory interneurons, whereas high-band filtering can be done by "specific" interneurons that are excited by one cell and inhibit one cell. These specific inhibitory interneurons can transform an input that varies over a large intensity range into an essentially "on-off" or bimodal output response, the alternative depending on the relative strengths of excitatory and inhibitory inputs. Analogous input-output transformations have been found experimentally in the ventral cochlear nucleus, for example (Whitfield, 1967, p. 80).

It is often important that excitatory and inhibitory signals interact only after they have been smoothed an equal number of times by prior stages of cellular processing. Otherwise, it is hard to achieve the proper relative onset times of excitatory and inhibitory signals, or the proper relative strengths of these signals, for purposes of pattern discrimination. Analogously, equal smoothing is also useful in processing the inputs to pairs of antagonistic "muscles", as in Figure 8, so that these muscles act in synchrony.

An alternative to equal smoothing exists. The inhibitory interneuron of Figure 2b can be used if it exponentially smooths its input with a decay rate which is large relative to the fluctuation rate of the input, *and* if the input is magnified before it is smoothed. Then the inhibitory output will be approximately as smooth as the excitatory input. Hence almost equal smoothing is possible by two pathways with different numbers of intermediate cells.

Small, rapidly-responding, non-recurrent inhibitory interneurons can accomplish high-band filtering. Rapid response is needed to forbid build-up of the postsynaptic potential to large values. Small interneuronal cell bodies can achieve rapid growth of interneuronal membrane potential by avoiding the dilution of interneuronal input in a large cellular volume. In principle, high-band filtering can be accomplished without an inhibitory interneuron, as the next paragraph notes.

High-band filtering can also be achieved if local postsynaptic response gets blocked as presynaptic spiking frequency increases. Also a switch-over as spiking frequency increases from net release of excitatory transmitter to net release of inhibitory transmitter would be a very effective mechanism. This last mechanism violates Dale's principle, but its efficiency could be so great that it should be kept in mind.

Non-specific inhibitory interneurons can produce pattern normalization if they terminate either at suitable cell bodies, or at the axon hillocks of prior cells, or even at the synaptic knobs of prior cells. The latter two locales for inhibitory interaction are, at least formally, better than the cell body termination for two reasons. First, a layer of cells bodies can then be eliminated. Second, the axonal response rate to inputs is presumably at least as rapid as the response at the axon's cell body, because the axons in our network faithfully replicate in their spiking frequencies the "slow potentials" fluctuating in the cell bodies. The inhibitory input is consequently less smoothed by axon hillock and synaptic knob potentials than by cell body potentials, and thus the cell's net output is more faithfully tuned to input events. In a similar fashion, axon hillock and synaptic knob inhibition is advantageously located to block totally the signal of a large cell body; the same inhibitory signal acting directly at the cell body could be lost in an ocean of excitatory influences. Experimental reports of axon hillock and synaptic knob inhibition have appeared (Eccles, 1964; Eccles, Ito, and Szentagothai, 1967).

The mathematical results below on pattern filtering are true under weak constraints on cell body parameters. The main constraints are: the build-up of inhibition is at least as rapid as the build-up of excitation; the inhibitory time lag—discounting threshold effects—is no longer than the excitatory time lag; the inhibitory threshold is higher than the excitatory threshold; and the axonal time scales are no slower than the time scales for slow potential fluctuation in cell bodies. Given these constraints, one can almost say that simply by "throwing together" excitatory and inhibitory components, some patterns will be selectively filtered. To guarantee that many patterns will be filtered, one can, for example, organize the cells into successive layers whose profusely branching axons flow mainly away from the periphery with a wide distribution of spiking thresholds. Some network examples which illustrate the above remarks are listed below, where $i = 1, 2, \ldots, n$.

Type I

$$\dot{x}_i(t) = -\alpha x_i(t) + \beta I_i(t), I_i(t) = \tilde{\theta}_i I(t), \tag{27}$$

$$\dot{x}_{n+1}(t) = -\gamma x_{n+1}(t) + \delta I(t), I(t) = \sum_{k=1}^{n} I_k(t), \tag{28}$$

$$\dot{x}_{n+1+i}(t) = -\zeta x_{n+1+i}(t) + \eta [x_i(t - \tau_1) - \Gamma_i]^+ \\ - \kappa [x_{n+1}(t - \tau_2) - \Gamma_{n+1}]^+ \tag{29}$$

$$\dot{x}_{2n+1+i}(t) = -\lambda x_{2n+1+i}(t) + \mu [x_{n+1+i}(t - \tau_3) - \Gamma_{n+1+i}]^+, \tag{30}$$

$$\dot{x}_{3n+1+i}(t) = -\nu x_{3n+1+i}(t) + \xi [x_{n+1+i}(t - \tau_4) - \Gamma_{n+1+i}]^+, \tag{31}$$

$$\dot{x}_{4n+1}(t) = -\rho x_{4n+1}(t) + \sigma \sum_{k=1}^{n} [x_{2n+1+k}(t - \tau_5) - \Gamma_{2n+1+k}]^+ \\ - \chi \sum_{k=1}^{n} [x_{3n+1+k}(t - \tau_6) - \Gamma_{3n+1+k}]^+, \tag{32}$$

and

$$O_{4n+1}(t) = \omega [x_{4n+1}(t) - \Gamma_{4n+1}]^+. \tag{33}$$

This network is pictured in Figure 9, where $n = 2$.

Type II illustrates what happens if some of the exponential averaging steps occur so quickly that they can be approximated by algebraic transformations.

Type II

Use (27), (28),

$$O_i(t) = \eta [x_i(t - \tau_1) - \Gamma_i]^+ - \kappa [x_{n+1}(t - \tau_2) - \Gamma_{n+1}]^+, \tag{34}$$

$$\dot{x}_{n+2}(t) = -\lambda x_{n+2}(t) + \mu \sum_{k=1}^{n} [O_k(t - \tau_3) - \Gamma_{n+1+k}]^+ \\ - \nu \sum_{k=1}^{n} [O_k(t - \tau_4) - \Gamma_{2n+1+k}]^+, \tag{35}$$

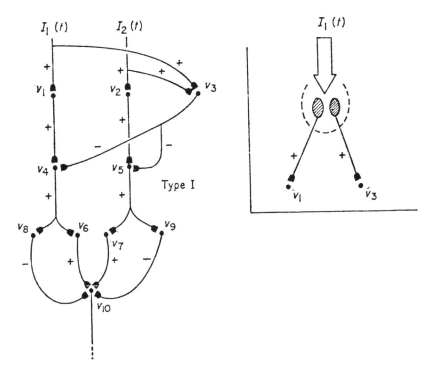

Figure 9.

and

$$O_{n+2}(t) = \xi[x_{n+2}(t) - \Gamma_{n+2}]^+. \tag{36}$$

Some Type II networks are illustrated in Figure 10, where $n = 2$. All axonal or synaptic knob inhibitions are presumed in Figure 10 to occur very rapidly compared to exponential averging rates at the cell bodies. Double synaptic knob inhibition is also possible, if (35) is changed to

$$\dot{x}_{n+2}(t) = -\lambda x_{n+2}(t) + \mu \sum_{k=1}^{n}[O_k(t - \tau_3) - \nu[O_k(t - \tau_4) - \Gamma_{2n+1+k}]^+ - \Gamma_{n+1+k}]^+.$$

The resultant network is shown in Figure 11.

Type III and IV networks illustrate some possibilities if *all* exponential averaging steps occur so quickly relative to the input fluctuation rate that they can be approximated by algebraic transformations.

Type III

Let

$$P_i(t) = \alpha[I_i(t - \tau_1) - \Gamma_i]^+ - \beta\left[\sum_{k=1}^{n} I_k(t - \tau_2) - \Gamma_{n+1}\right]^+, \tag{37}$$

$$Q_i(t) = \gamma[P_i(t - \tau_3) - \Gamma_{n+1+i}]^+ - \delta[P_i(t - \tau_4) - \Gamma_{2n+1+i}]^+, \tag{38}$$

and let the output be

$$O(t) = \zeta\left[\sum_{k=1}^{n} Q_k(t) - \Gamma_{3n+1}\right]^+. \tag{39}$$

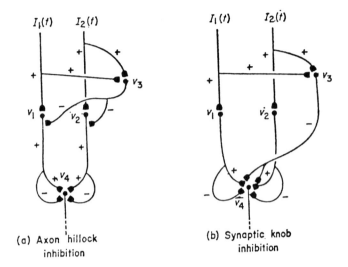

(a) Axon hillock
inhibition

(b) Synaptic knob
inhibition

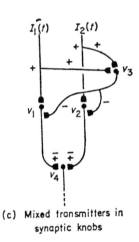

(c) Mixed transmitters in
synaptic knobs

Figure 10.

Type IV

Use (37) and (39) along with

$$Q_i(t) = \gamma[P_i(t - \tau_3) - \delta[P_i(t - \tau_4) - \Gamma_{2n+1+i}]^+ - \Gamma_{n+1+i}]^+. \tag{40}$$

A study of Type I networks will readily suggest how the other, simpler types behave. In a Type I network, the pattern $I_i(t) = \theta_i I(t)$, already neurally encoded, is transferred in a "specific" point-to-point representation along the excitatory pathways

$$I_i(t) \to^+ v_i \to^+ v_{n+1+i}.$$

Each $I_i(t)$ also reaches the "non-specific" inhibitory interneuron v_{n+1} via axon collaterals. Hence in (27), the input to v_i is $\theta_i I(t)$, whereas in (28), the input to v_{n+1} is $\sum_{k=1}^n \theta_k I(t) = I(t)$. The non-specific cell v_{n+1} thereupon inhibits each v_i, and the total input to v_{n+1+i} in (29) is given by

$$J_i(t) = \eta[x_i(t - \tau_1) - \Gamma_i]^+ - \kappa[x_{n+1}(t - \tau_2) - \Gamma_{n+1}]^+, \tag{41}$$

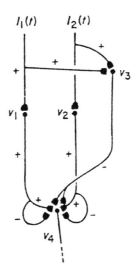

Figure 11.

which is also the net output $O_i(t)$ from v_i in (34). Each v_{n+1+i} sends excitatory signals to v_{2n+1+i} and v_{3n+1+i}. Each v_{2n+1+i}, in turn, excites the output cell v_{4n+1}, whereas each v_{3n+1+i} inhibits v_{4n+1}, as in (32). The output from v_{4n+1} is given in (33). The inset in Figure 9 points out that the input receptor itself can be a compound organ with excitatory and inhibitory components, cf. Ratliff (1965).

The general remarks of Section 10 are realized in Type I networks as follows.

(A) Non-Specific versus Specific Cells in Pattern Normalization

The cells v_i and v_{n+1+i} are "specific" cells, since they preserve the spatial separation and ordering of the individual inputs $I_i(t)$. The cell v_{n+1} is a "non-specific" cell, since it averages all inputs $I_i(t)$ and then diffusely inhibits all cells v_{n+1+i}. This non-specific cell will produce the pattern normalization.

(B) Output Thresholds as Low-Band Filters

The cut-off of outputs for which $\tilde{\theta}_i < \theta_i - \epsilon$ will be accomplished by the thresholds $\Gamma_i = \Gamma_{n+1}(\theta_i - \epsilon)$ in (29).

(C) Specific Inhibitory Interneurons Acting on a Common Output Cell as High-Band Filters

Equations (29) to (32) will forbid any $I_i(t)$ from creating a positive input to v_{4n+1} if $\tilde{\theta}_i > \theta_i + \epsilon$. The cut-off is accomplished by the inhibitory interneurons v_{3n+1+i}. This could also be accomplished by (34) and (35), or (37) amd (38), etc.

Thus a substantial conceptual difference exists between the non-specific inhibitory interneuron v_{n+1} and the specific ones v_{3n+1+i} : v_{n+1} normalizes patterns, whereas v_{3n+1+i} creates a high-band filter.

(D) The Continuum between "and" and "or" in the Terminal Threshold

The threshold Γ_{4n+1} in (33) can be chosen so large that the output from v_{4n+1} is positive only if all $I_i(t)$ create positive signals to v_{4n+1}. Then Γ_{4n+1} acts like an "and" switch. Were we to let Γ_{4n+1} approach zero, the "and" switch would be smoothly deformed into an "or" switch when $\Gamma_{4n+1} = 0$, and $O_{4n+1}(t)$ would be positive if any signal to v_{4n+1} were positive. This is one reason why the anatomy of the network by itself does not suffice to tell us what tasks the network is performing. In a similar way, all our results would change were the inhibitory signals too weak, or too slow, etc.

(E) Equal Smoothing

The excitatory cells v_i and the inhibitory cell v_{n+1} each smooth the signals reaching v_{n+1+i} once. The excitatory cells v_{2n+1+i} and the inhibitory cells v_{4n+1+i} each smooth the signals reaching v_{4n+1} once. Type II, III, and IV networks replace some of these smoothing steps by input amplification and rapid decay.

(F) Multiple-Threshold versus Single-Threshold Cells

A paper by Wickelgren (1969) appeared as this paper was being written, and describes some possible uses of neurons with multiple thresholds. From the vantage point of the present formalism, anything that a multiple-threshold neuron can discriminate or learn can also be discriminated or learned by a suitable juxtaposition of single-threshold units. The main formal advantage of a multiple-threshold unit is that, once its design as an input filter is perfected, it can readily be replicated wherever it is needed; e.g., the pyramidal cells of the cerebral cortex. The question therefore seems to be one of evolutionary efficiency and miniaturization of control rather than of absolute formal superiority of one or the other type of system. Our network operations can, in fact, be interpreted as interactions between small membrane patches and associated cell volume segments in multiple-threshold neurons if one so desires. If this is done, then several filtering steps could take place in the dendrites of the multiple-threshold cell, or in any region whose time scale is faster than the scale of slow potential fluctuations.

10. Pattern Normalization in Type I Networks

To prove that pattern normalization is accomplished by equations (27) and (28), we study the input $J_i(t)$ to v_{n+1+i}, as defined in (41), when the spatial pattern $\hat{\theta}$ is presented. Supposing that x_i and x_{n+1} have zero initial data (i.e., start out in equilibrium), $J_i(t)$ can be written in the form

$$J_i(t) = \eta[J(\alpha, \tilde{\theta}_i I, t - \tau_1) - \Gamma_i]^+ - \kappa[J(\gamma, I, t - \tau_2) - \Gamma_{n+1}]^+$$

by redefining several parameters and using the notation

$$J(\omega, K, t) = \begin{cases} 0, & t < 0 \\ \int_0^t e^{-\omega(t-v)} K(v) dv, & t \geq 0 \end{cases}.$$

The following Lemma illustrates pattern normalization in $J_i(t)$ for a convenient choice of parameters.

Lemma 3. Let $\alpha = \gamma, \tau_1 = \tau_2, \kappa \geq \eta$, and $\Gamma_i = \Gamma_{n+1}(\theta_i - \epsilon)$. Let $\tau_1 = 0$ for convenience. Let $I(t)$ be any bounded, monotone non-decreasing, and continuous function with $I(0) = 0$.

If $\tilde{\theta}_i \leq \theta_i - \epsilon$, then $J_i(t) \leq 0$ for all $t \geq 0$.

Suppose $\tilde{\theta}_i > \theta_i - \epsilon$. Then $J_i(t) = 0$ until the first time $t = T_1$ at which

$$J(\alpha, I, t) = \tilde{\theta}_i^{-1} \Gamma_{n+1}(\theta_i - \epsilon) \tag{42}$$

and

$$\frac{d}{dt} J(\alpha, I, t) > 0. \tag{43}$$

Thereafter $J_i(t)$ is monotone non-decreasing and satisfies the equation

$$J_i(t) = \eta[\tilde{\theta}_i J(\alpha, I, t) - \Gamma_{n+1}(\theta_i - \epsilon)]^+ \tag{44}$$

until the first time $t = T_2$ at which (43) and

$$J(\alpha, I, t) = \Gamma_{n+1} \tag{45}$$

hold. For $t > T_2, J_i(t)$ is monotone non-increasing. Thus

$$J_i(t) \leq \eta \Gamma_{n+1}[\tilde{\theta}_i - (\theta_i - \epsilon)]^+ \tag{46}$$

for $t \geq 0$, and

$$\lim_{t \to \infty} J_i(t) = \eta[\alpha^{-1}\tilde{\theta}_i I - \Gamma_{n+1}(\tilde{\theta}_i - \epsilon)]^+ - \kappa[\alpha^{-1}I - \Gamma_{n+1}]^+, \tag{47}$$

where $I = \lim_{t \to \infty} I(t)$.

Lemma 3 can easily be modified to include inputs which rise so rapidly that both excitation and inhibition set in before the input begins to decay, as Proposition 2 will show. The parameter choices $\alpha = \gamma$ and $\tau_1 = \tau_2$ will ultimately be generalized to $\alpha \geq \gamma$ and $\tau_1 \geq \tau_2$, since the excitatory and inhibitory cells cannot *in vivo* be certain to have equal parameters and time lags. The present case illustrates some basic phenomena with a minimum of technical detail, and is studied in Appendix D.

By Lemma 3, the input to v_{n+1+i} is positive only if $\tilde{\theta}_i > \theta_i - \epsilon$ and if $I(t)$ is sufficiently intense that $\sup_t J(\alpha, I, t) > \Gamma_{n+1}(\theta_i - \epsilon)$. Even for arbitrarily large I, the input is bounded above by $\Gamma_{n+1}[\tilde{\theta}_i - (\theta_i - \epsilon)]^+$ and oscillates at most once. Thus pattern normalization and low-band filtering have occurred.

For a general total input $I(t)$, the following proposition holds.

Proposition 2. Let $\alpha = \Gamma, \tau_1 = \tau_2 = 0, \kappa \geq \eta$, and $\Gamma_i = \Gamma_{n+1}(\theta_i - \epsilon)$. Let $I(t)$ be any bounded, non-negative, and continuous function with $I(0) = 0$.

If $\tilde{\theta}_i \leq \theta_i - \epsilon$, then $J_i(t) \leq 0$ for all $t \geq 0$.

Suppose $\tilde{\theta}_i > \theta_i - \epsilon$. Then corresponding to every rise and fall in $I(t)$, $J(\alpha, I, t)$ can rise and fall at most once, and thus the following oscillations in $J_i(t)$ can occur.

(a) (Unimodal). Suppose $J(\alpha, I, t)$ continues to rise until (42) and (43) hold, but falls before (45) holds. Then $J_i(t)$ rises and falls with

$$\text{sign } \frac{d}{dt} J_i(t) = \text{sign } \frac{d}{dt} J(\alpha, I, t).$$

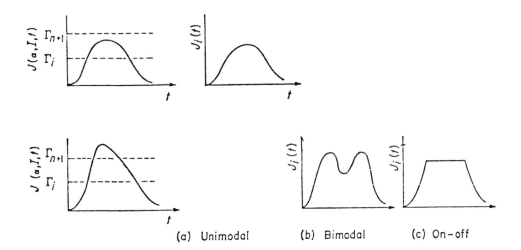

Figure 12.

(b) (Bimodal). Suppose $\eta\tilde{\theta}_i < \kappa$ and that $J(\alpha, I, t)$ continues to rise until (43) and (45) hold. Thereafter $J_i(t)$ decreases as $J(\alpha, I, t)$ increases, and $J_i(t)$ increases as $J(\alpha, I, t)$ decreases until (45) holds again, after which $J_i(t)$ decreases towards $J_i(t) = 0$.

(c) (On-Off). Suppose $\eta\tilde{\theta}_i = \kappa$; i.e., $\tilde{\theta}_i = 1$ until $\eta = \kappa$. Let $J(\alpha, I, t)$ rise and fall as in (b). Then $J_i(t)$ rises with $J(\alpha, I, t)$ until

$$J(\alpha, I, t) \geq \Gamma_{n+1}. \tag{49}$$

For all t such that (49) holds,

$$J_i(t) = \eta\Gamma(1 - \theta_i + \epsilon).$$

Thereafter $J_i(t)$ decreases until zero is reached. See Figure 12.

Proposition 2 is proved using the method of Lemma 3. The condition $\Gamma_i = \Gamma_{n+1}(\theta_i - \epsilon)$ in these statements amounts to nothing more than the inequality $\Gamma_i < \Gamma_{n+1}$ written in a convenient form that shows which pattern weights can pass through. The general case $\alpha \leq \gamma, \tau_1 \geq \tau_2, \kappa \geq \eta$, and $\Gamma_i < \Gamma_{n+1}$ requires a study of the input

$$J_i(t) = \eta[\tilde{\theta}_i J(\alpha, I, t - \tau_1) - \Gamma_{n+1}(\theta_i - \epsilon)]^+ - \kappa[J(\gamma, I, t - \tau_2) - \Gamma_{n+1}]^+. \tag{50}$$

The condition $\tau_1 \geq \tau_2$ is needed to avoid a gap of $\tau_2 - \tau_1$ time units during which $J_i(t)$ can approach ∞ as $I \to \infty$ before inhibition sets in. The condition $\alpha \geq \gamma$ guarantees that the inhibitory potential grows no slower than the excitatory potential, and therefore will be sufficiently strong to eventually drive $J_i(t)$ to zero if $\tau_1 \geq \tau_2$. The absolute, as well as the relative, sizes of α, γ, τ_1, and τ_2 influence the form of $J_i(t)$. If $\tau_1 = \tau_2$ but $\alpha \geq \gamma$, for example, then the inequality

$$J(\alpha, I, t - \tau_1) \leq J(\gamma, I, t - \tau_1),$$

which holds for any non-negative and continuous input I, guarantees that pattern normalization occurs. On the other hand, the difference $[J(\gamma, I, t - \tau_1) - J(\alpha, I, t - \tau_1)]$ at any time t can depend strongly on the past shape of the input, and thus $J_i(t)$ can remain non-positive even if the input is at times intense. $J_i(t)$ will better reflect instantaneous fluctuations of the input if the input is magnified and rapidly smoothed. The next proposition proves that this will happen if the input fluctuations have a certain amount of regularity; for example, if the input is the output of another cell.

Proposition 3. Given any $t \geq 0$ and $\epsilon > 0$ suppose that there exist functions $R(\epsilon) > 0$ and $T(t, \epsilon) \geq 0$ such that

$$t \geq R(\epsilon) + T(t, \epsilon) \tag{51}$$

and

$$|I(v) - I(t)| \leq \epsilon \quad \text{if } v\epsilon[T(t, \epsilon), t]. \tag{52}$$

Let $B(\alpha)$ be any nonnegative and continuous function such that $\omega = \lim_{\alpha \to \infty} \alpha^{-1} B(\alpha)$ exists with $0 < \omega < \infty$. Then

$$|\alpha J(\alpha, I, t) - I(t)| \leq \|I\| e^{-\alpha R(\epsilon)} + \epsilon, \tag{53}$$

where $\|I\| = \sup\{|I(t)| : t \geq 0\}$, and obviously

$$\lim_{\alpha \to \infty} J(\alpha, B(\alpha)I, t) = \omega I(t). \tag{54}$$

Remarks: The function $B(\alpha)$ magnifies the input as the decay rate α increases. Equation (53) shows that if $I(t)$ fluctuates ever more slowly, then less magnification and slower decay will suffice to keep $J(\alpha, B(\alpha)I, t)$ close to $\omega I(t)$. The simple proof is given in Appendix E.

Propositions 2 and 3 are applied to $J_i(t)$ below, where we vary $\eta = \eta(\alpha)$ and $\kappa = \kappa(\gamma)$ as functions of α and γ, respectively.

Corollary 1. Let $\alpha \geq \gamma, \kappa \geq \eta$, and $\Gamma_i = \Gamma_{n+1}(\theta_i - \epsilon)$. Suppose that the finite positive limits $\mu = \lim_{\alpha \to \infty} \alpha^{-1} \eta(\alpha)$ and $\nu = \lim_{\gamma \to \infty} \gamma^{-1} \kappa(\gamma)$ exist, and let

$$0 \leq \tau_1 - \tau_2 \leq \min\{R(\tfrac{\epsilon}{3}), R(\tfrac{\epsilon}{3\nu})\}. \tag{56}$$

Then for α and γ sufficiently large, $|J_i(t) - M_i(t)| \leq \epsilon$, where $M_i(t) \leq 0$ for all $t \geq 0$ unless $\tilde{\theta}_i > \alpha\gamma^{-1}(\theta_i - \epsilon)$. If $\tilde{\theta}_i > \alpha\gamma^{-1}(\theta_i - \epsilon)$, $M_i(t)$ is either unimodal, bimodal, or on-off on any one oscillation of $I(t - \tau_1)$.

The proof is given in Appendix F. Corollary 1 shows that increasing the relative growth rate of inhibition to excitation increases the minimal pattern weights $\tilde{\theta}_i$ which give rise to an output signal from v_i, unless the relative threshold size $\Gamma_i\Gamma_{n+1}^{-1}$ is changed to compensate. Also decreasing the input fluctuation rate allows an increase in the maximal permissible gap between the inhibitory and excitatory time lags. The decrease in input fluctuation rate can be achieved, other things equal, by letting the input source be an ever larger cell body. In other words, an increase in the spatial scale of the input source can allow an increase in the temporal scale of the relative excitatory and inhibitory signal onset times.

11. High-Band Filters

Specific inhibitory interneurons will now be used to cut off signals to the output cell when these signals become too large. It suffices to let $\Gamma_{n+1+i} = \Gamma^{(1)}$, $\Gamma_{2n+1+i} = \Gamma^{(2)}$, and $\Gamma_{3n+1+i} = \Gamma^{(3)}$ for all $i = 1, \ldots, n$. For convenience of exposition, we also introduce the notation $\tau^{(2)} = \tau_3 + \tau_5$ and $\tau^{(3)} = \tau_4 + \tau_6$. Then (30) to (32) can be written in terms of the functions

$$K_i(t) = [x_{n+1+i}(t) - \Gamma^{(1)}]^+ \tag{57}$$

and

$$L_i(t) = \sigma[\mu J(\lambda, K_i, t) - \Gamma^{(2)}]^+ - \chi[\xi J(\nu, K_i, t + \tau^{(2)} - \tau^{(3)}) - \Gamma^{(3)}]^+ \tag{58}$$

as

$$x_{2n+1+i}(t) = \mu J(\lambda, K_i, t - \tau_3), \tag{59}$$

$$x_{3n+1+i}(t) = \xi J(\nu, K_i, t - \tau_4), \tag{60}$$

and consequently

$$x_{4n+1}(t) = J(\rho, \sum_i L_i, t - \tau^{(2)}), \tag{61}$$

if x_{2n+1+i}, x_{3n+1+i}, and x_{4n+1} have zero initial data.

Suppose we could show that each summand $L_i(t)$ in (61) will be non-positive if K_i becomes too large. Then by choosing the threshold Γ_{4n+1} sufficiently large, the output $O_{4n+1}(t)$ in (33) would remain zero if any K_i is too large. We therefore consider $L_i(t)$ as a functional of K_i. $L_i(t)$ can be rewritten in the form

$$L_i(t) = \eta[J(\lambda, K_i, t) - \Omega]^+ - \kappa[J(\nu, K_i, t + \tau) - \Gamma]^+$$

where $\eta = \sigma\mu$, $\kappa = \chi\xi$, $\Omega = \sigma\Gamma^{(2)}$, $\Gamma = \chi\Gamma^{(3)}$, and $\tau = \tau^{(2)} - \tau^{(3)}$. To accomplish our aim, we approximate $L_i(t)$ by an input of the form

$$N_i(t) = \eta[\lambda^{-1}K_i(t)(1 - e^{-\lambda t}) - \Omega]^+ - \kappa[\nu^{-1}K_i(t)(1 - e^{-\nu(t+\tau)}) - \Gamma]^+.$$

As in Proposition 3, this can be done if $K_i(t)$ has uniformly small oscillations in very small intervals, by magnifying $K_i(t)$, smoothing it quickly, and choosing τ sufficiently small. In fact, for very fast smoothing rates, $N_i(t)$ can be further approximated in sufficiently small intervals by

$$P_i(t) = \eta[\lambda^{-1}I(1 - e^{-\lambda t}) - \Omega]^+ - \kappa[\nu^{-1}I(1 - e^{-\nu(t+\tau)}) - \Gamma]^+,$$

i.e. by a constant input I smoothed once by the excitatory and inhibitory cells. The approximation $P_i(t)$ holds even for slow smoothing rates if the input $K_i(t)$ is of "on-off" type, as we can guarantee by Proposition 3 at the pattern normalizing stage of non-recurrent inhibition. Hence we consider the function $P_i(t)$ below.

Proposition 4. Suppose $\lambda \geq \nu$, $\Gamma > \Omega$, $\nu\Gamma > \lambda\Omega$, $\kappa \geq \eta e^{\nu\tau}$, and $\tau > 0$. Then $P_i(t) \leq 0$ for all $t \geq 0$ unless $I < I_0$, where

$$\left(1 - \frac{\lambda\Omega}{I_0}\right)^{1/\lambda}\left(1 - \frac{\nu\Gamma}{I_0}\right)^{-1/\nu} = e^\tau. \tag{62}$$

The proof is given in Appendix G.

At least partial high-band filtering is also possible if the integrals

$$\int_0^t e^{-\omega(t-\nu)} K_i(\nu)\,dv$$

with $\omega = \lambda$, ν are not very close to $\omega^{-1} I(1 - e^{-\omega t})$, due to the following simple inequalities, which hold whenever $\lambda \geq \nu$ and $K_i(t)$ is monotone non-decreasing:

$$J(\lambda, K_i, t) \leq J(\lambda, K_i, t + \tau) \leq J(\nu, K_i, t + \tau)$$

and

$$\frac{d}{dt} J(\lambda, K_i, t) \leq \frac{d}{dt} J(\nu, K_i, t).$$

Nonetheless, a precise control of maximal output size is not readily available in the general case.

12. Discrimination of Space-Time Patterns

The above construction yields cells that can respond only to a given spatial pattern, or to patterns differing from the given one by a prescribed error, if these patterns are presented with sufficient intensity and duration. It is now simple in principle to construct cells which respond only to a prescribed space-time pattern. Let a space-time pattern with weights

$$\theta_i(t) = I_i(t) \left[\sum_{k=1}^n I_k(t) \right]^{-1}$$

be given. For sufficiently small values of $\xi > 0$, the continuous function $\theta_i(t)$ can be arbitrarily well approximated by a sequence

$$\{\theta_i(k\xi) : k = 0, 1, 2, \ldots, N\}$$

of its values. For each k, the weights

$$\theta(k\xi) = \{\theta_i(k\xi) : \quad i = 1, 2, \ldots, n\}$$

form a spatial pattern. To guarantee a good approximation of $\theta(t)$ by the patterns $\theta(k\xi)$, let ξ be chosen such that each $\theta_i(t)$ changes slowly in time intervals of length ξ. Given such a ξ, let total input intensities be specified—the "suprathreshold" intensities—which can create an output signal from a cell $v^{(k)}$ in response to the pattern $\theta(k\xi)$, and to no distinct pattern. In other words, the cells $v^{(k)}, k = 1, 2, \ldots, N$, divide all spatial patterns into $N + 1$ classes—the N classes which are close to some pattern $\theta(k\xi)$, and the class of all the other patterns.

It is now readily seen that the output cells $v^{(k)}, k = 1, 2, \ldots, N$, for any finite N, can receive their inputs from the same receptive cells (or "retina") v_i, $i = 1, 2, \ldots, n$, as in Figure 13, where we have chosen $n = N = 2$ for simplicity. In Figure 13, each receptive cell v_{n+1+i} sends out an axon with two axon collaterals. One collateral from each v_{n+1+i} will lead towards one of the cells $v^{(k)}$. The same normalizing cell v_{n+1}

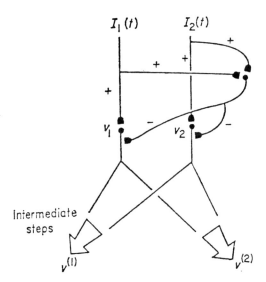

Figure 13.

can be used to normalize all the spatial patterns. This is not necessary, however; one normalizing cell can normalize several patterns, or several normalizing cells can normalize one pattern. Given a specific spatial distribution of normalizing cells, one can then determine from the thresholds of the v_{n+1+i} axon collaterals which pattern class will excite each $v^{(k)}$.

In a clear sense, this construction uses the fewest possible cells to filter spatial patterns. The n cells at the first layer characterize the level of sensory discrimination that is desired. The N cells at the last layer characterize the number of pattern classes to be discriminated. All intermediate cells can, if desired, be replaced by processes of smoothing, input additions and subtractions, and threshold cut-offs taking place on dendrites, axons, or synaptic knobs of these $n + N$ cells, perhaps at the price of violating Dale's principle.

Now that any finite number of spatial patterns $\theta(k\xi)$ can be discriminated by cells $v^{(k)}$ leading from the same receptors, discrimination of the space-time pattern $\theta(t)$ can be achieved by constructing a cell $\tilde{v}$ which produces an output signal only if all the cells $v^{(k)}$ are stimulated one after the other with a time lag of ξ. This can be done in many ways. The most direct way is to let $v^{(k)}$ send an axon to $\tilde{v}$ whose time lag is $\tau^{(k)}$. Suppose $\tau^{(k)} = \tau^{(k-1)} - \xi \geq 0$, $k = 1, 2, \ldots, N$, and use non-recurrent inhibitory interneurons to guarantee that $\tilde{v}$ fires only if it receives signals (almost) simultaneously from all cells $v^{(k)}$. This completes the construction.

Since any combination of events at the sensory periphery is a space-time pattern, any combination of events can be discriminated by an application of the above simple mechanisms. These mechanisms will not be used in precisely the given form in all sensory filters, if only due to differences in perceptual constancies between modalities, and because the above "passive" discriminations must be supplemented by "operant" discriminations in realistic behavioral interactions. Such refinements will be considered in another place, in suitable idealized cases.

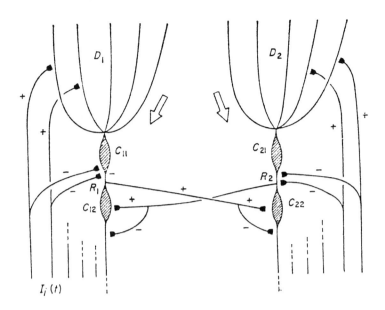

Figure 14.

13. Velocity and Orientation Detectors

To illustrate the above construction, we sketch a possible anatomy for two hypothetical cells that can respond only to lines of fixed length moving with a prescribed velocity and orientation (Figure 14). Each dendrite in the dendritic bush D_1 receives inputs from a different "retinal" cell, and the retinal cells fall under a straight line of fixed length and orientation on the retina. Each input $I_i(t)$ sends an excitatory signal to some dendrite and a normalizing non-recurrent inhibitory signal to the region R_1 at which local spike potentials carry excitatory signals from the cell body enlargement C_{11} to C_{12}. The threshold of R_1 can thus be chosen so that a signal reaches C_{12} from C_{11} only if all dendrites in D_1 have been almost simultaneously excited; i.e., if a line of prescribed length and orientation has perturbed the retinal cells. R_1 also sends an excitatory signal to C_{22}, which is normalized at the C_{22} axon hillock by a non-recurrent inhibitory interneuron. The time lag of this signal is ξ. The threshold of C_{22} is chosen so that an output occurs only if signals from R_1 and R_2 arrive almost simultaneously at C_{22}. Suppose that the line moves from the retinal cells that perturb D_1 to those that perturb D_2 in ξ time units—say at a velocity $V(\xi)$. Then $v^{(2)}$ will fire. If the motion is from D_2 receptors to D_1 receptors, then $v^{(1)}$ will fire. No other input can fire these cells.

One can in a similar way get $v^{(1)}$ to fire in response to a stationary line, $v^{(2)}$ to fire only in response to a line moving from $D^{(1)}$ to $D^{(2)}$ receptors at velocity $V(\xi)$, and $v^{(1)}$ *not* to fire if a line moves from $D^{(2)}$ to $D^{(1)}$ at velocity $V(\xi)$ but will fire if the motion proceeds at other velocities. Only minor changes in threshold, and the use of non-recurrent inhibition from R_2 to C_{12} are needed. More complicated discriminators can be imagined with equal ease.

14. Alternative Mechanisms of Pattern Normalization: Saturating Potentials in an On-Off Field, or Logarithmic Transducers

Pattern normalization by non-specific inhibitory interneurons can formally be replaced by at least two other mechanisms. In other words, a variety of mechanisms might seek a common functional goal *in vivo*.

(A) Saturating Potentials in an On-Off Field

Given n cells v_i, $i = 1, 2, \ldots, n$, let the excitatory input $I_i(t)$ to v_i be delivered with equal strength as an inhibitory input to all v_j, $j \neq i$ as in Figure 5a. Suppose that $x_i(t)$ responds linearly to the excitatory input $I_i(t)$ when $x_i(t)$ has small values, but approaches a finite constant M if $I_i(t)$ persists with very large values in the absence of competing inhibition. Also let $x_i(t)$ respond linearly to the inhibitory couplings $-x_i(t)I_j(t), j \neq i$, and let $x_i(t)$ decay exponentially to equilibrium $(= 0)$ in the absence of inputs. Then the output of each v_i is normalized.

By hypothesis,

$$\dot{x}_i(t) = [M - x_i(t)]I_i(t) - x_i(t)[\alpha + \sum_{k \neq i} I_k(t)]. \tag{63}$$

Let $I_i(t) = \theta_i I(t)$, and define the variables

$$x(t) = \sum_{k=1}^{n} x_k(t)$$

and

$$X_i(t) = x_i(t)x^{-1}(t).$$

Then (63) yields the equations

$$\dot{X}_i(t) = A(t)[\theta_i - X_i(t)] \tag{64}$$

and

$$\dot{x}(t) = MI(t) - [\alpha + I(t)]x(t), \tag{65}$$

where $A(t) = MI(t)x^{-1}(t)$. To illustrate our main point let $I(t)$ be monotone non-decreasing with $I = \lim_{t \to \infty} I(t) > 0$, and start the system in equilibrium. Now by (64), $X_i(t)$ monotonically approaches the limit θ_i. In particular, after initial transients decay,

$$x_i(t) \sim \theta_i \frac{MI(t)}{\alpha + I(t)} \leq \frac{\theta_i MI}{\alpha + I} \leq \theta_i M,$$

showing that pattern normalization occurs.

(B) Logarithmic Transducers

This alternative is ironic in that it works well formally, is compatible with some data about logarithmic transduction from inputs to frequencies in individual cells (Granit, 1955), but seems hard to build into the interaction between cells unless linear and logarithmic transduction laws are mixed.

Suppose that the peripheral input $I_i(t)$ is logarithmically transduced when it reaches v_i, $i = 1, 2, \ldots, n$. Also let all the peripheral inputs combine linearly at a cell v_{n+1}, whereupon the total input is logarithmically transduced. Let v_{n+1} linearly inhibit each v_i. Then the output from each v_i is normalized. By hypothesis, the transduced input to v_i is

$$\tilde{I}_i(t) = \log I_i(t)$$
$$= \log \theta_i I(t)$$
$$= \log \theta_i + \log I(t).$$

The total input to v_{n+1} is $\sum_{k=1}^{n} I_k(t) = I(t)$, which is logarithmically transduced yielding $\tilde{I}_{n+1}(t) = \log I(t)$. $\tilde{I}_{n+1}(t)$ then linearly inhibits v_i yielding the net potential

$$\tilde{I}_i(t) - \tilde{I}_{n+1}(t) = \log \theta_i,$$

which is normalized. The non-linearity of the transformation $\theta_i \to \log \theta_i$ does not interfere with the selectivity of the filter. It is only necessary that the transformation be one-to-one.

APPENDIX A

Proof of Proposition 1

Suppose $x_1(\infty)$ and $x_2(\infty)$ exist. If $x_1(\infty) \leq \Gamma$, then by (3), $x_2(\infty) = 0$. But then by (2), $x_1(\infty) = \alpha^{-1}I$, which is a contradiction since $I > \alpha\Gamma$ by hypothesis. Hence $x_1(\infty) > \Gamma$ if $x_1(\infty)$ and $x_2(\infty)$ exist.

In a similar fashion, $x_1(\infty) > \Gamma$ if either limit $x_1(\infty)$ or $x_2(\infty)$ exists, since the existence of one limit clearly implies the existence of the other by integrating (2) and (3).

Suppose neither limit $x_1(\infty)$ or $x_2(\infty)$ exists. Then by the above remarks, the inequality $x_1(t) > \Gamma$ must hold at arbitrarily large times, or else by integration of (3), the existence of $x_2(\infty)$ will follow. In fact $x_1(t)$ must oscillate above Γ infinitely often: if $\dot{x}_1(t)$ has fixed sign at all large t, then $x_1(\infty)$ exists, since the solution of (2) and (3) is clearly bounded and continuous.

APPENDIX B

Proof of Lemma 2

Clearly $x_0(t)$ is monotonely concave for $t \geq 0$. Integrating (6) yields

$$x_i(t) = \beta_i \int_0^t e^{-\alpha_i(t-v)}[x_{i-1}(v - \tau_i) - \Gamma_i]^+ dv. \tag{B1}$$

Given any integral of the form

$$f(t) = \int_0^t e^{-\alpha(t-v)}g(v)dv$$

with $g(v)$ piecewise twice differentiable and $g(0) = 0$, successive integration by parts yields

$$\dot{f}(t) = \int_0^t e^{-\alpha(t-v)}\dot{g}(v)dv \tag{B2}$$

and

$$\ddot{f}(t) = \dot{g}(0)e^{-\alpha t} + \int_0^t e^{-\alpha(t-v)}\ddot{g}(v)dv. \tag{B3}$$

By (B2), if $\dot{g}(v) \geq 0$ for $v \geq 0$, then $\dot{f}(0) \geq 0$ for $t \geq 0$. By (B3), $\ddot{f}(0) = \dot{g}(0) \geq 0$. Thus if $\ddot{g}(v)$ changes sign at most once from non-negative to non-positive the same is true of $\ddot{f}(t)$. Applying (B2) and (B3) to $f(t) = x_i(t)$ and $g(t) = \beta_i[x_{i-1}(v - \tau_i) - \Gamma_i]^+$ iteratively for $i = 1, 2, \ldots, n$ proves Lemma 2.

APPENDIX C

Proof of Theorem 1

Let

$$J(t) = I_{CS}(t) - \beta[K(t) - \Omega]^+, \tag{C1}$$

where

$$K(t) = \delta e^{-\gamma(t-\sigma)} \int_0^{t-\sigma} e^{\gamma v} I_{CS}(v) dv \qquad (C2)$$

for $t \geq \sigma$, and 0 otherwise. By (4) and (5)

$$x_1(t) = \int_0^t e^{-\alpha(t-v)} J(v) dv \qquad (C3)$$

since $x_1(0) = 0$.

If $I_{CS}(t)$ is asymptotically steady state, then (C3) implies

$$x_1(\infty) = \alpha^{-1} I(1 - \gamma^{-1}\beta\delta) + \alpha^{-1}\beta\Omega.$$

We must check that $x_1(\infty) < \Gamma$. Given $\beta\delta > \gamma$, this is equivalent to

$$I(\gamma^{-1}\beta\delta - 1) > \beta\Omega - \alpha\Gamma,$$

which is true for all $I > \alpha\Gamma$ if

$$\alpha\Gamma(\gamma^{-1}\beta\delta - 1) > \beta\Omega - \alpha\Gamma,$$

or $\alpha\delta\Gamma > \gamma\Omega$, as hypothesized.

Suppose $I_{CS}(t)$ is monotonely concave. To show that $\dot{x}_i(t)$ changes sign at most once from non-negative to non-positive, note by (C3) that

$$\dot{x}_1(t) = \int_0^t e^{-\alpha(t-v)} \dot{J}(v) dv,$$

since $x_1(0) = 0$. It thus suffices by Lemma 2 to show that $J(0) \geq 0$ and that $\dot{J}(t) \leq 0$ for $t \geq t_0$ if $\dot{J}(t_0) = 0$. Since $J(t) = \dot{I}_{CS}(0) \geq 0$ for $t\epsilon[0,\sigma]$, $\dot{J}(0) = \ddot{I}_{CS}(0) \leq 0$. The inhibitory term is eventually positive since $I > \delta^{-1}\gamma\Omega$. Let $t_1 = \max\{t : K(t) \leq \Omega\}$. Note that for all $t \leq t_1$, $K(t) \leq \Omega$, since by (11),

$$\dot{K}(t) = \delta e^{-\gamma(t-\sigma)} \int_0^{t-\sigma} e^{\gamma v} \dot{I}_{CS}(v) dv \geq 0.$$

For $t \geq t_1$, (C1) implies

$$\dot{J}(t) = \dot{I}_{CS}(t) - \beta\delta e^{-\gamma(t-\sigma)} \int_0^{t-\sigma} e^{\alpha v} \dot{I}_{CS}(v) dv. \qquad (C4)$$

Suppose $\dot{J}(t_0) = 0$ for some t_0. Then $\dot{J}(t) \leq 0$ for $t \geq t_0$ if $\ddot{J}(t_0) \leq 0$. Since

$$\ddot{J}(t) = \ddot{I}_{CS}(t) - \beta\delta\dot{I}_{CS}(t - \sigma) + \gamma\beta\delta e^{-\gamma(t-\sigma)} \int_0^{t-\sigma} e^{\gamma v} \dot{I}_{CS}(v) dv,$$

(C4) implies

$$\ddot{J}(t_0) = \ddot{I}_{CS}(t_0) + \gamma\dot{I}_{CS}(t_0) - \beta\delta\dot{I}_{CS}(t_0 - \sigma).$$

Since $\ddot{I}_{CS}(t) \leq 0$ for all $t \geq 0$,

$$\ddot{J}(t_0) \leq \gamma(1 - \gamma^{-1}\beta\delta)\dot{I}_{CS}(t_0 - \sigma),$$

and since $\beta\delta > \gamma$ and $\dot{I}_{CS}(t) \geq 0$, $\ddot{J}(t_0) \leq 0$. Thus $\dot{x}_1(t)$ changes sign at most once towards the non-positive.

Suppose $I_{CS}(t)$ is steady state. Then (C3) becomes

$$x_1(t, I) = \alpha^{-1}I(1 - e^{-\alpha t}) - \beta e^{-\alpha t}\int_0^t e^{\alpha v}[x_2(v - \sigma, I) - \Omega]^+ dv, \qquad (C5)$$

where by (5),
$$x_2(t, I) = \gamma^{-1}\delta I(1 - e^{-\gamma t}). \qquad (C6)$$

Substitution of (C6) into (C5) and integration of (C5) for $t \geq S \equiv S(I)$ yields

$$\begin{aligned} x_1(t, I) &= \alpha^{-1}I(1 - e^{-\alpha t}) - \alpha^{-1}\beta(\gamma^{-1}\delta I - \Omega)(1 - e^{-\alpha(t-S)}) \\ &+ \gamma^{-1}(\alpha - \gamma)^{-1}\beta\delta I e^{-\gamma(S-\sigma)}[e^{-\gamma(t-S)} - e^{-\alpha(t-S)}], \end{aligned} \qquad (C7)$$

where we have chosen $\alpha \neq \gamma$ to avoid the simpler case. By (C6) and the definition of S,

$$\gamma^{-1}\delta I[1 - e^{-\gamma(S-\sigma)}] = \Omega, \qquad (C8)$$

and thus
$$e^{-\gamma(S-\sigma)} = \delta^{-1}I^{-1}(\delta I - \gamma\Omega). \qquad (C9)$$

Substituting (C9) in (C7), we find

$$\begin{aligned} x_1(t, I) &= \alpha^{-1}I(1 - e^{-\alpha t}) + \gamma^{-1}\beta(\delta I - \gamma\Omega)[-\alpha^{-1}(1 - e^{-\alpha(t-S)}) \\ &+ (\alpha - \gamma)^{-1}(e^{-\gamma(t-S)} - e^{-\alpha(t-S)})]. \end{aligned} \qquad (C10)$$

To compute dS/dI, differentiate (C9) and find

$$\frac{dS}{dI} = -I^{-1}(\delta I - \gamma\Omega)^{-1}\Omega < 0. \qquad (C11)$$

To compute dT/dI, set $x_1(t, I) = \Gamma$ in (C10), let $t = T$, and differentiate with respect to I. The result, after some rearrangement of terms, is

$$\frac{dT}{dI} = AB^{-1}, \qquad (C12)$$

where

$$\begin{aligned} A &= -\alpha^{-1}(1 - e^{-\alpha T}) + \gamma^{-1}\beta\delta[\alpha^{-1}(1 - e^{-\alpha(T-S)}) \\ &+ (\alpha - \gamma)^{-1}(e^{-\alpha(T-S)} - e^{-\gamma(T-S)})] - (\alpha - \gamma)^{-1}I^{-1}\beta\Omega[e^{-\alpha(T-S)} - e^{-\gamma(T-S)}] \end{aligned}$$

and
$$B = Ie^{-\alpha T} + (\alpha - \gamma)^{-1}\beta(\delta I - \gamma\Omega)[e^{-\alpha(T-S)} - e^{-\gamma(T-S)}]. \qquad (C13)$$

A can be further simplified, since

$$-IA = \alpha^{-1}I(1 - e^{-\alpha T}) + \gamma^{-1}\beta(\delta I - \gamma\Omega)[-\alpha^{-1}(1 - e^{-\alpha(T-S)})$$
$$+ (\alpha - \gamma)^{-1}(e^{-\gamma(T-S)} - e^{-\alpha(T-S)})] - \alpha^{-1}\beta\Omega(1 - e^{-\alpha(T-S)}),$$

and thus by (C10)

$$A = -I^{-1}[\Gamma - \alpha^{-1}\beta\Omega(1 - e^{-\alpha(T-S)})].\tag{C14}$$

B can be simplified as well, since by (C10),

$$B = \frac{\partial}{\partial t}x_1(T, I)\tag{C15}$$

and thus $B < 0$ whenever T is defined. Letting

$$\text{sign}(w) = \begin{cases} 1, & w > 0 \\ 0, & w = 0 \\ -1, & w < 0 \end{cases},$$

(C12), (C14) and (C15) yield

$$\text{sign } \frac{dT}{dI} = \text{sign } [\Gamma - \alpha^{-1}\beta\Omega(1 - e^{-\alpha(T-S)})].\tag{C16}$$

In particular, $\alpha\Gamma \geq \beta\Omega$ implies $dT/dI \geq 0$. In general $(dT/dI)(I) \leq 0$ for $I \geq I_0$, if $(dT/dI)(I_0) \leq 0$, since by (C16) it suffices to show that

$$\frac{d}{dI}[\Gamma - \alpha^{-1}\beta\Omega(1 - e^{-\alpha(T-S)})] \leq 0$$

if $dT/dI = 0$, or that $(d/dI)(T - S) \geq 0$ if $dT/dI = 0$, which follows from (C11). In both cases, $T(I)$ is monotonic for large I. Thus $T(\infty) \equiv \lim_{I\to\infty} T(I) \leq \infty$ exists. To show that $T(\infty) < \infty$, set $t = T$ in (C10) and let $I \to \infty$. If $T(\infty) = \infty$, this yields the contradiction $\Gamma = -\infty$, since $\beta\delta > \gamma$.

To study the dependence of $(d/dI)(T - S)$ on the sign of $\alpha - \gamma$, manipulate (C11) to (C14) to find

$$\frac{d}{dI}(T - S) = -CB^{-1},$$

where

$$C = -(\delta I - \gamma\Omega)^{-1}\Omega e^{-\alpha T} + I^{-1}\{\Gamma - \alpha^{-1}\beta\Omega(1 - e^{-\alpha(T-S)})$$
$$+ (\alpha - \gamma)^{-1}\beta\Omega[e^{-\gamma(T-S)} - e^{-\alpha(T-S)}]\}\tag{C17}$$

and thus

$$\text{sign } \left[\frac{d}{dt}(T - S)\right] = \text{sign } C.\tag{C18}$$

To prove that

$$\text{sign } \left[(\alpha - \gamma)\frac{d}{dI}(T - S)(I_0)\right] \leq 0$$

implies

$$\text{sign } \left[(\alpha - \gamma)\frac{d}{dI}(T - S)(I)\right] \leq 0$$

.

for $I \geq I_0$, it suffices to show that

$$\text{sign } (\frac{dC}{dI}) = \text{sign } (\gamma - \alpha) \quad \text{if } C = 0, \qquad (C19)$$

since before $(d/dI)(T - S)$ can change sign from ± 1 to ∓ 1, it must pass through zero, where, by (C19), it will be deflected to the sign of $\gamma - \alpha$.

To prove (C19), write the first term on the right in (C17) as

$$(\delta I - \gamma \Omega)^{-1} \Omega e^{-\alpha T} = (\delta I - \gamma \Omega)^{-1} \Omega e^{-\alpha(T-S)} e^{-\alpha S}$$

and apply (C9). Then

$$(\delta I - \gamma \Omega)^{-1} \Omega e^{-\alpha T} = (\delta I)^{-\alpha/\gamma} \Omega e^{-\alpha \sigma} (\delta I - \gamma \Omega)^{(\alpha/\gamma)-1} e^{-\alpha(T-S)}. \qquad (C20)$$

Differentiate (C20) subject to the constraint $(d/dI)(T - S) = C = 0$. Then

$$-\frac{d}{dI}[(\delta I - \gamma \Omega)^{-1} \Omega e^{-\alpha T}] = \gamma^{-1}(\delta I - \gamma \Omega)^{-1} \Omega e^{-\alpha T}[\alpha I^{-1} - (\alpha - \gamma)\delta(\delta I - \gamma \Omega)^{-1}]$$

$$= I^{-1}(\delta I - \gamma \Omega)^{-1} \Omega e^{-\alpha T}[1 + (\gamma - \alpha)\Omega(\delta I - \gamma \Omega)^{-1}].$$

Also note by (C17) that $C = 0$ implies

$$\frac{d}{dI}\{I^{-1}[\Gamma - \alpha^{-1}\beta\Omega(1 - e^{-\alpha(T-S)}) + (\alpha - \gamma)^{-1}\beta\Omega(e^{-\gamma(T-S)} - e^{-\alpha(T-S)})]\}$$

$$= -I^{-1}(\delta I - \gamma \Omega)^{-1} \Omega e^{-\alpha T}.$$

Combining these identities shows that

$$\frac{dC}{dI} = (\gamma - \alpha)\Omega^2 e^{-\alpha T} I^{-1}(\delta I - \gamma \Omega)^{-2}$$

if $C = 0$, which yields (C19).

APPENDIX D

Proof of Lemma 3

Since $I(t)$ is monotone non-decreasing,

$$\frac{d}{dt} J(\alpha, I, t) \geq 0.$$

Thus once either of the terms

$$R_i(t) = [\tilde{\theta}_i J(\alpha, I, t) - \Gamma_{n+1}(\theta_i - \epsilon)]^+$$

or

$$S_i(t) = [J(\alpha, I, t) - \Gamma_{n+1}]^+$$

in $J_i(t)$ becomes positive, it remains positive.

If $\tilde{\theta}_i \leq \theta_i - \epsilon$, then $S_i(t)$ becomes positive no later than $R_i(t)$ does. Until $R_i(t) > 0$, $J_i(t) \leq 0$. Once $R_i(t)$ becomes positive,

$$\frac{d}{dt}J_i(t) = (\eta\tilde{\theta}_i - \kappa)\frac{d}{dt}J(\alpha, I, t) \leq 0, \tag{D1}$$

so that $J_i(t) \leq 0$ for all $t \geq 0$ in this case.

If $\tilde{\theta}_i > \theta_i - \epsilon$, then $S_i(t)$ becomes positive before $R_i(t)$ does. In fact, $S_i(t)$ becomes positive after $t = T_1$, and $R_i(t)$ becomes positive after $t = T_2$. The equation (44) thus holds for $t \leq T_2$, whence $J_i(t)$ is non-decreasing during these times, whereas for $t > T_2$, (D1) holds. The remaining assertions of the lemma follow readily from these facts.

APPENDIX E

Proof of Proposition 3

First we prove (53). Clearly

$$\alpha[J(\alpha, I, t) - I(t)J(\alpha, I, t)] = \alpha J(\alpha, I - I(t), t).$$

Thus

$$|\alpha J(\alpha, I, t) - I(t)| \leq \|I\|e^{-\alpha t} + \alpha J(\alpha, I - I(t), t). \tag{E1}$$

Denoting $T(t, \epsilon)$ by T, note that

$$\alpha J(\alpha, I - I(t), t) < \epsilon + \|I\|[e^{-\alpha(t-T)} - e^{-\alpha t}],$$

which along with (E1) implies (53).

By (E1),

$$|\alpha J(\alpha, \omega\ I, t) - \omega I(t)| \leq \omega\|I\|e^{-\alpha R(\epsilon)} + \omega\epsilon$$

for any $\omega > 0$. Given any $\delta > 0$, choose $\epsilon \leq \delta/2\omega$ and then

$$\alpha > R^{-1}(\epsilon)\log(2\delta^{-1}\omega\|I\|)$$

to find that

$$|\alpha J(\alpha, \omega I, t) - \omega I(t)| \leq \delta;$$

i.e.,

$$\lim_{\alpha \to \infty} \alpha J(\alpha, \omega I, t) = \omega I(t).$$

Since also

$$J(\alpha, B(\alpha), I, t) = \alpha J(\alpha, \alpha^{-1}B(\alpha)I, t)$$

and clearly

$$\lim_{\alpha \to \infty} \alpha J(\alpha, \alpha^{-1}B(\alpha)I, t) = \lim_{\alpha \to \infty} \alpha J(\alpha, \omega I, t),$$

(54) follows.

APPENDIX F

Proof of Corollary 1

By Proposition 3, for sufficiently large α and γ,

$$\|J_i(t) - K_i(t)\| \le \frac{\epsilon}{3},$$

where

$$K_i(t) = \eta[\tilde{\theta}_i \alpha^{-1} I(t - \tau_1) - \Gamma_{n+1}(\theta_i - \epsilon)]^+ - \kappa[\gamma^{-1} I(t - \tau_2) - \Gamma_{n+1}]^+.$$

Define

$$M_i(t) = \eta[\tilde{\theta}_i \alpha^{-1} I(t - \tau_1) - \Gamma_{n+1}(\theta_i - \epsilon)]^+ - \kappa[\gamma^{-1} I(t - \tau_1) - \Gamma_{n+1}]^+.$$

Since by (51), (52), and (56),

$$|I(t - \tau_1) - I(t - \tau_2)| \le \frac{\epsilon}{3} \min(1, \nu^{-1}),$$

for sufficiently large α and γ,

$$|K_i(t) - M_i(t)| \le \frac{2\epsilon}{3}.$$

We have therefore shown that $|J_i(t) - M_i(t)| \le \epsilon$ for sufficiently large α and γ. The properties of $M_i(t)$ as $I(t - \tau_1)$ oscillates once are easily proved as in Proposition 2.

APPENDIX G

Proof of Proposition 4

First we show that $P_i(t) > 0$ for some $t \ge 0$ only if the excitatory signal arrives before the inhibitory signal does; i.e., only if there exists a time $T \le t$ such that

$$\lambda^{-1} I(1 - e^{-\lambda T}) > \Omega$$

and

$$\nu^{-1} I(1 - e^{-\nu(T+\tau)}) \le \Gamma.$$

These two equations are equivalent to the inequality $f(I) > e^\tau$, where

$$f(I) = \left(1 - \frac{\lambda \Omega}{I}\right)^{1/\lambda} \left(1 - \frac{\nu \Gamma}{I}\right)^{-1/\nu}.$$

The only other way for $N_i(t)$ to become positive is for inhibition to set in before excitation does, but not so strongly as to keep $N_i(t)$ non-positive. If this were to happen, then $N_i(t)$ would remain non-positive until the first time $t = T$ at which

$$\lambda^{-1} I(1 - e^{-\lambda T}) = \Omega$$

and
$$\nu^{-1}I(1 - e^{-\nu(T+\tau)}) \geq \Gamma.$$

At such a time, however, we readily find that

$$\text{sign } \dot{N}_i(t) = \text{sign } [\eta e^{-\lambda T} - \kappa e^{-\nu(T+\tau)}]$$
$$\leq \text{sign } [\eta - \kappa e^{-\nu\tau}] \leq 0,$$

whence $N_i(t)$ is always non-positive. Thus $N_i(t) > 0$ for some $t \geq 0$ only if $f(I) > e^\tau$.
It is readily checked that for $I \geq \lambda\Omega$,

$$\text{sign } \dot{f}(I) = \text{sign } [\lambda\Omega - \nu\Gamma] < 0.$$

Thus if there exists an $I = I_0$ such that $f(I_0) = e^\tau$, as in (62), then $f(I) > e^\tau$ only if $I < I_0$. Such an I_0 exists, since $f(\nu\Gamma) = \infty$, $f(\infty) = 1$, and $\tau > 0$.

REFERENCES

Eccles, J.C. (1964). **The physiology of synapses.** Berlin: Springer-Verlag.

Eccles, J.C., Ito, M., and Szentagothai, J. (1967). **The cerebellum as a neuronal machine.** New York: Springer-Verlag.

Frank, M. and Pfaffmann, C. (1969). *Science,* **164,** 1183.

Granit, R. (1955). **Receptors and sensory perception.** New Haven: Yale University Press.

Grossberg, S. (1969a). *Journal of Mathematical Psychology,* **6,** 209.

Grossberg, S. (1969b). *Mathematical Biosciences,* **4,** 255.

Grossberg, S. (1969c). *Journal of Theoretical Biology,* **22,** 325.

Grossberg, S. (1969d). *Mathematical Biosciences,* **4,** 201.

Grossberg, S. (1969e). *Journal of Mathematics and Mechanics,* **19,** 53.

Grossberg, S. (1969f). *Journal of Statistical Physics,* **1,** 319.

Grossberg, S. (1969g). *Studies in Applied Mathematics,* **XLVIII,** 105.

Grossberg, S. (1970). *Studies in Applied Mathematics,* **49,** 135–166.

Hubel, D.H. and Wiesel, T.N. (1965). *Journal of Neurophysiology,* **28,** 229.

Kilmer, W.L. (1969). The reticular formation, II: The biology of the reticular formation. Interim Scientific Report 3, Division of Engineering Research, Michigan State University.

Kilmer, W.L., Blum, J., and McCulloch, W.S. (1969). The reticular formation, I: Modeling studies of the reticular formation. Interim Scientific Report 3, Division of Engineering Research, Michigan State University.

Lettvin, J.Y., Maturana, H.R., McCulloch, W.S., and Pitts, W.H. (1960). *Journal of General Physiology,* **43,** 129.

Ratliff, F. (1965). **Mach bands: Quantitative studies on neural networks in the retina.** San Francisco: Holden-Day.

Sterling, P. and Wickelgren, B.G. (1969). *Journal of Neurophysiology,* **32,** 1.

Whitfield, I.C. (1967). **The auditory pathway.** London: Edward Arnold Ltd.

Wickelgren, W.A. (1969). *Bulletin of Mathematical Biophysics,* **31,** 123.

CHAPTER 4

NEURAL EXPECTATION: CEREBELLAR AND RETINAL ANALOGS OF CELLS FIRED BY LEARNABLE OR UNLEARNED PATTERN CLASSES

by

Stephen Grossberg

Preface

This article from 1972 carried forward the classification of pattern recognition networks that was begun in the 1970 article that comprises Chapter 3. The 1972 article made three main points. First, it noted that some of the instar networks derived in Chapter 3 are strikingly similar to neural circuits that had recently been studied in vertebrate retinas. These are the instars whose first inhibitory layer, which carries out pattern normalization, is chosen to be a shunting on-center off-surround network. In this retinal interpretation, the first inhibitory layer is compared with the horizontal cell layer of the retina. The second inhibitory layer is compared with the amacrine cell layer of the retina. The Weber-law modulated ratio processing at the on-center of the shunting network is compared with Weber-law modulated reflectance processing at retinal bipolar cells. The instar output cells are compared with opponent-organized retinal ganglion cells.

This convergence between theory and data was surprising for several reasons. For one, the instar constructions were carried out before the data were published. More significantly, the instars were motivated by formal considerations of how to design a minimal network for selective discrimination of spatial patterns. The fact that retinas exhibit key features of this minimal design is of great conceptual interest.

Also of interest was the fact that a large conceptual gap existed between the heuristics of the instar construction and the apparent meaning of the neural data. It took almost two years to make the conceptual leap between the formal instar construction (Chapter 3) and its retinal interpretation (Chapter 4), which in retrospect seems so obvious. This fact is one of many illustrations of the gap that can exist between the functional meaning of behaviorally derived network mechanisms and the apparent meaning of the neural data that they eventually explain.

Stated in another way, neural network models do not merely summarize neural data in an obvious way. This is illustrated in the present case by the fact that the relevant neural data were published by Werblin and his colleagues in 1969. As of 1974, Werblin did not yet realize how his data could be explained by a shunting on-center off-surround network. In Werblin (1974, p. 78), he wrote "that surround antagonism in the bipolar is a subtractive phenomenon" after rejecting the alternative that "the surround acts to *attenuate* the signal reaching the bipolar cell by a constant multiplicative factor." Werblin here chose the lesser of two evils, but neither alternative is correct. Without an appropriate neural network formalism, the properties of shunting on-center off-surround networks are not easily understood.

The second task of the present article was to show how an instar could be made to *learn* the class of input patterns to which it would selectively respond. As a result of this construction, an instar could learn to respond to an arbitrary spatial pattern, or set of spatial patterns. These trained spatial patterns could, moreover, be switched on and off at will in a task-dependent fashion.

The article demonstrated the neural plausibility of this construction by showing that it could be realized using a type of anatomy that had been described in the cerbellum. In this interpretation, the learned bias, or *prime*, of the instar acted as a type of *motor expectation* which would lead to an instar output only if the expectation was approximately matched by the input pattern.

This new interpretation of learning in the cerebellum built upon previous neural network models of cerebellar learning (see Chapter 2). The earliest such models were those of Brindley (1964) and Grossberg (1964, 1969). Brindley's work inspired that of Marr (1969) and Albus (1971). The Grossberg (1969) model set the stage for the present work. The functional role of the cerebellum is still a topic of active research, as Chapter 2 has illustrated.

A secondary effect of this adaptive instar construction was to call attention to the importance of top-down learned expectations, and their matching with bottom-up input patterns, to control neural pattern recognition, This observation prepared the way for the discovery of Adaptive Resonance Theory (see Part III).

The third task of the present article was to offer an explicit construction of the first multi-layer neural network that could learn to self-organize an arbitrary mapping from vectors in $\Re^n$ to vectors in $\Re^m$ in real-time. This process was called *universal recoding*. The cells at which universal recoding was effected, called U cells, were at once the output cells of adaptive instars and the input cells, or source cells, of adaptive outstars. Examples of such multi-layer universal recoding networks are illustrated in Figures 6 and 8.

When the back propagation neural network became popular five years ago, some of its popularizers claimed that it was the first multi-layer neural network that was able to learn a multi-dimensional map. In reality, examples of self-organizing multi-level maps have been known since 1972. The 1972 construction makes no claims of optimality, but it does provide an explicit construction. Many recent analyses of multi-layer feedforward mapping networks are based on Kolmogorov's seminal theorem, and are either existence proofs which do not provide an explicit construction, or have not been shown to be learnable by any learning scheme, including back propagation. Only very recently have questions of "learnability" been broached in this literature (White, 1990). In contrast, three-layer instar-outstar mapping networks have provided explicit constructions of learnable networks for two decades. The remaining chapters in Parts II and III of the book provide explicit examples of increasingly powerful self-organizing instar-outstar mapping networks.

The reason why these literatures originally developed without better communication may perhaps be traced to the fact that the back propagation model grew out of the literature on perceptrons and LMS networks, which are typically operated off-line under supervision by an external controller, whereas the instar-outstar model grew out of the literature on associative and competitive networks, which are designed to operate autonomously in real time (see Chapter 1). How these parallel literatures will interact in the future is still an open question, but many practitioners are already building hybrid systems using results from both streams.

References

Albus, J.S. (1971). A theory of cerebellar function. *Mathematical Biosciences*, **10**, 25–61.

Brindley, G.S. (1964). The use made by the cerebellum of the information that it receives from sense organs. *International Brain Research Organizational Bulletin*, **3**, 80.

Grossberg, S. (1964). **The theory of embedding fields with applications to psychology and neurophysiology.** New York: Rockefeller Institute for Medical Research.

Grossberg, S. (1969). On learning of spatio-temporal patterns by networks with ordered sensory and motor components, I: Excitatory components of the cerebellum. *Studied in Applied Mathematics*, **48**, 105–132.

Marr, D. (1969). A theory of cerebellar cortex. *Journal of Physiology (London)*, **202**, 437–470.

Werblin, F.S. (1974). Control of retinal sensitivity, II: Lateral interactions at the outer plexiform layer. *Journal of General Physiology*, **63**, 62–87.

White, H. (1990). Connectionist nonparametric regression: Multilayer feedforward networks can learn arbitrary mappings. *Neural Networks*, **3**, 535–550.

Kybernetik
1972, **10**, 49–57
©1972 Springer-Verlag, Inc.

NEURAL EXPECTATION: CEREBELLAR AND RETINAL ANALOGS OF CELLS FIRED BY LEARNABLE OR UNLEARNED PATTERN CLASSES

Stephen Grossberg†

Abstract

Neural networks are introduced which can be taught by classical or instrumental conditioning to fire in response to arbitrary learned classes of patterns. The filters of output cells are biased by presetting cells whose activation prepares the output cell to "expect" prescribed patterns. For example, an animal that learns to expect food in response to a lever press becomes frustrated if food does not follow the lever press. Its expectations are thereby modified, since frustration is negatively reinforcing. A neural analog with aspects of cerebellar circuitry is noted, including diffuse mossy fiber inputs feeding parallel fibers that end in Purkinje cell dendrites, climbing fiber inputs ending in Purkinje cell dendrites and giving off collaterals to nuclear cells, and inhibitory Purkinje cell outputs to nuclear cells. The networks are motivated by studying mechanisms of pattern discrimination that require no learning. The latter often use two successive layers of inhibition, analogous to horizontal and amacrine cell layers in vertebrate retinas. Cells exhibiting hue (in)constancy, brightness (in)constancy, or movement detection properties are included. These results are relevant to Land's retinex theory and to the existence of opponent- and nonopponent-type cell responses in retinal cells. Some adaptation mechanisms, and arousal mechanisms for crispening the pattern weights that can fire a given cell, are noted.

† Supported in part by the Alfred P. Sloan Foundation and the Office of Naval Research (N00014-67-A0204-0051).

1. Introduction

This paper describes neural networks containing cells U that fire in response to arbitrary learnable classes of input patterns. These input patterns need not be precoded in the anatomy or physiology of the networks at their birth, and can be changed at will throughout their life. The cells U can also learn to control arbitrary output patterns. U cells are thus "universal" cells whose input and output properties are entirely flexible and changeable by classical and instrumental conditioning.

The learned class of input patterns which can fire a cell U is controlled by presetting cells P. The cells P send axons to the filtering mechanism (e.g., inhibitory interneurons and dendrites) that processes inputs to U. Each P cells can learn a particular pattern that will bias U's filter when P is active. A given P cell can bias several U cells, each with a different learned—or unlearned—pattern. If more than one P cell is active, then U's filter is biased by a pattern which is a weighted average of the patterns controlled separately by each active P cell. The weighting pattern can be changed by altering the relative firing intensities of the active P cells.

The need for such presetting mechanisms is suggested by learning experiments in which an animal O's expectations of future events are learned. For example, let O learn to lever press for food. On a recall trial, O "expects" food when it lever presses in response to hunger. If food is not delivered, O can become "frustrated". Frustration is negatively reinforcing (Kimble, 1961; Wagner, 1969) and can modify O's future expectations. Frustration is biologically useful, since it permits O to eliminate learned, but later unsuccessful, instrumental behavior before irreversible damage is done by the absence of primary reinforcement. On recall trials in the lever press example, lever press cures are presumed to also preset consummatory controls which can be released by expected sensory cues of the food reward. The presetting cells are analogous to the cells P and the consummatory control cells are analogous to the cells U. This paper approaches the study of neural expectation and its frustration by sketching some mathematical features of presetting mechanisms. Presetting mechanisms will later be merged with mechanisms of "negative incentive motivation", as developed in Grossberg (1972), to create a more global picture of the expectation-frustration mechanism.

Given a catalog of preset mechanisms, one naturally seeks analogies with known anatomies *in vivo*. This search is complicated by two factors. First, seemingly different anatomies can share common preset mechanisms; their differences might only be due to differences in arrangement ("symmetries") of P and U cells, and in the distribution of $P \to U$ axons. Second, the same preset mechanism can form part of different total processing schemes in different cell groups. A striking analogy with aspects of cerebellar anatomy is nonetheless discernible. This analogy includes the following cerebellar facts (Bell and Dow, 1967; Eccles, Ito, and Szentogothai, 1967): (1) existence of a diffuse excitatory mossy fiber input; (2) existence of a localized excitatory climbing fiber input that branches off from excitatory axons to cerebellar nuclear cells; (3) existence of an inhibitory Purkinje cell output to nuclear cells; (4) possibility of firing the Purkinje cell in response to either, or both, input sources; (5) possibility of plastic changes at parallel fiber–Purkinje spine contacts.

The network anatomies use inhibitory interneurons in several configurations. A particular configuration is partly determined by the physiology of its individual cells;

for example, by whether the inhibition is subtractive or shunting (multiplicative) (Creutzfeldt, Sakmann, Scheich, and Korn, 1970; Sperling, 1970; Sperling and Sondhi, 1968). Each configuration determines a characteristic time response of the network to test inputs; for example, transient "on-off" responses, or saturated "on" responses, or graded responses to rectangular inputs can occur. Alternatives to inhibitory interneurons exist in some cases; for example, blockade of postsynaptic potential response at higher than prescribed spiking frequencies, or switch-over from net excitation to net inhibition of postsynaptic sites as presynaptic spiking frequency exceeds a critical value (Bennett, 1971; Blackenship, Wachtel, and Kandel, 1971; Wachtel and Kandel, 1971). The present mechanisms include as special cases some mechanisms of sensory adaptation, and the possibility of "crispening" the pattern weights that can elicit a response from U by altering the ambient arousal level.

U cell anatomies are related to the anatomies of cells R which can discriminate patterns without prior learning or presetting. R cell anatomies were introduced in Grossberg (1970a). They also have neural analogs, for example in vertebrate retinas. Such cells can, for example, exhibit essentially perfect hue constancy or brightness constancy (Cornsweet, 1970). Two successive stages of lateral inhibitory interactions, reminiscent of horizontal cell and amacrine cell interactions (Dowling and Werblin, 1969; Werblin and Dowling, 1969), prepare the inputs to R cells to achieve this constancy. R cell response can also exhibit shifts in perceived hues and brightnesses as background illumination increases. Perfect constancy cells need differ from imperfect constancy cells only in the spatial distribution of the inhibitory interneurons that prepare their outputs. Logarithmic transformation of peripheral inputs is unnecessary to achieve hue or brightness constancy of the R cell variety.

2. Theoretical Review

A previous paper (Grossberg, 1970a) introduced neural networks which can discriminate arbitrary input patterns and learn to release arbitrary output patterns in response to prescribed input patterns. These discrimination mechanisms are ritualistic in the sense that a given output cell responds to the same class of patterns at all times. The ritualistic discrimination and learning mechanisms can be modified to construct the cells $\dot{U}$. They are therefore reviewed below.

Grossberg discusses the following situation. Let n cells v_i be given, $i = 1, 2 \ldots n$. Let the input to v_i be $C_i(t)$. A *spatial pattern* is an excitatory input to $V = \{v_i : i = 1, 2, \ldots, n\}$ of the form $C_i(t) = \tilde{\theta}_i C(t)$, where $\tilde{\theta}_i$ is the fixed relative intensity of the input at v_i (hence $\tilde{\theta}_i \geq 0$ and $\sum_{k=1}^{n} \tilde{\theta}_k = 1$), and $C(t)$ is the total input intensity. This concept of spatial pattern notes that recognition of a picture is invariant under considerable fluctuations in background illumination. Grossberg considers the following problem: what is the *minimal* anatomy and physiology of an input filtering device, fed by V, that fires an output cell R if and only if

$$\theta_i - \epsilon < \tilde{\theta}_i < \theta_i + \epsilon \qquad (1)$$

for all $i = 1, 2, \ldots, n$; that is, if and only if the pattern $\tilde{\theta} = (\tilde{\theta}_1, \ldots, \tilde{\theta}_n)$ differs by less than ϵ from a prescribed pattern $\theta = (\theta_1, \ldots, \theta_n)$? It will be shown that such a cell R can exhibit perfect hue constancy or brightness constancy, within an error of ϵ.

The above definition of spatial pattern is compatible with mathematical properties of neural networks (*embedding fields*) derived from psychological postulates about

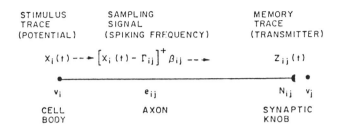

Figure 1. Network interpretation.

classical conditioning (Grossberg, 1969a, 1971). In their simplest form, these networks are defined as follows.

$$\dot{x}_i(t) = -\alpha_i x_i(t) + \sum_{k=1}^{N} [x_k(t-\tau_{ki}) - \Gamma_{ki}]^+ \beta_{ki} z_{ki}(t)$$

$$- \sum_{k=1}^{N} [x_k(t-\sigma_{ki}) - \Omega_{ki}]^+ \gamma_{ki} + C_i(t) \tag{2}$$

and

$$\dot{z}_{jk}(t) = -\delta_{jk} z_{jk}(t) + \epsilon_{jk}[x_j(t-\tau_{jk}) - \Gamma_{jk}]^+ x_k(t), \tag{3}$$

where $i, j, k = 1, 2, \ldots, N$ and $[\xi]^+ = \max(\xi, 0)$ for any real number ξ. $x_i(t)$ denotes the stimulus trace (or average membrane potential) at time t of the cell body (or cell body cluster) v_i, and $z_{jk}(t)$ denotes the memory trace (or associational strength, or excitatory transmitter production activity) at time t of the synaptic knob (or knobs) N_{jk} found at the end of the axon(s) e_{jk} from v_j to v_k. The term $[x_k(t-\tau_{ki})-\Gamma_{ki}]^+\beta_{ki}$ in (2) is proportional to the spiking frequency released into e_{ki} in the time interval $[t-\tau_{ki}, t-\tau_{ki}+dt]$. Γ_{ki} is the spiking threshold, β_{ki} is proportional to the anatomical connection strength from v_k to N_{ki}, and τ_{ki} is the time required for spikes to travel from v_k to N_{ki}. The term $\sum_{k=1}^{N}[x_k(t-\tau_{ki})-\Gamma_{ki}]^+\beta_{ki}z_{ki}(t)$ in (2) is the total excitatory input from other cells to v_i at time t. At an excitatory synapse ($\beta_{ki} > 0$), spiking frequency couples multiplicatively to transmitter to release transmitter that perturbs $x_i(t)$, and all such signals combine additively at v_i. The term

$$\sum_{k=1}^{N} [x_k(t-\sigma_{ki}) - \Omega_{ki}]^+ \gamma_{ki}$$

is the total inhibitory input from other cells to v_i at time t. The term $C_i(t)$ is the experimental input (or stimulus) to v_i at time t. See Figure 1.

In (3), the memory trace cross-correlates the presynaptic spiking frequency which reaches N_{jk} from v_j at time t with the value of average potential at v_k at this time.

To illustrate how the spatial pattern concept relates to learning in (2) and (3), consider the simplest embedding field that can learn by Pavlovian conditioning; namely, an *outstar* (Grossberg, 1969b, 1970b). Let a CS-activated cell v_{n+1} send equal signals to its synaptic knobs $N_{n+1,i}$, which abut the UCS-activated cells $V = \{v_i : i =$

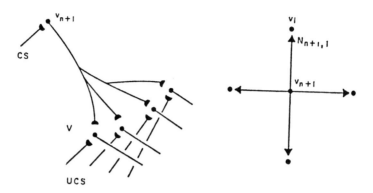

Figure 2. An outstar.

$1, 2, \ldots, n\}$; see Figure 2. v_1 can learn and perform at V a spatial pattern; that is, a UCS input to V of the form $C_i(t) = \tilde{\theta}_i C(t)$. The synaptic knobs $N_{n+1,i}$ encode the pattern, or "relative figure-to-ground," $\tilde{\theta} = (\tilde{\theta}_1, \tilde{\theta}_2, \ldots, \theta_n)$ in their transmitters $z_{n+1,i}$ at a rate which depends on $C(t)$, among other factors. The total amount $\sum_{k=1}^{n} z_{n+1,k}$ of transmitter accumulation is not constant, however. It can be potentiated either by presynaptic spikes from v_{n+1} to the knobs $N_{n+1,i}$, or by a combination of pre- and post-synaptic activity. It can also spontaneously decay. These fluctuations can occur in the absence of learning. Learning alters the relative sizes of the $z_{n+1,i}$ which are attracted to the pattern weights $\tilde{\theta}_i$.

The pattern $\tilde{\theta}$ at V is learned only at times when the synaptic knobs $N_{n+1,i}$ receive CS-activated spikes from v_{n+1}. This is the property of "stimulus sampling". The relative transmitters $Z_{n+1,i} = z_{n+1,i} \left(\sum_{k=1}^{n} z_{n+1,k} \right)^{-1}$ are the "stimulus sampling probabilities" of an outstar (Grossberg, 1970b). Whenever v_{n+1} samples V, its synaptic knobs begin to learn the spatial pattern playing on V at this time. If a sequence of spatial patterns plays on V while v_{n+1} is sampling, then all v_{n+1} learns a pattern which is a weighted average of all the patterns, rather than any single pattern in the sequence. Any nonnegative continuous input to V can be written as such a sequence of patterns.

During recall trials, an input to v_{n+1} reproduces at V the pattern which the outstar has learned. The total output to V can, however, vary wildly through time. For example, fluctuations in spiking frequency from v_{n+1} to the knobs $N_{n+1,i}$ can change the total output either directly, by altering the term

$$[x_{n+1}(t - \tau_{n+1}) - \Gamma_{n+1}]^+$$

in the v_{n+1}-to-v_i signals

$$\beta[x_{n+1}(t - \tau_{n+1}) - \Gamma_{n+1}]^+ z_{n+1,i}(t),$$

or indirectly, by changing the total transmitter level $\sum_{k=1}^{n} z_{n+1,k}(t)$. Such changes in total output do not destroy the encoded memory of pattern weights or the relative output to v_i (Grossberg, 1969b, 1970b). Nonetheless, v_i cannot discern what its pattern weight is if the total output fluctuates. It is therefore natural to seek anatomies, fed by outstar signals, which can discriminate the pattern that the outstar has learned in spite of fluctuations in total outstar output. This is the problem summarized by equation (1).

In the study of ritualistic pattern discrimination, no learning occurs. Hence $\delta_{jk} = \epsilon_{jk} = 0$ in (3) and $z_{ki}(t)$ is set equal to 1 in (2) for notational convenience. Two stages of inhibitory processing intermediate between V and a discriminative output cell R are needed to achieve the criterion in (1) (Grossberg, 1970a, Section 8):

I. Pattern Normalization and Low-Band Filtering

Pattern normalization guarantees that as the pattern intensity $C(t)$ becomes arbitrarily large, the potential $x_i(t)$ in the ith filtering channel remains bounded without losing the pattern weight due to saturation at the maximal potential. In other words, the first inhibitory layer limits the range of dynamical response to inputs without saturating pattern weights. For example, normalization occurs if $x_i(t) = \tilde{\theta}_i \Gamma(t)$ where $0 < \Gamma(t) \leq \Gamma < \infty$.

Given a mechanism of pattern normalization, a suitably chosen positive spiking threshold can prevent an output from the ith channel unless $\tilde{\theta}_i > \theta_i - \epsilon$. For example, if $x_i(t) = \tilde{\theta}_i \Gamma(t)$, choose the spiking threshold of the ith channel to equal

$$\Gamma_i = \Gamma(\theta_i - \epsilon). \tag{4}$$

Then $x_i(t) \leq \Gamma_i$ unless $\tilde{\theta}_i > \theta_i - \epsilon$. One half of the inequalities (1) is hereby achieved. By (4), given any pattern normalization device, it is necessary that

$$\max \sum_{k=1}^{n} x_k > \sum_{k=1}^{n} \Gamma_k,$$

in order that all low-band filtered channels be able to fire simultaneously.

II. High-Band Filtering

A second processing step is needed to guarantee the inequalities $\tilde{\theta}_i < \theta_i + \epsilon$ in (1). This step inhibits the ith low-band filtered signal when it exceeds a size corresponding to an input whose pattern weight $\tilde{\theta}_i$ exceeds $\theta_i + \epsilon$. The doubly inhibited output from the ith channel is therefore large only if (1) holds.

All n of these doubly inhibited signals summate at R. R's threshold is chosen so high that R can emit a signal only if it receives large signals almost simultaneously from all n channels; that is, only if (1) holds for all $i = 1, 2, \ldots, n$.

The pattern normalization and high-band filtering steps do not determine which pattern will pass through the filter. The choice of spiking threshold as in (4) does this. A U cell filter differs from an R cell filter only because active P cells can change the "threshold pattern" which must be overcome to fire U, and can learn arbitrary threshold patterns. The network that accomplishes this does not, however, use variable spiking thresholds. Rather it uses a physiologically more plausible mixture of excitatory and inhibitory signals. This mixing process will be motivated by a review of some concrete ways to realize steps (I) and (II) of the ritualistic filtering process.

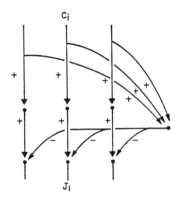

Figure 3. Subtractive nonspecific nonrecurrent interneuron.

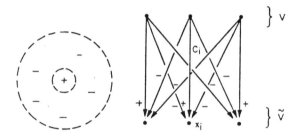

Figure 4. Shunting on-center off-surround field.

Pattern normalization and low-band filtering can be achieved in at least two ways.

(i) Subtractive Nonspecific Nonrecurrent Interneuron (see Figure 3). Let the net signal in the ith channel after operation of the inhibitory interneuron be

$$J_i(t) = [C_i(t) - \Gamma_i]^+ - \zeta[\sum_{k=1}^{n} C_k(t) - \Gamma]^+, \tag{5}$$

with $\Gamma > \sum_{k=1}^{n} \Gamma_k$ and $\zeta \geq 1$. Since $\Gamma > \sum_{k=1}^{n} \Gamma_k$, Γ_i can be written in the form $\Gamma_i = \Gamma(\theta_i - \epsilon)$, as in (4). Also write $C_i = \tilde{\theta}_i C$ where $C = \sum_{k=1}^{n} C_k$. By (5), $J_i(t) \leq 0$ for all $t \geq 0$ unless $\tilde{\theta}_i > \theta_i - \epsilon$. Thus no output occurs unless $\tilde{\theta}_i > \theta_i - \epsilon$. This is because $\tilde{\theta}_i \leq \theta_i - \epsilon$ implies that C exceeds Γ before C_i exceeds Γ_i, and that $dJ_i(t)/dt \leq 0$ whenever $C > \Gamma$. In the case $\tilde{\theta}_i > \theta_i - \epsilon$, Grossberg (1970a, Section 10) studies the function J_i as C oscillates, and extends the results to cases in which time lags and exponential averaging rates in the excitatory and inhibitory terms of (5) differ. For example, unless $\tilde{\theta}_i = \zeta = 1$ in (5), $J_i(t)$ responds to growth of C from zero to large values with a transient "on" response, and to decay of C from large values to zero with a transient "off" response. If $\tilde{\theta}_i = \zeta = 1$, then $J_i(t)$ saturates at a constant value when C takes on large values.

(ii) Multiplicative On-Off Field. The subtractive form of the interaction in (5) depends on inputs and thresholds which are small compared to the saturation level of

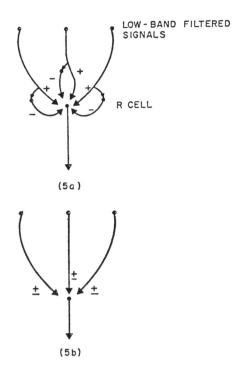

Figure 5. Some high-band filters.

cell body potentials. Given large inputs that drive the potentials towards saturation, a different inhibitory anatomy can preserve input pattern weights in the response of cell body potentials. Consider Figure 4. The ith cell in V excites the ith cell in $\tilde{V}$ and equally inhibits all other cells in $\tilde{V}$ by interacting multiplicatively with ("shunting") cell body potential. The potential x_i of the ith $\tilde{V}$ cell thus obeys the equation

$$\dot{x}_i = (M - x_i)C_i - \alpha x_i - x_i \sum_{k \neq i} C_k. \tag{6}$$

This is a passive membrane equation with equilibrium scaled to zero for convenience, and inputs C_i representing depolarizing or hyperpolarizing conductance changes (Sperling, 1970; Sperling and Sondhi, 1968). Grossberg (1970a, Section 14A) proves that each x_i is bounded and is attracted to $\tilde{\theta}_i$. If, in fact, C varies slowly relative to x_i, then

$$x_i \cong \tilde{\theta}_i \frac{MC}{\alpha + C}, \tag{7}$$

so that x_i is monotone increasing as a function of C. Contrast mechanism (i). Equation (7) accomplishes pattern normalization without low-band filtering. The next positive spiking threshold in the ith channel accomplishes low-band filtering.

High-band filtering can be achieved by a specific inhibitory interneuron, as in Figure 5a (Grossberg, 1970a, Section 11). For example, let the input in the ith low-band filtered channel have the form

$$K_i(t) = [O_i(t) - \Omega_i]^+ - \zeta[O_i(t) - \Gamma_i]^+, \tag{8}$$

where $O_i(t)$ is the ith output after low-band filtering, and the parameters satisfy $\Omega_i < \Gamma_i$ and $\zeta > 1$. K_i is monotone increasing as a function of O_i when $\Omega_i < O_i < \Gamma_i$, but decreases in O_i as soon as O_j exceeds Γ_j. In the present case, letting $\Gamma_i = \Omega_i + \eta$ suffices, where $O_i = \Gamma_i$ before $\hat{\theta}_i = \theta_i + \epsilon$. Other mechanisms accomplish the same functional goal; for example, blockade of postsynaptic potential response if presynaptic spiking frequency exceeds the level corresponding to $\theta_i = \theta_i + \epsilon$, or switch-over as spiking frequency reaches the $\hat{\theta}_i = \theta_i + \epsilon$ level from net excitation to net inhibition of postsynaptic response (Bennett, 1971; Blackenship, Wachtel, and Kandel, 1971; Wachtel and Kandel, 1971), as in Figure 5b.

3. Retinal Analog of R Cells

Cells of type R can exhibit hue constancy or brightness constancy because of the following considerations. Suppose, for example, that an R cell receives peripheral inputs from three classes of cones, v_1, v_2, and v_3, each class containing a pigment with different but overlapping absorption spectra (Cornsweet, 1970, p. 200). Suppose momentarily that a given hue is characterized by a fixed relative excitation of each cone class; that is, by a fixed spatial pattern $\theta = (\theta_1, \theta_2, \theta_3)$. An increase in background illumination by white light does not change the pattern of inputs to the three cone classes (Cornsweet, 1970, p. 243). Thus the cell R responds to the hue characterized by θ in spite of fluctuations in the background intensity of white light. In this example, output from a given cone class is inhibited by output from one or more other cone classes at the pattern normalization step. This fact is compatible with the existence of spectrally opponent cells at the ganglion cell layer of the macaque retina (Abramov, 1968).

A similar minimal construction exists for cells R exhibiting brightness constancy. It suffices to change the source cells in the above example. Thus let the pattern $\theta = (\theta_1, \theta_2, \ldots, \theta_n)$ describe the relative intensities of illumination at center cells v_1 and surround cells $v_2, \ldots, v_n$, such that the source cells are either all rods, or are all members of a single cone class. The R cells responding to these sources will yield a brightness constancy, respectively, to either white light or to a fixed wavelength to which the cone class responds. The brightness constancy dissolves as soon as the surround is no longer excited. The existence of inhibitory interactions between cells fed by cones and between cells fed by rods has been reported in the goldfish retina. Stell (1967) showed that the external horizontal layer is fed by rods. Kaneko (1970) recorded luminosity- and chromaticity-type S-potentials from the external and internal horizontal layers of the goldfish retina. Naka and Rushton (1966) reported that S-potentials from color units in the fish retina are influenced by at least one stage of shunting inhibition; cf. Equation (7). A shunt acts also at the level of the cones in the turtle retina (Baylor and Fuortes, 1970). In all these cases, the absolute range of dynamical response in retinal cells can be small, because relative responses at different spatial loci are the crucial quantities.

More sophisticated forms of color constancy are known, and some can be approached by modifying cell connections. The above simple form of color constancy is achieved by pattern normalization among cone classes, followed by low- and high-band filtering. Land (1964), in his retinex theory, notes data suggesting that each cone class establishes its own "lightness" scale before the cones interact. See also Land and McCann (1971). This idea is related to the following modified anatomy, which is included more as a directive for further studies than as a purported explanation of all lightness phenomena. First let each cone class interact within itself to yield pattern normalization. Choose a multiplicative on-off field as in Section 2(ii) for definiteness. Let the off-surround be of much broader spatial extent than the on-center. Each on-off field can, for example, feed the bipolar cell layer of the network. The normalization step reduces the variability of response due to variations in background illumination that excite each cone class, as Equation (7) illustrates. It can be followed by low- and high-band filtering to yield R cells exhibiting brightness constancy within each cone class. Even if it isn't, however, some degree of constancy is assured. The intracone class normalization step (perhaps followed by low- and high-band filtering) provides a "retinex" for our network. Each cone class is given its own retinex, as Land suggested. Then let the different retinexes interact "classically"—namely, as in the original color constancy construction—to yield spectrally-opponent cell types in the ganglion cell layer. This construction, were it to exist *in vivo*, could employ bipolar cells which respond to inputs derived from only one cone class in an on-center off-surround configuration. A more local color theory, without a "lightness" scale, could require less bipolar cell selectivity; namely, bipolars could respond to more than one cone class in an on-center off-surround configuration.

The mudpuppy retina exhibits analogs with the minimal mechanisms of Section 2. Since our constructions say little about the *global* properties of neuronal fields of discriminative cells, no more than qualitative similarities will be mentioned. An analog exists between mechanisms of pattern normalization followed by low-band filtering and processing in the horizontal cell layer of the mudpuppy retina (Dowling and Werblin, 1969). Consider the multiplicative on-off field in Section 2(ii) for definiteness. An on-center and off-surround response can be measured intracellularly from bipolar cells, at which mudpuppy receptor and horizontal cell inputs converge (Werblin and Dowling, 1969). The horizontal cells hyperpolarize bipolar cells and integrate receptor signals from a broad retinal area, as is also true of a pattern normalizer. Werblin and Dowling (pp. 347–348) stress the importance of the ratio of center-to-surround illumination in determining the bipolar cell response; cf. Equation (7). They note that horizontal cell inhibition counteracts the depolarizing effects of receptor input on bipolar cell response without hyperpolarizing the bipolar cell (p. 347), that the horizontal cell apparently operates in a nonrecurrent manner relative to its receptor input sources (p. 347), and that the bipolar potential can be maintained at graded sizes in response to graded inputs (pp. 347–348). These facts also hold in Equation (6). In principle, however, Equation (6) can also yield hyperpolarization if a tonic input term is added. Bipolar responses resemble color-coded C-type S-potentials (p. 347). This is compatible with the use of pattern normalization and low-band filtering to prepare inputs to cells R whose responses exhibit color constancy.

High-band filtering mechanisms can be compared with amacrine cell responses in the mudpuppy retina. Werblin (1970, p. 348) notes that an amacrine cell response can be elicited from a limited number of bipolar cells, much as a specific mixed excitatory-inhibitory connection forms a high-band filter. Werblin and Dowling (1969, p. 351) strengthen this interpretation by noting that the amacrine cell is activated by the initial part of the transient in the bipolar cell response. They hypothesize that a return synapse from amacrine cell to bipolar cell is inhibitory, and that the amacrine cell inhibits the excitation which it receives from the bipolar cell. Such a mechanism could suffice to high-band filter the amacrine cell input. Given this horizontal cell and amacrine cell analogy of R-cell filters, ganglion cells, receiving amacrine-bipolar output, would be a natural class of cells in which R cells, if they exist, might be sought in the mudpuppy retina. Grossberg (1970a) shows that other types of discriminative cells than hue or brightness constancy detectors can be constructed using similar mechanisms; e.g., movement detectors (Werblin, 1970).

The above constancies can be weakened by changing the relative strengths of inhibitory signals. For example, replacing (6) by

$$\dot{x}_i = (M - x_i)C_i\gamma_{ii} - \alpha x_i - x_i \sum_{k \neq i} C_k\gamma_{ki}, \tag{9}$$

where the γ_{ki} determine the strengths of signals (excitatory if $k = i$, inhibitory if $k \neq i$) from the kth to the ith cone class, yields an asymptotic response to the pattern $C_i(t) = \tilde{\theta}_i C(t)$ of the form

$$x_i \cong \frac{\tilde{\theta}_i \gamma_{ii} MC}{\alpha + (\sum_k \tilde{\theta}_k \gamma_{ki})C}. \tag{10}$$

Unless the sums $\sum_k \tilde{\theta}_k \gamma_{ki}$ are independent of i, the pattern recorded in the relative potentials $x_i(\sum_{k=1}^{n} x_k)^{-1}$ shifts as a function of total intensity C. This shift in pattern excites those R cells which are sensitive to the new pattern, and yields an analogous shift in perceived hue. Transformation of the form $A(C) = K_1 C(K_2 + C)^{-1}$ have been used to explain properties of hue and brightness inconstancies as a function of background illumination (Cornsweet, 1970, p. 252). The choices of coefficients in these examples differ from that in (10), which illustrates only one possible cause of hue shifts. The problem of choosing coefficients in $A(C)$ is complicated by the appearance of shunting terms at retinal layers beyond the cone and horizontal layers. Creutzfeldt, Sakmann, Scheich, and Korn (1970) use such a transformation to describe ganglion cell responses in the cat retina. They also reference earlier efforts.

4. A Learnable Preset Mechanism: Subtractive Case

To motivate the construction of U cells, consider, as in Section 1, the problem of learning to lever press for food. Activity of P cells is associated with the lever press response. Activity of U cells releases consummatory motor activity. During training trials, P cells learn the patterns which unconditionally activate the U cells. During recall trials, P cells prevent the U cell filter from firing U unless the learned input patterns re-occur. Thus we must answer three questions: (A) How does P learn input patterns at U? (B) Before learning, how do the input patterns at U unconditionally drive U cell firing? (C) After learning, how does P activity bias the U cell filter to prevent all but the learned patterns from activating U? We seek the *minimal* anatomies that answer these questions. Only the U cell analog of Equation (4) need be studied; all other properties of R-filters carry over to the U-filter case without change.

Consider question (A). Denote the collection of P cells generically by $V_1 = \{v_j : j = 1, 2, \ldots, m\}$. Let each P cell be the source cell of an outstar, whose axon collaterals terminate at the cells $V_2 = \{v_i : i = m+1,\ldots,m+n\}$. Let the cells V_2 receive the input patterns which unconditionally activate U from cells

$$V_3 = \{v_{i+n} : i = m+1,\ldots,m+n\}.$$

The $V_1 \to V_2$ synaptic knobs can learn these input patterns by Pavlovian conditioning.

Consider question (C). Denote by

$$V_4 = \{v_{i+2n} : i = m+1,\ldots,m+n\}$$

the cells at which the input pattern is low-band filtered by the output from P cells. As in (5), the difference between the input pattern and the threshold pattern must be computed. Hence excitatory $v_{i+n} \to v_{i+2n}$ axons deliver the input pattern from V_3 to V_4. Since the threshold pattern is reproduced at V_2 by active V_1 cells, inhibitory $v_i \to v_{i+2n}$ axons carry the threshold pattern from V_2 to V_4. Note that the input pattern is multiply represented at V_2 and V_4, and that two excitatory input sources converge at V_2 cells.

Consider question (B). In the absence of P cell activity, input patterns can unconditionally activate U. The ith input channel activates a net excitatory signal $v_{i+n} \to v_{i+2n}$ and a net inhibitory signal $v_{i+n} \to v_i \to v_{i+2n}$ from V_3 to V_4. Thus the absolute value of the excitatory signal exceeds the absolute value of the inhibitory signal. Moreover the spiking thresholds of $v_i \to v_{i+2n}$ axons are set equal to zero to avoid distortion of threshold pattern weights.

Output from V_4 cells is high-band filtered on the way to the output cell $V_5 = v_{m+3n+1}$, which is of type U. The spiking threshold of $V_4 \to V_5$ axons are set equal to zero to avoid distortion of low-band filtered signals. V_5 can be the source of an outstar which (say) samples motor control patterns at cells V_6; see Figure 6. In Figure 6, synaptic knobs at which classical conditioning occur are denoted by semicircles. All other knobs are denoted by arrows. A brief summary of network dynamics follows.

V_3 can create unconditional outputs from V_5 in the absence of V_1 activity. To see this, let the pattern weight $\tilde{\theta}_i$ be emitted from v_{i+n} to v_i and v_{i+2n}. Let the strength of the excitatory $v_{i+n} \to v_{i+2n}$ signal be $\tilde{\theta}_i I$. Then the net strength of the inhibitory $v_{i+n} \to v_i \to v_{i+2n}$ signal can be written in the form $\tilde{\theta}_i \eta I$, where $0 < \eta < 1$. By additivity of inputs, the net signal to v_{i+2n} created by V_3 is $\tilde{\theta}_i(1-\eta)I$, which is positive. An output from v_{i+2n} occurs because the v_{i+2n} spiking threshold is zero. The constraint on $v_{i+n} \to v_i \to v_{i+2n}$ signal size does not constrain the size of the $v_{i+n} \to v_i$ signal, nor consequently the rate of pattern learning in $V_1 \to V_2$ synaptic knobs.

To see how the presetting mechanism works, suppose that $v_j \to V_2$ synaptic knobs are active while the pattern $\theta = (\theta_1,\ldots,\theta_n)$ is emitted by V_3. Then the jth outstar learns this pattern by Pavlovian conditioning. On recall trials, let v_j be the only active cell in V_1. It reproduces the pattern θ at V_2. V_2 communicates this pattern as inhibitory signals to V_4. Let the net $v_j \to v_i \to v_{i+2n}$ inhibitory signal be $-\theta_i K$. Now let V_3 emit the test pattern $\tilde{\theta} = (\tilde{\theta}_1,\ldots,\tilde{\theta}_n)$. The $V_1 \to V_2 \to V_4$, $V_3 \to V_2 \to V_4$, and $V_2 \to V_4$ signals combine additively at V_4. The net signal to v_{i+2n} is

$$J_i = \tilde{\theta}_i(1-\eta)I - \theta_i K. \tag{11}$$

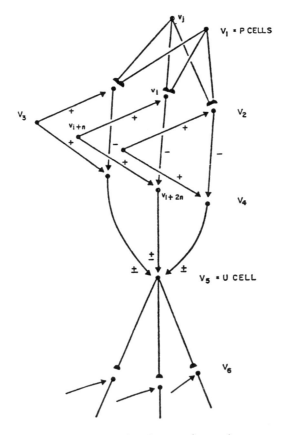

Figure 6. A learnable preset mechanism: subtractive case.

Since the spiking threshold of v_{i+2n} is zero, (11) implies that v_{i+2n} will fire only if

$$\tilde{\theta}_i > \theta_i K (1-n)^{-1} I^{-1}. \tag{12}$$

Equation (12) can hold for all i only if $(1-\eta)I > K$; that is, only if the V_3 channel is stronger than the V_1 channel. This achieves low-band filtering by the conditioned pattern θ. High-band filtering of *any* low-band filtered input is then automatically achieved by $V_4 \rightarrow V_5$ signals. Hence, when V_1 presets the U-filter with pattern θ, the U cell only fires if the test pattern emitted by V_3 is θ, within an error of ϵ. Note that increasing the total $v_j \rightarrow V_2$ input increases K, and thus the minimal pattern weights that can fire V_4. By contrast, increasing the total V_3 output increases I, and thereby decreases the minimal pattern weights that can fire V_3. This "crispening" effect can thus be controlled by varying the arousal, or adaptation, levels of V_1 and V_3, respectively.

Suppose that more than one cell in V_1 fires to V_2 at a given time. Let the $v_j \rightarrow v_i$ synaptic knob encode the pattern weight θ_{ji}. Then the net signal from v_j to v_{i+2n} has the form $-\theta_{ji} K_j$, where K_j depends on the spiking frequency in $v_j \rightarrow V_2$ axons. The total input to v_{i+2n} in response to all active V_1 cells and to V_3 output is

$$J_i = \tilde{\theta}_i (1-\eta)I - \sum_{j+1}^{m} \theta_{ji} K_j.$$

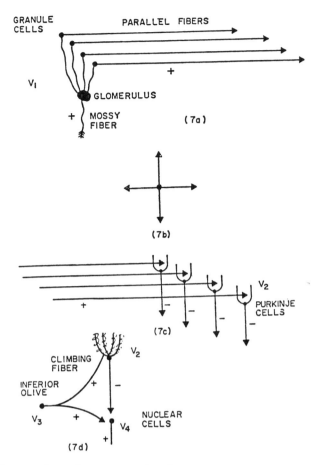

Figure 7. Cerebellar analog of preset mechanism.

Thus v_{i+2n} fires only if

$$\tilde{\theta}_i > \sum_{j=1}^{m} \theta_{ji} K_j (1 - \eta)^{-1} I^{-1}. \tag{13}$$

The right-hand side of (13) is a weighted average of all pattern weights in knobs abutting v_i. The weights are determined by the intensity of signals from each cell v_j. The above conclusions can be mathematically extended to consider the influence of time lags and exponential averaging rates using the analysis of the analogous ritualistic case in Grossberg (1970a).

5. Cerebellar Analogs of U Cells

By redrawing the network in Figure 6, a striking analogy with aspects of cerebellar anatomy emerges (Bell and Dow, 1967; Eccles, Ito, and Szentagothai, 1967). This analogy includes the following identifications: V_1 = mossy fiber glomeruli; V_2 = Purkinje cells; V_3 = inferior olive cells; V_4 = cerebellar nuclear cells; $V_1 \to V_2$ axons = excitatory parallel fibers; $V_2 \to V_4$ axons = inhibitory Purkinje cell axons; $V_3 \to V_2$ axons = excitatory climbing fibers; $V_3 \to V_4$ axons = excitatory collaterals of climbing fibers.

This analogy becomes more evident when Figure 6 is redrawn as follows. The $V_1 \rightarrow V_2$ outstar axons can be drawn as in Figure 7a, rather than as in Figure 7b. The mossy fiber ends in a glomerulus (rosette) that feeds the dendrites of a band of contiguous granule cells. The granule cell axons are parallel fibers, which activate Purkinje cell dendrites. The abstract outstar anatomy of Figure 7b is functionally identical with Figure 7a if the cluster of parallel fibers in Figure 7a is driven in phase by its glomerulus. In Figure 7c, the overlapping dendritic trees of Purkinje cells receive input from contiguous bands of parallel fibers. In Figure 7d, each Purkinje cell receives a climbing fiber input from V_3. V_3 also sends an input to a cluster of nuclear cells. Also in Figure 7d, Purkinje cells send inhibitory signals to those nuclear cells which mutually share the same V_3 sources. Suppose that this analogy with cerebellar anatomy also extends to cerebellar physiology, beyond a mere labelling of axons as excitatory and inhibitory. Then a possible functional reason for the convergence of excitatory mossy fiber and climbing fiber inputs on inhibitory Purkinje cells, and for diverging excitatory signals to Purkinje cells and nuclear cells, is the following: the mossy fiber input biases the nuclear cells to fire in response to prescribed patterns in the climbing fiber channel. If this interpretation is correct, then both mossy fiber and climbing fiber inputs can separately fire Purkinje cells, and simultaneous inputs from different channels can summate. Freeman (1970) reports analogous data. This interpretation is compatible with the suggestion (Grossberg, 1969c; Miller and Oscarsson, 1970) that cross-correlation of mossy fiber and climbing fiber inputs occurs at the Purkinje cells. Moreover, equation (12) requires that the climbing fiber channel exert a more profound influence on Purkinje firing than the mossy fiber channel. On the other hand, Bloedel and Roberts (1971) emphasize the possible functional importance of the refractory period in Purkinje cell spiking that follows a climbing fiber input. Possibly this refractory period helps to break up the temporal processing of cerebellar inputs into sequences of spatial patterns (Grossberg, 1969d, Section 12). Quantization of temporal processing seems to occur in some sensory systems. For example, exploratory sniffing and tactile input from facial vibrissae seem to be synchronized with the theta rhythm and heart beat in rats (Komisaruk, 1970). After the rat's head is fixed in position, the vibrissae twitch forward and a brief inhalation sniff occurs. The vibrissae are then retracted and the head moves to a nearby fixation point. Then the cycle of coordinated vibrissae motion and inhalation repeats itself. This mechanism seems to break up the sensory input into sequences of spatial patterns. Different sensory channels admit their next spatial pattern in phase with each other. Thus patterns in different modalities can be filtered simultaneously and correlated with each other. This interpretation of Purkinje refractoriness is at best speculative at the present time. Nonetheless, the anatomical analogy in Figure 7 clearly shows that the abstract minimal anatomy in Figure 6 is constructed using plausible anatomical principles.

6. A Learnable Present Mechanism: Multiplicative Case

A mechanism for low-band filtering and pattern normalization using shunting inhibition, such as that in Section 2(ii), will now be sketched. Consider Figure 8. V_1 consists of outstar sources. V_2 receives outstar signals. V_3 sends test inputs to V_2 and V_4. V_5 (V_6) receives signals from V_2 (V_4) that have been preprocessed by a multiplicative on-off field. V_6 sends excitatory signals to V_7, whereas V_5 sends inhibitory signals to V_7. The low-band comparison between the input patterns controlled by V_3 and the

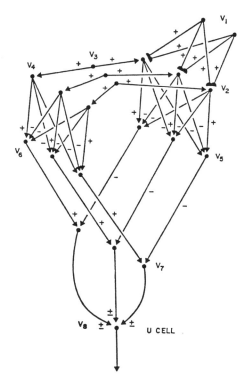

Figure 8. A learnable preset mechanism: shunting case.

threshold patterns controlled by V_1 thus occurs at V_7. Signals from V_7 to V_8 are high-band filtered. V_8 is a cell of type U. The inhibitory signal $V_3 \rightarrow V_2 \rightarrow V_5 \rightarrow V_7$ must be weaker than the excitatory signal $V_3 \rightarrow V_4 \rightarrow V_6 \rightarrow V_7$. This can be accomplished in several ways; for example, let the saturation level of V_5 potentials be smaller than the saturation level of V_6 potentials. The spiking thresholds of $V_2 \rightarrow V_5$, $V_4 \rightarrow V_6$, $V_5 \rightarrow V_7$, $V_6 \rightarrow V_7$, and $V_7 \rightarrow V_8$ axons are set equal to zero to avoid biasing filtered pattern weights. This completes the construction. Note that in all low-band filters of this paper, the statistical dispersion of signals in the excitatory channels is the same as the statistical dispersion of signals in the parallel inhibitory channels. This yields decision rules for cellular firing the retune themselves as the statistics of the input change; cf. Sperling (1970).

More elaborate variations on these themes readily suggest themselves. Given the existence of such striking retinal and cerebellar analogs to the minimal anatomies, it is to be hoped that some of these variations will have more quantitative neural analogs, whose functional meaning will be evident from an inspection of their psychologically derived counterparts. At the very least, the minimal anatomies show how different anatomies can be, even if they carry out similar discrimination tasks, one ritualistically and one with a learnable, or unlearned, preset mechanism.

REFERENCES

Abramov, I. (1968). Further analysis of the responses of LGN cells. *Journal of the Optical Society of America*, **58**, 574.

Baylor, D.A. and Fuortes, M.G.F. (1970). Electrical responses of single cones in the retina of the turtle. *Journal of Physiology (London)*, **207**, 77.

Bell, C.C. and Dow, R.S. (1967). Cerebellar circuity. In F.O. Schmitt, T. Melnechuk, G.C. Quarton, and G. Adelman (Eds.), **Neurosciences research symposium summaries, Volume 2**. Cambridge, MA: MIT Press.

Bennett, M.V.L. (1971). Analysis of parallel excitatory and inhibitory synaptic channels. *Journal of Neurophysiology*, **34**, 69.

Blackenship, J.E., Wachtel, H., and Kandel, E.R. (1971). Ionic mechanisms of excitatory, inhibitory, and dual synaptic actions mediated by an identified interneuron in abdominal ganglion of *Aplysia*. *Journal of Neurophysiology*, **34**, 76.

Bloedel, J.R. and Roberts, W.J. (1970). Action of climbing fibers in cerebellar cortex of the cat. *Journal of Neurophysiology*, **34**, 32.

Cornsweet, T.N. (1970). **Visual perception**. New York: Academic Press.

Creutzfeldt, O.D., Sakmann, B., Scheich, H., and Korn, A. (1970). Sensitivity distribution and spatial summation within receptive-field center of retinal on-center ganglion cells and transfer function of the retina. *Journal of Neurophysiology*, **33**, 654.

Dowling, J.E. and Werblin, F.S. (1969). Organization of retina of the mudpuppy *Necturus maculosus*, I: Synaptic structure. *Journal of Neurophysiology*, **32**, 315.

Eccles, J.C., Ito, M., and Szentagothai, J. (1967). **The cerebellum as a neuronal machine**. Berlin-Heidelberg-New York: Springer-Verlag.

Freeman, J.A. (1970). Responses of cat cerebellar Purkinje cells to convergent inputs from cerebral cortex and peripheral sensory systems. *Journal of Neurophysiology*, **33**, 697.

Grossberg, S. (1969a). Embedding fields: A theory of learning with physiological implications. *Journal of Mathematical Psychology*, **6**, 209.

Grossberg, S. (1969b). Some networks that can learn, remember, and reproduce any number of complicated space-time patterns, I. *Journal of Mathematics and Mechanics*, **19**, 53.

Grossberg, S. (1969c). On learning of spatiotemporal patterns by networks with ordered sensory and motor components, I: Excitatory components of the cerebellum. *Studies in Applied Mathematics*, **48**, 105.

Grossberg, S. (1970a). Neural pattern discrimination. *Journal of Theoretical Biology*, **27**, 291.

Grossberg, S. (1970b). Some networks that can learn, remember, and reproduce any number of complicated space-time patterns, II. *Studies in Applied Mathematics*, **49**, 135.

Grossberg, S. (1971). Pavlovian pattern learning in nonlinear neural networks. *Proceedings of the National Academy of Sciences*, **68**, 828.

Grossberg, S. (1972). A neural theory of punishment and avoidance, Parts I and II. *Mathematical Biosciences*, **15**, pp. 39–67 and pp. 253–285.

Kaneko, A. (1970). Physiological and morphological identification of horizontal, bipolar, and amacrine cells in goldfish retina. *Journal of Physiology (London)*, **207**, 623.

Kimble, G.A. (1961). **Conditioning and learning**, New York: Appleton-Century-Crofts.

Komisaruk, B.R. (1970). Synchrony between limbic system theta activity and rhythmical behavior in rats. *Journal of Comparative and Physiological Psychology*, **70**, 482.

Land, E.H. (1969). The retinex. *American Scientist*, **52**, 247.

Land, E.H. and McCann, J.J. (1971). Lightness theory. *Journal of the Optical Society of America*, **61**, 1.

Miller, S. and Oscarsson, O. (1970). Termination and functional organization of spino-olivocerebellar paths. In W.S. Fields and W.D. Willis (Eds.), **The cerebellum in health and disease**. St. Louis: W.H. Green.

Naka, K.I. and Rushton, W.A.H. (1966). S-potentials from color units in the retina of fish (*Cyprinidae*). *Journal of Physiology (London)*, **185**, 536.

Sperling, G. (1970). Model of visual adaptation and contrast detection. *Perception and Psychophysics*, **8**, 143.

Sperling, G. and Sondhi, M.M. (1968). Model for visual luminance discrimination and flicker detection. *Journal of the Optical Society of America*, **58**, 1133.

Stell, W.K. (1967). The structure and relationship of horizontal cells and photoreceptor-bipolar synaptic complexes in goldfish retina. *American Journal of Anatomy*, **121**, 401.

Wachtel, H. and Kandel, E.R. (1971). Conversion of synaptic excitation to inhibition at a dual chemical synapse. *Journal of Neurophysiology*, **34**, 56.

Wagner, A.R. (1969). Frustrative nonreward: A variety of punishment. In B.A. Campbell and R.M. Church (Eds.), **Punishment and aversive behavior**. New York: Appleton-Century-Crofts.

Werblin, F.S. (1970). Response of retinal cells to moving spots: Intracellular recording in *Necturus maculosus*. *Journal of Neurophysiology*, **33**, 342.

Werblin, F.S. and Dowling, J.E. (1969). Organization of the retina of the mudpuppy *Necturus maculosus*, II: Intracellular recording. *Journal of Neurophysiology*, **32**, 339.

CHAPTER 5

SELF-ORGANIZATION OF ORIENTATION SENSITIVE CELLS IN THE STRIATE CORTEX
by
Christoph von der Malsburg

Preface

This 1973 article by Malsburg is a seminal contribution to the neural network literature. It responded to the 1972 article that comprises Chapter 4 (see Section IIIa and Table 1 below) by introducing a new adaptive instar model. In this instar model, the adaptive thresholds and priming signals of Chapter 4 are replaced by adaptive weights within the bottom-up filter. The inhibitory signals that control pattern normalization and instar selectivity in Chapter 4 are replaced by an additive on-center off-surround feedback network. In this modelling context, Malsburg carried out computer simulations that demonstrated the first self-organizing feature map. His immediate goal was to clarify how a spatial map of orientationally tuned cells can self-organize in the visual cortex.

The excitatory and inhibitory interactions in this model are described by an additive network. The learning mechanism is not, however, a locally defined mechanism or a real-time law. This is true because Malsburg chose as his learning equation a Hebbian learning law. In the notation of equation (10) in Chapter 2, he assumed that

$$\frac{d}{dt}z_{ij} = Gf_i(x_i)h_j(x_j), \tag{1}$$

where $f_i \geq 0$ and $h_j \geq 0$. By this law, the adaptive weights z_{ij} must always increase, unlike the non-Hebbian learning laws (10) and (11) of Chapter 2. To prevent these adaptive weights from diverging without limit, Malsburg also assumed that

$$\sum_i z_{ij} = \text{constant}. \tag{2}$$

To implement this constraint in real time, it would be necessary to assume that

$$\sum_i f_i(x_i) = 0. \tag{3}$$

By the fact that all $f_i \geq 0$, (3) would imply that all

$$f_i \equiv 0, \tag{4}$$

so weights in (1) would never change. Instead, Malsburg implemented equations (1) and (2) in alternating time slices. This hybrid rule is not a real-time rule. In addition, it is not a local rule, because equation (2) requires that all values z_{ij} be instantaneously transmitted to node j. Notwithstanding the problems arising from using the normalizing mechanism (2), it was nonetheless clear that *some* mechanism of normalization was needed, as also the articles in Chapters 3 and 4 had previously shown.

These conceptual and computational tensions in the 1973 model led to the 1976 article that comprises Chapter 6, which describes the competitive learning model in its modern form and proves its basic coding properties.

Kybernetik
1973, **14**, 85–100
©1973 Springer-Verlag, Inc.

SELF-ORGANIZATION OF ORIENTATION SENSITIVE CELLS
IN THE STRIATE CORTEX

Christoph von der Malsburg†

Abstract

A nerve net model for the visual cortex of higher vertebrates is presented. A simple learning procedure is shown to be sufficient for the organization of some essential functional properties of single units. The rather special assumptions usually made in the literature regarding preorganization of the visual cortex are thereby avoided. The model consists of 338 neurones forming a sheet analogous to the cortex. The neurones are connected randomly to a "retina" of 19 cells. Nine different stimuli in the form of light bars were applied. The afferent connections were modified according to a mechanism of synaptic training. After twenty presentations of all the stimuli individual cortical neurones became sensitive to only one orientation. Neurones with the same or similar orientation sensitivity tended to appear in clusters, which are analogous to cortical columns. The system was shown to be insensitive to a background of disturbing input excitations during learning. After learning it was able to repair small defects introduced into the wiring and was relatively insensitive to stimuli not used during training.

I. Introduction

The task of the cortex for the processing of visual information is different from that of the peripheral optical system. Whereas eye, retina, and lateral geniculate body (LGB) transform the images in a "photographic" way, i.e. preserving essentially the spatial arrangement of the retinal image, the cortex transforms this geometry into a space of concepts.

Within the last decade electrophysiology took the first steps into discovering the way in which the visual cortex performs this transformation. This paper is mainly concerned with the following features, which have been found in the primary visual cortex (area 17) of cat and monkey (Hubel and Wiesel, 1962, 1963, 1968).

† Acknowledgements: The author would like to thank Professor Dr. Otto Creutzfeldt for providing excellent working conditions and for helpful suggestions, Dr. H. Wässle for critical remarks on the manuscript, and Dr. Jean Ennever for correcting my English. The numerical calculations have been done on the UNIVAC 1108 computer of the Gesellschaft für wissenschaftliche Datenverarbeitung, Göttingen.

1. There are neurones which are selectively sensitive to the presentation of light bars and edges of a certain orientation (Hubel and Wiesel, 1962).

2. The neurones seem to be organized in "functional columns", i.e. the neurones lying within one cylinder vertical to the cortical surface are sensitive to the same orientation (Hubel and Wiesel, 1963).

3. Neighbouring columns tend to respond to stimuli of similar orientation (Hubel and Wiesel, 1963, 1968).

Although these findings are interesting in themselves, they will yield their full potential profit only if two questions are answered:

I. For what reason and to what end is area 17 organized in this way?

II. By which mechanisms are these neuronal properties determined?

Ad I: The fibres of the optic radiation are most sensitive to phasic changes of light intensity. Such intensity changes are brought about by eye movements, which scan the receptive fields of individual retinal and geniculate neurones over the light and dark contours of an image. Moving light edges and bars are therefore the most important stimuli which lead to geniculate output, i. e. cortical input. This may be considered one of the conditions for the existence of edge and bar detectors at the first cortical levels.

Ad II: The only mechanism proposed so far in the literature is genetical predetermination of the required circuitry (Hubel and Wiesel, 1963). This view has several disadvantages.

First, it would cost the system an immense volume of genetic information to tell all the terminal branches of the afferent axons with which cortical neurone they have to make contact.

Second, a rigid, genetically determined circuit would not have a high degree of plasticity. Such plasticity was demonstrated by experiments, in which the trigger features of visual cortical cells of young kittens could be determined in various ways by visual experience (Hirsch and Spinelli, 1970; Blakemore and Cooper, 1970; Blakemore and Mitchell, 1973).

Finally, plasticity, i. e. a process of self-organization should be possible in later stages of information processing by the brain, when it has to deal with situations not foreseen by nature.

The aim of this paper is to propose a mechanism of self-organization of the visual cortex which is able to explain in a simple way the facts 1 to 3 above and which also reduces the genetical problem to a reasonable level.

II. The Model

We describe now a model structure for the visual cortex and its specific afferents, which is in principle in accord with the known anatomical data and which has the minimum degree of complication required for the purpose of this paper.

a) The Elements

The model consists of a network of cells. The information transmitting signal is thought to be the discharge rate of the cells, averaged over a small interval of time. Thus the signal we employ here is a smooth function of time. This avoids the problem of artificial pulse—synchronization caused by the quantization of time, which is necessary in computer simulations. The cells make contact via connections (synapses). The connections can differ in weight, and are characterized by a number called strength of connection. The strength of connection from a cell A to a cell B will be denoted by p_{AB}. This term would include excitatory effects such as the sum of the post-synaptic potentials caused in a cell B by all the synapses of cell A on the dendrites and cell body of B. No assumptions are being made about the morphological variables which might determine the strength of connection. It may be different effectiveness or position of single synapses or merely a variable number of synapses between cells A and B (probably both). There are excitatory (E) and inhibitory (I) cells which have positive and negative strengths of connection respectively.

It is a simplification to characterize the connection between two cells by one number (or actually two numbers, as there are two directions, $A \rightarrow B$ and $B \rightarrow A$). In reality there is at least the complication of a variable synaptic delay and of different time-courses of excitation in cell B caused by one pulse of cell A. But the simplification of one number is sufficient for our purpose. The excitation per second caused by A in B is equal to the output of A (i.e. its firing frequency) times the strength of connection $A \rightarrow B$. This may, of course, be negative or positive.

It is furthermore assumed that the excitation and inhibition of one cell caused by all its presynaptic elements are summed linearly. The resulting quantity constitutes the input to the cell. The internal state of the cell is described by a quantity $H(t)$, which is callled "excitatory state" (ES). As output signal of the cell we take that part of its ES which exceeds a threshold. It shall be denoted by $H^*(t)$ (see Table 1). The cells influence each other via their output signals. The total input into a cell k is $\sum_l p_{lk} H_l^*(t)$, the p_{lk} being the strength of connection from cell l to cell k.

In the absence of input to a cell its ES decays exponentially with time. This can be described by the differential equation $d/dt\,H(t) = -\alpha H(t)$. The decay constant α is introduced to represent two phenomena, the decay of the postsynaptic potential and the post-excitatory polarization following each action potential. A single decay constant is a crude but adequate approximation to these two processes. The cells used here are very simple models of real neurones. The most conspicuous simplification is the linear dependency of the output signal on the input, as long as the threshold is exceeded. This implies, in particular, that there is no intrinsic upper limitation to the output signal, as is imposed in reality by an absolute refractive period. Such an unlimited output can lead to instability in a network which contains circular excitatory pathways. Therefore, in this model, instabilities can only be avoided by a properly devised inhibitory system within the network. In real systems there seems also to exist a limited mechanism apart from the absolute refractive period, as cells rarely fire with maximum frequency for an extended period of time (above 100 msec).

b) The Wiring of the Model

The cells of the model form a two dimensional arrangement, the "cortical plane". Their distribution is uniform, E- and I-cells have equal density, although the relative proportions do not matter. The strength of connection between any two cells is a function $f(x)$ of their distance x. This function should be monotonically decreasing, e.g. bell-shaped. It is characterized by a range R and an amplitude A. There are functions $f(x)$ with different range R and amplitude A according to the different

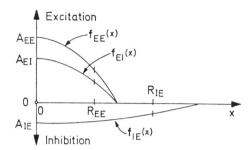

Figure 1. Schematic representation of the dependency of the intra-cortical connection strengths on cell distance x. Explanation of symbols in the text.

types of pairs of pre- and post-synaptic elements: $E \to E, E \to I, I \to E$ and $I \to I$ (see Figure 1):

$f_{EE}(x)$ with amplitude $A_{EE} > 0$ and range R_{EE},

$f_{EI}(x)$ with amplitude $A_{EI} > 0$ and range $R_{EI} = R_{EE}$,

$f_{IE}(x)$ with amplitude $A_{IE} < 0$ and range $R_{IE} > R_{EE}$.

No connection is assumed here between the I-cells ($A_{II} = 0$). This assumption and the restriction to $R_{EI} = R_{EE}$ do not lead to a loss of features essential for this paper. The intracortical connections described will serve to organize columns. For this it is essential that R_{IE} be larger than R_{EE}, as will become evident later on.

How does this model cortex compare with the cortex found in higher vertebrates? Firstly, it has only two kinds of cells, E- and I-cells. We do not try here to identify them with two of the many classes of neurones described in actual cortex. This identification may, in fact, be impossible, as perhaps no single cell of the cortex has the field of innervation we look for. The model could in this case be saved by the existence of multicellular units: clusters of cells integrated by strong mutual excitation. The individual arborizations of these cells could then add up to give the postulated field of innervation. It was Colonnier who introduced the concept of local fields of innervation to explain columnar organization. He also discussed histological evidence for this scheme (Colonnier, 1966).

It should be emphasized that the model described here certainly corresponds to only a part of the real cortex; for example long-range excitatory connections within the cortex are not represented. Also there may be several systems like the one described here, which occupy the same space and which are weakly linked to each other.

c) The Afferent Organization

There is a set of afferent fibres which provide the input to the model cortex. The fibres have circular receptive fields within a small area of the retina. Where the retina is hit by the light of a stimulus, it switches its optical fibres to an active state, i.e. a state of constant firing. All the other fibres are silent. The model retina is thus again a simplification as only one type of cell (on-cells) without a center-surround

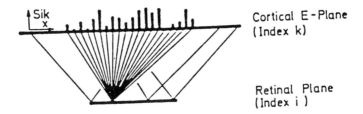

Figure 2. Schematic drawing to show the organization of the afferents. The lower horizontal line represents the retinal plane or a cross section through the bundle of afferent fibres. The upper horizontal line represents a section of the cortical plane. The vertical bars symbolize the different strengths of connection from one fibre i to many of the cortical E-cells k. The distribution of the heights of the bars is random. The connection of the other afferent fibres to one cortical cell are not shown.

organization and no off-cells are assumed. This simplification is possible, as only static light bars will be used as stimuli. Each afferent fibre projects to an area of the cortical plane and connects to all the E-cells within that area. A possible connection to I-cells is left out for the sake of simplicity.

Up to this point the wiring of the system is homogeneous: Each element is entirely equivalent to its neighbours of the same class, if one considers only relative coordinates. We now add an element of irregularity. Let s_{ik} be the strength of connection between the fibre i and the E-cell k. It is chosen to be an element of a set of random numbers (Figure 2). This set was arbitrarily assumed to have uniform distribution in an interval $[0, s]$. No correlation is assumed between the numbers s_{ik} for different k. (We will introduce later a correlation between the s_{ik} for different values of i.) If $A_i^*(t)$ denotes the signal on the afferent fibre i, then the afferent input into the cell k is $\sum_i s_{ik} A_i^*(t)$.

A word has to be said about retinotopic organization here: It is well known that there is a continuous mapping from the retina onto the visual cortex. Suppose that this is also true for the model in the sense that the receptive field position on the retina and the geometrical centers of the fields of projection of the afferent fibres correspond to a continuous mapping. But the probabilistic distribution of connection strengths within the field of projection will lead to a random scatter in the "centers of gravity" of the fields of projection and the retinotopic organization will be upset on a small scale. For the present study one can forget retinotopic organization altogether since the fields of projection of neighbouring retinal cells overlap considerably. Suppose that the small piece of cortex considered here lies entirely within the region of overlap of the fibres coming from the small piece of relevant retina, as is illustrated by Figure 3. Within this small cortical area all afferent fibres can then be regarded as equivalent in spite of their different position on the retina.

Several experimental findings on cat and monkey suggest that also in reality retintopical organization gives way to random scatter on a small scale: If one records during one cortical electrode penetration from successive neurones, one will find a large random scatter superimposed on the slow systematic displacement due to retinotopic organization (Hubel and Wiesel, 1962; Albus, 1973). In addition, if one maps the

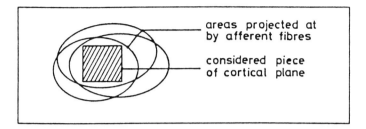

areas projected at
by afferent fibres

considered piece
of cortical plane

Figure 3. View onto the cortical plane, showing the overlap of the fields of projection of different fibres. The hatched area lies entirely within the region of overlap and so the information about the exact positions of the receptive fields of the afferent fibres is lost within this area.

two receptive fields of binocular units, one finds a disparity in their positions which changes unsystematically from cell to cell (Joshua and Bishop, 1970). This suggests a still larger individual scatter in the course of single afferent fibres, as the position of the receptive field corresponds to an average position of the fibres constituting it. An additional argument is the rather irregular course of afferent fibres seen on Golgi pictures (Ruiz-Marcos and Valverde, 1970; Ramon y Cajal, 1955, p. 613).

d) The Learning Principle

The system as it is described up to now is not yet able to explain the experimental facts stated in the introduction. For this, a process of self-organization is required, i.e. the system has to have the possibility to modify itself. This is done in the following way: if during a stimulation the afferent fibre i is active and if the stimulus leads to the firing of the E-cell k, then s_{ik}, the strength of connection between fibre i and cell k, is increased by an increment Δs_{ik}. This corresponds to synaptic learning as it was proposed earlier in one form or another (Hebb, 1949; Uttley, 1970; Brindley, 1969; Marr, 1971). The learning principle as defined here leaves the question open by which mechanism such type of synaptic learning may be brought about: by a chemical change within the existing synapses, by a change of their position, by an increase in the number of synapses, or by a change of their dimensions. There are morphological data which support the last two alternatives (Cragg, 1968; Møllgaard et al., 1971).

The principle, as it was just stated, leaves one main problem. If s_{ik} is increased by a constant amount Δs at each time when a coincidence $i - k$ takes place, then this will lead to synaptic strengths which will grow forever and eventually will cause instability of the circuit. One way out would be to let the s_{ik} saturate: the increments get smaller and smaller as s_{ik} approaches a maximum value. For this model we choose a different solution, which is stated in the form of a learning principle:

> If there is a coincidence of activity in an afferent fibre i and a cortical E-cell k, then s_{ik}, the strength of connection between the two, is increased to $s_{ik} + \Delta s$, Δs being proportional to the signal on the afferent fibre i and to the output signal of the E-cell k. Then all the s_{ik} leading to the same cortical cell k are renormalized to keep the sum $\sum_j s_{jk}$ constant.

This last step could correspond to the idea that the total synaptic strength con-

$H_k(t)$	Excitatory state (ES) of cell k at time t
θ_k	Threshold of cell k
$H_k^*(t)$	Signal of cell k

$$H_k^*(t) = \begin{cases} H_k(t) - \theta_k & \text{if } H_k(t) > \theta_k \\ 0 & \text{otherwise} \end{cases}$$

$A_i^*(t)$	Signal of afferent fibre i
N	Number of cortical cells
M	Number of afferent fibres
α_k	Decay constant of ES of cortical cell k
s_{ik}	Strength of connection between fibre i and cell k
p_{lk}	Strength of connection from cell l to cell k

$$\tfrac{d}{dt} H_k(t) = -\alpha_k H_k(t) + \sum_{l=1}^{N} p_{lk} H_l^*(t) + \sum_{i=1}^{M} s_{ik} A_i^*(t), \quad k = 1, \ldots, N$$

Table 1. Equations of evolution in time.

verging on one neurone is limited by the dendritic surface available. It means that some s_{ik} are increased at the expense of others.

III. The Function of the Model

a) Basic Equations of Evolution

What functional states are there for the model network described in the last section and how will it be influenced by stimulation? To answer these questions we have to write down the equations which govern the evolution of the system. They are summarized in Table 1 (compare Grossberg, 1972). At first sight they look like linear differential equations. But H_k^* is a nonlinear function of H_k and this nonlinearity is essential, i.e. one cannot get rid of it by approximations. There are no mathematical ways to solve these equations in a closed form and that is the reason we had to do numerical calculations on a computer.

In this paper we are interested only in static stimuli, i.e. stimuli which are switched on for a moment and switched off again. Ideally the network's response will be an initial transient settling down to a steady state, which lasts until the end of the stimulus period. As the details of the switching-on and -off periods are irrelevant for this paper, we will restrict our argument to the steady state, however short it might be in reality.

The specialization of the equation of Table 1 to the steady state, or $dH_k/dt = 0$, reads:

$$\alpha_k H_k = \sum_{l=1}^{N} p_{lk} H_l^* + \sum_{i=1}^{M} s_{ik} A_i^*, \quad k = 1, \ldots, N.$$

Here one can divide by α_k and absorb the factor $1/\alpha_k$ on the right side into the definition of the coefficients p_{lk} and s_{ik} giving p_{lk}' and s_{ik}':

$$H_k = \sum_{l=1}^{N} p_{lk}' H_l^* + \sum_{i=1}^{M} s_{ik}' A_i^*, \quad k = 1, \ldots, N.$$

E_k	ES of E-cell number k
I_k	ES of I-cell number k
E_k^*, I_k^*	Corresponding signals
N	Number of E-cells and number of I-cells
M	Number of afferent fibres

Strengths of Connections:

$p_{lk} > 0$	from E-cell l to E-cell k
$q_{lk} > 0$	from I-cell l to E-cell k
$r_{lk} > 0$	from E-cell l to I-cell k
$s_{ik} > 0$	from afferent fibre i to E-cell k

a) $E_k = \sum_{l=1; l \neq k}^{N} p_{lk} E_l^* - \sum_{l=1}^{N} q_{lk} I_l^* + \sum_{i=1}^{M} s_{ik} A_i^*, \quad k = 1, \ldots, N$

b) $I_k = \sum_{l=1}^{N} r_{lk} E_l^*, \quad k = 1, \ldots, N$

Table 2. Stationary equations.

These equations can be made more explicit, as according to the conventions of the model many of the p_{lk} and s_{ik} vanish and others are negative. By the introduction of more specialized symbols, the final set of equations of Table 2 is obtained. (The primes are dropped again, as no confusion can arise.)

b) Specification of Details

Many of the definitions used in the description of the model above were unprecise, because too many details would have obscured the principle. These details have now to be specified. Some of these features will still be found to be oversimplified, but their special form was dictated by the necessity to economize computer time and space.

A hexagonal array was chosen for E- and I-cells (see Figure 4). For every E-cell there is a corresponding I-cell occupying the same place. The hexagonal arrangement has the advantage of giving to each cell an almost circular surround of neighbouring cells. The total number of cells was chosen to be $2 \times 169 = 338$ cells, giving a network of a major diameter of 15 cells (Figure 6). The threshold of all the cells was made equal to 1.

The wiring of the network is explained in Figure 4: Each active E-cell directly excites the immediately neighbouring E-cells with strength p and the immediately neighbouring I-cells (including the one occupying the same place as the active cell) with strength r. Each active I-cell inhibits with strength q its next-to-immediate neighbours amongst the E-cells only.

These distributions are rather crude representations of the bell shaped curves of Figure 1. The fact that the I-cells do not inhibit their directly neighbouring E-cells has no major consequences on the function of the model, as was checked in separate calculations. It is a measure of economy.

The afferents are made up to 19 fibres. Each fibre is thought to fan out into 169 branches to contact the 169 E-cells. Correspondingly, a matrix of 19×169 numbers representing the strengths of connection had to be specified. This matrix was derived

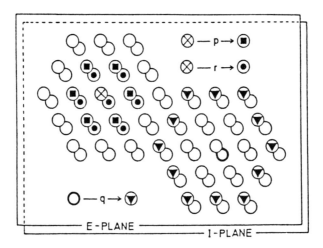

Figure 4. A small part of the simulated cortex, showing the hexagonal array of the *E*-cells (upper plane) and the *I*-cells (lower plane). The different symbols are used to designate those cells which are connected with strengths p, r, and q. Every cell is connected with its neighbors in the same way (except at the borders).

$$N = 169$$
$$M = 19$$
$$p = 0.4$$
$$q = 0.3$$
$$s = 0.25$$
$$r = 0.286$$
$$h = 0.05$$

Table 3. Numerical parameters (for definitions, see text and Table 2).

from a set $s'_{ik} (i = 1, \ldots, 19; k = 1, \ldots, 169)$ of random numbers with a flat distribution within an interval $[0, s]$. (For the values of s and all the other numerical parameters see Table 3.)

With the numbers s'_{ik} the total afferent synaptic strength s'_k leading to the *E*-cell k can be written $s'_k = \sum_{i=1}^{19} s'_{ik}$. This number has to be a constant during learning. For the sake of simplicity, all the s'_k were changed to their mean value, which is $19 \cdot s/2$. This was done by renormalizing the s'_{ik} according to:

$$s_{ik} = s'_{ik} \cdot 19 \cdot \frac{s}{2} / s'_k, \quad i = 1, \ldots, 19; \quad k = 1, \ldots, 169.$$

The s_{ik} thus derived are the starting values of the afferent strengths of connection. All the simulations of this paper are based on the same initial set of synaptic strengths.

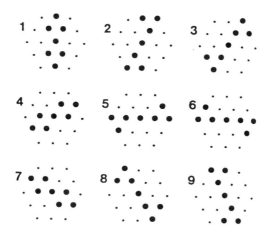

Figure 5. The standard set of stimuli used on the model "retina". Large and small dots represent active and non-active fibres respectively.

In each learning step the s_{ik} values are increased to

$$s'_{ik} = s_{ik} + h \cdot A^*_i \cdot E^*_k$$

after the stimulation. Then the s'_{ik} are renormalized in the way just described to give the s_{ik} of a next generation.

The stimuli always consisted of seven active afferent fibres, i.e. seven of the 19 A^*_i in equation a) of Table 2 were set to 1, the others to zero.

There was a standard set of nine stimuli, which was employed mainly. This set is shown in Figure 5. It was chosen to represent light bars of different orientation.

It should however be emphasized that in the absence of retinotopical organization the important property of the stimuli in Figure 5 is not their geometrical arrangement but rather their relationships established by mutual overlap.

c) The Procedure of the Numerical Calculations

The solutions to the equations of Table 2 were found by numerical calculation on a UNIVAC 1108. The method we employed was stepwise approximation by an iterative procedure. That means the equations we really used were those of Table 1, the different steps of the approximation corresponding to their solution at consecutive time steps. Not every set of parameters p, q, r and s lead to stable solutions. Those finally employed were found partly by trial and error.

The solution is not reached in a monotone and quick way. The ES of the cells will first follow a course of damped oscillations and then approach slowly their final values. To save time, this slow approximation was stopped after 20 iterative ("time") steps and the result taken as an approximate solution to the equation of Table 2. By then the change from step to step in the ES of most cells was smaller than 0.5%.

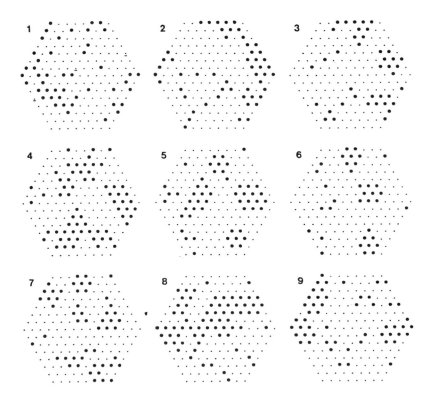

Figure 6. The reactions of the cortical E-cells to the stimuli of Figure 5. Large dots represent firing cells. The numbers to the upper left correspond to those of Figure 5.

After the solution was found, learning was done by the described manipulations on the s_{ik}. All the other parameters were held fixed.

d) The Results without Learning

Figure 6 shows in a qualitative way the reaction of the network to the nine stimuli (Figure 5), before any learning took place. The small and large dots represent E-cells with ES below and above threshold respectively. The I-cells are not shown. As can be seen, the cells have already the clear tendency to fire in clusters. To get a more quantitative impression of the reaction of the cells consider the left column of diagrams in Figures 7, 8, and 9, which summarize the behaviour of three typical cells, Nos. 50, 70, and 120 (for their positions see Figure 6). The vertical bars in the hexagon in the bottom row show the connection strengths s_{ik} of the 19 afferent fibres to the cell. Their hexagonal arrangement corresponds to the one in Figure 5. For each stimulus the afferent excitation (which corresponds to the sum of seven of the bars) is plotted in the middle row of Figures 7–9 against stimulus number. Notice that the points in these diagrams tend to form a continuous line, i.e. neighbouring points are correlated. This is a consequence of the retinal overlap between neighbouring stimuli.

The upper graphs of the left columns in Figures 7–9 show the ES of the particular cells in response to the nine stimuli. This plot could also be called the cells orien-

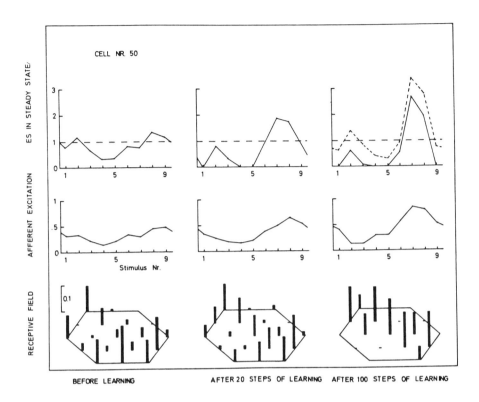

Figure 7. Receptive field organization, afferent excitation, and ES of the E-cell no. 50 in the steady state response to the nine stimuli. Left, middle, and right columns correspond to the system without learning, with 20 steps and with 100 steps of learning, respectively. The heights of the vertical bars in the hexagon in the lower row represent connection strengths s_{ik} of the 19 retinal fibres to the cell. Their arrangement corresponds to Figure 5. The position of this cell is underlined in the first diagram of Figure 6 in the fifth line from the top.

tational tuning curve. Its details are determined roughly by the efferent excitation, although it is modified by what goes on in the cortical neighbourhood.

A summary of the main features of the 169 tuning curves is shown in Table 4. Twelve cells never reach threshold. Seventy of them react to stimuli in a multimodal fashion, i.e. they fire within separate regions. This is exemplified by the cell in Figure 7 (left column). A large fraction, eighty-seven, of the cells could already be called orientation sensitive, as their tuning curves are unimodal, although not very sharp (e.g., cell number 70, Figure 8). In summary one can say that although there is no systematics in the organization of the afferents, we already get a tendency to firing in clusters ("columnar organization") and a considerable fraction of the cells (51%) with unimodal orientation tuning ("orientation specific units"), although the tuning curves may still be comparatively flat.

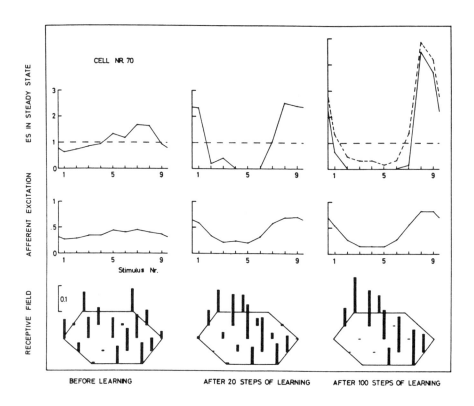

Figure 8. Receptive field organization, afferent excitation, and ES of the E-cell no. 70. Its position on the cortex is in the seventh line from the top (see Figure 6, 1). For explanation, see Figure 7.

e) The Results after a Learning Phase

A step of learning consists of one presentation of all the nine different stimuli and the learning manipulations on the s_{ik} subsequent to each presentation.

During the learning phase the sequence of presentation of the stimuli was 1, 6, 2, 7, 3, 8, 4, 9 instead of the natural one (1, 2, 3, ...). This was to avoid special effects resulting from the consecutive presentation of two maximally overlapping stimuli.

The behaviour of the system after 20 steps of learning is shown in Figure 10. The cells now show a much stronger tendency to fire in clusters than they did before learning (compare Figure 6). This can be interpreted in the following way: the intracortical connections give the cells a natural tendency to fire in separate clusters. At first the cells are disturbed in this tendency by the afferent excitation, which at the beginning does not favour clusters at all. Nevertheless the ES of the cortical cells will be highest, if they can exchange maximal intracortical excitation and minimal intracortical inhibition, which is the case with firing in patterns of small clusters. Now, the higher the ES of a cortical cell, the stronger will be its influence on the afferent organization via learning. Finally those patterns of afferent organization will persist which favour cortical clusters.

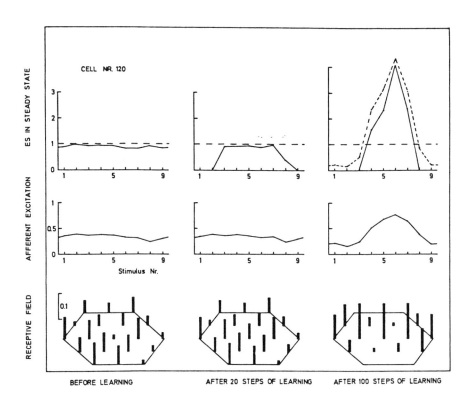

Figure 9. Receptive field organization, afferent excitation, and ES of the E-cell no. 120. Position in the eleventh line from the top (Figure 6, 1). For explanation, see Figure 7.

If the statistics of the afferent stimulations are stationary, the learning process in the system will saturate after some time. This saturation is not yet reached after 20 learning steps. Therefore the reactions of the system continue to change. Figure 11 shows the responses of the E-cells after 100 steps of learning, of which the last 40 were accelerated by doubling the learning constant h (its value being 0.1 instead of 0.05).

To see the effect of learning on the level of the single cells, consider the middle and right columns in Figures 7–9. In many cases the tuning curves are now much steeper, the cells being either strongly excited or little excited (e.g., Figures 7 and 8). This behaviour is more pronounced with more learning (see right columns). The cell of Figure 7 had at first two sensitive regions, one of which disappeared within the first 20 steps of learning. In the case of Figure 9 there was no reaction of the cell to any of the stimuli up to learning step 20. Later on, however, it was occasionally excited to the firing level by its neighbours. This led to a sudden modulation of its tuning curve, which is very steep after 100 learning steps.

The changes in the tuning curves of the cells with learning are the result of positive feedback: Whenever a cell fires, it will strengthen those afferent connections which

a) Classification of tuning curves

	No response	Unimodal	Multimodal
Before learning	12	87	70
20 steps of learning	43	118	8
100 steps of learning	21	147	1

b) Width of unimodal tuning curves (n is the number of neighbouring stimuli to which the cells responded)

n	1	2	3	4	5	6	7
Before learning	20	24	18	19	5	—	1
20 steps of learning	24	19	45	25	5	—	—
100 steps of learning	8	43	64	25	7	—	—

Table 4. Classification of cells according to reaction type.

were exciting the cell. This leads to increased afferent excitation of the cell, when the same stimulus is applied the next time. Increased afferent excitation will in its turn make the cell fire more strongly in response to the stimulus, and this will lead to accelerated learning as long as saturation is far. The corresponding modifications of the afferent organizations and of the excitation curves are apparent in Figures 7–9, bottom row. In the end, only those s_{ik} persist which are used by the effective stimuli (compare Figure 5 for the stimuli). The decrease of the unused connection strengths is a consequence of the condition that their sum be constant.

The chain of positive feedback described in the last paragraph is modified by the intracortical excitation and inhibition, which are added to the afferent excitation. This is the point where intracortical dynamics enters and leads to the clustering of firing.

The behaviour of all the E-cells with learning is summed up in Table 4. It shows that less and less cells have multimodal tuning curves (70 before learning, 8 after 20 steps, and one after 100 steps). Note also that very sharp tuning curves, i.e. reaction of a cell to only a single stimulus, seems not to be favoured by the system after extended learning (24 after 20 steps and only 8 after 100 steps).

The broken lines in the upper right graphs of Figures 7–9 show the excitation of the cells alone, no inhibition being subtracted. The inhibition is the difference between the two curves of each graph. As one can see, the tuning curves are made a bit narrower by the inhibition. In 20 cases a second separate sensitive region of a cell was suppressed by the inhibition, as in the example of the cell of Figure 7. Therefore in this model the inhibition takes part in the organization of the "cortex" in an essential way (apart from its stabilizing function), although it is homogeneously distributed and not modified by learning at all.

Two of the three aims we set for the model in the introduction of this paper are now accomplished: First, clusters of cortical activity are brought about by intracor-

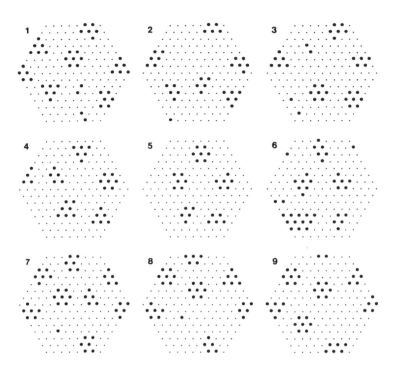

Figure 10. Reaction of the cortical E-cells after 20 steps of learning. The figure corresponds to Figure 6. In this and the following figure there is no learning between the nine stimulations shown.

tical dynamics. Second, organization of orientation specific units is brought about by a learning strategy rather than by genetical determination.

The third task was an explanation of the fact, that neighbouring cells have the tendency to react to stimuli of neighbouring orientation (Hubel and Wiesel, 1963, 1968). This now turns out to be a natural consequence of the existence of clusters and of their influence on the afferent synaptic strengths, as can be seen directly by inspection of Figure 12.

Each bar in this figure indicates the median of the orientations to which the corresponding cell responded. If, for instance, a cell fired in response to stimuli 1, 2, and 3, the orientation corresponding to stimulus 2 is plotted, regardless of the magnitude of the three answers. If the cell fired in response to stimuli 1 and 2, the plotted orientation lies halfway between those for 1 and 2. Two crossing bars indicate a "bimodal" reaction of the cell, i.e. responses to two orientations separated by one or more uneffective orientations.

It can be seen that the probability of similar orientations in adjacent cells is high. This tendency is emphasized in Figure 13, which shows the optimal orientations after 100 steps of learning. There are even series of cells with continuously turning

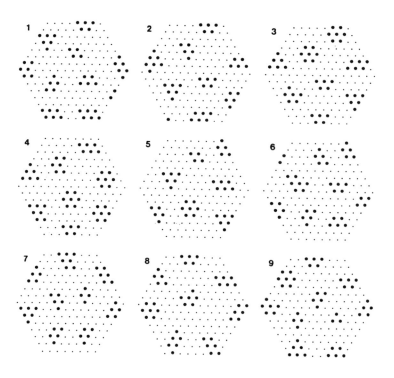

Figure 11. Reaction of the cortical E-cells after 100 steps of learning.

orientations (e.g., the seventh line in Figure 13) as described in the literature (Hubel and Wiesel, 1968).

The Effect of Non-Standard Stimuli

An important question one can pose now is how the trained system will react to stimuli which it does not know yet. To answer this question, the system was tested with 45 different stimuli $m_i, i = 1, \ldots, 45$. As the standard stimuli $n_k, k = 1, \ldots, 9$ of Figure 5, the m_i consisted of seven retinal points each. The m_i were characterized by the maximal overlap $V_{i\,\text{max}}$ they had with any of the n_k:

$$V_{i\,\text{max}} = \max_{k=1,\ldots,9}(m_i \cap n_k).$$

The m_i were chosen to form five groups of equal V_{max}, containing nine stimuli each. V_{max} varied from 2 in the first group to 6 in the fifth group. As the model retina is so small, no stimuli with $V_{\text{max}} = 1$ could be found. Within one group the stimuli were chosen to be as different as possible.

To judge the effect of a stimulus on the system, the mean output signal E of the E-cells was computed:

$$E = \frac{1}{N}\sum_k E_k^*.$$

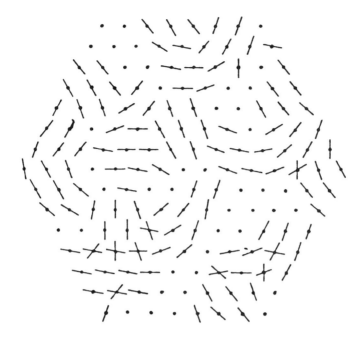

Figure 12. View onto the cortex. Each bar indicates the optimal orientation of the E-cell (for definition, see text). Dots without a bar are cells which never reacted to the standard set of stimuli. Two bars indicate two separate sensitive regions.

Figure 13. View onto the cortex after 100 steps of learning.

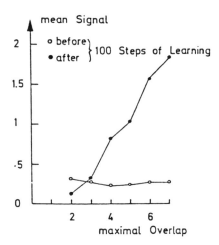

Figure 14. The mean output signal of the E-cells in response to different sets of stimuli. The stimuli of each set have a maximal overlap with stimuli of the standard set. This overlap is calculated as the number of fibres the stimuli have in common and it is shown on the abscissa. An overlap of seven corresponds to the standard set.

In Figure 14 the average of E for the nine stimuli in one group is plotted against the maximum overlap $V_{i\,max}$ with the standard stimuli. The overlap 7 means the standard set itself. The flat curve (o–o) is the effect of the stimuli on the "naive" network, before learning of any stimuli took place. No significant differences between the groups are found. The steeper curve (•–•) shows the effect of the different stimulus sets after the network went through 100 steps of learning the standard stimuli, which in Figure 14 corresponds to the group of overlap 7. The stimuli most similar to the stimuli used for training are clearly favoured. The response becomes smaller the less similar the test stimuli are to the standard set. In the case of overlap 2 there is even a suppression in comparison with the sensitivity before training. This indicates that the system responds less to "new" stimuli once it has been taught a given set.

It should be noted that the mean output signal of the cells increased after learning (e.g., from 0.25 to 1.8 for the standard stimuli in Figure 14). A more realistic model should be able to keep the mean excitation of the network constant in spite of learning. This could be done by an adapting inhibitory system. The trained network would then actively suppress the response to all stimuli with which it was not trained. With this modification, even more than in the present model, the network could be regarded as an effective filter.

g) The Sensitivity to Nonspecific Input

Up to now the task of the model was fairly simple: a set of stimuli which could be characterized by one parameter (their orientation) was presented. The problem for each cortical cell was to become selectively sensitive to a small range of the stimulus parameter only. In reality there are certainly different sources of perturbations:

1. There is a very large number of different stimuli which make up a large percentage of the information flow, but each individual stimulus occurs so rarely that no cortical cell would get specialized to it.

2. Those stimuli occurring frequently have small variations of composition, which can be regarded as a disturbance.

3. There is a nonspecific input to the cells, which is not related to the visual information.

To test the ability of the model to work in the presence of perturbations the following experiment was done. A random number t_k was added to the specific afferent excitation $\sum_i s_{ik} A_i^*$ (see Table 2) received by cell number k ($k = 1, \ldots, 169$). There was a new set of random numbers for every stimulation.

The first generation of the s_{ik} was chosen from the interval $[0, 0.175]$; the t_k from the interval $[0, 0.525]$, three times as large. Consequently the mean of the expressions $\sum_i s_{ik} A_i^*$ is 0.613 ± 0.095 (root mean square deviation) and the mean of the t_k is 0.263 ± 0.153. Their sum, $\sum_i s_{ik} A_i^* + t_k$, has a mean of 0.875 (as before) and its r. m. s. deviation is ± 0.180, which is largely determined by the perturbation t_k.

The most important feature of the afferent excitatory input to the cortical cells is its differentiation between different cells during one stimulation and for one cell between different stimulations. These differences have to be detected and enhanced by learning. However in the present experiment they are completely buried under the differences produced by the perturbative random excitation t_k.

How serious the perturbation is can be assessed from Figure 15, which shows the reactions of the untrained system to six times the same stimulus (number one of Figure 5). Without the perturbation the reactions would be identical. After 20 steps of learning (involving nine stimuli each and with $h = 0.1$, compare Table 3) the picture is quite different: Figure 16, also six presentations of stimulus one, shows much less variations.

To measure the decrease in variability from Figure 15 to Figure 16 by a number, the entropy of these variations was calculated. If E-cell k fired n times during m presentations of the same stimulus, then the probability of k to react can be defined as $p_k = n/m$, and h_k, the corresponding entropy can be calculated

$$h_k = -p_k ld p_k - (1 - p_k) ld (1 - p_k)$$

(ld is the binary logarithm). If k fires half the time, then the entropy is maximum, $h_k = 1.0$. The mean entropy of all the E-cells then is

$$H = \frac{1}{N} \sum_k h_k,$$

where N is the number of cells.

The entropy of the variability of reactions to one and the same stimulus before learning (Figure 15) is $H = 0.674$ and after 20 steps of learning (Figure 16) it is $H = 0.203$, considerably reduced.

In conclusion one can say: If there is a systematic structure in the information arriving at the cortical cells, it can be detected and enhanced by the learning system even if it is buried in nonstructured, random excitation.

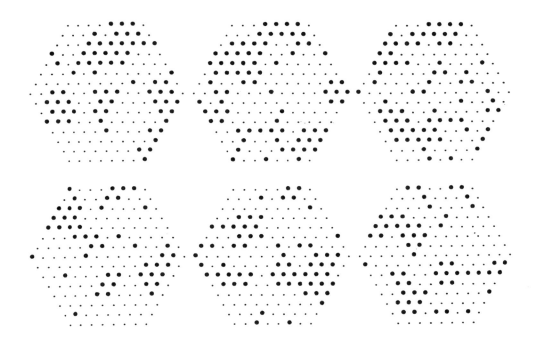

Figure 15. Six reactions of the E-cells to the same stimulus (1 of Figure 5) before learning. The differences are produced by extra random input.

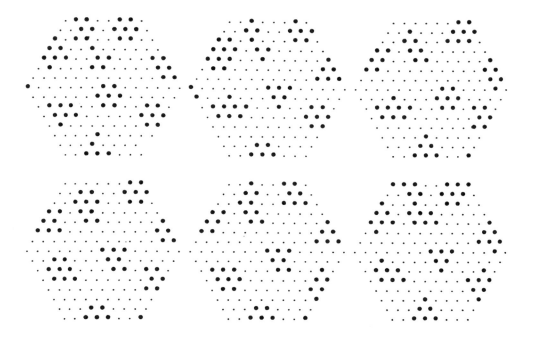

Figure 16. Six reactions of the E-cells to stimulus 1 after 20 steps of learning.

h) Redundancy of Information Storage

It has been demonstrated that the connectivity between two points of nervous tissue can change after simultaneous stimulation of these points (e.g., Bliss and Gardner-Medwin, 1970). These changes may be interpreted as synaptic learning. Unfortunately they were never longlasting and after some hours or sometimes days the connectivity had decayed to its previous value. This fact, which was also found in other preparations, has always been a serious argument against the interpretation of synaptic conditioning as a basis for permanent memory.

With our model we performed an experiment which may be relevant to this question. In the system as it was left after 100 steps of learning, twelve arbitrarily chosen afferent fibres were strengthened by increasing the corresponding synaptic strengths s_{ik} to triple value, and the synaptic input to the cortical cells was renormalized to keep their total synaptic input constant (section IIIb). This reduced the increased numbers s_{ik} to a somewhat lower value. Then the system was allowed to learn for 40 more steps (with $h = 0.1$). It was found that most of the connection strengths were brought back to a level which was close to the value before the added increase. Two of the increased s_{ik} were connected to cells which never reacted before, during, or after this experiment. Consequently no learning took place and these s_{ik} stayed high. The sum of the remaining 10 s_{ik} was 0.963 before the experiment. After the increase and renormalization it was 2.351, and after the 40 steps of learning it was back to 1.026, although saturation had not yet been reached.

The explanation of this result is that the characteristics of a pattern to which a cell responds are determined by all the effective connections leading to the cell. If the strength of only one of these connections is changed, the optimal pattern of the cell will not be changed very much. This one connection will then readapt by the process of learning to its previous value.

The experiment shows that the system has enough redundancy in its information storage to make it insensitive to such small defects as an arbitrary change in the strength of some connections. This kind of argument could be able to explain the failure of the experiments mentioned above: The conductivity changes artifically produced in the experiment may be considered as disturbances of the normal function of the neural structure and are therefore "repaired" by the nervous system.

IV. Discussion

It was the aim of this paper to show that there is at least one way to explain a large part of the functional organization in the visual cortex of cat and monkey without depending completely on a genetically predetermined connectivity between the cortex and its afferent fibres.

Most of the principles used here have been described before in the literature: the form of intracortical connectivity (Figure 1) (Colonnier, 1966; Wilson and Cowan, to be published), mechanisms of synaptical conditioning (Hebb, 1949; Rosenblatt, 1961; Brindley, 1969; Grossberg, 1972; Uttley, 1970; Marr, 1971), and random connections (Beurle, 1956; Rosenblatt, 1961; Marr, 1971). The equations used here are very similar to those of Grossberg (1972).

a) The Structure of the Model and Generalizations

This paper proposed two principal mechanisms: the development of pattern sensitive cortical cells by a self-organizing process involving synaptic learning, and the arrangement of functional columns as a consequence of intracortical connections rather than due to a predetermined distribution of afferents.

The two main directions of local intracortical fibre systems are tangential and vertical to the cortical surface. The model takes these two directions into account in a simplified way. The vertical connections are implicit in the representation of all the cells of one vertical cylinder by only two cells, an excitatory and an inhibitory. The underlying assumption is that all cells of this cylinder are so strongly connected by vertical fibres that they fire virtually simultaneously under most conditions.

The horizontal connections, on the other hand, have been represented explicitly. In contrast to the histological picture they spread symmetrically in all directions. This can be justified by the fact that each connection between two functional units represents an average over many fibres which connect a multitude of individual cells. The firing of cortical cells in clusters is due to the excitatory horizontal connections. As a consequence of the homogeneity of intracortical connection the borders between such clusters are not fixed and may shift slightly from one stimulation to the next. The inhibitory and excitatory interaction between cortical neurones makes it necessary to think in terms of collective networks rather than of isolated neurones. This means that the functional behaviour of a cortical neurone is not only a function of its receptive field in terms of its afferent input, but also of its intracortical connections.

To organize orientation specificity of the cortical cells a mechanism of adaptation, namely synaptic conditioning, is introduced. This mechanism is applied to a network with nonspecific, random interconnections and is able to transform it into a highly specialized system. Some of the special features of the "learning principle" employed here need discussion.

The total sum of synaptic strength converging onto one cell was kept constant: while some synapses grew stronger, others became weaker. This was introduced for several reasons. One is stability: a system with only growing excitatory synapses is unstable. A second reason is the requirement of high specificity of the cells: they should become insensitive to all stimuli for which they were not trained. Both of these functions can probably also be realized by replacing the principle of constant synaptic strengths by additional training of inhibitory connections.

Some of the limitations of the proposed model are caused not by the underlying principles but rather by the restricted number of cells and connections and the highly restricted sensory inputs used in the computer simulations. More cells would give the cortex more degrees of freedom and it could adapt to a greater range of stimuli. An obvious generalization would be the inclusion of moving stimuli. The important stimulus property selected for would then no longer be retinal position but rather a temporal sequence of positions. Another generalization would be the organization of a hierarchical system of feature detectors.

b) Comparison with Experiments

The learning principle was applied only to synapses of the afferent fibres. This may be taken as a special case of learning in early development such as the "learning" of binocularity (Wiesel and Hubel, 1965) or orientation tuning (Blakemore and Cooper, 1970).

Many neurones in the visual cortex of very young kittens are orientation sensitive before any visual experience has occurred, but they are not so sharply tuned as in adult animals (Hubel and Wiesel, 1963; Pettigrew, 1972). In the light of these findings it is interesting to note that also in the proposed model a high percentage of orientation sensitive cells is found before any training took place (Table 4). Narrowly tuned neuronal orientation specificity found during experiments on unexperienced kittens may be a consequence of fast learning during the experiments, a property also shown by the model (see below).

The model also leads to one important "prediction". If only a restricted set of stimuli is presented during the training period, the cortical neurones will specialize to these stimuli and will thereafter become insensitive to all other stimuli. This corresponds to experimental findings on training of young animals: if kittens are raised in an environment consisting entirely of horizontal or vertical stripes, they become virtually blind for contours perpendicular to the orientation they had experienced during the training period (Blakemore and Cooper, 1970). When testing the visual cortex cells of such animals a highly significant anisotropy in the distribution of preferred orientations was found. It was later shown that an exposure time as short as one hour during a sensitive period was sufficient to induce the anisotropy of preferred orientations (Blakemore and Mitchell, 1973). This compares well with the quick convergence of the self-organization in the model network, which became relatively insensitive to untrained stimuli after as little as a hundred presentations of the set of training stimuli. This phenomenon, like the corresponding experiments on unexperienced kittens, may be an analogue to imprinting rather than learning in the definition of ethologists.

Recent experiments in this laboratory make it doubtful that many geniculate fibres, the receptive fields of which are arranged in a line parallel to the optimal orientation, converge on individual cortical "simple" cells. The excitatory input of such cells appears to have a receptive field the form and size of which correspond to those of individual retinal ganglion cells rather than to lines (Benevento, Creutzfeldt, and Kuhnt, 1972). It seems that the temporal sequence of retinal excitation, i.e. the stimulus movement, is a more important aspect of cortical organization. In order to test this, the dynamic aspects rather than steady state conditions may have to be investigated with our model.

The results of this theoretical study are encouraging as they show that such simple assumptions about intracortical connections and the mechanism of synaptic conditioning as made in this model proved to be sufficient to explain some of the most striking functional properties of the visual cortex.

REFERENCES

Albus, K. (1973). Topology of orientation sensitivity in the cortical areas 17 and 18 of the cat. *Pflügers Arch. Supplement*, **339**, R91.

Benevento, L.A., Creutzfeldt, O.D., and Kuhnt, U. (1972). Significance of intracortical inhibition in the visual cortex. *Nature*, **238**, 124–126.

Beurle, R.L. (1956). Properties of a mass of cells capable of regenerating pulses. *Philosophical Transactions of the Royal Society of London B*, **240**, 55–94.

Blakemore, C. and Cooper, G.F. (1970). Development of the brain depends on the visual environment. *Nature*, **228**, 477–478.

Blakemore, C. and Mitchell, D.E. (1973). Environmental modification of the visual cortex and the neural basis of learning and memory. *Nature*, **241**, 467–468.

Bliss, T.V.P. and Gardner-Medwin, A.R. (1971). Long-lasting increases of synaptic influence in the unanaesthetized hippocampus. *Journal of Physiology (London)*, **216**, 32P–33P.

Brindley, G.S. (1969). Nerve net models of plausible size that perform many simple learning tasks. *Proceedings of the Royal Society of London B*, **174**, 173–191.

Colonnier, H.L. (1966). Structural design of the neocortex. In J.C. Eccles (Ed.), **Brain and conscious experience**. Berlin/Heidelberg/New York: Springer-Verlag, pp. 1–21.

Cragg, B.G. (1968). Are there structural alterations in synapses related to functioning? *Proceedings of the Royal Society of London B*, **171**, 319–323.

Grossberg, S. (1972). Neural expectation: Cerebellar and retinal analogs of cells fired by learnable or unlearned pattern classes. *Kybernetik*, **10**, 49–57.

Hebb, D.O. (1949). **Organization of behaviour**. New York: Wiley.

Hirsch, H.V.B. and Spinelli, D.N. (1970). Visual experience modifies distribuution of horizontally and vertically oriented receptive fields in cats. *Science*, **168**, 869–871.

Hubel, D.H. and Wiesel, T.N. (1962). Receptive fields, binocular interaction, and functional architecture in the cat's visual cortex. *Journal of Physiology (London)*, **160**, 106–154.

Hubel, D.H. and Wiesel, T.N. (1963). Receptive fields of cells in striate cortex of very young, visually inexperienced kittens. *Journal of Neurophysiology*, **26**, 994–1002.

Hubel, D.H. and Wiesel, T.N. (1968). Receptive fields and functional architecture of monkey striate cortex. *Journal of Physiology (London)*, **195**, 215–243.

Joshua, D.E. and Bishop, P.O. (1970). Binocular single vision and depth discrimination: Receptive field disparities for central and peripheral vision and binocular interactions on peripheral single units in cat striate cortex. *Experimental Brain Research*, **10**, 389–416.

Marr, D. (1971). Simple memory. *Philosophical Transactions of the Royal Society of London B*, **262**, 23–81.

Møllgaard, K., Diamond, M.C., Bennett, E.L., Rosenzweig, M.R., and Lindner, B. (1971). Quantitative synaptic changes with differential experience in rat brain. *International Journal of Neuroscience*, **2**, 113–128.

Pettigrew, J.D. (1972). The importance of early visual experience for neurones of the developing geniculostriate system. *Investigative Ophthalmology*, **11**, 386–392.

Ramon y Cajal, S. (1955). **Histologie du système nerveux, Vol. II**. Madrid: Consejo Superior de Investigaciones Científicas, Instituto Ramon y Cajal.

Rosenblatt, F. (1961). **Principles of neurodynamics: Perceptrons and the theory of brain mechanisms**. Washington, DC: Spartan Books.

Ruiz-Marcos, A. and Valverde, F. (1970). Dynamic architecture of the visual cortex. *Brain Research*, **19**, 25–39.

Uttley, A.M. (1970). The informon: A network for adaptive pattern recognition. *Journal of Theoretical Biology*, **27**, 31–67.

Wiesel, T.N. and Hubel, D.H. (1965). Comparison of the effects of unilateral and bilateral eye closure on cortical unit responses in kittens. *Journal of Neurophysiology*, **28**, 1029–1040.

CHAPTER 6

ADAPTIVE PATTERN CLASSIFICATION AND UNIVERSAL RECODING, I: PARALLEL DEVELOPMENT AND CODING OF NEURAL FEATURE DETECTORS

by

Stephen Grossberg

Preface

This 1976 article responded to Malsburg's 1973 article (Chapter 5), which in turn responded to the 1972 instar model (Chapter 4). The article was one of a series of three articles published in *Biological Cybernetics* in 1976 that developed the competitive learning, or self-organizing feature map, model.

The first article (Grossberg, 1976) described the competitive learning model's main concepts and mechanisms, and showed that they were strikingly similar to concepts that had been recently described in the field of morphogenesis. The goal of this comparison was to suggest that the mechanisms for neural self-organization were formally homologous to mechanisms used by non-neural developing tissues. This comparison suggested that both types of self-organization are manifestations of a universal developmental code. The Grossberg (1976) article also noted that models in the non-neural morphogenetic literature had been described using a chemical kinetics formalism that did not incorporate important properties of *cellular* mechanisms. It was suggested that cellular mechanisms, in particular shunting mechanisms, compute important developmental properties, and that some difficulties faced by the kinetic models could be overcome by using them. This morphogenetic analysis was extended in subsequent articles to discuss processes such as gastrulation, formation of Hydra's heads, slime mold aggregation, cell streaming and adhesion, and competitive flow-counterflow currents for the control of intracellular learning without saturation (Grossberg, 1978a, 1980). It was shown that all of these processes could be discussed using cellular network laws that are homologous to neural laws governing short term memory and long term memory dynamics. The third 1976 article in this *Biological Cybernetics* series introduced Adaptive Resonance Theory, and is Chapter 9 of this book.

The second 1976 article is the present one. It continued to carry out the program of universal recoding that was begun in 1970. As noted in its Abstract, it showed how "any set of arbitrary spatial patterns can be recoded, or transformed, into any other spatial patterns (universal recoding), if there are sufficiently many cells in the network's cortex." The present version of universal recoding replaced the 1972 adaptive instar model by a new competitive learning model which, unlike Malsburg's 1973 model, was defined by local mechanisms operating in real time.

Such a competitive learning model was based upon a synthesis of previous mathematical results concerning non-Hebbian associative learning and the dynamics of shunting on-center off-surround feedback networks. The gated steepest descent associative learning law (see equation 13 in Chapter 1 and equation 11 in Chapter 2) had been analysed in a series of theorems in the late 1960's and early 1970's; for example, in Grossberg (1969). The normalization properties of shunting on-center off-surround feedforward networks were known since 1970 (see Chapter 2, Section 13, and Chapter 3). The normalization, contrast-enhancement, and CAM properties of shunting on-center off-surround feedback networks were being discovered as Malsburg did his work (see Chapter 2, Section 15, and Grossberg, 1973).

In the 1976 article, a canonical ordering of operations for self-organizing feature maps is prescribed (see Figure 1) at and between the model's two levels F_1 and F_2 (then called V_1 and V_2): normalization of the input pattern at level F_1 of the network; adaptive filtering of the normalized pattern in $F_1 \rightarrow F_2$ pathways; contrast-enhancement at level F_2 of the spatially distributed input pattern from the $F_1 \rightarrow F_2$ pathways; associative learning at only those adaptive weights which abut the winning F_2 nodes; time-averaged tracking by these winning weights of the F_1 signals that are carried by their $F_1 \rightarrow F_2$ pathway. These rules have been used in essentially all subsequent competitive learning and self-organizing feature map models.

The article also notes that these competitive learning rules use two successive inhibitory levels whose functional role is formally analogous to the inhibitory levels in the retinal model of Chapter 3. The goal of such comparisons was to discover the broadest possible set of relevant constraints to guide what to compute, and how to compute it.

The article proves two simple, but basic, theorems that characterize the main properties of competitive learning. In order to do this, it selected the simplest example that possesses useful coding properties; namely, the "choice," "winner-take-all," or "maximal compression" case in which level F_2 chooses for storage in STM that node which receives the largest total input from F_1. This is the important limiting case of *categorical perception*; namely, all the input vectors that cause a particular F_2 node to fire are members of the same category, and the set of all inputs is partitioned into disjoint and exhaustive categories that are surrounded by categorical boundaries. The winner-take-all case also has the nice property, noted in Grossberg (1978b, Section 19; reprinted in Grossberg, 1982, Chapter 12) of computing a Bayesian estimator. The theorems show that if the number of input pattern received by level F_1 is not too great relative to the number of classifying nodes in F_2, or if there are not too many input clusters relative to the number of classifying nodes in F_2, then a temporally stable recognition code is learned such that the adaptive weights self-normalize, and their time-averaged values compute the best values consistent with the statistical distribution of their category's exemplars. A simple consequence of this result is that equiprobable input clusters tend to create recognition categories of equal size. These properties have played an important role in the competitive learning applications of Kohonen (1984), including his phonetic typewriter application in Chapter 7.

One way to guarantee that there are not too many input clusters compared with the number of categorical F_2 nodes is to assume that there exists a very large number of F_2 nodes. Otherwise expressed, let F_2 establish a "sparse code" of the input stream. Such an approach has been followed by Kanerva (1988).

In addition to the winner-take-all networks, networks that only partially contrast-enhance their input patterns are described in the article. These partially contrast-enhanced activity patterns are called "bubbles" by Kohonen in Chapter 7. In the 1976 model, these bubbles are self-sharpening during learning due to the interaction of the learning process at the $F_1 \rightarrow F_2$ adaptive weights with the contrast-enhancing property of the shunting feedback network at level F_2. A third type of network is also described in the article. This network combines winner-take-all competition with activity-dependent habituation of the selected F_2 nodes. It is similar to the model described by Bienenstock, Cooper, and Munro (1982) and instantiates a kind of "conscience" into the choice procedure as described by Hecht-Nielsen in Chapter 8.

The type of input normalization described herein uses an L_1 norm; that is $\|\mathbf{a}\|_1 = \sum_{i=1}^{n} |a_i|$, given any vector $\mathbf{a} = (a_1, a_2, \ldots, a_n)$. The L_1 norm was used because it is the type of norm computed by a shunting on-center off-surround feedforward network without any preprocessing of the input. In Grossberg (1978b, Section 58), the effects of using an arbitrary L_p norm $\|\mathbf{a}\|_p = (\sum_i |a_i|^p)^{1/p}$ was discussed, including the L_2 norm which processes the dot products $S_j = \theta \cdot z^{(j)}$ of the adaptive filter without bias due to vector lengths. The L_2 norm has often been used in subsequent competitive learning applications (see Chapter 7). It is also used in the ART 2 model (Chapter 12), although the L_1 norm is used in the ART 1 model (Chapter 10).

Theorem 2 in this chapter shows how a temporally stable code can be learned in the sparse coding case. Since sparse coding can be guaranteed, given any fixed set of inputs, by choosing enough F_2 nodes, this result provided a way to explicitly construct three-level instar-outstar maps capable of mapping (arbitrarily fine) categories of vectors in $\Re^n$ into arbitrary vectors in $\Re^m$ (universal recoding).

However, even a very large, but fixed, number of nodes in F_2 will never be enough if an arbitrary number of inputs can perturb the network. The article's final result was to construct input sequences that lead to temporally unstable learning, and to articulate the problems that needed to be solved to overcome this instability problem. This analysis set the stage for the third article in the series (Chapter 9), in which Adaptive Resonance Theory was introduced to show how a stable recognition code could be learned in response to an arbitrary input stream, given any number of nodes in F_2.

References

Bienenstock, E.L., Cooper, L.N., and Munro, P.W. (1982). Theory for the development of neuron selectivity: Orientation specification and binocular interaction in visual cortex. *Journal of Neuroscience*, **2**, 32–48.

Grossberg, S. (1969). On learning and energy-entropy dependence in recurrent and nonrecurrent signed networks. *Journal of Statistical Physics*, **1**, 319–350.

Grossberg, S. (1973). Contour enhancement, short-term memory, and constancies in reverberating neural networks. *Studies in Applied Mathematics*, **52**, 217–257.

Grossberg, S. (1976). On the development of feature detectors in the visual cortex with applications to learning and reaction-diffusion systems. *Biological Cybernetics*, **21**, 145–159.

Grossberg, S. (1978a). Communication, memory, and development. In R. Rosen and F. Snell (Eds.), **Progress in theoretical biology, Volume 5**. New York: Academic Press.

Grossberg, S. (1978b). A theory of human memory: Self-organization and performance of sensory-motor codes, maps, and plans. In R. Rosen and F. Snell (Eds.), **Progress in theoretical biology, Volume 5**. New York: Academic Press.

Grossberg, S. (1980). Intracellular mechanisms of adaptation and self-regulation in self-organizing networks; The role of chemical transducers. *Bulletin of Mathematical Biology*, **3**, 365–396.

Grossberg, S. (1982). **Studies of mind and brain: Neural principles of learning, perception, development, cognition, and motor control**. Boston: Reidel Press.

Kanerva, P. (1988). **Sparse distributed memory**. Cambridge, MA: MIT Press.

Kohonen, T. (1984). **Self-organization and associative memory**. New York: Springer-Verlag.

Biological Cybernetics
1976, **23**, 121–134
©1976 Springer-Verlag, Inc.

ADAPTIVE PATTERN CLASSIFICATION
AND UNIVERSAL RECODING, I:
PARALLEL DEVELOPMENT AND CODING
OF NEURAL FEATURE DETECTORS

Stephen Grossberg†

Abstract

This paper analyses a model for the parallel development and adult coding of neural feature detectors. The model was introduced in Grossberg (1976). We show how experience can retune feature detectors to respond to a prescribed convex set of spatial patterns. In particular, the detectors automatically respond to average features chosen from the set even if the average features have never been experienced. Using this procedure, any set of arbitrary spatial patterns can be recoded, or transformed, into any other spatial patterns (universal recoding), if there are sufficiently many cells in the network's cortex. The network is built from short term memory (STM) and long term memory (LTM) mechanisms, including mechanisms of adaptation, filtering, contrast enhancement, tuning, and nonspecific arousal. These mechanisms capture some experimental properties of plasticity in the kitten visual cortex. The model also suggests a classification of adult feature detector properties in terms of a small number of functional principles. In particular, experiments on retinal dynamics, including amacrine cell function, are suggested.

---

† Supported in part by the Advanced Research Projects Agency under ONR contract N00014-76-C-0185.

1. Introduction

This paper analyses a model for the development of neural feature detectors during an animal's early experience with its environment. The model also suggests mechanisms of adult pattern discrimination that remain after development has been completed. The model evolved from earlier experimental and theoretical work. Various data showed that there is a critical period during which experimental manipulations can alter the patterns to which feature detectors in the visual cortex are tuned (e. g., Barlow and Pettigrew, 1971; Blakemore and Cooper, 1970; Blakemore and Mitchell, 1973; Hirsch and Spinelli, 1970, 1971; Hubel and Wiesel, 1970; Wiesel and Hubel, 1963, 1965). This work led von der Malsburg (1973) and Pérez et al. (1974) to construct models of the cortical tuning process, which they analysed using computer methods. Their models are strikingly similar. Both use a mechanism of long term memory (LTM) to encode changes in tuning. This mechanism learns by classical, or Pavlovian, conditioning (Kimble, 1967) within a neural network. Such a concept was qualitatively described by Hebb (1949) and was rigorously analysed in its present form by Grossberg (e. g., 1967, 1970a, 1971, 1974). The LTM mechanism in a given interneuronal pathway is a plastic synaptic strength which has two crucial properties: (a) it is computed from a time average of the product of presynaptic signals and postsynaptic potentials; (b) it multiplicatively gates, or shunts, a presynaptic signal before it can perturb the postsynaptic cell.

Given this LTM mechanism, both models invoke various devices to regulate the retinocortical signals that drive the tuning process. On-center off-surround networks undergoing additive interactions, attenuation of small retinocortical signals at the cortex, and conservation of the total synaptic strength impinging on each cortical cell are used in both models. Grossberg (1976) realized that all of these mechanisms for distributing signals could be replaced by a minimal model for parallel processing of patterns in noise, which is realized by an on-center off-surround recurrent network whose interactions are of shunting type (Grossberg, 1973). Three crucial properties of this model are: (a) normalization, or adaptation, of total network activity; (b) contrast enhancement of input paterns; and (c) short term memory (STM) storage of the contrast-enhanced pattern. Using these properties, Grossberg (1976) eliminates the conservation of total synaptic strength—which is incompatible with classical conditioning—and shows that the tuning process can be derived from *adult* STM and LTM principles. The model is schematized in Figure 1. It describes the interaction via plastic synaptic pathways of two network regions, V_1 and V_2, that are separately capable of normalizaing patterns, but V_2 can also contrast enhance patterns and store them in STM. In the original models of von der Malsburg and Pérez et al., V_1 was interpreted as a "retina" or "thalamus" and V_2 as "visual cortex." In Part II, an analogous anatomy for V_1 as "olfactory bulb" and V_2 as "prepyriform cortex" will be noted. In Section 5, a more microscopic analysis of the model leads to a discussion of V_1 as a composite of retinal receptors, horizontal cells, and bipolar cells, and of V_2 as a composite of amacrine cells and ganglion cells. Such varied interpretations are possible because the same functional principles seem to operate in various anatomies.

Using this abstract structure, it was suggested in Grossberg (1976) how hierarchies of cells capable of discriminating arbitrary spatial patterns can be synthesized. Also a striking analogy was described between the structure and properties of certain reaction-diffusion systems that have been used to model development (Gierer

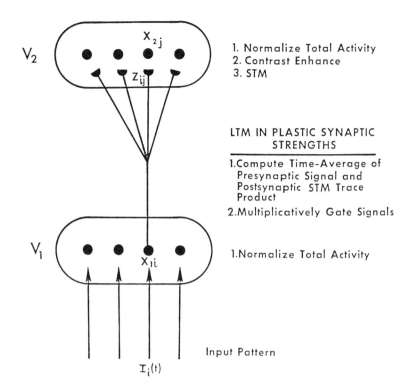

Figure 1. Minimal model of developmental tuning using STM and LTM mechanisms.

and Meinhardt, 1972; Meinhardt and Gierer, 1974) and of reverberating shunting networks. This paper continues this program by rigorously analysing mathematical properties of the model, which thereupon suggest other developmental and adult STM and LTM mechanisms that are related to it. The following sections will describe these connections with a minimum of mathematical detail. Mathematical proofs are contained in the Appendix.

2. The Tuning Process

This section reviews properties of the model that will be needed below. Suppose that V_1 consists of n states (or cells, or cell populations) $v_{1i}, i = 1, 2, \ldots, n$, which receive inputs $I_i(t)$ whose intensity depends on the presence of a prescribed feature, or features, in an external pattern. Let the population response (or activity, or average potential) of v_{i1} be $x_{1i}(t)$. The relative input intensity $\theta_i = I_i I^{-1}$, where $I = \sum_{k=1}^{n} I_k$, measures the relative importance of the feature coded by v_i in any given input pattern. If the θ_i's are constant during a given time interval, the inputs are said to form a *spatial pattern*. How can the laws governing the $x_{1i}(t)$ be determined so that $x_{1i}(t)$ is capable of accurately registering θ_i? Grossberg (1973) showed that a bounded, linear law for x_{1i}, in which x_{1i} returns to equilibrium after inputs cease, and in which neither input pathways nor populations v_{1i} interact, does not suffice; cf., Grossberg and Levine (1975) for a review. The problem is that as the total input I increases, given *fixed* θ_i values, each x_{1i} saturates at its maximial value. This does not happen if off-surround interactions also occur. For example, let the inputs I_i

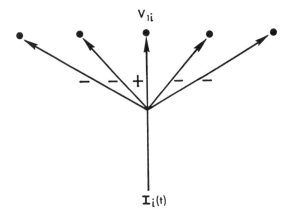

Figure 2. Nonrecurrent, or feedforward, on-center off-surround network.

be distributed via a nonrecurrent, or feedforward, on-center off-surround anatomy undergoing shunting (or mass action, or passive membrane) interactions, as in Figure 2. Then

$$\dot{x}_{1i} = -Ax_{1i} + (B - x_{1i})I_i - x_{1i}\sum_{k\neq i} I_k \tag{1}$$

with $0 \leq x_{1i}(0) \leq B$. At equilibrium (namely, $\dot{x}_{1i} = 0$),

$$x_{1i} = \theta_i \frac{BI}{A+I}, \tag{2}$$

which is proportional to θ_i no matter how large I becomes. Since also $BI(A+I)^{-1} \leq B$, the total activity $x_1 \equiv \sum_{k=1}^{n} x_{1k}$ never exceeds B; it is normalized, or adapts, due to automatic gain control by the inhibitory inputs. The normalization property in (2) shows that x_{1i} codes θ_i rather than instantaneous fluctuations in I.

To store patterns in STM, recurrent or feedback pathways are needed to keep signals active after the inputs cease. Again the problem of saturation must be dealt with, so that some type of recurrent on-center off-surround anatomy is suggested. The minimal solution is to let V_2 be governed by a system of the form

$$\dot{x}_{2j} = -Ax_{2j} + (B - x_{2j})[f(x_{2j}) + I_{2j}] - x_{2j}\sum_{k\neq j} f(x_{2k}), \tag{3}$$

where $f(w)$ is the average feedback signal produced by an average activity level w, and I_{2j} is the total excitatory input to v_{2j} (Figure 3a). In particular, v_{2j} excites itself via the term $(B - x_{2j})f(x_{2j})$, and v_{2k} inhibits v_{2j} via the term $-x_{2j}f(x_{2k})$, for every $k \neq j$. The choice of $f(w)$ dramatically influences how recurrent interactions within V_2 transform the input pattern $I^{(2)} = (I_{21}, I_{22}, \ldots, I_{2N})$ through time. Grossberg (1973) shows that a sigmoid, or S-shaped, $f(w)$ can reverberate important inputs in STM after contrast-enhancing them, yet can also suppress noise.

Various generalizations of recurrent networks have been studied, such as

$$\dot{x}_{2j} = -Ax_{2j} + (B - x_{2j})[\sum_{k=1}^{N} f(x_{2k})C_{kj} + I_{2j}]$$

$$-(x_{2j} + D)\sum_{k=1}^{N} f(x_{2k})E_{kj}, \tag{4}$$

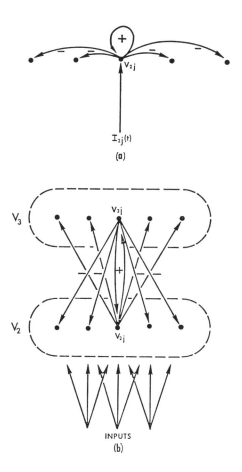

Figure 3. Some recurrent, or feedback, on-center off-surround networks.

$D \geq 0$, where the excitatory coefficients C_{kj} ("on-center") decrease with the distance between populations v_{2k} and v_{2j} more rapidly than do the inhibitory coefficients E_{kj} ("off-surround"). Levine and Grossberg (1976) show that, in such cases, the inhibitory off-surround signals $\sum_{k=1}^{N} f(x_{2k})E_{kj}$ to v_{2j} can be chosen strong enough to offset the saturating effects of inputs I_{2j} plus excitatory on-center signals $\sum_{k=1}^{N} f(x_{2k})C_{kj}$. Elias and Grossberg (1975) study generalizations of (4) in which inhibitory interneurons interact with their excitatory counterparts.

Below we will consider networks in which the excitatory signals I_{2j} to V_2 are sums of signals from many populations in V_1. Moreover, the synaptic strengths of these signals can be trained. This fact suggests another reason for making V_2 recurrent. A recurrent anatomy is needed within V_2 to prevent saturation in response to trainable signals. To see this, note in the nonrecurrent network (1) that each excitatory input to v_{1i} is replicated as an inhibitory input to all $v_{1k}, k \neq i$. The size of a trainable signal to v_{2j} depends on the activity of v_{2j}. This signal therefore cannot be replicated at populations $v_{2k}, k \neq j$, unless recurrent interactions within V_2 exist. Moreover, whether or not signals are trainable, whenever I_{2j} is a sum of signals from many populations, recurrent signals within V_2 prevent saturation at a large saving of extra signal pathways to the populations $v_{2k}, k \neq j$.

A related scheme for marrying sums of (trainable) signals with pattern normalization is illustrated in Figure 3b. Here a sum of signals I_{2j} from V_1 perturbs each v_{2j}. Population v_{2j} thereupon excites an on-center of cells near v_{3j}, and inhibits a broad off-surround of populations centered at v_{3j}. Thus, when a pattern $I^{(2)}$ arrives at V_2, it is normalized at V_3 before saturation can take place across V_2. Then feedback signals from V_3 to V_2 prevent saturation at V_2 from setting in as follows. Each population v_{3j} that receives a large net excitatory signal from V_2 excites its on-center of cells near v_{2j}, and inhibits a broad off-surround of populations centered at v_{2j}. This feedback inhibition prevents the pattern $I^{(2)}$ from saturating V_2, much as recurrent inhibition in equation (4) works. Figure 3b can also be expanded to explicitly include inhibitory interneurons, as in Ellias and Grossberg (1975).

Normalization in V_1 by (1) occurs gradually in time, as each x_{1i} adjusts to its new equilibrium value, but it will be assumed below to occur instantaneously with x_{1i} approaching θ_i rather than $\theta_i BI(A + I)^{-1}$. These simplifications yield theorems about the tuning process that avoid unimportant details. The assumption that normalization occurs instantaneously is tenable because the normalized pattern at V_1 drives slow changes in the strength of connections from V_1 to V_2. Instantaneous normalization means that the pattern at V_1 normalizes itself before the connection strengths have a chance to substantially change.

Let the synaptic strength of the pathways from v_{1i} to the jth population v_{2j} in V_2 be denoted by $z_{ij}(t)$ (see Figure 1). Let the total signal to v_{2j} due to the normalized pattern $\theta = (\theta_1, \theta_2, \ldots, \theta_n)$ at V_1 and the vector $z^{(j)}(t) = (z_{1j}(t), z_{2j}(t), \ldots, z_{nj}(t))$ of synaptic strengths be

$$S_j(t) \equiv \theta \cdot z^{(j)}(t) \equiv \sum_{k=1}^{n} \theta_k z_{kj}(t); \tag{5}$$

that is, each $z_{kj}(t)$ *gates* the signal θ_k from the v_{1k} on its way to v_{2j}, and these gated signals combine additively at v_{2j} (cf., Grossberg, 1967, 1970a, 1971, 1974). Since $z^{(j)}(t)$ determines the size of the input to v_{2j}, given any pattern θ, it is called the *classifying vector* of v_{2j} at time t. Every v_{2j}, $j = 1, 2, \ldots, N$, in V_2 receives such a signal when θ is active at V_1. In this way, θ creates a pattern of activity across V_2.

Given any activity pattern across V_2, it can be transformed in several ways as time goes on. Two main questions about this process are: (a) will the *total* activity of V_2 be suppressed, or will some of its activities be stored in STM? and (b) which of the *relative* activities across V_2 will be preserved, suppressed, or enhanced? Several papers (Ellias and Grossberg, 1975; Grossberg, 1973; Grossberg and Levine, 1975) analyse how the parameters of a reverberating shunting on-center off-surround network determine the answers to these questions. Below some of these facts are cited as they are needed. In particular, if all the activities are sufficiently small, then they will not be stored in STM. If they are sufficiently large, then they will be contrast enhanced, normalized, and stored in STM. Figure 4 schematizes two storage possibilities. Figure 4a depicts a pattern of activity across V_2 before it is transformed by V_2. Given suitable parameters, if some of the initial activities exceed a quenching threshold (QT), then V_2 will *choose* the population having maximal initial activity for storage in STM, as in Figure 4b. Under other circumstances, all initial activities below the QT are suppressed, whereas *all* initial activities above the QT are con-

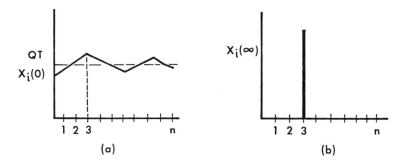

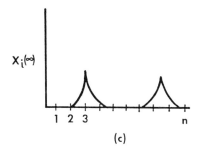

Figure 4. Contrast enhancement and STM by recurrent network: (a) initial pattern; (b) choice; (c) partial contrast.

trast enhanced, normalized, and stored in STM (Figure 4c); that is, *partial* contrast in STM is possible. Grossberg (1973) shows that partial contrast can occur if the signals between populations in a recurrent shunting on-center off-surround network are sigmoid (S-shaped) functions of their activity levels. Ellias and Grossberg (1975) show that partial contrast can occur if the self-excitatory signals of populations in V_2 are stronger than their self-inhibitory signals, and moreover if the excitatory signals between populations in V_2 decrease with inter-population distance faster than the inhibitory signals.

The enhancement and STM storage processes also occur much faster than the slow changes in connection strengths z_{ij}; hence, it is assumed below that these processes occur instantaneously in order to focus on the slow changes in z_{ij}.

The slow changes in z_{ij} are assumed to be determined by a time averaged product of the signal from v_{1i} to v_{2j} with the cortical response at v_{2j}; thus,

$$\dot{z}_{ij} = -C_{ij}z_{ij} + D_{ij}x_{2j},$$

where C_{ij} is the decay rate (possibly variable) of z_{ij}, and D_{ij} is the signal from v_{1i} to v_{2j}. For example, if $C_{ij} = 1$, the V_1 and V_2 patterns are normalized, and V_2 chooses only the population v_{2j} whose initial activity is maximal for storage in STM (Figure

4b), then while v_{2j} is active,

$$\dot{z}_{ij} = -z_{ij} + \theta_i, \quad \text{for all } i = 1, 2, \ldots, n.$$

It remains to determine how these z_{ij} and all other $z_{ik}, k \neq j$, change under other circumstances. To eliminate conceptual and mathematical difficulties that arise if z_{ij} can decay even when V_1 and V_2 are inactive, we let *all* changes in each z_{ij} be determined by which populations in V_2 have their activities chosen for storage in STM. In other words, all changes in z_{ij} are driven by *feedback* within the excitatory recurrent loops of V_2 that establish STM storage. Then

$$\dot{z}_{ij} = (-z_{ij} + \theta_i)x_{2j} \tag{6}$$

where $\sum_{k=1}^{N} x_{2k}(t) = 1$ if STM in V_2 is active at time t, whereas $\sum_{k=1}^{N} x_{2k}(t) = 0$ if STM in V_2 is inactive at time t.

If V_2 *chooses* a population for storage in STM, as in Figure 4b, then

$$x_{2j} = \begin{cases} 1 & \text{if } S_j > \max\{\epsilon, S_k : k \neq j\} \\ 0 & \text{if } S_j < \max\{\epsilon, S_k : k \neq j\}, \end{cases} \tag{7}$$

where, as in (5), $S_j = \theta \cdot z^{(j)}$ with $\theta_i = I_i(\sum_{k=1}^{n} I_k)^{-1}$. Equation (7) omits the cases where two or more signals S_j are equal, and are larger than all other signals and ϵ. In these cases, the x_{2j}'s of such S_j's are equal and add up to 1. Such a normalization rule for equal maximal signals will be tacitly assumed in all the cases below, but will otherwise be ignored to avoid tedious details. Equation (6) shows that z_{ij} can change only if $x_{2j} > 0$. Equation (7) shows that V_2 chooses the maximal activity for storage in STM. This activity is normalized ($x_{2j} = 0$ or 1), and it corresponds to the population with the largest initial signal ($S_j > \max\{S_k : k \neq j\}$). No changes in z_{ij} occur if all signals S_j are too small to be stored in STM (all $S_j \leq \epsilon$).

If partial contrast in STM holds, as in Figure 4c, then the dynamics of a reverberating shunting network can be approximated by a rule of the form

$$x_{2j} = \begin{cases} f(S_j)[\sum_{S_k > \epsilon} f(S_k)]^{-1} & \text{if } S_j > \epsilon \\ 0 & \text{if } S_j < \epsilon \end{cases} \tag{8}$$

where $f(w)$ is an increasing nonnegative function of w such that $w = 0$; e. g., $f(w) = w^2$. In (8), the positive constant ϵ represents the QT; the function $f(w)$ controls how suprathreshold signals S_j will be contrast enhanced; and the ratio of $f(S_j)$ to $\sum\{f(S_k) : S_k > \epsilon\}$ expresses the normalization of STM.

3. Ritualistic Pattern Classification

After developmental tuning has taken place, the above mechanisms describe a model of pattern classification in the "adult" network. These mechanisms will be described first as interesting in themselves, and as a helpful prelude to understanding the tuning process. They are capable of classifying arbitrarily complicated spatial patterns into mutually nonoverlapping, or partially overlapping, sets depending on whether (7) or (8) holds. These mechanisms realize basic principles of pattern discrimination using shunting interactions. An alternative scheme of pattern discrimination using a mixture of shunting and additive mechanisms has already been given

(Grossberg, 1970b, 1972). Together these schemes suggest numerous anatomical and physiological variations that embody the same small class of functional principles. Since particular anatomies imply that particular physiological rules should be operative, intriguing questions about the dynamics of various neural structures, such as retina, neocortex, hippocampus, and cerebellum, are suggested.

First consider what happens if V_2 chooses a population for storage in STM. After learning ceases (that is, $\dot{z}_{ij} \equiv 0$), all classifying vectors $z^{(j)}$ are constant in time, and equations (6) and (7) reduce to the statement that population v_{2j} is stored in STM if

$$S_j > \max\{\epsilon, S_k : k \neq j\}. \tag{9}$$

In other words, v_{2j} *codes* all patterns θ such that (9) holds; alternatively stated, v_{2j} is a *feature detector* in the sense that all patterns

$$P_j = \{\theta : \theta \cdot z^{(j)} > \max(\epsilon, \theta \cdot z^{(k)} : k \neq j)\} \tag{10}$$

are classified by v_{2j}. The set P_j defines a *convex cone* C_j in the space of nonnegative input vectors $J = (I_1, I_2, \ldots, I_n)$, since if two such vectors $J^{(1)}$ and $J^{(2)}$ are in C_j, then so are all the vectors $\alpha J^{(1)}$, $\beta J^{(2)}$, and $\gamma J^{(1)} + (1 - \gamma)J^{(2)}$, where $\alpha > 0$, $\beta > 0$, and $0 < \gamma < 1$. The convex cone C_j defines the *feature* coded by v_{2j}.

The classification rule in (10) has an informative geometrical interpretation in n-dimensional Euclidean space. The signal $S_j = \theta \cdot z^{(j)}$ is the inner product of θ and $z^{(j)}$ (Greenspan and Benney, 1973). Letting $\|\xi\| = \sqrt{\sum_{k=1}^n \xi_k^2}$ denote the Euclidean length of any real vector $\xi = (\xi_1, \xi_2, \ldots, \xi_n)$, and $\cos(\eta, \omega)$ denote the cosine between two vectors η and ω, it is elementary that

$$S_j = \|\theta\| \, \|z^{(j)}\| \cos(\theta, z^{(j)}).$$

In other words, the signal S_j is the length of the projection of the normalized pattern θ on the classifying vector $z^{(j)}$ times the length of $z^{(j)}$. Thus if all $z^{(j)}, j = 1, 2, \ldots, N$, have equal length, then among all patterns with the same length, (10) classifies all patterns θ in P_j whose angle with $z^{(j)}$ is smaller than the angles between θ and any $z^{(k)}, k \neq j$, is small enough to satisfy the ϵ-condition. In particular, patterns θ that are *parallel* to $z^{(j)}$ are classified in P_j. The choice of classifying vectors $z^{(j)}$ hereby determines how the patterns θ will be divided up. Section 8 will show that the tuning mechanism (6)–(7) makes the $z^{(j)}$ vectors more parallel to prescribed patterns θ, and thereupon changes the classifying sets P_j. In summary:

(i) the number of populations in V_2 determines the maximum number N of pattern classes P_j;

(ii) the choice of classifying vectors $z^{(j)}$ determines how different these classes can be; for example, choosing all vectors $z^{(j)}$ equal will generate one class that is redundantly represented by all v_{2j}; and

(iii) the size of ϵ determines how similar patterns must be to be classified by the same v_{2J}.

If the choice rule (7) is replaced by the partial contrast rule (8), then an important new possibility occurs, which can be described either by studying STM responses to all θ at fixed v_{2J}, or to a fixed θ at all v_{2j}. In the former case, each v_{2j} has a *tuning curve*, or *generalization gradient*; namely, a maximal response to certain patterns, and submaximal responses to other patterns. In the latter case, each pattern θ is *filtered* by V_2 in a way that shows how close θ lies to *each* of the classifying vectors $z^{(j)}$. The pattern will only be classified by v_{2j}—that is, stored in STM—if it lies sufficiently close to $z^{(j)}$ for its signal S_j to exceed the quenching threshold of V_2.

For example, suppose that some of the classifying vectors $z^{(j)}$ are chosen to create large signals at V_2 when vertical lines perturb V_1 and that other $z^{(j)}$ create large signals at V_2 when horizontal lines perturb V_1. If a pattern containing both horizontal and vertical lines perturbs V_1, then the population activities in V_2 corresponding to both types of lines can be stored in STM, unless competition between their populations drives all activity below the QT. Now let V_3 be another "cortex" that receives signals from V_2, in the same fashion that V_2 receives signals from V_1. Given an appropriate choice of classifying vectors for V_3, there can exist cells in V_3 that fire in STM only if horizontal *and* vertical lines perturb a prescribed region of V_1; e. g., hypercomplex cells. The existence of tuning curved in a given cortex V_i hereby increases the discriminative capabilities of the next cortex V_{i+1} in a hierarchy; cf., Grossberg (1976).

The above mechanisms will now be discussed as cases of a general scheme of pattern classification. This is done with two goals in mind: firstly, to emphasize that these mechanisms might well exist in other than "retinocortical" analogs; and secondly, to generate explicit experimental directives in a variety of neural structures. One such directive will be described in Section 5.

4. Shunts versus Additive Interactions as Mechanisms of Pattern Classification

The processing stages utilized in Section 3 are the following:

(A) Normalization

Input patterns are normalized in V_1 by an on-center off-surround anatomy undergoing shunting interactions.

(B) Partial Filtering by Signals

The signals S_j generated by V_2 by a normalized pattern on V_1 create the data base on which later computations are determined. The signal generating rule (5), for example, has the following important property. Suppose that an input $I_i(t) = \theta_i I(t)$ is normalized to x_{1i}, as in (2), rather than to the approximate value θ_i. The signal from V_1 to v_{2j} becomes

$$\tilde{S}_j = BI(A+I)^{-1}S_j$$

and (9) is replaced by the analogous rule

$$\tilde{S}_j > \max\{\epsilon, \tilde{S}_k : k \neq j\}.$$

Then V_2 will classify a given pattern into the same class P_j no matter how large I is chosen. In other words, the signal generating rule is invariant under suprathreshold variations of the total activity at V_1. If I_i is the transduced receptor response to an external input J_i—that is, $I_i = g(J_i)$—then the signal-generating rule is invariant, given *any* $z^{(j)}$'s, if $g(w) = w^p$ for some $p > 0$.

(C) Contrast Enhancement of Signals

The signals S_j are contrast enhanced by the recurrent on-center off-surround anatomy within V_2, and either a choice (Figure 4b) or a tuning curve (Figure 4c) results.

Two successive stages of lateral inhibition are needed in this model. The first stage normalizes input patterns. The second stage sharpens the filtering of signals.

Additive mechanisms can also achieve classification of arbitrarily complicated spatial patterns. These mechanisms also employ three successive stages (A)–(C) of pattern processing, with stage (A) normalizing input patterns, stages (A) and (C) using inhibitory interactions, and stage (C) completing the pattern classification that is begun by the signal generating rules of stage (B). The additive model can differ in several respects from the shunting model:

(i) its anatomy can be feedforward; that is, there need not be a recurrent network in stage (C);

(ii) threshold rules replace the inner product signal-generating rule (5) to determine partial filtering of signals; and

(iii) the responses in time of stages (A)–(C) to a sustained pattern at V_1 are not the same in the additive model. For example, sustained responses in the shunting model can be replaced by responses to the onset and offset of the pattern in the additive model (Grossberg, 1970b).

Mixtures of additive and shunting mechanisms are also possible. The additive mechanisms will now be summarized to illustrate the basic stages (A)–(C).

An additive nonspecific inhibitory interneuron normalizes patterns at V_1 (Figure 5). Many variations on this theme exist (Grossberg, 1970b) in which such parameters as the lateral spread of inhibition, the number of cell layers, and the rates of excitatory and inhibitory decay can be varied. The idea in its simplest form is this. The excitatory input I_i excites a bifurcating pathway. One branch of the pathway is specific, and the other branch is nonspecific. The lateral inhibitory interneuron $v_{1,n+1}$ lies in the nonspecific branch. It sums the excitatory inputs I_i, and generates a nonspecific signal back to all the specific pathways if a signal threshold Γ is exceeded. Each input I_i also generates a specific signal from v_{1i} that is a linear function of I_i above a signal threshold. Each pathway from v_{1i} in V_1 to v_{2j} in V_2 has its own signal threshold Γ_{ij}. The net signal from v_{1i} to v_{2j} is

$$K_{ij} = [I_i - \Gamma_{ij}]^+ - [\sum_{k=1}^{n} I_k - \Gamma]^+,$$

where the notation $[u]^+ = \max(u, 0)$ defines the threshold rule. Define $\theta_{ij} = \Gamma_{ij}\Gamma^{-1}$ and let the spatial pattern $I_i = \theta_i I$ perturb V_1. Then

$$K_{ij} = [\theta_i I - \theta_{ij}\Gamma]^+ - [I - \Gamma]^+. \tag{11}$$

The net signal K_{ij} has the following properties:

(i) $K_{ij} \le 0$ for all values of $I > 0$ if $\theta_i \le \theta_{ij}$;

(ii) $K_i > 0$ for $I > \theta_{ij}\theta_i^{-1}$ if $\theta_i > \theta_{ij}$; and

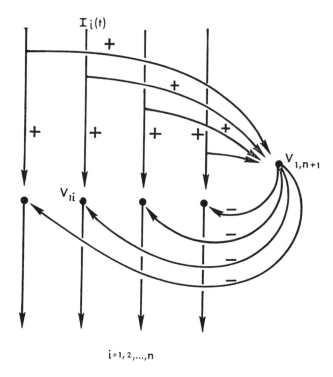

$$i = 1, 2, \ldots, n$$

Figure 5. Normalization and low-band filtering by subtractive nonspecific interneuron and signal threshold rules.

(iii) $K_{ij} \leq (\theta_i - \theta_{ij})\Gamma$ for all $I > 0$.

In other words, by (i), no signal is emitted from v_{1i} to v_{2j} if $\theta_i < \theta_{ij}$; by (ii) if $\theta_i > \theta_{ij}$, a signal is emitted from v_{1i} if I exceeds a threshold depending on θ_i and θ_{ij}; and by (iii), the total activity in the cells v_{1i} is normalized. Partial filtering of signals is thus achieved by the choice of threshold pattern $\theta^{(j)} = (\theta_{1j}, \theta_{2j}, \ldots, \theta_{nj})$ rather than by the choice of classifying vector $z^{(j)} = (z_{1j}, z_{2j}, \ldots, z_{nj})$.

Stage (C) is needed because the total signal to v_{2j} can be maximized by patterns θ which are very different from the threshold pattern $\theta^{(j)}$. This problem arises because the signals K_{ij} continue to grow linearly as a function of I after the threshold value $\theta_{ij}\theta_i^{-1}$ is exceeded. Grossberg (1970b) shows that the problem can be avoided by inhibiting each signal K_{ij} if it gets too large. For example, let the net signal from v_{1i} to v_{2j} be

$$S_{ij}^* = K_{ij} - \alpha[K_{ij} - \beta]^+, \tag{12}$$

where $\alpha > 1$ and $0 < \beta \ll 1$. This mechanism inhibits the signal from v_{1i} and v_{2j} if it represents a θ_i which is too much larger than θ_{ij}. Equation (12) can be realized by any of the several inhibitory mechanisms: a specific subtractive inhibitory interneuron (Figure 6a), a switchover from net excitation to net inhibition when the spiking frequency in the pathway from v_{1i} to v_{2j} becomes too large (Bennett, 1971; Blackenship *et al.*, 1971; Wachtel and Kandel, 1971), or postsynaptic blockade of the v_{2j} cell membrane at sufficiently high spiking frequences. Signal S_{ij}^* is positive

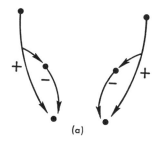

(a)

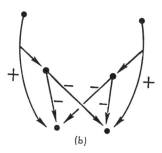

(b)

Figure 6. (a) Specific subtractive inhibitory interneurons; (b) Nonspecific inhibitory interneurons.

only if θ_i is sufficiently close to θ_{ij} in value. Stage (C) is completed by choosing the signal threshold of v_{2j} so high that v_{2j} only fires if *all* signals S_{ij}^*, $i = 1, 2, \ldots, n$, are positive; that is, only if the input pattern θ is close to the threshold pattern $\theta^{(j)}$. The second stage of inhibition hereby completes the partial filtering process by choosing a population v_{2j} in V_2 to code $\theta^{(j)}$, as in Figure 4b. If the specific inhibitory interneurons of Figure 6a are replaced by a lateral spread of inhibition, as in Figure 6b, then a tuning curve is generated, as in Figure 4c.

5. What Do Retinal Amacrine Cells Do?

This section illustrates how the principles (A)–(C) can generate interesting questions about particular neural processes. Grossberg (1970b, 1972) introduces a retinal model in which shunting and additive interactions both occur. In this model, retinal amacrine cells are examples of the inhibitory interaction in stage (C). We will note that amacrine cells have *opposite* effects on signals if they realize a shunting rather than an additive model. In the retinal model of Grossberg (1972), normalization is accomplished by an on-center off-surround anatomy undergoing shunting interactions. Analogously, *in vivo* receptors excite bipolar cells (on-center) as well as horizontal cells, and the horizontal cells inhibit bipolar cells via their lateral interactions (off-surorund). Partial filtering of the normalized inputs is accomplished by signal thresholds; for example, using the normalized x_{1i} activities in (2), the simplest signal function from v_{1i} to v_{2j} is $K_{ij} = [x_{1i} - \Gamma_{ij}]^+$. Stage (C) is then accomplished by a mechanism such as (12), by which large signals are inhibited. Whether a choice

(Figure 4b) or a tuning curve (Figure 4c) is generated depends, in part, on how broadly these lateral inhibitory signals that complete stage (C) are distributed. This second stage of inhibition is identified with the inhibition that amacrine cells, fed by bipolar cell activity, generate at ganglion cells. Grossberg (1972) notes data that support the idea that stage (C) is realized by an additive mechanism such as (12). In particular, amacrine cells often respond when an input pattern is turned on, or off, or both. Two questions about amacrine cells now suggest themselves.

(i) If this interpretation of amacrine cells is true, then they will shut off signals from the bipolar cells to the ganglion cells when these signals become too *large*; that is, they act as high-band filters. By contrast, inhibition in stage (C) of the shunting model shuts off signals if they become too *small*. Opposite effects due to the second inhibitory stage can hereby create a similar functional transformation of the input pattern. If a shunting role for amacrine cells is sought, then the following types of anatomy would be anticipated: inhibitory bipolar-to-amacrine-to-bipolar cell feedback that contrast enhances the receptor-to-bipolar signals, or inhibitory ganglion-to-amacrine-to-ganglion cell feedback that contrast enhances the bipolar-to-ganglion cell signals, or some functionally similar feedback loop. To decide between these two possible roles for amacrine cells, one must test whether amacrine cells suppress large signals or small ones; in either case, if the model is applicable, contrast enhancement of the normalized and filtered retinal pattern is the result, so that this property cannot be used as a criterion.

(ii) Does the spatial extent of lateral amacrine interaction determine the amount of contrast, or the breadth of the tuning curves, in ganglion cell responses, as in Figures 4b or 4c? For example, there exist narrow field diffuse amacrine cells, wide field diffuse amacrine cells, stratified diffuse amacrine cells, and unstratified amacrine cells (Boycott and Dowling, 1969). Do these specializations guarantee particular tuning characteristics in the corresponding ganglion cells?

Grossberg (1972) also suggests a cerebellar analog based on the same principles. Thus at least formal aspects of various neural structures seem to be emerging as manifestations of common principles. These results suggest a program of classifying seemingly different anatomical and physiological data according to whether they realize similar functional transformations of patterned neural activity, such as total activity normalization, partial filtering by signals, and contrast enhancement of the signal pattern. Below are described certain properties of the shunting mechanism that will be needed when development is discussed.

6. Arousal as a Tuning Mechanism

The recurrent networks in V_2 all have a quenching threshold (QT); namely, a criterion activity level that must be exceeded before a population's activity can reverberate in STM. Changing the QT or, equivalently, changing the size of signals to V_2, can retune the responsiveness of populations in V_2 to prescribed patterns at V_1. For example, suppose that an unexpected, or novel, event triggers a nonspecific arousal input to V_2, which magnifies all the signals from V_1 to V_2 (see Part II). Then certain signals, which could not otherwise be stored in STM, will exceed the QT and be stored. For example, if V_2 is capable of partial contrast in STM and also receives a nonspecific arousal input, then (8) can be replaced by

$$x_{2j} = \begin{cases} f(\phi S_j)[\sum_{\phi S_k > \epsilon} f(\phi S_k)]^{-1} & \text{if } \phi S_j > \epsilon \\ 0 & \text{if } \phi S_j < \epsilon \end{cases} \tag{13}$$

where ϕ is an increasing function of the arousal level. Note that an increase in ϕ allows more V_2 populations to reverberate in STM; cf., Grossberg (1973) for mathematical proofs. In a similar fashion, if an unexpected event triggers nonspecific shunting inhibition of the inhibitory interneurons in the off-surrounds of V_2, then the QT will decrease (Grossberg, 1973; Ellias and Grossberg, 1975), yielding an equivalent effect. Equation (8) can then be changed to

$$x_{2j} = \begin{cases} f(S_j)[\sum_{S_k > \phi^* \epsilon} f(S_k)]^{-1} & \text{if } S_j > \phi^* \epsilon \\ 0 & \text{if } S_j < \phi^* \epsilon \end{cases} \tag{14}$$

where ϕ^* is a decreasing function of the arousal level.

Reductions in arousal level have the opposite effect. For example, if (13) holds, and arousal is lowered until only one population in V_2 exceeds the QT, then a choice will be made in STM, as in Figure 4b. Thus a choice in STM can be due either to *structural* properties of the network, such as the rules for generating signals between populations in V_2 [cf., the faster-than-linear signal function in Grossberg (1973)], or to an arousal level that is not high enough to create a tuning curve. Similarly, if arousal is too small, then all functions x_{2j} in (13) will always equal zero, and no STM storage will occur.

Changes in arousal can have a profound influence on the time course of LTM, as in (6), because they change the STM patterns that drive the learning process. For example, if during development arousal level is chosen to produce a choice in STM, then the tuning of classifying vectors $z^{(j)}$ will be sharper than if the arousal level were chosen to generate partial contrast in STM.

The influence of arousal on tuning of STM patterns can also be expressed in another way, which suggests a mechanism that will be needed in Part II when universal recoding is discussed.

7. Arousal as a Search Mechanism

Suppose that arousal level is fixed during learning trials, and that a given pattern θ at V_1 does not create any STM storage at V_2 because all the inner products $\theta \cdot z^{(j)}$ are too small. If arousal level is then increased in (13) until some $x_{2j} > 0$, STM storage will occur. In other words, changing the arousal level can facilitate *search* for a suitable classifying population in V_2.

Why does arousal level increase if no STM storage occurs at V_2? This is a property of the expectation mechanism that is developed in Part II. Also in Part II a pattern θ at V_1 that is not classified by V_2 will use this mechanism to release a subliminal search routine that terminates when an admissible classification occurs.

8. Development of an STM Code

System (6)–(7) will be analysed mathematically because it illustrates properties of the model in a particularly simple and lucid way. The first result describes how this system responds to a single pattern that is iteratively presented through time.

Theorem 1 (One Pattern)

Given a pattern θ, suppose that there exists a unique j such that

$$S_j(0) > \max\{\epsilon, S_k(0) : k \neq j\}. \tag{15}$$

Let θ be practiced during a sequence of nonoverlapping intervals $[U_k, V_k]$, $k = 1, 2, \ldots$. Then the angle between $z^{(j)}(t)$ and θ monotonically decreases, the signal $S_j(t)$ is monotonically attracted towards $\|\theta\|^2$ and $\|z^{(j)}\|^2$ oscillates at most once as it pursues $S_j(t)$. In particular, if $\|z^{(j)}(0)\| \leq \|\theta\|$, then $S_j(t)$ is monotone increasing. Except in the trivial case that $S_j(0) = \|\theta\|^2$, the limiting relations

$$\lim_{t \to \infty} \|z^{(j)}(t)\|^2 = \lim_{t \to \infty} S_j(t) = \|\theta\|^2 \tag{16}$$

hold if and only if

$$\sum_{k=1}^{\infty}(V_k - U_k) = \infty. \tag{17}$$

Remark. If $z^{(j)}(0)$ is small, in the sense that $\|z^{(j)}(0)\| \leq \|\theta\|$, then by Theorem 1, as time goes on, the learning process maximizes the inner product signal $S_j(t) = \theta \cdot z^{(j)}(t)$ over all possible choices of $z^{(j)}$ such that $\|z^{(j)}\| \leq \|\theta\|$. This follows from the obvious fact that

$$\sup\{\theta \cdot \psi : \|\psi\| \leq \|\theta\|\} = \|\theta\|^2.$$

Otherwise expressed, learning makes $z^{(j)}$ parallel to θ, and normalizes the length of $z^{(j)}$.

What happens if several different spatial patterns $\theta^{(k)} = (\theta_1^{(k)}, \theta_2^{(k)}, \ldots, \theta_n^{(k)})$, $k = 1, 2, \ldots, M$, all perturb V_1 at different times? How are changes in the z_{ij}'s due to one pattern prevented from contradicting changes in the z_{ij}'s due to a different pattern? The choice-making property of V_2 does this for us; it acts as a sampling device that prevents contradictions from occurring. A heuristic argument will now be given to suggest how sampling works. This argument will then be refined and made rigorous. For definiteness, suppose that M spatial patterns $\theta^{(k)}$ are chosen, $M \leq N$, such that their signals at time $t = 0$ satisfy

$$\theta^{(k)} \cdot z^{(k)}(0) > \max\{\epsilon, \theta^{(k)} \cdot z^{(j)}(0) : j \neq k\} \tag{18}$$

for all $k = 1, 2, \ldots, M$. In other words, at time $t = 0$, $\theta^{(k)}$ is coded by v_{2k}. Let $\theta^{(1)}$ be the first pattern to perturb V_1. By (18), population v_{21} receives the largest signal from V_1. All other populations v_{2j}, $j \neq 1$, are thereupon inhibited by the off-surround of v_{21}, whereas v_{21} reverberates in STM. By (6), none of the synaptic strengths $z^{(j)}(t)$, $j \neq 1$, can learn while $\theta^{(1)}$ is presented. As in Theorem 1, presenting $\theta^{(1)}$ makes $z^{(1)}(t)$ more parallel to $\theta^{(1)}$ as t increases. Consequently, if a different pattern, say $\theta^{(2)}$, perturbs V_1 on the next learning trial, then it will excite v_{22} more than any other v_{2j}, $j \neq 2$: it cannot excite v_{21} because the coefficients $z^{(1)}(t)$ are more parallel to $\theta^{(1)}$ than before; and it cannot excite any v_{2j}, $j \neq 1, 2$ because the v_{2j} coefficients $z^{(j)}(t)$ still equal $z^{(j)}(0)$. In response to $\theta^{(2)}$, v_{22} inhibits all other v_{2j}, $j \neq 2$. Consequently none of the v_{2j} coefficients $z^{(j)}(t)$ can learn, $j \neq 2$; learning makes the coefficients $z^{(2)}(t)$

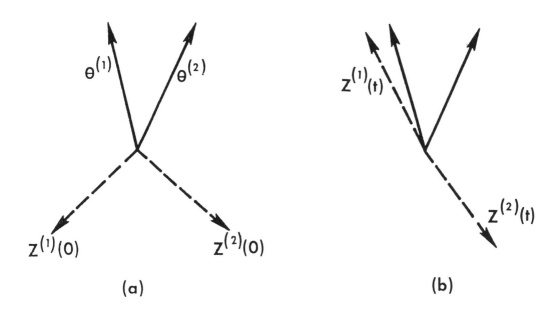

Figure 7. Practicing $\theta^{(1)}$ brings $z^{(1)}(t)$ closer to $\theta^{(1)}$ and $\theta^{(2)}$ than $z^{(2)}(0)$.

become more parallel to $\theta^{(2)}$ as t increases. The same occurs on all learning trials. By inhibiting the postsynaptic part of the learning mechanism in all but the chosen V_2 population, the on-center off-surround network in V_2 samples one vector $z^{(j)}(t)$ of trainable coefficients at any time. In this way, V_2 can learn to distinguish as many as N patterns if it contains N populations.

This argument is almost correct. It fails, in general, because by making (say) $z^{(1)}(t)$ more parallel to $\theta^{(1)}$, it is also possible to make $z^{(1)}(t)$ more parallel to $\theta^{(2)}$ than $z^{(2)}(0)$ is. Thus when $\theta^{(2)}$ is presented, it will be coded by v_{21} rather than v_{22}. In other words, practicing one pattern can recode other patterns. A typical example of this property is illustrated in Figure 7. Figure 7a depicts the two dimensional patterns $\theta^{(1)}$ and $\theta^{(2)}$ as solid vectors, and the two classifying vectors $z^{(1)}(0)$ and $z^{(2)}(0)$ as dotted vectors. Clearly (18) holds for $j = 1, 2$. As a result of practicing $\theta^{(1)}$ during a fixed interval, Figure 7b is produced. Note that $\theta^{(2)} \cdot z^{(1)}(t) > \theta^{(2)} \cdot z^{(2)}(t)$ after the practice interval terminates. Consequently, v_{21}, rather than v_{22}, codes $\theta^{(2)}$ when $\theta^{(2)}$ is practiced. This property can be iterated to show how systematic trends in the sequence of practiced patterns can produce systematic drifts in recoding. Consider Figure 8. Again two dimensional patterns are denoted by solid vectors and classifying vectors are denoted by dotted vectors. Let the patterns be practiced in the order $\theta^{(1)}, \theta^{(2)}, \ldots, \theta^{(M)}$, where $M \gg N$. By successively practicing $\theta^{(1)}, \theta^{(2)}, \ldots, \theta^{(r-1)}$, the vector $z^{(1)}(t)$ is dragged along clockwise until it almost reaches $\theta^{(r-1)}$. Then $\theta^{(r)}$ is practiced, and since $\theta^{(r)}$ is coded by v_{22}, $z^{(1)}(t)$ stops moving and $z^{(2)}(t)$ begins to move clockwise; $z^{(2)}(t)$ continues to move clockwise while $\theta^{(r+1)}, \theta^{(r+2)}, \ldots, \theta^{(2r-1)}$ are practiced. Then $z^{(3)}(t)$ begins to move clockwise, and so on. The clockwise drift in the practice schedule hereby shifts each $z^{(j)}(t), j = 1, 2, \ldots, M - 1$, to a position that is close to the one $z^{(j+1)}(0)$ occupied. In other words, essentially *all* vectors in V_2 are

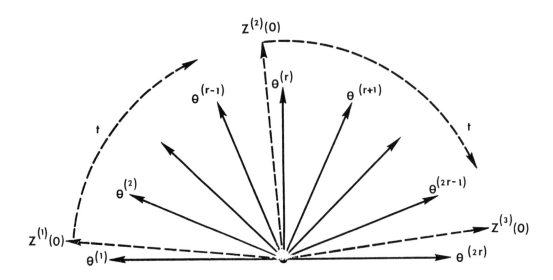

Figure 8. Practicing a sequence of spatial patterns can recode all the populations.

reclassified. If the same practice schedule $\theta^{(1)}, \theta^{(2)}, \ldots, \theta^{(M)}$ is repeated on a second learning trial, then essentially all v_{2i} are recoded by $v_{2,i+2}$, and so on. Each learning trial recodes V_2 until all the N populations in V_2 code one of the N most clockwise vectors $\theta^{(k)}$. This asymptotic coding of V_2 is stable, except for a wild oscillation in the coding of v_{21} on each learning trial, if the same practice schedule is always repeated. If, however, a counter-clockwise drift in practiced patterns is then imposed, all of V_2 will be recoded until the N most counter-clockwise vectors $\theta^{(k)}$ are coded. In general, if there are many patterns relative to the number of populations in V_2, and if the statistical structure of the practice sequences continually changes, then there need not exist a stable coding rule in V_2. This is quite unsatisfactory.

By contrast, if there are few, or sparse, patterns relative to the number of populations in V_2, then a stable coding rule does exist, and the STM choice rule in V_2 does provide an effective sampling technique. Such a situation is exposed to a "visually deprived" environment, in imitation of experiments on young animals. A theorem concerning this case will now be stated, if only to suggest what auxiliary mechanisms will be needed to establish a stable coding rule in the general case. This theorem shows how populations learn to code convex regions of features. In particular, if v_{2j} learns to code a certain set of features, then it automatically codes *average* features derived from this set.

The following nomenclature will be needed to state the theorem. A *partition* $\oplus_{k=1}^{K} \mathcal{P}_k$ of a finite set $\mathcal{P}$ is a subdivision of $\mathcal{P}$ into nonoverlapping and exhaustive subsets $\mathcal{P}_j$. The *convex hull* $\mathcal{H}(\mathcal{P})$ of a finite set $\mathcal{P}$ is the set of all convex combinations of elements in $\mathcal{P}$; for example, if $\mathcal{P} = \{\theta^{(1)}, \theta^{(2)}, \ldots, \theta^{(M)}\}$, then

$$\mathcal{H}(\mathcal{P}) = \{\sum_{k=1}^{M} \lambda_k \theta^{(k)} : \text{each } \lambda_k \geq 0 \text{ and } \sum_{k=1}^{M} \lambda_k = 1\}.$$

Given a set $\mathcal{P}$ with subset $\mathcal{Q}$, let $\mathcal{R} = \mathcal{P} \backslash \mathcal{Q}$ denote the set of elements in $\mathcal{P}$ that are not in $\mathcal{Q}$. If the classifying vector $z^{(j)}(t)$ codes the set of patterns $\mathcal{P}_j(t)$, let $\mathcal{P}_j^*(t) = \mathcal{P}_j(t) \cup \{z^{(j)}(t)\}$. The *distance* between a vector P and a set of vectors $\mathcal{Q}$, denoted by $\|P - \mathcal{Q}\|$, is defined by

$$\|P - \mathcal{Q}\| = \inf\{\|P - Q\| : Q \in \mathcal{Q}\}.$$

Theorem 2 (Sparse Patterns)

Let the network practice any set $\mathcal{P} = \{\theta^{(i)} : i = 1, 2, \ldots, M\}$ of patterns for which there exists a partition $\mathcal{P} = \bigoplus_{k=1}^{N} \mathcal{P}_k(0)$ such that

$$\min\{u \cdot v : u \in \mathcal{P}_j(0), v \in \mathcal{P}_j^*(0)\} > \max\{u \cdot v : u \in \mathcal{P}_j(0), v \in \mathcal{P}^*(0) \backslash \mathcal{P}_j^*(0)\} \quad (19)$$

for all $j = 1, 2, \ldots, N$. Then $\mathcal{P}_j(t) = \mathcal{P}_j(0)$ and the functions

$$D_j(t) = \|z^{(j)}(t) - \mathcal{H}(\mathcal{P}^{(j)}(t))\| \quad (20)$$

are monotone decreasing for $t \geq 0$ and $j = 1, 2, \ldots, N$. If moreover the patterns in $\mathcal{P}^{(j)}(0)$ are practiced in intervals $[U_{jm}, V_{jm}], m = 1, 2, \ldots$, such that

$$\sum_{m=1}^{\infty} (V_{jm} - U_{jm}) = \infty \quad (21)$$

then

$$\lim_{t \to \infty} D_j(t) = 0. \quad (22)$$

Remarks. In other words, if the classifying vectors initially code the patterns into sparse classes, in the sense of (19), then this code persists through time, and the classifying vectors approach a convex combination of their coded patterns. As (20) and (22) show, learning permits each v_{2j} to respond as vigorously as possible to its class of coded patterns.

The above results indicate that, given a fixed number of patterns, it becomes easier to establish a stable code for them as the number of populations in V_2 increases. Once V_2 is constructed, however, it is not possible to increase its number of populations at will. Moreover, *in vivo*, an enormous variety of patterns typically barrages the visual system. How can a stable code be guaranteed no matter how many patterns perturb V_1?

One way is to assume that a biochemically determined *critical period* exists during which the z_{ij}'s are capable of learning; once the critical period terminates, some chemical factor is removed and the z_{ij}'s remain fixed in the last code to be established. The existence of a critical period has been reported (Hubel and Wiesel, 1970), but whether it is due to a chemical factor, or *merely* to a chemical factor, is as yet unknown. From a formal point of view, such a mechanism suffers from several significant related disadvantages. The most obvious one is that all the code information that is learned throughout the critical period can be obliterated if its last phase exhibits an unlikely statistical trend. In addition, a repetitive statistical trend can prevent many patterns from being coded at all. For example, in Figure 8, once the classifying vectors code the N most clockwise patterns, many of the other $M - N$ patterns might be too far away from $z^{(1)}$ to satisfy the ϵ-condition in (7); they will then not be coded by any population. Yet each of these $M - N$ patterns has been presented as frequently as the N patterns that are coded. More generally, because populations which are already coded can be recoded so easily, it is hard to search for as yet uncommitted populations to code as yet uncoded patterns. This problem prevents a universal recoding from being achieved (see Part II).

These negative remarks can be supplemented by intriguing positive observations. Stabilizing the code seems to require the same formal machinery that is needed in models of adult attention and discrimination learning (Grossberg, 1975). This machinery, in turn, is highly evocative of data concerning attentional modulation of olfactory patterns by the prepyriform cortex of cats (Freeman, 1974). Auxiliary mechanisms for stabilizing the code will therefore be motivated below. It is understood that a biochemically triggered critical period can coexist with these mechanisms, or indeed can preempt them in sufficiently primitive organisms.

Various mechanisms can be contemplated which partially stabilize the code, but which are not sufficient. A satiation mechanism will be sketched below to clarify what is needed. Consider (6) with

$$x_{2j}(t) = \begin{cases} G_j(t) & \text{if } S_j(t)G_j(t) > \max\{\epsilon, S_k(t)G_k(t) : k \neq j\} \\ 0 & \text{if } S_j(t)G_j(t) < \max\{\epsilon, S_k(t)G_k(t) : k \neq j\} \end{cases} \tag{23}$$

where

$$G_j(t) = g\left(1 - \int_0^t x_{2j}(v)K(t-v)dv\right). \tag{24}$$

In (24), $g(w)$ is a monotone increasing function such that $g(0) = 0$ and $g(1) = 1$. $K(w)$ is a monotone decreasing function such that $K(0) = 1$ and $K(\infty) = 0$; for example, $K(w) = e^{-w}$. Equation (23) says that persistent activation of v_{2j} causes its STM response to satiate, or adapt; if v_{2j} is active during a sufficiently long interval, its activity approaches zero. Correspondingly, $z^{(j)}$'s fluctuations are damped within a time interval of fixed length. Such a mechanism is inadequate if the training schedule allows v_{2j} to recover its maximal strength. Figure 9 shows, for example, an ordering of patterns that permits recoding of essentially all populations in V_2.

This problem is only made worse by replacing the choice rule in (23) by a partial contrast rule such as

$$x_{2j} = \begin{cases} \dfrac{f(S_j G_j)}{\sum_{S_k G_k > \epsilon} f(S_k G_k)} & \text{if } S_j G_j > \epsilon \\ 0 & \text{if } S_j G_j < \epsilon. \end{cases}$$

Here, if a prescribed pattern θ causes a maximal STM response at v_{2j}, then the activity x_{2j} is suppressed by G_j more rapidly than the activities of other θ-activated

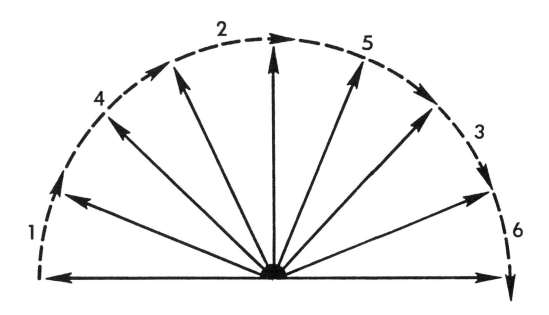

Figure 9. Practicing in the order 1, 2, 3, 4, 5, 6 can recode all the populations even if satiation exists.

populations. There can consequently be a shift in the locus of maximal responsiveness even to a single pattern—that is, recoding—in addition to the difficulty cited in Figure 9.

Such examples clarify what is essential:

(A) *Before* $z^{(j)}(t)$ learns a pattern, or class of related patterns, it must be able to fluctuate freely in response to pattern inputs in search of a classification.

(B) *After* $z^{(j)}(t)$ learns a pattern, it must be prevented from coding very different patterns, no matter what the training schedule is. In particular, satiating $z^{(j)}$'s ability to change through time does not suffice, since a very different pattern can still be coded by $z^{(j)}$ if this pattern elicits a larger signal at v_{2j}, say due to the size of $\|z^{(j)}\|$ rather than the direction of vector $z^{(j)}$, than at any of the uncommitted populations.

Requirements (A) and (B) constrain the interaction of STM and LTM mechanisms, given that (6) holds. For example, by (6), if a pattern θ creates signals while v_{2j} is active in STM, then $z^{(j)}(t)$ will change. Suppose that a sequence $\theta^{(1)}, \theta^{(2)}$ of two very different patterns is successively presented to V_1, and that $z^{(1)}(t)$ codes $\theta^{(1)}$. In response to $\theta^{(1)}$, v_{21} is activated, but $z^{(1)}(t)$ does not substantially change because it already codes $\theta^{(1)}$. Now let $\theta^{(2)}$ perturb V_1. By requirement (B), $z^{(1)}(t)$ must not be allowed to change. By (6), $z^{(1)}(t)$ will change unless either no signal is emitted from V_1 when v_{21} is active, or a signal is emitted from V_1 only after v_{21} is inactivated. These two cases will be separately considered in the next two paragraphs.

In the former case, some type of feedback to V_1 must suppress the V_1-to-V_2 signals that would otherwise be generated by $\theta^{(2)}$. This feedback somehow tells V_1 that $\theta^{(2)}$ is very different from the pattern $\theta^{(1)}$ that is presently coded in STM. By (A), however,

$\theta^{(2)}$ can generate V_1-to-V_2 signals at *some* time, either to search for a classifying vector, or to activate its already learned STM representation. Thus after V_1-to-V_2 signals are suppressed long enough for STM activity in v_{21} to also be suppressed, then V_1-to-V_2 signals are reactivated.

In the latter case, changing $\theta^{(1)}$ to $\theta^{(2)}$ somehow suppresses the STM activity that codes $\theta^{(1)}$; in particular, somehow the network can tell when the spatial patterns that perturb V_1 are changed. In both cases, the same general issue is raised: how does the network process a temporal succession $\theta^{(1)}, \theta^{(2)}, \ldots, \theta^{(k)}, \ldots$ of spatial patterns $\theta^{(k)} = (\theta_1^{(k)}, \theta_2^{(k)}, \ldots, \theta_n^{(k)})$; that is, a *space-time pattern*. Space-time patterns are the typical inputs to a receptive field *in vivo*. The problem of stabilizing the STM code forces us to consider their processing in some detail. Part II of this paper considers this problem.

APPENDIX

Proof of Theorem 1. Consider the case in which

$$\|\theta\|^2 > S_j(0) > \max\{\epsilon, S_k(0) : k \neq j\}. \tag{A1}$$

The case in which $S_j(0) \geq \|\theta\|^2$ can be treated similarly. First it will be shown that if the inequalities

$$\|\theta\|^2 > S_j(t) > \max\{\epsilon, S_k(t) : k \neq j\} \tag{A2}$$

hold at any time $t = T \in \bigcup_{m=1}^{\infty}[U_m, V_m]$, then they hold at all times $t \in [T, \infty) \cap \bigcup_{m=1}^{\infty}[U_m, V_m]$. By (A2), $x_{2j}(T) = 1$ and $x_{2k}(T) = 0$, $k \neq j$. Consequently, by (6),

$$\dot{z}_{ij}(T) = -z_{ij}(T) + \theta_i \tag{A3}$$

and

$$\dot{z}_{ik}(T) = 0 \tag{A4}$$

for $k \neq j$ and $i = 1, 2, \ldots, n$. By (A2)–(A4),

$$\dot{S}_j(T) = -S_j(T) + \|\theta\|^2 > 0 = \dot{S}_k(T), \tag{A5}$$

$k \neq j$. Thus (A2) holds for all $t \in [T, \infty) \cap \bigcup_{m=1}^{\infty}[U_m, V_m]$. By (A2) and (A5), for all $t \in \bigcup_{m=1}^{\infty}[U_m, V_m]$, $S_j(t)$ increases monotonically towards $\|\theta\|^2$ and (16) holds if and only if (17) holds. For $t \notin \bigcup_{m=1}^{\infty}[U_m, V_m]$, all $\dot{S}_k(t) = 0$, $k = 1, 2, \ldots, n$.

Letting $N_j = \|z^{(j)}\|^2$ and $C_j = \cos(z^{(j)}, \theta) \equiv S_j N_j^{-1/2}\|\theta\|^{-1}$, it readily follows from (A5) that for all $t \in \bigcup_{m=1}^{\infty}[U_m, V_m]$,

$$\dot{N}_j = 2(-N_j + S_j) \tag{A6}$$

and

$$\dot{C}_j = \|\theta\|N_j^{-1/2}(1 - C_j^2). \tag{A7}$$

Equation (A7) shows that the angle between $z^{(j)}(t)$ and θ closes monotonically as θ is practiced. Since $S_j(t)$ is a monotonic function, (A6) shows that $N_j(t)$ oscillates at most once.

In particular, suppose $\|z^{(j)}(0)\| \leq \|\theta\|$. Then $S_j(0) \leq \|\theta\|^2$, since otherwise

$$\theta \cdot z^{(j)}(0) > \theta \cdot \theta \geq z^{(j)}(0) \cdot z^{(j)}(0)$$

which implies

$$1 \geq C_j(0) > \|\theta\| \, \|z^{(j)}(0)\|^{-1} \geq \|z^{(j)}(0)\| \, \|\theta\|^{-1},$$

and thus

$$\|z^{(j)}(0)\| > \|\theta\| > \|z^{(j)}(0)\|,$$

which is a contradiction. By (A5), therefore $\|z^{(j)}(0)\| \leq \|\theta\|$ implies that $S_j(t)$ is monotone increasing.

Proof of Theorem 2. Inequality (19) is based on the fact that, if a fixed set of patterns $\theta^{(j_1)}, \theta^{(j_2)}, \ldots, \theta^{(j_k)}$ is classified by $z^{(j)}(t)$ for all $t \geq 0$, then

$$z^{(j)}(t) \in \mathcal{H}(\theta^{(j_1)}, \theta^{(j_2)}, \ldots, \theta^{(j_k)}, z^{(j)}(0)), \tag{A8}$$

for all $t \geq 0$. For example, suppose that the patterns are practiced in the order $\theta^{(j_1)}, \theta^{(j_2)}, \ldots, \theta^{(j_k)}$ during the nonoverlapping intervals $[U_1, V_1], [U_2, V_2], \ldots, [U_k, V_k]$. Except during these intervals, $\dot{z}^{(j)} = 0$. Thus for $t \in [U_1, V_1]$,

$$\dot{z}^{(j)} = -z^{(j)} + \theta^{(j_1)},$$

or

$$z^{(j)}(t) = z^{(j)}(0)e^{-(t-U_1)} + \theta^{(j_1)}(1 - e^{-(t-U_1)}),$$

so that

$$z^{(j)}(t) \in \mathcal{H}(\theta^{(j_1)}, z^{(j)}(0)) \subset \mathcal{H}(\theta^{(j_1)}, \ldots, \theta^{(j_k)}, z^{(j)}(0)).$$

For $t \in [U_2, V_2]$,

$$z^{(j)}(t) = [z^{(j)}(0)e^{-(V_1-U_1)} + \theta^{(j_1)}(1 - e^{-(V_1-U_1)})]e^{-(t-U_2)} + \theta^{(j_2)}(1 - e^{-(t-U_2)}). \tag{A9}$$

Hence

$$z^{(j)} \in \mathcal{H}(\theta^{(j_1)}, \theta^{(j_2)}, z^{(j)}(0)) \subset \mathcal{H}(\theta^{(j_1)}, \ldots, \theta^{(j_k)}, z^{(j)}(0)),$$

and so on.

Condition (19) is then applied using the fact that, for any $U \in P_j(0)$, $V \in \mathcal{H}(P_j^*(0))$, and $W \in \mathcal{H}(P^*(0) \backslash P_j^*(0))$,

$$U \cdot V > \max\{\epsilon, U \cdot W\} \tag{A10}$$

because

$$U \cdot V \geq \min\{u \cdot v : u \in P_j(0), v \in P_j^*(0)\}$$

and

$$\max\{u \cdot v : u \in P_j(0), v \in P^*(0) \backslash P_j^*(0)\} \geq U \cdot W.$$

Until a pattern is reclassified, however, (A8) shows that $z^{(j)}(t) \in \mathcal{H}(P_j^*(0))$ and that $z^{(k)}(t) \in \mathcal{H}(P^*(0) \backslash P_j^*(0))$ for any $k \neq j$. But then, by (A10), reclassification is impossible.

That $D_j(t)$ in (20) is monotone decreasing follows from iterations of (A9). That (21) implies (22) follows just as in the proof of Theorem 1.

REFERENCES

Barlow, H.B. and Pettigrew, J.D. (1971). Lack of specificity of neurons in the visual cortex of young kittens. *Journal of Physiology (London)*, **218**, 98–100.

Bennett, M.V.L. (1971). Analysis of parallel excitatory and inhibitory synaptic channels. *Journal of Neurophysiology*, **34**, 69–75.

Blackenship, J.E., Wachtel, H., and Kandel, E.R. (1971). Ionic mechanisms of excitatory, inhibitory, and dual synaptic actions mediated by an identified interneuron in abdominal ganglion of *Aplysia*. *Journal of Neurophysiology*, **34**, 76–92.

Blakemore, C. and Cooper, G.F. (1970). Development of the brain depends on the visual environment. *Nature*, **228**, 477–478.

Blakemore, C. and Mitchell, D.E. (1973). Environmental modification of the visual cortex and the neural basis of learning and memory. *Nature*, **241**, 467–468.

Boycott, B.B. and Dowling, J.E. (1969). Organization of the primate retina: Light miscroscopy. *Philosophical Transactions of the Royal Society (B)*, **255**, 109–184.

Ellias, S.A. and Grossberg, S. (1975). Pattern formation, contrast control, and oscillations in the short term memory of shunting on-center off-surround networks. *Biological Cybernetics*, **20**, 69–98.

Freeman, W.J. (1974). Neural coding through mass action in the olfactory system. *Proceedings of the IEEE Conference on Biologically Motivated Automata Theory*.

Gierer, A. and Meinhardt, H. (1972). A theory of biological pattern formation. *Kybernetik*, **12**, 30–39.

Greenspan, H.P. and Benney, D.J. (1973). **Calculus**. New York: McGraw-Hill.

Grossberg, S. (1967). Nonlinear difference-differential equations in prediction and learning theory. *Proceedings of the National Academy of Sciences*, **58**, 1329–1334.

Grossberg, S. (1970a). Some networks that can learn, remember, and reproduce any number of complicated space-time patterns, II. *Studies in Applied Mathematics*, **49**, 135–166.

Grossberg, S. (1970b). Neural pattern discrimination. *Journal of Theoretical Biology*, **27**, 291–337.

Grossberg, S. (1971). Pavlovian pattern learning by nonlinear neural networks. *Proceedings of the National Academy of Sciences*, **68**, 828–831.

Grossberg, S. (1972). Neural expectation: Cerebellar and retinal analogs of cells fired by learnable or unlearned pattern classes. *Kybernetik*, **10**, 49–57.

Grossberg, S. (1973). Contour enhancement, short term memory, and constancies in reverberating neural networks. *Studies in Applied Mathematics*, **52**, 213–257.

Grossberg, S. (1974). Classical and instrumental learning by neural networks. In R. Rosen and F. Snell (Eds.), **Progress in theoretical biology**. New York: Academic Press, 51–141.

Grossberg, S. (1975). A neural model of attention, reinforcement, and discrimination learning. *International Review of Neurobiology*, **18**, 263–327.

Grossberg, S. (1976). On the development of feature detectors in the visual cortex with applications to learning and reaction-diffusion systems. *Biological Cybernetics*, **21**, 145–159.

Grossberg, S. and Levine, D.S. (1975). Some developmental and attentional biases in the contrast enhancement and short term memory of recurrent neural networks. *Journal of Theoretical Biology*, **53**, 341–380.

Hebb, D.O. (1949). **The organization of behavior**. New York: Wiley and Sons.

Hirsch, H.V.B. and Spinelli, D.N. (1970). Visual experience modifies distribution of horizontally and vertically oriented receptive fields in cats. *Science*, **168**, 869–871.

Hirsch, H.V.B. and Spinelli, D.N. (1971). Modification of the distribution of receptive field orientation in cats by selective visual exposure during development. *Experimental Brain Research*, **12**, 509–527.

Hubel, D.H. and Wiesel, T.N. (1970). The period of susceptibility to the physiological effects of unilateral eye closure in kittens. *Journal of Physiology (London)*, **206**, 419–436.

Kimble, G.A. (1967). **Foundations of conditioning and learning**. New York: Appleton-Century-Crofts.

Levine, D.S. and Grossberg, S. (1976). Visual illusions in neural networks: Line neutralization, tilt aftereffects, and angle expansion. *Journal of Theoretical Biology*, **61**, 477–504.

Meinhardt, H. and Gierer, A. (1974). Applications of a theory of biological pattern formation based on lateral inhibition. *Journal of Cell Science*, **15**, 321–346.

Pérez, R., Glass, L., and Shlaer, R. (1974). Development of specificity in the cat visual cortex. *Journal of Mathematical Biology*.

von der Malsburg, C. (1973). Self-organization of orientation sensitive cells in the striate cortex. *Kybernetik*, **14**, 85–100.

Wachtel, H. and Kandel, E.R. (1971). Conversion of synaptic excitation to inhibition at a dual chemical synapse. *Journal of Neurophysiology*, **34**.

Wiesel, T.N. and Hubel, D.H. (1963). Single-cell responses in striate cortex of kittens deprived of vision in one eye. *Journal of Neurophysiology*, **26**, 1003–1017.

Wiesel, T.N. and Hubel, D.H. (1965). Comparison of the effects of unilateral and bilateral eye closure on cortical unit responses in kittens. *Journal of Neurophysiology*, **28**, 1029–1040.

CHAPTER 7

THE "NEURAL" PHONETIC TYPEWRITER
by
Teuvo Kohonen

Preface

In this 1988 article, Kohonen describes a neural phonetic typewriter whose goal is to transcribe spoken language into typed text. This application of neural networks to a very important technological problem illustrates characteristics of many applications that are being developed at the present time. Perhaps the most notable fact is that neural networks are usually parts of a larger system that may contain components drawn from several technologies.

In the present example, the neural network part of the application is the competitive learning, or self-organizing feature map, model (see Chapter 6). Kohonen notes that the winner-take-all process, which selects the maximum dot product of the normalized input vector with all the normalized adaptive weight vectors, is equivalent to selecting the minimum distance of the normalized input vector to all the normalized adaptive weight vectors. He uses this observation to facilitate comparison of the Bayesian, self-normalizing classification properties of competitive learning with other classification processes that are often used in speech processing, such as Voronoi tessellation and vector quantization. In fact, although scalar quantization has long been known within the engineering community, learned vector quantization gained prominence there in the 1980's (Gray, 1984). The development of competitive learning within the neural network community in the 1970's was carried out as an independent stream of research whose advantages have been assimilated into the engineering literature during the past few years. From this perspective, the ART networks may be viewed as learned vector quantization models whose control structures can function autonomously to achieve absolutely stable learning and hypothesis testing properties.

In the phonetic typewriter application, the neural network is used to learn phonemic representations. In addition, there is also a non-neural preprocessor and postprocessor. The preprocessor uses, as Kohonen remarks, "standard digital signal processing" techniques, including a fast Fourier transform, that were developed for just such acoustic engineering problems. He discusses how the preprocessor was set up to cope with both sustained and transient phonemic information.

Postprocessing uses a technique called "redundant hash addressing" that builds up a database of 15,000–20,000 rules to disambiguate quasiphonemes into true phonemes. By combining these methods, a "phonotopic map" is generated of spoken words. Such a map generates a type of working memory representation of the temporal order information that links the phonemic representations (also see Chapter 18).

Kohonen goes on to describe a hardware implementation of the system, which includes a virtual implementation of the neural network. The characteristics of using neural network components as key processing stages of a complete, but hybrid, system, and implementing the whole system using available hardware, is typically how neural networks are being applied in technology today. Systems are also starting to be implemented that use increasing numbers of neurally-inspired components, and whose hardware implementations attempt to more closely emulate the parallel neural computations to take fuller advantage of the intrinsic computational advantages of a physically natural hardware realization.

Reference

Gray, R.M. (1984). Vector quantization. *IEEE ASSP Magazine*, April, 4–29.

Computer
1988, **21**, 11–22
©1988 IEEE

THE "NEURAL" PHONETIC TYPEWRITER

Teuvo Kohonen

In 1930 a Hungarian scientist, Tihamér Nemes, filed a patent application in Germany for the principle of making an optoelectrical system automatically transcribe speech. His idea was to use the optical sound track on a movie film as a grating to produce diffraction patterns (corresponding to speech spectra), which then could be identified and typed out. The application was turned down as "unrealistic." Since then the problem of automatic speech recognition has occupied the minds of scientists and engineers, both amateur and professional.

Research on speech recognition principles has been pursued in many laboratories around the world, academic as well as industrial, with various objectives in mind[1]. One ambitious goal is to implement automated query systems that could be accessed through public telephone lines, because some telephone companies have observed that telephone operators spend most of their time answering queries. An even more ambitious plan, adopted in 1986 by the Japanese national ATR (Advanced Telecommunication Research) project, is to receive speech in one language and to synthesize it in another, on line. The dream of a phonetic typewriter that can produce text from arbitrary dictation is an old one; it was envisioned by Nemes and is still being pursued today. Several dozen devices, even special microcircuits, that can recognize isolated words from limited vocabularies with varying accuracy are now on the market. These devices have important applications, such as the operation of machines by voice, various dispatching services that employ voice-activated devices, and aids for seriously handicapped people. But in spite of big investments and the work of experts, the original goals have not been reached. High-level speech recognition has existed so far only in science fiction.

Recently, researchers have placed great hopes on artificial neural networks to perform such "natural" tasks as speech recognition. This was indeed one motivation for us to start research in this area many years ago at Helsinki University of Technology. This article describes the result of that research—a complete "neural" speech recognition system, which recognizes phonetic units, called *phonemes*, from a continuous speech signal. Although motivated by neural network principles, the choices in its design must be regarded as a compromise of many technical aspects of those principles. As our system is a genuine "phonetic typewriter" intended to transcribe orthographically edited text from an unlimited vocabulary, it cannot be directly compared with any more conventional, word-based system that applies classical concepts such as dynamic time warping[1] and hidden Markov models[2].

Why is speech recognition difficult?

Automatic recognition of speech belongs to the broader category of pattern recognition tasks[3], for which, during the past 30 years or so, many heuristic and even sophisticated methods have been tried. It may seem strange that while progress in many other fields of technology has been astoundingly rapid, research investments in these "natural" tasks have not yet yielded adequate dividends. After initial optimism, the researchers in this area have gradually become aware of the many difficulties to be surmounted.

Human beings' recognition of speech consists of many tasks, ranging from the detection of phonemes from speech waveforms to the high-level understanding of messages. We do not actually hear all speech elements; we realize this easily when we try to decipher foreign or uncommon utterances. Instead, we continuously relate fragmentary sensory stimuli to contexts familiar from various experiences, and we unconsciously test and reiterate our perceptions at different levels of abstraction. In other words, what we believe we *hear*, we in fact *reconstruct* in our minds from pieces of received information.

Even in clear speech from the same speaker, distributions of the spectral samples of different phonemes overlap. Their statistical density functions are not Gaussian, so they cannot be approximated analytically. The same phonemes spoken by different persons can be confused too; for example, the $/\varepsilon/$ of one speaker might sound like the $/n/$ of another. For this reason, absolutely speaker-independent detection of phonemes is possible only with relatively low accuracy.

Some phonemes are spectally clearer and stabler than others. For speech recognition purposes, we distinguish three acoustically different categories:

(1) Vocal (voiced, nonturbulent) phonemes, including the vowels, semivowels ($/j/$, $/v/$), nasals ($/m/$, $/n/$, $/\eta/$), and liquids ($/l/$, $/r/$);

(2) Fricatives ($/s/$, $/š/$, $/z/$, etc.);

(3) Plosives ($/k/$, $/p/$, $/t/$, $/b/$, $/d/$, $/g/$, etc.).

The phonemes of the first two categories have rather well-defined, stationary spectra, whereas the plosives are identifiable only on the basis of their transient properties. For instance, for $/k,p,t/$ there is a silence followed by a short, faint burst of voice characteristic of each plosive, depending on its point of articulation (lips, tongue, palate). The transition of the speech signal to the next phoneme also varies among the plosives.

A high-level automatic speech recognition system should also interpret the semantic context of utterances so that it can maintain selective attention to particular portions of speech. This ability would call for higher thinking processes, not only imitation of the operation of the preattentive sensory system. The first large experimental speech-understanding systems followed this line of thought (see the report of the ARPA project[4], which was completed around 1976), but for commercial application such solutions were too expensive. Machine interpretation of the meaning of complete sentences is a very difficult task; it has been accomplished only when the syntax has been artificially limited. Such "party tricks" may have led the public to believe that practical speech recognition has reached a more advanced level than it has. Despite decades of intensive research, no machine has yet been able to recognize general, continuous speech produced by an arbitrary speaker, when no speech samples have been supplied.

Recognition of the speech of arbitrary speakers is much more difficult than generally believed. Existing commercial speaker-independent systems are restricted to isolated words from vocabularies not exceeding 40 words. Reddy and Zue estimated in 1983 that for speaker-independent recognition of connected speech, based on a 20,000-word vocabulary, a computing power of 100,000 MIPS, corresponding to 100 supercomputers, would be necessary[5]. Moreover, the detailed programs to perform these operations have not been devised. The difficulties would be even greater if the vocabularies were unlimited, if the utterances were loaded with emotions, or if speech were produced under noisy or stressful conditions.

We must, of course, be aware of these difficulties. On the other hand, we would never complete any practical speech recognizer if we had to attack all the problems simultaneously. Engineering solutions are therefore often restricted to particular tasks. For instance, we might wish to recognize isolated commands from a limited vocabulary, or to type text from dictation automatically. Many satisfactory techniques for speaker-specific, isolated-word recognition have already been developed. Systems that type English text from clear dictation with short pauses between the words have been demonstrated[6]. Typing unlimited dictation in English is another intriguing objective. Systems designed for English recognize words as complete units, and various grammatical forms such as plural, possessive, and so forth can be stored in the vocabulary as separate word tokens. This is not possible in many other languages—Finnish and Japanese, for example—in which the grammar is implemented by inflections and there may be dozens of different forms of the same root word. For inflectional languages the system must construct the text from recognized phonetic units, taking into account the transformations of these units due to coarticulation effects (i.e., a phoneme's acoustic spectrum varies in the context of different phonemes).

Especially in image analysis, but in speech recognition too, many newer methods concentrate on structural and syntactic relationships between the pattern elements, and special grammars for their analysis have been developed. It seems, however, that the first step, preanalysis and detection of primary features such as acoustic spectra, is still often based on rather coarse principles, without careful consideration of the very special statistical properties of the natural signals and their clustering. Therefore, when new, highly parallel and adaptive methods such as artificial neural networks are introduced, we assume that their capacities can best be utilized if the networks are made to adapt to the real data, finding relevant features in the signals. This was in fact one of the central assumptions in our research.

To recapitulate, speech is a very difficult stochastic process, and its elements are not unique at all. The distributions of the different phonemic classes overlap seriously, and to minimize misclassification errors, careful statistical as well as structural analyses are needed.

The promise of neural computers

Because the brain has already implemented the speech recognition function (and many others), some researchers have reached the straightforward conclusion that artificial neural networks should be able to do the same, regarding these networks as a panacea for such "natural" problems. Many of these people believe that the only bottleneck is computing power, and some even expect that all the remaining problems will be solved when, say, optical neural computers, with a vast computing capacity, become feasible. What these people fail to realize is that *we may not yet have discovered what biological neurons and neural systems are like.* Maybe the machines we call neural networks and neural computers are too simple. Before we can utilize such computing capacities, we must know *what* and *how* to compute.

It is true that intriguing simulations of new information-processing functions, based on artificial neural networks, have been made, but most of these demonstrations have been performed with artificial data that are separable into disjoint classes. Difficulties multiply when natural, stochastic data are applied. In my own experience the quality of a neural network must be tested in an on-line connection with a natural environment. One of the most difficult problems is dealing with input data whose statistical density functions overlap, have awkward forms in high-dimensional signal spaces, and are not even stationary. Furthermore, in practical applications the number of samples of input data used for training cannot be large; for instance, we cannot expect that every user has the patience to dictate a sufficient number of speech samples to guarantee ultimate accuracy.

On the other hand, since digital computing principles are already in existence, they should be used wherever they are superior to biological circuits, as in the syntactic analysis of symbolic expressions and even in the spectral analysis of speech waveforms. The discrete Fourier transform has very effective digital implementations.

Our choice was to try neural networks in a task in which the most demanding statistical analyses are performed—namely, in the optimal detection of the phonemes. In this task we could test some new learning methods that had been shown to yield a recognition accuracy comparable to the decision-theoretic maximum, while at the same time performing the computations by simple elements, using a minimal amount of sample data for training.

Acoustic preprocessing

Physiological research on hearing has revealed many details that may or may not be significant to artificial speech recognition. The main operation carried out in human hearing is a frequency analysis based on the resonances of the basilar membrane of the inner ear. The spectral decomposition of the speech signal is transmitted to the brain through the auditory nerves. Especially at lower frequencies, however, each peak of the pressure wave gives rise to separate bursts of neural impulses; thus, some kind of time-domain information also is transmitted by the ear. On the other hand, a certain degree of synchronization of neural impulses to the acoustic signals seems to occur at all frequencies, thus conveying phase information. One therefore might stipulate that the artificial ear contain detectors that mimic the operation of the sensory receptors as fully as possible.

Biological neural networks are able to enhance signal transients in a nonlinear fashion. This property has been simulated in physical models that describe the mechanical properties of the inner ear and chemical transmission in its neural cells[7,8]. Nonetheless, we decided to apply conventional frequency analysis techniques, as such, to the preprocessing of speech. The main motivations for this approach were that the digital Fourier analysis is both accurate and fast and the fundamentals of digital filtering are well understood. Standard digital signal processing has been considered sufficient in acoustic engineering and telecommunication. Our decision was thus a typical engineering choice. We also believed the self-organizing neural network described here would accept many alternative kinds of preprocessing and compensate for modest imperfections, as long as they occur consistently. Our final results confirmed this belief; at least there were no large differences in recognition accuracies between stationary and transient phonemes.

Briefly, the complete acoustic preprocessor of our system consists of the following stages:

(1) Noise-canceling microphone;

(2) Preamplifier with a switched-capacitor, 5.3-kHz low-pass filter;

(3) 12-bit analog-to-digital converter with 13.02-kHz sampling rate;

(4) 256-point fast Fourier transform, computed every 9.83 ms using a 256-point Hamming window;

(5) Logarithmization and filtering of spectral powers by fourth-order elliptic low-pass filters;

(6) Grouping of spectral channels into a 15-component real-pattern vector;

(7) Subtraction of the average from all components;

(8) Normalization of the resulting vector into constant length.

Operations 3 through 8 are computed by the signal processor chip TMS 32010 (our design is four years old; much faster processors are now available).

In many speech recognition systems acoustic processing encodes the speech signal into so-called LPC (linear predictive coding) coefficients[1], which contain approximately the same information as the spectral decomposition. We preferred the FFT because, as will be shown, one of the main operations of the neural network that recognizes the phonemes is to perform metric clustering of the phonemic samples. The FFT, a transform of the signal, reflects its clustering properties better than a parametric code.

We had the option of applying the overall root-mean-square value of the speech signal as the extra sixteenth component in the pattern vector; in this way we expected to obtain more information on the transient signals. The recognition accuracy remained the same, however, within one percent. We believe that the acoustic processor can analyse many other speech features in addition to the spectral ones. Another trick that improved accuracy on the order of two percent was to make the true pattern vector out of two spectra 30 ms apart in the time scale. Since the two samples represent two different stages of the signal, dynamic transformation is added to the preanalysis.

Because the plosives must be distinguished on the basis of the fast, transient parts of the speech waveform, we selected the spectral samples of the plosives from the transient regions of the signal, on the basis of the constancy of the waveform. On the other hand, there is evidence that the biological auditory system is sensitive not only to the spectral representations of speech but to their particular transient features too, and apparently it uses the nonlinear adaptive properties of the inner ear, especially its hair cells, the different transmission delays in the neural fibers, and many kinds of neural gating in the auditory nuclei (processing stations between the ear and the brain). For the time being, these nonlinear, dynamic neural functions are not understood well enough to warrant the design of standard electronic analogies for them.

Vector quantization

The instantaneous spectal power values on the 15 channels formed from the FFT can be regarded as a 15-dimensional real vector in a Euclidean space. We might think that the spectra of the different phonemes of speech occupy different regions of this space, so that they could be detected by some kind of multidimensional discrimination method. In reality, several problems arise. One of them, as already stated, is that the distributions of the spectra of different phonemic classes overlap, so that it is not possible to distinguish the phonemes by any discrimination method with 100 percent certainty. The best we can do is to divide the space with optimal discrimination borders, relative to which, on the average, the rate of misclassifications is minimized. It turns out that analytical definition of such (nonlinear) borders is far from trivial, whereas neural networks can define them very effectively. Another problem is presented by the coarticulation effects discussed later.

A concept useful for the illustration of these so-called vector space methods for pattern recognition and neural networks is called *Voronoi tessellation*. For simplicity, consider that the dissimilarity of two or more spectra can be expressed in terms of their vectorial difference (actually the norm of this difference) in an n-dimensional Euclidean space. Figure 1 exemplifies a two-dimensional space in which a finite number of *reference vectors* are shown as points, corresponding to their coordinates. This space is partitioned into regions, bordered by lines (in general, hyperplanes) such that each partition contains a reference vector that is the nearest neighbor to any vector within the same partition. These lines, or the midplanes of the neighboring reference vectors, constitute the Voronoi tessellation, which defines a set of *discrimination* or *decision surfaces*. This tessellation represents one kind of *vector quantization*, which generally means quantization of the vector space into discrete regions.

One or more neighboring reference vectors can be made to define a category in the vector space as the union of their respective partitions. Determination of such reference vectors was the main problem on which we concentrated in our neural network research. There are, of course, many classical mathematical approaches to this problem[3]. In very simple and straightforward pattern recognition, samples, or prototypes, of earlier observed vectors are used as such for the reference vectors. For the new or unknown vector, a small number of its nearest prototypes are sought; then majority voting is applied to them to determine classification. A drawback of this method is that for good statistical accuracy an appreciable number of reference vectors are needed. Consequently, the comparison computations during classification, especially if they are made serially, become time-consuming; the unknown vector must be compared with all the reference vectors. Therefore, our aim was to describe the samples by a much smaller representative set of reference vectors without loss of accuracy.

Imagine now that a fixed number of discrete neurons is in parallel, looking at the speech spectrum, or the set of input signals. Imagine that each neuron has a template, a reference spectrum with respect to which the degree of matching with the input spectrum can be defined. Imagine further that the different neurons compete, the neuron with the highest matching score being regarded as the "winner." The input

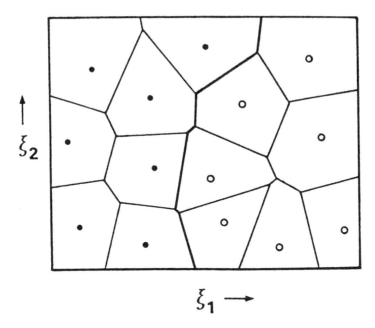

Figure 1. Voronoi tessellation partitions a two-dimensional (ξ_1, ξ_2) "pattern space" into regions around reference vectors, shown as points in this coordinate system. All vectors (ξ_1, ξ_2) in the same partition have the same reference vector as their nearest neighbor and are classified according to it. The solid and open circles, respectively, represent reference vectors of two classes, and the discrimination "surface" between them is drawn in bold.

spectrum would then be assigned to the winner in the same way that an arbitrary vector is assigned to the closest reference vector and classified according to it in the above Voronoi tessellation. There are neural networks in which such templates are formed adaptively, and which perform this comparison in parallel, so that the neuron whose template matches best with the input automatically gives an active response to it. Indeed, the self-organizing process described below defines reference vectors for the neurons such that their Voronoi tessellation sets near-optimal decision borders between the classes—i.e., the fraction of input vectors falling on the wrong side of the borders is minimized. In classical decision theory, theoretical minimization of the probability for misclassification is a standard procedure, and the mathematical setting for it is the Bayes theory of probability. In what follows, we shall thus point out that the vector quantization and nearest neighbor classification resulting in the neural network defines the reference vectors in such a way that their Voronoi tessellation very closely approximates the theoretical Bayesian decision surfaces.

The neural network

Detailed biophysical analysis of the phenomena taking place at the cell membrane of biological neurons leads to systems of nonlinear differential equations with dozens of state variables for each neuron; this would be untenable in a computational application. Obviously it is necessary to simplify the mathematics, while retaining some

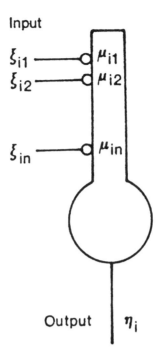

Figure 2. Symbol of a theoretical neuron and the signal and system variables relating to it. The small circles correspond to the input connections, the synapses.

essentials of the real dynamic behavior. The approximations made here, while reasonably simple, are still rather "neural" and have been influential in many intriguing applications.

Figure 2 depicts one model neuron and defines its signal and state variables. The input signals are connected to the neuron with different, variable "transmittances" corresponding to the coupling strengths of the neural junctions called *synapses*. The latter are noted by μ_{ij} (here i is the index of the neuron and j that of its input). Correspondingly, ξ_{ij} is the signal value (signal activity, actually the frequency of the neural impulses) at the jth input of the ith neuron.

Each neuron is thought to act as a pulse-frequency modulator, producing an output activity η_i (actually a train of neural impulses with this repetition frequency), which is obtained by integrating the input signals according to the following differential equation. (The biological neurons have an active membrane with a capacitance that integrates input currents and triggers a volley of impulses when a critical level of depolarization is achieved.)

$$\frac{d\eta_i}{dt} = \sum_{j=1}^{n} \mu_{ij}\xi_{ij} - \gamma(\eta_i) \tag{1}$$

The first term on the right corresponds to the coupling of input signals to the neuron through the different transmittances; a linear, superpositive effect was assumed for simplicity. The last term, $-\gamma(\eta_i)$, stands for a nonlinear leakage effect that describes all nonideal properties, such as saturation, leakage, and shunting effects of the neuron, in a simple way. It is assumed to be a stronger than linear function of η_i. It is further assumed that the inverse function γ^{-1} exists. Then if the ξ_{ij} are held stationary, or they are changing slowly, we can consider the case $d\eta_i/dt \sim 0$, whereby the output will follow the integrated input as in a nonlinear, saturating amplifier according to

$$\eta_i = \sigma[\sum_{j=1}^{n} \mu_{ij}\xi_{ij}] \qquad (2)$$

Here $\sigma[.]$ is the inverse function of γ, and it usually has a typical sigmoidal form, with low and high saturation limits and a proportionality range between.

The settling of activity according to Equation 1 proceeds very quickly; in biological circuits it occurs in tens of milliseconds. Next we consider an adaptive process in which the transmittances μ_{ij} are assumed to change too. This is the effect regarded as "learning" in neural circuits, and its time constants are much longer. In biological circuits this process corresponds to changes in proteins and neural structures that typically take weeks. A simple, natural adaptation law that already has suggested many applications is the following: First, we must stipulate that parametric changes occur very selectively; thus dependence on the signals must be nonlinear. The classical choice made by most modelers is to assume that changes are proportional to the *product* of input and output activities (the so-called law of Hebb). However, this choice, as such, would be unnatural because the parameters would change in one direction only (notice that the signals are positive). Therefore it is necessary to modify this law—for example, by including some kind of nonlinear "forgetting" term. Thus we can write

$$\frac{d\mu_{ij}}{dt} = \alpha\eta_i\xi_{ij} - \beta(\eta_i)\mu_{ij} \qquad (3)$$

where α is a positive constant, the first term is the "Hebbian" term, and the last term represents the nonlinear "forgetting" effect, which depends on the activity η_i; forgetting is thus "active." As will be pointed out later, the first term defines changes in the μ_{ij} in such a direction that the neuron tends to become more and more sensitive and selective to the particular combination of signals ξ_{ij} presented at the input. This is the basic adaptive effect.

On the other hand, to stabilize the output activity to a proper range it seems very profitable for $\beta(\eta_i)$ to be a scalar function with a Taylor expansion in which the constant term is zero. Careful analyses have shown that this kind of neuron becomes selective to the so-called *largest principal component* of input[9]. For many choices of the functional form, it can further be shown that the μ_{ij} will automatically become normalized such that the vector formed from the μ_{ij} during the process tends to a constant length (norm) independent of the signal values that occur in the process[9]. We shall employ this effect a bit later in a further simplification of the model.

One cannot understand the essentials of neural circuits unless one considers their behavior as a *collective* system. An example occurs in the "self-organizing feature maps" in our speech recognition application. Consider Figure 3a, where a set of neurons forms a layer, and each neuron is connected to its neighbors in the lateral direction. We have drawn the network one-dimensionally for clarity, although in all practical applications it has been two-dimensional. The external inputs, in the simplest model used for pattern recognition, are connected in parallel to all the neurons

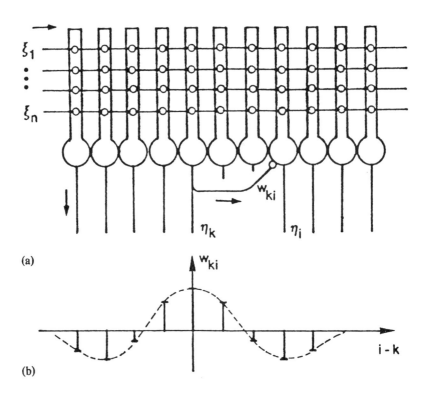

Figure 3. (a) Neural network underlying the formation of the phonotopic maps used in speech recognition. (b) The strengths of lateral interaction as a function of distance (the "Mexican hat" function).

of this network so that each neuron can simultaneously "look" at the same input. (Certain interesting but much more complex effects result if the input connections are made to different portions of the network and the activation is propagated through it in a sequence.)

The feedback connections are coupled to the neurons in the same way as the external inputs. However, for simplicity, only the latter are assumed to have adaptive synapses. If the feedbacks were adaptive, too, this network would exhibit other more complex effects[9]. It should also be emphasized that the biological synaptic circuits of the feedbacks are different from those of the external inputs. The time-invariant coupling coefficient of the feedback connections, as a function of distance, has roughly the "Mexican hat" form depicted in Figure 3b, as in real neural networks. For negative coupling, signal-inverting elements are necessary; in biological circuits inversion is made by a special kind of inhibitory interneuron. If the external input is denoted

$$I_i = \sum_{j=1}^{n} \mu_{ij} \xi_{ij} \qquad (4)$$

then the system equation for the network activities η_i, denoting the feedback coupling

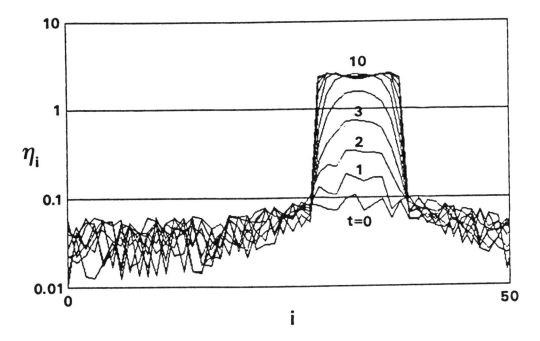

Figure 4. Development of the distribution of activity over time (t) into a stable "bubble" in a laterally interconnected neural network (cf. Figure 3). The activities of the individual neurons (η_i) are shown in the logarithmic scale.

from neuron k to neuron i by w_{ki}, can be written

$$\frac{d\eta_i}{dt} = I_i + \sum_{k \in S_i} w_{ki}\eta_k - \gamma(\eta_i) \tag{5}$$

where k runs over the subset S_i of those neurons that have connections with neuron i. A characteristic phenomenon, due to the lateral feedback interconnections, will be observed first: The initial activity distribution in the network may be more or less random, but over time the activity develops into clusters or "bubbles" of a certain dimension, as shown in Figures 4 and 5. If the interaction range is not much less than the diameter of the network, the network activity seems to develop into a single bubble, located around the maximum of the (smoothed) initial activity.

Consider now that there is no external source of activation other than that provided by the input signal connections, which extend in parallel over the whole network. According to Equations 1 and 2, the strength of the initial activation of a neuron is proportional to the dot product $m_i^T x$ where m_i is the vector of the μ_{ij}, x is the vector of the ξ_{ij}, and T is the transpose of a vector. (We use here concepts of matrix algebra whereby m_i and x are column vectors.) Therefore, the bubble is formed around those units at which $m_i^T x$ is maximum.

The saturation limits of $\sigma[.]$ defined by Equation 2 stabilize the activities η_i to either a low or a high value. Similarly, $\beta(\eta_i)$ takes on either of two values. Without loss of generality, it is possible to rescale the variables ξ_{ij} and μ_{ij} to make $\eta_i \in \{0, 1\}$, $\beta(\eta_i) \in \{0, \alpha\}$, whereby Equation 3 will be further simplified and split into two

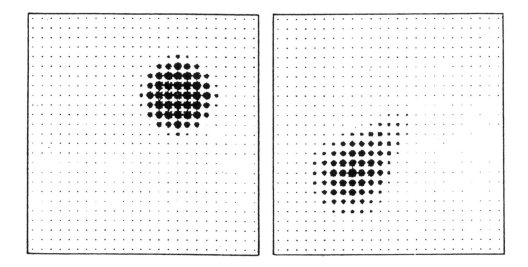

Figure 5. "Bubbles" formed in a two-dimensional network viewed from the top. The dots correspond to neurons, and their sizes correspond to their activity. In the picture on the right, the input was changing slowly, and the motion of the bubble is indicated by its "tail."

equations:

$$\frac{d\mu_{ij}}{dt} = \alpha(\xi_{ij} - \mu_{ij}) \tag{6a}$$

if $\eta_i = 1$ and $\beta = \alpha$ (inside the bubble), and

$$\frac{d\mu_{ij}}{dt} = 0 \tag{6b}$$

for $\eta_i = \beta = 0$ (outside the bubble).

It is evident from Equation 6 that the transmittances μ_{ij} then adaptively tend to follow up the input signals ξ_{ij}. In other words, these neurons start to become selectively sensitized to the prevailing input pattern. But this occurs only when the bubble lies over the particular neuron. For another input, the bubble lies over other neurons, which then become sensitized to that input. In this way different parts of the network are automatically "tuned" to different inputs.

The network will indeed be tuned to different inputs in an ordered fashion, as if a continuous map of the signal space were formed over the network. The continuity of this mapping follows from the simple fact that the vectors m_i of contiguous units (within the bubbles) are modified in the same direction, so that during the course of the process the neighboring values become smoothed. The ordering of these values, however, is a very subtle phenomenon, the proof or complete explanation of which is mathematically very sophisticated[9] and cannot be given here. The effect is difficult to visualize without, say, an animation film. A concrete example of this kind of ordering is the phonotopic map described later in this article.

Shortcut learning algorithm

In the time-continuous process just described, the weight vectors attain asymptotic values, which then define a vector quantization of the input signal space, and thus a classification of all its vectors. In practice, the same vector quantization can be computed much more quickly from a numerically simpler algorithm. The bubble is equivalent to a neighborhood set N_c of all those network units that lie within a certain radius form a certain unit c. It can be shown that the size of the bubble depends on the interaction parameters, and so we can reason that the radius of the bubble is controllable, eventually being definable as some function of time. For good self-organizing results, it has been found empirically that the radius indeed should decrease in time monotonically. Similarly $\alpha = \alpha(t)$ ought to be a monotonically decreasing function of time. Simple but effective choices for these functions have been determined in a series of practical experiments[9].

As stated earlier, the process defined by Equation 1 normalizes the weight vectors m_i to the same length. Since the bubble is formed around those units at which $m_i^T x$ is maximum, its center also coincides with that unit for which the norm of the vectorial difference $x - m_i$ is minimum.

Combining all the above results, we obtain the following shortcut algorithm. Let us start with random initial values $m_i = m_i(0)$. For $t = 0, 1, 2, \ldots$, compute:

(1) Center of the bubble (c):

$$\|x(t) - m_c(t)\| = \min_i\{\|x(t) - m_i(t)\|\} \tag{7a}$$

(2) Updated weight vectors:

$$\begin{aligned} m_i(t+1) &= m_i(t) + \alpha(t)(x(t) - m_i(t)) \quad \text{for } i \in N_c, \\ m_i(t+1) &= m_i(t) \quad \text{for all other indices } i \end{aligned} \tag{7b}$$

As stated above, $\alpha = \alpha(t)$ and $N_c = N_c(t)$ are empirical functions of time. The asymptotic values of the m_i define the vector quantization. Notice, too, that Equation 7a defines the classification of input according to the closest weight vector to x.

We must point out that if N_c contained the index i only, Equations 7a and 7b would superficially resemble the classical vector quantization method called *k-means clustering*[10]. The present method, however, is more general because the corrections are made over a wider, dynamically defined neighborhood set, or bubble N_c, so that an *ordered* mapping is obtained. Together with some fine adjustments of the m_i vectors[9], spectral recognition accuracy is improved significantly.

Phonotopic maps

For this discussion we assume that a lattice of hexagonally arranged neurons forms a two-dimensional neural network of the type depicted in Figure 3. As already described, the microphone signal is first converted into a spectral representation, grouped into 15 channels. These channels together constitute the 15-component stochastic input vector x, a function of time, to the network. The self-organizing process has been used to create a "topographic" two-dimensional map of speech elements onto the network.

Superficially the network seems to have only one layer of neurons; due to the lateral interactions in the network, however, its topology is in effect even more complicated than that of the famous multilayered Boltzmann machines or backpropagation networks[11]. Any neuron in our network is also able to create an internal representation of input information in the same way as the "hidden units" in the backpropagation networks eventually do. Several projects have recently been launched to apply Boltzmann machines to speech recognition. We should learn in the near future how they compete with the design described here.

The input vectors x, representing short-time spectra of the speech waveform, are computed in our system every 9.83 milliseconds. These samples are applied in Equations 7a and 7b as input data in their natural order, and the self-organizing process then defines the m_i, or the weight vectors of the neurons. One striking result is that the various neurons of the network become sensitized to spectra of different phonemes and their variations in a two-dimensional order, although teaching was not done by the phonemes; only spectral samples of input were applied. The reason is that the input spectra are clustered around phonemes, and the process finds these clusters. The maps can be calibrated using spectra of known phonemes. If then a new or unknown spectrum is presented at the inputs, the neuron with the closest transmittance vector m_i gives the response, and so the classification occurs in accordance with the Voronoi tessellation in which the m_i act as reference vectors. The values of these vectors very closely reflect the actual speech signal statistics[11]. Figure 6 shows the calibration result for different phonemic samples as a gray-level histogram of such responses, and Figure 7 shows the map when its neurons are labeled according to the majority voting for a number of different responses.

The speech signal is a continuous waveform that makes transitions between various states, corresponding to the phonemes. On the other hand, as stated earlier, the plosives are detectable only as transient states of the speech waveform. For that reason their labeling in Figure 7 is not reliable. Recently we solved the problem of more accurate detection of plosives and certain other phonemic categories by using special, auxiliary maps in which only a certain category of phonemes was represented, and which were trained by a subset of samples. For this purpose we first detect the presence of such phonemes (as a group) from the waveform, and then we use this information to activate the corresponding map. For instance, the occurrence of /k,p,t/ is indicated by low signal energy, and the corresponding spectral samples are picked from the transient regions following silence. The nasals as a group are detectable by responses obtained form the middle area of the main map.

Another problem is *segmentation* of the responses from the map into a standard phonemic transcription. Consider that the spectral samples are taken at regular intervals every 9.83 milliseconds, and they are first labeled in accordance with the corresponding phonemic spectra. These labeled samples are called *quasiphonemes*; in contrast, the duration of a true phoneme is variable, say, from 40 to 400 milliseconds. We have used several alternative rules for the segmentation of quasiphoneme sequences into true phonemes. One of them is based on the degree of stability of the waveform; most phonemes, let alone plosives, have a unique stationary state. An-

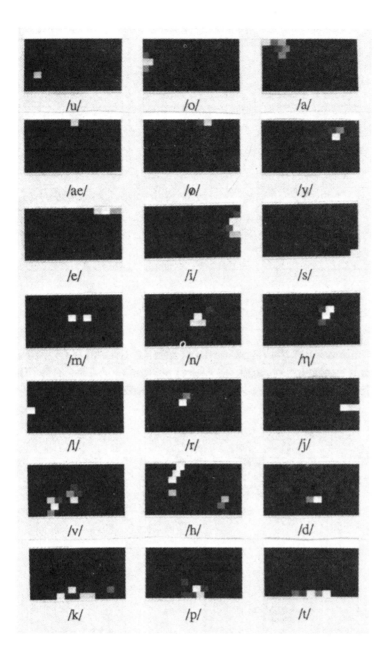

Figure 6. The signal of natural speech is preanalysed and represented on 15 spectral channels ranging from 200 Hz to 5 kHz. The spectral powers of the different channel outputs are presented as input to an artificial neural network. The neurons are tuned automatically, without any supervision or extra information, to the acoustic units of speech identifiable as phonemes. In this set of pictures the neurons correspond to the small rectangular subareas. Calibration of the map was made with 50 samples of each test phoneme. The shaded areas correspond to histograms of responses from the map to certain phonemes (white: maximum).

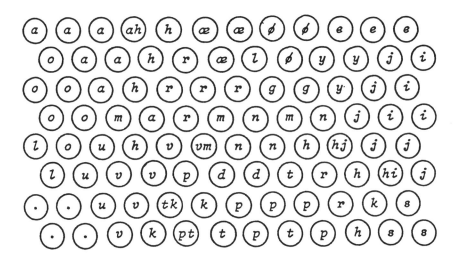

Figure 7. The neurons, shown as circles, are labeled with the symbols of the phonemes to which they "learned" to give best responses. Most neurons give a unique answer; the double labels here show neurons that respond to two phonemes. Distinction of /k,p,t/ from this map is not reliable and needs the analysis of the transient spectra of these phonemes by an auxiliary map. In the Japanese version there are auxiliary maps for /k,p,t/, /b,d,g/, and /m,n,η/ for more accurate analysis.

other, more heuristic method is to decide that if m out of n successive quasiphonemes are the same, they correspond to a single phoneme; e.g., $m = 4$ and $n = 7$ are typical values.

The sequences of quasiphonemes can also be visualized as trajectories over the main map, as shown in Figure 8. Each arrowhead represents one spectral sample, For clarity, the sequence of coordinates shown by arrows has been slightly smoothed to make the curves more continuous. It is clearly discernible that convergence points of the speech waveform seem to correspond to certain (stationary) phonemes.

This kind of graph provides a new means, in addition to some earlier ones, for the visualization of the phonemes of speech, which may be used for speech training and therapy. Profoundly deaf people may find it advantageous to have an immediate visual feedback from their speech.

It may be necessary to point out that the phonotopic map is not the same thing as the so-called formant maps used in phonetics. The latter display the speech signal in coordinates that correspond to the two lowest formants, or resonant frequencies of the vocal tract. Neither is this map any kind of principal component graph for phonemes. The phonotopic map displays the images of the complete spectra as points on a plane, the distances of which approximately correspond to the *vectorial differences* between the original spectra; so this map should rather be regarded as a *similarity graph*, the coordinates of which have no explicit interpretation.

Actually, the phoneme recognition accuracy can still be improved by three or four percent if the templates m_i are fine-tuned; small corrections to the responding

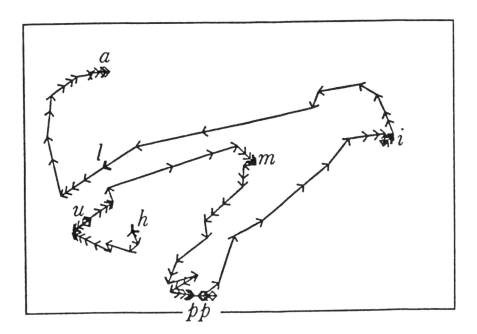

Figure 8. Sequence of the responses obtained from the phonotopic map when the Finnish word *humppila* was uttered. The arrows correspond to intervals of 9.83 milliseconds, at which the speech waveform was analyzed spectrally.

neurons can be made automatically by turning their template vectors toward x if a tentative classification was correct, and away from x if the result was wrong.

Postprocessing in symbolic form

Even if the classification of speech spectra were error-free, the phonemes would not be identifiable from them with 100-percent reliability. This is because there are *coarticulation effects* in speech: the phonemes are influenced by neighboring phonemes. One might imagine it possible to list and take into account all such variations. But there may be many hundreds of different *frames* or *contexts* of neighboring phonemes in which a particular phoneme may occur. Even this, however, is an optimistic figure since the neighbors too may be transformed by other coarticulation effects and errors. Thus, the correction of such transformed phonemes should be made by reference to some kind of *context-sensitive stochastic grammar*, the rules of which are derived from real examples. I have developed a program code that automatically constructs the grammatical transformation rules on the basis of speech samples and their correct reference transcriptions[12]. A typical error grammar may contain 15,000 to 20,000 rules (productions), and these rules can be encoded as a data structure or stored in an associative memory. The optimal amount of context is determined automatically for each rule separately. No special hardware is needed; the search of the matching rules and their application can be made in real time by efficient and fast software methods, based on so-called hash coding, without slowing down the recognition operation.

The two-stage speech recognition system described in this article is a genuine phonetic typewriter, since it outputs orthographic transcriptions for unrestricted utterances, the forms of which only approximately obey certain morphological rules or regularities of a particular language. We have implemented this system for both Finnish and (romanized) Japanese. Both of these languages, like Latin, are characterized by the fact that their orthography is almost identical to their phonemic transcription.

As a complete speech recognition device, our system can be made to operate in either of two modes: (1) transcribing dictation of *unlimited* text, whereby the words (at least in some common idioms) can be connected, since similar rules are applicable for the editing of spaces between the words (at pesent short pauses are needed to insert spaces); and (2) isolated-word recognition from a large vocabulary.

In isolated-word recognition we first use the phonotopic map and its segmentation algorithm to produce a raw phonemic transcription of the uttered word. Then this transcription is compared with reference transcriptions earlier collected from a great many words. Comparison of partly erroneous symbolic expressions (strings) can be related to many standard similarity criteria. Rapid prescreening and spotting of the closest candidates can again be performed by associative or hash-coding methods; we have introduced a very effective error-tolerant searching scheme called *redundant hash addressing*, by which a small number of the best candidates, selected from vocabularies of thousands of items, can be located in a few hundred milliseconds (on a personal computer). After that, the more accurate final comparison between the much smaller number of candidates can be made by the best statistical methods.

Hardware implementations and performance

The system's neural network could, in principle, be built up of parallel hardware components that behave according to Equations 5 and 6. For the time being, no such components have been developed. On the other hand, for many applications the equivalent functions from Equations 7a and 7b are readily computable by fast digital signal processor chips; in that case the various neurons only exist *virtually*, as the signal processors are able to solve their equations by a timesharing principle. Even this operation, however, can be performed in real time, especially in speech processing.

The most central neural hardware of our system is contained on the coprocessor board shown in Figure 9. Its block diagram is shown in Figure 10. Only two signal processors have been necessary: one for the acoustic preprocessor that produces the input pattern vectors x, and another for timeshared computation of the responses from the neural network. For the time being, the self-organized computation of the templates m_i, or "learning," is made in an IBM PC AT-compatible host processor, and the transmittance parameters (synaptic transmittances) are loaded onto the coprocessor board. Newer designs are intended to operate as stand-alone systems. A standard microprocessor CPU chip on our board takes care of overall control and data routing and performs some preprocessing operations after FFT (such as logarithmization and normalization), as well as segmenting the quasiphoneme strings and deciding whether the auxiliary transient maps are to be used. Although the 80186 is a not-so-effective CPU, it still has extra capacity for postprocessing operations: it can be programmed to apply the context-sensitive grammar for unlimited text or to perform the isolated-word recognition operations.

Figure 9. The coprocessor board for the neural network and the postprocessing functions.

The personal computer has been used during experimentation for all postprocessing operations. Nonetheless, the overall recognition operations take place in near real time. In the intended mode of operation the speech recognizer will only assist the keyboard operations and communicate with the CPU through the same channel.

One of the most serious problems with this system, as well as with any existing speech recognizer, is recognition accuracy, especially for an arbitrary speaker. After postprocessing, the present transcription accuracy varies between 92 and 97 percent, depending on speaker and difficulty of text. We performed most of the experiments reported here with half a dozen male speakers, using office text, names, and the most frequent words of the language. The number of tests performed over the years is inestimable. Typically, thousands of words have been involved in a particular series of tests. Enrollment of a new speaker requires dictation of 100 words, and the learning processes can proceed concurrently with dictation. The total learning time on the PC is less than 10 minutes. During learning, the template vectors of the phonotopic map are tuned to the new samples.

Isolated-word recognition from a 1000-word vocabulary is possible with an accuracy of 96 to 98 percent. Since the recognition system forms an intermediate symbolic transcription that can be compared with any standard reference transcriptions, the vocabulary or its active subsets can be defined in written form and changed dynamically during use, without the need of speaking any samples of these words.

All output, for unlimited text as well as for isolated words, is produced in near real time: the mean delay is on the order of 250 milliseconds per word. It should be noticed

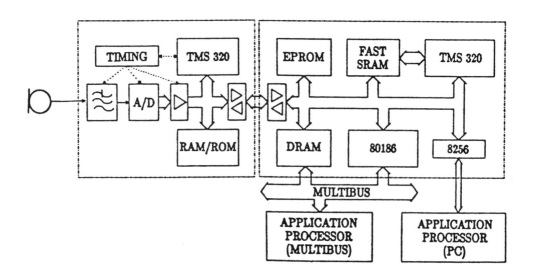

Figure 10. Block diagram of the coprocessor board. A/D: analog-to-digital converter. TMS320: Texas Instruments 32010 signal processor chip. RAM/ROM: 4K-word random-access memory, 256-word programmable read-only memory. EPROM: 64K-byte electrically erasable read-only memory. DRAM: 512K-byte dual-port random-access memory. SRAM: 96K-byte paged dual-port random-access memory. 80186: Intel microprocessor CPU. 8256: parallel interface.

that contemporary microprocessors already have much higher speeds (typically five times higher) than the chips used in our design.

To the best of our knowledge, this system is the only existing complete speech recognizer that employs neural computing principles and has been brought to a commercial stage, verified by extensive tests. Of course, it still falls somewhat short of expectations; obviously some kind of linguistic postprocessing model would improve its performance. On the other hand, our principal aim was to demonstrate the highly adaptive properties of neural networks, which allow a very accurate, nonlinear statistical analysis of real signals. These properties ought to be a goal of all practical "neurocomputers."

REFERENCES

1. Lea, W.A. (Ed.) (1980). **Trends in speech recognition.** Englewood Cliffs, NJ: Prentice-Hall.

2. Levinson, S.E., Rabiner, L.R., and Sondhi, M.M. (1983). An introduction to the application of the theory of probabilistic functions of a Markov process to automatic speech recognition. *Bell Systems Technical Journal*, April, 1035–1073.

3. Devijver, P.A. and Kittler, J. (1982). **Pattern recognition: A statistical approach.** London: Prentice-Hall.

4. Klatt, D.H. (1977). Review of the ARPA speech understanding project. *Journal of the Acoustical Society of America*, December, 1345–1366.

5. Reddy, R. and Zue, V. (1983). Recognizing continuous speech remains an elusive goal. *IEEE Spectrum*, November, 84–87.

6. Petre, P. (1985). Speak, master: Typewriters that take dictation. *Fortune*, January, 56–60.

7. Schroeder, M.R. and Hall, J.L. (1974). Model for mechanical to neural transduction in the auditory receptor. *Journal of the Acoustical Society of America*, May, 1055-1060.

8. Meddis, R. (1986). Simulation of mechanical to neural transduction in the auditory receptor. *Journal of the Acoustical Society of America*, March, 703–711.

9. Kohonen, T. (1984). **Self-organization and associative memory.** Series in Information Sciences, Volume 8, Berlin-Heidelberg-New York-Tokyo: Springer-Verlag (second edition, 1988).

10. Makhoul, H., Roucos, S., and Gish, H. (1985). Vector quantization in speech coding. *Proceedings IEEE*, November, 1551–1588.

11. Rumelhart, D.E., Hinton, G.E., and Williams, R.J. (1986). Learning internal representations by error propagation. In D.E. Rumelhart, J.L. McClelland, and the PDP Research Group (Eds.), **Parallel distributed processing, Explorations in the microstructure of cognition, Volume 1: Foundations.** Cambridge, MA: MIT Press, 318–362.

12. Kohonen, T. (1986). Dynamically expanding context, with application to the correction of symbol strings in the recognition of continuous speech. *Proceedings of the eighth international conference on pattern recognition*, IEEE Computer Society, Washington DC, 1148–1151.

CHAPTER 8

COUNTERPROPAGATION NETWORKS
by
Robert Hecht-Nielsen

Preface

In this 1987 article, Hecht-Nielsen notes that the three-level instar-outstar map of Chapter 6 can be used "as a statistically optimal self-programming look-up table." In this context, a set of examples $(\mathbf{x}_1, \mathbf{y}_1)$, $(\mathbf{x}_2, \mathbf{y}_2), \ldots$ of a function $\mathbf{y}_i = \phi(\mathbf{x}_i)$ or $\mathbf{y}_i = \phi(\mathbf{x}_i) + \mathbf{n}$ is given, where $\mathbf{n}$ is a stationary noise process such that $\mathbf{x}_i \in \Re^n$ and $\mathbf{y}_i \in \Re^m$. The network self-organizes a learned approximation to this $\Re^n \to \Re^m$ map.

Hecht-Nielsen defines the instar input vectors as $X_i = (\mathbf{x}_i, \mathbf{y}_i)$ and the outstar input vectors as $Y_i = (\mathbf{x}_i, \mathbf{y}_i)$ during learning. Using this definition, very different $\mathbf{y}_i$ vectors can, for example, help the network to choose different winner-take-all category nodes even if the corresponding $\mathbf{x}_i$ vectors are similar, and very similar $\mathbf{y}_i$ vectors can help the network to choose the same category node if the $\mathbf{x}_i$ vectors are not too different. This way of defining inputs helps to "supervise" node selection within the "unsupervised" competitive learning module that constitutes the first two layers of the network. On test trials inputs such as $X_i^* = (\mathbf{x}_i, 0)$ are presented and the map makes its best prediction Y_i^* to these data.

Hecht-Nielsen notes the importance of controlling the densities of inputs corresponding to each category (see Theorem 2 of Chapter 6) and the usefulness of employing some sort of "conscience" method to desensitize nodes that are chosen too often if the densities are not equidistributed. This conscience idea is illustrated by the "habituating choice" model of Chapter 6 (equations 23 and 24), but as noted there, this model can become unstable given certain input orderings. All of these remarks attempt to cope in one way or another with the inability of competitive learning models to learn, by themselves, about arbitrary data streams in a temporally stable and predictively reliable way, even though they work well in the sparse learning case. It should be emphasized, however, that other popular learning models, such as backpropagation and the Boltzmann machine, experience even more severe learning instabilities (see Chapter 2).

Hecht-Nielsen called the instar-outstar model the *counterpropagation* network (CPN). He also named the instar-outstar model, where the the standard inputs $\mathbf{x}_i$ and $\mathbf{y}_i$ are used, *forward-only counterpropagation*. These models are suggested to be "a new type of mapping network." However, the equations in Figure 2 are the standard equations of the instar-outstar map. The only difference between counterpropagation and the instar-outstar map is the use of augmented input and output vectors $(\mathbf{x}_i, \mathbf{y}_i)$.

A change of inputs or parameters is not the accepted usage of the term "new model." The new name perhaps seemed more plausible in the light of other new names that Hecht-Nielsen gave in this article to the competitive learning model and the outstar model. He called the competitive learning model, which was developed in the 1970's by Malsburg (Chapter 5) and Grossberg (Chapters 4 and 6), "Kohonen learning," although the first published use by Kohonen of the model in Figure 2 appears to occur in Kohonen (1984). Hecht-Nielsen also called the outstar model, which was developed in the 1960's by Grossberg (1968a, 1968b, 1969, 1970), "Grossberg learning." These newly named parts are then joined together using the additional new name of "counterpropagation."

These new names seem to reflect problems that arose in the field of neural networks when it became popular due to the paradigm shift that was described in the Editorial Preface. As noted there, the pressures leading to this shift had been building for some time across several fields, and when they exceeded threshold, the type of rapid surge occurred that is characteristic of many autocatalytic processes.

As a result of this rapid transition, spokesmen in several fields began to lecture about many known, but previously insufficiently assimilated, results and to encourage their colleagues to develop them. The colleagues then named the models after their spokesmen. In this way, the classical McCulloch-Pitts model and additive model were renamed the Hopfield model by physicists and engineers new to the field (see Chapter 2). These historical revisions caused serious stresses across the field. Hecht-Nielsen's response was to rename established models, whose previous names were based on functional properties, after investigators who helped to develop them, before these models could be named after yet another new spokesman. That is how the Cohen-Grossberg model was named (Chapter 2). This name was suggested by a number of groups to acknowledge that Grossberg had discovered the additive model in the 1960's and that Cohen and Grossberg had discovered the Liapunov function for the additive, shunting, and many other symmetric CAM models before Hopfield did.

Our own group's philosophy has been to give models functional names—such as additive, shunting, instar, outstar, avalanche, and adaptive resonance models—and to encourage researchers to broaden their historical citations of these functional names as they better understand the field's history. In the present heated state of the field's development, this philosophy is not always easy to implement.

On a broader plane, we are concerned that the types of misleading marketing in science, that one reads about too regularly in the popular press, be vigorously resisted in the field of neural networks while we still have the chance to establish good scientific values on which to build a healthy field. The confusing proliferation of new names for old models with perfectly good functional names is one sign that this problem has yet to be fully solved.

References

Grossberg, S. (1968a). Some nonlinear networks capable of learning a spatial pattern of arbitrary complexity. *Proceedings of the National Academy of Sciences*, **59**, 368–372.

Grossberg, S. (1968b). A prediction theory for some nonlinear functional-differential equations, II: Learning of patterns. *Journal of Mathematical Analysis and Applications*, **22**, 490–522.

Grossberg, S. (1969). On learning and energy-entropy dependence in recurrent and nonrecurrent signed networks. *Journal of Statistical Physics*, **1**, 319–350.

Grossberg, S. (1970). Some networks that can learn, remember, and reproduce any number of complicated space-time patterns, II. *Studies in Applied Mathematics*, **49**, 135–166.

Kohonen, T. (1984). **Self-organization and associative memory**. New York: Springer-Verlag.

Applied Optics
1987, **26**, 4979–4984

COUNTERPROPAGATION NETWORKS

Robert Hecht-Nielsen

Abstract

By combining Kohonen learning and Grossberg learning a new type of mapping neural network is obtained. This counterpropagation network (CPN) fucntions as a statistically optimal self-programming lookup table. The paper begins with some introductory comments, followed by the definition of the CPN. Then a closed-form formula for the error of the network is developed. The paper concludes with a discussion of CPN variants and comments about CPN convergence and performance. References and a neurocomputing bibliography with a combined total of eighty entries are provided.

I. Introduction

Of all the practical information processing operations that neural networks can currently carry out, one of the most useful is the ability to learn a mathematical mapping by self-organization in response to examples of the mapping's action. Typically, one generates a set of examples $(\mathbf{x}_1, \mathbf{y}_1)$, $(\mathbf{x}_2, \mathbf{y}_2), \ldots$ of the action of a function ϕ, where $\mathbf{y}_i = \phi(\mathbf{x}_i)$ or $\mathbf{y}_i = \phi(\mathbf{x}_i) + \mathbf{n}$ (where $\mathbf{n}$ is a stationary noise process). These examples statistically define the desired input/output relationship.

A network that self-organizes itself to implement an approximation to a function or mapping is called a mapping neural network. Currently, the most popular mapping neural network is the backpropagation network of Rumelhart[1]. The backpropagation network has been shown to be capable of implementing approximations to a variety of mappings from $\mathbf{R}^n$ to $\mathbf{R}^m$. Although most applications of backpropagation to date have been to mappings that have binary input and output vectors (i.e., each vector component is essentially either one or zero), there is ample evidence that backpropagation also works for at least some non-binary vector mappings.

In this paper a new type of mapping neural network, called the counterpropagation network (CPN), is introduced. It is shown that (under nonpathological conditions) this network will self-organize a near-optimal (in the sense that the entries in the table are statistically equiprobable) lookup table approximation to the mapping used to generate its data. The method works equally well for both binary and continuous vector mappings. It is shown that for a sufficiently large network the mapping approximation can be made essentially as accurate as desired. The counterpropagation network architecture is a combination of a portion of the self-organizing map of Kohonen[2] and the outstar structure of Grossberg[3].

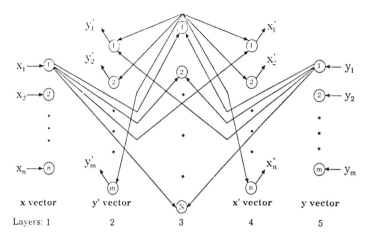

x vector   y' vector   x' vector   y vector

Layers: 1   2   3   4   5

Figure 1. Topology of the counterpropagation network.

Although most pure mapping network problems are best attacked by use of back-propagation, those applications that require statistically equiprobable feature vectors or where a lookup table structure is desirable should be approached using the counterpropagation network. Problems such as vector quantization code development, high-dimensional probability density function estimation and characterization, and pattern recognition for continuously variable pattern vectors are often best solved using counterpropagation networks.

II. Counterpropagation Network

Figure 1 presents the topology of the CPN and Figure 2 presents the transfer functions and learning laws of each of the five layers of the network. The basic idea is that, during adaptation, pairs of example vectors $(\mathbf{x},\mathbf{y})$ (both assumed to be of unit length) are presented to the network at layers 1 and 5, respectively. These vectors then propagate through the network in a counterflow manner to yield output vectors $\mathbf{x}'$ and $\mathbf{y}'$ that are intended to be approximations of $\mathbf{x}$ and $\mathbf{y}$. Thus the name counterpropagation.

As shown in Figure 1, the full $\mathbf{x}$ and $\mathbf{y}$ input vectors are supplied to each processing element of layer 3, whereas the processing elements of layers 2 and 4 only get their corresponding component of these vectors. The processing elements of layers 2 and 4 also receive inputs from each processing element of layer 3 (the layer 3 processing element output signals, of which there are N, are labeled z_i).

When an $\mathbf{x}$ and $\mathbf{y}$ vector pair is presented to the network the processing elements of layer 3 compete with one another as shown in the z_i equation of Figure 2. The processing element with the highest average weight vector correlations with $\mathbf{x}$ and $\mathbf{y}$ (i.e., the highest value of I_i) has its output signal (z_i) set to one. All $N-1$ other z_i outputs are set to zero. Ties are broken on the basis of the smallest processing element index. By virtue of the form of the layer 3 weight change law (shown at the bottom of Figure 2), only the best matching processing element on layer 3 gets to adjust its weight vector in response to each vector pair input during training.

As shown by Kohonen[2], the $(\mathbf{u}_i, \mathbf{v}_i)$ weight vectors of layer 3 (which start out as unit vectors) will self-organize in response to the input vector pairs so that these

Layers 1 & 5: Fanouts

Layers 2 & 4:

$$y'_i = \sum_{j=1}^{n} w_{ij} z_j$$

$$\dot{w}_{ij} = (-a w_{ij} + b y_i) z_j$$

$$(x'_i \text{ similar})$$

Layer 3:

$$z_i = \begin{cases} 1 & \text{if } I_i > I_j, \quad \forall j \\ 0 & \text{otherwise} \end{cases}$$

$$I_i = \sum_{j=1}^{n} u_{ij} x_j + \sum_{j=1}^{m} v_{ij} y_j = \mathbf{u}_i \cdot \mathbf{x} + \mathbf{v}_i \cdot \mathbf{y}$$

$$\dot{\mathbf{u}}_i = \alpha(\mathbf{x} - \mathbf{u}_i) z_i$$

$$\dot{\mathbf{v}}_i = \beta(\mathbf{y} - \mathbf{v}_i) z_i$$

Figure 2. CPN mathematics.

vectors will, after statistical equilibration, have the following two properties:

(1) The vectors $\mathbf{u}_i$ and $\mathbf{v}_i$ will remain approximately unit vectors.

(2) The weight vectors $\mathbf{u}_i$, $\mathbf{v}_i$ will be distributed on the Cartesian product unit sphere in such a way that the probability of a given randomly chosen $(\mathbf{x},\mathbf{y})$ (the $\mathbf{x}$ vectors are assumed to be chosen in accordance with a fixed probability density function ρ and this then induces a density for the $\mathbf{y}$ vectors) being closest to any one of these weight vectors is equal to approximately $1/N$. In other words, the win regions of these weight vectors are equally likely to contain an input vector pair chosen in accordance with ρ (see Section III and Reference 4 for the definition of a win region). [Note: Proposition 5. 1 in Chapter 5 of Reference 2 is not exactly correct (personal communication from Kohonen). A density correlation factor is required because the weight vectors tend to oversample high density areas and undersample low density areas. A practical cure for this problem is suggested below.]

Figure 3 clarifies this behavior. The weight vectors $\mathbf{u}_i$ and $\mathbf{v}_i$ of the winning processing element on layer 3 are moved toward $\mathbf{x}$ and $\mathbf{y}$, respectively, by an amount equal to the fraction α of the distance between them and their targets. Since these vectors are all normalized, these movements are approximately perpendicular to the directions of $\mathbf{u}_i$ and $\mathbf{v}_i$, and thus do not change their length much. In fact, if either of these vectors gets significantly longer or shorter than unit length, this weight adjustment process will act to restore their length to one by dragging them up or down radially as well as turning them. This process ends up moving the weight vectors of layer 3 around to an equilibrium configuration that represents the average of the effects of a huge number of adjustments. Thus, they become representative of the distribution of the input data vector pairs. Thus, the weight vectors of the processing elements of layer 3 become organized as a more or less statistically optimal

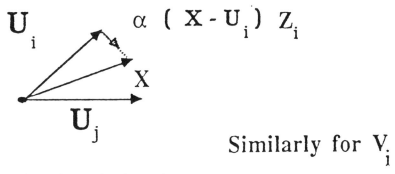

Similarly for V_i

Figure 3. Kohonen's weight change law.

set of examples of the relationships between the **x** and **y** vectors. Note that, if the function ϕ is invertible, layer 3 will be equally sensitive to both the forward and backward mappings. Weight changes with layer 3 processing elements take place in accordance with the two equations at the bottom of Figure 2. This Kohonen learning law rotates the closest matching weight vectors around toward the latest input vectors. This movement is typically almost perpendicular to the weight vector and thus has the effect of keeping the vector approximately normalized (see Reference 2 for details on Kohonen learning).

Layers 2 and 4 of the network learn the average **x** and **y** vector values that occur when each of the processing elements of layer 3 wins the closeness competition. Such a structure is called and outstar and was invented by Grossberg[3]. Grossberg has shown that, if the constants a and b in the layer 2 and 4 equations of Figure 2 are set equal to each other at a positive value less than one, the **x**' and **y**' values emitted by layers 2 and 4 will, after statistical equilibrium, equal approximately the average value of the **x** and **y** vectors that historically allowed that particular layer 3 element to win the competition of that layer.

In summary, after both layer 3 and layers 2 and 4 equilibrate, an input vector pair **x** and **y** will cause the network to emit **x**' and **y**' vectors that are approximately the same as the nearest matching layer 3 weight vector pair. If the pair **x** and **0** (i.e., the **y** vector is set to zero) are entered, the output pair will again be essentially the same as the layer 3 weight vector pair with a first vector element that best matches **x**. If ϕ is invertible the same sort of result will hold if a pair **0** and **y** is entered. If a pair having some components of both the **x** and **y** vectors zeroed out is entered, the network will complete the vector pair and the outputs will be approximately the same as the best matching layer 3 weight vector's elements. Thus, CPN functions very much like a lookup table. The overall CPN can be viewed as a modular element that will self-organize to form such a table and then respond to partial inputs as outlined above. Figure 4 shows a schematic representation for the CPN module. This module can be used as a building block for creating more complex and more capable networks.

III. CPN Error Analysis

Since the output of a CPN is almost exactly equal to one of the weight vectors (this is also true for the forward-only CPN version considered below), let us analyze the mean-squared error of a CPN system on this basis. To stay within the confines of conventional notation (and to emphasize the universality of the discussion) the layer

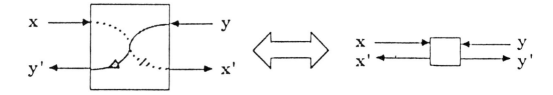

Figure 4. The CPN module.

3 weight vectors are named $\mathbf{w}_i$ even though this contradicts the notation of Section II. In fact, several of the variables (e.g., $n, \mathbf{z}, \mathbf{v}$) used previously will be reused in this section with different meanings.

The first issue is to define the input/output behavior of the CPN system. The basic idea is that an input vector $\mathbf{z}$ (consisting perhaps of the input vector pair $\mathbf{x}$ and $\mathbf{y}$ of Section II) comes into the system. The network then compares $\mathbf{z}$ with all the weight vectors $\mathbf{w}_i, i = 1, 2, \ldots, N$ of the system and emits the nearest matching vector $\mathbf{w}_k$ as its output. This is the basic function of the CPN. As in the previous section, $\mathbf{z}$ is assumed to be randomly selected in accordance with a fixed probability density function ρ.

Given the above definitions, the mean-squared error $F(W)$ of this system is the average of the square of the distance between an arbitrary input vector $\mathbf{z}$ and the nearest matching $\mathbf{w}_i$, weighted by the probability $\rho(\mathbf{z})$, which is given by

$$F(W) = \int_{\Omega^n} \theta(W, \mathbf{z})\rho(\mathbf{z})dA(\mathbf{z}),$$

where

$$W = [\mathbf{w}_1, \mathbf{w}_2, \ldots, \mathbf{w}_N]$$
$$\mathbf{z}, \mathbf{w}_i \in \Omega^n \equiv \{\mathbf{x} \in \mathbf{R}^n : \|\mathbf{x}\| = 1\},$$
$$\theta(W, \mathbf{z}) \equiv \min(\|\mathbf{z} - \mathbf{w}_1\|^2, \|\mathbf{z} - \mathbf{w}_2\|^2, \ldots, \|\mathbf{z} - \mathbf{w}_N\|^2).$$

This can be simplified by noting that

$$\|\mathbf{z} - \mathbf{w}_i\|^2 = \|\mathbf{z}\|^2 + \|\mathbf{w}_i\|^2 - 2\mathbf{z} \cdot \mathbf{w}_i,$$

and thus

$$\theta(W, \mathbf{z}) = 2 - 2\max(\mathbf{z} \cdot \mathbf{w}_1, \mathbf{z} \cdot \mathbf{w}_2, \ldots, \mathbf{z} \cdot \mathbf{w}_N).$$

By defining the win region of $\mathbf{w}_i$ to be

$$B_i \equiv \{\mathbf{z} \in \Omega^n | i \text{ is the smallest integer } 1 \le i \le N$$

$$\text{such that } \mathbf{z} \cdot \mathbf{w}_i \ge \mathbf{z} \cdot \mathbf{w}_j \quad \forall j\},$$

we can reexpress the integral for $F(W)$ as

$$F(W) = 2 - 2\sum_{i=1}^{N} \mathbf{w}_i \cdot \int_{B_i} \mathbf{z}\rho(\mathbf{z})dA(\mathbf{z}),$$

since for $\mathbf{z} \in B_i$,

$$\mathbf{z} \cdot \mathbf{w}_i = \max(\mathbf{z} \cdot \mathbf{w}_1, \mathbf{z} \cdot \mathbf{w}_2, \ldots, \mathbf{z} \cdot \mathbf{w}_N),$$

and since $\mathbf{w}_i$ is a constant vector. Note that if m_i is defined to be

$$m_i \equiv \int_{B_i} \rho(\mathbf{z}) dA(\mathbf{z})$$

and $\mathbf{v}_i$ (the centroid of the sphere subset B_i) is defined to be

$$\mathbf{v}_i \equiv (1/m_i) \int_{B_i} \mathbf{z}\rho(\mathbf{z}) dA(\mathbf{z})$$

we can rewrite $F(W)$ as

$$F(W) = 2 - 2\sum_{i=1}^{N} m_i(\mathbf{w}_i \cdot \mathbf{v}_i).$$

Note that

$$\sum_{i=1}^{N} m_i = 1.$$

The geometry of $F(W)$ is that it gets smaller as the B_i regions get smaller and more uniform in importance (as determined by m_i). Note that $\mathbf{v}_i$ can be thought of as the average vector in B_i. If B_i is a small, localized, almost planar region, $\mathbf{v}_i$ will be almost a unit vector that points to the probability-weighted center of B_i. This will make the dot product $\mathbf{w}_i \cdot \mathbf{v}_i$ almost one, since $\mathbf{w}_i$ is a unit vector that also points at the center of B_i. However, if B_i is very large and significantly curved, $\mathbf{v}_i$ will be significantly shorter than a unit vector and the dot product $\mathbf{w}_i \cdot \mathbf{v}_i$ will be smaller, thus increasing $F(W)$. Finally, note that the sum of the $\mathbf{v}_i$ vectors is a constant vector that only depends on ρ and not on the weight vectors:

$$\sum_{i=1}^{N} \mathbf{v}_i = \int_{\Omega^n} \mathbf{z}\rho(\mathbf{z}) dA(\mathbf{z}).$$

In conclusion, a relatively simple formula exists for the mean-squared error $F(W)$ of the CPN. By virtue of the generality of the approach taken in this definition this formula applies to both the full CPN and the forward-only version defined below. As is clear from the form of the equation, the dependence of the error on each coordinate of the input vectors is uniform across all the coordinates. Thus, no matter how important or unimportant a coordinate is for the implementation of a mapping its contribution to the adjustment of the Kohonen units is approximately the same (this is particularly so for the forward-only version of the network). This effect fundamentally limits the accuracy of any lookup table approximation.

IV. CPN Variants and Evolutes

Multiple types of counterpropagation network have been defined, with the CPN module defined above being the most important example. One useful CPN variant

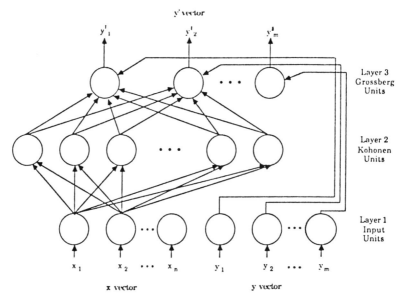

Figure 5. Forward-only CPN.

is illustrated in Figure 5. In this network layer 4 of the basic CPN has been excised, as have the interconnects from the **y** input vector to layer 3 (this last change is optional). The net result is a CPN variant (called the forward-only CPN module) that is ideal for problems in which only transformations from **x** to **y** are of interest (and implementation of the inverse mapping and completions of partial **x**–**y** input pairs are not of interest).

Finally, by modifying the competition process on layer 3 of the CPN, there can be K winning processing elements (corresponding to the K nearest matching w_i vectors) instead of one (see Reference 4 for additional discussion about the advantages of this). If the outputs of these K processing elements are set so that they sum to one (i.e., the former single output signal of one is now divided among the K units in some manner directly dependent on their relative I_i values) the outstars of layers 2 and 4 will blend their usual output values. This interpolation process can lead to significantly increased mapping approximation accuracy for no increase in network size. A CPN using this approach is operating in an interpolative mode, as opposed to the accretive mode discussed above.

V. Discussion

One of the problems with CPN (returning now to the notation of Figures 1 and 2) is that Kohonen learning only works well when ρ is nonzero only in a single connected region. If this is not true, weight vectors can get stuck in isolated regions and cannot move to where they are needed. A number of solutions have been developed for this. One is called convex combination. In this approach, one starts off with all the (unit) weight vectors equal to the vector $\mathbf{1} = (1/\sqrt{n}, 1\sqrt{n}, \ldots, 1/\sqrt{n})$. The **x**–**y** data inputs then start out as normalized convex combinations, i.e.,

$$\alpha\mathbf{x} + (1 - \alpha)\mathbf{1}$$

of their actual values and this same vector. Initially, the combinations start off with a very low value of α (near zero). This forces all the data vectors to be close to the weight vectors. As time goes on the value of α is raised slowly to one. As this happens, the weight vectors are peeled off and follow the input data vectors as they move away from $\mathbf{1}$. This works very well but it slows down adaptation. Another approach is to add noise to the data, which has the effect of making ρ positive everywhere. This works all right but is much slower than convex combination. Finally, another approach is to build a conscience into each Kohonen processing element to monitor its success in the layer 3 competition. If it wins the competition substantially more often than $1/N$ of the time, have that unit take itself out of the competition for a while, allowing stuck units to win their way out of captivity. Initial work suggests that this approach works well and may solve the problems with Kohonen's Proposition 5. 1. This idea of adding a conscience to the layer 3 processing elements is due to Duane DeSieno of Logical Designs in San Diego.

Given its simple lookup table function, CPN is obviously inferior to backpropagation for most mapping network applications. Its advantages are that it is simple and that it forms a good statistical model of its input vector environment (i.e., of ρ). Another potential advantage is the existence of a closed-form formula for the mean-squared error of the network's mapping function. As with all lookup table approaches, CPN requires a number of entries (Kohonen units) to achieve high mapping approximation accuracy. However, because CPN adjusts its weights to conform to the statistics of the input vectors the number of Kohonen processing elements required to reach a particular level of mapping approximation accuracy depends primarily on the complexity of the mapping and the statistics of the $\mathbf{x}$ and $\mathbf{y}$ vector selections, and not very much on the dimensionality of the spaces involved. Thus, CPN avoids the worst part of Richard Bellman's "curse of high dimensionality". The use of CPN in an interpolation mode can also help accuracy considerably. CPN seems to be well suited to situations where the relationships between the input data components are more important than the implementation of a mapping (although it does fairly well as a mapping network). The network is also useful for rapid prototyping of neurocomputing systems (even if a backpropagation or some other mapping network will be used in its place late after the rest of the system is working) because it typically converges 1 or 2 orders of magnitude faster than backpropagation. The CPN module can be used during early development and can later be replaced by a plug-compatible network such as backpropagation.

Finally, CPN illustrates a key point about neurocomputing system design, namely that many of the existing network paradigms can be viewed as building block components that can be assembled into new configurations that offer new information processing capabilities.

REFERENCES

1. Rumelhart, D.E. and McClelland, J.L. (1986, 1987). **Parallel distributed processing: Explorations in the microstructure of cognition, Volumes 1, 2, 3**. Cambridge, MA: MIT Press.

2. Kohonen, T. (1984). **Self-organization and associative memory**. New York: Springer-Verlag.

3. Grossberg, S. (1982). **Studies of mind and brain**. Boston: Reidel Press.

4. Hecht-Nielsen, R. (1987). Combinatorial hypercompression. In **Proceedings of the IEEE international conference on neural networks**. New York: IEEE.

BIBLIOGRAPHY

Amari, S. (1983). Field theory of self-organizing neural networks. *IEEE Transactions on Systems, Man and Cybernetics*, **SMC-13**, 741.

Amari, S. and Arbib, M.A. (1982). **Competition and cooperation in neural nets**. New York: Springer-Verlag.

Amari, S. (1974). A method of statistical neurodynamics. *Biological Cybernetics*, **14**, 201.

Amari, S. (1971). Characteristics of randomly connected threshold-element networks and network systems. *IEEE Proceedings*, **59**, 35.

Anderson, J.A. (1983). Cognitive and psychological computation with neural models. *IEEE Transactions on Systems, Man and Cybernetics*, **SMC-13**, 799.

Anderson, J.A. (1972). A simple neural network generating an interactive memory. *Mathematical Biosciences*, **14**, 197.

Barto, A.G. and Sutton, R.S. (1984). Stimulation experiments with goal-seeking adaptive elements. AFWAL-TR-84-1022, DTIC Document ADA 140295.

Barto, A.G. and Sutton, R.S. (1981). Landmark learning: An illustration of associative search. *Biological Cybernetics*, **42**, 1.

Carpenter, G.A. and Grossberg, S. (1987). A massively parallel architecture for a self-organizing neural pattern recognition machine. *Computer Vision, Graphics, and Image Processing*, **37**, 54.

Casasent, D. (1986). Scene analysis research: Optical pattern recognition and artificial intelligence. *Proceedings of the Society for Photo-Optical Instrumentation Engineering*, **634**, 439.

Cohen, M.A. and Grossberg, S. (1986). Neural dynamics of speech and language coding: Developmental programs, perceptual grouping, and competition for short term memory. *Human Neurobiology*, **5**, 1.

Cohen, M.A. and Grossberg, S. (1983). Absolute stability of global pattern formation and parallel memory storage by competitive neural networks. *IEEE Transactions on Systems, Man and Cybernetics*, **SMC-13**, 815.

Cover, T.M. and Hart, P.E. (1967). Nearest neighbor pattern classification. *IEEE Transactions on Information Theory*, **IT-13**.

Cruz, C. and Tam, J.Y. (1985). NEP: An emulation-assist processor for parallel associative networks. IBM Palo Alto Scientific Center Report G320-2374.

Cruz, C. and Myers, H.J. (1983). Associative networks II. IBM Palo Alto Scientific Center Report G320-3446.

Cruz, C. and Myers, H.J. (1982). Associative networks. IBM Palo Alto Scientific Center Report G320-3474.

Daugman, J.G. (1985). Uncertainty relation for resolution in space, spatial frequency, and orientation optimized by two-dimensional visual cortical filters. *Journal of the Optical Society of America*, **2**, 1160.

Denker, J. (1986). **Proceedings of the second annual conference on neural networks**, AIP Conference Proceedings, **151**. New York: American Institute of Physics.

Dunning, G.J., Marom, E., Owechko, Y., and Soffer, B.H. (1986). Optical holographic associative memory using a phase conjugate resonator. *Proceedings of the Society of Photo-Optical Instrumentation Engineering*, **625**, 205.

Farlow, S.J. (Ed.) (1984). **Self-organizing methods in modeling: GMDH type algorithms**. New York: Marcel Dekker.

Fisher, A.D., Fukuda, R.C., and Lee, J.N. (1986). Implementations of adaptive associative optical computing elements. *Proceedings of the Society for Photo-Optical Instrumentation Engineering*, **625**, 1.

Fisher, A.D. and Giles, C.L. (1985). Optical adaptive associative computer architectures. *Proceedings IEEE COMPCOM meeting*, IEEE catalog CH2135-2/85, pp. 342–344.

Fisher, A.D., Giles, C.L., and Lee, J.N. (1984). Associative processor architectures for optical computing. *Journal of the Optical Society of America A*, **1**, 1337.

Fukushima, K. and Miyake, S. (1984). Neocognitron: A new algorithm for pattern recognition tolerant of deformations and shifts in position. *Pattern Recognition*, **15**, 455.

Geman, S. (1981). The law of large numbers in neural modeling. In S. Grossberg (Ed.), **Mathematical psychology and psychophysiology**. Providence, RI: American Mathematical Society.

Grossberg, S. and Stone, G. (1986). Neural dynamics of word recognition and recall: Attentional priming, learning, and resonance. *Psychological Review*, **93**, 46.

Grossberg, S. and Kuperstein, M. (1986). **Neural dynamics of adaptive sensory-motor control**. Amsterdam: Elsevier/North-Holland.

Grossberg, S. and Mingolla, E. (1985). Neural dynamics of perceptual grouping: Textures, boundaries, and emergent segmentations. *Perception and Psychophysics*, **38**, 141.

Grossberg, S. and Cohen, M.A. (1984). Some global properties of binocular resonances: Disparity matching, filling-in, and figure-ground separation. In T. Caelli and P. Dodwell (Eds.), **Figural synthesis**. Hillsdale, NJ: Erlbaum Associates.

Grossberg, S. (1971). Embedding fields: Underlying philosophy, mathematics, and applications to psychology, physiology, and anatomy. *Journal of Cybernetics*, **1**, 28.

Grossberg, S. (1970). Some networks that can learn, remember, and reproduce any number of complicated space-time patterns, II. *Studies in Applied Mathematics,* **49**, 135.

Grossberg, S. (1969). Embedding fields: A theory of learning with physiological implications. *Journal of Mathematical Psychology,* **6**, 209.

Grossberg, S. (1969). Some networks that can learn, remember, and reproduce any number of complicated space-time patterns, I. *Journal of Mathematics and Mechanics,* **19**, 53.

Grossberg, S. (1967). Nonlinear difference-differential equations in prediction and learning theory. *Proceedings of the National Academy of Sciences USA,* **58**, 1329.

Hecht-Nielsen, R. (1987). Kolmogorov's mapping neural network existence theorem. In **Proceedings of the IEEE international conference on neural networks.** New York: IEEE.

Hecht-Nielsen, R. (1987). Counterpropagation networks. In **Proceedings of the IEEE international conference on neural networks.** New York: IEEE.

Hecht-Nielsen, R. (1987). Neurocomputer applications. In **Proceedings of the national computer conference 1987.** Reston, VA: American Federation of Information Processing Societies.

Hecht-Nielsen, R. (1987). Neural network nearest matched filter classification of spatiotemporal patterns. *Applied Optics,* **26**, 1892.

Hecht-Nielsen, R. (1986). Performance limits of optical, electro-optical, and electronic artificial neural system processors. *Proceedings of the Society of Photo-Optical Instrumentation Engineering,* **634**, 277.

Hecht-Nielsen, R. (1983). Book review of Grossberg's **Studies of mind and brain.** *Journal of Mathematical Psychology,* **27**, 335.

Hecht-Nielsen, R. (1982). Neural analog processing. *Proceedings of the Society of Photo-Optical Instrumentation Engineering,* **360**, 180.

Hecht-Nielsen, R. (1981). Neural analog information processing. *Proceedings of the Society of Photo-Optical Instrumentaiton Engineering,* **298**, 138.

Hinton, G.E. and Anderson, J.A. (Eds.) (1981). **Parallel models of associative memory.** Hillsdale, NJ: Erlbaum Associates.

Hopfield, J.J. and Tank, D.W. (1985). Neural computation of decisions in optimization problems. *Biological Cybernetics,* **52**, 141.

Hopfield, J.J. (1984). Neurons with graded response have collective computational properties like those of two-state neurons. *Proceedings of the National Academy of Sciences USA,* **81**.

Hopfield, J.J. (1982). Neural networks and physical systems with emergent collective computational abilities. *Proceedings of the National Academy of Sciences USA,* **79**, 2254.

Klopf, A.H. (1982). **The hedonistic neuron.** Washington, DC: Hemisphere.

Klopf, A.H. and Gose, E. (1969). An evolutionary pattern recognition network. *IEEE Transactions on Systems, Man and Cybernetics,* **SMC-5**, 247.

Kosko, B. (in press). Bidirectional associative memories.

Kosko, B. (1987). Fuzzy associative memories. In A. Kandel (Ed.), **Fuzzy expert systems**. Reading, MA: Addison-Wesley.

Kosko, B. (1986). Fuzzy entropy and conditioning. *Information Science*, **40**, 165.

Kosko, B. (1986). Fuzzy knowledge combination. *International Journal of Intelligent Systems*, **1**, 293.

Kosko, B. and Limm, J. (1985). Vision as causal activation and association. *Proceedings of the Society of Photo-Optical Instrumentation Engineering*, **579**, 104.

McClelland, D.E. and Rumelhart, D.E. (1985). Distributed memory and the representation of general and specific information. *Journal of Experimental Psychology*, **114**, 159.

McEliece, R.J., Posner, E.C., Rodemich, E.R., and Venkatesh, S.S. (1986). The capacity of the Hopfield associative memory. California Institute of Technology.

Mitchell, R.L. (1978) Helicopter blade modulation model (revised). Defense Technical Information Center, DTIC AD 1089574, March.

Palm, G. (1980). On associative memory. *Biological Cybernetics*, **36**, 19.

Psaltis, D. and Venkatesh, S.S. (1985). Information storage and retrieval in two associative nets. California Institute of Technology.

Psaltis, D. and Abu-Mostafa, Y.S. (1985). Computation power of parallelism in optical computers. California Institute of Technology.

Psaltis, D. and Farhat, N. (1985). Optical information procesing based on an associative-memory model of neural networks with thresholding and feedback. *Optical Letters*, **10**, 98.

Rumelhart, D.E., Hinton, G.E., and Williams, R.J. (1985). Learning internal representation by error propagation. Institute for Cognitive Science Report 85-6, UCSD.

Rumelhart, D.E. and Zipser, D. (1985). Feature discovery by competitive learning. *Cognitive Science*, **9**, 75.

Sejnowski, T.J. and Rosenberg, C.R. (1986). NETalk: A parallel network that learns to read aloud. Johns Hopkins University.

Sejnowski, T.J. (1981). Skeleton filters in the brain. In G.E. Hinton and J.A. Anderson (Eds.), **Parallel models of associative memory**. Hillsdale, NJ: Erlbaum Associates.

Soffer, B.H., Dunning, G.J., Owechko, Y., and Marom, E. (1986). Associative holographic memory with feedback using phase-conjugate mirrors. *Optical Letters*, **11**, 118.

Steinbuch, K. amd Piske, U.A.W. (1963). Learning matrices and their applications. *IEEE Transactions on Electronics and Computing*, **EC-12**, 846.

Steinbuch, K. (1961). Die Lernmatrix. *Kybernetik*, **1**, 36.

Thakoor, A. (1987). Content-addressable, high density memories based on neural networks models. JPL Report D-4166, March.

Widrow, B. and Stearns, D. (1985). **Adaptive signal processing**. Englewood Cliffs, NJ: Prentice-Hall.

Widrow, B. (1962). Generalization information storage in networks of ADALINE neurons. In G.T. Yovitts (Ed.), **Self-organizing systems**. Washington, DC: Spartan.

Widrow, B. and Hoff, M. Jr. (1960). Adaptive switching circuits. IRE WESCON Convention Record, Part 4, 96.

Willshaw, D.J. (1971). Models of distributed associative memory. PhD Thesis, University of Edinburgh.

Willshaw, D.J. and Longuet-Higgins, H.C. (1970). Associative memory models. In B. Meltzer and O. Michie (Eds.), **Machine intelligence**. Edinburgh U.P.

Willshaw, D.J., Buneman, O.P., and Longuet-Higgins, H.C. (1969). Non-holographic associative memory. *Nature*, **222**, 960.

Woodward, P.M. (1953). **Probability and information theory with applications to radar**. New York: Pergamon Press.

ADAPTIVE PATTERN CLASSIFICATION AND UNIVERSAL RECODING, II: FEEDBACK, EXPECTATION, OLFACTION, AND ILLUSIONS

by

Stephen Grossberg

Preface

This 1976 article introduced Adaptive Resonance Theory, or ART, and suggested that the competitive learning model of Chapter 6 be replaced by an ART model to design an instar-outstar mapping system capable of autonomously learning a stable $\Re^n \to \Re^m$ map until the network's full memory capacity is utilized. The article described many of the themes that energized subsequent developments of ART as a physical theory and as a self-organizing pattern recognition device for technology. A number of the theory's main physical predictions have since received experimental support (see below).

This 1976 article unified the analysis and interpretation of concepts and models that had been undergoing development since 1970. These models included competitive networks, associative learning laws, and self-organizing feature maps (Chapters 1–6). The remaining models grew out of an analysis of classical conditioning, operant discrimination learning, and the control of attention during learning and recognition (Grossberg, 1972a, 1972b, 1975). In the 1976 ART article, these themes were joined together into a unified processing framework.

An attentional subsystem, which carries out the learning, was distinguished from an orienting subsystem, which helps to control hypothesis testing and memory search of the attentional subsystem. Learning of top-down expectations was added to bottom-up learning. These top-down expectations help to establish an adaptive resonance which carves out an attentional focus when bottom-up inputs and the top-down expectations are well enough matched. Thus, the selection of a recognition code at level F_2 (denoted here by V_2) became interpretable as the selection of a hypothesis, or symbolic representation of the data, that could be tested by read-out of a learned top-down expectation. In this way, pattern recognition was subsumed under the more general themes of knowledge discovery and hypothesis testing during cognitive information processing.

Recognition learning was dynamically stabilized by the top-down learned expectations, as well as by rapid search for a better category except when the top-down expectation is well-enough matched to the bottom-up data to risk refining its category's adaptive weights. Thus ART learning occurs in an *approximate match* mode, not the mismatch mode of LMS or backpropagation (see Chapters 1 and 2).

The process of memory search was suggested to be mediated by a different type of memory than the fast STM of cell activation and the slow LTM of adaptive weight change. This medium term memory, or MTM, was predicted to be realized by a habituating chemical transmitter, suggested to be norepinephrine, and examples of its possible role were predicted in cortical plasticity, negative aftereffects, and spatial frequency adaptation. The control of habituating transmitters for MTM is still a topic of current research in the design of search mechanisms for ART recognition systems (see ART 3 in Chapter 14), as well as in the design of reset mechanisms during cortical visual processing (Grossberg, 1991).

Some of the 1976 ART predictions that are of current interest include the following: In 1972, it was predicted that norepinephrine and acetylcholine jointly control brain plasticity during learning of reinforcement and recognition codes (Grossberg, 1972b). This analysis was extended in Chapter 6 and the present chapter to predict that norepinephrine and acetylcholine control cortical plasticity during the critical period in visual cortex. Several experimental studies have described relevant data (Bear and Singer, 1986; Kasamatsu and Pettigrew, 1976; Pettigrew and Kasamatsu, 1978). A role for attention in the regulation of cortical plasticity was also predicted, and subsequently reported (Singer, 1982). Standing waves of resonant cortical activity (also called order-preserving limit cycles) were predicted to subserve these cortical dynamics (see also Grossberg, 1978). Several labs have recently reported the existence of resonant standing waves (Eckhorn et al., 1988; Gray et al., 1989). These theoretical results built upon earlier predictions that synaptic plasticity is controlled by processes in which an inward Na^+ current and an outward K^+ current interact synergetically with an inward Ca^{++} current that competes with an Mg^{++} current (Grossberg, 1968, 1969a). Recent data about the role of NMDA receptors have refined contemporary understanding of such synergetic interactions (Kleinschmidt, Bear, and Singer, 1987). An associative learning law was introduced in which synaptic efficacy is gated by post-synaptic activity such that, with the learning gate open, synaptic strength can either increase or decrease (see also Grossberg, 1969b, 1978, and Chapter 6). Such a gated learning law has since been reported in visual cortex and hippocampus (Levy, 1985; Levy, Brassel, and Moore, 1983; Levy and Desmond, 1985; Rauschecker and Singer, 1979; see also Singer, 1983 in Chapter 16). It is the basic learning law used in the ART models.

A top-down learned expectation that is matched against bottom-up data to regulate selective attention was derived herein. It has the properties of the Processing Negativity event-related potential that was reported by Näätänen, Gaillard, and Mäntysalo (1978). See also Näätänen (1982) and Chapter 17. A hippocampal generator of the P300 event-related potential, as distinct from possible neocortical generators, was predicted in Grossberg (1980, p.25) from an analysis of how short term memory in an ART model is reset by novel events. A hippocampal P300 generator was experimentally reported in Halgren et al. (1980). An analysis of how the emotional meaning of cues modulates attention led to a complementary prediction. Grossberg (1975) predicted that both negative and positive emotions generate positive attentional feedback (see Figure 2). Experimental support for this prediction was found by Bower (1981) and Bower, Gilligan, and Monteiro (1981). The pathway subserving this attentional feedback process, called incentive motivation, was interpreted in Grossberg (1975) and herein (also see Chapter 20) as a pathway from hippocampus to neocortex. Such a pathway was discovered by Rosene and Hoesen (1977).

A reciprocal pathway for associative learning of conditioned reinforcers was predicted to pass from neocortical sensory representations to hippocampal pyramidal cells (see Figure 2 and Grossberg, 1971, 1972a, 1972b, 1975). Experimental evidence was reported by Berger and Thompson (1978) who first interpreted their results as the discovery of a general neural "engram." Subsequent experiments considered the effects of selective ablations on learning both in hippocampus and in cerebellum, leading to the conclusion that hippocampal learning is indeed a variant of the predicted conditioned reinforcer learning, whereas the cerebellum carries out a type of motor learning (Thompson *et al.*, 1984). These experimental results concerning differences between reinforcement learning and motor learning are related to a prediction concerning the control of motivated instrumental behavior; namely, that hippocampal processes bifurcate into the aforementioned positive attentional feedback pathway to neocortex and into a motivationally signed motor mapping subsystem for control of approach and avoidance behavior (Grossberg, 1975). Experimental evidence for spatial mapping properties of the hippocampus was described by O'Keefe and Nadel (1978). A reciprocal cortico-hippocampal interaction between conditioned reinforcers and incentive motivational sources was also suggested (see Figure 2 and Grossberg, 1975), along with the implication that the hippocampus mediates stimulus-reinforcement contingencies whose mismatch with sensory processing in the cortex prevents readout of cortical commands. Gabriel, Foster, Orona, Saltwick, and Stanton (1980) have reported compatible data.

A study of how reinforcing cues are forgotten, or extinguished, led to a network design in which opponent processes are gated by slowly varying chemical transmitters (Grossberg, 1972b). These opponent processes were interpreted in terms of the dynamics of hypothalamus and medial forebrain bundle, and the chemical transmitters were interpreted to be catecholaminergic. These habituating chemical transmitters are used as a mechanism of MTM and memory search herein. A mathematical study of these opponent processes led to the discovery in Grossberg (1972b, 1975) of the transmitter properties that could be used for memory search. The same analysis disclosed in Grossberg (1972b) a formal behavioral syndrome wherein catecholaminergic underarousal could cause an elevated behavioral threshold to coexist with suprathreshold hypersensitivity. Moreover, an arousing drug could transform this underaroused syndrome into an overaroused syndrome by moving the system over an inverted U whose peak corresponds to normal sensitivity. The overaroused syndrome has formal emotional properties symptomatic of certain schizophrenias. A similar underaroused syndrome in hyperactive children has been described by Shaywitz, Cohen, and Bowers (1977) and Shekim, DeKirmenjian, and Chapel (1977), notably the elevated threshold (Weber and Sulzbacher, 1975). Amphetamine is an arousing therapeutic drug which improves symptoms in small enough quantities (Swanson and Kinsbourne, 1976; Weiss and Hechtmann, 1979), but which is capable of causing schizophrenic syndromes in large enough doses (Ellinwood and Kilbey, 1980; MacLennan and Maier, 1983).

This partial list of predictions and supportive data illustrates the difficulty of understanding and evaluating interdisciplinary brain theories and their experimental implications from the perspective of traditional specialties. Simultaneous analysis of multiple levels of brain organization is characteristic of the theoretical development of neural architectures. Experimental evidence from multiple levels of brain organization is thus needed, from biochemical data about membrane channels and neurotransmitters, to emergent network properties about resonance and attention. Organizational principles and their mechanistic realizations need to simultaneously satisfy constraints on multiple levels of design in order to rule out the many hypotheses which seem plausible in the light of a limited set of data, but are incompatible with more global theoretical constraints. Fortunately, due to the paradigm shift described in the Editorial Preface, the organization of the brain sciences is rapidly adapting to meet the intellectual challenge posed by the explanations and predictions of interdisciplinary brain theories, although experimental tests are still often reported without reference to their theoretical antecedents. As the infrastructure needed for cooperative work between theorists and experimentalists matures, more efficient and critical tests of theories can be anticipated.

Such a development is much to be desired, since many theoretical predictions have not yet been tested at all. One such neurophysiologically untested ART prediction is that cortical recognition codes are regulated by a matching law called the 2/3 Rule (see Chapter 10).

References

Bear, M.F. and Singer, W. (1986). Modulation of visual cortical plasticity by acetylcholine and noradrenaline. *Nature*, **320**, 172–176.

Berger, T.W. and Thompson, R.F. (1978). Neuronal plasticity in the limbic system during classical conditioning of the rabbit nictitating membrane response, I: The hippocampus. *Brain Research*, **145**, 323–346.

Bower, G.H. (1981). Mood and memory. *American Psychologist*, **36**, 129–148.

Bower, G.H., Gilligan, S.G., and Monteiro, K.P. (1981). Selectivity of learning caused by adaptive states. *Journal of Experimental Psychology: General*, **110**, 451–473.

Eckhorn, R., Bauer, R., Jordan, W., Brosch, M., Kruse, W., Munk, M., and Reitboeck, H.J. (1988). Coherent oscillations: A mechanism of future linking in the visual cortex? *Biological Cybernetics*, **60**, 121–130.

Ellinwood, E.H. and Kilbey, M.M. (1980). Fundamental mechanisms underlying altered behavior following chronic administration of psychomotor stimulants. *Biological Psychiatry*, **15**, 749–757.

Gabriel, M., Foster, K., Orona, E., Saltwick, S.E., and Stanton, M. (1980). Neuronal activity of cingulate cortex, anteroventral thalamus, and hippocampal formation in discriminative conditioning: Encoding and extraction of the significance of conditional stimuli. *Progress in Psychobiology and Physiological Psychology*, **9**, 125–231.

Gray, C.M., Konig, P., Engel, A.K., and Singer, W. (1989). Oscillatory responses in cat visual cortex exhibit inter-columnar synchronization which reflects global stimulus properties. *Nature*, **338**, 334–337.

Grossberg, S. (1968). Some physiological and biochemical consequences of psychological postulates. *Proceedings of the National Academy of Sciences*, **60**, 758–765.

Grossberg, S. (1969a). On the production and release of chemical transmitters and related topics in cellular control. *Journal of Theoretical Biology*, **22**, 325–364.

Grossberg, S. (1969b). On learning and energy-entropy dependence in recurrent and nonrecurrent signed networks. *Journal of Statistical Physics*, **1**, 319–350.

Grossberg, S. (1971). On the dynamics of operant conditioning. *Journal of Theoretical Biology*, **33**, 225–255.

Grossberg, S. (1972a). A neural theory of punishment and avoidance, I: Qualitative theory. *Mathematical Biosciences*, **15**, 39–67.

Grossberg, S. (1972b). A neural theory of punishment and avoidance, II: Quantitative theory. *Mathematical Biosciences*, **15**, 253–285.

Grossberg, S. (1975). A neural model of attention, reinforcement, and discrimination learning. *International Review of Neurobiology*, **18**, 263–327.

Grossberg, S. (1978). A theory of visual coding, memory, and development. In E. Leeuwenberg and H. Buffart (Eds.), **Formal theories of visual perception**. New York: Wiley and Sons.

Grossberg, S. (1991). Why do parallel cortical systems exist for the perception of static form and moving form? *Perception and Psychophysics*, in press.

Halgren, E., Squires, N.K., Wilson, C.L., Rohrbaugh, J.W., Babb, T.L., and Crandall, P.H. (1980). Endogenous potentials generated in the human hippocampal formation and amygdala by infrequent events. *Science*, **210**, 803–805.

Kasamatsu, T. and Pettigrew, J.D. (1976). Depletion of brain catecholamines: Failure of ocular dominance shift after monocular occlusion in kittens. *Science*, **194**, 206–208.

Kleinschmidt, A., Bear, M.F., and Singer, W. (1987). Blockade of "NMDA" receptors disrupts experience-dependent plasticity of kitten striate cortex. *Science*, **238**, 355–358.

Levy, W.B. (1985). Associative changes at the synapse: LTP in the hippocampus. In W.B. Levy, J. Anderson, and S. Lehmkuhle (Eds.), **Synaptic modification, neuron selectivity, and nervous system organization**. Hillsdale, NJ: Erlbaum, 5–33.

Levy, W.B., Brassel, S.E., and Moore, S.D. (1983). Partial quantification of the associative synaptic learning rule of the dentate gyrus. *Neuroscience*, **8**, 799–808.

Levy, W.B. and Desmond, N.L. (1985). The rules of elemental synaptic plasticity. In W.B. Levy, J. Anderson, and S. Lehmkuhle (Eds.), **Synaptic modification, neuron selectivity, and nervous system organization**. Hillsdale, NJ: Erlbaum, 105–121.

MacLennan, A.J. and Maier, S.F. (1983). Coping and the stress-induced potentiation of stimulant stereotypy in the rat. *Science*, **219**, 1091–1093.

Näätänen, R. (1982). Processing negativity: An evoked potential reflection of selective attention. *Psychological Bulletin*, **92**, 605–640.

Näätänen, R., Gaillard, A., and Mäntysalo, S. (1978). The N1 effect of selective attention reinterpreted. *Acta Psychologica*, **42**, 313–329.

O'Keefe, J. and Nadel, L. (1978). **The hippocampus as a cognitive map**. Oxford: Oxford University Press.

Pettigrew, J.D. and Kasamatsu, T. (1978). Local perfusion of noradrenaline maintains visual cortical plasticity. *Nature*, **271**, 761–763.

Rauschecker, J.P. and Singer, W. (1979). Changes in the circuitry of the kitten's visual cortex are gated by postsynaptic activity. *Nature*, **280**, 58–60.

Rosene, D.L. and Hoesen, G.W. van (1977). Hippocampal efferents reach widespread areas of cerebral cortex and amygdala in the rhesus monkey. *Science*, **198**, 315–317.

Shaywitz, B.A., Cohen, D.J., and Bowers, M.B. Jr. (1977). CSF monoamine metabolites in children with minimal brain dysfunction: Evidence for alteration of brain dopamine. *Journal of Pediatrics*, **90**, 67–71.

Shekim, W.O., DeKirmenjian, H., and Chapel, J.L. (1977). Urinary catecholamine metabolites in hyperkinetic boys treated with d-amphetamine. *American Journal of Psychiatry*, **134**, 1276–1279.

Singer, W. (1982). The role of attention in developmental plasticity. *Human Neurobiology*, **1**, 41–43.

Singer, W. (1983). Neuronal activity as a shaping factor in the self-organization of neuron assemblies. In E. Basar, H. Flohr, H. Haken, and A.J. Mandell (Eds.), **Synergetics of the brain**. New York: Springer-Verlag.

Swanson, J.M. and Kinsbourne, M. (1976). Stimulant-related state-dependent learning in hyperactive children. *Science*, **192**, 1354–1356.

Thompson, R.F., Barchas, J.D., Clark, G.A., Donegan, N., Kettner, R.E., Lavond, D.G., Madden, J., Mauk, M.D., and McCormick, D.A. (1984). Neuronal substrates of associative learning in the mammalian brain. In D.L. Alkon and J. Farley (Eds.), **Primary neural substrates of learning and behavioral change**. New York: Cambridge University Press.

Weber, B.A. and Sulzbacher, S.I. (1975). Use of CNS stimulant medication in averaged electroencephalic audiometry with children with MBD. *Journal of Learning Disabilities*, **8**, 300–303.

Weiss, G. and Hechtman, L. (1979). The hyperactive child syndrome. *Science*, **205**, 1348–1354.

Biological Cybernetics
1976, **23**, 187–202
©1976 Springer-Verlag, Inc.

ADAPTIVE PATTERN CLASSIFICATION
AND UNIVERSAL RECODING, II:
FEEDBACK, EXPECTATION, OLFACTION, ILLUSIONS

Stephen Grossberg†

Abstract

Part I of this paper describes a model for the parallel development and adult coding of neural feature detectors. It shows how any set of arbitrary spatial patterns can be recoded, or transformed, into any other spatial patterns (universal recoding), if there are sufficiently many cells in the network's cortex. This code is, however, unstable through time if arbitrarily many patterns can perturb a fixed number of cortical cells. This paper shows how to stabilize the code in the general case using feedback between cellular sites. A biochemically defined critical period is not necessary to stabilize the code, nor is it sufficient to ensure useful coding properties.

We ask how short term memory can be reset in response to temporal sequences of spatial patterns. This leads to a context-dependent code in which no feature detector need uniquely characterize an input pattern; yet unique classification by the pattern of activity across feature detectors is possible. This property uses learned expectation mechanisms whereby unexpected patterns are temporarily suppressed and/or activate nonspecific arousal. The simplest case describes reciprocal interactions via trainable synaptic pathways (long term memory traces) between two recurrent on-center off-surround networks undergoing mass action (shunting) interactions. This unit can establish an *adaptive resonance*, or reverberation, between two regions if their coded patterns match, and can suppress the reverberation if their patterns do not match. This concept yields a model of olfactory coding within the olfactory bulb and prepyriform cortex. The resonance idea also includes the establishment of reverberation between conditioned reinforcers and generators of contingent negative variation if presently available sensory cues are compatible with the network's drive requirements at that time; and a search and lock mechanism whereby the disparity between two patterns can be minimized and the minimal disparity images locked into position. Stabilizing the code uses attentional mechanisms, in particular non-specific arousal as a tuning and search device. We suggest that arousal is gated by a chemical transmitter system—for example, norepinephrine—whose relative states of

---

† Supported in part by the Advanced Research Projects Agency under ONR contract N00014-76-C-0185.

accumulation at antagonistic pairs of on-cells and off-cells through time can shift the spatial pattern of STM activity across a field of feature detectors. For example, a sudden arousal increment in response to an unexpected pattern can reverse, or rebound, these relative activities, thereby suppressing incorrectly classified populations. The rebound mechanism has formal properties analogous to negative afterimages and spatial frequency adaptation.

1. Introduction

In Part I of this paper (Grossberg, 1976b) a model for the parallel development and adult coding of neural feature detectors was analysed. In this model, a network region V_1 sends signals to region V_2 via trainable pathways. Region V_1 is capable of normalizing its total activity. Region V_2 can normalize its total activity, contrast enhance the V_1-to-V_2 signals, and store the contrast-enhanced pattern in short term memory (STM). The STM pattern thereupon causes slow changes in the long term memory (LTM) traces of the V_1-to-V_2 pathways. These LTM changes are the basis for reclassification by V_2 of spatial patterns at V_1.

Part I shows that the code that develops in this way is unstable if arbitrarily many patterns at V_1 perturb a fixed number of cells in V_2. This paper attacks the problem of stabilizing network responses to arbitrarily chosen space-time patterns at V_1; in particular, to classes of spatial patterns of arbitrary size. We continue where Part I left off. The ith equation from Part I will be denoted by the notation (Ii) below. A similar notation will be used to denote the ith Section in Part I.

2. Adaptive Resonance: Stable Coding and Reset of STM

When a temporal succession $\theta^{(1)}, \theta^{(2)}, \ldots, \theta^{(k)}, \ldots$ of spatial patterns $\theta^{(k)} = (\theta_1^{(k)}, \theta_2^{(k)}, \ldots, \theta_n^{(k)})$ perturbs V_1, how does each pattern $\theta^{(k)}$ *inhibit* the STM pattern on V_2 that was elicited by the previous pattern $\theta^{(k-1)}$, and *reset* V_2 to store data derived from $\theta^{(k)}$ without bias? This question can be reversed in an information way: can V_2 be protected from continual inhibition of its STM throughout the time interval during which a *fixed* $\theta^{(k-1)}$ is presented to V_1? In other words, how does the network know the spatial pattern $\theta^{(k-1)}$ is *changed* to a different pattern $\theta^{(k)}$? The assumption that STM must be actively inhibited in order to shut it off is a mathematical property of reverberating shunting networks (Grossberg, 1973; Ellias and Grossberg, 1975; Grossberg and Levine, 1975). Otherwise there would be an averaging in STM of the codes for all the patterns $\theta^{(1)}, \theta^{(2)}, \ldots, \theta^{(k)}, \ldots$, and no useful coding of any one pattern.

Section I8 shows that there are two possible ways to stabilize STM in response to a space-time pattern. Both possible ways will be considered below; namely, inhibition of V_1-to-V_2 signals by feedback from V_2 to V_1, followed by a shift in the spatial locus of STM activity at V_2; and a direct shift in STM locus at V_2 when the input pattern at V_1 changes. Both mechanisms seem to have important practical applications.

The former mechanism has a minimal realization in which V_1 and V_2 send each other conditionable excitatory signals, and recurrent on-center off-surrounds exist in both V_1 and V_2, as in Figure 1. To derive this mechanism, let two distinct patterns $\theta^{(1)}$ and $\theta^{(2)}$ successively perturb V_1, and let $\theta^{(i)}$ be coded by v_{2i}, $i = 1, 2$, in V_2.

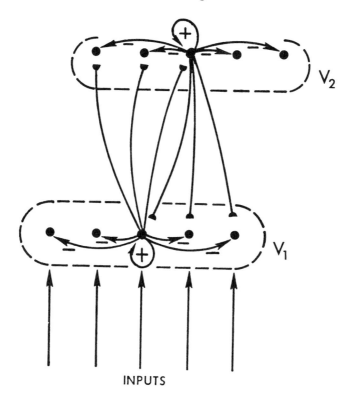

Figure 1. Minimal anatomy of an adaptive resonance.

The mechanism will have the following properties. When $\theta^{(1)}$ perturbs V_1, V_1-to-V_2 signals activate STM at v_{21}. Population v_{21} remains active when $\theta^{(2)}$ perturbs V_1, but V_1-to-V_2 signals are suppressed. Then v_{21}'s activity is also suppressed, whereupon $\theta^{(2)}$ can generate V_1-to-V_2 signals that activate STM at v_{22}. We already know how $\theta^{(1)}$ activates v_{21}, and how v_{21} remains active in STM. How are V_1-to-V_2 signals suppressed when $\theta^{(2)}$ perturbs V_1? If v_{21} were not active in STM when $\theta^{(2)}$ perturbs V_1, then suppression would not occur, since $\theta^{(2)}$ would activate STM just as $\theta^{(1)}$ did. Moreover, if v_{22} were active in STM, rather than v_{21}, then V_1-to-V_2 signals would not be suppressed, just as signals are not suppressed after $\theta^{(1)}$ excites v_{21}. Thus, V_1-to-V_2 signals are suppressed because feedback signals from v_{21} to V_1 somehow reproduce $\theta^{(1)}$ at V_1, and these signals compete with the $\theta^{(2)}$ input to suppress V_1-to-v_{21} signals.

How can v_{21}-to-V_1 signals reproduce $\theta^{(1)}$ at V_1? There is only one way in the present setup. While V_1-to-v_{21} signals are learning to code $\theta^{(1)}$, feedback signals from v_{21}-to-V_1 also learn to reproduce $\theta^{(1)}$ at V_1; that is, the pathways from V_1 to V_2 and from V_2 to V_1 are both trainable.

Given this much, how does mixing two different patterns, such as $\theta^{(1)}$ and $\theta^{(2)}$, at V_1 suppress V_1-to-V_2 signals, whereas either of these patterns separately does not? More generally, what class of patterns at V_1, whether due to pattern mixture or to external perturbation, suppresses V_1-to-V_2 signals? The following constraints motivate the construction:

(A) V_1 is a shunting network;

(B) signals typically add up in such a network; and

(C) feedback signals from v_{2i} to V_1 do not shut off V_1-to-v_{2i} signals when input $\theta^{(i)}$ also perturbs V_1, $i = 1, 2$.

Given these constraints, the class of *uniform* patterns across V_1 ($\theta_i = 1/n, i = 1, 2, \ldots, n$) will suppress output from V_1; in other words, only spatial *differences* in pattern intensity will generate outputs from V_1. This property emerges naturally in shunting networks, and is familiar, for example, in visual physiology.

How does this property accomplish our goal? When $\theta^{(1)}$ is presented at V_1, signals from V_1 to V_2 excite v_{21}. Feedback from v_{21} to V_1 adds learned signals that are proportional to $\theta^{(1)}$ to the external $\theta^{(1)}$ input. By additivity, the mixture of signals is again the pattern $\theta^{(1)}$, albeit with a different total activity. Hence V_1-to-V_2 signals continue to excite v_{21}. A *resonance* between V_1 and V_2 develops that sustains STM activity at v_{21}.

When $\theta^{(2)}$ appears at V_1, the v_{21}-to-V_1 signals still are proportional to $\theta^{(1)}$. If the sum of $\theta^{(2)}$ inputs and $\theta^{(1)}$ signals at V_1 is (approximately) uniform, then V_1-to-V_2 signals are inhibited, or at least damped. [All that is needed is a V_1-to-V_2 signal that is too small to exceed the quenching threshold (QT).] This event inhibits STM activity at v_{21}, so that v_{21}-to-V_1 signals terminate. Then only the $\theta^{(2)}$ input is active at V_1, so that V_1-to-V_2 signals are elicited, but now activate v_{22}.

How does inhibition of V_1-to-v_{21} signals inhibit STM activity at v_{21}? This will not happen if recurrent excitatory signals within V_2 can sustain activity in STM. Hence we assume that the QT is chosen sufficiently high to prevent STM reverberation at v_{21} unless V_1-to-v_{21} signals are sufficiently large. Reverberation in STM is now accomplished by an excitatory resonance of signals between V_1 and V_2. The inhibitory off-surrounds in V_1 and V_2 continue to normalize and contrast enhance activity within these regions, but the STM itself is now carried by reverberation between them.

It remains to develop the above ideas mathematically. First we show how a uniform pattern is suppressed. This will be done by developing equation (I1), for simplicity; namely,

$$\dot{x}_{1i} = -Ax_{1i} + (B - x_{1i})I_i - x_{1i}\sum_{k \neq i} I_k. \qquad (I1)$$

In (I1), an assumption is made that does not hold in all membranes; namely, that the passive equilibrium potential (namely 0 in $\dot{x}_{1i} = -Ax_{1i}$) equals the inhibitory equilibrium potential (namely 0 in $\dot{x}_{1i} = -x_{1i}\sum_{k \neq i} I_k$). More generally,

$$\dot{x}_{1i} = -Ax_{1i} + (B - x_{1i})I_i - (x_{1i} + C)\sum_{k \neq i} I_k, \qquad (1)$$

where $C > 0$. The constant C is related to the Nernst potential for potassium (Hodgkin, 1964; Katz, 1966). Consider the equilibrium value of (1) in response to spatial pattern $I_i = \theta_i I$. Then

$$x_{1i} = \frac{(B + C)I}{A + I}\left[\theta_i - \frac{C}{B + C}\right]. \qquad (2)$$

Suppose for definiteness that

$$B = (n - 1)C. \qquad (3)$$

Then

$$x_{1i} = \frac{nCI}{A+I}\left(\theta_i - \frac{1}{n}\right). \tag{4}$$

Also suppse that signals $h(x_{1i})$ from v_{1i} to V_2 are generated only if $x_{1i} > 0$; e.g., set $h(x_{1i}) = [x_{1i}^p]^+$ for some $p > 0$, where $[u]^+ = \max(u, 0)$. Now let I_i be a uniform pattern (all $\theta_i = 1/n$). By (4), all $x_{1i} = 0$ so that no signals are generated. In effect, setting $C > 0$ contrast-enhances the signals from V_1 to V_2 by chopping off the "uniform part" of inputs to V_1. Condition (3) can be weakened to

$$B \le (n-1)C \tag{5}$$

since then, in (2), $C(B+C)^{-1} \ge 1/n$ and signals are even harder to generate. Generalizations to situations in which the on-center and off-surround connection strengths depend on distance can also be made, as in

$$\dot{x}_{1i} = -Ax_{1i} + (B - x_{1i})\sum_k I_k C_{ki} - (x_{1i} + D)\sum_k I_k E_{ki}. \tag{6}$$

Levine and Grossberg (1975) show how the behavior of these nonrecurrent networks, and analogous recurrent networks, such as (I4), can formally model certain visual illusions, such as line neutralization, tilt aftereffect, and angle expansion. The size of D in (6) influences how pronounced the angle expansion will be, for example; this is again a contrast enhancement effect.

Equation (1) describes how V_1 processes external patterns $(I_1, I_2, \ldots, I_n)$. Now add on the influence of feedback signals from V_2, again in an on-center off-surround anatomy. Denote the total feedback signal from V_2 to v_{1i} by J_i. Then (1) becomes

$$\dot{x}_{1i} = -Ax_{1i} + (B - x_{1i})(I_i + J_i) - (x_{1i} + C)\sum_{k \ne i}(I_k + J_k). \tag{7}$$

We will check that, both before and after learning occurs, feedback does not interfere with coding by V_2 of a pattern $(I_1, I_2, \ldots, I_n)$ at V_1. Before learning occurs, feedback is uniformly distributed; that is, $J_i = \frac{1}{n}J$. By (7), in response to a spatial pattern, $I_i = \theta_i I$, the equilibrium value of v_{1i} is then

$$x_{1i} = \frac{nCI}{A+I+J}\left(\theta_i - \frac{1}{n}\right), \tag{8}$$

which differs from (4) only by a reduction in total activity due to J. At time $t = 0$, therefore, feedback signals begin to learn the pattern θ. Will this be true at all times $t \ge 0$? That is, if feedback is proportional to θ, will the pattern at V_1 be θ? Additivity of inputs to V_1 guarantees this: if $I_i = \theta_i I$ and $J_i = \theta_i J$, then the equilibrium value of v_{1i} is

$$x_{1i} = \frac{nC(I+J)}{A+I+J}\left(\theta_i - \frac{1}{n}\right), \tag{9}$$

which differs from (4) only by an amplification in total activity due to J. Adding feedback signals to a shunting on-center off-surround anatomy does not change the coding by V_2 of signals from V_1. A similar analysis holds for the system in which recurrent on-center off-surround signals replace the nonrecurrent on-center off-surround inputs of (7). The recurrent system will be needed herein, because the feedback signals J_i will contain summands whose trainable synaptic strengths are determined by the postsynaptic activities at x_{1i}. See Section I2 for an explanation. Thus we let V_1 be governed by the system

$$\dot{x}_{1i} = -Ax_{1i} + (B - x_{1i})\left[\sum_{k=1}^{n} f(x_{1k})C_{ki} + I_i + J_i\right]$$

$$- (x_{1i} + D)\sum_{k=1}^{n} f(x_{1k})E_{ki}. \tag{10}$$

The feedback signals J_i are defined as follows. The signals from each v_{2j} to V_1 are trainable. Denote the synaptic strength of the path p_{ji} from v_{2j} to v_{1i} by y_{ji}. The total signal from V_2 to v_{1i} is then (simplest case)

$$J_i = x^{(2)} \cdot y^{(i)} = \sum_{k=1}^{N} x_{2j} y_{ji}.$$

In case V_2 chooses a population for STM storage, say v_{2j}, then $J_i = x_{2j} y_{ji}$, and the feedback pattern across V_1 is determined by the vector $y^{(i)} = (y_{j1}, y_{2j}, \ldots, y_{jn})$ of synaptic strengths.

What rule governs the training of each $y^{(i)}$? As usual, y_{ji} will learn by computing a time average of multiplied presynaptic signals and postsynaptic activities. Two comments are in order:

(i) As in (I6), let training terminate if no STM activation occurs at V_2;

(ii) Since x_{1i} can be driven to negative values, which do not generate V_1-to-V_2 signals, and since we want feedback to reproduce the V_1 pattern that is coded by V_2, restrict learning by the feedback synaptic strengths to supraequilibrium x_{1i} values. By (i) and (ii),

$$\dot{y}_{ji} = \{-y_{ji} + [x_{1i}]^+\}x_{2j}. \tag{11}$$

These equations obviously code the pattern $I_i = \theta_i I$ at V_1 if the $y^{(i)}(0)$ patterns are uniform and V_2 makes a choice.

Finally, we choose the QT of V_2 sufficiently large so that termination of V_1-to-v_{2j} signals suppresses v_{2j}'s STM reverberation. Then excitatory signals from V_1 generate recurrent signals within V_2 that contrast enhance, or even choose, V_2 populations for STM storage. As in (I6), let $S_j \equiv I_{2j}$ be the total V_1-to-v_{2j} signal; thus

$$S_j = x^{(1)} \cdot z^{(j)} \equiv \sum_{k=1}^{N} x_{1k} z_{kj}, \tag{12}$$

and let V_2 obey a system of the same form as (I4); namely

$$\dot{x}_{2j} = -Ax_{2j} + (B - x_{2j})\left[\sum_{k=1}^{N} f(x_{2k})C_{kj} + I_{2j}\right]$$

$$- (x_{2j} + D)\sum_{k=1}^{N} f(x_{2k})E_{kj}. \tag{13}$$

In summary, recurrent on-center off-surround interactions exist within both V_1 and V_2, and excitatory trainable signals exist in both directions between V_1 and V_2. In particular, V_1 must be a higher-order network processing station than a retina. Generalizations of equations (10)–(13) are readily accomplished, by explicitly including the finite reaction rates of inhibitory interneurons, or by using more complicated signal functions. The papers by Ellias and Grossberg (1975), Grossberg and Levine (1975), and Levine and Grossberg (1976) indicate how these changes will influence network dynamics. The following two comments might also be useful. First, when $\theta^{(1)}$ is changed to $\theta^{(2)}$, suppression of V_1-to-V_2 signals occurs before the trainable coefficients can substantially change. In other words, the stability of STM coding in an adaptive resonance depends heavily on the existence of different reaction rates for STM and LTM traces. Second, even if there is no biochemically triggered critical period, a critical period exists in an adaptively resonating network while the STM code is being established. The critical period terminates when learned feedback from V_2 to V_1 prevents recoding from occurring at any population in V_2.

3. Adaptive Resonance in Reinforcement, Motivation, and Attention

A case can be made for adaptive resonance as a general organizational principle *in vivo*. One important example will be noted in this section, and related examples in the next two sections. The first example describes an adaptive resonance whose trainable synaptic strengths can change during adulthood.

Grossberg (1975a) describes a neuropsychological theory of attention that builds on earlier work concerning reinforcement (Grossberg, 1971, 1972a, 1972b). Without redeveloping this theory herein, we sketch a part of it in which an adaptive resonance occurs. Consider Figure 2. This figure idealizes an adaptive resonance in which V_1 and V_2 both possess recurrent on-center off-surround interactions, and both V_1-to-V_2 and V_2-to-V_1 synaptic strengths are conditionable. Region V_1 receives (precoded) external sensory cues, and region V_2 receives inputs generated by internal drives. Signals from V_1-to-V_2 are trained when rewards act at V_2; their patterns code the balance of drives and rewards across V_2 populations when their V_1 sampling cells are active. Signals from V_2-to-V_1 learn "psychological sets," or classes of cues that have regularly occurred contiguously in time with a given active drive center.

The V_1-to-V_2 signals embody the *conditioned reinforcer* properties of a cue that activates V_1. The V_2-to-V_1 signals are interpreted as idealizations of the *contingent negative variations*, or CNV (Cohen, 1969). Such a wave has been associated with an animal's expectancy, decision (Walter, 1964), motivation (Cant and Bickford, 1967; Irwin *et al.*, 1966), volition (McAdam *et al.*, 1966), preparatory set (Low *et al.*, 1966), and arousal (McAdam, 1969). When this network is embedded into a more complete system of interactions, an interpretation of V_1 as neocortex and of V_2 as hippocampus is suggested.

Since both V_1 and V_2 receive external inputs in this example, both regions have inhibitory equilibrium potentials that can suppress (close to) uniform patterns. Adaptive resonance here means that the conditioned reinforcer properties of presently available sensory cues are compatible with the network's drive requirements at that time. When resonance is established, motor activity that consummates this consensus can be triggered further downstream in the network (Grossberg, 1975). Note that no feature detectors in V_1 need uniquely determine an input pattern; yet resonance will

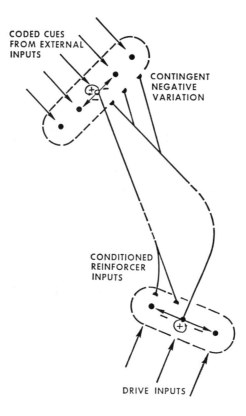

CODED CUES
FROM EXTERNAL
INPUTS

CONTINGENT
NEGATIVE
VARIATION

CONDITIONED
REINFORCER
INPUTS

DRIVE INPUTS

Figure 2. An adaptive resonance that helps to regulate attention to external cues that are compatible with internal needs.

not be established unless the pattern of activity in V_1 accurately codes the input. The code is *context-dependent*.

4. Search and Lock Mechanism

Each of our eyes looks out on visual space from a different position. To focus an object at a finite depth, the eyes verge together until a good match of their separate images is achieved. Then fixation on the object can be maintained. How do our eyes know when this match has been achieved, so that searching eye movements can cease and a fixated position can be maintained?

A resonance mechanism much like the one in Section 3 can achieve this. Let recurrent on-center off-surround signals exist within V_1 and V_2 separately. Replace the trainable interfield signals of Section 3 either by untrainable on-center off-surround signals, or just on-center signals if the recurrent intrafield off-surround interactions are sufficiently strong. Thus each v_{1i} (v_{2i}) is the center of signals from v_{2i} (v_{1i}). As in Section 3, suppose that signals and inputs must match to initiate reverberation between V_1 and V_2. In Section 3, this meant that the coded signals released by one input pattern have to match the other input pattern. Here it means that the two input patterns themselves must match. Thus, only if the two eyes are correctly verged, thereby receiving matched patterns, will V_1 and V_2 reverberate. Now assume that output from V_1 and V_2 inhibits the arousal source that drves the eye movements. Fixation is hereby achieved. See Julesz (1971) for a discussion of interacting fields of dipoles that have a search and lock capability.

5. Olfactory Coding and Learned Expectation

In this example, three regions V_1, V_2, and V_3 interact in a way that suggests comparison with data on the neural processing of olfactory stimuli. The main points will be made using the simplest network realizations of relevant mechanisms.

Let V_1 be endowed with recurrent shunting on-center off-surround interactions. Thus

$$
\dot{x}_{1i} = - A^{(1)}x_{1i} + (B^{(1)} - x_{1i})\left[\sum_{k=1}^{N_1} f_1(x_{1k})C_{ki}^{(1)} + I_i\right]
$$
$$
- (x_{1i} + D^{(1)})\sum_{k=1}^{N_1} f_1(x_{1k})E_{ki}^{(1)};
$$

(14)

V_1 can normalize and contrast-enhance input patterns if the signal function $F_1(w)$ and/or interaction coefficients $C_{ki}^{(1)}$ and $E_{ki}^{(1)}$ are properly chosen.

Region V_2 is also endowed with recurrent shunting on-center off-surround interactions, as in

$$
\dot{x}_{2j} = - A^{(2)}x_{2j} + (B^{(2)} - x_{2j})\left[\sum_{k=1}^{N_2} f_2(x_{2k})C_{kj}^{(2)} + S_j\right]
$$
$$
- (x_{2j} + D^{(2)})\sum_{k=1}^{N_2} f_2(x_{2k})E_{kj}^{(2)}
$$

(15)

where $D^{(2)} > 0$. The total signal S_j is the sum of two parts, $S_j^{(1)}$ and $S_j^{(3)}$. Signal $S_j^{(1)}$ is the total signal from V_1 to v_{2j}; it codes patterns at V_1 using an inner-product signal-generating rule, such as

$$
S_j^{(1)} = \sum_{k=1}^{N_1} h_1(x_{1k})z_{kj},
$$

(16)

where $h_1(w)$ is the excitatory V_1-to-V_2 signal function—for example, $h_1(w) = [w^p]^+$, $p > 0$—and z_{kj} is the synaptic strength from v_{1k} to v_{2j}. Signal $S_j^{(3)}$ is the total signal from a third region V_3 to v_{2j}; these signals will be trainable. In effect, V_3 will have a similar relationship to V_2 here as V_2 had to V_1 in Section 2. The signal $S_j^{(3)}$ also has an inner-product form, namely

$$
S_j^{(3)} = \sum_{k=1}^{N_3} h_3(x_{3k})y_{kj},
$$

(17)

where $h_3(w)$ is the excitatory V_3-to-V_2 signal function, and y_{kj} is the trainable synaptic strength from v_{3k} to v_{2j}.

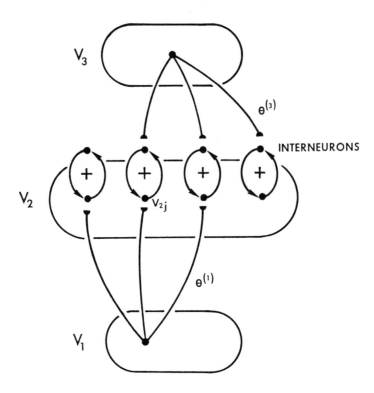

Figure 3. Expectation signals from V_3-to-V_2 inhibit V_2's response to signals from V_1-to-V_2 unless $\theta^{(1)}$ is approximately parallel to $\theta^{(3)}$.

As in Section 2, if the pattern $\theta = (\theta_1, \theta_2, \ldots, \theta_N)$ is approximately uniform, where $\theta_j = S_j(\sum_{k=1}^{N_2} S_k)^{-1}$, then V_2's output will be suppressed. The signal pattern $\theta^{(3)} = (\theta_1^{(3)}, \theta_2^{(3)}, \ldots, \theta_{N_1}^{(3)})$ from V_3 to V_2 such that $\theta_j^{(3)} = S_j^{(3)}(\sum_{k=1}^{N_2} S_k^{(3)})^{-1}$ constitutes an expectation, or expected pattern, that is learned when activity in certain V_3 populations coincides with the elicitation of $\theta^{(3)}$ at V_2. If the afferent signal pattern $\theta^{(1)} = (\theta_1^{(1)}, \theta_2^{(1)}, \ldots, \theta_{N_1}^{(1)})$ from V_1 to V_2, defined by $\theta_j^{(1)} = S_j^{(1)}(\sum_{k=1}^{N_2} S_k^{(1)})^{-1}$, is parallel to $\theta^{(3)}$, then V_2 is allowed to transfer this pattern to higher network centers, with perhaps some contrast control due to fluctuations in total signal strength at V_2, as between (4) and (9). However, if $\theta^{(1)}$ is complementary to $\theta^{(3)}$, then V_2's output is quenched, and higher centers do not receive the pattern.

Some further comment about the pathways from V_3 to V_2 is in order. One provocative connection scheme is the following: let V_3-to-V_2 signals terminate on the excitatory on-center interneurons of V_2, as in Figure 3. Signals from V_3 to V_2 sample the pattern, say $\theta^{(3)}$, at these interneurons during learning trials. Later activation of V_3 can then reproduce $\theta^{(3)}$ at the interneurons on performance trials. The input pattern $\theta^{(1)}$ to V_2, after being averaged by the populations v_{2j}, is then added to $\theta^{(3)}$ at the interneurons. If the net pattern θ is parallel to $\theta^{(1)}$, then interneuronal feedback to V_2 gradually normalizes and contrast enhances $\theta^{(1)}$ until it achieves a stable asymptotic configuration. If θ is approximately uniform, however, then interneuronal feedback tends to suppress the reverberation. If the amplification of interneuronal feedback signals is large compared to the size of V_1-to-V_2 signals, then this feedback will determine whether or not $\theta^{(1)}$ is quenched at V_2.

There exist numerous variations on the above theme. For example, let V_2 be an *unlumped* recurrent on-center off-surround network, in which the inhibitory interneurons average their excitatory inputs at a finite rate. Then V_2 is capable of an approximately periodic oscillation of activity, or *limit cycle*, in response to afferent signals (Ellias and Grossberg, 1975). The expected pattern can then quench the limit cycle if the afferent pattern is unexpected, or can amplify an expected afferent pattern, as in (9), until it triggers limit cycle activity. For the unlumped system to code a spatial pattern, the same ordering of STM activities should (approximately) hold through time, except possibly for phase leads due to the shunt. By Ellias and Grossberg (1975, Section 18), such a limit cycle can exist if the expected pattern serves as an input source and the test pattern (approximately) matches it. In particular, order-preserving limit cycles can exist in an unlumped adaptive resonance. I conjecture also that in unlumped systems whose inhibitory gain is sufficiently large (fast oscillations), a limit cycle can be approximately order-preserving in a finite time interval, since the lumped system (infinitely fast oscillations) is asymptotically order-preserving. Indeed by "perturbing off the fast manifold"—that is decreasing inhibitory gain—an infinite range of oscillation frequencies can be achieved.

Is there a physical advantage to letting the expectation operate from V_3 to V_2 rather than from V_2 to V_1, as in Section 2? There is. In the former case, the expectation is compared to *coded* patterns; for example, to the *generalization gradient* of a pattern at V_1; cf., Section I3. If a set of patterns at V_1 has a similar generalization gradient at V_2, then a *single* expectation from V_3 can quench, or amplify, them as a class. In other words, if an expectation is learned in response to one pattern at V_1, then it will act similarly on any *equivalent* pattern at V_1. In this sense, the generalization gradient, or code, of a pattern defines the pattern features that are behaviorally important to the network.

The above network suggests an analogue with olfactory coding such that V_1 idealizes the olfactory bulb and V_2 idealizes the prepyriform, or primary olfactory, cortex (Freeman, 1972). In this analogy, granule cells in both the olfactory bulb and prepyriform cortex subserve recurrent inhibitory interactions, the mitral and tufted cells in the olfactory bulb act as excitatory populations, and superficial pyramidal cells in the prepyriform cortex act as excitatory populations. Signals from V_1 to V_2 idealize the lateral olfactory tract; see Figure 4.

Given this interpretation, the model generates several implications. In the *lumped* model, wherein inhibitory cells equilibrate rapidly, the generalization gradient at V_2 of a smell-induced pattern at V_1 determines the olfactory code. In other words, a "place theory" (Somjen, 1972, p. 304) or "activity density function" (Freeman, 1972, p. 112) at V_2 determines the code. This suggestion is similar to the idea that the afferent taste message is coded by the relative amount (or spatial pattern) of neural activity across many neurons (Pfaffman, 1955), in particular across chorda tympani fibers (Erickson, 1963). In the *unlumped* model, where limit cycle activity is possible, the coded spatial pattern becomes a space-time pattern of activity. In the special case that *all* populations in V_2 are inhibited by each population in V_2, this limit cycle might merely describe cyclic changes in contrast enhancement which do not invert the relative *ordering* of activities of the populations in V_2 (Ellias and Grossberg, 1975).

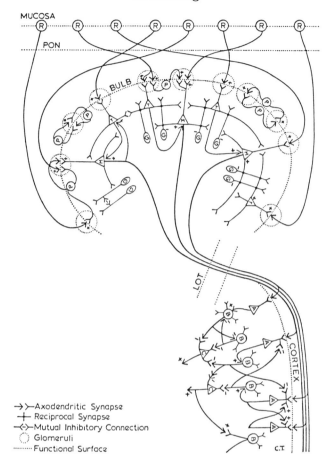

Figure 4. Anatomy of olfactory bulb, lateral olfactory tract, and prepyriform cortex (from Freeman, 1972).

More commonly, a given population in V_2 can only inhibit a subset of populations in V_2. Then the limit cycle behavior can be more complex. Because spatially localized feedback signals can change the net gain of each population's activity to different values at different positions, the frequency, phase, and the peak amplitude of oscillation at a given population can be correlated; cf., the Hughes-Hendrix frequency theory of coding (Hughes and Hendrix, 1967; Somjen, 1972).

The inner-product signal-generating rule (16) requires that signals from each v_{1i} be dispersed broadly across V_2. We therefore expect each mitral cell to send divergent signals across large prepyriform regions via its axons in the lateral olfactory tract. See Freeman (1972, p. 133) for a review of confirming evidence.

With these conventions in mind, an interesting possibility emerges. If the olfactory system were found to have a critical period in which its code can be retuned by experience, then one place to look for trainable synapses in a sensory cortex is at lateral olfactory synaptic knobs in the prepyriform cortex during the critical period.

Emery and Freeman (1969) show that the prepyriform cortex can filter its olfactory messages by a mechanism of selective attention, which is based on the formation of a spatial pattern of excitability in the excitatory feedback gains of the cortical superficial pyramidal cells; see Freeman (1974, p. 3) for a summary. This spatial pattern acts like an expectation, since if the olfactory pattern to the cortex matches the expected pattern, then the cortex can sustain the pattern. Otherwise, the pattern is quenched. We suggest that the expectation mechanism works as described above, where also the expectation modifies the excitatory feedback gain of the cells in V_2.

Several interesting questions about olfactory processing are now suggested. What brain region acts like V_3? Given that such a region exists, then the V_3-to-V_2 synaptic knobs should provide trainable preparations in an *adult* mammalian sensory cortex. If V_3 exists, does it sustain an adaptive resonance with V_2, as V_2 and V_1 do in Section 2? If so, then a critical period could exist at V_2-to-V_3 synaptic knobs, rather than V_1-to-V_2 synaptic knobs. Indeed, is V_3 a formal prepyriform cortex, V_2 its olfactory bulb, and V_1 the source of olfactory messages? Or is V_3 simply a source of extramodality signals that can preset the system to expect a given class of patterns?

6. Modulation of Nonspecific Arousal by a Learned Expectation Mechanism

The mechanism in Section 2 cannot be the only ones that reset STM. An adaptive resonance, for example, can code only one class of patterns at a time in STM. By contrast, sequential STM buffer effects are familiar *in vivo*; for example, repeating a telephone number, or other sequence of events, that has temporarily been stored in STM. An adaptive resonance is incapable of building a hierarchy of command states that are simultaneously active in STM; such a hierarchy is needed to control a behavioral *plan*, or goal-oriented series of sensory-motor coordinations (Grossberg, 1978). If we imagine that V_3 in Section 5, or higher network regions, participate in such sequential and/or hierarchical STM structures, then we must find a way to regulate the pattern of STM activities across these structures in response to new sensory data.

A basic property of such a mechanism is illustrated by the following example. A telephone number can be stored in STM without rehearsing all of its digits at the same time, or indeed any of its digits at certain times. Such unrehearsed but stored items are "opaque" to the learning subject. Yet presentation of a new digit can reset the storage of *all* of these items to make room for the new digit. The mechanism that does this therefore *nonspecifically* influences all the items coded in the neural field; cf., Grossberg (1978).

The expectation mechanisms of Sections 2 and 5 delete present coding of all patterns in a field to code a new pattern. To synthesize mechanisms that can influence all coded patterns without necessarily deleting them, the input patterns in some examples below will be replicated in two parallel representations. The pattern in one representation will be coded as before. The pattern in the other representation will provide data to the nonspecific mechanism that reorganizes the opaque field of STM activities. This latter mechanism will act as a correlation filter, or decision function, that releases nonspecific activity at prescribed times; it does not pass the patterns themselves to higher centers.

There exist both additive and shunting versions of the mechanism. Both are included to develop the themes of Section I4. The minimal additive version was derived in Grossberg (1972c, 1975). The basic idea is as follows. The STM pattern generated by an input pattern θ is typically not θ, but is rather a coded version of

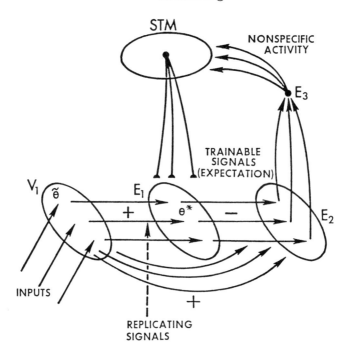

Figure 5. An additive model for gating nonspecific arousal using expectation signals.

θ. This coded activity will preset the network to expect a pattern θ^*. The expected pattern θ^* will then be compared with the test pattern $\tilde{\theta}$ that concurrently perturbs V_1. If θ^* is close to $\tilde{\theta}$, then a signal will be elicited from a prescribed network population. This signal will control nonspecific arousal of the network populations that subserve STM.

To show how an expectation develops, suppose that θ is followed by θ^* on several learning trials. Consider the time interval on each trial when θ is coded in STM and θ^* is active at V_1. Then θ^* will be replicated at E_1, and the coded STM representation of θ will elicit signals to E_1 that learn θ^* using trainable synaptic strengths, as in Figure 5. Thereafter, when θ is coded in STM, pattern θ^* will be elicited at E_1 by θ's STM representation. The pattern at E_1 is then transferred to E_2 as proportional inhibitory signals, which take the place of the threshold pattern of Section I4. Thus, the pattern of inhibitory signals represents the pattern θ^* that is expected by the network.

These inhibitory signals will be compared with the pattern weights of the test pattern $\tilde{\theta}$. To accomplish this, when a pattern is presented to V_1, it is also replicated at E_2 as proportional excitatory signals.

The inhibitory $V_1 \rightarrow E_1 \rightarrow E_2$ signals that the pattern creates are chosen weaker than the direct excitatory $V_1 \rightarrow E_2$ signals to achieve net excitatory signals at E_2 from V_1. Given this structure, let θ be active in STM when $\tilde{\theta}$ is presented to V_1. Only if each excitatory pattern weight at E_2 (of θ) exceeds the corresponding inhibitory pattern weight (of θ^*) by a suitable proportionality constant will the output signals from that pathway be positive, as in equation (I11). A high-band filter adjoined to each such pathway ensures that the net signal in each pathway from E_2 to E_3

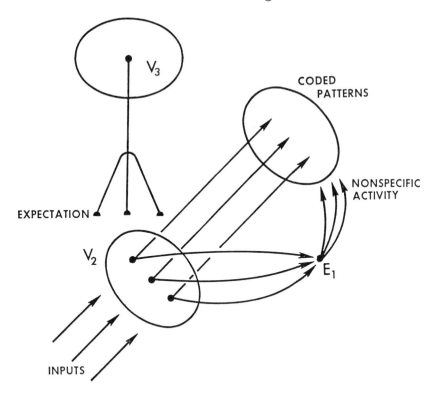

Figure 6. A postsynaptic shunting model for gating nonspecific arousal using expectation signals.

is positive only if the excitatory pattern weight is sufficiently close to its inhibitory pattern weight, as in equation (I12). The firing threshold of the population E_3 in the final common path of these signals is chosen so high that all signals must be positive to fire E_3. Thus E_3 fires only if $\tilde{\theta}$ is close to θ^*. If no expected pattern θ^* is active, then *any* test pattern $\tilde{\theta}$ can elicit a signal unless further structure is added; for example, add tonically active cells that inhibit E_2 until a prescribed pattern is coded in STM, and thereupon inhibits the tonically active cells via a recurrent off-surround. Grossberg (1972c, 1975) discusses this mechanism in greater detail.

Two shunting analogues of the expectation mechanism are possible. The simpler shunting mechanism works as in Section 5. A region V_3 presets a region V_2 with an expectation pattern. Signals from V_2 bifurcate; one pathway carries coded patterns, as in Sections 2 and 5; the other path E_1, which acts like E_3 in Figure 5, sums up the signals from V_2. Thus if the test pattern at V_1 is unexpected, the output from E_3 will be quenched, whereas if the test pattern is expected, the output from E_3 will be large. This mechanism does not require a replication of pattern representations. See Figure 6.

Another shunting version is more complicated, but is included for completeness. Consider learning trials on which θ^* follows θ. Let θ be coded in STM while θ^* is replicated at E_1. The signals to E_1 generated by θ's representation will shunt the θ^*-generated output signals from E_1 on their way to E_2 (Figure 7). For example, suppose that only population v_i is active in STM, that the jth population in E_1 is e_j, and

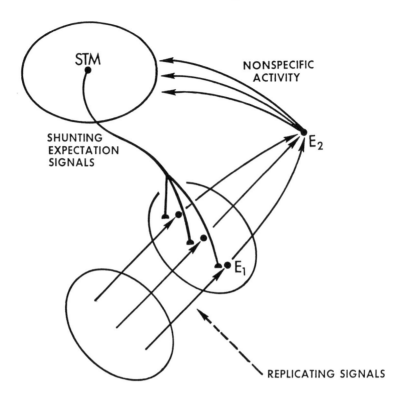

Figure 7. A presynaptic shunt for gating nonspecific arousal using expectation signals.

that the synaptic strength from v_i to the pathway from e_j to E_2 is z_{ij}. Then the total output signal from E_1 to E_2 is proportional to $\theta^* \cdot z^{(i)}$, where $z^{(i)} = (z_{i1}, z_{i2}, \ldots, z_{in})$. While this signal is on, the plastic synaptic strengths $z^{(i)}$ will learn the pattern θ^*. In other words, the plastic synaptic strengths shunt signals as they compute a time average of presynaptic signals and postsynaptic activity. After learning takes place, present pattern $\tilde{\theta}$ to V_1 while θ is coded in STM at V_2. Then the total output signal from E_1 will be proportional to $\tilde{\theta} \cdot z^{(i)}$, which is proportional to $\tilde{\theta} \cdot \theta^*$ as a result of prior learning. Only if this inner-product signal is sufficiently large will the final common path E_2 fire. Again an output signal is generated only if $\tilde{\theta}$ is sufficiently similar to θ^*.

This shunting expectation mechanism has the additional property that it can filter patterns. Suppose that several populations $v_{i_1}, v_{i_2}, \ldots, v_{i_k}$ are simultaneously active in STM, and have STM activities $x_{i_1}, x_{i_2}, \ldots, x_{i_k}$. Then the total signal from E_1 to E_2 is proportional to

$$\tilde{\theta} \cdot \sum_{j=1}^{k} x_{i_j} z^{(i_j)}. \tag{18}$$

Thus E_2 can fire if $\tilde{\theta}$ is sufficiently close to *any* $z^{(i_j)}$ that has a sufficiently large activity x_{ij}.

In both the additive and shunting models, a signal is elicited from the final common path of the expectation mechanism only if the test pattern $\tilde{\theta}$ is close to the expected pattern θ^*. Grossberg (1975) assumes that *every* pattern which is processed by the network is capable of eliciting nonspecific arousal, but that the output from the expectation mechanism inhibits the source of nonspecific activity when an expected event occurs. The net output generates nonspecific arousal in response to unexpected events, as in Section I6, or to events that occur when there is no prior STM activity, as in Section I7. Grossberg (1975) also uses these properties to develop a model of attention and discrimination learning.

The above mechanisms suggest that, in addition to the specific pathways that code prescribed patterns, there exist other pathways that release arousal in response to unexpected events. What are these pathways in the olfactory system? We suggest that they are among the multisynaptic pathways that project from the olfactory bulb into the reticular formation (Noback, 1967, pp. 131–133, 221–230).

7. Universal Recoding

By universal recoding is meant a process whereby any k spatial patterns in R^m can be recoded into any k spatial patterns in R^n, for any fixed $k \geq 1, m \geq 2$, and $n \geq 2$. Computer studies aimed at this objective have been reported by Kilmer and Olinski (1974) in their model of hippocampal dynamics.

To accomplish universal recoding, three regions V_1, V_2, and V_3 will be needed. Let V_1 have m populations and let V_3 have n populations. The patterns $\theta^{(1)}, \theta^{(2)}, \ldots, \theta^{(k)}$ in R^m will be serially presented to V_1 as the corresponding patterns $\tilde{\theta}^{(1)}, \tilde{\theta}^{(2)}, \ldots, \tilde{\theta}^{(k)}$ in R^n are presented to V_3. Each pattern $\theta^{(i)}$ at V_1 will be coded at V_2 by a unique population v_{2i}. Thus V_2 contains at least k populations. Then v_{2i} can sample the pattern $\tilde{\theta}^{(i)}$ at V_3 until its trainable v_{2i}-to-V_3 synapses learn this pattern. Consequently, on performance trials, presenting $\theta^{(i)}$ at V_1 excites v_{2i}, which thereupon reproduces $\tilde{\theta}^{(i)}$ at V_3.

To realize these properties, V_1 and V_3 will be endowed with recurrent shunting on-center off-surrounds in order to normalize their patterns. Both the V_1-to-V_2 and the V_2-to-V_3 synaptic strengths will be trainable; the former to code patterns $\theta^{(i)}$, the latter to learn patterns $\tilde{\theta}^{(i)}$. It remains to show how V_2 chooses a unique v_{2i} in response to each $\theta^{(i)}$. A simple, but inefficient, way to do this is to use the Sparse Pattern Theorem (Theorem 2) of Part I; namely, let the number K of populations in V_2 be so much larger than k that at most one pattern $\theta^{(i)}$ is in each set P_i defined by equation (I10). In fact, if this is done, then the V_1-to-V_2 coefficients need not be trainable. For example, let

$$\dot{x}_{2j} = -Ax_{2j} + (B - x_{2j})S_j - (x_{2j} + B)\sum_{l \neq j} S_l \qquad (19)$$

where $S_j = \sum_{l=1}^{m} x_{1l}z_{1j}$ is the V_1-to-v_{2j} signal. By (2), the equilibrium point of (19) is

$$x_{2j} = \frac{BS}{A+S}\left(\phi_j - \frac{1}{2}\right) \qquad (20)$$

where $S = \sum_{l=1}^{K} S_l$ and $\phi_j = S_j S^{-1}$. By (20), at most one x_{2j} is positive, and this occurs only if $S_j > \max\{S_l : l \neq j\}$; that is, only if v_{2j} is chosen by V_2. Let K be chosen so large that, in response to any $\theta^{(i)}$ at V_1, inequality $\phi_i > 1/2$ holds. Also let the threshold of V_2-to-V_3 signals equal 0. Then, in response to $\theta^{(i)}$ at V_1, only v_{2i} in V_2 can sample $\tilde{\theta}^{(i)}$ at V_3. Universal recoding is hereby accomplished in this case.

This method fails if K is fixed and k is chosen too large. The following difficulty must be overcome. Suppose that two patterns $\theta^{(1)}$ and $\theta^{(2)}$ would ordinarily be coded by the same population v_{21} in V_2; that is

$$\theta^{(i)} \cdot z^{(1)}(0) > \max\{\epsilon, \theta^{(i)} \cdot z^{(j)}(0) : j \neq 1\}, \quad i = 1, 2. \tag{21}$$

If $\theta^{(1)}$ is presented sufficiently often before $\theta^{(2)}$ is presented, how can $\theta^{(2)}$ be prevented from being coded by v_{21}, and yet be allowed to search for and find an as yet unpracticed population in V_2? An adaptive resonance between V_1 and V_2 does not suffice. Then activity in v_{21} generates V_2-to-V_1 feedback that quenches V_1-to-V_2 signals when $\theta^{(2)}$ is first presented to V_1; but when v_{21} is hereby inactivated and V_1-to-V_2 signals resume in response to $\theta^{(2)}$ alone, they again activate v_{21}, by (21). Somehow presentation of $\theta^{(2)}$ must inhibit v_{21}—including the large excitatory V_1-to-v_{21} signal generated by $\theta^{(2)}$—until $\theta^{(2)}$ can find an uncommitted population among the uninhibited, or *renormalized*, populations of V_2. in particular, there must be at least two sources of input to V_2: the excitatory signals that code the patterns at V_1, and the signals that are elicited by a mismatch of patterns. The latter signals differentially inhibit populations which are currently active in STM. These inputs are nonspecific because the STM code is opaque. How does nonspecific arousal interact with current STM activity to differentially inhibit active populations?

Some additional prerequisites are now also evident. Differential inhibition must last long enough for a new population v_{22} to start reverberating in STM. After v_{21} is initially inhibited in this way, it no longer triggers the expectation mechanism. Nonspecific arousal consequently ceases. What prevents the large V_1-to-v_{21} signals due to $\theta^{(2)}$ from reactivating v_{21}? Only the STM activity of other cells is available to do this. Thus inhibition of v_{21} is maintained by recurrent inhibitory signals from active populations in V_2, such as v_{22}.

Before synthesizing this mechanism, several comments will be made to put it in a broader perspective. Firstly, Grossberg (1975) shows the need for a similar mechanism to achieve attentional shifts and discrimination learning. In a clear intuitive sense, searching for an uncommitted population is a type of attentional shift. Secondly, a universal recoding mechanism is capable of making arbitrarily fine discriminations; even if two patterns $\theta^{(1)}$ and $\theta^{(2)}$ are very similar, they can be recoded into two patterns $\tilde{\theta}^{(1)}$ and $\tilde{\theta}^{(2)}$ that are very dissimilar. It is this latter property that requires the full power of the mechanism described in Grossberg (1975). Thirdly, universal recoding represents a limiting case of situations that often occur *in vivo*. In this limiting case, *any* change of input pattern is treated like an unexpected event, because no matter how similar $\theta^{(1)}$ and $\theta^{(2)}$ are, they can, by universality, be conditioned to arbitrarily different patterns $\tilde{\theta}^{(1)}$ and $\tilde{\theta}^{(2)}$. A weaker condition often holds *in vivo*, where unexpected consequences (e.g., no reward) of treating two patterns the same provides a basis for discriminating between them. Nonetheless, similar patterns can be differentially reinforced *in vivo*, and the mechanism described below has this capability. In effect, different reinforcement contingencies will generate different cognitive structures by triggering nonspecific arousal at different times. A more thorough analysis of a reinforcement theory in which the conditioning and activation of nonspecific arousal is central is given in Grossberg (1971, 1972a, 1972b).

8. Search

It is now easy to supply formal rules capable of universal recoding. However, the physical substrates of these rules will require a much deeper understanding. Firstly, sufficient formal rules will be noted, and then an analysis of their physical substrates will be begun. This analysis will open a path to many related subjects, such as cholinergic versus noadrenergic interactions in neocortex, spatial frequency adaptation, and negative afterimages.

Speaking formally, the following properties suffice:

(i) inhibition of active stages $v_{21}, v_{22}, \ldots, v_{2i}$ in V_2 if a mismatch occurs in the expectation mechanism between their coded patterns and externally presented pattern $\theta^{(1)}$ at V_1;

(ii) reduction of the QT, or amplification of nonspecific arousal, until the activity of *some* uninhibited and unclassified population $v_{2,i+1}$ exceeds the QT;

(iii) maintenance of $v_{2,i+1}$'s STM activity, and of inhibition of $v_{21}, v_{22}, \ldots, v_{2i}$, until $v_{2,i+1}$'s classifying vector $z^{(i+1)}$ can be trained. On later trials, presentation of $\theta^{(1)}$ at V_1 will therefore elicit a maximal signal at $v_{2,i+1}$, whence $v_{2,i+1}$ will classify $\theta^{(1)}$.

These rules imply that a *search* routine will continue until an uncommitted population is found. In particular, suppose that at time $t = 0$, the signals $S_j^{(1)}(0)$ from V_1 to v_{2j} satisfy $S_j^{(1)}(0) > S_{j+1}^{(1)}(0), j = 1, 2, \ldots, N_2 - 1$. Thus, in response to $\theta^{(1)}$ at V_1, v_{21} will be activated. Suppose, however, that v_{21} codes $\theta^{*(1)} \neq \theta^{(1)}$. Then a mismatch occurs in the expectation mechanism, and nonspecific arousal is elicited. Consequently, v_{21} is inhibited as the QT decreases, or equivalently, as the amplification of V_1-to-V_2 signals increases. Among the uninhibited populations $v_{22}, v_{23}, \ldots, v_{2N_2}$, v_{22} now receives the largest net signal, and is therefore activated. Suppose, however, that v_{22} codes $\theta^{*(2)} \neq \theta^{(1)}$; again a mismatch occurs in the expectation mechanism. Nonspecific arousal is again elicited, v_{22} is inhibited, and the process repeats itself until a population $v_{2,i+1}$ is found which does not already code a discordant pattern $\theta^{*(i+1)}$. Then STM activity at $v_{2,i+1}$ can be maintained while the classifying vector $z^{(i+1)}$ learns $\theta^{(1)}$. The need for reducing the QT, or equivalenty increasing nonspecific arousal, is clarified by this description, since the signal $S_{i+1}^{(1)}(0)$ might otherwise be too small to elicit sustained STM activity at $v_{2,i+1}$, especially if i is large.

The maximal length of the search routine depends on how long inhibition of previously active populations lasts. An uncommitted population $v_{2,i+1}$ can be found only if *all* the populations $v_{21}, v_{22}, \ldots, v_{2i}$ are inhibited when nonspecific arousal is triggered by $\theta^{*(i)}$. If inhibition wears off gradually as i increases, eventually $S_1^{(1)}$ will be large enough to re-excite v_{21} in STM, say after population v_{2j} fails to code $\theta^{(1)}$. Then a cyclic reactivation of $v_{21}, v_{22}, \ldots, v_{2j}$ will ensue. Since some residual inhibition remains, as the cycle repeats itself, the amount of residual accumulation will accumulate. On successive search cycles, j can therefore increase until an asymptotic search cycle length j^* is reached, whose size depends on how fast inhibition decays.

There exists an inverse relationship between j^* and the number of cortical populations needed to achieve a prescribed level of discrimination between two patterns. This is because it becomes easier to discriminate two similar patterns as the number of cortical populations with distinct classifying vectors increases. Consequently, the expected search duration will be smaller if the number of cortical populations is larger, and then the decay rate of inhibition can be faster.

9. Slow Noradrenergic Transmitter Accumulation-Depletion as a Search Mechanism

We will suggest that the search mechanism is part of a broader scheme of pattern processing that exhibits remarkable structure symmetries. In previous work on reinforcement, Grossberg (1972b) synthesizes networks in which pairs of populations code drive states of opposite sign; e.g., fear versus relief, hunger versus frustration. These population pairs, or "dipoles," compete with each other to generate a net incentive motivational signal that regulates compatible motor output, among other things. If a persistent input to one dipole population is sufficiently turned off, then a transient *rebound*, or reversal, occurs in the relative activities of the two dipole populations; e.g., offset of shock elicits relief. This rebound is also generated if an unexpected event causes a sudden increment of arousal equally to both populations in a dipole.

Grossberg (1972a) discusses the existence of analogous dipoles in sensory cortex, wherein one population ("on-cells") is elicited when its stimulus is on, and its antagonistic population ("off-cells") is transiently excited when the stimulus is turned off. The off-cells are then capable of sampling sensory or motor patterns elsewhere in the network, and hereby the offset of a cue can be used as a basis for learned action.

Grossberg (1972a, 1972b, 1975) suggests that both types of dipole are examples of a general network design, and synthesizes both with similar formal rules. This synthesis uses a slowly varying transmitter accumulation-depletion mechanism to drive the dipole rebound. Grossberg (1972b) notes data suggesting norepinephrine as a possible candidate for this transmitter. Experiments by Wise *et al.* (1973) compatibly report that norepinephrine and serotonin act as parallel transmitters in reward and punishment centers of the rat. Grossberg (1972b) also suggests that the reticular formation is a likely source of nonspecific arousal in response to unexpected events, and there are at least three major ascending norepinephrine fiber systems in the rat brainstem (Fuxe *et al.*, 1970; Jacobowitz, 1973; Lindvall and Björklund, 1974; Stein, 1974; Ungerstedt, 1971) that reach neocortex, hippocampus, limbic system, and hypothalamus, among other regions.

We now suggest that this transmitter system is also used to help search for uncommitted cortical populations. This proposal requires only an explication of previous mechanisms for new purposes, rather than an additional construction. The reader is referred to Grossberg (1972b, 1975) for a detailed analysis of the rebound mechanism. The simplest version is described in Figure 8 and Table 1. Below some properties that suggest the mechanism in the present context will be sketched.

It is clear how nonspecific arousal reduces the QT or, equivalently, amplifies input signals, as in equation (I13) or equation (I14). But how does nonspecific arousal, which is distributed *uniformly* across all populations in V_2, alter the balance of excitation in favor of previously inactive populations? This problem is particularly evident in adaptive resonances. Here a mismatch between the pattern (say $\theta^{*(1)}$) coded by a population (say v_{21}) and a test pattern at V_1 (say $\theta^{(1)}$) suppresses the V_1-to-v_{21} signal, and causes x_{21} to decay *before* nonspecific arousal arrives. Clearly a more slowly decaying trace must remain to indicate that v_{21} has just been active. This trace

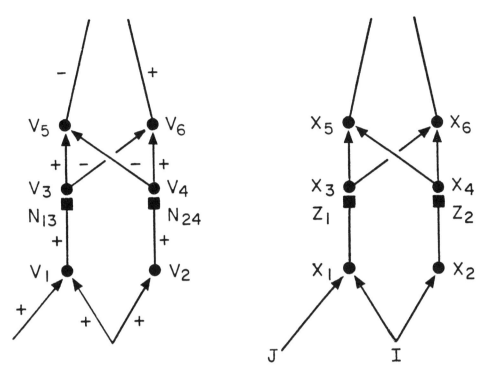

Figure 8. The minimal nonrecurrent rebound mechanism for a dipole of populations.

$$\dot{x}_1 = -\alpha x_1 + I + J$$

$$\dot{x}_2 = -\alpha x_2 + I$$

$$\dot{z}_1 = \beta(\gamma - z_1) - \delta f(x_1(t - \tau))z_1$$

$$\dot{z}_2 = \beta(\gamma - z_2) - \delta f(x_2(t - \tau))z_2$$

$$\dot{x}_3 = -\epsilon x_3 + \zeta f(x_1(t - \tau))z_1$$

$$\dot{x}_4 = -\epsilon x_4 + \zeta f(x_2(t - \tau))z_2$$

$$\dot{x}_5 = -\eta x_5 + \kappa[x_3(t - \sigma) - x_4(t - \sigma)]$$

$$\dot{x}_6 = -\eta x_6 + \kappa[x_4(t - \sigma) - x_3(t - \sigma)]$$

Table 1

must also be slowly decaying to maintain inhibition of incorrect populations during a search routine. More precisely, STM activity at v_{21} depletes the slow trace in v_{21}'s arousal pathway, while the trace accumulates at inactive populations. Then equal arousal signals to all populations are gated, or shunted, by their slow traces, so that previously inactive populations receive larger arousal signals. Figure 9 schematizes one such arrangement.

Figure 9 depicts two dipoles D_1 and D_2 of on-cells and off-cells. Nonspecific

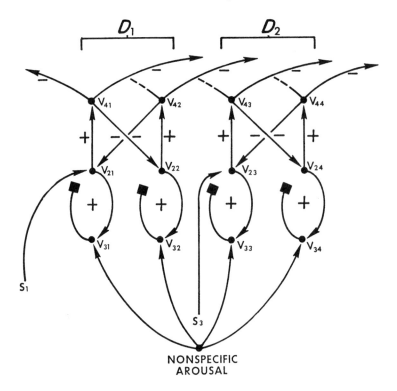

Figure 9. Nonspecific arousal is gated by slow transmitter accumulation-depletion in an on-center off-surround network of dipoles.

arousal perturbs all of the excitatory interneurons $v_{3i}, i = 1, 2, 3, 4$. Slowly varying transmitter exists in the pathways $v_{3i} \rightarrow v_{2i}$. Thus, arousal signals on their way to the populations v_{2i} are gated at the v_{3i}-to-v_{2i} synapses by the pattern of accumulated transmitter at that time. The on-cell populations v_{21} and v_{23} also receive signals S_1 and S_3, respectively, that are driven by patterns at V_1. If (say) S_1 is large enough to activate v_{21} in STM, then excitatory activity reverberates through the loop $v_{21} \rightarrow v_{31} \rightarrow v_{21}$ and partially depletes its transmitter. Such reverberation is possible because the net $v_{21} \rightarrow v_{31} \rightarrow v_{21}$ signal is a monotone *increasing* function of signal size S_1, even though transmitter accumulation is a monotone *decreasing* function of signal size (Grossberg, 1972b). This is a consequence of the gating effect of transmitter on the signal. The second effect of gating occurs when the reverberation terminates and a uniform arousal signal perturbs all v_{3i}. Since previously active channels have less transmitter than inactive ones, the inactive populations, including off-cells like v_{22}, receive larger gated signals than the active ones. After v_{22} is activated, it inhibits v_{21} via the inhibitory interneuron v_{42}. The inhibitory interneurons v_{4i} also scatter inhibition across the field of populations, with on-cells inhibiting on-cells, and off-cells inhibiting off-cells, to normalize their respective total activities.

If such an anatomy exists *in vivo*, it would not be surprising if the transmitter at on-cells differs from that at off-cells; cf., norepinephrine and serotonin. Such a difference might provide a chemical substrate whereby the off-surrounds of on-cells and of off-cells could be segregated to include only cells of their own type, much as horizontal cells are segregated in certain retinas (Kaneko, 1970; Stell, 1967). Such an arrangement will also be used to discuss afterimages in Section 11.

The synaptic strengths of S_i-to-v_{2i} pathways, $i = 1, 3$, are trainable during the critical period. As in previous papers, these synaptic strengths will be assumed to reflect transmitter production rates in the corresponding synaptic knobs; see Grossberg (1974) for a review. Arguing by analogy with Grossberg (1972b), we suggest that this transmitter system is cholinergic, rather than adrenergic. The present model is therefore compatible with the idea that adrenergic changes merely set the stage for learning by cholinergic synapses, rather than causing memory fixation themselves. The latter stronger view is compatible with indirect evidence reviewed by Stein (1974). The present model is not incompatible with the stronger view; but given the parallel course of formal cholinergic and adrenergic changes in rebound-encoding transitions, it seems that deciding between the two alternatives will require delicate experimentation.

The mechanism in Figure 9 is appealing because of its simplicity. Relatively localized excitatory signals emerge from the cells v_{2i} ("on-center"), and more broadly distributed inhibitory signals emerge from the cells v_{4i} ("off-surround"). These are standard adaptational mechanisms plus slow transmitter accumulation-depletion. See Ellias and Grossberg (1975) for a study of STM in a related class of networks. Variations on this theme containing more processing stages are possible; cf., Grossberg (1972b, Sections 7 and 8) for generalizations in the case of drive dipoles, including variations wherein the accumulation-depletion transmitter is inhibitory.

10. Spatial Frequency Adaptation

The rebound mechanism has other formal properties that are analogous to sensory phenomena. To the extent that the rebound mechanism really explains these phenomena, they become manifestations of basic constraints on neural coding, rather than merely curious accidents of nature.

Wilson (1975) proposes a neural model to explain various data about spatial frequency adaptation to sine wave gratings, square wave gratings, tilted gratings, and single bars. In his model, signals are feedforward from retina to cortex, and are distributed in an on-center off-surround interaction pattern whose connection strengths decrease monotonically with distance. Wilson uses trainable synaptic strengths as his mechanism of adaptation. Only the inhibitory synapses of the model are modifiable: their changes are determined by a product of presynaptic signal size and postsynaptic potential. If the net postsynaptic potential of a given cell is large, then the inhibitory synaptic strengths of active synapses impinging on the cell get stronger, and tend to inhibit the potential more vigorously. This negative feedback mechanism produces good fits to various data on adaptation. Wilson also assumes that a synaptic conservation law holds; namely, the total inhibitory synaptic strength impinging on each excitatory neuron is constant through time. This mechanism correctly predicts that elevation of perceptual threshold should be greater at higher spatial frequencies of the adapting grating, and it overcomes the otherwise unduly great depression of the modulation transfer function at all frequencies below 3 cycles/degree, given an adapting spatial frequency of 3 cycles/degree. Grossberg (1975) notes that synaptic conservation rules are incompatible with classical conditioning, and suggests that normalization of the total retinal output due to its on-center off-surround interactions can be used instead. In effect, good fits to spatial frequency adaptation can be achieved given two regions V_1 and V_2, each endowed with shunting on-center off-surround interactions, excitatory signals from V_1 to V_2 that code the patterns at V_1, and a mechanism of signal gating whereby the most active populations are slowly suppressed.

We now note that adaptational effects can formally be generated by slow accumulation-depletion, rather than by learned cross-correlation, of transmitter. When a pattern at V_1 maximally excites a certain population v_{2i} for a long time, the transmitters associated with *all* of the populations in v_{2i}'s generalization gradient will gradually become depleted, thereby causing a shift in excitability in response to similar patterns. In other words, imbalances in accumulation-depletion due to persistent activity can change the spatial distribution of inhibition across populations. If this mechanism is valid, then the rate of spatial frequency adaptation might depend on the level of nonspecific arousal. In particular, after the inspection pattern is viewed, do parametric increases in arousal level when a test pattern is imposed influence the amount of adaptation by influencing the size of the rebound?

11. Afterimages

An excellent review of this venerable subject is given by Brown (1965). Here we show how the rebound mechanism can generate negative afterimages, and summarize compatible experimental evidence concerning the effect of background illumination on the course of afterimages. The general ideas that afterimages depend on effects of "fatigue" (Fechner, 1840) or antagonistic activity (Plateau, 1834) are very old, but the concept of a tonically driven accumulation-depletion mechanism operating in linked shunting recurrent on-center off-surround fields of dipoles considerably sharpens these ideas. Consider Figure 10. Suppose that the pattern in Figure 10a perturbs a network whose populations code the orientation of lines in prescribed retinal regions (Hubel and Wiesel, 1963; Szentagothai and Arbib, 1974, p. 419). Suppose that the orientationally tuned populations corresponding to a given retinal region interact via a recurrent shunting on-center off-surround network, such that populations that code nearby orientations excite each other, but populations that code very different orientations inhibit each other, as is compatible with the developmental model of this paper. See also Levine and Grossberg (1976) for a discussion of relevant experimental data and an explanation of certain visual illusions in such a network. Given this interaction scheme between populations, when the pattern of Figure 10a is active, the maximally inhibited orientations are the ones perpendicular to the orientations of line fragments in the pattern (Figure 10b). When the pattern is shut off, these perpendicular orientations will be the ones that experience the greatest rebounds. These rebounding populations code a series of concentric circles, or rather the flickering fragments of concentric circles, as in Figure 10c; cf., MacKay (1957).

Negative afterimages in color are also known to occur (Brown, 1965), and will arise using a rebound mechanism if each dipole codes a pair of complementary colors, and the off-surround of each color-coded cell perturbs only similarly color-coded cells, as in Figure 9, thereby generating a lightness scale; cf., Grossberg (1972c).

The effects of changing background illumination, or the *secondary field*, on afterimages are remarkably similar to the effects of changing arousal level on the rebound. If a secondary field is turned on during the observation of a positive afterimage in darkness, a rapid transition to a negative afterimage can be generated (Brown, 1965,

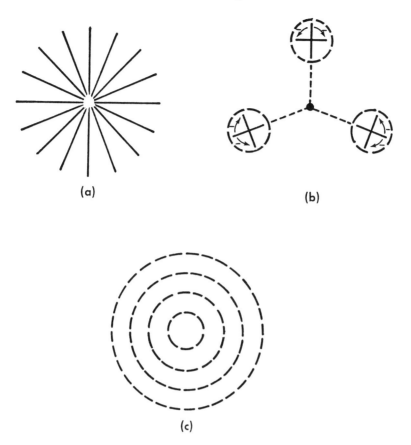

(a)   (b)

(c)

Figure 10. Negative afterimage in space: (a) the test figure; (b) maximal inhibition of orthogonal orientations; (c) rebound generates afterimage.

p. 483; Helmholtz, 1866). If the secondary field is then turned off, the afterimage can revert in appearance to that of the stage when the secondary field was first turned on. In the rebound mechanism, an increase in uniform input to the dipole tends to reverse the relative dipole activities. If the uniform input is shut off, the slowly varying transmitter levels can still be close to their original values, so that the original relative dipole activities are rapidly restored. The higher the luminance of the secondary field, the shorter is the afterimage latency, and the more rapidly is the afterimage extinguished (Juhasz, 1920). In a dipole, a higher uniform input more rapidly equalizes the amounts of transmitter in the two dipole channels by depleting them both at a faster, more uniform rate. When approximately equal levels of transmitter are achieved, the inhibitory interneurons between the dipole's populations kill any relative advantage of one population over the other. The duration of an afterimage increases with an increase in primary stimulus luminance (Brown, 1965, p. 493). In a dipole, increasing the intensity of an input to one population increases the rebound at the other population when the input terminates, much as termination of a more intense shock causes greater relief (Grossberg, 1972b).

The brightness of the positive afterimage has been found to be greater and the latency shorter if the primary stimulus is relatively brief. A longer stimulus results in a decrease of both the duration and the brightness of the positive afterimage. In the accumulation-depletion mechanism, there is a transient overshoot in transmitter release when an input is first turned on, followed by a decrease in transmitter release to an asymptotic level that depends on input intensity (Grossberg, 1964, Section IX (O), (P)).

Helmholtz (1866, 1924) observed that if the primary stimulus is 4 to 8 seconds in duration, then the duration of a negative afterimage may be increased to as long as 8 minutes. Such long effects unambiguously implicate a slowly varying process, and indeed a process slow enough to facilitate search for uncommitted populations during the interim interval.

12. Conclusion

The above results hope to show that a small class of network mechanisms can be used to unify the discussion of a variety of seemingly disparate phenomena that are related to sensory processing. For example, the results on negative afterimages and spatial frequency adaptation can be appended to those of Levine and Grossberg (1976), which show that recurrent shunting on-center off-surround networks also enjoy formal properties analogous to other visual illusions, such as hysteresis, line neutralization, tilt aftereffect, and angle expansion. All these results suggest that seeming idiosyncracies in sensory processing are unaviodable epiphenomena of useful design constraints on the development and maintenance of our wonderful sensory endowment.

REFERENCES

Brown, J.L. (1965). Afterimages. In C.H. Graham (Ed.), **Vision and visual perception**. New York: Wiley, 479–503.

Cant, B.R. and Bickford, R.G. (1967). The effect of motivation on the contingent negative variation (CNV). *Electroencephalography and Clinical Neurophysiology*, **23**, 594.

Cohen, J. (1969). Very slow brain potentials relating to expectancy: The CNV. In E. Donchin and D.B. Lindsley (Eds.), **Average evoked potentials**. Washington, DC: National Aeronautics and Space Administration, 143–198.

Ellias, S.A. and Grossberg, S. (1975). Pattern formation, contrast control, and oscillations in the short term memory of shunting on-center off-surround networks. *Biological Cybernetics*, **20**, 69–98.

Emery, J.D. and Freeman, W.J. (1969). Pattern analysis of cortical evoked potential parameters during attention charges. *Physiological Behavior*, **4**, 69–77.

Erickson, R.P. (1963). Sensory neural patterns and gustation. In Y. Zotterman (Ed.), **Olfaction and taste**. New York: Pergamon Press, 205–213.

Fechner, G.T. (1840). Ueber die subjectiven Nachbilder und Nebenbilder, I. *Poggendorf Ann. Phys. Chem.*, **50**, 193–221.

Freeman, W.J. (1972). Waves, pulses, and the theory of neural masses. In R. Rosen and F. Snell (Eds.), **Progress in theoretical biology**. New York: Academic Press, 87–165.

Freeman, W.J. (1974). Neural coding through mass action in the olfactory system. *Proceedings of the IEEE Conference on Biologically Motivated Automata Theory*.

Fuxe, K., Hökfelt, T., and Ungerstedt, U. (1970). Morphological and functional aspects of central monoamine neurons. *International Review of Neurobiology*, **13**, 93–126.

Grossberg, S. (1971). On the dynamics of operant conditioning. *Journal of Theoretical Biology*, **33**, 225–255.

Grossberg, S. (1972a). A neural theory of punishment and avoidance, I: Qualitative theory. *Mathematical Biosciences*, **15**, 39–67.

Grossberg, S. (1972b). A neural theory of punishment and avoidance, II: Quantitative theory. *Mathematical Biosciences*, **15**, 253–285.

Grossberg, S. (1972c). Neural expectation: Cerebellar and retinal analogs of cells fired by learnable or unlearned pattern classes. *Kybernetik*, **10**, 49–57.

Grossberg, S. (1974). Classical and instrumental learning by neural networks. In R. Rosen and F. Snell (Eds.), **Progress in theoretical biology**. New York: Academic Press, 51–141.

Grossberg, S. (1975). A neural model of attention, reinforcement, and discrimination learning. *International Review of Neurobiology*, **18**, 263–327.

Grossberg, S. (1976a). On the development of feature detectors in the visual cortex with applications to learning and reaction-diffusion systems. *Biological Cybernetics*, **21**, 145–159.

Grossberg, S. (1976b). Adaptive pattern classification and universal recoding, I: Parallel development and coding of neural feature detectors. *Biological Cybernetics*, **23**, 121–134.

Grossberg, S. (1978). Human memory: Self-organization of sensory-motor codes, maps, and plans. In R. Rosen and F. Snell (Eds.), **Progress in theoretical biology, Volume 5**. New York: Academic Press.

Grossberg, S. and Levine, D.S. (1975). Some developmental and attentional biases in the contrast enhancement and short term memory of recurrent neural networks. *Journal of Theoretical Biology*, **53**, 341–380.

Helmholtz, H. von (1866). **Handbuch der physiologischen Optik**. Hamburg, Leipzig: Voss.

Helmholtz, H. von (1924). **Physiological optics, Volume II**, J.P.C. Southall (Ed.). Optical Society of America.

Hodgkin, A.L. (1964). **The conduction of the nervous impulse**. Springfield, IL: C.C. Thomas.

Hubel, D.H. and Wiesel, T.N. (1963). Receptive fields of cells in striate cortex of very young, visually inexperienced kittens. *Journal of Neurophysiology*, **26**, 994–1002.

Hughes, J.R. and Hendrix, D.E. (1967). The frequency component hypothesis in relation to the coding mechanism in the olfactory bulb. In T. Hayashi (Ed.), **Olfaciton and taste II**. Oxford: Pergamon Press, 51–87.

Irwin, D.A., Rebert, C.S., McAdam, D.W., and Knott, J.R. (1966). Slow potential changes (CNV) in the human EEG as a function of motivational variables. *Electroencephalography and Clinical Neurophysiology*, **21**, 412–413.

Jacobowitz, D.M. (1973). Effects of 6-hydroxydopa. In E. Usdin and H.S. Snyder (Eds.), **Frontiers in catecholamine research**. New York: Pergamon Press, 729–739.

Juhasz, A. (1920). Über die komplementärgefärbten Nachbilder. *Z. Psychologie*, **51**, 233–263.

Julesz, B. (1971). **Foundations of cyclopean perception**. Chicago: University of Chicago Press.

Kaneiko, A. (1970). Physiological and morphological identification of horizontal, bipolar, and amacrine cells in goldfish retina. *Journal of Physiology (London)*, **207**, 623.

Katz, B. (1966). **Nerve, muscle, and synapse**. New York: McGraw-Hill.

Kilmer, W. and Olinski, M. (1974). Model of a plausible learning scheme for CA3 hippocampus. *Kybernetik*, **16**, 133–143.

Levine, D.S. and Grossberg, S. (1976). Visual illusions in neural networks: Line neutralization, tilt aftereffects, and angle expansion. *Journal of Theoretical Biology*, **61**, 477–504.

Lindvall, O. and Björklund, A. (1974). The organization of the ascending catecholamine neuron systems in the rat brain as revealed by the glyoxylic acid flourescence method. *Acta Phsyiol. Scan. Supplement*, **412**, 1–48.

Low, M.D., Borda, R.P., Frost, J.D., and Kellaway, P. (1966). Surface negative slow potential shift associated with conditioning in man. *Neurology*, **16**, 771–782.

MacKay, D.M. (1957). Moving visual images produced by regular stationary patterns. *Nature*, **180**, 849–850.

McAdam, D.W. (1969). Increases in CNV excitability during negative cortical slow potentials in man. *Electroencephalography and Clinical Neurophysiology*, **26**, 216–219.

McAdam, D.W., Irwin, D.A., Rebert, C.S., and Knott, J.R. (1966). Conative control of the contingent negative variation. *Electroencephalography and Clinical Neurophysiology*, **21**, 194–195.

Noback, C.R. (1967). **The human nervous system**. New York: McGraw-Hill.

Plateau, J. (1834). Über das Phänomen der zufälligen Farben. *Poggendorff Ann. Phys. Chem.*, **32**, 543–554.

Pfaffman, C. (1955). Gustatory nerve impulses in rat, cat, and rabbit. *Journal of Neurophysiology*, **18**, 429–440.

Somjen, G. (1972). **Sensory coding in the mammalian nervous system**. New York: Meredith Corporation.

Stein, L. (1974). Norepinephrine reward pathways: Role in self-stimulation, memory consolidation and schizophrenia. In *Nebraska Symposium on Motivation*, **22**.

Stell, W.K. (1967). The structure and relationship of horizontal cells and photo-receptor-bipolar synaptic complexes in goldfish retina. *American Journal of Anatomy*, **121**, 401.

Szentagothai, J. and Arbib, M.A. (1974). Conceptual models of neural organization. *Neurosciences Research Program Bulletin*, **12**.

Ungerstedt, U. (1971). Stereotaxic mapping of the monoamine pathways in the rat brain. *Acta Physiol. Scan. Supplement*, **82**, 1–48.

Walter, W.G. (1964). Slow potential waves in the human brain associated with expectancy, attention and decision. *Arch. Psychiat. Nervenkr.*, **206**, 309–322.

Wilson, H. (1975). A synaptic model for spatial frequency adaptation. *Journal of Theoretical Biology*, **49**.

Wise, C.D., Berger, B.D., and Stein, L. (1973). Evidence of α-noradrenergic reward receptors and serotonergic punishment receptors in the rat brain. *Biological Psychiatry*, **6**, 3–21.

CHAPTER 10

A MASSIVELY PARALLEL ARCHITECTURE
FOR A SELF-ORGANIZING NEURAL PATTERN
RECOGNITION MACHINE
by
Gail A. Carpenter and Stephen Grossberg

Preface

During the decade following 1976, ART was progressively developed as a physical theory to explain and predict ever larger behavioral and neural databases in a principled manner. The main articles in this development have been brought together in several books (Grossberg, 1982, 1987a, 1987b, 1988). The present article initiated a parallel stream of research activity aimed at rigorous development and computational analysis of ART architectures as systems of differential equations, or algorithmic approximations thereto. This research stream introduced key new elements into the ART theoretical framework while also specifying the systems in such a way as to make them suitable for applications in technology. The present article defines and analyses the ART 1 architecture. This architecture is designed to rapidly and stably learn recognition categories in response to arbitrary sequences of binary input patterns, until the full memory capacity of the architecture is utilized.

The ART 1 architecture uses a 2/3 Rule to match bottom-up data with top-down learned expectations. It is proved that the 2/3 Rule is sufficient to achieve stable learning in response to arbitrary binary input sequences. It is also shown, by example, that infinitely many input sequences exist that are not stably coded if the 2/3 Rule is violated.

This result is of interest for several reasons. The 2/3 Rule was derived as a way to reconcile the property of automatic activation of level F_1 by bottom-up inputs, with the property of *attentive priming*, or sensitization without firing, of level F_1 by a top-down expectation. The attentive priming event is a form of "intentionality" in the network. The network hereby "gets ready" for future events that may or may not occur. The 2/3 Rule achieves both properties by using a third source of input to F_1; namely, a nonspecific *attentional gain control* channel. Alternative ART priming mechanisms are developed in Chapters 12 and 15.

The 2/3 Rule computes a type of analog spatial logic. Thus, "intentionality implies logic" in ART. This conclusion stands in interesting contrast with the Searle (1983) critique that traditional AI uses logic at the cost of eliminating intentionality. ART hereby helps to overcome an old controversy by eliminating one of its most irritating antimonies.

The central result that leads ART to achieve this synthesis is its solution of the *stability-plasticity dilemma*. Namely, an ART system can dynamically buffer useful memories against unselective forgetting due to the "blooming buzzing confusion" of irrelevant events, yet can trigger rapid learning of new recognition codes, or selective refinement of old recognition codes, in response to novel behavioral demands. From this perspective, "adaptive stability implies intentionality" is a more fundamental statement than its consequence that "intentionality implies logic."

ART 1 computes a nonstandard type of logic which is used to learn recognition categories of arbitrary coarseness, or "fuzziness." A *vigilance* parameter was introduced in ART 1 to control how fuzzy each category could become. The vigilance calibrates the network's "attentive sensitivity" to disconfirmed expectations. High vigilance leads to learning of fine categories; low vigilance to coarse categories. In Chapter 15, it is shown how vigilance can be controlled on a trial-by-trial basis to learn categories whose coarseness is determined by their predictive consequences.

The ART 1 design does not instantiate ART heuristics in their most general form. In particular, no preprocessing is described, either for spatially organized data, as in vision, or temporally organized data, as in speech. Such preprocessing or postprocessing structures are described in other articles about ART (see Carpenter, Grossberg, and Mehanian, 1989; Grossberg, 1982, 1987a, 1987b, 1988, and Part III). ART 1 restricts its processing to the important special case of winner-take-all categories and binary input streams, albeit inputs of arbitrarily high dimension that may be presented in an arbitrary order. These design restrictions permitted a rigorous analysis of ART 1 dynamics to be carried out. In particular, it was proved that the adaptive weights oscillate at most once through time, in response to an *arbitrary* input sequence, yet a familiar input can directly access the *globally best* category, without any search, after learning self-stabilizes. These ART properties are rigorously proved herein.

In a subsequent article (Carpenter and Grossberg, 1988), it was pointed out that a formal lesion of the ART 1 orienting subsystem creates a memory disturbance whose formal symptoms are similar to those of medial temporal amnesia, including unlimited anterograde amnesia; limited retrograde amnesia; failure of consolidation; abnormal reactions to novelty, including perseverative reactions; normal priming; and normal information processing of familiar events.

Subsequent ART networks progressively relax the constraints on ART 1 without eliminating the main architectural elements needed to solve the stability-plasticity dilemma.

References

Carpenter, G.A. and Grossberg, S. (1988). Neural dynamics of category learning and recognition: Attention, memory consolidation, and amnesia. In J. Davis, R. Newburgh, and E. Wegman (Eds.), **Brain structure, learning, and memory**. AAAS Symposium Series.

Carpenter, G.A., Grossberg, S., and Mehanian, C. (1989). Invariant recognition of cluttered scenes by a self-organizing ART architecture: CORT-X boundary segmentation. *Neural Networks*, **2**, 169–181.

Grossberg, S. (1982). **Studies of mind and brain: Neural principles of learning, perception, development, cognition, and motor control**. Boston: Reidel Press.

Grossberg, S. (Editor) (1987a). **The adaptive brain, I: Cognition, learning, reinforcement, and rhythm**. Amsterdam: Elsevier/North-Holland.

Grossberg, S. (Editor) (1987b). **The adaptive brain, II: Vision, speech, language, and motor control**. Amsterdam: Elsevier/North-Holland.

Grossberg, S. (Editor) (1988). **Neural networks and natural intelligence.** Cambridge, MA: MIT Press.

Searle, J.R. (1983). **Intentionality, an essay in the philosophy of mind.** Cambridge: Cambridge University Press.

Computer Vision, Graphics, and Image Processing
1987, **37**, 54–115

A MASSIVELY PARALLEL ARCHITECTURE
FOR A SELF-ORGANIZING
NEURAL PATTERN RECOGNITION MACHINE

Gail A. Carpenter† and Stephen Grossberg‡

Abstract

A neural network architecture for the learning of recognition categories is derived. Real-time network dynamics are completely characterized through mathematical analysis and computer simulations. The architecture self-organizes and self-stabilizes its recognition codes in response to arbitrary orderings of arbitrarily many and arbitrarily complex binary input patterns. Top-down attentional and matching mechanisms are critical in self-stabilizing the code learning process. The architecture embodies a parallel search scheme which updates itself adaptively as the learning process unfolds. After learning self-stabilizes, the search process is automatically disengaged. Thereafter input patterns directly access their recognition codes without any search. Thus recognition time does not grow as a function of code complexity. A novel input pattern can directly access a category if it shares invariant properties with the set of familiar invariant properties with the set of familiar exemplars of that category. These invariant properties emerge in the form of learned critical feature patterns, or prototypes. The architecture possesses a context-sensitive self-scaling property which enables its emergent critical feature patterns to form. They detect and remember statistically predictive configurations of featural elements which are derived from the set of all input patterns that are ever experienced. Four types of attentional process—priming, gain control, vigilance, and intermodal competition—are mechanistically characterized. Top-down priming and gain control are needed for code matching and self-stabilization. Attentional vigilance determines how fine the learned categories will be. If vigilance increases due to an environmental disconfirmation, then the system automatically searches for and learns finer recognition categories. A new nonlinear matching law (the 2/3 Rule) and new nonlinear associative laws (the Weber Law Rule, the Associative Decay Rule, and the Template Learning Rule) are needed to achieve these properties. All the rules describe emergent properties of parallel network interactions. The architecture circumvents the

† Supported in part by the Air Force Office of Scientific Research (AFOSR F49620-86-C0037 and AFOSR F49620-87-C0018), the Army Research Office (ARO DAAG-29-85-K0095), and the National Science Foundation (NSF DMS-84-13119).

‡ Supported in part by the Air Force Office of Scientific Research (AFOSR F49620-86-C0037 and AFOSR F49620-87-C0018) and the Army Research Office (ARO DAAG-29-85-K0095). We wish to thank Cynthia Suchta and Carol Yanakakis for their valuable assistance in the preparation of the manuscript.

noise, saturation, capacity, orthogonality, and linear predictability constraints that limit the codes which can be stably learned by alternative recognition models.

1. Introduction: Self-Organization of Neural Recognition Codes

A fundamental problem of perception and cognition concerns the characterization of how humans discover, learn, and recognize invariant properties of the environments to which they are exposed. When such recognition codes spontaneously emerge through an individual's interaction with an environment, the processes are said to undergo *self-organization* (Basar, Flohr, Haken, and Mandell, 1983). This article develops a theory of how recognition codes are self-organized by a class of neural networks whose qualitative features have been used to analyse data about speech perception, word recognition and recall, visual perception, olfactory coding, evoked potentials, thalamocortical interactions, attentional modulation of critical period termination, and amnesias (Banquet and Grossberg, 1986; Carpenter and Grossberg, 1985a, 1985b, 1986a, 1986b; Grossberg, 1976a, 1976b, 1978a, 1980, 1986a; Grossberg and Stone, 1986a, 1986b). These networks comprise the *adaptive resonance theory* (ART) which was introduced in Grossberg (1976b).

This article describes a system of differential equations which completely characterizes one class of ART networks. The network model is capable of self-organizing, self-stabilizing, and self-scaling its recognition codes in response to arbitrary temporal sequences of arbitrarily many input patterns of variable complexity. These formal properties, which are mathematically proven herein, provide a secure foundation for designing a real-time hardware implementation of this class of massively parallel ART circuits.

Before proceeding to a description of this class of ART systems, we summarize some of their major properties and some scientific problems for which they provide a solution.

A. Plasticity

Each system generates recognition codes adaptively in response to a series of environmental inputs. As learning procceeds, interactions between the inputs and the system generate new steady states and basins of attraction. These steady states are formed as the system discovers and learns *critical feature patterns*, or prototypes, that represent invariants of the set of all experienced input patterns.

B. Stability

The learned codes are dynamically buffered against relentless recoding by irrelevant inputs. The formation of steady states is internally controlled using mechanisms that suppress possible sources of system instability.

C. Stability-Plasticity Dilemma: Multiple Interacting Memory Systems

The properties of plasticity and stability are intimately related. An adequate system must be able to adaptively switch between its stable and plastic modes. It must be capable of plasticity in order to learn about significant new events, yet it must also remain stable in response to irrelevant or often repeated events. In order to prevent the relentless degradation of its learned codes by the "blooming, buzzing confusion" of irrelevant experience, an ART system is sensitive to *novelty*. It is capable of distinguishing between familiar and unfamiliar events, as well as between expected and unexpected events.

Multiple interacting memory systems are needed to monitor and adaptively react to the novelty of events. Within ART, interactions between two functionally complementary subsystems are needed to process familiar and unfamiliar events. Familiar events are processed within an attentional subsystem. This subsystem establishes ever more precise internal representations of and responses to familiar events. It also builds up the learned top-down expectations that help to stabilize the learned bottom-up codes of familiar events. By itself, however, the attentional subsystem is unable simultaneously to maintain stable representations of familiar categories and to create new categories for unfamiliar patterns. An isolated attentional subsystem is either rigid and incapable of creating new categories for unfamiliar patterns, or unstable and capable of ceaselessly recoding the categories of familiar patterns in response to certain input environments.

The second subsystem is an orienting subsystem that resets the attentional subsystem when an unfamiliar event occurs. The orienting subsystem is essential for expressing whether a novel pattern is familiar and well represented by an existing recognition code, or unfamiliar and in need of a new recognition code. Figure 1 schematizes the architecture that is analysed herein.

D. Role of Attention in Learning

Within an ART system, attentional mechanisms play a major role in self-stabilizing the learning of an emergent recognition code. Our mechanistic analysis of the role of attention in learning leads us to distinguish between four types of attentional mechanism: attentional priming, attentional gain control, attentional vigilance, and intermodality competition. These mechanisms are characterized below.

E. Complexity

An ART system dynamically reorganizes its recognition codes to preserve its stability-plasticity balance as its internal representations become increasingly complex and differentiated through learning. By contrast, many classical adaptive pattern recognition systems become unstable when they are confronted by complex input environments. The instabilities of a number of these models are identified in Grossberg (1976a, 1978b, 1986a). Models which become unstable in response to nontrivial input environments are not viable either as brain models or as designs for adaptive machines.

Unlike many alternative models (e.g., Anderson, Silverstein, Ritz, and Jones, 1977; Fukushima, 1980; Hopfield, 1982; Kohonen, 1977; McClelland and Rumelhart, 1985), the present model constraints arbitrary combinations of binary input patterns. In particular, it places no orthogonality or linear predictability constraints upon its input patterns. The model computations remain sensitive no matter how many input patterns are processed. The model does not require that very small, and thus noise-degradable, increments in memory be made in order to avoid saturation of its cumulative memory. The model can store arbitrarily many recognition categories in response to input patterns that are defined on arbitrarily many input channels. Its memory matrices need not be square, so that no restrictions on memory capacity are imposed by the number of input channels. Finally, all the memory of the system can be devoted to stable recognition learning. It is not he case that the number of

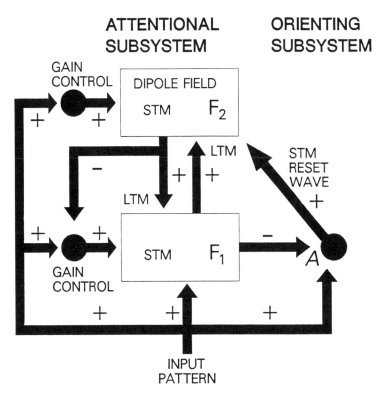

Figure 1. Anatomy of the attentional-orienting system: Two successive stages, F_1 and F_2, of the attentional subsystem encode patterns of activation in short term memory (STM). Bottom-up and top-down pathways between F_1 and F_2 contain adaptive long term memory (LTM) traces which multiply the signals in these pathways. The remainder of the circuit modulates these STM and LTM processes. Modulation by gain control enables F_1 to distinguish between bottom-up input patterns and top-down priming, or template, patterns, as well as to match these bottom-up and top-down patterns. Gain control signals also enable F_2 to react supraliminally to signals from F_1 while an input pattern is on. The orienting subsystem generates a reset wave to F_2 when mismatches between bottom-up and top-down patterns occur at F_1. This reset wave selectively and enduringly inhibits active F_2 cells until the input is shut off. Variations of this architecture are depicted in Figure 14.

stable classifications is bounded by some fraction of the number of input channels or patterns.

Thus a primary goal of the present article is to characterize neural networks capable of self-stabilizing the self-organization of their recognition codes in response to an arbitrarily complex environment of input patterns in a way that parsimoniously reconciles the requirements of plasticity, stability, and complexity.

2. Self-Scaling Computational Units, Self-Adjusting Memory Search, Direct Access, and Attentional Vigilance

Four properties are basic to the workings of the networks that we characterize herein.

A. Self-Scaling Computational Units: Critical Feature Patterns

Properly defining signal and noise in a self-organizing system raises a number of subtle issues. Pattern context must enter the definition so that input features which are treated as irrelevant noise when they are embedded in a given input pattern may be treated as informative signals when they are embedded in a different input pattern. The system's unique learning history must also enter the definition so that portions of an input pattern which are treated as noise when they perturb a system at one stage of its self-organization may be treated as signals when they perturb the same system at a different stage of its self-organization. The present systems automatically self-scale their computational units to embody context- and learning-dependent definitions of signal and noise.

One property of these self-scaling computational units is schematized in Figure 2. In Figure 2a, each of the two input patterns is composed of three features. The patterns agree at two of the three features, but disagree at the third feature. A mismatch of one out of three features may be designated as informative by the system. When this occurs, these mismatched features are treated as signals which can elicit learning of distinct recognition codes for the two patterns. Moreover, the mismatched features, being informative, are incorporated into these distinct recognition codes.

In Figure 2b, each of the two input patterns is composed of thirty-one features. The patterns are constructed by adding identical subpatterns to the two patterns in Figure 2a. Thus the input patterns in Figure 2b disagree at the same features as the input patterns in Figure 2a. In the patterns of Figure 2b, however, this mismatch is less important, other things being equal, than in the patterns of Figure 2a. Consequently, the system may treat the mismatched features as noise. A single recognition code may be learned to represent both of the input patterns in Figure 2b. The mismatched features would not be learned as part of this recognition code because they are treated as noise.

The assertion that *critical feature patterns* are the computational units of the code learning process summarizes this self-scaling property. The term *critical feature* indicates that not all features are treated as signals by the system. The learned units are *patterns* of critical features because the perceptual context in which the features are embedded influences which features will be processed as signals and which features will be processed as noise. Thus a feature may be a critical feature in one pattern (Figure 2a) and an irrelevant noise element in a different pattern (Figure 2b).

The need to overcome the limitations of featural processing with some type of contextually sensitive pattern processing has long been a central concern in the human pattern recognition literature. Experimental studies have led to the general conclusions that "The trace system which underlies the recognition of patterns can be characterized by a central tendency and a boundary" (Posner, 1973, p.54), and that "just listing features does not go far enough in specifying the knowledge represented in a concept. People also know something about the relations between the features of a concept, and about the variability that is permissible on any feature" (Smith and Medin, 1981, p.83). We illustrate herein how these properties may be achieved using self-scaling computational units such as critical feature patterns.

B. Self-Adjusting Memory Search

No pre-wired search algorithm, such as a search tree, can maintain its efficiency

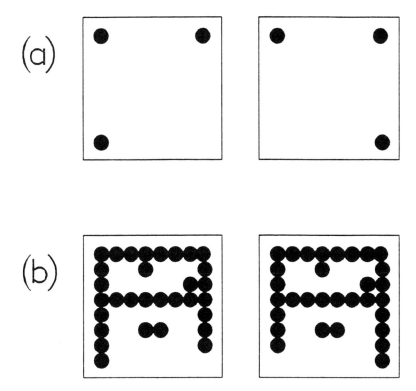

Figure 2. Self-scaling property discovers critical features in a context-sensitive way: (a) Two input patterns of 3 features mismatch at 1 feature. When this mismatch is sufficient to generate distinct recognition codes for the two patterns, the mismatched features are encoded in LTM as part of the critical feature patterns of these recognition codes. (b) Identical subpatterns are added to the two input patterns in (a). Although the new input patterns mismatch at the same one feature, this mismatch may be treated as noise due to the additional complexity of the two new patterns. Both patterns may thus learn to activate the same recognition code. When this occurs, the mismatched feature is deleted from LTM in the critical feature pattern of the code.

as a knowledge structure evolves due to learning in a unique input environment. A search order that may be optimal in one knowledge domain may become extremely inefficient as that knowledge domain becomes more complex due to learning.

The ART system considered herein is capable of a parallel memory search that adaptively updates its search order to maintain efficiency as its recognition code becomes arbitrarily complex due to learning. This self-adjusting search mechanism is part of the network design whereby the learning process self-stabilizes by engaging the orienting subsystem (Section 1C).

None of these mechanisms is akin to the rules of a serial computer program. Instead, the circuit architecture as a whole generates a self-adjusting search order and self-stabilization as emergent properties that arise through system interactions. Once the ART architecture is in place, a little randomness in the initial values of its memory traces, rather than a carefully wired search tree, enables the search to carry on until the recognition code self-stabilizes.

C. Direct Access to Learned Codes

A hallmark of human recognition performance is the remarkable rapidity with which familiar objects can be recognized. The existence of many learned recognition codes for alternative experiences does not necessarily interfere with rapid recognition of an unambiguous familiar event. This type of rapid recognition is very difficult to understand using models wherein trees or other serial algorithms need to be searched for longer and longer periods as a learned recognition code becomes larger and larger.

In an ART model, as the learned code becomes globally self-consistent and pre-dictively accurate, the search mechanism is automatically disengaged. Subsequently, no matter how large and complex the learned code may become, familiar input pat-terns *directly access*, or activate, their learned code, or category. Unfamiliar patterns can also directly access a learned category if they share invariant properties with the critical feature pattern of the category. In this sense, the critical feature pattern acts as a prototype for the entire category. As in human pattern recognition experiments, an input pattern that matches a learned critical feature pattern may be better rec-ognized than any of the input patterns that gave rise to the critical feature pattern (Posner, 1973; Posner and Keele, 1968, 1970).

Unfamiliar input patterns which cannot stably access a learned category engage the self-adjusting search process in order to discover a network substrate for a new recognition category. After this new code is learned, the search process is automati-cally disengaged and direct access ensues.

D. Environment as a Teacher: Modulation of Attentional Vigilance

Although an ART system self-organizes its recognition code, the environment can also modulate the learning process and thereby carry out a teaching role. This teach-ing role allows a system with a fixed set of feature detectors to function successfully in an environment which imposes variable performance demands. Different environ-ments may demand either coarse discriminations or fine discriminations to be made among the same set of objects. As Posner (1973, pp.53–54) has noted:

> "If subjects are taught a tight concept, they tend to be very careful about classifying any particular pattern as an instance of that concept. They tend to reject a relatively small distortion of the prototype as an instance, and they rarely classify a pattern as a member of the concept when it is not. On the other hand, subjects learning high-variability concepts often falsely classify patterns as members of the concept, but rarely reject a member of the concept incorrectly...The situation largely determines which type of learning will be superior."

In an ART system, if an erroneous recognition is followed by negative reinforce-ment, then the system becomes more *vigilant*. This change in vigilance may be inter-preted as a change in the system's attentional state which increases its sensitivity to mismatches between bottom-up input patterns and active top-down critical feature patterns. A vigilance change alters the size of a single parameter in the network. The *interactions* within the network respond to this parameter change by learning recognition codes that make finer distinctions. In other words, if the network erro-neously groups together some input patterns, then negative reinforcement can help the network to learn the desired distinction by making the system more vigilant. The system then behaves *as if* it has a better set of feature detectors.

The ability of a vigilance change to alter the course of pattern recognition illustrates a theme that is common to a variety of neural processes: a one-dimensional parameter change that modulates a simple nonspecific neural process can have complex specific effects upon high-dimensional neural information processing.

Sections 3–7 outline qualitatively the main operations of the model. Sections 8–11 describe computer simulations which illustrate the model's ability to learn categories. Section 12 defines the model mathematically. The remaining sections characterize the model's properties using mathematical analysis and more computer simulations, with the model hypotheses summarized in Section 18.

3. Bottom-Up Adaptive Filtering and Contrast-Enhancement in Short Term Memory

We begin by considering the typical network reactions to a single input pattern I within a temporal stream of input patterns. Each input pattern may be the output pattern of a preprocessing stage. Different preprocessing is given, for example, to speech signals and to visual signals before the outcome of such modality-specific preprocessing ever reaches the attentional subsystem. The preprocessed input pattern I is received at the stage F_1 of an attentional subsystem. Pattern I is transformed into a pattern X of activation across the nodes, or abstract "feature detectors", of F_1 (Figure 3). The transformed pattern X represents a pattern in short term memory (STM). In F_1 each node whose activity is sufficiently large generates excitatory signals along pathways to target nodes at the next processing stage F_2. A pattern X of STM activities across F_1 hereby elicits a pattern S of output signals from F_1. When a signal from a node in F_1 is carried along a pathway to F_2, the signal is multiplied, or *gated*, by the pathway's long term memory (LTM) trace. The LTM-gated signal (i.e., signal times LTM trace), not the signal alone, reaches the target node. Each target node sums up all of its LTM-gated signals. In this way, pattern S generates a pattern T of LTM-gated and summed input signals to F_2 (Figure 4a). The transformation from S to T is called an *adaptive filter*.

The input pattern T to F_2 is quickly transformed by interactions among the nodes of F_2. These interactions contrast-enhance the input pattern T. The resulting pattern of activation across F_2 is a new pattern Y. The contrast-enhanced pattern Y, rather than the input pattern T, is stored in STM by F_2.

A special case of this contrast-enhancement process is one in which F_2 chooses the node which receives the largest input. The chosen node is the only one that can store activity in STM. In general, the contrast enhancing transformation from T to Y enables more than one node at a time to be active in STM. Such transformations are designed to simultaneously represent in STM several groupings, or chunks, of an input pattern (Cohen and Grossberg, 1986a, 1986b, 1986c; Grossberg, 1978a, 1986a). When F_2 is designed to make a choice in STM, it selects that global grouping of the input pattern which is preferred by the adaptive filter. This process automatically enables the network to partition all the input patterns which are received by F_1 into disjoint sets of recognition categories, each corresponding to a particular node (or "pointer," or "index") in F_2. Such a categorical mechanism is both interesting in itself and a necessary prelude to the analysis of recognition codes in which multiple groupings of X are simultaneously represented by Y. In the example that is characterized in this article, level F_2 is designed to make a choice.

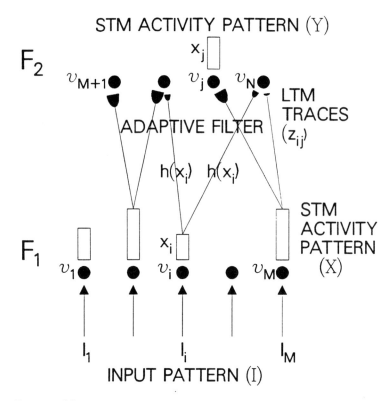

Figure 3. Stages of bottom-up activation: The input pattern I generates a pattern of STM activation X across F_1. Sufficiently active F_1 nodes emit bottom-up signals to F_2. This signal pattern S is gated by long term memory (LTM) traces within the $F_1 \rightarrow F_2$ pathways. The LTM gated signals are summed before activating their target nodes in F_2. This LTM-gated and summed signal pattern T generates a pattern of activation Y across F_2. The nodes in F_1 are denoted by $v_1, v_2, \ldots, v_M$. The nodes in F_2 are denoted by $v_{M+1}, v_{M+2}, \ldots v_N$. The input to node v_i is denoted by I_i. The STM activity of node v_i is denoted by x_i. The LTM trace of the pathway from v_i to v_j is denoted by z_{ij}.

All the LTM traces in the adaptive filter, and thus all learned past experiences of the network, are used to determine the recognition code Y via the transformation $I \rightarrow X \rightarrow S \rightarrow T \rightarrow Y$. However, only those nodes of F_2 which maintain stored activity in the STM pattern Y can elicit new learning at contiguous LTM traces. Because the recognition code Y is a more contrast-enhanced pattern than T, many F_2 nodes which receive positive inputs ($I \rightarrow X \rightarrow S \rightarrow T$) may not store any STM activity ($T \rightarrow Y$). The LTM traces in pathways leading to these nodes thus influence the recognition event but are not altered by the recognition event. Some memories which influence the focus of attention are not themselves attended.

4. Top-Down Template Matching and Stabilization of Code Learning

As soon as the bottom-up STM transformation $X \rightarrow Y$ takes place, the STM activities Y in F_2 elicit a top-down excitatory signal pattern U back to F_1 (Figure 4b). Only sufficiently large STM activities in Y elicit signals in U along the feedback

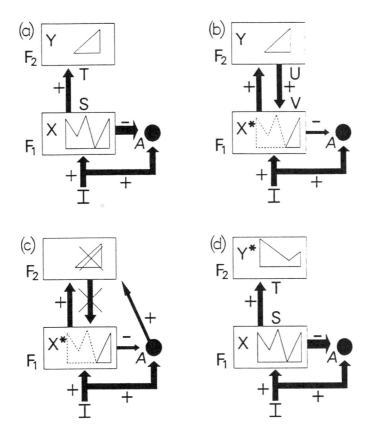

Figure 4. Search for a correct F_2 code: (a) The input pattern I generates the specific STM activity pattern X at F_1 as it nonspecifically activates A. Pattern X both inhibits A and generates the output signal pattern S. Signal pattern S is transformed into the input pattern T, which activates the STM pattern Y across F_2. (b) Pattern Y generates the top-down signal pattern U which is transformed into the template pattern V. If V mismatches I at F_1, then a new STM activity pattern X* is generated at F_1. The reduction in total STM activity which occurs when X is transformed into X* causes a decrease in the total inhibition from F_1 to A. (c) Then the input-driven activation of A can release a nonspecific arousal wave to F_2, which resets the STM pattern Y at F_2. (d) After Y is inhibited, its top-down template is eliminated, and X can be reinstated at F_1. Now X once again generates input pattern T to F_2, but since Y remains inhibited T can activate a different STM pattern Y* at F_2. If the top-down template due to Y* also mismatches I at F_1, then the rapid search for an appropriate F_2 code continues.

pathways $F_2 \rightarrow F_1$. As in the bottom-up adaptive filter, the top-down signals U are also gated by LTM traces and the LTM-gated signals are summed at F_1 nodes. The pattern U of output signals from F_2 hereby generates a pattern V of LTM-gated and summed input signals to F_1. The transformation from U to V is thus also an adaptive filter. The pattern V is called a *top-down template*, or *learned expectation*.

Two sources of input now perturb F_1: the bottom-up input pattern I which gave rise to the original activity pattern X, and the top-down template pattern V that resulted from activating X. The activity pattern X^* across F_1 that is induced by I and V taken together is typically different from the activity pattern X that was previously induced by I alone. In particular, F_1 acts to match V against I. The result of this matching process determines the future course of learning and recognition by the network.

The entire activation sequence

$$I \rightarrow X \rightarrow S \rightarrow T \rightarrow Y \rightarrow U \rightarrow V \rightarrow X^* \tag{1}$$

takes place very quickly relative to the rate with which the LTM traces in either the bottom-up adaptive filter $S \rightarrow T$ or the top-down adaptive filter $U \rightarrow V$ can change. Even though none of the LTM traces changes during such a short time, their prior learning strongly influences the STM patterns Y and X^* that evolve within the network by determining the transformations $S \rightarrow T$ and $U \rightarrow V$. We now discuss how a match or mismatch of I and V at F_1 regulates the course of learning in response to the pattern I, and in particular solves the stability-plasticity dilemma (Section 1C).

5. Interactions between Attentional and Orienting Subsystems: STM Reset and Search

In Figure 4a, an input pattern I generates an STM activity pattern X across F_1. The input pattern I also excites the orienting subsystem A, but pattern X at F_1 inhibits A before it can generate an output signal. Activity pattern X also elicits an output pattern S which, via the bottom-up adaptive filter, instates an STM activity pattern Y across F_2. In Figure 4b, pattern Y reads a top-down template pattern V into F_1. Template V mismatches input I, thereby significantly inhibiting STM activity across F_1. The amount by which activity in X is attenuated to generate X^* depends upon how much of the input pattern I is encoded within the template pattern V.

When a mismatch attenuates STM activity across F_1, the total size of the inhibitory signal from F_1 to A is also attenuated. If the attenuation is sufficiently great, inhibition from F_1 to A can no longer prevent the arousal source A from firing. Figure 4c depicts how disinhibition of A releases an arousal burst to F_2 which equally, or nonspecifically, excites all the F_2 cells. The cell populations of F_2 react to such an arousal signal in a state-dependent fashion. In the special case that F_2 chooses a single population for STM storage, the arousal burst selectively inhibits, or resets, the active population in F_2. This inhibition is long-lasting. One physiological design for F_2 processing which has these properties is a *gated dipole field* (Grossberg, 1980, 1984a). A gated dipole field consists of opponent processing channels which are gated by habituating chemical transmitters. A nonspecific arousal burst induces selective and enduring inhibition of active populations within a gated dipole field.

In Figure 4c, inhibition of Y leads to removal of the top-down template V, and thereby terminates the mismatch between I and V. Input pattern I can thus reinstate the original activity pattern X across F_1, which again generates the output pattern S from F_1 and the input pattern T to F_2. Due to the enduring inhibition at F_2, the input pattern T can no longer activate the original pattern Y at F_2. A new pattern Y^* is thus generated at F_2 by I (Figure 4d). Despite the fact that some F_2 nodes may remain inhibited by the STM reset property, the new pattern Y^* may encode large STM activities. This is because level F_2 is designed so that its total suprathreshold activity remains approximately constant, or normalized, despite the fact that some of its nodes may remain inhibited by the STM reset mechanism. This property is related to the limited capacity of STM. A physiological process capable of achieving the STM normalization property is based upon on-center off-surround feedback interactions among cells obeying membrane equations (Grossberg, 1980, 1983).

The new activity pattern Y* reads-out a new top-down template pattern V*. If a mismatch again occurs at F_1, the orienting subsystem is again engaged, thereby leading to another arousal-mediated reset of STM at F_2. In this way, a rapid series of STM matching and reset events may occur. Such an STM matching and reset series controls the system's search of LTM by sequentially engaging the novelty-sensitive orienting subsystem. Although STM is reset sequentially in time via this mismatch-mediated, self-terminating LTM search process, the mechanisms which control the LTM search are all parallel network interactions, rather than serial algorithms. Such a parallel search scheme continuously adjusts itself to the system's evolving LTM codes. In general, the spatial configuration of LTM codes depends upon both the system's initial configuration and its unique learning history, and hence cannot be predicted *a priori* by a pre-wired search algorithm. Instead, the mismatch-mediated engagement of the orienting subsystem realizes the type of self-adjusting search that was described in Section 2B.

The mismatch-mediated search of LTM ends when an STM pattern across F_2 reads-out a top-down template which matches I, to the degree of accuracy required by the level of attentional vigilance (Section 2D), or which has not yet undergone any prior learning. In the latter case, a new recognition category is then established as a bottom-up code and top-down template are learned.

6. Attentional Gain Control and Attentional Priming

Further properties of the top-down template matching process can be derived by considering its role in the regulation of attentional priming. Consider, for example, a situation in which F_2 is activated by a level other than F_1 before F_1 can be activated by a bottom-up input (Figure 5a). In such a situation, F_2 can generate a top-down template V to F_1. The level F_1 is then primed, or sensitized, to receive a bottom-up input that may or may not match the active expectancy. As depicted in Figure 5a, level F_1 can be primed to receive a bottom-up input without necessarily eliciting suprathreshold output signals in response to the priming expectancy.

On the other hand, an input pattern I must be able to generate a suprathreshold activity pattern X even if no top-down expectancy is active across F_1 (Figures 4a and 5b). How does F_1 know that it should generate a suprathreshold reaction to a bottom-up input pattern but not to a top-down input pattern? In both cases, excitatory input signals stimulate F_1 cells. Some auxiliary mechanism must exist to distinguish between bottom-up and top-down inputs. This auxiliary mechanism is called *attentional gain control* to distinguish it from *attentional priming* by the top-down template itself (Figure 5a). While F_2 is active, the attentional priming mechanism delivers *excitatory specific learned* template patterns to F_1. The attentional gain control mechanism has an *inhibitory nonspecific unlearned* effect on the sensitivity with which F_1 responds to the template pattern, as well as to other pat-

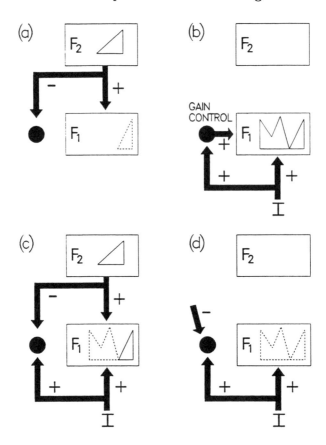

Figure 5. Matching by the 2/3 Rule: (a) A top-down template from F_2 inhibits the attentional gain control source as it subliminally primes target F_1 cells. (b) Only F_1 cells that receive bottom-up inputs and gain control signals can become supraliminally active. (c) When a bottom-up input pattern and a top-down template are simultaneously active, only those F_1 cells that receive inputs from both sources can become supraliminally active. (d) Intermodality inhibition can shut off the F_1 gain control source and thereby prevent a bottom-up input from supraliminally activating F_1. Similarly, disinhibition of the F_1 gain control source may cause a top-down prime to become supraliminal.

terns received by F_1. The attentional gain control process enables F_1 to tell the difference between bottom-up and top-down signals.

7. Matching: The 2/3 Rule

A rule for pattern matching at F_1, called the 2/3 Rule, follows naturally from the distinction between attentional gain control and attentional priming. It says that two out of three signal sources must activate an F_1 node in order for that node to generate suprathreshold output signals. In Figure 5a, during top-down processing, or priming, the nodes of F_1 receive inputs from at most one of their three possible input sources. Hence no cells in F_1 are supraliminally activated by the top-down template. In Figure 5b, during bottom-up processing, a suprathreshold node in F_1 is one which receives both a specific input from the input pattern I and a nonspecific excitatory signal from the gain control channel. In Figure 5c, during the matching of simultaneous bottom-up and top-down patterns, the nonspecific gain control signal to F_1 is inhibited by the top-down channel. Nodes of F_1 which receive sufficiently large inputs from both the bottom-up and the top-down signal patterns generate suprathreshold activities. Nodes which receive a bottom-up input or a top-down input, but not both, cannot become suprathreshold: mismatched inputs cannot generate suprathreshold activities. Attentional gain control thus leads to a matching process whereby the addition of top-down excitatory inputs to F_1 can lead to an overall decrease in F_1's STM activity (Figures 4a and 4b). Figure 5d shows how competitive interactions across modalities can prevent F_1 from generating a supraliminal reaction to bottom-up signals when attention shifts from one modality to another.

8. Code Instability and Code Stability

The importance of using the 2/3 Rule for matching is now illustrated by describing how its absence can lead to a temporally unstable code (Figure 6a). The system becomes unstable when the inhibitory top-down attentional gain control signals (Figure 5c) are too small for the 2/3 Rule to hold at F_1. Larger attentional gain control signals restore code stability by reinstating the 2/3 Rule (Figure 6b). Figure 6b also illustrates how a novel exemplar can directly access a previously established category; how the category in which a given exemplar is coded can be influenced by the categories which form to encode very different exemplars; and how the network responds to exemplars as coherent groupings of features, rather than to isolated feature matches or mismatches.

Code Instability Example

In Figure 6, four input patterns, A, B, C, and D, are periodically presented in the order ABCAD. Patterns B, C, and D are all subsets of A. The relationships among the inputs that make the simulation work are as follows: $D \subset C \subset A$; $B \subset A$; $B \cap C = \phi$; and $| D | < | B | < | C |$, where $| I |$ denotes the number of features in input pattern I. The choice of input patterns in Figure 6 is thus one of infinitely many examples in which, without the 2/3 Rule, an alphabet of four input patterns cannot be stably coded.

The numbers 1, 2, 3, ... listed at the left in Figure 6 itemize the presentation order. The next column, labeled BU for Bottom-Up, describes the input pattern that was presented on each trial. Each Top-Down Template column corresponds to a different node in F_2. If M nodes $v_1, v_2, \ldots, v_M$ exist in F_1, then the F_2 nodes are denoted by $v_{M+1}, v_{M+2}, \ldots v_N$. Column 1 corresponds to node v_{M+1}, column 2 corresponds to node v_{M+2}, and so on. Each row summarizes the network response to its input pattern. The symbol RES, which stands for *resonance*, designates the node in F_2 which codes the input pattern on that trial. For example, v_{M+2} codes pattern C on trial 3, and v_{M+1} codes pattern B on trial 7. The patterns in a given row describe the templates after learning has equilibrated on that trial.

In Figure 6a, input pattern A is periodically recoded. On trial 1, it is coded by v_{M+1}; on trial 4, it is coded by v_{M+2}; on trial 6, it is coded by v_{M+1}; on trial 9, it is coded by v_{M+2}. This alternation in the nodes v_{M+1} and v_{M+2} which code pattern A repeats indefinitely.

Violation of the 2/3 Rule occurs on trials 4, 6, 8, 9, and so on. This violation

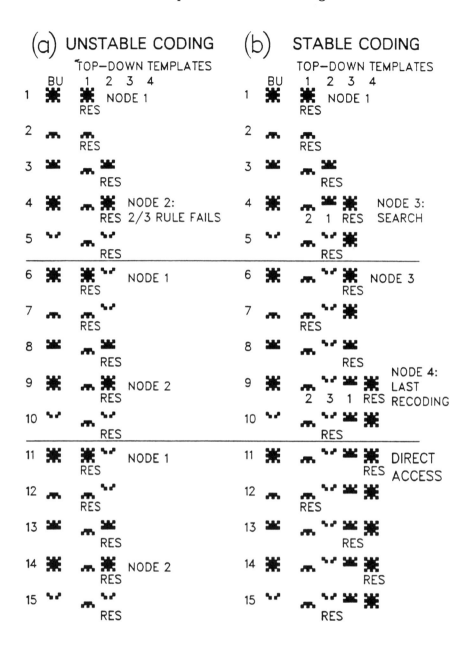

Figure 6. Stabilization of categorical learning by the 2/3 Rule: In both (a) and (b), four input patterns A, B, C, and D are presented repeatedly in the list order ABCAD. In (a), the 2/3 Rule is violated because the top-down inhibitory gain control mechanism is weak (Figure 5c). Pattern A is periodically coded by v_{M+1} and v_{M+2}. It is never coded by a single stable category. In (b), the 2/3 Rule is restored by strengthening the top-down inhibitory gain control mechanism. After some initial recoding during the first two presentations of ABCAD, all patterns directly access distinct stable categories. A black square in a template pattern designates that the corresponding top-down LTM trace is large. A blank square designates that the LTM trace is small.

is illustrated by comparing the template of v_{M+2} on trials 3 and 4. On trial 3, the template of v_{M+2} is coded by pattern C, which is a subset of pattern A. On trial 4, pattern A is presented and directly activates node v_{M+2}. Since the inhibitory top-down gain control is too weak to quench the mismatched portion of the input, pattern A remains supraliminal in F_1 even after the template C is read-out from v_{M+2}. No search is elicited by the mismatch of pattern A and its subset template C. Consequently the template of v_{M+2} is recoded from pattern C to its superset pattern A.

Code Stability Example

In Figure 6b, the 2/3 Rule does hold because the inhibitory top-down attentional gain control channel is strengthened. Thus the network experiences a sequence of recodings that ultimately stabilizes. In particular, on trial 4, node v_{M+2} reads-out the template C, which mismatches the input pattern A. Here, a search is initiated, as indicated by the numbers beneath the template symbols in row 4. First, v_{M+2}'s template C mismatches A. Then v_{M+1}'s template B mismatches A. Finally A activates the uncommitted node v_{M+3}, which resonates with F_1 as it learns the template A.

In Figure 6b, pattern A is coded by v_{M+1} on trial 1; by v_{M+3} on trials 4 and 6; and by v_{M+4} on trial 9. Note that the self-adjusting search order in response to A is different on trials 4 and 9 (Section 2B). On all future trials, input pattern A is coded by v_{M+4}. Moreover, all the input patterns A, B, C, and D have learned a stable code by trial 9. Thus the code self-stabilizes by the second run through the input list ABCAD. On trials 11 through 15, and on all future trials, each input pattern chooses a different code ($A \rightarrow v_{M+4}$; $B \rightarrow v_{M+1}$; $C \rightarrow v_{M+3}$; $D \rightarrow v_{M+2}$). Each pattern belongs to a separate category because the vigilance parameter (Section 2D) was chosen to be large in this example. Moreover, after code learning stabilizes, each input pattern directly activates its node in F_2 without undergoing any additional search (Section 2C). Thus after trial 9, only the "RES" symbol appears under the top-down templates. The patterns shown in any row between 9 and 15 provide a complete description of the learned code.

Examples of how a novel exemplar can activate a previously learned category are found on trials 2 and 5 in Figures 6a and 6b. On trial 2 pattern B is presented for the first time and directly accesses the category coded by v_{M+1}, which was previously learned by pattern A on trial 1. In other words, B activates the same categorical "pointer," or "marker," or "index" as A. In so doing, B may change the categorical template, which determines which input patterns will also be coded by this index on future trials. The category does not change, but its invariants may change.

9. Using Context to Distinguish Signal from Noise in Patterns of Variable Complexity

The simulation in Figure 7 illustrates how, at a fixed vigilance level, the network automatically rescales its matching criterion in response to inputs of variable complexity (Section 2A). On the first four trials, the patterns are presented in the order ABAB. By trial 2, coding is complete. Pattern A directly accesses node v_{M+1} on trial 3, and pattern B directly accesses node v_{M+2} on trial 4. Thus patterns A and B are coded by different categories. On trials 5–8, patterns C and D are presented in the order CDCD. Patterns C and D are constructed from patterns A and B, respectively, by adding identical upper halves to A and B. Thus, pattern C differs from pattern D at the same locations where pattern A differs from pattern B. Due to the addition of these upper halves, the network does not code C in the category v_{M+1} of A and does not code D in the category v_{M+2} of B. Moreover, because patterns C and D represent many more features than patterns A and B, the difference between C and D is treated as noise, whereas the identical difference between A and B is considered significant. In particular, both patterns C and D are coded within the same category v_{M+3} on trials 7 and 8, and the critical feature pattern which forms the template of v_{M+3} does not contain the subpatterns at which C and D are mismatched. In contrast, these subpatterns are contained within the templates of v_{M+1} and v_{M+2} to enable these nodes to differentially classify A and B.

Figure 7 illustrates that the matching process compares whole activity patterns across a field of feature-selective cells, rather than activations of individual feature detectors, and that the properties of this matching process which enable it to stabilize network learning also automatically rescale the matching criterion. Thus the network can both differentiate finer details of simple input patterns and tolerate larger mismatches of complex input patterns. This rescaling property also defines the difference between irrelevant features and significant pattern mismatches.

If a mismatch within the attentional subsystem does not activate the orienting subsystem, then no further search for a different code occurs. Thus on trial 6 in Figure 7, mismatched features between the template of v_{M+3} and input pattern D are treated as noise in the sense that they are rapidly suppressed in short term memory (STM) at F_1, and are eliminated from the critical feature pattern learned by the v_{M+3} template. If the mismatch does generate a search, then the mismatched features may be included in the critical feature pattern of the category to which the search leads. Thus on trial 2 of Figure 6, the input pattern B mismatches the template of node v_{M+1}, which causes the search to select node v_{M+2}. As a result, A and B are coded by the distinct categories v_{M+1} and v_{M+2}, respectively. If a template mismatches a simple input pattern at just a few features, a search may be elicited, thereby enabling the network to learn fine discriminations among patterns composed of few features, such as A and B. On the other hand, if a template mismatches the same number of features within a complex input pattern, then a search may not be elicited and the mismatched features may be suppressed as noise, as in the template of v_{M+3}. Thus the pattern matching process of the model automatically exhibits properties that are akin to attentional focussing, or "zooming in."

10. Vigilance Level Tunes Categorical Coarseness: Disconfirming Feedback

The previous section showed how, given each fixed vigilance level, the network automatically rescales its sensitivity to patterns of variable complexity. The present section shows that changes in the vigilance level can regulate the coarseness of the categories that are learned in response to a fixed sequence of input patterns. First we need to define the vigilance parameter ρ.

Let $|I|$ denote the number of input pathways which receive positive inputs when I is presented. Assume that each such input pathway sends an excitatory signal of fixed size P to A whenever I is presented, so that the total excitatory input to A is $P|I|$. Assume also that each F_1 node whose activity becomes positive due to I generates an inhibitory signal of fixed size Q to A, and denote by $|X|$ the number of

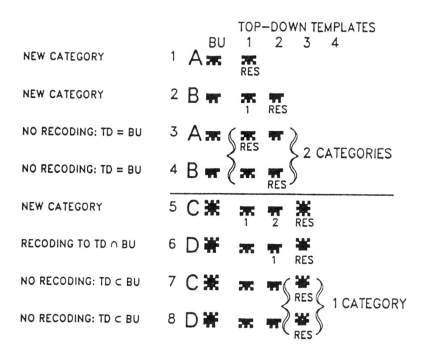

Figure 7. Distinguishing noise from patterns for inputs of variable complexity: Input patterns A and B are coded by the distinct category nodes v_{M+1} and v_{M+2}, respectively. Input patterns C and D include A and B as subsets, but also possess identical subpatterns of additional features. Due to this additional pattern complexity, C and D are coded by the same category node v_{M+3}. At this vigilance level ($\rho = .8$), the network treats the difference between C and D as noise, and suppresses the discordant elements in the v_{M+3} template. By contrast, it treats the difference between A and B as informative, and codes the difference in the v_{M+1} and v_{M+2} templates, respectively.

active pathways from F_1 to A that are activated by the F_1 activity pattern X. Then the total inhibitory input from F_1 to A is $Q\,|\,X\,|$. When

$$P\,|\,I\,| > Q\,|\,X\,|, \tag{2}$$

the orienting subsystem A receives a net excitatory signal and generates a nonspecific reset signal to F_2 (Figure 4c). The quantity

$$\rho \equiv \frac{P}{Q} \tag{3}$$

is called the *vigilance parameter* of A. By (2) and (3), STM reset is initiated when

$$\rho > \frac{|\,X\,|}{|\,I\,|}. \tag{4}$$

STM reset is prevented when

$$\rho \leq \frac{|X|}{|I|}. \tag{5}$$

In other words, the proportion $|X|/|I|$ of the input pattern I which is matched by the top-down template to generate X must exceed ρ in order to prevent STM reset at F_2.

While F_2 is inactive (Figure 5b), $|X| = |I|$. Activation of A is always forbidden in this case to prevent an input I from resetting its correct F_2 code. By (5), this constraint is achieved if

$$\rho \leq 1; \tag{6}$$

that is, if $P \leq Q$.

In summary, due to the 2/3 Rule, a bad mismatch at F_1 causes a large collapse of total F_1 activity, which leads to activation of A. In order for this to happen, the system maintains a measure of the original level of total F_1 activity and compares this criterion level with the collapsed level of total F_1 activity. The criterion level is computed by summing bottom-up inputs from I to A. This sum provides a stable criterion because it is proportional to the initial activation of F_1 by the bottom-up input, and it remains unchanged as the matching process unfolds in real-time.

We now illustrate how a low vigilance level leads to learning of coarse categories, whereas a high vigilance level leads to learning of fine categories. Suppose, for example, that a low vigilance level has led to a learned grouping of inputs which need to be distinguished for successful adaptation to a prescribed input environment, but that a punishing event occurs as a consequence of this erroneous grouping (Section 2D). Suppose that, in addition to its negative reinforcing effects, the punishing event also has the cognitive effect of increasing sensitivity to pattern mismatches. Such an increase in sensitivity is modelled within the network by an increase in the vigilance parameter, ρ, defined by (3). Increasing this single parameter enables the network to discriminate patterns which previously were lumped together. Once these patterns are coded by different categories in F_2, the different categories can be associated with different behavioral responses. In this way, environmental feedback can enable the network to parse more finely whatever input patterns happen to occur without altering the feature detection process *per se*. The vigilance parameter is increased if a punishing event amplifies all the signals from the input pattern to A so that parameter P increases. Alternatively, ρ may be increased either by a nonspecific decrease in the size Q of signals from F_1 to A, or by direct input signals to A.

Figure 8 describes a series of simulations in which four input patterns—A, B, C, D—are coded. In these simulations, $A \subset B \subset C \subset D$. The different parts of the figure show how categorical learning changes with changes of ρ. When $\rho = .8$ (Figure 8a), 4 categories are learned: (A)(B)(C)(D). When $\rho = .7$ (Figure 8b), 3 categories are learned: (A)(B)(C,D). When $\rho = .6$ (Figure 8c), 3 different categories are learned: (A)(B,C)(D). When $\rho = .5$ (Figure 8d), 2 categories are learned: (A,B)(C,D). When $\rho = .3$ (Figure 8e), 2 different categories are learned: (A,B,C)(D). When $\rho = .2$ (Figure 8f), all the patterns are lumped together into a single category.

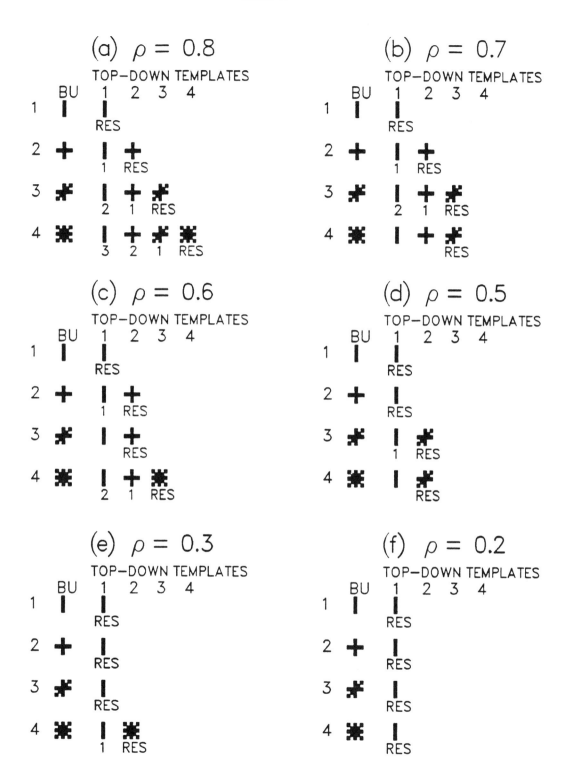

Figure 8. Influence of vigilance level on categorical groupings: As the vigilance parameter ρ decreases, the number of categories progressively decreases.

11. Rapid Classification of an Arbitrary Type Font

In order to illustrate how an ART network codifies a more complex series of patterns, we show in Figure 9 the first 20 trials of a simulation using alphabet letters as input patterns. In Figure 9a, the vigilance parameter $\rho = .5$. In Figure 9b, $\rho = .8$. Three properties are notable in these simulations. First, choosing a different vigilance parameter can determine different coding histories, such that higher vigilance induces coding into finer categories. Second, the network modifies its search order on each trial to reflect the cumulative effects of prior learning, and bypasses the orienting subsystem to directly access categories after learning has taken place. Third, the templates of coarser categories tend to be more abstract because they must approximately match a larger number of input pattern exemplars.

Given $\rho = .5$, the network groups the 26 letter patterns into 8 stable categories within 3 presentations. In this simulation, F_2 contains 15 nodes. Thus 7 nodes remain uncoded because the network self-stabilizes its learning after satisfying criteria of vigilance and global self-consistency. Given $\rho = .8$ and 15 F_2 nodes, the network groups 25 of the 26 letters into 15 stable categories within 3 presentations. The 26th letter is rejected by the network in order to self-stabilize its learning while satisfying its criteria of vigilance and global self-consistency. Given a choice of ρ closer to 1, the network classifies 15 letters into 15 distinct categories within 2 presentations. In general, if an ART network is endowed with sufficiently many nodes in F_1 and F_2, it is capable of self-organizing an arbitrary ordering of arbitrarily many and arbitrarily complex input patterns into self-stabilizing recognition categories subject to the constraints of vigilance and global code self-consistency.

We now turn to a mathematical analysis of the properties which control learning and recognition by an ART network.

12. Network Equations: Interactions between Short Term Memory and Long Term Memory Patterns

The STM and LTM equations are described below in dimensionless form (Lin and Segal, 1974), where the number of parameters is reduced to a minimum.

A. STM Equations

The STM activity x_k of any node v_k in F_1 or F_2 obeys a membrane equation of the form

$$\epsilon\frac{d}{dt}x_k = -x_k + (1 - Ax_k)J_k^+ - (B + Cx_k)J_k^-, \tag{7}$$

where J_k^+ is the total excitatory input to v_k, J_k^- is the total inhibitory input to v_k, and all the parameters are nonnegative. If $A > 0$ and $C > 0$, then the STM activity $x_k(t)$ remains within the finite interval $[-BC^{-1}, A^{-1}]$ no matter how large the nonnegative inputs J_k^+ and J_k^- become.

We denote nodes in F_1 by v_i, where $i = 1, 2, \ldots, M$. We denote nodes in F_2 by v_j, where $j = M + 1, M + 2, \ldots, N$. Thus by (7),

$$\epsilon\frac{d}{dt}x_i = -x_i + (1 - A_1x_i)J_i^+ - (B_1 + C_1x_i)J_i^- \tag{8}$$

and

$$\epsilon\frac{d}{dt}x_j = -x_j + (1 - A_2x_j)J_j^+ - (B_2 + C_2x_j)J_j^-. \tag{9}$$

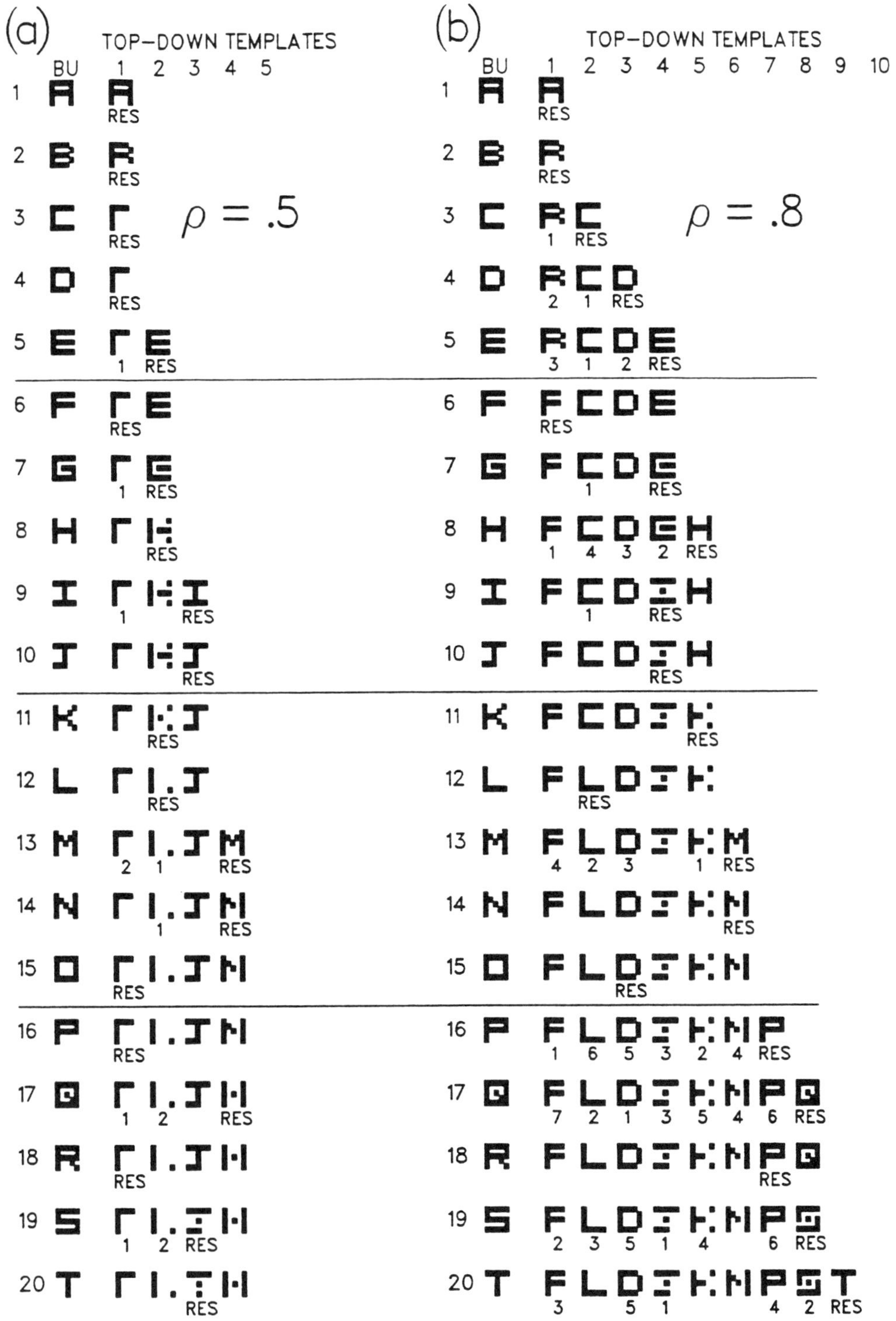

Figure 9. Alphabet learning: Different vigilance levels cause different numbers of letter categories and different critical feature patterns, or templates, to form.

In the notation of (1) and Figure 4a, the F_1 activity pattern $X = (x_1, x_2, \ldots, x_M)$ and the F_2 activity pattern $Y = (x_{M+1}, x_{M+2}, \ldots, x_N)$.

The input J_i^+ to the ith node v_i of F_1 is a sum of the bottom-up input I_i and the top-down template input V_i:

$$V_i = D_1 \sum_j f(x_j) z_{ji}; \tag{10}$$

that is,

$$J_i^+ = I_i + V_i, \tag{11}$$

where $f(x_j)$ is the signal generated by activity x_j of v_j, and z_{ji} is the LTM trace in the top-down pathway from v_j to v_i. In the notation of Figure 4b, the input pattern $I = (I_1, I_2, \ldots, I_M)$, the signal pattern $U = (f(x_{M+1}), f(x_{M+2}), \ldots, f(x_N))$, and the template pattern $V = (V_1, V_2, \ldots, V_M)$.

The inhibitory input J_i^- governs the attentional gain control signal:

$$J_i^- = \sum_j f(x_j). \tag{12}$$

Thus $J_i^- = 0$ if and only if F_2 is inactive. When F_2 is active, $J_i^- > 0$ and hence term J_i^- in (8) has a nonspecific inhibitory effect on all the STM activities x_i of F_1. In Figure 5c, this nonspecific inhibitory effect is mediated by inhibition of an active excitatory gain control channel. Such a mechanism is formally described by (12). The attentional gain control signal can be implemented in any of several formally equivalent ways. See the Appendix for some alternative systems.

The inputs and parameters of STM activities in F_2 are chosen so that the F_2 node which receives the largest input from F_1 wins the competition for STM activity. Theorems in Ellias and Grossberg (1975), Grossberg (1973), and Grossberg and Levine (1975) provide a basis for choosing these parameters. The inputs J_j^+ and J_j^- to the F_2 node v_j have the following form.

Input J_j^+ adds a positive feedback signal $g(x_j)$ from v_j to itself to the bottom-up adaptive filter input T_j, where

$$T_j = D_2 \sum_i h(x_i) z_{ij}. \tag{13}$$

That is,

$$J_j^+ = g(x_j) + T_j, \tag{14}$$

where $h(x_i)$ is the signal emitted by the F_1 node v_i and z_{ij} is the LTM trace in the pathway from v_i to v_j. Input J_j^- adds up negative feedback signals $g(x_k)$ from all the other nodes in F_2:

$$J_j^- = \sum_{k \neq j} g(x_k). \tag{15}$$

In the notation of (1) and Figure 4a, the output pattern $S = (h(x_1), h(x_2), \ldots, h(x_M))$ and the input pattern $T = (T_{M+1}, T_{M+2}, \ldots, T_N)$.

Taken together, the positive feedback signal $g(x_j)$ in (14) and the negative feedback signal J_j^- in (15) define an on-center off-surround feedback interaction which contrast-enhances the STM activity pattern Y of F_2 in response to the input pattern T. When F_2's parameters are chosen properly, this contrast-enhancement process enables F_2 to choose for STM activation only the node v_j which receives the largest input T_j. In particular, when parameter ϵ is small in equation (9), F_2 behaves approximately like a binary switching, or choice, circuit:

$$f(x_j) = \begin{cases} 1 & \text{if } T_j = \max\{T_k\} \\ 0 & \text{otherwise.} \end{cases} \tag{16}$$

In the choice case, the top-down template in (10) obeys

$$V_i = \begin{cases} D_1 z_{ji} & \text{if the } F_2 \text{ node } v_j \text{ is active} \\ 0 & \text{if } F_2 \text{ is inactive.} \end{cases} \tag{17}$$

Since V_i is proportional to the LTM trace z_{ji} of the active F_2 node v_j, we can define the template pattern that is read-out by each active F_2 node v_j to be $V^{(j)} \equiv D_1(z_{j1}, z_{j2}, \ldots, z_{jM})$.

B. LTM Equations

The equations for the bottom-up LTM traces z_{ij} and the top-down LTM traces z_{ji} between pairs of nodes v_i in F_1 and v_j in F_2 are formally summarized in this section to facilitate the description of how these equations help to generate useful learning and recognition properties.

The LTM trace of the bottom-up pathway from v_i to v_j obeys a learning equation of the form

$$\frac{d}{dt} z_{ij} = K_1 f(x_j)[-E_{ij} z_{ij} + h(x_i)]. \tag{18}$$

In (18), term $f(x_j)$ is a postsynaptic sampling, or learning, signal because $f(x_j) = 0$ implies $\frac{d}{dt} z_{ij} = 0$. Term $f(x_j)$ is also the output signal of v_j to pathways from v_j to F_1, as in (10).

The LTM trace of the top-down pathway from v_j to v_i also obeys a learning equation of the form

$$\frac{d}{dt} z_{ji} = K_2 f(x_j)[-E_{ji} z_{ji} + h(x_i)]. \tag{19}$$

In the present model, the simplest choice of K_2 and E_{ji} was made for the top-down LTM traces:

$$K_2 = E_{ji} = 1. \tag{20}$$

A more complex choice of E_{ij} was made for the bottom-up LTM traces in order to generate the Weber Law Rule of Section 14. The Weber Law Rule requires that the positive bottom-up LTM traces learned during the encoding of an F_1 pattern X with a smaller number $|X|$ of active nodes be larger than the LTM traces learned during the encoding of an F_1 pattern with a larger number of active nodes, other things being equal. This inverse relationship between pattern complexity and bottom-up LTM trace strength can be realized by allowing the bottom-up LTM traces at each node v_j to compete among themselves for synaptic sites. The Weber Law Rule can also be generated by the STM dynamics of F_1 when competitive interactions are assumed to occur among the nodes of F_1. Generating the Weber Law Rule at F_1 rather than at the bottom-up LTM traces enjoys several advantages, and this model will be developed elsewhere (Carpenter and Grossberg, 1987). In particular, implementing the Weber Law Rule at F_1 enables us to choose $E_{ij} = 1$.

Competition among the LTM traces which abut the node v_j is modelled herein by defining

$$E_{ij} = h(x_i) + L^{-1} \sum_{k \neq i} h(x_k) \qquad (21)$$

and letting $K_1 =$ constant. It is convenient to write K_1 in the form $K_1 = KL$. A physical interpretation of this choice can be seen by rewriting (18) in the form

$$\frac{d}{dt} z_{ij} = K f(x_j)[(1 - z_{ij})Lh(x_i) - z_{ij} \sum_{k \neq i} h(x_k)]. \qquad (22)$$

By (22), when a postsynaptic signal $f(x_j)$ is positive, a positive presynaptic signal from the F_1 node v_i can commit receptor sites to the LTM process z_{ij} at a rate $(1 - z_{ij})Lh(x_i)K f(x_j)$. In other words, uncommitted sites—which number $(1 - z_{ij})$ out of the total population size 1—are committed by the joint action of signals $Lh(x_i)$ and $K f(x_j)$. Simultaneously signals $h(x_k)$, $k \neq i$, which reach v_j at different patches of the v_j membrane, compete for the sites which are already committed to z_{ij} via the mass action competitive terms $-z_{ij}h(x_k)K f(x_j)$. In other words, sites which are committed to z_{ij} lose their commitment at a rate $-z_{ij} \sum_{k \neq i} h(x_k)K f(x_j)$ which is proportional to the number of committed sites z_{ij}, the total competitive input $-\sum_{k \neq i} h(x_k)$, and the postsynaptic gating signal $K f(x_j)$.

Malsburg and Willshaw (1981) have used a different type of competition among LTM traces in their model of retinotectal development. Translated to the present notation, Malsburg and Willshaw postulate that for each fixed F_1 node v_i, competition occurs among all the bottom-up LTM traces z_{ij} in pathways emanating from v_i in such a way as to keep the total synaptic strength $\sum_j z_{ij}$ constant through time. This model does not generate the Weber Law Rule. We show in Section 14 that the Weber Law Rule is essential for achieving direct access to learned categories of arbitrary input patterns in the present model.

C. STM Reset System

A simple type of mismatch-mediated activation of A and STM reset of F_2 by A were implemented in the simulations. As outlined in Section 10, each active input pathway sends an excitatory signal of size P to the orienting subsystem A. Potentials x_i of F_1 which exceed zero generate an inhibitory signal of size Q to A. These constraints lead to the following Reset Rule.

Reset Rule:

Population A generates a nonspecific reset wave to F_2 whenever

$$\frac{|X|}{|I|} < \rho = \frac{P}{Q} \qquad (23)$$

where I is the current input pattern and $|X|$ is the number of nodes across F_1 such that $x_i > 0$. The nonspecific reset wave successively shuts off active F_2 nodes until the search ends or the input pattern I shuts off. Thus (16) must be modified as follows to maintain inhibition of all F_2 nodes which have been reset by A during the presentation of I:

F_2 Choice and Search

$$f(x_j) = \begin{cases} 1 & \text{if } T_j = \max\{T_k : k \in \mathbf{J}\} \\ 0 & \text{otherwise} \end{cases} \tag{24}$$

where $\mathbf{J}$ is the set of indices of F_2 nodes which have not yet been reset on the present learning trial. At the beginning of each new learning trial, $\mathbf{J}$ is reset at $\{M+1 \dots N\}$. (See Figure 1.) As a learning trial proceeds, $\mathbf{J}$ loses one index at a time until the mismatch-mediated search for F_2 nodes terminates.

13. Direct Access to Subset and Superset Patterns

The need for a Weber Law Rule can be motivated as follows. Suppose that a bottom-up input pattern $I^{(1)}$ activates a network in which pattern $I^{(1)}$ is perfectly coded by the adaptive filter from F_1 to F_2. Suppose that another pattern $I^{(2)}$ is also perfectly coded and that $I^{(2)}$ contains $I^{(1)}$ as a subset; that is, $I^{(2)}$ equals $I^{(1)}$ at all the nodes where $I^{(1)}$ is positive. If $I^{(1)}$ and $I^{(2)}$ are sufficiently different, they should have access to distinct categories at F_2. However, since $I^{(2)}$ equals $I^{(1)}$ at their intersection, and since all the F_1 nodes where $I^{(2)}$ does not equal $I^{(1)}$ are inactive when $I^{(1)}$ is presented, how does the network decide between the two categories when $I^{(1)}$ is presented?

To accomplish this, the node $v^{(1)}$ in F_2 which codes $I^{(1)}$ should receive a bigger signal from the adaptive filter than the node $v^{(2)}$ in F_2 which codes a superset $I^{(2)}$ of $I^{(1)}$. In order to realize this constraint, the LTM traces at $v^{(2)}$ which filter $I^{(1)}$ should be smaller than the LTM traces at $v^{(1)}$ which filter $I^{(1)}$. Since the LTM traces at $v^{(2)}$ were coded by the superset pattern $I^{(2)}$, this constraint suggests that larger patterns are encoded by smaller LTM traces. Thus the absolute sizes of the LTM traces projecting to the different nodes $v^{(1)}$ and $v^{(2)}$ reflect the overall scale of the patterns $I^{(1)}$ and $I^{(2)}$ coded by the nodes. The quantitative realization of this inverse relationship between LTM size and input pattern scale is called the Weber Law Rule.

This inverse relationship suggests how a subset $I^{(1)}$ may selectively activate its node $v^{(1)}$ rather than the node $v^{(2)}$ corresponding to a superset $I^{(2)}$. On the other hand, the superset $I^{(2)}$ must also be able to directly activate its node $v^{(2)}$ rather than the node $v^{(1)}$ of a subset $I^{(1)}$. To achieve subset access, the positive LTM traces of $v^{(1)}$ become larger than the positive LTM traces of $v^{(2)}$. Since presentation of $I^{(2)}$ activates the entire subset pattern $I^{(1)}$, a further property is needed to understand why the subset node $v^{(1)}$ is not activated by the superset $I^{(2)}$. This property—which we call the Associative Decay Rule—implies that some LTM traces decay toward zero during learning. Thus the associative learning laws considered herein violate Hebb's (1949) learning postulate.

In particular, the relative sizes of the LTM traces projecting to an F_2 node reflect the internal structuring of the input patterns coded by that node. During learning of $I^{(1)}$, the LTM traces decay toward zero in pathways which project to $v^{(1)}$ from F_1 cells where $I^{(1)}$ equals zero (Figure 10a). Simultaneously, the LTM traces become large in the pathways which project to $v^{(1)}$ from F_1 cells where $I^{(1)}$ is positive (Figure 10a). In contrast, during learning of $I^{(2)}$, the LTM traces become large in all the pathways which project to $v^{(2)}$ from F_1 cells where $I^{(2)}$ is positive (Figure 10b), including those cells where $I^{(1)}$ equals zero. Since $I^{(2)}$ is a superset of $I^{(1)}$, the Weber Law Rule implies that LTM traces in pathways to $v^{(2)}$ (Figure 10b) do not grow as large as LTM traces in pathways to $v^{(1)}$ (Figure 10a). On the other hand, after learning occurs, more positive LTM traces exist in pathways to $v^{(2)}$ than to $v^{(1)}$. Thus a trade-off exists between the individual sizes of LTM traces and the number of positive LTM traces which lead to each F_2 node. This trade-off enables $I^{(1)}$ to access $v^{(1)}$ (Figure 10c) and $I^{(2)}$ to access $v^{(2)}$ (Figure 10d).

14. Weber Law Rule and Associative Decay Rule for Bottom-Up LTM Traces

We now describe more precisely how the conjoint action of a Weber Law Rule and an Associative Decay Rule allow direct access to both subset and superset F_2 codes. To fix ideas, suppose that each input pattern I to F_1 is a pattern of 0's and 1's. Let $|\,I\,|$ denote the number of 1's in the input pattern I. The two rules can be summarized as follows.

Associative Decay Rule:

As learning of I takes place, LTM traces in the bottom-up coding pathways and the top-down template pathways between an inactive F_1 node and an active F_2 node approach 0. Associative learning within the LTM traces can thus cause decreases as well as increases in the sizes of the traces. This is a non-Hebbian form of associative learning.

Weber Law Rule:

As learning of I takes place, LTM traces in the bottom-up coding pathways which join active F_1 and F_2 nodes approach an asymptote of the form

$$\frac{\alpha}{\beta+|\,I\,|,} \tag{25}$$

where α and β are positive constants. By (25), larger $|\,I\,|$ values imply smaller positive LTM traces in the pathways encoding I.

Direct access by the subset $I^{(1)}$ and the superset $I^{(2)}$ can now be understood as follows. By (25), the positive LTM traces which code $I^{(1)}$ have size

$$\frac{\alpha}{\beta+|\,I^{(1)}\,|} \tag{26}$$

and the positive LTM traces which code $I^{(2)}$ have size

$$\frac{\alpha}{\beta+|\,I^{(2)}\,|,} \tag{27}$$

where $|\,I^{(1)}\,|<|\,I^{(2)}\,|$. When $I^{(1)}$ is presented at F_1, $|\,I^{(1)}\,|$ nodes in F_1 are suprathreshold. Thus the *total* input to $v^{(1)}$ is proportional to

$$T_{11} = \frac{\alpha\,|\,I^{(1)}\,|}{\beta+|\,I^{(1)}\,|} \tag{28}$$

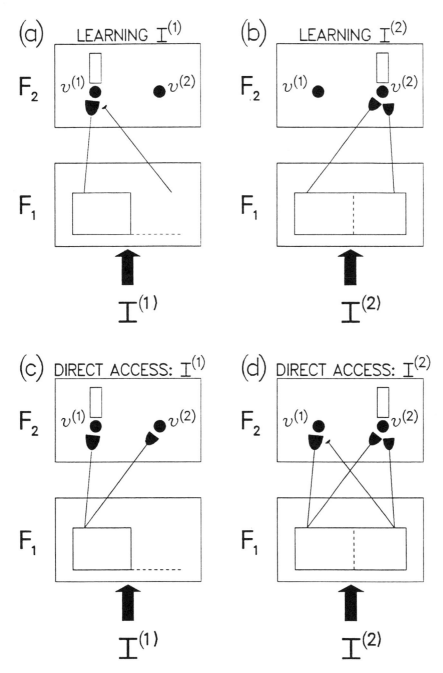

Figure 10. The Weber Law Rule and the Associative Decay Rule enable both subset and superset input patterns to directly access distinct F_2 nodes: (a) and (b) schematize the learning induced by presentation of $I^{(1)}$ (a subset pattern) and $I^{(2)}$ (a superset pattern). Larger path endings designate larger learned LTM traces. (c) and (d) schematize how $I^{(1)}$ and $I^{(2)}$ directly access the F_2 nodes $v^{(1)}$ and $v^{(2)}$, respectively. This property illustrates how distinct, but otherwise arbitrary, input patterns can directly access different categories. No restrictions on input orthogonality or linear predictability are needed.

and the *total* input to $v^{(2)}$ is proportional to

$$T_{12} = \frac{\alpha \mid I^{(1)} \mid}{\beta + \mid I^{(2)} \mid}. \tag{29}$$

Because (25) defines a *decreasing* function of $\mid I \mid$ and because $\mid I^{(1)} \mid < \mid I^{(2)} \mid$, it follows that $T_{11} > T_{12}$. Thus $I^{(1)}$ activates $v^{(1)}$ instead of $v^{(2)}$.

When $I^{(2)}$ is presented at F_1, $\mid I^{(2)} \mid$ nodes in F_1 are suprathreshold. Thus the *total* input to $v^{(2)}$ is proportional to

$$T_{22} = \frac{\alpha \mid I^{(2)} \mid}{\beta + \mid I^{(2)} \mid}. \tag{30}$$

We now invoke the Associative Decay Rule. Because $I^{(2)}$ is a superset of $I^{(1)}$, only those F_1 nodes in $I^{(2)}$ that are also activated by $I^{(1)}$ project to positive LTM traces at $v^{(1)}$. Thus the *total* input to $v^{(1)}$ is proportional to

$$T_{21} = \frac{\alpha \mid I^{(1)} \mid}{\beta + \mid I^{(1)} \mid}. \tag{31}$$

Both T_{22} and T_{21} are expressed in terms of the Weber function

$$W(\mid I \mid) = \frac{\alpha \mid I \mid}{\beta + \mid I \mid}, \tag{32}$$

which is an *increasing* function of $\mid I \mid$. Since $\mid I^{(1)} \mid < \mid I^{(2)} \mid$, $T_{22} > T_{21}$. Thus the superset $I^{(2)}$ activates its node $v^{(2)}$ rather than the subset node $v^{(1)}$. In summary, direct access to subsets and supersets can be traced to the opposite monotonic behavior of the functions (25) and (32).

It remains to show how the Associative Decay Rule and the Weber Law Rule are generated by the STM and LTM laws (8)–(22). The Associative Decay Rule for bottom-up LTM traces follows from (22). When the F_1 node v_i is inactive, $h(x_i) = 0$. When the F_2 node v_j is active, $f(x_j) = 1$. Thus if z_{ij} is the LTM trace in a bottom-up pathway from an inactive F_1 node v_i to an active F_2 node v_j, (22) reduces to

$$\frac{d}{dt} z_{ij} = -K z_{ij} \sum_{k \neq i} h(x_k). \tag{33}$$

The signal function $h(x_k)$ is scaled to rise steeply from 0 to the constant 1 when x_k exceeds zero. For simplicity, suppose that

$$h(x_k) = \begin{cases} 1 & \text{if } x_k > 0 \\ 0 & \text{otherwise.} \end{cases} \tag{34}$$

Thus during a learning trial when v_i is inactive,

$$\sum_{k \neq i} h(x_k) = \mid X \mid \tag{35}$$

where $|X|$ is the number of positive activities in the F_1 activity pattern X. By (33) and (35), when v_i is inactive and v_j is active,

$$\frac{d}{dt}z_{ij} = -Kz_{ij}\,|\,X\,| \tag{36}$$

which shows that z_{ij} decays exponentially toward zero.

The Weber Law Rule for bottom-up LTM traces z_{ij} follows from (22), (24), and (34). Consider an input pattern I of 0's and 1's that activates $|I|$ nodes in F_1 and node v_j in F_2. Then, by (34),

$$\sum_{k=1}^{M} h(x_k) = |\,I\,|. \tag{37}$$

For each z_{ij} in a bottom-up pathway from an active F_1 node v_i to an active F_2 node v_j, $f(x_j) = 1$ and $h(x_i) = 1$, so

$$\frac{d}{dt}z_{ij} = K[(1 - z_{ij})L - z_{ij}(|\,I\,| - 1)]. \tag{38}$$

At equilibrium, $dz_{ij}/dt = 0$. It then follows from (38) that at equilibrium

$$z_{ij} = \frac{\alpha}{\beta + |\,I\,|} \tag{39}$$

as in (25), with $\alpha = L$ and $\beta = L - 1$. Both α and β must be positive, which is the case if $L > 1$. By (22), this means that each lateral inhibitory signal $-h(x_k)$, $k \neq i$, is weaker than the direct excitatory signal $Lh(x_i)$, other things being equal.

When top-down signals from F_2 to F_1 supplement a bottom-up input pattern I to F_1, the number $|\,X\,|$ of positive activities in X may become smaller than $|\,I\,|$ due to the 2/3 Rule. If v_i remains active after the F_2 node v_j becomes active, (38) generalizes to

$$\frac{d}{dt}z_{ij} = K[(1 - z_{ij})L - z_{ij}(|\,X\,| - 1)]. \tag{40}$$

By combining (36) and (40), both the Associative Decay Rule and the Weber Law Rule for bottom-up LTM traces may be understood as consequences of the LTM equation

$$\frac{d}{dt}z_{ij} = \begin{cases} K[(1 - z_{ij})L - z_{ij}(|\,X\,| - 1)] & \text{if } v_i \text{ and } v_j \text{ are active} \\ -K\,|\,X\,|\,z_{ij} & \text{if } v_i \text{ is inactive and } v_j \text{ is active}. \\ 0 & \text{if } v_j \text{ is inactive} \end{cases} \tag{41}$$

Evaluation of term $|\,X\,|$ in (41) depends upon whether or not a top-down template perturbs F_1 when a bottom-up input pattern I is active.

15. Template Learning Rule and Associative Decay Rule for Top-Down LTM Traces

The Template Learning Rule and the Associative Decay Rule together imply that the top-down LTM traces in all the pathways from an F_2 node v_j encode the critical feature pattern of all input patterns which have activated v_j without triggering F_2

reset. To see this, as in Section 14, suppose that an input pattern I of 0's and 1's is being learned.

Template Learning Rule:

As learning of I takes place, LTM traces in the top-down pathways from an active F_2 node to an active F_1 node approach 1.

The Template Learning Rule and the Associative Decay Rule for top-down LTM traces z_{ji} follow by combining (19) and (20) to obtain:

$$\frac{d}{dt}z_{ji} = f(x_j)[-z_{ji} + h(x_i)]. \tag{42}$$

If the F_2 node v_j is active and the F_1 node v_i is inactive, then $h(x_i) = 0$ and $f(x_j) = 1$, so (42) reduces to

$$\frac{d}{dt}z_{ji} = -z_{ji}. \tag{43}$$

Thus z_{ji} decays exponentially toward zero and the Associative Decay Rule holds. On the other hand, if both v_i and v_j are active, then $f(x_j) = h(x_i) = 1$, so (42) reduces to

$$\frac{d}{dt}z_{ji} = -z_{ji} + 1. \tag{44}$$

Thus z_{ji} increases exponentially toward 1 and the Template Learning Rule holds.

Combining equations (42)-(44) leads to the learning rule governing the LTM traces z_{ji} in a top-down template:

$$\frac{d}{dt}z_{ji} = \begin{cases} -z_{ji}+1 & \text{if } v_i \text{ and } v_j \text{ are active} \\ -z_{ji} & \text{if } v_i \text{ is inactive and } v_j \text{ is active} \\ 0 & \text{if } v_j \text{ is inactive} \end{cases} \tag{45}$$

Equation (45) says that the template of v_j tries to learn the activity pattern across F_1 when v_j is active.

The 2/3 Rule controls which nodes v_i in (45) remain active in response to an input pattern I. The 2/3 Rule implies that if the F_2 node v_j becomes active while the F_1 node v_i is receiving a large bottom-up input I_i, then v_i will remain active only if z_{ji} is sufficiently large. Hence there is some critical strength of the top-down LTM traces such that if z_{ji} falls below that strength, then v_i will never again be active when v_j is active, even if I_i is large. As long as z_{ji} remains above the critical LTM strength, it will increase when I_i is large and v_j is active, and decrease when I_i is small and v_j is active. Once z_{ji} falls below the critical LTM strength, it will decay toward 0 whenever v_j is active; that is, the feature represented by v_i drops out of the critical feature pattern encoded by v_j.

These and related properties of the network can be summarized compactly using the following notation.

Let **I** denote the set of indices of nodes v_i which receive a positive input from the pattern I. When I is a pattern of 0's and 1's, then

$$I_i = \begin{cases} 1 & \text{if } i \in \mathbf{I} \\ 0 & \text{otherwise} \end{cases}, \tag{46}$$

where $\mathbf{I}$ is a subset of the F_1 index set $\{1 \ldots M\}$. As in Section 12, let $V^{(j)} = D_1(z_{j1} \ldots z_{ji} \ldots z_{jM})$ denote the template pattern of top-down LTM traces in pathways leading from the F_2 node v_j. The index set $\mathbf{V}^{(j)} = \mathbf{V}^{(j)}(t)$ is defined as follows: $i \in \mathbf{V}^{(j)}$ iff z_{ji} is larger than the critical LTM strength required for v_i to be active when v_j is active and $i \in \mathbf{I}$. For fixed t, let $\mathbf{X}$ denote the subset of indices $\{1 \ldots M\}$ such that $i \in \mathbf{X}$ iff the F_1 node v_i is active at time t.

With this notation, the 2/3 Rule can be summarized by stating that when a pattern I is presented,

$$\mathbf{X} = \begin{cases} \mathbf{I} & \text{if } F_2 \text{ is inactive} \\ \mathbf{I} \cap \mathbf{V}^{(j)} & \text{if the } F_2 \text{ node } v_j \text{ is active.} \end{cases} \tag{47}$$

The link between STM dynamics at F_1 and F_2 and LTM dynamics between F_1 and F_2 can now be succinctly expressed in terms of (47),

$$\frac{d}{dt} z_{ij} = \begin{cases} K[(1 - z_{ij})L - z_{ij}(|\mathbf{X}| - 1)] & \text{if } i \in \mathbf{X} \text{ and } f(x_j) = 1 \\ -K |\mathbf{X}| z_{ij} & \text{if } i \notin \mathbf{X} \text{ and } f(x_j) = 1 \\ 0 & \text{if } f(x_j) = 0 \end{cases} \tag{48}$$

and

$$\frac{d}{dt} z_{ji} = \begin{cases} -z_{ji} + 1 & \text{if } i \in \mathbf{X} \text{ and } f(x_j) = 1 \\ -z_{ji} & \text{if } i \notin \mathbf{X} \text{ and } f(x_j) = 1 . \\ 0 & \text{if } f(x_j) = 0 \end{cases} \tag{49}$$

A number of definitions that were made intuitively in Sections 3–9 can now be summarized as follows.

Definitions

Coding: An active F_2 node v_J is said to *code* an input I on a given trial if no reset of v_J occurs after the template $V^{(J)}$ is read out at F_1.

Reset could, in principle, occur due to three different factors. The read-out of the template $V^{(J)}$ can change the activity pattern X across F_1. The new pattern X could conceivably generate a maximal input via the $F_1 \rightarrow F_2$ adaptive filter to an F_2 node other than v_J. The theorems below show how the 2/3 Rule and the learning rules prevent template read-out from undermining the choice of v_J via the $F_1 \rightarrow F_2$ adaptive filter. Reset of v_J could also, in principle, occur due to the learning induced in the LTM traces z_{iJ} and z_{Ji} by the choice of v_J. In a real-time learning system whose choices are determined by a continuous flow of bottom-up and top-down signals, one cannot take for granted that the learning process, which alters the sizes of these signals, will maintain a choice within a single learning trial. The theorems in the next sections state conditions which prevent either template readout or learning from resetting the F_2 choice via the adaptive filter from F_1 to F_2.

Only the third possible reset mechanism—activation of the orienting subsystem A by a mismatch at F_1—is allowed to reset the F_2 choice. Equations (5) and (47) imply that if v_J becomes active during the presentation of I, then inequality

$$|\mathbf{I} \cap \mathbf{V}^{(J)}| \geq \rho |\mathbf{I}| \tag{50}$$

is a necessary condition to prevent reset of v_J by activation of A. Sufficient conditions are stated in the theorems below.

Direct Access: Pattern I is said to have *direct access* to an F_2 node v_J if presentation of I leads at once to activation of v_J and v_J codes I on that trial.

By equations (13) and (34), input I chooses node v_J first if, for all $j \neq J$,

$$\sum_{i \in I} z_{iJ} > \sum_{i \in I} z_{ij}. \tag{51}$$

The conditions under which v_J then codes I are characterized in the theorems below.

Fast Learning: For the remainder of this article we consider the *fast learning case* in which learning rates enable LTM traces to approximately reach the asymptotes determined by the STM patterns on each trial. Given the fast learning assumption, at the end of a trial during which v_J was active, (48) implies that

$$z_{iJ} \cong \begin{cases} \frac{L}{L-1+|\mathbf{X}|} & \text{if } i \in \mathbf{X} \\ 0 & \text{if } i \notin \mathbf{X} \end{cases} \tag{52}$$

and (49) implies that

$$z_{Ji} \cong \begin{cases} 1 & \text{if } i \in \mathbf{X} \\ 0 & \text{if } i \notin \mathbf{X} \end{cases}. \tag{53}$$

Thus although $z_{ij} \neq z_{ji}$ in (52) and (53), z_{ij} is large iff z_{ji} is large and $z_{ij} = 0$ iff $z_{ji} = 0$. We can therefore introduce the following definition.

Asymptotic Learning: An F_2 node v_j has *asymptotically learned* the STM pattern X if its LTM traces z_{ij} and z_{ji} satisfy (52) and (53).

By (47), **X** in (52) and (53) equals either **I** or $\mathbf{I} \cap \mathbf{V}^{(j)}$. This observation motivates the following definition.

Perfect Learning: An F_2 node v_j has *perfectly learned* an input pattern I iff v_j has asymptotically learned the STM pattern X $=$ I.

16. Direct Access to Nodes Coding Perfectly Learned Patterns

We can now prove the following generalization of the fact that subset and superset nodes can be directly accessed (Section 13).

Theorem 1 (Direct Access by Perfectly Learned Patterns): An input pattern I has direct access to a node v_J which has perfectly learned I if $L > 1$ and all initial bottom-up LTM traces satisfy the

Direct Access Inequality

$$0 < z_{ij}(0) < \frac{L}{L-1+M}, \tag{54}$$

where M is the number of nodes in F_1.

Proof:

In order to prove that I has direct access to v_J we need to show that: (i) v_J is the first F_2 node to be chosen; (ii) v_J remains the chosen node after its template $V^{(J)}$ is read-out at F_1; (iii) read-out of $V^{(J)}$ does not lead to F_2 reset by the orienting subsystem; and (iv) v_J remains active as fast learning occurs.

To prove property (i), we must establish that, at the start of the trial, $T_J > T_j$ for all $j \neq J$. When I is presented, $|\mathbf{I}|$ active pathways project to each F_2 node. In particular, by (13) and (34),

$$T_J = D_2 \sum_{i \in \mathbf{I}} z_{iJ} \tag{55}$$

and

$$T_j = D_2 \sum_{i \in \mathbf{I}} z_{ij}. \tag{56}$$

Because node v_J perfectly codes I at the start of the trial, it follows from (52) that

$$z_{iJ} = \begin{cases} \frac{L}{L-1+|\mathbf{I}|} & \text{if } i \in \mathbf{I} \\ 0 & \text{if } i \notin \mathbf{I}. \end{cases} \tag{57}$$

By (55) and (57),

$$T_J = \frac{D_2 L |\mathbf{I}|}{L-1+|\mathbf{I}|}. \tag{58}$$

In order to evaluate T_j in (56), we need to consider nodes v_j which have asymptotically learned a different pattern than I, as well as nodes v_j which are as yet uncommitted. Suppose that v_j, $j \neq J$, has asymptotically learned a pattern $V^{(j)} \neq I$. Then by (52),

$$z_{ij} = \begin{cases} \frac{L}{L-1+|\mathbf{V}^{(j)}|} & \text{if } i \in \mathbf{V}^{(j)} \\ 0 & \text{if } i \notin \mathbf{V}^{(j)}. \end{cases} \tag{59}$$

By (59), the only positive LTM traces in the sum $\sum_{i \in \mathbf{I}} z_{ij}$ in (56) are the traces with indices $i \in \mathbf{I} \cap \mathbf{V}^{(j)}$. Moreover, all of these positive LTM traces have the same value. Thus (59) implies that

$$T_j = \frac{D_2 L |\mathbf{I} \cap \mathbf{V}^{(j)}|}{L-1+|\mathbf{V}^{(j)}|}. \tag{60}$$

We now prove that T_J in (58) is larger than T_j in (60) if $L > 1$; that is,

$$\frac{|\mathbf{I}|}{L-1+|\mathbf{I}|} > \frac{|\mathbf{I} \cap \mathbf{V}^{(j)}|}{L-1+|\mathbf{V}^{(j)}|}. \tag{61}$$

Suppose first that $|\mathbf{V}^{(j)}| > |\mathbf{I}|$. Then $|\mathbf{I}| \geq |\mathbf{I} \cap \mathbf{V}^{(j)}|$ and $(L-1+|\mathbf{I}|) < (L-1+|\mathbf{V}^{(j)}|)$, which together imply (61).

Suppose next that $|\mathbf{V}^{(j)}| \leq |\mathbf{I}|$. Then, since $\mathbf{V}^{(j)} \neq \mathbf{I}$, it follows that $|\mathbf{I}| > |\mathbf{I} \cap \mathbf{V}^{(j)}|$. Thus, since the function $w/(L-1+w)$ is an increasing function of w,

$$\frac{|\mathbf{I}|}{L-1+|\mathbf{I}|} > \frac{|\mathbf{I} \cap \mathbf{V}^{(j)}|}{L-1+|\mathbf{I} \cap \mathbf{V}^{(j)}|}. \tag{62}$$

Finally, since $|\mathbf{V}^{(j)}| \geq |\mathbf{I} \cap \mathbf{V}^{(j)}|$,

$$\frac{|\mathbf{I} \cap \mathbf{V}^{(j)}|}{L-1+|\mathbf{I} \cap \mathbf{V}^{(j)}|} \geq \frac{|\mathbf{I} \cap \mathbf{V}^{(j)}|}{L-1+|\mathbf{V}^{(j)}|}. \tag{63}$$

Inequalities (62) and (63) together imply (61). This completes the proof that I first activates v_J rather than any other previously coded node v_j.

It remains to prove that I activates v_J rather than an uncommitted node v_j which has not yet been chosen to learn any category. The LTM traces of each uncommitted node v_j obey the Direct Access Inequality (54), which along with $|\mathbf{I}| \leq M$ implies that

$$T_J = \frac{D_2 L\,|\mathbf{I}|}{L-1+|\mathbf{I}|} \geq \frac{D_2 L\,|\mathbf{I}|}{L-1+M} > D_2 \sum_{i \in \mathbf{I}} z_{ij} = T_j. \tag{64}$$

This completes the proof of property (i).

The proof of property (ii), that v_J remains the chosen node after its template $V^{(J)}$ is read-out, follows immediately from the fact that $\mathbf{V}^{(J)} = \mathbf{I}$. By (47), the set $\mathbf{X}$ of active nodes remains equal to $\mathbf{I}$ after $V^{(J)}$ is read-out. Thus T_J and T_j are unchanged by read-out of $V^{(J)}$, which completes the proof of property (ii).

Property (iii) also follows immediately from the fact that $\mathbf{I} \cap \mathbf{V}^{(J)} = \mathbf{I}$ in the inequality

$$|\mathbf{I} \cap \mathbf{V}^{(J)}| \geq \rho\,|\mathbf{I}|. \tag{50}$$

Property (iv) follows from the fact that, while v_J is active, no new learning occurs, since v_J had already perfectly learned input pattern I before the trial began. This completes the proof of Theorem 1.

17. Initial Strengths of LTM Traces

A. Direct Access Inequality: Initial Bottom-Up LTM Traces are Small

Theorem 1 shows that the Direct Access Inequality (54) is needed to prevent uncommitted nodes from interfering with the direct activation of perfectly coded nodes. We now show that violation of the Direct Access Inequality may force all uncommitted nodes to code a single input pattern, and thus to drastically reduce the coding capacity of F_2.

To see this, suppose that for all v_j in F_2 and all $i \in \mathbf{I}$,

$$z_{ij}(0) > \frac{L}{L-1+|\mathbf{I}|}. \tag{65}$$

Suppose that on the first trial, v_{j_1} is the first F_2 node to be activated by input I. Thus $T_{j_1} > T_j$, where $j \neq j_1$, at the start of the trial. While activation of v_{j_1} persists, T_{j_1} decreases towards the value $D_2 L\,|\mathbf{I}|\,(L-1+|\mathbf{I}|)^{-1}$ due to learning. However, for all $j \neq j_1$,

$$T_j = D_2 \sum_{i \in \mathbf{I}} z_{ij}(0) > \frac{D_2 L\,|\mathbf{I}|}{L-1+|\mathbf{I}|}. \tag{66}$$

By (66), T_{j_1} eventually decreases so much that $T_{j_1} = T_{j_2}$ for some other node v_{j_2} in F_2. Thereafter, T_{j_1} and T_{j_2} both approach $D_2 L\,|\mathbf{I}|\,(L-1+|\mathbf{I}|)^{-1}$ as activation alternates between v_{j_1} and v_{j_2}. Due to inequality (65), all F_2 nodes v_j eventually are activated and their T_j values decrease towards $D_2 L\,|\mathbf{I}|\,(L-1+|\mathbf{I}|)^{-1}$. Thus *all* the F_2 nodes asymptotically learn the same input pattern I. The Direct Access Inequality (54) prevents these anomalies from occurring. It makes precise the idea that the initial values of the bottom-up LTM traces $z_{ij}(0)$ must not be too large.

B. Template Learning Inequality: Initial Top-Down Traces are Large

In contrast, the initial top-down LTM traces $z_{ji}(0)$ must not be too small. The 2/3 Rule implies that if the initial top-down LTM traces $z_{ji}(0)$ were too small, then no uncommitted F_2 node could ever learn any input pattern, since all F_1 activity would be quenched as soon as F_2 became active.

To understand this issue more precisely, suppose that an input I is presented. While F_2 is inactive, $\mathbf{X} = \mathbf{I}$. Suppose that, with or without a search, the uncommitted F_2 node v_J becomes active on that trial. In order for v_J to be able to encode I given an arbitrary value of the vigilance parameter ρ, it is necessary that $\mathbf{X}$ remain equal to I after the template $V^{(J)}$ has been read out; that is,

$$\mathbf{I} \cap \mathbf{V}^{(J)}(0) = \mathbf{I} \quad \text{for any I.} \tag{67}$$

Because I is arbitrary, the 2/3 Rule requires that $\mathbf{V}^{(J)}$ initially be the entire set $\{1, \dots, M\}$. In other words, the initial strengths of all the top-down LTM traces $z_{J1} \dots z_{JM}$ must be greater than the critical LTM strength, denoted by $\bar{z}$, that is required to maintain suprathreshold STM activity in each F_1 node v_i such that $i \in \mathbf{I}$. Equation (49) and the 2/3 Rule then imply that, as long as I persists and v_J remains active, $z_{Ji} \to 1$ for $i \in \mathbf{I}$ and $z_{Ji} \to 0$ for $i \notin \mathbf{I}$. Thus $\mathbf{V}^{(J)}$ contracts from $\{1, \dots, M\}$ to I as the node v_J encodes the pattern I.

It is shown in the Appendix that the following inequalities imply the 2/3 Rule:

2/3 Rule Inequalities

$$\max\{1, D_1\} < B_1 < 1 + D_1; \tag{68}$$

and that the critical top-down LTM strength is

$$\bar{z} \equiv \frac{B_1 - 1}{D_1}. \tag{69}$$

Then the

Template Learning Inequality

$$1 \geq z_{ji}(0) > \bar{z} \tag{70}$$

implies that $\mathbf{V}^{(j)}(0) = \{1 \dots M\}$ for all j, so (67) holds.

C. Activity-Dependent Nonspecific Tuning of Initial LTM Values

Equations (52) and (53) suggest a simple developmental process by which the opposing constraints on $z_{ij}(0)$ and $z_{ji}(0)$ of Sections 17A and 17B can be achieved. Suppose that at a developmental stage prior to the category learning stage, all F_1 and F_2 nodes become endogenously active. Let this activity nonspecifically influence F_1 and F_2 nodes for a sufficiently long time interval to allow their LTM traces to approach their asymptotic values. The presence of noise in the system implies that the initial z_{ij} and z_{ji} values are randomly distributed close to these asymptotic values. At the end of this stage, then,

$$z_{ij}(0) \cong \frac{L}{L - 1 + M} \tag{71}$$

and

$$z_{ji}(0) \cong 1 \tag{72}$$

for all $i = 1 \ldots M$ and $j = M+1 \ldots N$. The bottom-up LTM traces $z_{ij}(0)$ and the top-down LTM traces $z_{ji}(0)$ are then as large as possible, and still satisfy the Direct Access Inequality (54) and the Template Learning Inequality (70). Switching from this early developmental stage to the category learning stage could then be viewed as a switch from an endogenous source of broadly-distributed activity to an exogenous source of patterned activity.

18. Summary of the Model

Below, we summarize the hypotheses that define the model. All subsequent theorems in the article assume that these hypotheses hold.

Binary Input Patterns

$$I_i = \begin{cases} 1 & \text{if } i \in \mathbf{I} \\ 0 & \text{otherwise} \end{cases} \tag{46}$$

Automatic Bottom-Up Activation and 2/3 Rule

$$\mathbf{X} = \begin{cases} \mathbf{I} & \text{if } F_2 \text{ is inactive} \\ \mathbf{I} \cap \mathbf{V}^{(j)} & \text{if the } F_2 \text{ node } v_j \text{ is active} \end{cases} \tag{47}$$

Weber Law Rule and Bottom-Up Associative Decay Rule

$$\frac{d}{dt} z_{ij} = \begin{cases} K[(1 - z_{ij})L - z_{ij}(|\mathbf{X}| - 1)] & \text{if } i \in \mathbf{X} \text{ and } f(x_j) = 1 \\ -K|\mathbf{X}| z_{ij} & \text{if } i \notin \mathbf{X} \text{ and } f(x_j) = 1 \\ 0 & \text{if } f(x_j) = 0 \end{cases} \tag{48}$$

Template Learning Rule and Top-Down Associative Decay Rule

$$\frac{d}{dt} z_{ji} = \begin{cases} -z_{ji} + 1 & \text{if } i \in \mathbf{X} \text{ and } f(x_j) = 1 \\ -z_{ji} & \text{if } i \notin \mathbf{X} \text{ and } f(x_j) = 1 \\ 0 & \text{if } f(x_j) = 0 \end{cases} \tag{49}$$

Reset Rule

An active F_2 node v_j is reset if

$$\frac{|\mathbf{I} \cap \mathbf{V}^{(j)}|}{|\mathbf{I}|} < \rho \equiv \frac{P}{Q}. \tag{73}$$

Once a node is reset, it remains inactive for the duration of the trial.

F_2 Choice and Search

If $\mathbf{J}$ is the index set of F_2 nodes which have not yet been reset on the present learning trial, then

$$f(x_j) = \begin{cases} 1 & \text{if } T_j = \max\{T_k : k \in \mathbf{J}\} \\ 0 & \text{otherwise} \end{cases} \tag{24}$$

where

$$T_j = D_2 \sum_{i \in \mathbf{X}} z_{ij}. \tag{74}$$

In addition, all STM activities x_i and x_j are reset to zero after each learning trial. The initial bottom-up LTM traces $z_{ij}(0)$ are chosen to satisfy the

Direct Access Inequality

$$0 < z_{ij}(0) < \frac{L}{L-1+M}. \tag{54}$$

The initial top-down LTM traces are chosen to satisfy the

Template Learning Inequality

$$1 \geq z_{ji}(0) > \overline{z} \equiv \frac{B_1 - 1}{D_1}. \tag{75}$$

Fast Learning

It is assumed that fast learning occurs so that, when v_j in F_2 is active, all LTM traces approach the asymptotes,

$$z_{ij} \cong \begin{cases} \frac{L}{L-1+|\mathbf{X}|} & \text{if } i \in \mathbf{X} \\ 0 & \text{if } i \in \mathbf{X} \end{cases} \tag{52}$$

and

$$z_{ji} \cong \begin{cases} 1 & \text{if } i \in \mathbf{X} \\ 0 & \text{if } i \notin \mathbf{X} \end{cases} \tag{53}$$

on each learning trial. A complete listing of parameter constraints is provided in Table 1 of the Appendix.

19. Order of Search and Stable Choices in Short-Term Memory

We will now analyze further properties of the class of ART systems which satisfy the hypotheses in Section 18. We will begin by characterizing the order of search. This analysis provides a basis for proving that learning self-stabilizes and leads to recognition by direct access.

This discussion of search order does not analyse where the search ends. Other things being equal, a network with a higher level of vigilance will require better F_1 matches, and hence will search more deeply, in response to each input pattern. The set of learned filters and templates thus depends upon the prior levels of vigilance, and the same ordering of input patterns may generate different LTM encodings due to the settings of the nonspecific vigilance parameter. The present discussion considers the order in which search will occur in response to a single input pattern which is presented after an arbitrary set of prior inputs has been asymptotically learned.

We will prove that the values of the F_2 input functions T_j at the start of each trial determine the order in which F_2 nodes are searched, assuming that no F_2 nodes are active before the trial begins. To distinguish these initial T_j values from subsequent T_j values, let O_j denote the value of T_j at the start of a trial. We will show that, if these values are ordered by decreasing size, as in

$$O_{j_1} > O_{j_2} > O_{j_3} > \dots, \tag{76}$$

then F_2 nodes are searched in the order $v_{j_1}, v_{j_2}, v_{j_3}, \ldots$ on that trial. To prove this result, we first derive a formula for O_j.

When an input I is first presented on a trial,

$$O_j = D_2 \sum_{i \in I} z_{ij}, \tag{77}$$

where the z_{ij}'s are evaluated at the start of the trial. By the Associative Decay Rule, z_{ij} in (77) is positive only if $i \in \mathbf{V}^{(j)}$, where $\mathbf{V}^{(j)}$ is also evaluated at the start of the trial. Thus by (77),

$$O_j = D_2 \sum_{i \in I \cap \mathbf{V}^{(j)}} z_{ij}. \tag{78}$$

If the LTM traces z_{ij} have undergone learning on a previous trial, then (52) implies

$$z_{ij} = \frac{L}{L - 1 + |\mathbf{V}^{(j)}|} \tag{79}$$

for all $i \in \mathbf{V}^{(j)}$. If v_j is an uncommitted node, then the Template Learning Inequality implies that $I \cap \mathbf{V}^{(j)} = I$. Combining these facts leads to the following formula for O_j.

Order Function

$$O_j = \begin{cases} \dfrac{D_2 L \, |I \cap \mathbf{V}^{(j)}|}{L - 1 + |\mathbf{V}^{(j)}|} & \text{if } v_j \text{ has been chosen on a previous trial} \\ D_2 \sum_{i \in I} z_{ij}(0) & \text{if } v_j \text{ is an uncommitted node.} \end{cases} \tag{80}$$

In response to input pattern I, (76) implies that node v_{j_1} is initially chosen by F_2. After v_{j_1} is chosen, it reads-out template $V^{(j_1)}$ to F_1. When $V^{(j_1)}$ and I both perturb F_1, a new activity pattern X is registered at F_1, as in Figure 4b. By the 2/3 Rule, $\mathbf{X} = \mathbf{I} \cap \mathbf{V}^{(j_1)}$. Consequently, a new bottom-up signal pattern from F_1 to F_2 will then be registered at F_2. How can we be sure that v_{j_1} will continue to receive the largest input from F_1 after its template is processed by F_1? In other words, does read-out of the top-down template $V^{(j_1)}$ confirm the choice due to the ordering of bottom-up signals O_j in (76)? Theorem 2 provides this guarantee. Then Theorem 3 shows that the ordering of initial T_j values determines the order of search on each trial despite the fact that the T_j values can fluctuate dramatically as different F_2 nodes get activated.

Theorem 2 (Stable Choices in STM)

Assume the model hypotheses of Section 18. Suppose that an F_2 node v_J is chosen for STM storage instead of another node v_j because $O_J > O_j$. Then read-out of the top-down template $V^{(J)}$ preserves the inequality $T_J > T_j$ and thus confirms the choice of v_J by the bottom-up filter.

Proof: Suppose that a node v_J is activated due to the input pattern I, and that v_J is not an uncommitted node. When v_J reads out the template $V^{(J)}$ to F_1, $\mathbf{X} = \mathbf{I} \cap \mathbf{V}^{(J)}$ by the 2/3 Rule. Then

$$T_j = D_2 \sum_{i \in I \cap \mathbf{V}^{(J)}} z_{ij}. \tag{81}$$

Since $z_{ij} > 0$ only if $i \in \mathbf{V}^{(j)}$,

$$T_j = D_2 \sum_{i \in \mathbf{I} \cap \mathbf{V}^{(J)} \cap \mathbf{V}^{(j)}} z_{ij}. \tag{82}$$

By (79), if T_j is not an uncommitted node,

$$T_j = \frac{D_2 L \mid \mathbf{I} \cap \mathbf{V}^{(J)} \cap \mathbf{V}^{(j)} \mid}{L - 1 + \mid \mathbf{V}^{(j)} \mid}. \tag{83}$$

By (80) and (83),

$$T_j \leq O_j. \tag{84}$$

Similarly, if v_j is an uncommitted node, the sum T_j in (82) is less than or equal to the sum O_j in (80). Thus read-out of template $V^{(J)}$ can only cause the bottom-up signals T_j, other than T_J, to decrease. Signal T_J, on the other hand, remains unchanged after read-out of $V^{(J)}$. This can be seen by replacing $V^{(j)}$ in (83) by $V^{(J)}$. Then

$$T_J = \frac{D_2 L \mid \mathbf{I} \cap \mathbf{V}^{(J)} \mid}{L - 1 + \mid \mathbf{V}^{(J)} \mid}. \tag{85}$$

Hence, after $V^{(J)}$ is read-out

$$T_J = O_J. \tag{86}$$

Combining (84) and (86) shows that inequality $T_J > T_j$ continues to hold after $V^{(J)}$ is read-out, thereby proving that top-down template read-out confirms the F_2 choice of the bottom-up filter.

The same is true if v_J is an uncommitted node. Here, the Template Learning Inequality shows that $\mathbf{X} = \mathbf{I}$ even after $v^{(J)}$ is read-out. Thus *all* bottom-up signals T_j remain unchanged after template read-out in this case. This completes the proof of Theorem 2.

Were the 2/3 Rule not operative, read-out of the template $V^{(j_1)}$ might activate many F_1 nodes that had not previously been activated by the input I alone. For example, a top-down template could, in principle, activate all the nodes of F_1, thereby preventing the input pattern, as a pattern, from being coded. Alternatively, disjoint input patterns could be coded by a single node, despite the fact that these two patterns do not share any features. The 2/3 Rule prevents such coding anomalies from occurring.

Theorem 3 (Initial Filter Values Determine Search Order)

The Order Function O_j determines the order of search no matter how many times F_2 is reset during a trial.

Proof: Since $O_{j_1} > O_{j_2} > \ldots$, node v_{j_1} is the first node to be activated on a given trial. After template $V^{(j_1)}$ is read-out, Theorem 2 implies that

$$T_{j_1} = O_{j_1} > \max \{O_j : j \neq j_1\} \geq \max\{T_j : j \neq j_1\}, \tag{87}$$

even though the full ordering of the T_j's may be different from that defined by the O_j's. If v_{j_1} is reset by the orienting subsystem, then template $V^{(j_1)}$ is shut off for the remainder of the trial and subsequent values of T_{j_1} do not influence which F_2 nodes will be chosen.

As soon as v_{j_1} and $V^{(j_1)}$ are shut off, $T_j = O_j$ for all $j \neq j_1$. Since $O_{j_2} > O_{j_3} > \ldots$, node v_{j_2} is chosen next and template $V^{(j_2)}$ is read-out. Theorem 2 implies that

$$T_{j_2} = O_{j_2} > \max\{O_j : j \neq j_1, j_2\} \geq \max\{T_j : j \neq j_1, j_2\}. \tag{88}$$

Thus $V^{(j_2)}$ confirms the F_2 choice due to O_{j_2} even though the ordering of T_j values may differ both from the ordering of O_j values and from the ordering of T_j values when $V^{(j_1)}$ was active.

This argument can now be iterated to show that the values $O_{j_1} > O_{j_2} > \ldots$ of the Order Function determine the order of search. This completes the proof of Theorem 3.

20. Stable Category Learning

Theorems 2 and 3 describe choice and search properties which occur on such a fast time scale that no new learning can occur. We now analyse properties of learning throughout an entire trial, and use these properties to show that code learning self-stabilizes across trials in response to an arbitrary list of binary input patterns. In Theorem 2, we proved that read-out of a top-down template confirms the F_2 choice made by the bottom-up filter. In Theorem 4, we will prove that learning also confirms the F_2 choice and does not trigger reset by the orienting subsystem. In addition, learning on a single trial causes monotonic changes in the LTM traces.

Theorem 4 (Learning on a Single Trial)

Assume the model hypotheses of Section 18. Suppose that an F_2 node v_J is chosen for STM storage and that read-out of the template $V^{(J)}$ does not immediately lead to reset of node v_J by the orienting subsystem. Then the LTM traces z_{iJ} and z_{Ji} change monotonically in such a way that T_J increases and all other T_j remain constant, thereby confirming the choice of v_J by the adaptive filter. In addition, the set $\mathbf{I} \cap \mathbf{V}^{(J)}$ remains constant during learning, so that learning does not trigger reset of v_J by the orienting subsystem.

Proof: We first show that the LTM traces $z_{Ji}(t)$ can only change monotonically and that the set $\mathbf{X}(t)$ does not change as long as v_J remains active. These conclusions follow from the learning rules for the top-down LTM traces z_{Ji}. Using these facts, we then show that the $z_{iJ}(t)$ change monotonically, that $T_J(t)$ can only increase, and that all other $T_j(t)$ must be constant while v_J remains active. These conclusions follow from the learning rules for the bottom-up LTM traces z_{iJ}. Together, these properties imply that learning confirms the choice of v_J and does not trigger reset of v_J by the orienting subsystem.

Suppose that read-out of $V^{(J)}$ is first registered by F_1 at time $t = t_0$. By the 2/3 Rule, $\mathbf{X}(t_0) = \mathbf{I} \cap \mathbf{V}^{(J)}(t_0)$. By (49), $z_{Ji}(t)$ begins to increase towards 1 if $i \in \mathbf{X}(t_0)$, and begins to decrease towards 0 if $i \notin \mathbf{X}(t_0)$. The Appendix shows that when v_J is active at F_2, each activity x_i in F_2 obeys the equation

$$\epsilon \frac{dx_i}{dt} = -x_i + (1 - A_1 x_i)(I_i + D_1 z_{Ji}) - (B_1 + C_1 x_i). \tag{89}$$

By (89), $x_i(t)$ increases if $z_{Ji}(t)$ increases, and $x_i(t)$ decreases if $z_{Ji}(t)$ decreases. Activities x_i which start out positive hereby become even larger, whereas activities x_i which start out non-positive become even smaller. In particular, $\mathbf{X}(t) = \mathbf{X}(t_0) = \mathbf{I} \cap \mathbf{V}^{(J)}(t_0)$ for all times $t \geq t_0$ at which v_J remains active.

We next prove that $T_J(t)$ increases, whereas all other $T_j(t)$ remain constant, while v_J is active. We suppose first that v_J is not an uncommitted node before considering the case in which v_J is an uncommitted node. While v_J remains active, the set $\mathbf{X}(t) = \mathbf{I} \cap \mathbf{V}^{(J)}(t_0)$. Thus

$$T_J(t) = D_2 \sum_{i \in \mathbf{I} \cap \mathbf{V}^{(J)}(t_0)} z_{iJ}(t). \tag{90}$$

At time $t = t_0$, each LTM trace in (90) satisfies

$$z_{iJ}(t_0) \cong \frac{L}{L - 1 + |\mathbf{V}^{(J)}(t_0)|} \tag{91}$$

due to (79). While v_J remains active, each of these LTM traces responds to the fact that $\mathbf{X}(t) = \mathbf{I} \cap \mathbf{V}^{(J)}(t_0)$. By (47) and (52), each $z_{iJ}(t)$ with $i \in \mathbf{I} \cap \mathbf{V}^{(J)}(t_0)$ increases towards

$$\frac{L}{L - 1 + |\mathbf{I} \cap \mathbf{V}^{(J)}(t_0)|}, \tag{92}$$

each $z_{iJ}(t)$ with $i \notin \mathbf{I} \cap \mathbf{V}^{(J)}(t_0)$ decreases towards 0, and all other bottom-up LTM traces $z_{ij}(t)$ remain constant. A comparison of (91) with (92) shows that $T_J(t)$ in (90) can only increase while v_J remains active. In contrast, all other $T_j(t)$ are constant while v_J remains active.

If v_J is an uncommitted node, then no LTM trace $z_{iJ}(t)$ changes before time $t = t_0$. Thus

$$z_{iJ}(t_0) = z_{iJ}(0), \quad i = 1, 2, \dots, M. \tag{93}$$

By the Template Learning Inequality (75), $\mathbf{I} \cap \mathbf{V}^{(J)}(t_0) = \mathbf{I}$, so that (90) can be written as

$$T_J(t) = D_2 \sum_{i \in \mathbf{I}} z_{iJ}(t). \tag{94}$$

By (93) and the Direct Access Inequality (54),

$$z_{iJ}(t_0) < \frac{L}{L - 1 + M}, \quad i = 1, 2, \dots, M. \tag{95}$$

While v_J remains active, $\mathbf{X}(t) = \mathbf{I} \cap \mathbf{V}^{(J)}(t_0) = \mathbf{I}$, so that each $z_{iJ}(t)$ in (94) approaches the value

$$\frac{L}{L - 1 + |\mathbf{I}|}. \tag{96}$$

Since $|\mathbf{I}| \leq M$ for any input pattern $\mathbf{I}$, a comparison of (95) and (96) shows that each $z_{iJ}(t)$ with $i \in \mathbf{I}$ increases while v_J remains active. In contrast, each $z_{iJ}(t)$ with $i \notin \mathbf{I}$ decreases towards zero and all other $z_{ij}(t)$ remain constant. Consequently, by (94), $T_J(t)$ increases and all other $T_j(t)$ are constant while v_J remains active. Thus learning confirms the choice of v_J. Hence the set $\mathbf{X}(t)$ remains constant and equal to $\mathbf{I} \cap \mathbf{V}^{(J)}(t_0)$ while learning proceeds.

This last fact, along with the hypothesis that read-out of $V^{(J)}$ does not immediately cause reset of v_J, implies that learning cannot trigger reset of v_J. By the Reset Rule (73), the hypothesis that read-out of $V^{(J)}$ does not immediately cause reset of v_J implies that

$$| \mathbf{I} \cap \mathbf{V}^{(J)}(t_0) | = | \mathbf{X}(t_0) | \geq \rho | \mathbf{I} | . \tag{97}$$

The fact that $\mathbf{X}(t)$ does not change while v_J remains active implies that

$$| \mathbf{X}(t) | = | \mathbf{X}(t_0) | \geq \rho | \mathbf{I} | \tag{98}$$

and hence that learning does not trigger reset of v_J. Thus v_J remains active and learning in its LTM traces $z_{iJ}(t)$ and $z_{Ji}(t)$ can continue until the trial is ended. This completes the proof of Theorem 4.

Theorems 2-4 immediately imply the following important corollary, which illustrates how 2/3 Rule matching, the learning laws, and the Reset Rule work together to prevent spurious reset events.

Corollary 1 (Reset by Mismatch)

An active F_2 node v_J can be reset only by the orienting subsystem. Reset occurs when the template $V^{(J)}$ causes an F_1 mismatch such that

$$| \mathbf{I} \cap \mathbf{V}^{(J)} | < \rho | \mathbf{I} | . \tag{99}$$

Reset cannot be caused within the attentional subsystem due to reordering of adaptive filter signals T_j by template read-out or due to learning.

Theorem 4 implies another important corollary which characterizes how a template changes due to learning on a given trial.

Corollary 2 (Subset Recoding)

If an F_2 node v_J is activated due to an input I and if read-out of $V^{(J)}$ at time $t = t_0$ implies that

$$| \mathbf{I} \cap \mathbf{V}^{(J)}(t_0) | \geq \rho | \mathbf{I} | , \tag{100}$$

then v_J remains active until I shuts off, and the template set $\mathbf{V}^{(J)}(t)$ contracts from $\mathbf{V}^{(J)}(t_0)$ to $\mathbf{I} \cap \mathbf{V}^{(J)}(t_0)$.

With these results in hand, we can now prove that the learning process self-stabilizes in response to an arbitrary list of binary input patterns.

Theorem 5 (Stable Category Learning)

Assume the model hypotheses of Section 18. Then in response to an arbitrary list of binary input patterns, all LTM traces $z_{ij}(t)$ and $z_{ji}(t)$ approach limits after a finite number of learning trials. Each template set $\mathbf{V}^{(j)}$ remains constant except for at most $M-1$ times $t_1^{(j)} < t_2^{(j)} < \ldots < t_{r_j}^{(j)}$ at which it progressively loses elements, leading to the

Subset Recoding Property

$$\mathbf{V}^{(j)}(t_1^{(j)}) \supset \mathbf{V}^{(j)}(t_2^{(j)}) \supset \ldots \supset \mathbf{V}^{(j)}(t_{r_j}^{(j)}). \tag{101}$$

All LTM traces oscillate at most once due to learning. The LTM traces $z_{ij}(t)$ and $z_{ji}(t)$ such that $i \notin \mathbf{V}^{(j)}(t_1^{(j)})$ decrease monotonically to zero. The LTM traces $z_{ij}(t)$ and $z_{ji}(t)$ such that $i \in \mathbf{V}^{(j)}(t_{r_j}^{(j)})$ are monotone increasing functions. The LTM traces $z_{ij}(t)$ and $z_{ji}(t)$ such that $i \in \mathbf{V}^{(j)}(t_k^{(j)})$ but $i \notin \mathbf{V}^{(j)}(t_{k+1}^{(j)})$ can increase at times $t \le t_{k+1}^{(j)}$ but can only decrease towards zero at times $t > t_{k+1}^{(j)}$.

Proof:

Suppose that an input pattern I is presented on a given trial and the Order Function satisfies

$$O_{j_1} > O_{j_2} > O_{j_3} > \ldots. \tag{76}$$

Then no learning occurs while F_2 nodes are searched in the order $v_{j_1}, v_{j_2}, \ldots$, by Theorem 3. If all F_2 nodes are reset by the search, then no learning occurs on that trial. If a node exists such that

$$|\mathbf{I} \cap \mathbf{V}^{(j)}| \ge \rho\,|\mathbf{I}|, \tag{102}$$

then search terminates at the first such node, v_{j_k}. Only the LTM traces z_{ij_k} and $z_{j_k i}$ can undergo learning on that trial, by Theorem 4. In particular, if an uncommitted node v_{j_k} is reached by the search, then the Template Learning Inequality implies

$$|\mathbf{I} \cap \mathbf{V}^{(j_k)}| = |\mathbf{I} \cap \mathbf{V}^{(j_k)}(0)| = |\mathbf{I}| \ge \rho\,|\mathbf{I}| \tag{103}$$

so that its LTM traces undergo learning on that trial. In summary, learning on a given trial can change only the LTM traces of the F_2 node v_{j_k} at which the search ends.

Corollary 2 shows that the template set $\mathbf{V}^{(j_k)}$ of the node v_{j_k} is either constant or contracts due to learning. A contraction can occur on only a finite number of trials, because there are only finitely many nodes in F_1. In addition, there are only finitely many nodes in F_2, hence only finitely many template sets $\mathbf{V}^{(j)}$ can contract. The Subset Recoding Property is hereby proved.

The monotonicity properties of the LTM traces follow from the Subset Recoding Property and Theorem 4. Suppose for definiteness that the search on a given trial terminates at a node v_J in response to an input pattern I. Suppose moreover that the template set $\mathbf{V}^{(J)}(t)$ contracts from $\mathbf{V}^{(J)}(t_k^{(J)})$ to $\mathbf{V}^{(J)}(t_{k+1}^{(J)}) = \mathbf{I} \cap \mathbf{V}^{(J)}(t_k^{(J)})$ due to read-out of the template $V^{(J)}(t_k^{(J)})$ on that trial. A comparison of (91) and (92) shows that each $z_{iJ}(t)$ with $i \in \mathbf{V}^{(J)}(t_{k+1}^{(J)})$ increases from

$$\frac{L}{L - 1 + |\mathbf{V}^{(J)}(t_k^{(J)})|} \tag{104}$$

to

$$\frac{L}{L - 1 + |\mathbf{V}^{(J)}(t_{k+1}^{(J)})|}, \tag{105}$$

that each $z_{iJ}(t)$ with $i \notin \mathbf{V}^{(J)}(t_{k+1}^{(J)})$ decreases towards zero, and that all other bottom-up LTM traces $z_{ij}(t)$ remain constant. In a similar fashion, each $z_{Ji}(t)$ with

$i \in \mathbf{V}^{(J)}(t^{(J)}_{k+1})$ remains approximately equal to one, each $z_{Ji}(t)$ with $i \notin \mathbf{V}^{(J)}(t^{(J)}_{k+1})$ decreases towards zero, and all other top-down LTM traces $z_{ji}(t)$ remain constant.

Due to the Subset Recoding Property (101),

$$| \mathbf{V}^{(J)}(t^{(J)}_1) | > | \mathbf{V}^{(J)}(t^{(J)}_2) | > \ldots > | \mathbf{V}^{(J)}(t^{(J)}_{r_J}) |. \tag{106}$$

Thus each LTM trace $z_{iJ}(t)$ with $i \in \mathbf{V}^{(J)}(t^{(J)}_{r_J})$ increases monotonically, as from (104) to (105), on the r_J trials where search ends at v_J and the template set $\mathbf{V}^{(J)}(t)$ contracts. On all other trials, these LTM traces remain constant. The other monotonicity properties are now also easily proved by combining the Subset Recoding Property (101) with the learning properties on a single trial. In particular, by the Subset Recoding Property, no LTM traces change after time

$$t = \max \{t^{(j)}_{r_j} : j = M+1, M+2, \ldots, N\}. \tag{107}$$

Thus all LTM traces approach their limits after a finite number of learning trials. This completes the proof of Theorem 5.

21. Critical Feature Patterns and Prototypes

The property of stable category learning can be intuitively summarized using the following definitions.

The *critical feature pattern* at time t of a node v_j is the template $V^{(j)}(t)$. Theorem 5 shows that the critical feature pattern of each node v_j is progressively refined as the learning process discovers the set of features that can match all the input patterns which v_j codes. Theorem 5 also says that the network discovers a set of *self-stabilizing* critical feature patterns as learning proceeds. At any stage of learning, the set of all critical feature patterns determines the order in which previously coded nodes will be activated, via the Order Function

$$O_j = \frac{D_2 L \, | \, \mathbf{I} \cap \mathbf{V}^{(j)} \, |}{L - 1 + | \, \mathbf{V}^{(j)} \, |}. \tag{108}$$

The *Reset Function*

$$R_j = \frac{| \, \mathbf{I} \cap \mathbf{V}^{(j)} \, |}{| \, \mathbf{I} \, |} \tag{109}$$

determines how many of these nodes will actually be searched, and thus which node may be recoded on each trial. In particular, an unfamiliar input pattern which has never before been experienced by the network will directly access a node v_{j_1} if the

Direct Access Conditions

$$O_{j_1} > \max(O_j : j \neq j_1) \quad \text{and} \quad R_{j_1} \geq \rho. \tag{110}$$

are satisfied.

An important example of direct access occurs when the input pattern I^* satisfies $\mathbf{I}^* = \mathbf{V}^{(j)}$, for some $j = M+1, M+2, \ldots, N$. Such an input pattern is called a *prototype*. Due to the Subset Recoding Property (101), at any given time a prototype pattern includes all the features common to the input patterns which have previously been coded by node v_j. Such a prototype pattern may never have been experienced itself. When an unfamiliar prototype pattern is presented for the first time, it will directly access its category v_j and is thus recognized. This property follows from Theorem 1, since v_j has perfectly learned I^*. Moreover, because $\mathbf{I}^* = \mathbf{V}^{(j)}$, a prototype is optimally matched by read-out of the template $V^{(j)}$.

A prototype generates an optimal match in the bottom-up filter, in the top-down template, and at F_1, even though it is unfamiliar. This is also true in human recognition data (Posner, 1973; Posner and Keele, 1968, 1970). Theorem 5 thus implies that an ART system can discover, learn, and recognize stable prototypes of an arbitrary list of input patterns. An ART system also supports direct access by unfamiliar input patterns which are not prototypes, but which share invariant properties with learned prototypes, in the sense that they satisfy the Direct Access Conditions.

22. Direct Access after Learning Self-Stabilizes

We can now prove that all patterns directly access their categories after the recognition learning process self-stablizes. In order to discuss this property precisely, we define three types of learned templates with respect to an input pattern I: subset templates, superset templates, and mixed templates. The LTM traces of a subset template V satisfy $\mathbf{V} \subseteq \mathbf{I}$: they are large only at a subset of the F_1 nodes which are activated by the input pattern I (Figure 11a). The LTM traces of a superset template V satisfy $\mathbf{V} \supset \mathbf{I}$: they are large at all the F_1 nodes which are activated by the input pattern I, as well as at some F_1 nodes which are not activated by I (Figure 11b). The LTM traces of a mixed template V are large at some, but not all, the F_1 nodes which are activated by the input pattern I, as well as at some F_1 nodes which are not activated by I: the set $\mathbf{I}$ is neither a subset nor a superset of $\mathbf{V}$ (Figure 11c).

Theorem 6 (Direct Access After Learning Self-Stabilizes)

Assume the model hypotheses of Section 18. After recognition learning has self-stabilized in response to an arbitrary list of binary input patterns, each input pattern I either has direct access to the node v_j which possesses the largest subset template with respect to I, or I cannot be coded by any node of F_2. In the latter case, F_2 contains no uncommitted nodes.

Remark: The possibility that an input pattern cannot be coded by any node of F_2 is a consequence of the fact that an ART network self-stabilizes its learning in response to a list containing arbitrarily many input patterns no matter how many coding nodes exist in F_2. If a list contains many input patterns and F_2 contains only a few nodes, one does not expect F_2 to code all the inputs if the vigilance parameter ρ is close to 1.

Proof:

Since learning has already stabilized, I can be coded only by a node v_j whose template $V^{(j)}$ is a subset template with respect to I. Otherwise, after template $V^{(j)} = V$ was read-out, the set $\mathbf{V}^{(j)}$ would contract from $\mathbf{V}$ to $\mathbf{I} \cap \mathbf{V}$ by Corollary 2 (Section 20), thereby contradicting the hypothesis that learning has already stabilized. In particular, input I cannot be coded by a node whose template is a superset template or a mixed template with respect to I. Nor can I be coded by an uncommitted node.

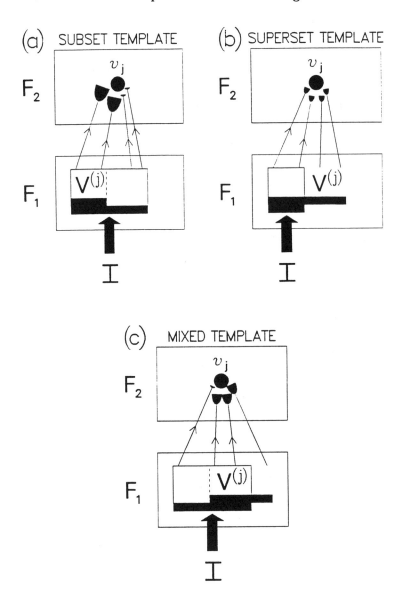

Figure 11. Subset, superset, and mixed templates $V^{(j)}$ with respect to an input pattern I: In (a), (b), and (c), the lower black bar designates the set of F_1 nodes that receive positive bottom-up inputs due to I. The upper black bar designates the set of F_1 nodes that receive positive top-down inputs due to the template $V^{(j)}$. (a) denotes a subset template $V^{(j)}$ with respect to I. (b) denotes a superset template $V^{(j)}$ with respect to I. (c) denotes a mixed template $V^{(j)}$ with respect to I. When node v_j in F_2 is not an uncommitted node, the top-down LTM traces in the template $V^{(j)}$ are large if and only if the LTM traces in the corresponding bottom-up pathways are large (Section 15). The absolute bottom-up LTM trace size depends inversely upon the size $|\mathbf{V}^{(j)}|$ of $V^{(j)}$, due to the Weber Law Rule (Section 14). Larger LTM traces are drawn as larger endings on the bottom-up pathways. The arrow heads denote the pathways that are activated by I before any top-down template influences F_1.

Thus if I activates any node other than one with a subset template, that node must be reset by the orienting subsystem.

For the remainder of the proof, let v_J be the first F_2 node activated by I. We show that if $V^{(J)}$ is a subset template, then it is the subset template with the largest index set; and that if the orienting subsystem resets v_J, then it also resets all nodes with subset templates which get activated on that trial. Thus either the node with maximal subset template is directly accessed, or all nodes in F_2 that are activated by I are quickly reset by the orienting subsystem because learning has already self-stabilized.

If v_j is any node with a subset template $V^{(j)}$ with respect to I, then the Order Function

$$O_j = \frac{D_2 L \mid V^{(j)} \mid}{L - 1 + \mid V^{(j)} \mid},$$ (111)

by (108). Function O_j in (111) is an increasing function of $\mid V^{(j)} \mid$. Thus if the first chosen node v_J has a subset template, then $V^{(J)}$ is the subset template with the largest index set.

If v_j is any node with a subset template $V^{(j)}$ with respect to I, then the Reset Function

$$R_j = \frac{\mid \mathbf{I} \cap \mathbf{V}^{(j)} \mid}{\mid \mathbf{I} \mid} = \frac{\mid \mathbf{V}^{(j)} \mid}{\mid \mathbf{I} \mid},$$ (112)

by (109). Once activated, such a node v_j will be reset if

$$R_j < \rho.$$ (113)

Thus if the node with the largest index set $\mathbf{V}^{(j)}$ is reset, (112) and (113) imply that all other nodes with subset templates will be reset.

Finally, suppose that v_J, the first node activated, does not have a subset template, but that some node v_j with a subset template is activated in the course of search. We need to show that $\mid \mathbf{I} \cap \mathbf{V}^{(j)} \mid = \mid \mathbf{V}^{(j)} \mid < \rho \mid \mathbf{I} \mid$, so that v_j is reset. Since v_j has a subset template,

$$O_j = \frac{D_2 L \mid \mathbf{V}^{(j)} \mid}{L - 1 + \mid \mathbf{V}^{(j)} \mid}.$$ (111)

Since $\mid \mathbf{I} \cap \mathbf{V}^{(J)} \mid \leq \mid \mathbf{V}^{(J)} \mid$,

$$O_J = \frac{D_2 L \mid \mathbf{I} \cap \mathbf{V}^{(J)} \mid}{L - 1 + \mid \mathbf{V}^{(J)} \mid} \leq \frac{D_2 L \mid \mathbf{V}^{(J)} \mid}{L - 1 + \mid \mathbf{V}^{(J)} \mid}.$$ (114)

Since v_J was chosen first, $O_J > O_j$. Comparison of (111) and (114) thus implies that $\mid \mathbf{V}^{(J)} \mid > \mid \mathbf{V}^{(j)} \mid$. Using the properties $O_j < O_J, \mid \mathbf{I} \cap \mathbf{V}^{(J)} \mid < \rho \mid \mathbf{I} \mid$, and $\mid \mathbf{V}^{(J)} \mid > \mid \mathbf{V}^{(j)} \mid$ in turn, we find

$$\frac{\mid \mathbf{V}^{(j)} \mid}{L - 1 + \mid \mathbf{V}^{(j)} \mid} < \frac{\mid \mathbf{I} \cap \mathbf{V}^{(J)} \mid}{L - 1 + \mid \mathbf{V}^{(J)} \mid} < \frac{\rho \mid \mathbf{I} \mid}{L - 1 + \mid \mathbf{V}^{(J)} \mid} < \frac{\rho \mid \mathbf{I} \mid}{L - 1 + \mid \mathbf{V}^{(j)} \mid},$$ (115)

which implies that

$$\mid \mathbf{I} \cap \mathbf{V}^{(j)} \mid = \mid \mathbf{V}^{(j)} \mid < \rho \mid \mathbf{I} \mid.$$ (116)

Therefore all F_2 nodes are reset if v_J is reset. This completes the proof of Theorem 6.

Theorem 6 shows that, in response to any familiar input pattern I, the network knows how to directly access the node v_j whose template $V^{(j)}$ corresponds to the prototype $I^* = V^{(j)}$ which is closest to I among all prototypes learned by the network. Because direct access obviates the need for search, recognition of familiar input patterns and of unfamiliar patterns that share categorical invariants with familiar patterns is very rapid no matter how large or complex the learned recognition code may have become. Grossberg and Stone (1986a) have, moreover, shown that the variations in reaction times and error rates which occur during direct access due to prior priming events are consistent with data collected from human subjects in lexical decision experiments and word familiarity and recall experiments.

Theorems 5 and 6 do not specify how many list presentations and F_2 nodes are needed to learn and recognize an arbitrary list through direct access. We make the following conjecture: in the fast learning case, if F_2 has at least n nodes, then each member of a list of n input patterns which is presented cyclically will have direct access to an F_2 node after at most n list presentations.

Given arbitrary lists of input patterns, this is the best possible result. If the vigilance parameter ρ is close to 1 and if a nested set of n binary patterns is presented in order of decreasing size, then exactly n list presentations are required for the final code to be learned. On the other hand, if a nested set of n patterns is presented in order of increasing size, then only one list presentation is required for the final code to be learned. Thus the number of trials needed to stabilize learning in the fast learning case depends upon both the ordering and the internal structure of the input patterns, as well as upon the vigilance level.

23. Order of Search: Mathematical Analysis

The Order Function

$$O_j = \frac{D_2 L \mid \mathbf{I} \cap \mathbf{V}^{(j)} \mid}{L - 1 + \mid \mathbf{V}^{(j)} \mid} \tag{108}$$

for previously coded nodes v_j shows that search order is determined by two opposing tendencies. A node v_j will be searched early if $\mid \mathbf{I} \cap \mathbf{V}^{(j)} \mid$ is large and if $\mid \mathbf{V}^{(j)} \mid$ is small. Term $\mid \mathbf{I} \cap \mathbf{V}^{(j)} \mid$ is maximized if $V^{(j)}$ is a superset template of I. Term $\mid \mathbf{V}^{(j)} \mid$ is small if $V^{(j)}$ codes only a few features. The relative importance of the template intersection $\mid \mathbf{I} \cap \mathbf{V}^{(j)} \mid$ and the template size $\mid \mathbf{V}^{(j)} \mid$ is determined by the size of $L - 1$ in (108). If $L - 1$ is small, both factors are important. If $L - 1$ is large, the template intersection term dominates search order. The next theorem completely characterizes the search order in the case that $L - 1$ is small.

Theorem 7 (Search Order)

Assume the model hypotheses of Section 18. Suppose that input pattern I satisfies

$$L - 1 \leq \frac{1}{\mid \mathbf{I} \mid} \tag{117}$$

and

$$\mid \mathbf{I} \mid \leq M - 1. \tag{118}$$

Then F_2 nodes are searched in the following order, if they are reached at all.

Subset templates with respect to I are searched first, in order of decreasing size. If the largest subset template is reset, then all subset templates are reset. If all subset templates have been reset and if no other learned templates exist, then the first uncommitted node to be activated will code I. If all subset templates are searched and if there exist learned superset templates but no mixed templates, then the node with the smallest superset template will be activated next and will code I. If all subset templates are searched and if both superset templates $V^{(J)}$ and mixed templates $V^{(j)}$ exist, then v_j will be searched before v_J if and only if

$$| \mathbf{V}^{(j)} | < | \mathbf{V}^{(J)} | \quad \text{and} \quad \frac{|\mathbf{I}|}{|\mathbf{V}^{(J)}|} < \frac{|\mathbf{I} \cap \mathbf{V}^{(j)}|}{|\mathbf{V}^{(j)}|}. \tag{119}$$

If all subset templates are searched and if there exist mixed templates but no superset templates, then a node v_j with a mixed template will be searched before an uncommitted node v_J if and only if

$$\frac{L\,|\mathbf{I} \cap \mathbf{V}^{(j)}|}{L - 1 + |\mathbf{V}^{(j)}|} > \sum_{i \in \mathbf{I}} z_{iJ}(0). \tag{120}$$

The proof is based upon the following lemma.

Lemma 1: If (117) holds, then for any pair of F_2 nodes v_J and v_j with learned templates, $O_J > O_j$ if either

$$\frac{|\mathbf{I} \cap \mathbf{V}^{(J)}|}{|\mathbf{V}^{(J)}|} > \frac{|\mathbf{I} \cap \mathbf{V}^{(j)}|}{|\mathbf{V}^{(j)}|} \tag{121}$$

or

$$\frac{|\mathbf{I} \cap \mathbf{V}^{(J)}|}{|\mathbf{V}^{(J)}|} = \frac{|\mathbf{I} \cap \mathbf{V}^{(j)}|}{|\mathbf{V}^{(j)}|} \quad \text{and} \quad |\mathbf{V}^{(J)}| > |\mathbf{V}^{(j)}|. \tag{122}$$

Proof of Lemma 1: We need to show that if either (121) or (122) holds, then $O_J > O_j$. By (108), $O_J > O_j$ is equivalent to

$$\begin{aligned} |\mathbf{I} \cap \mathbf{V}^{(J)}| \cdot |\mathbf{V}^{(j)}| - |\mathbf{I} \cap \mathbf{V}^{(j)}| \cdot |\mathbf{V}^{(J)}| \\ + (L-1)[|\mathbf{I} \cap \mathbf{V}^{(J)}| - |\mathbf{I} \cap \mathbf{V}^{(j)}|] > 0. \end{aligned} \tag{123}$$

Suppose that (121) holds. Then:

$$|\mathbf{I} \cap \mathbf{V}^{(J)}| \cdot |\mathbf{V}^{(j)}| - |\mathbf{I} \cap \mathbf{V}^{(j)}| \cdot |\mathbf{V}^{(J)}| > 0. \tag{124}$$

Since $L > 1$, inequality (123) then follows at once if $[|\mathbf{I} \cap \mathbf{V}^{(J)}| - |\mathbf{I} \cap \mathbf{V}^{(j)}|] \geq 0$.

Suppose that $|\mathbf{I} \cap \mathbf{V}^{(j)}| > |\mathbf{I} \cap \mathbf{V}^{(J)}|$. Each term in (124) is an integer. The entire left-hand side of (124) is consequently a positive integer, so

$$|\mathbf{I} \cap \mathbf{V}^{(J)}| \cdot |\mathbf{V}^{(j)}| - |\mathbf{I} \cap \mathbf{V}^{(j)}| \cdot |\mathbf{V}^{(J)}| \geq 1 > \frac{|\mathbf{I}| - 1}{|\mathbf{I}|}. \tag{125}$$

Inequality (124) also implies that $|\mathbf{I} \cap \mathbf{V}^{(J)}| \geq 1$, and in general $|\mathbf{I}| \geq |\mathbf{I} \cap \mathbf{V}^{(j)}|$. Thus by (117) and (125),

$$
\begin{aligned}
|\mathbf{I} \cap \mathbf{V}^{(J)}| \cdot |\mathbf{V}^{(j)}| - |\mathbf{I} \cap \mathbf{V}^{(j)}| \cdot |\mathbf{V}^{(J)}| &> (L-1)(|\mathbf{I}|-1) \\
&\geq (L-1)[|\mathbf{I} \cap \mathbf{V}^{(j)}| - |\mathbf{I} \cap \mathbf{V}^{(J)}|]
\end{aligned}
\tag{126}
$$

Inequality (126) implies (123), and hence $O_J > O_j$.

Suppose next that (122) holds. Then

$$
|\mathbf{I} \cap \mathbf{V}^{(J)}| \cdot |\mathbf{V}^{(j)}| - |\mathbf{I} \cap \mathbf{V}^{(j)}| \cdot |\mathbf{V}^{(J)}| = 0.
\tag{127}
$$

Also, $|\mathbf{V}^{(J)}| > |\mathbf{V}^{(j)}|$, so

$$
\frac{|\mathbf{I} \cap \mathbf{V}^{(J)}|}{|\mathbf{I} \cap \mathbf{V}^{(j)}|} = \frac{|\mathbf{V}^{(J)}|}{|\mathbf{V}^{(j)}|} > 1.
\tag{128}
$$

Equations (127) and (128) imply (123), thereby completing the proof of Lemma 1.

We can now prove the theorem.

Proof of Theorem 7: First we show that a node v_J with a subset template is searched before any node v_j with a mixed or superset template. Since $\mathbf{I} \cap \mathbf{V}^{(J)} = \mathbf{V}^{(J)}$ but $\mathbf{I} \cap \mathbf{V}^{(j)}$ is a proper subset of $\mathbf{V}^{(j)}$,

$$
\frac{|\mathbf{I} \cap \mathbf{V}^{(J)}|}{|\mathbf{V}^{(J)}|} = \frac{|\mathbf{V}^{(J)}|}{|\mathbf{V}^{(J)}|} = 1 > \frac{|\mathbf{I} \cap \mathbf{V}^{(j)}|}{|\mathbf{V}^{(j)}|}.
\tag{129}
$$

By (121) in Lemma 1, $O_J > O_j$. Thus all subset templates are searched before mixed templates or learned superset templates.

We next show that a node v_J with a subset template is also searched before any uncommitted node v_j. Since

$$
O_j = D_2 \sum_{i \in \mathbf{I}} z_{ij},
\tag{130}
$$

the Direct Access Inequality (54) implies that

$$
O_j < \frac{D_2 L |\mathbf{I}|}{L - 1 + M}.
\tag{131}
$$

The right-hand side of (131) is an increasing function of L. Thus by (117),

$$
\frac{D_2 L |\mathbf{I}|}{L - 1 + M} \leq \frac{D_2(|\mathbf{I}|^{-1} + 1) |\mathbf{I}|}{|\mathbf{I}|^{-1} + M} = \frac{D_2(1 + |\mathbf{I}|)}{|\mathbf{I}|^{-1} + M}.
\tag{132}
$$

Inequality (118) implies that

$$
\frac{D_2(1 + |\mathbf{I}|)}{|\mathbf{I}|^{-1} + M} \leq \frac{D_2 M}{|\mathbf{I}|^{-1} + M} < D_2.
\tag{133}
$$

On the other hand, since $|\mathbf{V}^{(J)}| \geq 1$,

$$
O_J = \frac{D_2 L |\mathbf{V}^{(J)}|}{L - 1 + |\mathbf{V}^{(J)}|} \geq \frac{D_2 L \cdot 1}{L - 1 + 1} = D_2.
\tag{134}
$$

Inequalities (131)–(134) together imply $O_J > O_j$.

If v_J has a subset template, then $|\mathbf{I} \cap \mathbf{V}^{(J)}| = |\mathbf{V}^{(J)}|$. Thus all nodes with subset templates have the same ratio $|\mathbf{I} \cap \mathbf{V}^{(J)}| |\mathbf{V}^{(J)}|^{-1} = 1$. By (122) in Lemma 1, nodes with subset templates are searched in the order of decreasing template size.

If all subset templates are searched and if no other learned templates exist, then an uncommitted node will be activated. This node codes I because it possesses an unlearned superset template that does not lead to F_2 reset.

Suppose all subset templates have been searched and that there exist learned superset templates but no mixed templates. If node v_J has a superset template $V^{(J)}$, then

$$O_J = \frac{D_2 L |\mathbf{I}|}{L - 1 + |\mathbf{V}^{(J)}|}. \tag{135}$$

By (135), the first superset node to be activated is the node v_J whose template is smallest. Node v_J is chosen before any uncommitted node v_j because, by (54),

$$O_J \geq \frac{D_2 L |\mathbf{I}|}{L - 1 + M} > D_2 \sum_{i \in \mathbf{I}} z_{ij}(0) = O_j. \tag{136}$$

If v_J is activated, it codes I because its template satisfies

$$|\mathbf{I} \cap \mathbf{V}^{(J)}| = |\mathbf{I}| \geq \rho |\mathbf{I}|. \tag{137}$$

Suppose that all subset templates are searched and that a superset template $V^{(J)}$ and a mixed template $V^{(j)}$ exist. We prove that $O_j > O_J$ if and only if (119) holds. Suppose that (119) holds. Then also

$$\frac{|\mathbf{I} \cap \mathbf{V}^{(J)}|}{|\mathbf{V}^{(J)}|} = \frac{|\mathbf{I}|}{|\mathbf{V}^{(J)}|} < \frac{|\mathbf{I} \cap \mathbf{V}^{(j)}|}{|\mathbf{V}^{(j)}|}. \tag{138}$$

By condition (121) of Lemma 1, $O_j > O_J$. Conversely, suppose that $O_j > O_J$. Then

$$\frac{|\mathbf{I} \cap \mathbf{V}^{(j)}|}{L - 1 + |\mathbf{V}^{(j)}|} > \frac{|\mathbf{I} \cap \mathbf{V}^{(J)}|}{L - 1 + |\mathbf{V}^{(J)}|} = \frac{|\mathbf{I}|}{L - 1 + |\mathbf{V}^{(J)}|}. \tag{139}$$

Since $V^{(j)}$ is a mixed template with respect to I, $|\mathbf{I} \cap \mathbf{V}^{(j)}| < |\mathbf{I}|$. Thus (139) implies that $|\mathbf{V}^{(j)}| < |\mathbf{V}^{(J)}|$ as well as

$$|\mathbf{I} \cap \mathbf{V}^{(j)}| \cdot |\mathbf{V}^{(J)}| - |\mathbf{I}| \cdot |\mathbf{V}^{(j)}| > (L-1)[|\mathbf{I}| - |\mathbf{I} \cap \mathbf{V}^{(j)}|] > 0, \tag{140}$$

from which (119) follows. This completes the proof of Theorem 7.

Note that Lemma 1 also specifies the order of search among mixed templates. If all the activated mixed template nodes are reset, then the node v_J with the minimal superset template will code I. Unless (120) holds, it is possible for an uncommitted node v_J to code I before a node with a mixed template v_j is activated. Inequality (120) does not automatically follow from the Direct Access Inequality (54) because $|\mathbf{I} \cap \mathbf{V}^{(j)}|$ may be much smaller than $|\mathbf{I}|$ when $V^{(j)}$ is a mixed template.

24. Order of Search: Computer Simulations

Figures 12 and 13 depict coding sequences that illustrate the order of search specified by Theorem 7 when $(L-1)$ is small and when the vigilance parameter ρ is close to 1. In Figure 12, each of nine input patterns was presented once. Consider the order of search that occurred in response to the final input pattern I that was presented on trial 9. By trial 8, nodes v_{M+1} and v_{M+2} had already encoded subset templates of this input pattern. On trial 9, these nodes were therefore searched in order of decreasing template size. Nodes v_{M+3}, v_{M+4}, v_{M+5}, and v_{M+6} had encoded mixed templates of the input pattern. These nodes were searched in the order $v_{M+3} \rightarrow v_{M+5} \rightarrow v_{M+4}$. This search order was not determined by template size *per se*, but was rather governed by the ratio $|\mathbf{I} \cap \mathbf{V}^{(j)}| \, |\mathbf{V}^{(j)}|^{-1}$ in (121) and (122). These ratios for nodes v_{M+3}, v_{M+5}, and v_{M+4} were 9/10, 14/16, and 7/8, respectively. Since $14/16 = 7/8$, node v_{M+5} was searched before node v_{M+4} because $|\mathbf{V}^{(M+5)}| = 16 > 8 = |\mathbf{V}^{(M+4)}|$. The mixed template node v_{M+6} was not searched. After searching v_{M+5}, the network activated the node v_{M+7} which possessed the smallest superset template. A comparison of rows 8 and 9 in column 7 shows how the superset template of v_{M+7} was recoded to match the input pattern. By (119), the superset template node v_{M+7} was searched before the mixed template node v_{M+6} because the ratio $|\mathbf{I}| \, |\mathbf{V}^{(M+7)}|^{-1} = 17/21$ was larger than $|\mathbf{I} \cap \mathbf{V}^{(M+6)}| \, |\mathbf{V}^{(M+6)}|^{-1} = 14/18$.

The eight input patterns of Figure 13 illustrate a search followed by coding of an uncommitted node. The last input pattern I in Figure 13 is the same as the last input pattern in Figure 12. In Figure 13, however, there are no superset templates corresponding to input pattern I. Consequently I was coded by a previously uncommitted node v_{M+8} on trial 8. On trial 8 the network searched nodes with subset templates in the order $v_{M+2} \rightarrow v_{M+1}$ and the mixed template nodes in the order $v_{M+4} \rightarrow v_{M+6} \rightarrow v_{M+5} \rightarrow v_{M+7}$. The mixed template node v_{M+3} was not searched because its template badly mismatched the input pattern I and thus did not satisfy (120). Instead, the uncommitted node v_{M+8} was activated and learned a template that matched the input pattern. If $(L-1)$ is not small enough to satisfy inequality (117), then mixed templates or superset templates may be searched before subset templates. For all $L > 1$, however, Theorem 6 implies that all input patterns have direct access to their coding nodes after the learning process equilibrates.

25. Biasing the Network towards Uncommitted Nodes

Another effect of choosing L large is to bias the network to choose uncommitted nodes in response to unfamiliar input patterns I. To understand this effect, suppose that for all i and j,

$$z_{ij}(0) \cong \frac{L}{L-1+M}. \tag{71}$$

Then when I is presented, an uncommitted node is chosen before a coded node v_j if

$$\frac{|\mathbf{I} \cap \mathbf{V}^{(j)}|}{L-1+|\mathbf{V}^{(j)}|} < \frac{|\mathbf{I}|}{L-1+M}. \tag{141}$$

This inequality is equivalent to

$$\frac{|\mathbf{I} \cap \mathbf{V}^{(j)}|}{|\mathbf{I}|} < \frac{L-1+|\mathbf{V}^{(j)}|}{L-1+M}. \tag{142}$$

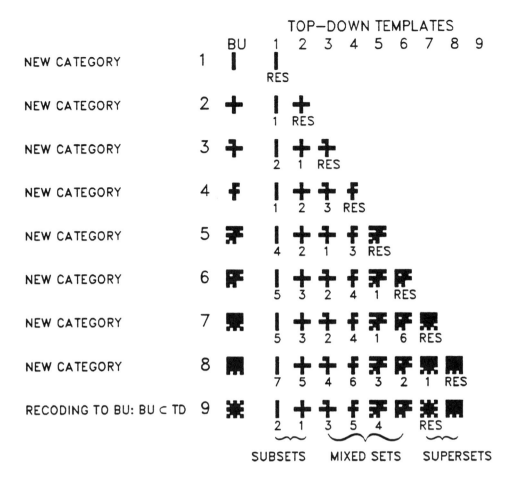

Figure 12. Computer simulation to illustrate order of search: On trial 9, the system first searches subset templates, next searches some, but not all, mixed templates, and finally recodes the smallest superset template. A smaller choice of vigilance parameter could have terminated the search at a subset template or mixed template node.

As L increases, the ratio

$$\frac{L-1+|\mathbf{V}^{(j)}|}{L-1+M} \to 1, \tag{143}$$

whereas the left-hand side of (142) is always less than or equal to 1. Thus for large values of L, the network tends to code unfamiliar input patterns into new categories, even if the vigilance parameter ρ is small. As L increases, the automatic scaling property (Section 2A) of the network also becomes weaker, as does the tendency to search subset templates first.

Recall that parameter L describes the relative strength of the bottom-up competition among LTM traces which gives rise to the Weber Law Rule (Section 12B), with smaller L corresponding to stronger LTM competition. Thus the structural process of LTM competition works with the state-dependent process of attentional vigilance to control how coarse the learned categories will be.

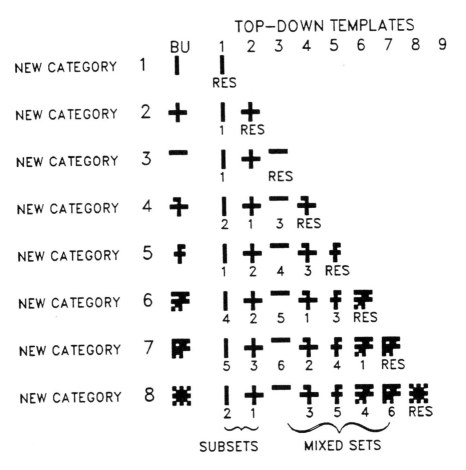

Figure 13. Computer simulation to illustrate order of search: Unlike the search described in Figure 12, no learned superset template exists when the search begins on trial 8. Consequently, the system first searches subset templates, next searches mixed templates, and finally terminates the search by coding a previously uncommitted node.

26. Computer Simulation of Self-Scaling Computational Units: Weighing the Evidence

We can now understand quantitatively how the network automatically rescales its matching and signal-to-noise criteria in the computer simulations of Figure 7. On the first four presentations, the input patterns are presented in the order ABAB. By trial 2, learning is complete. Pattern A directly accesses node v_{M+1} on trial 3, and pattern B directly accesses node v_{M+2} on trial 4. Thus patterns A and B are coded within different categories. On trials 5–8, patterns C and D are presented in the order CDCD. Patterns C and D are constructed from patterns A and B, respectively, by adding identical upper halves to A and B. Thus, pattern C differs from pattern D at the same locations where pattern A differs from pattern B. However, because patterns C and D represent many more active features than patterns A and B, the difference between C and D is treated as noise and is deleted from the critical feature pattern of v_{M+3} which codes both C and D, whereas the difference between A and B is considered significant and is included within the critical feature patterns of v_{M+1} and v_{M+2}.

The core issue in the network's different categorization of patterns A and B vs. patterns C and D is the following: Why on trial 2 does B reject the node v_{M+1} which has coded A, whereas D on trial 6 accepts the node v_{M+3} which has coded C? This occurs despite the fact that the mismatch between B and $V^{(M+1)}$ equals the mismatch between D and $V^{(M+3)}$:

$$|\mathbf{B}| - |\mathbf{B} \cap \mathbf{V}^{(M+1)}| = 3 = |\mathbf{D}| - |\mathbf{D} \cap \mathbf{V}^{(M+3)}|. \tag{144}$$

The reason is that

$$\frac{|\mathbf{B} \cap \mathbf{V}^{(M+1)}|}{|\mathbf{B}|} = \frac{8}{11} \tag{145}$$

whereas

$$\frac{|\mathbf{D} \cap \mathbf{V}^{(M+3)}|}{|\mathbf{D}|} = \frac{14}{17}. \tag{146}$$

In this simulation, the vigilance parameter $\rho = .8$. Thus

$$\frac{|\mathbf{B} \cap \mathbf{V}^{(M+1)}|}{|\mathbf{B}|} < \rho < \frac{|\mathbf{D} \cap \mathbf{V}^{(M+3)}|}{|\mathbf{D}|}. \tag{147}$$

By (73), pattern B resets v_{M+1} on trial 2 but D does not reset v_{M+3} on trial 6. Consequently, B is coded by a different category than A, whereas D is coded by the same category as C.

27. Concluding Remarks: Self-Stabilization and Unitization within Associative Networks

Two main conclusions of our work are especially salient. First, the code learning process is one of progressive refinement of distinctions. The distinctions that emerge are the resultant of all the input patterns which the network ever experiences, rather than of some preassigned features. Second, the matching process compares whole patterns, not just separate features. It may happen that two different input patterns to F_1 overlap a template at the same set of feature detectors, yet the network will reset the F_2 node in response to one input but not the other. The degree of mismatch of template pattern and input pattern *as a whole* determines whether coding or reset will occur. Thus the learning of categorical invariants resolves two opposing tendencies. As categories grow larger, and hence code increasingly global invariants, the templates which define them become smaller, as they discover and base the code on sets of critical feature patterns, or prototypes, rather than upon familiar pattern exemplars. This article shows how these two opposing tendencies can be resolved within a self-organizing system, leading to dynamic equilibration, or self-stabilization, of recognition categories in response to an arbitrary list of arbitrarily many binary input patterns. This self-stabilization property is of major importance for the further development of associative networks and the analysis of cognitive recognition processes.

Now that properties of self-organization, self-stabilization, and self-scaling are completely understood within the class of ART networks described herein, a number of generalizations also need to be studied. Within this article, an input pattern to level F_1 is globally grouped at F_2 when the F_2 population which receives the maximal input from the $F_1 \to F_2$ adaptive filter is chosen for short term memory (STM) storage. Within the total architecture of an ART system, even this simple type of F_2 reaction to the $F_1 \to F_2$ adaptive filter leads to powerful coding properties. On the other hand, a level F_2 which makes global choices must be viewed as a special case of a more general design for F_2.

If the second processing stage F_2 makes a choice, then later processing stages which are activated by F_2 alone could not further analyse the input pattern across F_1. The coding hierarchy for individual input patterns would end at the choice, or global grouping, stage. By contrast, a coding scheme wherein F_2 generates a spatially distributed representation of the F_1 activity pattern, rather than a choice, could support subsequent levels F_3, F_4, ..., F_n for coding multiple groupings, or chunks, and thus more abstract invariants of an input pattern. This possibility raises many issues concerning the properties of these configurations and their invariants, and of the architectural constraints which enable a multi-level coding hierarchy to learn and recognize distributed invariants in a stable and globally self-consistent fashion.

A parallel neural architecture, called a *masking field* (Cohen and Grossberg, 1986a, 1986b, 1986c; Grossberg, 1978a, 1984b, 1986a; Grossberg and Stone, 1986a) is a type of circuit design from which F_2—and by extension higher levels F_3, F_4, ..., F_n—may be fashioned to generate distributed representations of filtered input patterns. Masking field properties are of value for visual object recognition, speech recognition, and higher cognitive processes. Indeed, the same circuit design can be used for the development of general spatially distributed self-organizing recognition codes. The purpose of a masking field is to detect simultaneously, and weight properly in STM, all salient parts, or groupings, of an input pattern. The pattern as a whole is but one such grouping. A masking field generates a spatially distributed, yet unitized, representation of the input pattern in STM. Computer simulations of how a masking field can detect and learn unitized distributed representations of an input are found in Cohen and Grossberg (1986a, 1986b, 1986c). Much further work needs to be done to understand the design of ART systems all of whose levels F_i are masking fields.

Other useful generalizations of the ART system analysed herein include systems whose learning rate is slow relative to the time scale of a single trial; systems in which forgetting of LTM values can occur; systems which process continuous as well as binary input and output patterns; and systems in which Weber Law processing is realized through competitive STM interactions among F_1 nodes rather than competitive LTM interactions among bottom-up LTM traces (Section 12B). All of these generalizations will be considered in our future articles of this series.

Preprocessing of the input patterns to an ART system is no less important than choosing levels F_i capable of supporting a hierarchy of unitized codes of parts and wholes. In applications to visual object recognition, neural circuits which generate pre-attentively completed segmentations of a visual image before these completed segmentations generate inputs to an ART network have recently been constructed. (Grossberg, 1986b; Grossberg and Mingolla, 1985a, 1985b, 1986). In applications to adaptive speech recognition, inputs are encoded as STM patterns of temporal order information across item representations before these STM patterns generate inputs to an ART network (Grossberg, 1978a, 1984b, 1986a; Grossberg and Stone, 1986a, 1986b). Further work needs to be done to characterize these preprocessing stages and how they are joined to their ART coding networks. Although a great deal of work remains to be done, results such as those in the present article amply illustrate that the whole is much greater than the sum of its parts both in human experience and in self-organizing models thereof.

APPENDIX

Table 1 lists the constraints on the dimensionless model parameters for the system summarized in Section 18. We will now show that the 2/3 Rule holds when these constraints are satisfied. Then we describe four alternative, but dynamically equivalent, systems for realizing the 2/3 Rule and attentional gain control.

TABLE 1

Parameter Constraints

$$A_1 \geq 0$$

$$C_1 \geq 0$$

$$\max\{1, D_1\} < B_1 < 1 + D_1$$

$$0 < \epsilon << 1$$

$$K = O(1)$$

$$L > 1$$

$$0 < \rho \leq 1$$

$$0 < z_{ij}(0) < \frac{L}{L-1+M}$$

$$1 > z_{ji}(0) > \bar{z} \equiv \frac{B_1 - 1}{D_1}$$

$$0 \leq I_i, f, g, h \leq 1$$

Recall that x_i ($i = 1 \ldots M$) denotes the STM activity of an F_1 node v_i; that x_j ($j = M+1 \ldots N$) denotes the STM activity of an F_2 node v_j; that z_{ij} denotes the strength of the LTM trace in the bottom-up pathway from v_i to v_j; that z_{ji} denotes the strength of the LTM trace in the top-down pathway from v_j to v_i; that I_i denotes the bottom-up input to x_i; that $\mathbf{I}$ denotes the set of indices $i \in \{1 \ldots M\}$ such that $I_i > 0$; that $\mathbf{X} = \mathbf{X}(t)$ denotes the set of indices i such that $x_i(t) > 0$; and that $\mathbf{V}^{(j)} = \mathbf{V}^{(j)}(t)$ denotes the set of indices i such that $z_{ji}(t) > \bar{z}$.

Combining equations (8), (10), (11), and (12), we find the following equation for the ith STM trace of F_1:

$$\epsilon \frac{dx_i}{dt} = -x_i + (1 - A_1 x_i)(I_i + D_1 \sum_j f(x_j) z_{ji}) - (B_1 + C_1 x_i) \sum_j f(x_j). \qquad (A1)$$

When F_2 is inactive, all top-down signals $f(x_j) = 0$. Hence by (A1),

$$\epsilon \frac{dx_i}{dt} = -x_i + (1 - A_1 x_i) I_i. \qquad (A2)$$

When the F_2 node v_J is active, only the top-down signal $f(x_J)$ is non-zero. Since $f(x_J) = 1$,

$$\epsilon \frac{dx_i}{dt} = -x_i + (1 - A_1 x_i)(I_i + D_1 z_{Ji}) - (B_1 + C_1 x_i). \qquad (A3)$$

Since each x_i variable changes rapidly relative to the rate of change of the LTM trace z_{Ji} (since $0 < \epsilon << 1$), then x_i is always close to its steady state, $\frac{dx_i}{dt} = 0$. By (A2), then

$$x_i \cong \frac{I_i}{1 + A_1 I_i} \quad \text{if } F_2 \text{ is inactive} \tag{A4}$$

and, by (A3),

$$x_i \cong \frac{I_i + D_1 z_{Ji} - B_1}{1 + A_1(I_i + D_1 z_{Ji}) + C_1} \quad \text{if the } F_2 \text{ node } v_J \text{ is active.} \tag{A5}$$

The 2/3 Rule, as defined by:

$$\mathbf{X} = \begin{cases} \mathbf{I} & \text{if } F_2 \text{ is inactive} \\ \mathbf{I} \cap \mathbf{V}^{(J)} & \text{if the } F_2 \text{ node } v_J \text{ is active} \end{cases}, \tag{47}$$

can be derived as follows. Note first that (A4) implies that, when F_2 is inactive, $x_i > 0$ iff $I_i > 0$; i.e., $\mathbf{X} = \mathbf{I}$. On the other hand, if v_J is active, (A5) implies that :

$$x_i > 0 \text{ iff } z_{Ji} > \frac{B_1 - I_i}{D_1}. \tag{A6}$$

The 2/3 Rule requires that x_i be positive when the F_1 node v_i is receiving large inputs, both top-down and bottom-up. Thus setting $z_{Ji} = 1$ and $I_i = 1$ (their maximal values) in (A6) implies the constraint:

$$1 > \frac{B_1 - 1}{D_1}. \tag{A7}$$

The 2/3 Rule also requires that x_i be negative if v_i receives no top-down input, even if the bottom-up input is large. Thus setting $z_{Ji} = 0$ and $I_i = 1$ in (A6) implies the constraint:

$$0 < \frac{B_1 - 1}{D_1}. \tag{A8}$$

Finally, the 2/3 Rule requires that x_i be negative if v_i receives no bottom-up input, even if the top-down input is large. Thus setting $I_i = 0$ and $z_{Ji} = 1$ in (A6) implies the constraint:

$$1 < \frac{B_1}{D_1}. \tag{A9}$$

Inequalities (A7), (A8), and (A9) are summarized by the
2/3 Rule Inequalities:

$$\max\{1, D_1\} < B_1 < 1 + D_1. \tag{68}$$

Since $0 \leq I_i \leq 1$, (A6) also shows that if v_J is active and if

$$z_{Ji}(t) \leq \frac{B_1 - 1}{D_1}, \tag{A10}$$

then $x_i(t) \leq 0$; i.e., $i \notin X$. However if $i \notin X$, z_{Ji} decays toward 0 whenever v_J is active. Thus if (A10) is true at some time $t = t_0$, it remains true for all $t \geq t_0$. Therefore

$$\bar{z} \equiv \frac{B_1 - 1}{D_1} \tag{69}$$

is the critical top-down LTM strength such that if $z_{Ji}(t_0) \leq \bar{z}$, then $z_{Ji}(t) \leq \bar{z}$ for all $t \geq t_0$. Whenever v_J is active and $t \geq t_0$, the F_1 node v_i will be inactive.

Figure 14 depicts four ways in which attentional gain control can distinguish bottom-up and top-down processing to implement the 2/3 Rule. All of these systems generate the same asymptote (A5) when F_2 is active, and the same asymptotes, up to a minor change in parameters, when F_2 is inactive. The parameters in all four systems are defined to satisfy the constraints in Table 1.

In Figure 14a, F_2 can phasically excite the gain control channel, which thereupon nonspecifically inhibits the cells of F_1. Thus

$$\epsilon \frac{dx_i}{dt} = -x_i + (1 - A_1 x_i)(I_i + D_1 \sum_j f(x_j) z_{ji}) - (B_1 + C_1 x_i) G_1 \tag{A11}$$

where

$$G_1 = \begin{cases} 0 & \text{if } I \text{ is active and } F_2 \text{ is inactive} \\ 1 & \text{if } I \text{ is inactive and } F_2 \text{ is active} \\ 1 & \text{if } I \text{ is active and } F_2 \text{ is active} \\ 0 & \text{if } I \text{ is inactive and } F_2 \text{ is inactive.} \end{cases} \tag{A12}$$

In other words $G_1 = \sum_j f(x_j)$. Thus (A11) is just (A1) in a slightly different notation.

In Figure 14b, the plus sign within an open circle in the gain control channel designates that the gain control cells, in the absence of any bottom-up or top-down signals, are endogenously maintained at an equilibrium potential which exceeds their output threshold. Output signals from the gain control cells nonspecifically inhibit the cells of F_1. In short, the gain control channel tonically, or persistently, inhibits F_1 cells in the absence of bottom-up or top-down signals. Bottom-up and top-down signals phasically modulate the level of nonspecific inhibition. In particular, a bottom-up input alone totally inhibits the gain control channel, thereby disinhibiting the cells of F_1. A top-down signal alone maintains the inhibition from the gain control channel, because the inhibition is either on or off, and is thus not further increased by F_2. When both a bottom-up input and a top-down signal are active, their inputs to the gain control channel cancel, thereby again maintaining the same level of inhibition to F_1. The STM equations at F_1 are

$$\epsilon \frac{dx_i}{dt} = -x_i + (1 - A_1 x_i)(I_i + D_1 \sum_j f(x_j) z_{ji}) - (B_1 + C_1 x_i) G_2, \tag{A13}$$

where

$$G_2 = \begin{cases} 0 & \text{if } I \text{ is active and } F_2 \text{ is inactive} \\ 1 & \text{if } I \text{ is inactive and } F_2 \text{ is active} \\ 1 & \text{if } I \text{ is active and } F_2 \text{ is active} \\ 1 & \text{if } I \text{ is inactive and } F_2 \text{ is inactive.} \end{cases} \tag{A14}$$

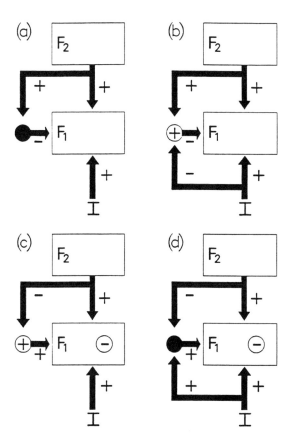

Figure 14. Design variations for realizing 2/3 Rule matching properties at F_1: In (a) and (b), F_2 excites the gain control channel, whereas in (c) and (d), F_2 inhibits the gain control channel. In (b), the input pattern I inhibits the gain control channel, whereas in (d), I excites the gain control channel. In (a) and (d), the gain control channel phasically reacts to its inputs (closed circles). Activation of the gain control channel in (a) nonspecifically inhibits F_1, and in (d) nonspecifically excites F_1. In (b) and (c), the gain control channel is tonically, or persistently, active in the absence of inputs (open circles surrounding plus signs). Activation of the gain control channel in (b) nonspecifically inhibits F_1, and in (c) nonspecifically excites F_1. In (c) and (d), the F_1 cells are maintained in a state of tonic hyperpolarization, or inhibition, in the absence of external inputs (open circles surrounding minus signs). All four cases lead to equivalent dynamics.

The equilibrium activities of x_i are as follows. If I is active and F_2 is inactive, then (A4) again holds. If I is inactive and F_2 is active, then (A5) again holds. Equation (A5) also holds if I is active and F_2 is active. If I is inactive and F_2 is inactive, then

$$x_i \cong \frac{-B_1}{1+C_1},\qquad (A15)$$

which is negative; hence no output signals are generated.

In Figure 14c, as in Figure 14b, the gain control cells are tonically active (plus sign in open circle). In Figure 14c, however, these cells nonspecifically excite the cells of F_1. In the absence of any external signals, F_1 cells are maintained in a state of tonic hyperpolarization, or negative activity (denoted by the minus sign in the open circle). The tonic excitation from the gain control cells balances the tonic inhibition due to hyperpolarization and thereby maintains the activity of F_2 cells near their output threshold of zero. A bottom-up input can thereby excite F_1 cells enough for them to generate output signals. When top-down signals are active, they inhibit the gain control cells. Consequently those F_1 cells which do not receive bottom-up or top-down signals become hyperpolarized. Due to tonic hyperpolarization, F_1 cells which receive a bottom-up signal or a top-down signal, but not both, cannot exeed their output threshold. Only F_1 cells at which large top-down and bottom-up signals converge can generate an output signal.

The STM equations at F_1 are

$$\epsilon \frac{dx_i}{dt} = -x_i + (1 - A_1 x_i)(I_i + D_1 \sum_j f(x_j) z_{ji} + B_1 G_3) - (B_1 + C_1 x_i), \qquad (A16)$$

where

$$G_3 = \begin{cases} 1 & \text{if } I \text{ is active and } F_2 \text{ is inactive} \\ 0 & \text{if } I \text{ is inactive and } F_2 \text{ is active} \\ 0 & \text{if } I \text{ is active and } F_2 \text{ is active} \\ 1 & \text{if } I \text{ is inactive and } F_2 \text{ is inactive} \end{cases} \qquad (A17)$$

The equilibrium activities of x_i are as follows. If I is active and F_2 is inactive, then

$$x_i \cong \frac{I_i}{1 + A_1 I_i + A_1 B_1 + C_1}. \qquad (A18)$$

Thus $x_i > 0$ iff $I_i > 0$. If I is inactive and F_2 is active, then (A5) holds. If I is active and F_2 is active, then (A5) holds. If I is inactive and F_2 is inactive, then

$$x_i \cong \frac{B_1 - B_1}{1 + A_1 B_1 + C_1} = 0. \qquad (A19)$$

Hence no output signals are generated from F_1. The coefficient B_1 in term $B_1 G_3$ of (A16) may be decreased somewhat without changing system dynamics.

In Figure 14d, the gain control cells are phasically excited by bottom-up signals and inhibited by top-down signals. Once active, they nonspecifically excite F_1 cells. In the absence of any external signals, F_1 cells are maintained in a state of tonic hyperpolarization, or negativity. In response to a bottom-up input, the gain control channel balances the tonic hyperpolarization of F_1 cells, thereby allowing those cells which receive bottom-up inputs to fire. When a top-down signal is active, no gain control outputs occur. Hence top-down signals alone cannot overcome the tonic hyperpolarization enough to generate output signals from F_1. Simultaneous convergence of an excitatory bottom-up signal and an inhibitory top-down signal at the gain control cells prevents these cells from generating output signals to F_1. Consequently, only those F_1 cells at which a bottom-up input and top-down template signal converge can overcome the tonic hyperpolarization to generate output signals.

The STM equations of F_1 are

$$\epsilon \frac{dx_i}{dt} = -x_i + (1 - A_1 x_i)(I_i + D_1 \sum_j f(x_j) z_{ji} + B_1 G_4) - (B_1 + C_1 x_i), \qquad (A20)$$

where

$$G_4 = \begin{cases} 1 & \text{if } I \text{ is active and } F_2 \text{ is inactive} \\ 0 & \text{if } I \text{ is inactive and } F_2 \text{ is active} \\ 0 & \text{if } I \text{ is active and } F_2 \text{ is active} \\ 0 & \text{if } I \text{ is inactive and } F_2 \text{ is inactive} \end{cases} \qquad (A21)$$

The equilibrium activities of x_i are as follows. If I is active and F_2 is inactive, then (A18) holds. If I is inactive and F_2 is active, then (A5) holds. Equation (A5) also holds if I is active and F_2 is active. If I is inactive and F_2 is inactive, then (A15) holds.

In all four cases, an F_1 cell fires only if the number of active excitatory pathways which converge upon the cell exceeds the number of active inhibitory pathways which converge upon the cell, where we count a source of tonic hyperpolarization as one input pathway. A similar rule governs the firing of the gain control channel in all cases.

REFERENCES

Anderson, J.A., Silverstein, J.W., Ritz, S.R., and Jones, R.S. (1977). Distinctive features, categorical perception, and probability learning: some applications of a neural model. *Psychological Review*, **84**, 413–451.

Banquet, J.P. and Grossberg, S. (1986). Probing cognitive processes through the structure of event-related potentials during learning: An experimental and theoretical analysis. Submitted for publication.

Basar, E., Flohr, H., Haken, H., and Mandell, A.J. (Eds.) (1983). **Synergetics of the brain**. New York: Springer-Verlag.

Carpenter, G.A. and Grossberg, S. (1985a). Category learning and adaptive pattern recognition: A neural network model. *Proceedings of the Third Army Conference on Applied Mathematics and Computing*, **ARO 86-1**, 37–56.

Carpenter, G.A. and Grossberg, S. (1985b). Neural dynamics of adaptive pattern recognition: Priming, search, attention, and category formation. *Society for Neuroscience Abstracts*, **11**, 1110.

Carpenter, G.A. and Grossberg, S. (1986a). Neural dynamics of category learning and recognition: Attention, memory consolidation, and amnesia. In J. Davis, R. Newburgh, and E. Wegman (Eds.), **Brain structure, learning, and memory**. AAAS Symposium Series.

Carpenter, G.A. and Grossberg, S. (1986b). Neural dynamics of category learning and recognition: Structural invariants, reinforcement, and evoked potentials. In M.L. Commons, S.M. Kosslyn, and R.J. Herrnstein (Eds.), **Pattern recognition and concepts in animals, people, and machines**. Hillsdale, NJ: Erlbaum.

Carpenter, G.A. and Grossberg, S. (1987). ART 2: Stable self-organization of pattern recognition codes for analog input patterns. *Applied Optics*, **26**, 4919–4930.

Cohen, M.A. and Grossberg, S. (1986a). Neural dynamics of speech and language coding: Developmental programs, perceptual grouping, and competition for short term memory. *Human Neurobiology*, **5**, 1–22.

Cohen, M.A. and Grossberg, S. (1986b). Unitized recognition codes for parts and wholes: The unique cue in configural discriminations. In M.L. Commons, S.M. Kosslyn, and R.J. Herrnstein (Eds.), **Pattern recognition and concepts in animals, people, and machines**. Hillsdale, NJ: Erlbaum.

Cohen, M.A. and Grossberg, S. (1986c). Masking fields: A massively parallel architecture for discovering learning, and recognizing multiple groupings of patterned data. *Applied Optics*, in press.

Ellias, S. and Grossberg, S. (1975). Pattern formation, contrast control, and oscillations in the short term memory of shunting on-center off-surround networks. *Biological Cybernetics*, **20**, 69–98.

Fukushima, K. (1980). Neocognitron: A self-organizing neural network model for a mechanism of pattern recognition unaffected by shift in position. *Biological Cybernetics*, **36**, 193–202.

Grossberg, S. (1973). Contour enhancement, short-term memory, and constancies in reverberating neural networks. *Studies in Applied Mathematics*, **52**, 217–257.

Grossberg, S. (1976a). Adaptive pattern classification and universal recoding, I: Parallel development and coding of neural feature detectors. *Biological Cybernetics*, **23**, 121–134.

Grossberg, S. (1976b). Adaptive pattern classification and universal recoding, II: Feedback, expectation, olfaction, and illusions. *Biological Cybernetics*, **23**, 187–202.

Grossberg, S. (1978a). A theory of human memory: Self-organization and performance of sensory-motor codes, maps, and plans. In R. Rosen and F. Snell (Eds.), **Progress in theoretical biology**, Vol. 5, pp. 233–374. New York: Academic Press.

Grossberg, S. (1978b). Do all neural networks really look alike? A comment on Anderson, Silverstein, Ritz, and Jones. *Psychological Review*, **85**, 592–596.

Grossberg, S. (1980). How does a brain build a cognitive code? *Psychological Review*, **87**, 1–51.

Grossberg, S. (1983). The quantized geometry of visual space: The coherent computation of depth, form, and lightness. *Behavioral Brain Sciences*, **6**, 625–692.

Grossberg, S. (1984a). Some psychophysiological and pharmacological correlates of a developmental, cognitive and motivational theory. In R. Karrer, J. Cohen, and P. Tueting (Eds.), **Brain and information: Event related potentials**, pp. 58–151. New York: New York Academy of Sciences.

Grossberg, S. (1984b). Unitization, automaticity, temporal order, and word recognition. *Cognition and Brain Theory*, **7**, 263–283.

Grossberg, S. (1986a). The adaptive self-organization of serial order in behavior: Speech, language, and motor control. In E.C. Schwab and H.C. Nusbaum (Eds.), **Pattern recognition by humans and machines**, Vol. 1. New York: Academic Press.

Grossberg, S. (1986b). Cortical dynamics of three-dimensional form, color, and brightness perception: Parts I and II. *Perception and Psychophysics*, in press.

Grossberg, S. and Levine, D. (1975). Some developmental and attentional biases in the contrast enhancement and short term memory of recurrent neural networks. *Journal of Theoretical Biology*, **53**, 341–380.

Grossberg, S. and Mingolla, E. (1985a). Neural dynamics of form perception: Boundary completion, illusory figures, and neon color spreading. *Psychological Review*, **92**, 173–211.

Grossberg, S. and Mingolla, E. (1985b). Neural dynamics of perceptual grouping: Textures, boundaries, and emergent segmentations. *Perception and Psychophysics*, **38**, 141–171.

Grossberg, S. and Mingolla, E. (1986). Neural dynamics of surface perception: Boundary webs, illuminants, and shape-from-shading. *Computer Vision, Graphics, and Image Processing*, in press.

Grossberg, S. and Stone, G.O. (1986a). Neural dynamics of word recognition and recall: Attentional priming, learning, and resonance. *Psychological Review*, **93**, 46–74.

Grossberg, S. and Stone, G.O. (1986b). Neural dynamics of attention switching and temporal order information in short term memory. *Memory and Cognition*, **14**, 451–468.

Hebb, D.O. (1949). **The organization of behavior**. New York: Wiley.

Hopfield, J.J. (1982). Neural networks and physical systems with emergent collective computational abilities. *Proceedings of The National Academy of Sciences USA*, **79**, 2554–2558.

Kohonen, T. (1977). **Associative memory: A System-theoretical approach**. New York: Springer-Verlag.

Lin, C.C. and Segal, L.A. (1974). **Mathematics applied to deterministic problems in the natural sciences**. New York: Macmillan.

Malsburg, C. von der and Willshaw, D.J. (1981). Differential equations for the development of topological nerve fibre projections. In S. Grossberg (Ed.), **Mathematical psychology and psychophysiology**, pp. 39–47. Providence, RI: American Mathematical Society.

McClelland, J.I. and Rumelhart, D.E. (1985). Distributed memory and the representation of general and specific information. *Journal of Experimental Psychology, General*, **114**, 159–188.

Posner, M.I. (1973). **Cognition: An introduction**. Glenview, IL: Scott, Foresman, and Company.

Posner, M.I. and Keele, S.W. (1968). On the genesis of abstract ideas. *Journal of Experimental Psychology*, **77**, 353–363.

Posner, M.I. and Keele, S.W. (1970). Retention of abstract ideas. *Journal of Experimental Psychology*, **83**, 304–308.

Smith, E.E. and Medin, D.L. (1981). **Categories and concepts**. Cambridge, MA: Harvard University Press.

VARIATIONS ON ADAPTIVE RESONANCE
by
T.W. Ryan and C.L. Winter

Preface

In 1987, Ryan and Winter, at SAIC, were among the first investigators to show ways in which a basic ART 1 system can be adapted for individual applications. They began with a special case of ART 1 and then showed how variations on this system led to new processing characteristics. Some of these characteristics are present in ART 1 in parameter ranges other than the one selected by Ryan and Winter. Other characteristics point to some of the computational requirements that led to the development of the ART 2 and ART 3 modules and the supervised ARTMAP system described later in this volume.

The ART 1 system that is the starting point for Ryan and Winter is constrained by their choice of parameters governing the bottom-up weights z_{ij}, here called b_{ij}. For this parameter range, implicitly defined by the choice of 1 in the denominator in equation (4), ART 1 memories are apt to be recoded, particularly when an input $\mathbf{I}$ activates a category whose learned expectation vector contains $\mathbf{I}$ as a subset pattern. This parameter range can be useful because it tends to maximize generalization in the category structure. When ART 1 is embedded in a supervised learning system such as ARTMAP, feedback to the orienting subsystem can prevent recoding errors while taking advantage of this generalization property. On the other hand, without benefit of such feedback, it is useful to be able to buffer learned codes using properties of the module itself. This may be done by choosing bottom-up weight parameters in such a way as to bias the system toward selection of uncoded nodes. This prevents selection of poorly matched categories, thus protecting those categories against recoding when the ART 1 vigilance parameter ρ (here called v) is small and when the category structure is still sparse, as occurs early in the coding process.

Ryan and Winter introduce an alternative device called the *adaptive threshold* (q_j). This device provides ART 1 with code buffering capabilities similar to the parameter choices that lead to selection of uncoded nodes by creating a large category activation threshold when large inputs are coded by the category. Subsequent small or poorly matched inputs then become unable to access nodes that code large inputs. This type of category-specific adaptation is reminiscent of the ART 3 Medium Term Memory for analog distributed search.

Ryan and Winter also introduce a symmetric adaptive threshold (equation 19) that buffers against code selection by large patterns as well as by small ones. They thus address an inherent asymmetry in ART 1 processing of inputs that are subsets of learned expectation vectors as opposed to processing of supersets. The symmetric adaptive threshold reduces this asymmetry, as does the Euclidean norm in ART 2. Selection from among these various design possibilities depends upon the requirements of a particular application. The ART 1 subset/superset asymmetry reflects the different category recognition response we might make to a fragment ($\mathbf{I}^{(1)}$) of a familiar item (z_J) versus our response to that familiar item appearing with other significant items ($I^{(2)}$), even if the absolute difference between $I^{(1)}$ and z_J is the same as the difference between $I^{(2)}$ and z_J. For example, input $I^{(1)}$ might signify an occluded z_J, while $I^{(2)}$ signifies an entirely new category.

**IEEE First International Conference
on Neural Networks**
M. Caudill and C. Butler (Eds.)
San Diego: IEEE, 1987, 767–775
©1987 IEEE

VARIATIONS ON ADAPTIVE RESONANCE

T.W. Ryan and C.L. Winter

In the process of implementing Adaptive Resonance Circuits (ARCs) [1] for a particular application [2], several circuit modifications and alternative processing conditions were considered. The objective of this paper is to report on some of these variations. First, we consider an adaptive thresholding technique that prevents inadvertent recoding of recognition nodes which can occur when novel patterns are presented. Next, we examine the behavior of an ARC when patterns are iteratively presented for relatively short periods of time. Finally, we consider the case of continuous ARC operation in which "neural" activity is not reinitialized with each new pattern presentation (as done in [1]). The adaptive thresholding technique provides a novel clustering algorithm applicable to both binary and mutilevel data.

Background

The Adaptive Resonance Circuit is a dynamic, parallel, self-organizing, competitive learning machine [1]. The circuit consists of four slabs: input (**I**), comparison (**C**), recognition (**R**), and Reset (**Re**) with interconnections as shown in Figure 1. The differential equations that govern the circuit are as follows:

Comparison activity:

$$\tau \dot{x}_i = -x_i + (1 - A_C x_i)[\sum_j f(y_j)t_{ji} + I_i] - (B_C + C_C x_i)\sum_j f(y_j) \tag{1}$$

Recognition activity:

$$\tau \dot{y}_j = -y_j + (1 - A_R y_j)[\sum_i f(x_i)b_{ij} + f(y_j)] - (B_R + C_R y_j)[\sum_{k \neq j} f(y_k) + r_j] \tag{2}$$

Top-down weights:

$$\dot{t}_{ji} = f(y_j)[f(x_i) - t_{ji}] \tag{3}$$

Bottom-up weights:

$$\dot{b}_{ij} = f(y_j)[f(x_i)/(1 + |C|) - b_{ij}] \tag{4}$$

Reset activity:

$$\tau_r \dot{r}_j = f(y_j)[Df(v|I| - |C|) - r_j] \tag{5}$$

In equations (1)–(5), τ is the time constant for short term memory (STM), I_i is the activity of I_i (the ith component of the input pattern), A, B, C, and D are constants and $f(\cdot)$ is a sigmoid function (Figure 2). $f(y_j)$ is referred to as the "output" of R_j. The quantity $|I| = \sum_i I_i$ is the total activity of I. For the standard ARC, we set $\tau_r = 1$ but other choices are more appropriate for the ARC variations considered. For the purposes of this paper, all input patterns are binary.

Equations (1), (3), and (4) are essentially the same as those found in [1]. Equation (5) and the incorporation of r_j into equation (2) are our interpretation of the "arousal" concept given in [1] in which the "vigilance" parameter v is used to control the clustering of input patterns.

The reader is referred to [1] for a complete description of the ARC and to [2] and [3] for summaries. In order to place the ARC variations in context, however, we present the salient features that apply in the "Fast-Learn" mode of operation in which all the differential equations are allowed to reach their asymptotic solutions with each input pattern presentation:

1. The forcing functions for the comparison and recognition slabs are

Comparison:

$$F_i = \sum_j f(y_j)t_{ji} + I_i - B_C \sum_j f(y_j) \tag{6}$$

Recognition:

$$F_j = \sum_i f(x_i)b_{ij} + f(y_j) - B_R[\sum_{k \neq j} f(y_k) + r_j]. \tag{7}$$

2. When $|R| = 0$, the recognition slab responds only to $\sum_i f(x_i)b_{ij}$, the correlation between the pattern on C, i. e., $\{f(x_i)\}$, and the bottom-up weights. The largest correlation determines the "winning" recognition node, R_j, which then inhibits all other recognition nodes.

3. If R_j is active, the forcing function for C_i is

$$F_i = t_{ji} + I_i - B_C. \tag{8}$$

With an appropriate sigmoid function, $C_i \to 1$ if $F_i > 0$. If $1 < B_C < 2$ then C converges to the intersection (bitwise AND) of the input patterns and the top-down pattern $T_j(C \to I \cap T_j)$. T_j is initialized so that $t_{ij}(0) = 1$ for all i and j.

4. The top-down pattern converges to the intersection of all patterns that are "coded" by R_j. A pattern P is coded by R_j if $P \cap T_j = T_j$ and $|T_j|/|P| > v$. If the set of patterns $\{P_1, P_2, \ldots, P_n\}$ are coded by R_k, then

$$\cap_i P_i = T_k, \tag{9}$$

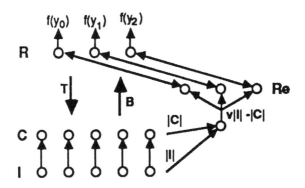

Figure 1. The major components of the ARC. T and B are the sets of top-down and bottom-up weights respectively. All nodes on C are interconnected with all nodes on R by both T and B.

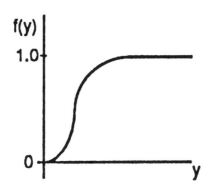

Figure 2. Typical sigmoid function.

and

$$|T_k| \geq v|P_i| \text{ for } i = 1,\ldots,n. \tag{10}$$

The top-down pattern T_j is called a "template" or prototype pattern for pattern class j.

5. The bottom-up weights are initialized to be randomly distributed on the interval $(0, 1/(1 + N_C))$ where N_C is the number of nodes on **C**. These weights converge to a normalized version of the template T (equation (4)).

6. Only those weights associated with active recognition codes are modified. This is assured by the $f(y_j)$ factors in equations (3) and (4). This is typical of competitive learning systems [4, 5].

7. The reset mechanism inhibits the active recognition node $\mathbf{R}_j$ whenever $|\mathbf{C}|/|\mathbf{I}| = |\mathbf{I} \cap T_j|/|\mathbf{I}| < v$. Thus if the input pattern is a "large" superset of T_j, then $\mathbf{R}_j$ will reject the pattern and the system will activate a new node. In this way, the system sequentially activates (cycles through) all coded nodes whose templates intersect T_j before selecting an unused node to code a novel pattern.

8. After training, the system provides "direct access" to coded patterns. This means that an input pattern previously learned by $\mathbf{R}_j$ will activate $\mathbf{R}_j$ first; no other recognition nodes will be activated. If $\mathbf{R}_j$ activates without causing a reset, the circuit is said to be in a "resonant" state. The number of possible pattern clusters is limited only by the number of nodes on $\mathbf{R}$.

Below we show that the learning behavior is significantly different if the system only sees brief "snapshots" of the various input patterns, a mode which is common to the training of most competitive learning systems such as back-propagation [4].

Adaptive Thresholding

One potential problem with the ARC as described above is that a recognition node $\mathbf{R}_k$ can be recoded by any input pattern P for which $|P \cap T_k| > v|P|$. For example, if $T_k \supset P$ (T_k contains P) then $|P \cap T_k| = |P|$. If P is resident on **C** for a sufficiently long time, then $T_k \to P$ and the memory of patterns previously coded by $\mathbf{R}_k$ is lost. During training, this is not critical as long as all patterns are presented repeatedly until coding stabilizes. The problem becomes acute, however, during recall operations when the input patterns cannot be guaranteed to come from the training set. This condition can be avoided without losing any other properties of the ARC by introducing an adaptive threshold, q_j, into equation (2):

$$\tau \dot{y}_j = -y_j + (1 - A_R y_j)[\sum_i f(x_i)b_{ij} - \delta q_j + f(y_j)] - (B_R + C_R y_j)[\sum_{k \neq j} f(y_k) + r_j] \tag{11}$$

where q_j is chosen to reflect the size of the pattern activating $\mathbf{R}_j$:

$$\dot{q}_j = f(y_j)[|\mathbf{C}|/(1 + |\mathbf{C}|) - q_j] \tag{12}$$

and δ is a fixed parameter that controls the extent of the pattern subspace that can excite $\mathbf{R}_j$. In [1] it is shown that presentation of a pattern P on **I** results in

$$F_j = \sum_i f(x_i)b_{ij} = |P \cap T_j|/(1 + |T_j|) \tag{13}$$

for a node $\mathbf{R}_j$ whose weights have reached equilibrium. If P is a pattern coded by $\mathbf{R}_j$, then $P \supset T_j$. Thus $\mathbf{C} = T_j$ and q_j converges to

$$q_j = |T_j|/(1 + |T_j|). \tag{14}$$

Now if P is any arbitrary pattern, the excitation of a coded node $\mathbf{R}_k$ is governed by the forcing function

$$F_k = \sum_i f(x_i) b_{ik} - \delta q_k = [|P \cap T_k| - \delta|T_k|]/(1 + |T_k|). \tag{15}$$

Thus $\mathbf{R}_k$ can be activated only if $|P \cap T_k| > \delta|T_k|$. If q_j is initially set to zero, then an uncoded node $\mathbf{R}_u$ with unmodified weights b_{iu} will receive the signal

$$\sum_i f(x_i) b_{iu} - \delta q_u = \sum_i f(x_i) b_{iu} < |P| b_{\max} \tag{16}$$

where $b_{\max}$ is the maximum allowable value of the initialized bottom-up weights. With an appropriate choice of $b_{\max}$, the direct access property is not lost.

Theorem. An ARC with adaptive thresholding characterized by equations (11) and (12) provides direct access to previously coded patterns as long as the distribution of initial bottom-up weights satisfies

$$b_{ij}(0) < v(1 - \delta)/(1 + N_C) \quad \forall i, j, \tag{17}$$

where N_C is the number of nodes on $\mathbf{C}$ and $0 < v, \delta < 1$.

Although the proof is straightforward, it is not critical to the following discussion and is omitted for the sake of brevity. The point to be made is that the addition of the adaptive thresholding term prevents recoding without jeopardizing direct access to coded patterns.

Figure 3 shows the results of training the standard and the modified ARC on a sequence of patterns in the Fast-Learn mode. The patterns for this experiment are shown in Figure 3a. Figure 3b presents the system parameter values used for all experiments described in this paper. In Figure 3c, the table entries indicate the recognition node that responded to the input. The symbol "r" indicates that the circuit reset before achieving resonance. The presence of the adaptive threshold reduces the number of resets needed to reach resonance and prevents later recoding by extraneous patterns.

The addition of the adaptive threshold also makes it possible for the system to self-organize when pattern presentations are relatively short (a few STM time constants). Learning in this "snapshot" mode is not possible with the standard ARC as we now show.

Learning with Iterative Short-Time Pattern Presentations

Consider an ARC without adaptive thresholding in an initialized state with $\{b_{ij}\}$ small but random. Presentation of a pattern A on $\mathbf{I}$ causes some recognition node, say $\mathbf{R}_A$, to activate and remain in a stable state. During the time that A is resident on $\mathbf{I}$, the bottom-up weights from non-zero elements of $\mathbf{I}$ to $\mathbf{R}_A$ increase and those from

(a) Pattern definitions:

P_2	1 1 0 0 0 0 0 0 0 0
P_3	1 1 1 0 0 0 0 0 0 0
P_7	1 1 1 1 1 1 1 0 0 0
P_8	1 1 1 1 1 1 1 1 0 0

(b) ARC parameter settings:

comparison:	N_C=10, τ=.05, A_C=0.0, B_C=1.2, C_C=1.0
recognition:	N_R=6, τ=.05, A_R=1.0, B_R=2.0, C_R=4.0
reset:	τ_r=1, D=20 for "Fast-Learn"
	τ_r=.05, D=1 for Continuous mode

(c)

	Standard ARC (v=.8)	Standard ARC (v=.5)	Simple Adaptive Threshold (v=.8, δ=.7)	Simple Adaptive Threshold (v=.5, δ=.45)
P_8	3, 3r5 , 5r3r1 , 1	4, 4r0 , 0	0	5
P_7	3, 5 , 1 , 1	4, 0 , 0	0	5
P_3	3, 3r5 , 5 , 5	4, 4 , 4	4	4
P_2	3, 3 , 3 , 3	4, 4 , 4	5	4
P_2	0 , 0	2 , 2	4 , 4	3 , 3
P_3	0r4 , 4	2 , 2	4r3 , 3	3 , 3
P_7	4r0r3 , 3	2r0 , 0	3r4r0 , 0	3r0 , 0
P_8	3 , 3	0 , 0	0 , 0	0 , 0

iterations →

Figure 3. Fast-Learn training behavior. (a) The set of binary training samples. (b) ARC parameter settings. (c) Training sequences for the standard ARC and the ARC with adaptive thresholding. Results for two presentation orders (P_8, P_7, P_3, P_2 and P_2, P_3, P_7, P_8) are shown. Activity is set to zero prior to each pattern presentation. The numbers in the tables refer to the resulting active recognition node index (0–5). Codings do not change with additional iterations. Adaptive thresholding reduces the number of resets (r) in establishing a stable code.

zero-valued weights decrease according to equation (4). Now suppose A is replaced by B after only a few STM time constants. If $|A \cap B| = 0$ (i. e., the patterns are orthogonal), then each node on $\mathbf{R}$, excluding $\mathbf{R}_A$, is equally likely to activate. If, however, A and B are not orthogonal, then $\mathbf{R}_A$ is more likely to respond than any other node due to the learning that occurred during the brief presentation of pattern A. If the top-down weights t_{Ai} associated with positions $A_i = 0$ have not changed to the point where (from equation (8))

$$t_{Ai} < B_C - 1 \tag{18}$$

then the reset mechanism will not activate. Thus a sequence of intersecting patterns will be coded by the same recognition node. One possible solution to this problem is to set $t_{ij}(0) = B_C - 1 + \epsilon$ for some small ϵ so that equation (18) is satisfied after only a brief presentation time. In this way, the circuit can be made to reset. With

	Standard ARC		Simple Adaptive Threshold	
	$(v=.8)$	$(v=.5)$	$(\delta = .8)$	$(\delta = .5)$
P_2	44	22	3100000000	344
P_3	44	22	3111111100	344
P_7	44	22	3333333111	333
P_8	44	22	3333333333	333
P_8	00	44	22	00
P_7	00	44	22	00
P_3	00	44	00	22
P_2	00	44	44	22
iteration	01	01	0123456789	012

Figure 4. Learning with short-time pattern presentations (3 STM time constants for each pattern presentation) and zero-reset for two presentation orders. Each column indicates the active recognition code for that trial. The final configuration is stable. For this pattern set, the standard ARC never forms clusters and the adaptive thresholding produces order dependent clustering.

short presentation times, however, there may not be sufficient time to cycle through the previously coded patterns, particularly if there is a large number of them.

An alternative solution is provided by adaptive thresholding. In this case, the brief presentation of pattern A causes the threshold q_A to increase slightly. If pattern B satisfies $\sum_i b_{iA} f(x_i) < \delta q_A$, then activation of $\mathbf{R}_A$ is prevented while some other node, $\mathbf{R}_B$, responds.

Figure 4 shows the results of iterative pattern learning with and without adaptive thresholding for the case when patterns are iteratively presented for only three STM time constants†. Adaptive thresholding makes it possible to form stable categories under these conditions. The top-down weights associated with a recognition node converge in this case to the *centroid* of the patterns coded by that node, rather than the intersection of the patterns. Note that for $\delta = .5$, two stable categories are obtained. For the case $\delta = .8$, three stable categories are formed, with the coding dependent on the order in which the patterns were presented. When the patterns were presented in increasing size, the classification, while stable, is not the categorization obtained using the Fast-Learn conditions‡. The recoding of $\mathbf{R}_1$ at iteration 7 (to include P_7) occurs, in part, because the forcing function (equation (15)) is not symmetrical with respect to pattern size mismatches. Small patterns may be rejected, but a pattern P that is a superset of a previously coded pattern A will excite $\mathbf{R}_A$ just as pattern A

---

† For the parameters in Figure 4b, this corresponds to .15 LTM time constants for each pattern presentation.

‡ With respect to the similarity criterion defined by equation (5), patterns P_2 and P_3 are less similar than P_7 and P_8.

would.

A symmetrical thresholding scheme can be achieved if the δq term is modified to reject large patterns as well as small ones. This occurs with the forcing function

$$F_j = \sum_i b_{ij} f(x_i) - \lambda g(z_j|\mathbf{C}| - q_j) \tag{19}$$

where z_j learns the mean bottom-up weight, $g(\cdot)$ is a symmetric nonlinear mapping with $g(0) = 0$ and $g(|x|)$ monotone increasing in $|x|$, and λ is a parameter that controls the size of the pattern clusters, having the same effect as the vigilance parameter (and δ in the previous discussion). In equation (19), and in the following discussion, we are only concerned with the bottom-up signal. All forcing terms involving $\mathbf{R}$ have been eliminated for clarity. To track the mean bottom-up weight, we let

$$\dot{z}_j = f(y_j)[1/(1 + |\mathbf{C}|) - z_j]. \tag{20}$$

Then, by comparison with equation (12) we see that $z_j = u_j - q_j$ where

$$\dot{u}_j = f(y_j)[1 - u_j]. \tag{21}$$

Then we modify equation (18) to read

$$F_j = \sum_i b_{ij} f(x_i) - \lambda u_j g[(u_j - q_j)|\mathbf{C}| - q_j]. \tag{22}$$

In equations (19) and (20), $|\mathbf{C}|$ is the size of the current pattern on $\mathbf{C}$. Note that q_j maintains a memory of all past values of $|\mathbf{C}|$ and u_j records the amount of time that node $\mathbf{R}_j$ has been active. The u_j term that multiplies the adaptive threshold has been introduced so that the recognition node behaves as a standard ARC recognition node initially but becomes increasingly discriminatory as $\mathbf{R}_j$ responds. To see how equation (22) works, consider the equilibrium state for F_j when $\mathbf{R}_j$ has learned only one pattern, J, and pattern P is presented:

$$\begin{aligned} F_j &\to |P \cap J|/(1 + |J|) - \lambda g[(1 - |J|/(1 + |J|))|P| - |J|/(1 + |J|)] \\ &\to |P \cap J|/(1 + |J|) - \lambda g((|P| - |J|)/(1 + |J|)). \end{aligned} \tag{23}$$

With this formulation, it is clear that for $|P| = |J|$, the forcing function is equivalent to that for the standard ARC (equation (13)). Figure 5 shows how the forcing function is affected by discrepancies in pattern size from the size "learned" by the q_j term. For the case shown in Figure 5, $g(x)$ is the absolute value of x. Note that the "receptive field" of pattern sizes becomes more discriminatory with respect to size mismatches as node $\mathbf{R}_j$ learns. Furthermore, the width of this region increases as $|J|$ increases. For binary patterns, this has the desirable property that a fixed Hamming distance is less significant for large patterns. Since u_j and q_j are bounded above, however, there is a limit to the rejection level. The pattern clusters formed with this algorithm achieve the same stable coding as the standard ARC does when operating in the "Fast-Learn" mode. For the short pattern presentation case, however, no reset occurs and the coding is robust against novel input patterns.

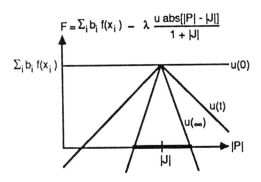

Figure 5. Size discrimination obtained by symmetric adaptive thresholding. The thick line segment shows the size "receptive field" at equilibrium.

	$\lambda=2$	$\lambda=6$	$\lambda=12$	$\lambda=20$
P_8	55	33333	000000	0000
P_7	55	33333	000033	0033
P_3	44	55555	222222	2222
P_2	44	55511	255555	1111
P_2	000	44444	2222222	0000
P_3	000	44422	2555555	2222
P_7	011	33333	0000011	1133
P_8	111	33333	0000000	1111
iteration	012	01234	0123456	0123

Figure 6. Training sequences for symmetric adaptive thresholding, zero-reset, and short presentations.

Figure 6 shows the training sequence for two pattern presentation orders. Note that in certain cases (e. g., $\lambda = 12$) the system first forms coarse clusters, then refines them as the participating recognition nodes log more activation time. As before, the circuit is reset to zero activity prior to each presentation. With the symmetric adaptive thresholding mechanism, however, it is not necessary to use the zero-reset option, as we show in the following section.

Continuous ARC Operation

The direct access theorems above and in [1] assume that the system is reinitialized to a zero-activity state prior to the presentation of each pattern on **I**. Since it seems unlikely that nature's learning systems exhibit this property, we investigated the behavior of the ARC in continuous dynamic operation as patterns were presented for short time periods.

	Standard ARC (v=.8)			Symmetric Adaptive Threshold (v=.8, λ=6)
P$_8$	3, r5, r3			0, r0
P$_7$	3, 5, 3		unstable	0, 0
P$_3$	r5, r3, r5			r4, r3
P$_2$	r3, r5, r3			r5, r5
P$_8$	0, r0			3, r3, r3, r3, r3, r3
P$_3$	r2, r2			r4, r4, r4, r4, r4, r4
P$_7$	r0, r0			r3, r3, r3, r3, r3, r3
P$_2$	r2, r2			r4, r4, r4, r4, r0, r0
iteration	0, 1, 2			0, 1, 2, 3, 4, 5

Figure 7. Training sequences for continuous operation, short pattern presentation (4 STM time constants). The reset mechanism detects significant changes in input and suppresses the active recognition node.

The reset mechanism serves to detect significant changes in the input pattern relative to the pattern residing on **C** (equation (5)) and subsequently suppresses activity of the active recognition node at the time a mismatch occurs. The reset mechanism in equation (5), however, is sensitive only to the case $|\mathbf{C}|/|\mathbf{I}| < v$. In order to operate in a continuous mode, it is also necessary to detect the inverse mismatch, that is, when $|\mathbf{I}|/|\mathbf{C}| < v$. This is easily done by introducing an auxiliary node whose activity is given by

$$\alpha = f(v|\mathbf{I}| - |\mathbf{C}|) + f(v|\mathbf{C}| - |\mathbf{I}|) + \alpha|\mathbf{R}| \tag{24}$$

where α is initially set to zero. Then equation (5) becomes

$$\tau_r \dot{r}_j = f(y_j)\{D\alpha - r_j\}. \tag{25}$$

Note that once α is activated by a mismatch, it will remain active until $|\mathbf{R}| = 0$ and the new input pattern is established on $|\mathbf{C}|$.

Example training sequences for the continuous operation mode are shown in Figure 7. Note that the pattern clustering sequences are slightly different here than for the zero-initialization case. In the continuous mode, reset causes a change in recognition node if two successive input patterns do not match according to the vigilance criterion implemented in equation (24). In the zero-initialization short-presentation mode, however, reset is never activated. Recoding only occurs as the size of the pattern clusters gradually decrease. Figure 7 shows that the standard ARC may produce unstable coding in the continuous mode. With the symmetric threshold, however, stable consistent coding is produced in all cases.

Conclusions

The Adaptive Resonance Circuit is a massively parallel pattern recognition machine capable of forming stable categories over a training set of binary patterns.

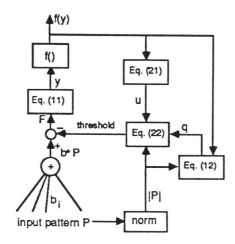

Figure 8. A "neuron" model that provides symmetric adaptive thresholding. Replace the threshold in equation (11) with the threshold from equation (22).

During operation, an arbitrary input pattern may activate a coded recognition node whose prototype pattern (the top-down pattern) bears no significant resemblance to the input pattern and there is no guarantee that the circuit will reset. In this case, the ARC will be recoded by the input pattern unless the set of weights is prevented from changing.

These shortcomings of the ARC can be overcome by using adaptive thresholding. To accomplish this, the basic neuron model acquires additional complexity. In order to prevent the spurious recoding condition, we introduced a term, q_j, which learns a measure of the "size" of the input patterns recognized by node $\mathbf{R}_j$ (see equation (12)). This addition prevents recoding in the Fast-Learn mode in which all quantities, including weights, are allowed to reach their equilibrium values before presenting a new pattern. This addition also allows stable codes to form when patterns are presented for only short periods, but the resulting clusters occasionally violate the desired "vigilance" level. The addition of another term, u_j, which tracks the amount of time that recognizer node $\mathbf{R}_j$ has been active, provides a means of implementing a symmetric adaptive threshold which prevents response to patterns that mismatch in size.

The resulting neuron model, shown in Figure 8, when connected in an ARC configuration, is able to produce stable categorizations of input patterns in Fast-Learn, Zero-Reset, and Continuous operation modes. This new "neuron" model is described by equation (22) for the binary data case but it can be easily generalized to non-binary data by treating the quantity $|\mathbf{C}|$ in equations (12) and (22) as a vector norm (e. g., let $|X| = X \cdot X$). As such the algorithm can be used for general purpose data clustering. Also, if the zero-reset mode is used for short-time pattern presentations, reset never occurs so the comparison slab serves no purpose and can be eliminated. In this configuration, the top-down and bottom-up weights are connected directly to the input slab. After learning in the short time presentation mode, the top-down weights converge to the centroids of the clustered patterns and are thus appropriate representatives of the pattern classes.

REFERENCES

[1] G. Carpenter and S. Grossberg (1987). A massively parallel architecture for a self-organizing neural pattern recognition machine. *Computer Vision, Graphics, and Image Processing*, **37**, 54.

[2] T. W. Ryan, C. L. Winter, and C. J. Turner (1987). Dynamic control of an artificial neural system: The property inheritance network. *Applied Optics*, **26**(23), 4961–4971.

[3] R. P. Lippmann (1987). An introduction to computing with neural nets. *IEEE ASSP Magazine*, **4**(**2**), April.

[4] D. E. Rumelhart and J. L. McClelland (Eds.) (1986). **Parallel distributed processing, Volume 1**. Cambridge, MA: MIT Press.

[5] T. Kohonen (1984). **Self-organization and associative memory**. New York: Springer-Verlag.

CHAPTER 12

ART 2: SELF-ORGANIZATION OF STABLE CATEGORY RECOGNITION CODES FOR ANALOG INPUT PATTERNS

by

Gail A. Carpenter and Stephen Grossberg

Preface

The ART 2 architecture was introduced and analysed in this article. Unlike the ART 1 architecture, it was designed to handle both analog and binary input patterns. Like the ART 1 architecture, it uses winner-take-all categorization at level F_2 in order to do so.

A number of new design constraints need to be satisfied in order to autonomously learn and perform arbitrary sequences of analog patterns at any level of vigilance. Whereas pairs of binary inputs differ by at least $+1$ in some vector entry, analog patterns may differ by arbitrarily small numbers and may be distorted by variable levels of background noise. Tasks such as conjointly suppressing a criterion level of input noise, using a quenching threshold (see Chapter 2), while distinguishing very similar input patterns at high vigilance, impose strict constraints on network design. For example, at high vigilance, spurious resets could occur due to the nonlinear processing of signals as they increase due to learning. The ART 2 design shows how these problems can be overcome by an autonomous learning system.

This article describe three variants of the ART 2 architecture. Each of these architectures employs more than one processing level in F_1. In the realizations described herein, three internal levels of F_1 are used, one to preprocess bottom-up inputs, one to preprocess top-down expectations, and the middle level to match the preprocessed bottom-up and top-down data and to modify the preprocessing levels based upon the outcome. Development of an algorithmic version of ART 2, called ART 2-A, has provided ART 2 capabilities that run three orders of magnitude faster in simulations (Carpenter, Grossberg, and Rosen, 1991), making ART 2 computations for both fast learning and slow learning nearly as rapid as those of fast-learn ART 1.

Reference

Carpenter, G.A., Grossberg, S., and Rosen, D. (1991). ART2-A: An adaptive resonance algorithm for rapid category learning and recognition. Submitted for publication.

Applied Optics
1987, **26**, 4919–4930

ART 2: SELF-ORGANIZATION OF STABLE CATEGORY RECOGNITION CODES FOR ANALOG INPUT PATTERNS

Gail A. Carpenter and Stephen Grossberg†

Abstract

Adaptive resonance architectures are neural networks that self-organize stable pattern recognition codes in real-time in response to arbitrary sequences of input patterns. This article introduces ART 2, a class of adaptive resonance architectures which rapidly self-organize pattern recognition categories in response to arbitrary sequences of either analog or binary input patterns. In order to cope with arbitrary sequences of analog input patterns, ART 2 architectures embody solutions to a number of design principles, such as the stability-plasticity tradeoff, the search-direct access tradeoff, and the match-reset tradeoff. In these architectures, top-down learned expectation and matching mechanisms are critical in self-stabilizing the code learning process. A parallel search scheme updates itself adaptively as the learning process unfolds, and realizes a form of real-time hypothesis discovery, testing, learning, and recognition. After learning self-stabilizes, the search process is automatically disengaged. Thereafter input patterns directly access their recognition codes without any search. Thus recognition time for familiar inputs does not increase with the complexity of the learned code. A novel input pattern can directly access a category if it shares invariant properties with the set of familiar exemplars of that category. A parameter called the attentional vigilance parameter determines how fine the categories will be. If vigilance increases (decreases) due to environmental feedback, then the system automatically searches for and learns finer (coarser) recognition categories. Gain control parameters enable the architecture to suppress noise up to a prescribed level. The architecture's global design enables it to learn effectively despite the high degree of nonlinearity of such mechanisms.

† This research was supported in part by the Air Force Office of Scientific Research (AFOSR F49620-86-C-0037 and AFOSR F49620-87-C-0018), the Army Research Office (ARO DAAG-29-85-K-0095), and the National Science Foundation (NSF DMS-86-11959 (G.A.C.) and NSF IRI-84-17756 (S.G.)). We wish to thank Cynthia Suchta and Carol Yanakakis for their valuable assistance in the preparation of the manuscript.

1. Adaptive Resonance Architectures

Adaptive resonance architectures are neural networks that self-organize stable recognition codes in real time in response to arbitrary sequences of input patterns. The basic principles of adaptive resonance theory (ART) were introduced in Grossberg[1]. A class of adaptive resonance architectures, called ART 1, has since been characterized as a system of ordinary differential equations in Carpenter and Grossberg[2,3]. Theorems have been proved that trace the real-time dynamics of ART 1 networks in response to arbitrary sequences of binary input patterns. These theorems predict both the order of search, as a function of the learning history of the network, and the asymptotic category structure self-organized by arbitrary sequences of binary input patterns. They also prove the self-stabilization property and show that the system's adaptive weights oscillate at most once, yet do not get trapped in spurious memory states or local minima.

This article describes a new class of adaptive resonance architectures, called ART 2. ART 2 networks self-organize stable recognition categories in response to arbitrary sequences of analog (gray-scale, continuous-valued) input patterns, as well as binary input patterns. Computer simulations are used to illustrate system dynamics. One such simulation is summarized in Figure 1, which shows how a typical ART 2 architecture has quickly learned to group 50 inputs into 34 stable recognition categories after a single presentation of each input. The plots below each number show all those input patterns ART 2 has grouped into the corresponding category. Equations for the system used in the simulation are given in Sections 5–8.

ART networks encode new input patterns, in part, by changing the weights, or long term memory (LTM) traces, of a bottom-up adaptive filter (Figure 2). This filter is contained in pathways leading from a feature representation field (F_1) to a category representation field (F_2) whose nodes undergo cooperative and competitive interactions. Such a combination of adaptive filtering and competition, sometimes called *competitive learning*, is shared by many other models of adaptive pattern recognition and associative learning. See Grossberg[4] for a review of the development of competitive learning models. In an ART network, however, it is a second, top-down adaptive filter that leads to the crucial property of code self-stabilization. Such top-down adaptive signals play the role of learned expectations in an ART system. They enable the network to carry out attentional priming, pattern matching, and self-adjusting parallel search. One of the key insights of the ART design is that top-down attentional and intentional, or expectation, mechanisms are necessary to self-stabilize learning in response to an arbitrary input environment.

The fields F_1 and F_2, as well as the bottom-up and top-down adaptive filters, are contained within ART's *attentional subsystem* (Figure 2). An auxiliary *orienting subsystem* becomes active when a bottom-up input to F_1 fails to match the learned top-down expectation read-out by the active category representation at F_2. In this case, the orienting subsystem is activated and causes rapid reset of the active category representation at F_2. This reset event automatically induces the attentional subsystem to proceed with a parallel search. Alternative categories are tested until either an adequate match is found or a new category is established. The search remains efficient because the search strategy is updated adaptively throughout the learning process. The search proceeds rapidly, relative to the learning rate. Thus significant changes in the bottom-up and top-down adaptive filters occur only when a search ends and

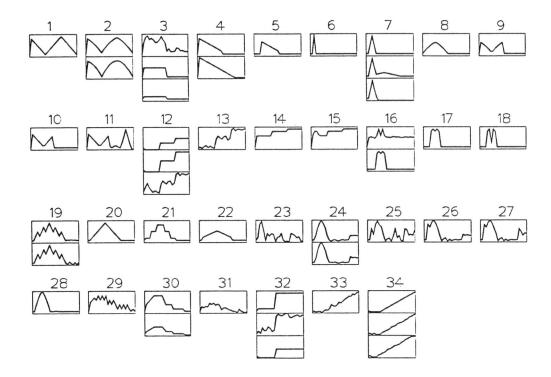

Figure 1. Category grouping of 50 analog input patterns into 34 recognition categories. Each input pattern I is depicted as a function of i ($i = 1 \ldots M$), with successive I_i values connected by straight lines. The category structure established upon one complete presentation of the 50 inputs remains stable thereafter if the same inputs are presented again.

a matched F_1 pattern resonates within the system. For the simulation illustrated in Figure 1, the ART 2 system carried out a search during many of the initial 50 input presentations.

The processing cycle of bottom-up adaptive filtering, code (or hypothesis) selection, read-out of a top-down learned expectation, matching, and code reset shows that, within an ART system, adaptive pattern recognition is a special case of the more general cognitive process of discovering, testing, searching, learning, and recognizing hypotheses. Applications of ART systems to problems concerning the adaptive processing of large abstract knowledge bases are thus a key goal for future research.

The fact that learning within an ART system occurs only within a resonant state enables such a system to solve the design tradeoff between plasticity and stability. Plasticity, or the potential for rapid change in the LTM traces, remains intact indefinitely, thereby enabling an ART architecture to learn about future unexpected events until it exhausts its full memory capacity.

Learning within a resonant state either refines the code of a previously established recognition code, based upon any new information that the input pattern may contain, or initiates code learning within a previously uncommitted set of nodes. If, for example, a new input were added at any time to the set of 50 inputs in Figure

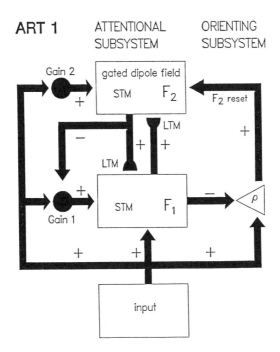

Figure 2. A typical ART 1 architecture. Rectangles represent fields where STM patterns are stored. Semicircles represent adaptive filter pathways and arrows represent paths which are not adaptive. Filled circles represent gain control nuclei, which sum input signals. Their output paths are nonspecific in the sense that at any given time a uniform signal is sent to all nodes in a receptor field. Gain control at F_1 and F_2 coordinates STM processing with input presentation rate.

1, the system would search the established categories. If an adequate match were found, possibly on the initial search cycle, the LTM category representation would be refined, if necessary, to incorporate the new pattern. If no match were found, and the full coding capacity were not yet exhausted, a new category would be formed, with previously uncommitted LTM traces encoding the STM pattern established by the input.

The architecture's adaptive search enables it to discover and learn appropriate recognition codes without getting trapped in spurious memory states or local minima. In other search models, such as search trees, the search time can become increasingly prolonged as the learned code becomes increasingly complex. In an ART architecture, by contrast, search takes place only as a recognition code is being learned, and the search maintains its efficiency as learning goes on.

Self-stabilization of prior learning is achieved via the dynamic buffering provided by read-out of a learned top-down expectation, not by switching off plasticity or restricting the class of admissible inputs. For example, after the initial presentation of 50 input patterns in the simulation illustrated by Figure 1, learning self-stabilized. In general, within an ART architecture, once learning self-stabilizes within a particular

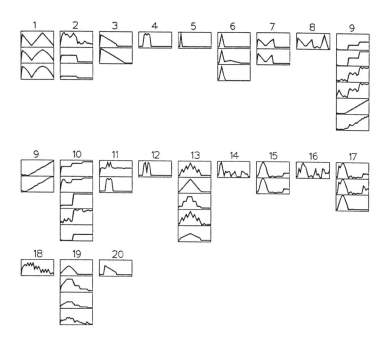

Figure 3. Lower vigilance implies coarser grouping. The same ART 2 system as used in Figure 1 has here grouped the same 50 inputs into 20 recognition categories. Note, for example, that categories 1 and 2 of Figure 1 are here joined in category 1; categories 14, 15, and 32 are here joined in category 10; and categories 19–22 are here joined in category 13.

recognition category, the search mechanism is automatically disengaged. Thereafter, that category can be directly activated, or accessed, with great rapidity and without search by any of its input exemplars.

The criterion for an adequate match between an input pattern and a chosen category template is adjustable in an ART architecture. The matching criterion is determined by a *vigilance parameter* that controls activation of the orienting subsystem. All other things being equal, higher vigilance imposes a stricter matching criterion, which in turn partitions the input set into finer categories. Lower vigilance tolerates greater top-down/bottom-up mismatches at F_1, leading in turn to coarser categories (Figure 3). In addition, at every vigilance level, the matching criterion is self-scaling: a small mismatch may be tolerated if the input pattern is complex, while the same featural mismatch would trigger reset if the input represented only a few features.

Even without any search, as when vigilance is low or the orienting subsystem is removed, ART 2 can often establish a reasonable category structure (Figure 4).

In this case, however, the top-down learned expectations assume the full burden of code self-stabilization by generating the attentional focus to dynamically buffer the emergent code. Although mismatch of bottom-up and top-down patterns at F_1 can attenuate unmatched features at F_1, such a mismatch does not elicit a search for a more appropriate F_2 code before learning can occur. Such learning will incorporate the unattenuated F_1 features into the initially selected category's recognition code. In this situation, more input trials may be needed before the code self-stabilizes; false groupings may occur during the early trials, as in category 1 of Figure 4a; and the flexible matching criterion achieved by variable vigilance is lost. Nonetheless, the top-down expectations can actively regulate the course of learning to generate a stable asymptotic code with desirable properies. For example, despite the initial anomalous coding in the example of Figure 4a, Figure 4b shows that a stable category structure is established by the third round of inputs in which the false groupings within category 1 in Figure 4a have been corrected by splitting grossly dissimilar inputs into the separate categories 1 and 7.

The top-down learned expectations and the orienting subsystem are not the only means by which an ART network carries out active regulation of the learning process. Attentional gain control at F_1 and F_2 also contributes to this active regulation (Section 2). Gain control acts to adjust overall sensitivity to patterned inputs and to coordinate the separate, asynchronous functions of the ART subsystems. Gain control nuclei are represented as large filled circles in the figures.

2. ART 1: Binary Input Patterns

Figure 2 illustrates the main features of a typical ART 1 network. Two successive stages, F_1 and F_2, of the attentional subsystem encode patterns of activation in short term memory (STM). Each bottom-up or top-down pathway between F_1 and F_2 contains an adaptive LTM trace that multiplies the signal in its pathway. The rest of the circuit modulates these STM and LTM processes. Modulation by Gain 1 enables F_1 to distinguish between a bottom-up input pattern and a top-down priming or template pattern, as well as to match these bottom-up and top-down patterns. In particular, bottom-up inputs can supraliminally activate F_2; top-down expectations in the absence of bottom-up inputs can subliminally sensitize, or prime, F_1; and a combination of bottom-up and top-down inputs is matched according to a 2/3 Rule which activates the nodes within the intersection of the bottom-up and top-down patterns (Figure 5). Thus, within the context of a self-organizing ART architecture, intentionality (or the action of learned top-down expectations) implies a spatial logic matching rule. Carpenter and Grossberg[3] prove that 2/3 Rule matching is necessary for self-stabilization of learning within ART 1 in response to arbitrary sequences of binary input patterns.

The orienting subsystem generates a reset wave to F_2 when the bottom-up input pattern and top-down template pattern mismatch at F_1, according to the vigilance criterion. The reset wave selectively and enduringly inhibits active F_2 cells until the current input is shut off. Offset of the input pattern terminates its processing at F_1 and triggers offset of Gain 2. Gain 2 offset causes rapid decay of STM at F_2, and thereby prepares F_2 to encode the next input pattern without bias.

An ART 1 system is fully defined by a system of differential equations that determine STM and LTM dynamics in response to an arbitrary temporal sequence of

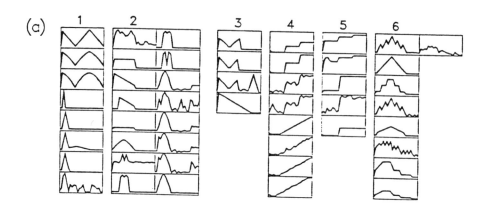

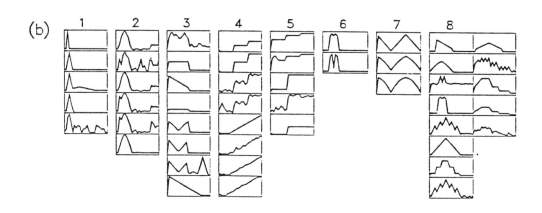

Figure 4. Category learning by an ART 2 model without orienting subsystem. (a) The same ART 2 system as used in Figures 1 and 3, but with vigilance level set equal to zero, has here grouped the same 50 inputs into 6 recognition categories after one presentation of each pattern. Without the full ART 2 system's ability to reset upon mismatch, transitory groupings occur, as in category 1. (b) By the third presentation of each input, a coarse but stable category structure has been established.

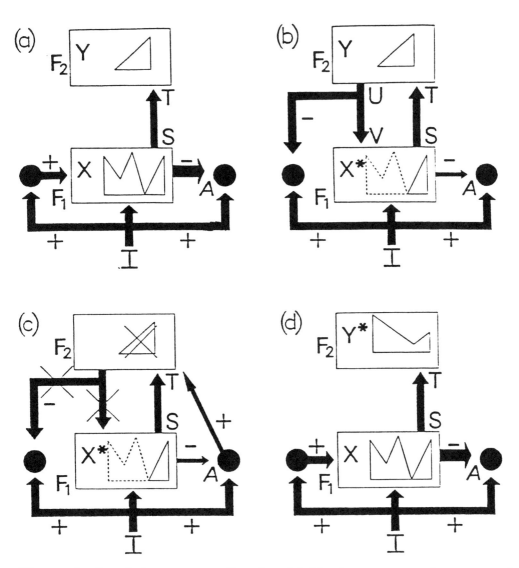

Figure 5. Search for a correct F_2 code. (a) The input pattern I generates the specific STM activity pattern X at F_1 as it nonspecifically activates A. Pattern X both inhibits A and generates the output signal pattern S. Signal pattern S is transformed into the input pattern T, which activates the STM pattern Y across F_2. (b) Pattern Y generates the top-down signal pattern U which is transformed into the template pattern V. If V mismatches I at F_1, then a new STM activity pattern X^* is generated at F_1. The reduction in total STM activity which occurs when X is transformed into X^* causes a decrease in the total inhibition from F_1 to A. (c) Then the input-driven activation of A can release a nonspecific arousal wave to F_2, which resets the STM pattern Y at F_2. (d) After Y is inhibited, its top-down template is eliminated, and X can be reinstated at F_1. Now X once again generates input pattern T to F_2, but since Y remains inhibited T can activate a different STM pattern Y^* at F_2. If the top-down template due to Y^* also mismatches I at F_1, then the rapid search for an appropriate F_2 code continues.

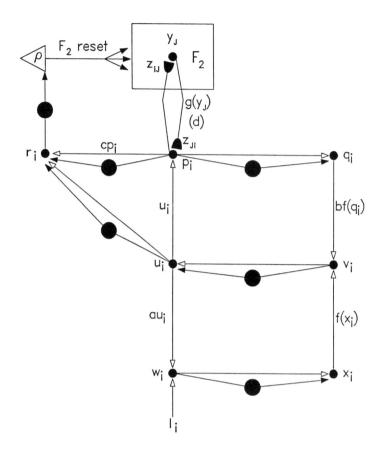

Figure 6. A typical ART 2 architecture. Open arrows indicate specific patterned inputs to target nodes. Filled arrows indicate nonspecific gain control inputs. The gain control nuclei (large filled circles) nonspecifically inhibit target nodes in proportion to the L_2-norm of STM activity in their source fields (equations (5), (6), (9), (20), and (21)). When F_2 makes a choice, $g(y_J) = d$ if the Jth F_2 node is active and $g(y_J) = 0$ otherwise. As in ART 1, gain control (not shown) coordinates STM processing with input presentation rate.

binary input patterns. Theorems characterizing these dynamics have been proved in the case where "fast learning" occurs; that is, where each trial is long enough for the LTM traces to approach equlibrium values[3]. Variations of the ART 1 architecture exhibit similar dynamics. Hence the term ART 1 designates a family, or class, of functionally equivalent architectures rather than a single model.

3. ART 2: Analog Input Patterns

ART 2 architectures are designed for the processing of analog, as well as binary, input patterns. A category representation system for analog inputs needs to be able to pick out and enhance similar signals embedded in various noisy backgrounds, as in category 16 of Figure 1.

Figure 6 illustrates a typical ART 2 architecture. A comparison of Figures 2 and 6 illustrates some of the principal differences between ART 1 and ART 2 networks. In order for ART 2 to match and learn sequences of analog input patterns in a stable fashion, its feature representation field F_1 includes several processing levels and gain control systems. Bottom-up input patterns and top-down signals are received at different locations in F_1. Positive feedback loops within F_1 enhance salient features and suppress noise. Although F_1 is more complex in ART 2 than in ART 1, the LTM equations of ART 2 are simpler.

How the signal functions and parameters of the various ART 2 architectures can best be chosen to categorize particular classes of analog input patterns for specialized applications is the subject of ongoing research. In particular, since ART 2 architectures are designed to categorize arbitrary sequences of analog or digital input patterns, an arbitrary preprocessor can be attached to the front end of an ART 2 architecture. This property is being exploited to design a self-organizing architecture for *invariant* recognition and recall using laser radar, boundary segmentation, and invariant filter methods to generate preprocessed inputs to ART 2^{5-8}.

4. ART 2 Design Principles

ART 2 architectures satisfy a set of design principles derived from an analysis of neural networks that form recognition categories for arbitrary sequences of analog input patterns. ART 2 systems have been developed to satisfy the multiple design principles or processing constraints that give rise to the architecture's emergent properties. At least three variations on the ART 2 architecture have been identified that are capable of satisfying these constraints. Indeed, the heart of the ART 2 analysis consists of discovering how different combinations of network mechanisms work together to generate particular combinations of desirable emergent properties. That is why theoretical ablation experiments on ART 2 architectures have proved to be so useful, since they reveal which emergent properties are spared and which are lost in reduced architectures.

In each ART 2 architecture, combinations of normalization, gain control, matching, and learning mechanisms are interwoven in generally similar ways. Although how this is done may be modified to some extent, in all of the ART 2 variations that we have discovered, F_1 needs to include different levels to receive and transform bottom-up input patterns and top-down expectation patterns, as well as an interfacing level of interneurons that matches the transformed bottom-up and top-down information and feeds the results back to the bottom and top F_1 levels. How the particular F_1 levels shown in Figure 6 work will be described in Sections 9–12. Alternative ART 2 models are illustrated in Section 13 and in Carpenter and Grossberg[5].

We will now describe the main ART 2 design principles.

Stability-Plasticity Tradeoff: An ART 2 system needs to be able to learn a stable recognition code in response to an arbitrary sequence of analog input patterns. Since the plasticity of an ART system is maintained for all time, and since input presentation times can be of arbitrary duration, STM processing must be defined in such a way that a sustained new input pattern does not wash away previously learned information. Section 12 shows how removal, or ablation, of one part of the F_1 internal feedback loop in Figure 6 can lead to a type of instability in which a single input, embedded in a particular input sequence, can jump between categories indefinitely.

Search-Direct Access Tradeoff: An ART 2 system carries out a parallel search in order to regulate the selection of appropriate recognition codes during the learning process, yet automatically disengages the search process as an input pattern becomes familiar. Thereafter the familiar input pattern directly accesses its recognition code no matter how complex the total learned recognition structure may have become, much as we can rapidly recognize our parents at different stages of our life even though we may learn much more as we grow older.

Match-Reset Tradeoff: An ART 2 system needs to be able to resolve several potentially conflicting properties which can be formulated as variants of a design tradeoff between the requirements of sensitive matching and formation of new codes.

The system should on the one hand, be able to recognize and react to arbitrarily small differences between an active F_1 STM pattern and the LTM pattern being read-out from an established category. In particular, if vigilance is high, the F_1 STM pattern established by a bottom-up input exemplar should be nearly identical to the learned top-down $F_2 \rightarrow F_1$ expectation pattern in order for the exemplar to be accepted as a member of an established category. On the other hand, when an uncommitted F_2 node becomes active for the first time, it should be able to remain active, without being reset, so that it can encode its first input exemplar, even though in this case there is no top-down/bottom-up pattern match whatsoever. Section 9 shows how a combination of an appropriately chosen ART 2 reset rule and LTM initial values work together to satisfy both of these processing requirements. In fact, ART 2 parameters can be chosen to satisfy the more general property that learning increases the system's sensitivity to mismatches between bottom-up and top-down patterns.

STM Invariance under Read-out of Matched LTM: Further discussion of match-reset tradeoff clarifies why F_1 is composed of several internal processing levels. Suppose that before an uncommitted F_2 node is first activated, its top-down $F_2 \rightarrow F_1$ LTM traces are chosen equal to zero. On the node's first learning trial, its LTM traces will progressively learn the STM pattern that is generated by the top level of F_1. As noted above, such learning must not be allowed to cause a mismatch capable of resetting F_2, because the LTM traces have not previously learned any other pattern. This property is achieved by designing the bottom and middle levels of F_1 so that their STM activity patterns are not changed at all by the read-out of these LTM traces as they learn their first positive values.

More generally, F_1 is designed so that read-out by F_2 of a previously learned LTM pattern that matches perfectly the STM pattern at the top level of F_1 does not change the STM patterns circulating at the bottom and middle levels of F_1. Thus, in a perfect match situation, or in a situation where a zero-vector of LTM values learns a perfect match, the STM activity patterns at the bottom and middle F_1 levels are left invariant; hence, no reset occurs.

This invariance property enables the bottom and middle F_1 levels to nonlinearly transform the input pattern in a manner that remains stable during learning. In particular, the input pattern may be contrast enhanced while noise in the input is suppressed. If read-out of a top-down LTM pattern could change even the baseline of activation at the F_1 levels which execute this transformation, then the degree of contrast enhancement and noise suppression could be altered, thereby generating a new STM pattern for learning by the top-down LTM traces. The STM invariance property prevents read-out of a perfectly matched LTM pattern from causing reset by preventing any change whatsoever from occurring in the STM patterning at the lower F_1 levels.

Coexistence of LTM Read-out and STM Normalization: The STM invariance property leads to the use of multiple F_1 levels because the F_1 nodes at which top-down LTM read-out occurs receive an additional input when top-down signals are active than when they are not. The extra F_1 levels provide enough degrees of computational freedom to both read-out top-down LTM and normalize the total STM pattern at the top F_1 level before this normalized STM pattern can interact with the middle F_1 level at which top-down and bottom-up information are matched.

In a similar fashion, the bottom F_1 level enables an input pattern to be normalized before this normalized STM pattern can interact with the middle F_1 level. Thus separate bottom and top F_1 levels provide enough degrees of computational freedom to compensate for fluctuations in baseline activity levels. In the absence of such normalization, confusions between useful pattern differences and spurious baseline fluctuations could easily upset the matching process and cause spurious reset events to occur, thereby destabilizing the network's search and learning processes.

No LTM Recoding by Superset Inputs: Although read-out of a top-down LTM pattern that perfectly matches the STM pattern at F_1's top level never causes F_2 reset, even a very small mismatch in these patterns is sufficient to reset F_2 if the vigilance parameter is chosen sufficiently high. The middle F_1 level plays a key role in causing the attenuation of STM activity that causes such a reset event to occur.

An important example of such a reset-inducing mismatch occurs when one or more, but not all, of the top-down LTM traces equal zero or very small values and the corresponding F_1 nodes have positive STM activities. When this occurs, the STM activities of these F_1 nodes are suppressed. If the total STM suppression is large enough to reset F_2, then the network searches for a better match. If the total STM suppression is not large enough to reset F_2, then the top-down LTM traces of these nodes remain small during the ensuing learning trial, because they sample the small STM values that their own small LTM values have caused.

This property is a version of the 2/3 Rule that has been used to prove stability of learning by an ART 1 architecture in response to an arbitrary sequence of binary input patterns[3]. It also is necessary in order for ART 2 to achieve stable learning in response to an arbitrary sequence of analog input patterns (Section 12). In the jargon of ART 1, a *superset* bottom-up input pattern cannot recode a *subset* top-down expectation. In ART 1, this property was achieved by an intentional gain control channel (Figure 2). In the versions of ART 2 developed so far, it is realized as part of F_1's internal levels. These design variations are still a subject of ongoing research.

Stable Choice until Reset: Match-reset trade-off also requires that only a reset event that is triggered by the orienting subsystem can cause a change in the chosen F_2 code. This property is imposed at any degree of mismatch between a top-down $F_2 \to F_1$ LTM pattern and the circulating F_1 STM pattern. Thus all the network's real-time pattern processing operations, including top-down $F_2 \to F_1$ feedback, the fast nonlinear feedback dynamics within F_1, and the slow LTM changes during learning must be organized to maintain the original $F_1 \to F_2$ category choice, unless F_2 is actively reset by the orienting subsystem.

Contrast Enhancement, Noise Suppression, and Mismatch Attenuation by Nonlinear Signal Functions: A given class of analog signals may be embedded in variable levels of background noise (Figure 1). A combination of normalization and nonlinear feedback processes within F_1 determines a noise criterion and enables the system to separate signal from noise. In particular, these processes contrast enhance the F_1 STM pattern, and hence also the learned LTM patterns. The degree of contrast enhancement and noise suppression is determined by the degree of nonlinearity in the feedback signal functions at F_1.

A nonlinear signal function operating on the sum of normalized bottom-up and top-down signals also correlates these signals, just as squaring a sum $A+B$ of two L_2-normalized vectors generates $2(1 + A \cdot B)$. Nonlinear feedback signalling hereby helps to attenuate the total activation of F_1 in response to mismatched bottom-up input and top-down expectation patterns, as well as to contrast-enhance and noise-suppress bottom-up input patterns. Figure 8e below shows that the absence of nonlinearity in the F_1 feedback loop can lead to all subpatterns of a pattern being coded in the same category under conditions of low vigilance.

Rapid Self-Stabilization: A learning system that is unstable in general can be made more stable by making the learning rate so slow that LTM traces change little on a single input trial. In this case, many learning trials are needed to encode a fixed set of inputs. Learning in an ART system needs to be slow relative to the STM processing rate (Section 5), but no restrictions are placed on absolute rates. Thus ART 2 is capable of stable learning in the "fast learning" case, in which LTM traces change so quickly that they can approach new equilibrium values on every trial. The ART 2 simulations in this article were all carried out under fast learning conditions, and rapid code self-stabilization occurs in each case. Self-stabilization is also sped up by the action of the orienting subsystem, but can also occur rapidly even without it (Figures 4 and 8).

Normalization: Several different schemes may be used to normalize activation patterns across F_1. In this article, we used nonspecific inhibitory interneurons (schematized by large black disks in Figure 6). Each such normalizer uses $O(M)$ connections where M is the number of nodes to be normalized. Alternatively, a shunting on-center off-surround network could be used as a normalizer[9], but such a network uses $O(M^2)$ connections.

Local Computations: ART 2 system STM and LTM computations use only information available locally and in real-time. There are no assumptions of weight transport, as in back propagation, nor of an *a priori* input probability distribution, as in simulated annealing. Moreover, all ART 2 local equations have a simple form (Sections 5–8). It is the architecture as a whole that endows the model with its desirable emergent computational properties.

5. ART 2 STM Equations: F_1

The potential, or STM activity, V_i of the ith node at any one of the F_1 processing stages obeys a membrane equation[10] of the form

$$\epsilon \frac{d}{dt} V_i = -A V_i + (1 - B V_i) J_i^+ - (C + D V_i) J_i^- \tag{1}$$

$(i = 1 \ldots M)$. Term J_i^+ is the total excitatory input to the ith node and J_i^- is the total inhibitory input. In the absence of all inputs, V_i decays to 0. The dimensionless parameter ϵ represents the ratio between the STM relaxation time and the LTM relaxation time. With the LTM rate $O(1)$, then

$$0 < \epsilon \ll 1. \tag{2}$$

Also, $B \equiv 0$ and $C \equiv 0$ in the F_1 equations of the ART 2 example in Figure 6. Thus the STM equations, in the singular form as $\epsilon \to 0$, reduce to

$$V_i = \frac{J_i^+}{A + DJ_i^-}. \tag{3}$$

In this form, the dimensionless equations (4)–(9) characterize the STM activities, p_i, q_i, u_i, v_i, w_i, and x_i, computed at F_1:

$$p_i = u_i + \sum_j g(y_j) z_{ji} \tag{4}$$

$$q_i = \frac{p_i}{e + \| p \|} \tag{5}$$

$$u_i = \frac{v_i}{e + \| v \|} \tag{6}$$

$$v_i = f(x_i) + b f(q_i) \tag{7}$$

$$w_i = I_i + a u_i \tag{8}$$

$$x_i = \frac{w_i}{e + \| w \|} \tag{9}$$

where $\| V \|$ denotes the L_2-norm of a vector V, y_j is the STM activity of the jth F_2 node, and z_{ji} is the LTM weight in the pathway from the jth F_2 node to the ith F_1 node. The nonlinear signal function f in equation (7) is typically of the form

$$f(x) = \begin{cases} \frac{2\theta x^2}{(x^2 + \theta^2)} & \text{if } 0 \le x \le \theta \\ x & \text{if } x \ge \theta, \end{cases} \tag{10}$$

which is continuously differentiable, or

$$f(x) = \begin{cases} 0 & \text{if } 0 \le x < \theta \\ x & \text{if } x \ge \theta, \end{cases} \tag{11}$$

which is piecewise linear. The graph of function $f(x)$ in equation (10) may also be shifted to the right, making $f(x) = 0$ for small x, as in (11). Since the variables x_i and q_i are always between 0 and 1 (equations (5) and (9)), the function values $f(x_i)$ and $f(q_i)$ also stay between 0 and 1. Alternatively, the signal function $f(x)$ could also be chosen to saturate at high x values. This would have the effect of flattening pattern details like those in category 17 of Figure 1, sitting on the top of an activity peak.

6. ART 2 STM Equations: F_2

The category representation field F_2 is the same in ART 2 as in ART 1[3] The key properties of F_2 are contrast enhancement of the filtered $F_1 \to F_2$ input pattern, and reset, or enduring inhibition, of active F_2 nodes whenever a pattern mismatch at F_1 is large enough to activate the orienting subsystem.

Contrast enhancement is carried out by competition within F_2. Choice is the extreme case of contrast enhancememt. F_2 makes a choice when the node receiving the largest total input quenches activity in all other nodes. In other words, let T_j be the summed filtered $F_1 \to F_2$ input to the jth F_2 node:

$$T_j = \sum_i p_i z_{ij} \tag{12}$$

$(j = M+1 \ldots N)$. Then F_2 is said to make a choice if the Jth F_2 node becomes maximally active, while all other nodes are inhibited, when

$$T_J = \max\{T_j : j = M+1 \ldots N\}. \tag{13}$$

F_2 reset may be carried out in several ways, one being use of a *gated dipole field* network in F_2. When a nonspecific arousal input reaches an F_2 gated dipole field, nodes are inhibited or reset (Section 8) in proportion to their former STM activity levels. Moreover this inhibition endures until the bottom-up input to F_1 shuts off. Such a nonspecific arousal wave reaches F_2, via the orienting subsystem, when a sufficiently large mismatch occurs at F_1.

When F_2 makes a choice, the main elements of the gated dipole field dynamics may be characterized as:

$$g(y_J) = \begin{cases} d & \text{if } T_J = \max\{T_j : \text{the } j^{th} \ F_2 \text{ node has not} \\ & \text{been reset on the current trial}\} \\ 0 & \text{otherwise.} \end{cases} \tag{14}$$

Equation (14) implies that (4) reduces to

$$p_i = \begin{cases} u_i & \text{if } F_2 \text{ is inactive} \\ u_i + dz_{Ji} & \text{if the } J^{th} \ F_2 \text{ node is active.} \end{cases} \tag{15}$$

7. ART 2 LTM Equations

The top-down and bottom-up LTM trace equations for ART 2 are given by

$$\text{Top} - \text{down } (F_2 \to F_1): \quad \frac{d}{dt} z_{ji} = g(y_j)[p_i - z_{ji}] \tag{16}$$

$$\text{Bottom} - \text{up } (F_1 \to F_2): \quad \frac{d}{dt} z_{ij} = g(y_j)[p_i - z_{ij}]. \tag{17}$$

If F_2 makes a choice, (14)–(17) imply that, if the Jth F_2 node is active, then

$$\frac{d}{dt} z_{Ji} = d[p_i - z_{Ji}] = d(1 - d)\left[\frac{u_i}{1 - d} - z_{Ji}\right] \tag{18}$$

and

$$\frac{d}{dt}z_{iJ} = d[p_i - z_{iJ}], \tag{19}$$

with $0 < d < 1$. For all $j \neq J$, $dz_{ji}/dt = 0$ and $dz_{ij}/dt = 0$. Sections 9 and 11 give admissible bounds on the initial values of the LTM traces.

8. ART 2 Reset Equations: The Orienting Subsystem

Since a binary pattern match may be computed by counting matched bits, ART 1 architectures do not require patterned information in the orienting subsystem (Figure 2). In contrast, computation of an analog pattern match does require patterned information. The degree of match between an STM pattern at F_1 and an active LTM pattern is determined by the vector $r = (r_1 \ldots r_M)$, where for the ART 2 architecture of Figure 6,

$$r_i = \frac{u_i + cp_i}{e + \| u \| + \| cp \|}. \tag{20}$$

The orienting subsystem is assumed to reset F_2 whenever an input pattern is active and

$$\frac{\rho}{e + \| r \|} > 1, \tag{21}$$

where the vigilance parameter ρ is set between 0 and 1.

For simplicity, we will henceforth consider an ART 2 system in which F_2 makes a choice and in which e is set equal to 0. Thus $\| x \| = \| u \| = \| q \| = 1$. Simulations use the piecewise linear signal function f in equation (11).

9. The Match-Reset Tradeoff: Choice of Top-down Initial LTM Values

Vector r gives rise to all the properties required to satisfy the match-reset tradeoff described in Section 4. Note first that, when the Jth F_2 node is active, equation (20) implies that

$$\| r \| = \frac{[\, 1 + 2 \| cp \| \cos(u,p) + \| cp \|^2 \,]^{1/2}}{1 + \| cp \|}, \tag{22}$$

where $\cos(u,p)$ denotes the cosine of the angle between the vector u and the vector p. Also, by equation (15), the vector p equals the sum $u + dz_J$, where $z_J \equiv (z_{J1} \ldots z_{JM})$ denotes the top-down vector of LTM traces projecting from the Jth F_2 node. Since $\| u \| = 1$, the geometry of the vector sum $p = u + dz_J$ implies that

$$\| p \| \cos(u,p) = 1 + \| dz_J \| \cos(u, z_J). \tag{23}$$

Also,

$$\| p \| = [\, 1 + 2 \| dz_J \| \cos(u, z_J) + \| dz_J \|^2 \,]^{1/2}. \tag{24}$$

Equations (22)–(24) imply that

$$\| r \| = \frac{[\, (1+c)^2 + 2(1+c) \| cd \, z_J \| \cos(u, z_J) + \| cd \, z_J \|^2 \,]^{1/2}}{1 + [\, c^2 + 2c \| cd \, z_J \| \cos(u, z_J) + \| cd \, z_J \|^2 \,]^{1/2}}. \tag{25}$$

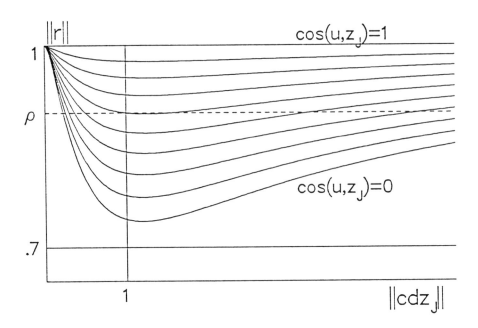

Figure 7. Graph of $\| r \|$ as a function of $\| cd \ z_J \|$ for values of $\cos(u, z_J)$ between 0 and 1 and for $c = .1$ and $d = .9$. F_2 reset occurs whenever $\| r \|$ falls below the vigilance parameter ρ.

Both numerator and denominator equal $1 + c + \| cd \ z_J \|$ when $\cos(u, z_J) = 1$. Thus $\| r \| = 1$ when the STM pattern u exactly matches the LTM pattern z_J, up to a constant multiple.

Figure 7 graphs $\| r \|$ as a function of $\| cdz_J \|$ for various values of $\cos(u, z_J)$. The Jth F_2 node remains active only if $\rho \leq \| r \|$. Since $\rho < 1$, Figure 7 shows that this will occur either if $\cos(u, z_J)$ is close to 1 or if $\| z_J \|$ is close to 0. That is, no reset occurs if the STM vector u is nearly parallel to the LTM vector z_J or if the top-down LTM traces z_{Ji} are all small. By equation (18), z_J becomes parallel to u during learning, thus inhibiting reset. Reset must also be inhibited, however, while a new category is being established. Figure 7 shows that this can be accomplished by making all $\| z_j \|$ small before any learning occurs; in particular, we let the top-down initial LTM values satisfy:

$$z_{ji}(0) = 0, \tag{26}$$

for $i = 1 \ \ldots \ M$ and $j = M + 1 \ \ldots \ N$.

Condition (26) ensures that no reset occurs when an uncommitted F_2 node first becomes active. Hence learning can begin. Moreover, the learning rule (18) and the LTM initial value rule (26) together imply that z_J remains parallel to u as learning proceeds, so $\| r(t) \| \equiv 1$. Thus no reset ever occurs during a trial in which an uncommitted F_2 node is first activated.

10. Learning Increases Mismatch Sensitivity and Confirms Category Choice

Figure 7 suggests how to implement the property that learning increases sensitivity to mismatches between bottom-up and top-down patterns. Figure 7 indicates that, for fixed $\cos(u, z_J)$, $\| r \|$ is a decreasing function of $\| cd\, z_J \|$ for $\| cd\, z_J \| \leq 1$. In fact, in the limit as $c \to 0$, the minimum of each curve approaches the line $\| cd\, z_J \| = 1$. By equations (18) and (26), $\| z_J \| < 1/(1 - d)$ and $\| z_J \| \to 1/(1 - d)$ during learning. Therefore implementation of the property that learning increases mismatch sensitivity translates into the parameter constraint

$$\frac{cd}{1 - d} \leq 1. \tag{27}$$

The closer the ratio $cd/(1 - d)$ is chosen to 1 the more sensitive the system is to mismatches, all other things being equal.

Parameter constraint (27) helps to ensure that learning on a given trial confirms the intial category choice on that trial. To see this note that, if an established category is chosen, $\| z_J \|$ is close to $1/(1 - d)$ at the beginning and end of a "fast learning" trial. However $\| z_J \|$ typically decreases and then increases during a learning trial. Therefore if $cd/(1-d)$ were greater than 1, the reset inequality (21) could be satisfied while $\| z_J \|$ was decreasing. Thus, without (27), it would be difficult to rule out the possibility of unexpected F_2 reset in the middle of a learning trial.

11. Choosing a New Category: Bottom-up LTM Initial Values

Section 9 discusses the fact that the top-down initial LTM values $z_{ji}(0)$ need to be chosen small, or else top-down LTM read-out by an uncommitted node could lead to immediate F_2 reset rather than learning of a new category. The bottom-up LTM initial values $z_{ij}(0)$ also need to be chosen small, but for different reasons.

Let $z^J \equiv (z_{1J} \, \ldots \, z_{MJ})$ denote the bottom-up vector of LTM traces that project to the Jth F_2 node. Equation (19) implies that $\| z^J \| \to 1/(1 - d)$ during learning. If $\| z^J(0) \|$ were chosen greater than $1/(1-d)$, an input that first chose an uncommitted node could switch to other uncommitted nodes in the middle of a learning trial. It is thus necessary to require that

$$\| z^J(0) \| \leq \frac{1}{1 - d}. \tag{28}$$

Inequality (28) implies that if each $z^J(0)$ is uniform, then each LTM trace must satisfy the constraint

$$z_{ij}(0) \leq \frac{1}{(1 - d)\sqrt{M}} \tag{29}$$

for $i = 1 \, \ldots M$ and $j = M + 1 \, \ldots \, N$. Alternatively, random numbers or trained patterns could be taken as initial LTM values. If bottom-up input is the sole source of F_2 activation, at least some $z_{iJ}(0)$ values need to be chosen positive if the Jth F_2 node is ever to become active.

Choosing equality in (29) biases the ART 2 system as much as possible toward choosing uncommitted nodes. A typical input would search only those nodes with which it is fairly well matched, and then go directly to an uncommitted node. If no learned category representation forms a good match, an uncommitted node will be directly accessed. Setting the initial bottom-up LTM trace values as large as possible, therefore, helps to stabilize the ART 2 network by ensuring that the system will form a new category, rather than recode an established but badly mismatched one, when vigilance is too low to prevent recoding by active reset via the orienting subsystem. Thus construction of the instability example in Figure 8c requires, in addition to the removal of the orienting subsystem and the internal feedback at F_1, that the initial bottom-up LTM trace values be significantly less than the maximum allowed by condition (29).

12. The Stability-Plasticity Tradeoff

ART 2 design principles permit arbitrary sequences of patterns to be encoded during arbitrarily long input trials, and the ability of the LTM traces to learn does not decrease with time. Some internal mechanism must therefore buffer established ART category structures against ceaseless recoding by new input patterns. ART 1 architectures buffer category structures by means of the 2/3 Rule for pattern matching (Figure 5). During matching, an F_1 node in ART 1 can remain active only if it receives significant inputs both bottom-up and top-down. ART 1 implements the 2/3 Rule using an inhibitory attentional gain control signal that is read out with the top-down LTM vector (Figure 2).

ART 2 architectures implement a weak version of the 2/3 Rule in which, during matching, an F_1 node can remain active only if it receives significant top-down input. It is possible, however, for a node receiving large top-down input to remain stored in memory even if bottom-up input to that node is absent on a given trial. The corresponding feature, which had been encoded as significant by prior exemplars, would hence remain part of the category representation although unmatched in the active exemplar. It would, moreover, be partially restored in STM. During learning, the relative importance of that feature would decline, but it would not necessarily be eliminated. However, a feature consistently absent from most category exemplars would eventually be removed from the category's expectation pattern z_J. The ART 2 matching rule implies that the feature would then not be relearned; if present in a given exemplar, it would be treated as noise.

All parts of the F_1 feedback loop in Figure 6 work together to implement this ART 2 matching rule. The five simulations in Figure 8 illustrate the roles of different components of the ART 2 system. Each column shows the ART 2 response to a sequence of 4 input patterns (A, B, C, and D) presented in the order ABCAD on trials 1–5 and again on trials 6–10. The ART 2 system dynamics established on the second round are stable, and thus would be repeated indefinitely if the same input sequence was repeated. Parameters c and d are held fixed throughout. The simulations explore the role of the remaining parameters, a, b, θ, and ρ.

Figure 8a shows a simulation with parameters a, b, and θ in a normal range, but with the vigilance parameter, ρ, set so high that the 4 inputs establish 4 categories. Two graphs are depicted for each trial: the top graph shows the input pattern ($I = A, B, C$, or D) and the bottom graph shows the LTM expectation pattern (z_J) at the end of the trial. The category number is shown beside the graph of z_J. On trial 1, input A establishes category 1. Note that pattern A is contrast-enhanced in LTM, due to the fact that the pattern troughs are below the noise level defined by the signal

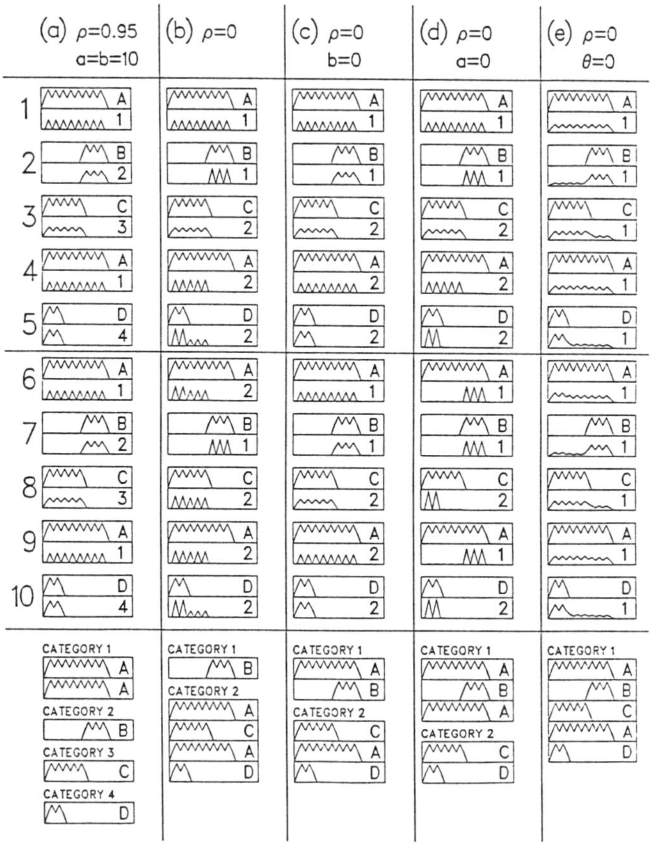

Figure 8. ART 2 matching processes. The ART 2 system of Figure 6 was used to generate the five simulations shown in columns (a)–(e). Each column shows the first 10 simulation trials, in which four input patterns (A, B, C, D) are presented in order ABCAD on trials 1–5, and again on trials 6–10. Details are given in the text (Section 12). (a) The full ART 2 system, with $\rho = .95$, separates the 4 inputs into 4 categories. Search occurs on trials 1–5; thereafter each input directly accesses its category representation. Parameters $a = 10, b = 10, c = .1, d = .9, \theta = .2$, and $M = 25$. The initial $z_{ij}(0)$ values, 1, are half the maximum, 2, allowed by constraint (27). The piecewise linear signal function (11) is used throughout. (b) Vigilance is here set so low $(\rho = 0)$ that no search can ever occur. The coarse category structure established on trials 6–10 is, however, stable and consistent. All system parameters except ρ are as in (a). (c) With $b = 0$, the ART 2 system here generates an unstable, or inconsistent, category structure. Namely, input A goes alternatively to categories 1 and 2, and will continue to do so for as long as the sequence ABCAD repeats. All parameters except b are as in (b). Similar instability can occur when d is close to 0. (d) With $a = 0$, the ART 2 matching process differs from that which occurs when a is large; namely, the input pattern I is stronger, relative to the top-down pattern z_J, than in (b). All parameters except a are as in (b). Similar processing occurs when d is small (~ 0.1) but not close to 0. (e) With $\theta = 0$, the F_1 signal function f becomes linear. Without the noise suppression/contrast enhancement provided by a nonlinear f, the completely different inputs B and D are here placed in a single category. All parameters except θ are as in (b).

threshold θ (equations (7) and (11)). In fact, θ is set equal to $1/\sqrt{M}$. This is the level at which uniform patterns are treated as pure noise but any nonuniform pattern can be contrast enhanced and stored in STM.

On trial 2, pattern B, which shares all its features with A, first searches category 1. The high vigilance level leads to F_2 reset, and B establishes the new category 2. On trial 3, pattern C also searches category 1; having nothing in common with pattern B, it then goes directly to an uncommitted node and establishes category 3. When A is again presented on trial 4, it directly accesses its original category 1. On trial 5, pattern D searches category 3, then category 1, then establishes the new category 4. Learning is stabilized on the first trial. Thus, on the second set of trials, A, B, C, and D choose the same categories as before, but without any search. Hereafter, each input directly accesses its category node. The bottom portion of the column summarizes the category structure established on trials 6–10. Pattern A is shown twice because it is presented twice every 5 trials. The categorization is stable, or consistent, in the sense that each pattern recognizes its unique category every time it appears.

For the four remaining simulations in Figures 8b–8e, the vigilance parameter ρ is chosen so small that no search can ever occur. Whatever category is chosen first by the bottom-up input must accept and learn the matched F_1 STM pattern for as long as the input remains active. By eliminating reset by choosing vigilance low, one can directly test how much top-down matching can accomplish on its own. For example, in Figure 8b, low vigilance enables pattern B to be accepted on trial 2 into the category 1 that was established by pattern A on trial 1. By the weak 2/3 Rule, the critical feature pattern learned in response to B causes the collapse of LTM traces that do not correspond to B. When pattern A is presented again on trial 4, it is recoded into the category 2 that was established by pattern C on trial 3, since A is more similar to the critical feature pattern established by pattern C than to the critical feature pattern established jointly by pattern B and itself. Thereafter, the code is stable under periodic presentation of the sequence ABCAD.

Note, however, that patterns A and D are classified together, whereas B is not, even though B is more similar to A than is D. This is a consequence of eliminating reset and of fast learning during periodic presentation. In particular, the critical feature pattern learned on trial 10 illustrates the tendency for D to attenuate LTM traces outside its range. Were this tendency strengthened by increasing contrast or changing presentation order, D would have also been classified separately from A. This simulation thus shows how the ART 2 system can self-stabilize its learning in the absence of reset. In combination with Figure 8a, it also illustrates how active reset and search can generate stable categories which better reflect the similarity relationships among the input patterns.

Figure 8b also illustrates some finer details of ART 2 matching properties. Here, the F_1 feedback parameters a and b (see equations (7) and (8) and Figure 6) are large enough so that a feature once removed from the category representation (z_J) is not reinstated even if present in a category exemplar (I). Thus on trial 4, features present in the right-hand portion of pattern A are not encoded in the LTM pattern of category 2, due to the weak 2/3 Rule. However on trial 5, features absent from pattern D but initially coded in z_J are nevertheless able to remain coded, although they are weakened. Since these features are again present in the exemplars of category

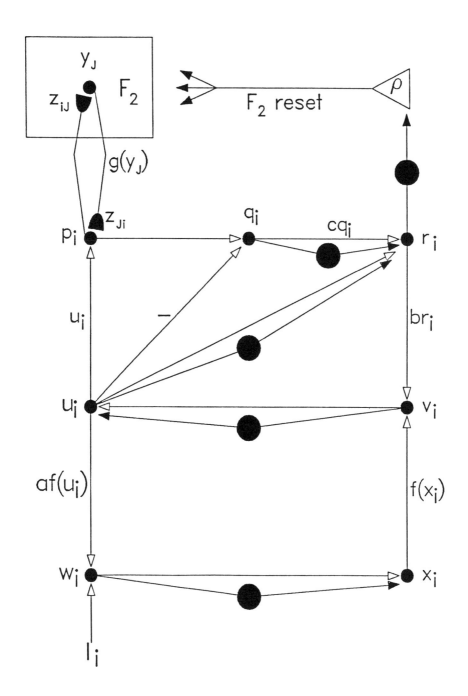

Figure 9. Alternative ART 2 architecture.

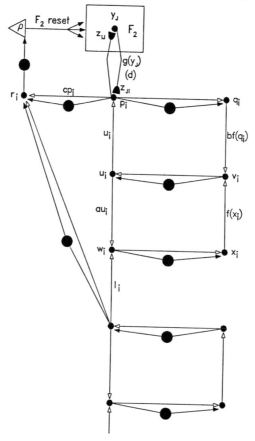

Figure 10. Alternative ART 2 architecture.

2 on trials 6, 8, and 9, they are periodically restored in LTM.

Finally, compare trial 7 in Figure 8b with trial 7 in Figure 8a. In each case pattern B has been established as the sole exemplar of a category. However in Figure 8b category 1 had contained pattern A on one previous trial. Memory of pattern A persists in the contrast-enhanced LTM pattern in Figure 8b. If the input set were more complex, this difference in learning history could possibly lead to subsequent differences in category structure.

Figure 8c illustrates that unstable coding can occur when the feedback parameter b is set equal to zero. Pattern A is placed in category 1 on trials 1, 6, etc.; and in category 2 on trials 4, 9, etc. It jumps to a new category every time it appears. With fast learning, previous LTM patterns are washed away by subsequent input patterns. Failure of the weak 2/3 Rule on trials 4, 6, 9, etc., combined with the small initial bottom-up LTM values and the absence of the orienting subsystem, leads to the instability. A large class of similar input sequences that share the subset-superset relationships of patterns A, B, C, and D also lead to unstable coding. However, if the class of input patterns were suitably restricted or if slow learning is imposed on each trial, then satisfactory results could still be obtained. Similar unstable dynamics occur if the top-down $F_2 \rightarrow F_1$ feedback parameter (d), instead of the internal F_1 feedback parameter (b), is chosen small (see Figure 6).

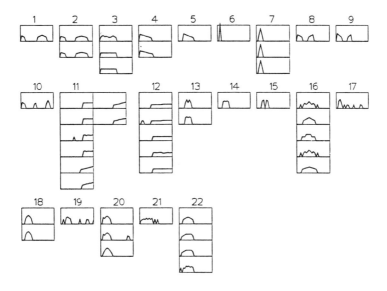

Figure 11. Recognition category summary for the ART 2 system in Figure 10. System parameters and vigilance level are the same as in Figure 3, which was generated using the ART 2 model of Figure 6. Because of the constant I input to the orienting subsystem, the ART 2 system of Figure 10 is here seen to be slightly more sensitive to pattern mismatch at a given vigilance level, all other things being equal.

Figure 8d illustrates how the lower feedback loop of the F_1 circuit in Figure 6 also buffers learned category representations against unstable recoding by bottom-up inputs. In this simulation, parameter a is set equal to 0. Similar dynamics occur if the top-down $F_2 \rightarrow F_1$ feedback parameter (d) is small, but not so small that instability occurs. Setting a equal to 0 (or making d small) has the effect of weakening the importance of the $F_2 \rightarrow F_1$ expectation feedback relative to the bottom-up input. In Figure 8d, therefore, the weak 2/3 Rule is partially violated. Note in particular the slight reinstatement on trials 4, 6, 8, and 9 of features present in I but not z_J at the start of the trial. An ART 2 system with a large and d close to 1 is better protected against potential instability than is the system of Figure 8d.

Finally, Figure 8e illustrates the role of nonlinearity in the F_1 feedback loop of ART 2. Here, the threshold parameter θ is set equal to 0 (equation (11)) so that the signal function f in equation (7) and Figure 6 is linear. Level F_1 therefore loses the properties of contrast enhancement and noise suppression. Even though the feedback parameters a, b, and d are all large, trial 2 shows that mismatched features in I, while attenuated, are never eliminated. The result is that, given the zero vigilance value, completely mismatched patterns, such as B and D, can be placed in the same category because they are parts of the superset pattern A that established the category.

TABLE 1

Corresponding Categories

Figure 3	Figure 11
1	1 and 2
2	3
3	4
4	14
5	6
6	7
7	8 and 9
8	10
9	11
10	12
11	13
12	15
13	16
14	17
15	18
16	19
17	20
18	21
19	22
20	5

13. Alternative ART 2 Architectures

Two alternative ART 2 models are shown in Figures 9 and 10. In Figure 9, the orienting subsystem pattern (r) is also part of F_1. In this model, $q = p - u$ so that $q = dz_J$ if the Jth F_2 node is active. Thus r directly computes the cosine of the angle between u and z_J. In contrast, vector r in the F_2 model of Figure 6 indirectly computes this angle by computing the angle between u and p, which is a linear combination of u and z_J. In addition the nonlinear signal function f appears twice in the lower F_1 loop in Figure 9; in Figure 6, f appears once in each F_1 loop, so that all matched input pathways projecting to any given node have the same signal function. Dynamics of the two ART 2 systems are similar. Equations for the ART 2 model of Figure 9 are given in Carpenter and Grossberg[5].

The ART 2 model in Figure 10 is also similar to the one in Figure 6, except here the input vector I is the output of a preprocessing stage that imitates the lower and upper loops of F_1. This allows I itself to be used as an input to the orienting subsystem, rather than the vector u, which is more like the architecture of ART 1 (Figure 2). The advantage of this is that I does not change when F_2 becomes active, and so provides a more stable input to the orienting subsystem throughout the trial than does u in Figure 6. Figure 11 summarizes one category structure established by the ART 2 system of Figure 10. All parameters, including vigilance, are the same in the simulations of Figures 3 and 11. The input patterns depicted in Figure 11 are the result of preprocessing the inputs of Figure 3. Table 1 shows which categories of Figure 3 correspond to categories in Figure 11. Except for categories 1 and 7 of Figure 3, which are each split into two in Figure 11, the category structure generated by the two models is identical.

REFERENCES

1. Grossberg, S. (1976). Adaptive pattern classification and universal recoding, II: Feedback, expectation, olfaction, and illusions. *Biological Cybernetics,* **23**, 187–202.

2. Carpenter, G.A. and Grossberg, S. (1985). Category learning and adaptive pattern recognition: A neural network model. *Proceedings of the Third Army Conference on Applied Mathematics and Computing,* **ARO 86-1**, 37–56.

3. Carpenter, G.A. and Grossberg, S. (1987a). A massively parallel architecture for a self-organizing neural pattern recognition machine. *Computer Vision, Graphics, and Image Processing,* **37**, 54–115.

4. Grossberg, S. (1987). Competitive learning: From interactive activation to adaptive resonance. *Cognitive Science,* **11**, 23–63.

5. Carpenter G.A. and Grossberg, S. (1987b). ART 2: Stable self-organization of pattern recognition codes for analog inputs patterns. In M. Caudill and C. Butler (Eds.), **Proceedings of the IEEE international conference on neural networks, II,** 727–736.

6. Carpenter, G.A. and Grossberg, S. (1987c). Invariant pattern recognition and recall by an attentive self-organizing ART architecture in a nonstationary world. In M. Caudill and C. Butler (Eds.), **Proceedings of the IEEE international conference on neural networks, II,** 737–746.

7. Hartley, K. (1987). Seeing the need for "ART". *Science News,* **132**, 14.

8. Kolodzy, P. (1987). Multidimensional machine vision using neural networks. In M. Caudill and C. Butler (Eds.), **Proceedings of the IEEE international conference on neural networks,** San Diego.

9. Grossberg, S. (1982). **Studies of mind and brain: Neural principles of learning, perception, development, cognition, and motor control.** Boston: Reidel Press.

10. Hodgkin, A.L. and Huxley, A.F. (1952). A quantitative description of membrane current and its applications to conduction and excitation in nerve. *Journal of Physiology,* **117**, 500–544.

ADAPTIVE BIDIRECTIONAL ASSOCIATIVE MEMORIES
by
Bart Kosko

Preface

In this 1987 article, Kosko discusses global Content-Addressable Memory (CAM) in two-level networks whose levels communicate with each other by both bottom-up and top-down signals. He calls such a network a Bidirectional Associative Memory, or BAM. A BAM thus embodies some of the properties of an ART network. In cases where the weights in the signal pathways do not change through time, the type of memory considered is STM. In cases where the weights are adaptive, Kosko calls the circuit an *adaptive* BAM.

Kosko uses the Cohen-Grossberg model and theorem (see Chapter 2) to establish global convergence of a BAM. He writes that the Cohen-Grossberg model considers "symmetric unidirectional autoassociators ... which we extend ... to arbitrary heteroassociators." This is a potentially confusing statement because the Cohen-Grossberg model and theorem consider an *arbitrary* symmetric connection matrix. *Any* network that satisfies its constraints is covered by the theorem, no matter how many levels it may have.

Kosko points out that if two levels in a network have activity vectors $(x_1, x_2, \ldots, x_n)$ and $(y_1, y_2, \ldots, y_m)$ with symmetric connections c_{ij} between the levels, then a network with the augmented activity vector $(w_1, w_2, \ldots, w_{n+m}) \equiv (x_1, x_2, \ldots, x_n, y_1, y_2, \ldots, y_m)$ can be defined wherein the connections c_{ij} form symmetric off-diagonal blocks in the new system's $(n+m) \times (n+m)$ *square* connection matrix. If the $n \times n$ and $m \times m$ on-diagonal blocks in the new connection matrix are then filled in by other symmetric matrices, then the entire connection matrix is symmetric. Here Kosko fills in with matrices with all entries equal to zero. All network trajectories will then converge to equilibrium points if the other constraints of the Cohen-Grossberg theorem also hold.

These remarks easily generalize to networks with arbitrarily many levels, connected by symmetric coefficients, whose intra-level connections are also symmetric. For example, the intra-level connections may represent additive or shunting on-center off-surround networks (see Chapters 2, 3, and 6). All such networks are special cases of the Cohen-Grossberg model. In particular, in Kosko's equations (18) and (19), the two sums over i and j collapse into one sum over the $(n+m)$ – dimensional vector $\mathbf{w}$. The BAM convergence proof described herein for additive and shunting networks is thus an application of the original Cohen-Grossberg proof.

Kosko provides a generalization of the Cohen-Grossberg theorem when he adds adaptive weights to a network's bidirectional pathways. In order to keep the coefficients symmetric, he uses the passive decay LTM equation (see Chapter 2, equation 10) with symmetric signal functions. He calls this classical learning equation by the new name *signal Hebb law*, and shows that a learning-dependent term can be added to the Cohen-Grossberg Liapunov function to define an augmented Liapunov function for the adaptive BAM.

Kosko next discusses properties of learning by an adaptive BAM. Because this network does not have an ART-style control structure that can solve the stability-plasticity dilemma, its stable learning properties depend either on the sparseness of the input patterns, or on a slow learning rate. Kosko's remarks concerning diminishing the input durations used to establish successive associations are one response to the network's instability when inputs are not sufficiently sparse. His remarks concerning the use of brief input presentations can be translated into the constraint of slow learning rates; in particular, the inputs are presented too briefly for the network to fully equilibrate to them, which could force undesired forgetting. A similar slow-learning constraint is used to help stabilize back propagation learning (see Chapters 1 and 2). Kosko's final remarks about "abstraction" by the network use the fact that balanced fluctuations tend to average out when slow learning is used.

What is the mathematical relationship between the ART 1 absolute stability proved in Chapter 10 for learning in response to an arbitrary *sequence* of binary input patterns and the Cohen-Grossberg model of CAM learning used by Kosko to prove convergence in response to an *individual* input? One important relationship is as follows. It is assumed in the ART 1 proof that the activation patterns at levels F_1 and F_2 quickly converge to an equilibrium pattern in response to any fixed input, or to any relatively slow change in system parameters due to learning. The ART 1 proof implicitly uses the Cohen-Grossberg theorem to guarantee stability of short term memory, in particular F_2 choice, in response to each fixed input. The heart of the proof uses special control mechanisms of the full ART 1 architecture to analyse how stable learning and categorization are achieved in response to an arbitrary sequence of inputs. Several of these mechanisms are not incorporated into the adaptive BAM design; hence, its susceptibility to a larger number of learning instabilities when presented with arbitrary input sequences.

Applied Optics
1987, **26**, 4947–4960
©1987 Optical Society of America

ADAPTIVE BIDIRECTIONAL ASSOCIATIVE MEMORIES

Bart Kosko†

Abstract

Bidirectionality, forward and backward information flow, is introduced in neural networks to produce two-way associative search for stored stimulus-response associations (A_i, B_i). Two fields of neurons, F_A and F_B, are connected by an $n \times p$ synaptic matrix M. Passing information through M gives one direction, passing information through its transpose M^T gives the other. Every matrix is bidirectionally stable for bivalent and for continuous neurons. Paired data (A_i, B_i) are encoded in M by summing bipolar correlation matrices. The bidirectional associative memory (BAM) behaves as a two-layer hierarchy of symmetrically connected neurons. When the neurons in F_A and F_B are activated, the network quickly evolves to a stable state of two-pattern reverberation, or pseudoadaptive resonance, for every connection topology M. The stable reverberation corresponds to a system energy local minimum. An adaptive BAM allows M to rapidly learn associations without supervision. Stable short-term memory reverberations across F_A and F_B gradually seep pattern information into the long-term memory connections M, allowing input associations (A_i, B_i) to dig their own energy wells in the network state space. The BAM correlation encoding scheme is extended to a general Hebbian learning law. Then every BAM adaptively resonates in the sense that all nodes and edges quickly equilibrate in a system energy local minimum. A sampling adaptive BAM results when many more training samples are presented than there are neurons in F_A and F_B, but presented for brief pulses of learning, not allowing learning to fully or nearly converge. Learning tends to improve with sample size. Sampling adaptive BAMs can learn some simple continuous mappings and can rapidly abstract bivalent associations from several noisy gray-scale samples.

---

† This research was supported by the Air Force Office of Scientific Research (AFOSR F49620-86-C-0070) and the Advanced Research Projects Agency of the Department of Defense under ARPA Order 5794. The author thanks Robert Sasseen for developing all software and graphics.

I. Introduction: Storing Data Pairs in Associative Memory Matrices

An $n \times p$ real matrix M can be interpreted as a matrix of synapses between two fields of neurons. The input or bottom-up field F_A consists of n neurons $\{a_1, \ldots, a_n\}$. The output or top-down field F_B consists of p neurons $\{b_1, \ldots, b_p\}$. The neurons a_i and b_j are the units of short-term memory (STM). For convenience, we shall use a_i and b_j to indicate neuron names and neuron states. Matrix entry m_{ij} is the synaptic connection from a_i to b_j. It is the unit of long-term memory (LTM). The sign of m_{ij} determines the type of synaptic connection: excitatory if $m_{ij} > 0$, inhibitory if $m_{ij} < 0$. The magnitude of m_{ij} determines the strength of the connection. A real n-dimensional row vector $\mathbf{A}$ represents a state of F_A, an STM pattern of activity across the neurons $a_1, \ldots, a_n$. A real p-dimensional row vector $\mathbf{B}$ represents a state of F_B. An associative memory is any vector space transformation $T : R^n \rightarrow R^p$. Usually T is nonlinear. The matrix mapping $M : R^n \rightarrow R^p$ is a linear associative memory. When F_A and F_B are distinct, M is a heteroassociative memory. It stores vector data pairs $(\mathbf{A}_i, \mathbf{B}_i)$. In the special case when $F_A = F_B$, M is an autoassociative associative memory. It stores data vectors $\mathbf{A}_i$.

Recall proceeds through vector-matrix multiplication and nonlinear state transition. The p-vector $\mathbf{A} M$ is a fan-in vector of input sums to the neurons in F_B: $\mathbf{A} M = (I_{b1}, \ldots, I_{bp})$. Specifically, each neuron a_i fans out its numeric output a_i across each synaptic pathway m_{ij}, sending the gated product $a_i m_{ij}$ to each neuron b_j in F_B. Each neuron b_j receives a fan-in of n gated products $a_i m_{ij}$, arriving independently and perhaps asynchronously, and sums them to compute its input $I_{bj} = a_1 m_{1j} + \ldots + a_n m_{nj}$. Neuron b_j processes input I_{bj} to produce the output signal $S(I_{bj})$. In general the signal function S is nonlinear, usually sigmoidal or S-shaped. The associative memory M recalls the vector of output signals $[S(I_{b1}), \ldots, S(I_{bp})]$ when presentred with input key A. In the simplest associative memories, linear associative memories, each neuron's output signal is simply its input signal: $S(I_{bj}) = I_{bj}$. Then associative recall is simply vector multiplication: $\mathbf{B} = \mathbf{A} M$.

What is the simplest way to store m data pairs $(A_1, B_1), (A_2, B_2), \ldots, (A_m, B_m)$ in an $n \times p$ associative memory matrix M? The simplest storage procedure is to convert each association (A_i, B_i) into an $n \times p$ matrix M_i, then combine each association matrix M_i pointwise. The simplest pointwise combination technique is addition: $M = M_1 + \ldots + M_m$. The simplest operation for converting two row vectors $\mathbf{A}_i$ and $\mathbf{B}_i$ of dimensions n and p into an $n \times p$ matrix M_i is the vector output product $\mathbf{A}_i^T \mathbf{B}_i$. So the simplest way to store m $(\mathbf{A}_i, \mathbf{B}_i)$ is to sum output product or correlation matrices:

$$M = \mathbf{A}_1^T \mathbf{B}_1 + \ldots \mathbf{A}_m^T \mathbf{B}_m. \tag{1}$$

This is the familiar storage method used in the theory of linear associative memories, studied by Kohonen[1,2] and Anderson et al.[3]. If the input patterns $\mathbf{A}_1, \ldots, \mathbf{A}_m$ are orthogonal—$\mathbf{A}_i \mathbf{A}_j^T = 1$ if $i = j$, 0 if not—perfect recall of the associated output patterns $\{\mathbf{B}_1, \ldots, \mathbf{B}_m\}$ is achieved in the forward direction

$$\mathbf{A}_i M = \mathbf{A}_i \mathbf{A}_i^T \mathbf{B}_i + \sum_{i \neq j} (\mathbf{A}_i \mathbf{A}_i^T) \mathbf{B}_j = \mathbf{B}_i. \tag{2}$$

If $\mathbf{A}_1, \ldots, \mathbf{A}_m$ are not orthonormal, as in general they are not, the second term on the right-hand side of equation (2), the noise term, contributes crosstalk to the recalled pattern by additively modulating the signal term. More generally, as Kohonen[2] has shown, the least-squares optimal linear associative memory (OLAM) M is given by $M = A^*B$, where A is the $m \times n$ matrix whose ith row is A_i, B is the $m \times p$ matrix whose ith row is B_i, and A^* is the Moore-Penrose pseudoinverse of A. If $\{A_1, \ldots, A_m\}$ are orthonormal, the OLAM $M = A^T B$, which is equivalent to the memory scheme in equation (1).

II. Discrete Bidirectional Associative Memory (BAM) Stability

Suppose we wish to synchronously feed back the recalled output B to an associative memory M to improve our recall accuracy. The recalled output B is some nonlinear transformation S of the input sum $A\,M$: $B = S(A\,M) = [S(A\,M^1), \ldots, S(A\,M^p)]$, where M^j is the jth column of M. What is the simplest way to feed B back to the associative memory? Since M has dimensions $n \times p$ and $\mathbf{B}$ is a p vector, $\mathbf{B}$ cannot vector multiply M, but it can multiply the M matrix transpose (adjoint) M^T. Thus the simplest feedback scheme is to pass $\mathbf{B}$ backward through M^T. Any other feedback scheme requires more information in the form of a $p \times n$ matrix N different from M^T. Field F_A receives the top-down message $\mathbf{B}\,M^T$ and produces the new STM pattern $A' = S(\mathbf{B}\,M^T) = [S(\mathbf{B}\,M_1^T), \ldots, S(\mathbf{B}\,M_n^T)]$ across F_A, where M_i is the ith row (column) of $M(M^T)$. Carpenter[4] and Grossberg[5-9] interpret top-down signals as expectations in their adaptive resonance theory (ART). Intuitively A' is what the field F_B expects to see when it receives bottom-up input B.

If A' is fed back through M, a new B' results, which can be fed back through M^T to produce A'', and so on. Ideally this back-and-forth flow of distributed information will quickly equilibrate or resonate on a fixed data pair (A_f, B_f):

$$A \to M \to B,$$

$$A' \leftarrow M^T \leftarrow B,$$

$$A' \to M \to B',$$

$$A'' \leftarrow M^T \leftarrow B',$$

$$\vdots$$

$$A_f \to M \to B_f,$$

$$A_f \leftarrow M^T \leftarrow B_f,$$

$$\vdots$$

If an associative memory matrix M equilibrates in this fashion for every input pair (A, B), then M is said to be bidirectionally stable[10,11].

Which matrices are bidirectionally stable to which signal functions S? Linear associative memory matrices are obviously in general not bidirectionally stable. We shall limit our discussion to sigmoidal or S-shaped signal functions S, such as $S(x) = (1 + e^{-x})^{-1}$, or more generally, to bounded monotone increasing signal functions. Grossberg[12] long ago showed that this is not a limitation at all. He proved that, roughly speaking, a sigmoidal signal function is optimal in the sense that, in unidirectional competitive networks, it computes a quenching threshold below which neural activity is suppressed as noise and above which neural activity is contrast enhanced and then stored as a stable reverberation in STM. In particular, linear signal functions amplify noise as faithfully as they amplify signals. This theoretical fact reflects the evolutionary fact that real neuron firing frequency is sigmoidal.

First we consider bivalent, or McCulloch-Pitts[13], neurons. Each neuron a_i and b_j is either on (+1) or off (0 or −1) at any time. Hence a state A of F_A is a point in the Boolean n-cube $B^n = \{0,1\}^n$ or $\{-1,1\}^n$. A state B of F_B is a point in $B^p = \{0,1\}^p$ or $\{-1,1\}^p$. A state of the bidirectional associative memory (BAM) (F_A, M, F_B) is a point (A, B) in the bivalent product space $B^n \times B^p$. Topologically, a BAM can be viewed as a two-layer hierarchy of symmetrically connected fields:

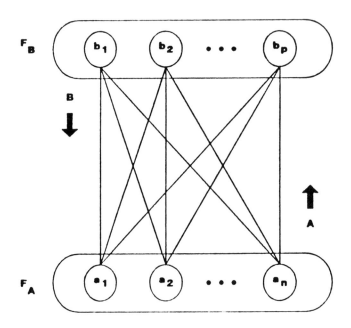

What is the simplest signal function S for a bivalent BAM (F_A, M, F_B)? The simplest S is a threshold function:

$$a_i = \begin{cases} 1 & \text{if } \mathbf{B} \, M_i^T > 0, \\ 0 & \text{if } \mathbf{B} \, M_i^T < 0. \end{cases} \tag{3}$$

$$b_j = \begin{cases} 1 & \text{if } \mathbf{A} \, M^j > 0, \\ 0 & \text{if } \mathbf{A} \, M^j < 0, \end{cases} \tag{4}$$

where once again M_i is the ith row (column) of $M(M^T)$ and M^j is the jth column (row) of $M(M^T)$. If the input sum to each neuron equals its threshold 0, the neuron maintains its current state. It stays on if it already is on, off if already off. For simplicity, each neuron has threshold 0 and no external inputs. In general, a_i has a numeric threshold T_i and constant numeric input I_i; b_j has threshold S_j and input J_j. A bivalent BAM is then specified by the vector 7-tuple $(F_A, T, I, M, F_B, S, J)$ and the threshold laws (3) and (4) are modified accordingly; e.g., $a_i = 1$ if $\mathbf{B} M_i^T + I_i > T_i$.

Which matrices M are bidirectionally stable for bivalent BAMs? All matrices. Every synaptic connection topology rapidly equilibrates, no matter how large the dimensions n and p. This surprising theorem is proved in References 11 and 14 and generalizes the well-known unidirectional stability for autoassociative networks with square symmetric M, as popularized by Hopfield[15] and reviewed below. Bidirectionality, forward and backward information flow, in neural nets produces two-way associative search for the nearest stored pair $(\mathbf{A}_i, \mathbf{B}_i)$ to an input key. Since every matrix is bidirectionally stable, many more matrices can be decoded than those in which information has been deliberately encoded.

When the BAM neurons are activated, the network quickly evolves to a stable state of two-pattern reverberation, or nonadaptive resonance[4,7]. The resonance is nonadaptive because no learning occurs. The weights m_{ij} are fixed. This behavior approximates equilibrium behavior in a learning context since changes in the synapses (LTM traces) m_{ij} are invariably slower than changes in the neuron activations (STM traces) a_i and b_j. Below we shall exploit this property to construct adaptive BAMs.

The stable reverberation corresponds to a system energy local minimum. Geometrically, an input pattern is placed on the BAM energy surface as a ball bearing in the bivalent product space $B^n \times B^p$. In paritcular, the bipolar correlation encoding scheme described below sculpts the energy surface so that the data pairs (A_i, B_i) are stored as local energy minima. The input ball bearing rolls down into the nearest basin of attraction, dissipating energy as it rolls. Frictional damping brings it to rest at the bottom of the energy well, and the pattern is classified or misclassified accordingly. Thus the BAM behaves as a programmable dissipative dynamic system.

For completeness we review the proof[10,11] that every matrix is bivalently bidirectionally stable. The proof technique is to show that some system functional $E : B^n \times B^p \to R$ is a Lyapunov function or bounded monotone decreasing energy function for the network. The energy function decreases if state changes occur. System stability occurs when the functional E rapidly obtains its lower bound, where it stays forever. Lyapunov functionals provide a shortcut to the global analysis of nonlinear dynamic systems, sidestepping the often hopeless task of solving the many coupled nonlinear difference or differential equations. The most general Lyapunov stability result is the Cohen-Grossberg theorem[16] for symmetric unidirectional autoassociators, which we extend in this and the next section to arbitrary bidirectional heteroassociators. The Lyapunov trick of the Cohen-Grossberg theorem is to substitute the neuron state-transition equations into the derivative of the appropriate energy function, and then use a sign argument to show that the derivative is always nonpositive. Hopfield[15] used the discrete version of this Lyapunov trick to show that zero-diagonal symmetric unidirectional autoassociators are stable for asynchronous or serial state changes, i.e., where at any moment at most one neuron changes state. The argument we now present subsumes this case when $F_A = F_B$ and $M = M^T$ in simple asynchronous operation. An appropriate measure of the energy of the bivalent (A, B) is the sum (average) of two energies: the energy $A\,M\,B^T$ of the forward pass and the energy $B\,M^T\,A^T$ of the backward pass. Taking the negative of these quadratic forms gives

$$
\begin{aligned}
E(A, B) &= -\frac{1}{2} A M B^T - \frac{1}{2} B M^T A^T \\
&= -A M B^T \\
&= -\sum_i \sum_j a_i b_j m_{ij},
\end{aligned}
\tag{5}
$$

provided all thresholds $T_i = S_j = 0$ and inputs $I_i = J_j = 0$, which we shall assume for simplicity. In general the appropriate energy function includes thresholds and inputs linearly:

$$E(A, B) = -AMB^T - IA^T + TA^T - JB^T + SB^T.$$

BAM convergence is proved by showing that synchronous or asynchronous state changes decrease the energy and that the energy is bounded below, so the BAM monotonically gravitates to fixed points. E is trivially bounded below for all A and B:

$$E(A, B) \geq -\sum_i \sum_j |m_{ij}|.$$

Synchronous versus asynchronous state changes must be clarified. Synchronous behavior occurs when all or some neurons within a field change their state at the same clock cycle. Asynchronous behavior is a special case. Simple asynchronous behavior occurs when only one neuron per field changes state per cycle. Subset asynchronous behavior occurs when some proper subset of neurons within a field changes state per cycle. These definitions of asynchrony are cross sectional. The resultant time-series interpretation of asynchronous behavior is that each neuron in a field randomly and independently changes state, converting the BAM network into a stochastic process. In the proof below we do not assume that changes occur concurrently in the two fields F_A and F_B. Otherwise, in principle the energy function might increase. Examination of the argument below shows, though, that this is very unlikely in a large network since so many additive terms in the energy differential are always negative. In any event, the BAM model of back-and-forth information flow we have been developing implicitly assumes that state changes are occurring in at most one field F_A or F_B at a time. Further, the Lyapunov argument below shows that synchronous operation produces sums of pointwise (neuronwise) energy changes that can be large. In practice this means synchronous updates produce much faster convergence than asynchronous updates.

First we consider state changes in field F_A. A similar argument will hold for changes in F_B. Field F_A change is denoted by $\Delta A = A_2 - A_1 = (\Delta a_1, \ldots, \Delta a_n)$ and energy change by $\Delta E = E_2 - E_1$. Hence $\Delta a_i = -1, 0,$ or $+1$ for a binary neuron. Then

$$
\begin{aligned}
\Delta E &= -\Delta AMB^T \\
&= -\sum_i \Delta a_i \sum_j b_j m_{ij} \\
&= -\sum_i \Delta a_i BM_i^T.
\end{aligned}
\tag{6}
$$

We need only consider nonzero state changes. If $\Delta a_i > 0$, the state transition law (3) above implies $B\ M_i^T > 0$. If $\Delta a_i < 0$, equation (3) implies $B\ M_i^T < 0$. Hence state change and input sum agree in sign. Hence their product is positive: $\Delta a_i B\ M_i^T > 0$. Hence $\Delta E < 0$. Similarly, the sign law (4) for b_j implies $\Delta E = -AM\Delta B^T < 0$. Since M was an arbitrary $n \times p$ real matrix, this proves that every matrix is bivalently bidirectionally stable.

III. BAM Correlation Encoding

Which BAM matrix M best encodes m binary pairs (A_i, B_i)? The correlation encoding scheme in equation (1) suggest adding the outer-product matrices $A_i^T B_i$ pointwise, at least to facilitate forward recall. Will this work for backward recall? The linearity of the transpose operator implies that it will:

$$
\begin{aligned}
M^T &= (A_1^T B_1)^T + \ldots (A_m^T B_m)^T \\
    &= B_1^T A_1 + \ldots B_m^T A_m.
\end{aligned}
\tag{7}
$$

However, the additive scheme (1) implies that if we use only binary vectors, M will contain no inhibitory synapses. So the input sums $B\, M_i^T$ and $A\, M^j$ can never be negative. So the state transition laws (3) and (4) imply that $a_i = b_j = 1$ once a_i and b_j turn on, which they probably will after the first update. Exceptions can occur for initial null vectors or a null matrix M, when $a_i = b_j = 0$.

Bipolar state vectors do not produce this problem. Suppose (X_i, Y_i) is the bipolar version of the binary pair (A_i, B_i), i.e., binary zeros are replaced with minus ones, i.e., $X_i = 2A_i - I$ and $Y_i = 2B_i - I$, where I is a unit vector of n-many or p-many ones. Then the ijth entry of $X_k^T Y_k$ is excitatory $(+1)$ if the vector elements x_i^k and y_j^k agree in sign, inhibitory (-1) if they disagree in sign. This is simple conjunctive or Hebbian correlation learning. Thus the sum M of bipolar outer-product matrices

$$
M = X_1^T Y_1 + \ldots + X_m^T Y_m
\tag{8}
$$

naturally weights the excitatory and inhibitory connections. Multiplying M or M^T by binary or bipolar vectors produces input sums of different signs, so equations (3) and (4) are not trivialized.

Note that to encode m binary vectors $\mathbf{A}_1, \ldots, \mathbf{A}_m$ in a unidirectional autoassociative memory matrix, equation (8) reduces to the symmetric matrix $X_1^T X_1 + \ldots + X_m^T X_m$, which is the storage mechanism used by Hopfield[15] (who also zeros the main diagonal to improve recall). Note also that the pair (A_i, B_i) can be unlearned or forgotten (erased) by summing $-X_i^T Y_i$, or, equivalently, by encoding (A_i^c, B_i) or (A_i, B_i^c) since bipolar complements are given by $X_i^c = -X_i$ and $Y_i^c = -Y_i$. Equation (8) allows data to be read, written, or erased from memory. Further,, $(X_i^c)^T Y_i^c = X_i^T Y_i$, so storing (A_i, B_i) through equation (8) implies storing (A_i^c, B_i^c) as well.

Strictly speaking bipolar correlation learning laws such as equation (8) can be biologically implausible. They imply that synapses can change character from excitatory to inhibitory, or inhibitory to excitatory, with successive experience. This is seldom observed with real synapses. However, when the number of stored patterns m is fairly large, $|m_{ij}| > 0$ tends to hold. So the addition or deletion of relatively few patterns does not on average change the sign of m_{ij}.

Is it better to use binary or bipolar state vectors for recall from equation (8)? In Reference 10 we prove that bipolar coding is better on average. Much of the argument can be seen from the properties of the bipolar signal-noise expansion

$$X_i M = (X_i X_i^T) Y_i + \sum_{j \neq i} (X_i X_j^T) Y_j$$

$$= n Y_i + \sum_{j \neq i} (X_i X_j^T) Y_j \tag{9}$$

$$= \sum_j c_{ij} Y_j,$$

where $c_{ij} = c_{ji} = X_i X_j^T$.

The c_{ij} are correction coefficients. Ideally the c_{ij} will behave in sign and magnitude so as to move Y_j closer to Y_i and give Y_j more positive weight the closer Y_j is to Y_i. Then the right-hand side of equation (9) will tend to equal a positive multiple of Y_i and thus threshold to Y_i or B_i. When the input X is nearer X_i than all other X_j, the subsequent output Y should tend to be nearer Y_i than all other Y_j. When Y is fed back through M^T, the output X' should tend to be even closer to X_i than X was, and so on. Combining this argument with the signal-noise expansion (9) and its transpose-based backward analog, we obtain an estimate of the BAM storage capacity for reliable recall: $m < \min(n, p)$. No more data pairs can be stored and accurately recalled than the lesser of the vector dimensions used.

This analysis explains much BAM behavior without Lyapunov techniques. However, such accurate decoding implicitly assumes that if stored input patterns are close, stored output patterns are close. Specifically we make the continuity assumption:

$$\frac{1}{n} H(A_i, A_j) \sim \frac{1}{p} H(B_i, B_j), \tag{10}$$

where $H(\ldots)$ denotes Hamming or l^1 distance. This is an implicit assumption of continuous mapping networks. When a data set substantially violates it, as in the parity mapping, which indicates whether there is an even or odd number of ones in a bit vector, supervised learning techniques such as backward error propagation[17-20] are preferable.

Do the correction coefficients c_{ij} behave as desired? They do, when (10) holds, in the sense that the naturally connect bipolar and binary spaces:

$$c_{ij} \underset{>}{\overset{<}{\lessgtr}} 0 \iff H(A_i, A_j) \underset{<}{\overset{>}{\gtrless}} n/2. \tag{11}$$

Expression (11) follows from

$$c_{ij} = X_i X_j^T$$

$$= (\text{number of common elements})$$

$$- (\text{number of different elements}) \tag{12}$$

$$= [n - H(A_i, A_j)] - H(A_i, A_j)$$

$$= n - 2H(A_i, A_j).$$

If A_j is more than half the space away, so to speak, from A_i, and thus by (10) if B_j is approximately more than half the space away from B_i, the negative sign of c_{ij}

corrects Y_j by converting it to Y_j^c, which is a better approximation of Y_i since B_j^c is approximately less than half the space away from B_i. The magnitude of c_{ij} then further corrects Y_j by directly approaching the maximum signal amplification factor, n, as $H(B_i B_j^c)$ approaches 0. If A_j is less than half the space away from A_i, then $c_{ij} > 0$ and c_{ij} approaches n as $H(B_i, B_j)$ approaches 0. If A_j is equidistant between A_i and A_i^c, then $c_{ij} = 0$. Finally, bipolar coding of state vectors is better on average than binary coding in the sense that on average

$$A_i X_i^T \overset{\geq}{\underset{<}{}} c_{ij} \iff H(A_i, A_j) \overset{\geq}{\underset{<}{}} n/2 \qquad (13)$$

tends to hold. So on avercage the c_{ij} always correct better in magnitude than the mixed coefficients $A_i X_j^T$ and sometimes the mixed coefficients can have the wrong sign.

Consider a simple example. Suppose we wish to store two pairs given by

$$A_1 = (1\ 0\ 1\ 0\ 1\ 0) \qquad B_1 = (1\ 1\ 0\ 0),$$

$$A_2 = (1\ 1\ 1\ 0\ 0\ 0) \qquad B_2 = (1\ 0\ 1\ 0).$$

Note that the vectors are nonorthogonal and that the continuity assumption (10) holds since $1/6 H(A_1, A_2) = 1/3 \sim 1/2 = 1/4 H(B_1, B_2)$. Convert these binary pairs to bipolar pairs:

$$X_1 = (1\ -1\ 1\ -1\ 1\ -1) \qquad Y_1 = (1\ 1\ -1\ -1),$$

$$X_2 = (1\ 1\ 1\ -1\ -1\ -1) \qquad Y_2 = (1\ -1\ 1\ -1).$$

Convert the bipolar pairs (X_i, Y_i) to correlation matrices $X_i^T Y_i$:

$$X_1^T Y_1 = \begin{pmatrix} 1 & 1 & -1 & -1 \\ -1 & -1 & 1 & 1 \\ 1 & 1 & -1 & -1 \\ -1 & -1 & 1 & 1 \\ 1 & 1 & -1 & -1 \\ -1 & -1 & 1 & 1 \end{pmatrix}.$$

$$X_2^T Y_2 = \begin{pmatrix} 1 & -1 & 1 & -1 \\ 1 & -1 & 1 & -1 \\ 1 & -1 & 1 & -1 \\ -1 & 1 & -1 & 1 \\ -1 & 1 & -1 & 1 \\ -1 & 1 & -1 & 1 \end{pmatrix}.$$

Then M is given by $M = X_1^T Y_1 + X_2^T Y_2$:

$$M = \begin{pmatrix} 2 & 0 & 0 & -2 \\ 0 & -2 & 2 & 0 \\ 2 & 0 & 0 & -2 \\ -2 & 0 & 0 & 2 \\ 0 & 2 & -2 & 0 \\ -2 & 0 & 0 & 2 \end{pmatrix}.$$

Then, using binary vectors for recall for ease of computing, we see that

$$A_1 M = (4 \ 2 \ -2 \ -4) \to (1 \ 1 \ 0 \ 0) = B_1,$$

$$A_2 M = (4 \ -2 \ 2 \ -4) \to (1 \ 0 \ 1 \ 0) = B_2,$$

on using the threshold signal function (4) and, on using equation (3),

$$B_1 M^T = (2 \ -2 \ 2 \ -2 \ 2 \ -2) \to (1 \ 0 \ 1 \ 0 \ 1 \ 0) = A_1,$$

$$B_2 M^T = (2 \ 2 \ 2 \ -2 \ -2 \ -2) \to (1 \ 1 \ 1 \ 0 \ 0 \ 0) = A_2.$$

The use of synchronous updates, combined with satisfying the continuity assumption and the memory capacity constraint [2 < min(6,4)], produced instant convergence to the local energy minima $E(A_1, B_1) = -A_1 M B_1^T = -(42 - 2 - 4)(1100)^T = -6 = E(A_2, B_2)$. Suppose we perturb A_2 by 1 bit. In particular, suppose we present an input $A = (011000)$ to the BAM. Then

$$A \ M = (2 \ -2 \ 2 \ -2) \to (1 \ 0 \ 1 \ 0) = B_2,$$

and thus A evokes the resonant pair (A_2, B_2) with initial energy $E(A, B_2) = -4$. Now suppose an input $A = (000110)$ is presented to the BAM. Since $H(A, A_1) = 3 < 5 = H(A, A_2)$, we might expect A to evoke the resonant pair (A_1, B_1). In fact

$$A \ M = (-2 \ 2 \ -2 \ 2) \to (0 \ 1 \ 0 \ 1) = B_2^c,$$

and B_2^c in turn recalls A_2^c, which recalls B_2^c, etc., with energies $E(A, B_2^c) = -4 > -6 = E(A_2^c, B_2^c)$ since $H(A, A_2^c) = 1$. We recall that the bipolar correlation encoding scheme (8) stores (A_i^c, B_i^c) when it stores (A_i, B_i).

Figure 1 displays snapshots of asynchronous BAM recall. Approximately six neurons update between snapshots. The spatial alphabetic associations (S, E), (M, V), and (G, N) are stored. F_A contains $n = 10 \times 14 = 140$ neurons. F_B contains $p = 9 \times 12 = 108$ neurons. A 40% noise corrupted version (99 bits randomly flipped) of (S, E) is presented to the BAM and (S, E) is perfectly recalled, illustrating the global order-from-chaos aesthetic appeal of asynchronous BAM operation.

BAMs are also natural structures for optical implementation. Perhaps the simplest all-optical implementation is a holographic resonator with M housed in a transmission hologram sandwiched between two phase-conjugate mirrors. Figures 2 and 3 display two different optical BAMs discussed in Reference 21. Figure 2 displays a simple matrix-vector multiplier BAM with M represented by a 2-D grid of pixels with varying transmittances. Figure 3 displays a BAM based on a volume reflection hologram. The box labeled threshold device accepts a weak signal image on one side and produces an intensified and contrast-enhanced version of the image on its output side. The Hughes liquid crystal light valve or two-wave mixing are two ways to implement such a device. Note that the configuration requires the hologram to be read with light of two different polarizations. Hence diffraction efficiency of holograms recorded as birefringence patterns in photorefractive crystals will be somewhat compromised.

 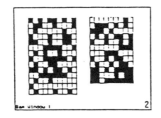 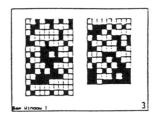

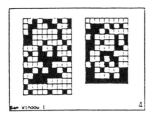 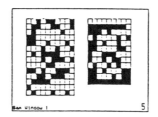 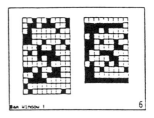

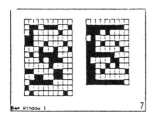 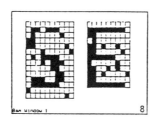 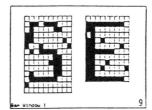

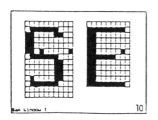 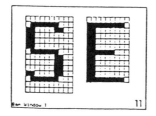

Figure 1. Asynchronous BAM recall. Approximately six neurons update per snapshot. The associated spatial patterns $(S, E), (M, V)$, and (G, N) are stored. Field F_A contains 140 neurons; F_B, 108. Perfect recall of (S, E) is achieved when recall is initiated with a 40% noise-corrupted version of (S, E).

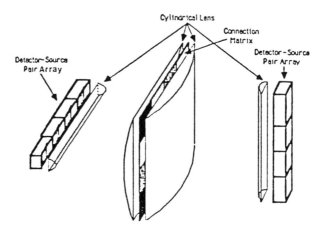

Figure 2. Matrix-vector multiplier BAM.

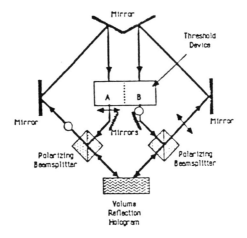

Figure 3. BAM voluume reflection hologram.

IV. Continuous BAMs

A continuous BAM[10,11] is specified by, for example, the additive dynamic system

$$\dot{a}_i = -a_i + \sum_j S(b_j)m_{ij} + I_i, \tag{14}$$

$$\dot{b}_j = -b_j + \sum_i S(a_i)m_{ij} + J_j, \tag{15}$$

where the overdot denotes time differentiation. The activations a_i and b_j can take on arbitrary real values. S is a sigmoid signal function. More generally, we shall only assume that S is bounded and strictly monotone increasing, so that $S' = dS(x)/dx > 0$. For definiteness, we assume all signals $S(x)$ are in $[0, 1]$ or $[-1, 1]$, so that the output (observable) state of the BAM is a trajectory in the product unit hypercube $I^n \times I^p$ where $I^n = [0, 1]^n$ or $[-1, 1]^n$. For example, in the simulations below we use the bipolar logistic sigmoid $S(x) = 2(1 + e^{-cx})^{-1} - 1$ for $c > 0$. I_i and J_j are constant external inputs.

The first term on the right-hand sides of equations (14) and (15) are STM passive decay terms. The second term is the endogenous feedback term. It sums gated bipolar signals from all neurons in the opposite field. The third term is the exogenous input, which is assumed to change so slowly relative to the STM reaction times that it is constant. Of course both right-hand sides of equations (14) and (15) are in general multiplied by time constants, as is each term. We omit these constants for notational convenience.

The additive model [equations (14) and (15)] can be extended to a shunting[8] or multiplicative model that allows multiplicative self-excitation through the term $(A_i - a_i)[S(a_i) + I_i^E]$ and multiplicative cross-inhibition through a similar term, where A_i (B_j) is the positive upper bound on the activation of a_i (b_j), and I_i^I (J_j^I) and I_i^E (J_j^E) are the respective constant non-negative inhibitory and excitatory inputs to a_i (b_j). The shunting model can then be written

$$\dot{a}_i = -a_i + (A_i - a_i)[S(a_i) + I_i^E] - a_i[\sum_j m_{ij}S(b_j) + I_i^I], \tag{16}$$

$$\dot{b}_j = -b_j + (B_j - b_j)[S(b_j) + J_j^E] - b_j[\sum_i m_{ij}S(a_i) + J_j^I]. \tag{17}$$

The inhibitory shunt a_i (b_j) can be replaced with $C_i + a_i$ ($D_j + b_j$) where C_i (D_j) is a non-negative constant. Then the range of a_i (b_j) is the interval $[-C_i, A_i]$ ($[D_j, B_j]$). The bidirectional stability of systems (16) and (17) follows from the same source of stability as the additive model, the bidirectional/heteroassociative extension of the Cohen-Grossberg theorem[16]. The thrust of this extension is to symmetrize an arbitrary rectangular connection matrix M by forming the zero-block diagonal matrix N:

$$\begin{pmatrix} 0 & M \\ M^T & 0 \end{pmatrix},$$

so that $N = N^T$. Thus the bidirectional heteroassociative procedure is converted to a large-scale unidirectional autoassociative procedure acting on the augmented state vectors $\mathbf{C} = [\mathbf{A}|\mathbf{B}]$, for which the Cohen-Grossberg theorem applies. The subsumption of the unidirectional version of equations (16) and (17) by fixed-weight competitive networks is discussed in reference 16. The Cohen-Grossberg theorem is further extended in the next section when we prove the stability of adaptive BAMs. For simplicity we shall continue to analyse only the additive model, which subsumes the symmetric unidirectional autoassociative circuit model put forth by Hopfield[22] when $M = M^T$.

As shown by Kosko[10,11], the appropriate bounded Lyapunov or energy function E for the additive BAM system [equations (14) and (15)] is

$$E(A, B) = \sum_i \int_0^{a_i} S'(x_i)x_i\,dx_i - \sum_i \sum_j S(a_i)S(b_j)m_{ij}$$
$$- \sum_i S(a_i)I_i + \sum_j \int_0^{b_j} S'(y_j)y_j\,dy_j - \sum_j S(b_j)J_j. \tag{18}$$

The time derivative of E is computed term by term. The objective is to factor out $S'(a_i)\dot{a}_i$ from terms involving inputs to a_i and $S'(b_j)\dot{b}_j$ from terms involving inputs to b_j, regroup, then substitute in the STM equations (15) and (16). The time derivative of the integrals is equivalent to the sum of the time derivative of $F[a_i(t)]$ for F_A terms, of $G[b_j(t)]$ for F_B terms. The chain rule gives $dF/dt = (dF/da_i)(da_i/dt) = S'(a_i)\dot{a}_i a_i$. The F_A input term gives $S'(a_i)\dot{a}_i I_i$. The product rule of differentiation is used to compute the time derivative of the quadratic form, which gives the sum of the two endogenous feedback terms in equations (14) and (15) modulated by the respective terms $S'(a_i)\dot{a}_i$ and $S'(b_j)\dot{b}_j$. Rearrangement then gives

$$
\begin{aligned}
\dot{E} = &- \sum_i S'(a_i)\dot{a}_i[-a_i + \sum_j S(b_j)m_{ij} + I_i] \\
&- \sum_j S'(b_j)\dot{b}_j[-b_j + \sum_i S(a_i)m_{ij} + J_j] \\
= &- \sum_i S'(a_i)\dot{a}_i^2 - \sum_j S'(b_j)\dot{b}_j^2 \\
\leq &\ 0,
\end{aligned}
\tag{19}
$$

on substituting equations (14) and (15) for the terms in brackets. Since $S' > 0$, equation (19) implies that $\dot{E} = 0$ if and only if $\dot{a}_i = \dot{b}_j = 0$ for all i and j. At equilibrium all activations and signals are constant. Since M was an arbitrary $n \times p$ real matrix, this proves that every matrix is continuously bidirectionally stable.

As Hopfield[22] has noted, in the high-gain case when the sigmoid signal function S is steep, the integral terms vanish from equation (18). Then the equilibria of the continuous energy E in equation (18) are the same as those of the bivalent energy E in equation (5), namely, the vertices of the product unit hypercube $I^n \times I^p$ or, equivalently, the binary points in $B^n \times B^p$. Continuous BAM convergence then has an intuitive fuzzy set interpretation. A fuzzy set is simply a point in the unit hypercube I^n or I^p. Each component of the fuzzy set is a fit[14] (rather than bit) value, indicating the degree to which that element fits in or belongs to the subset. In a unit hypercube, the midpoint of the hypercube, $M = (1/2, 1/2, \ldots, 1/2)$ has maximum fuzzy entropy[14] and binary vertices have minimum fuzzy entropy. In a continuous BAM the trajectory of an initial input pattern—an ambiguous or fuzzy key vector—if from somewhere inside $I^n \times I^p$ to the nearest product-space binary vertex. Hence this disambiguation process is precisely the minimization of fuzzy entropy[11,14].

V. Adaptive BAMs

BAM convergence is quick and robust when M is constant. Any connection topology always rapidly produces a stable contrast-enhanced STM reverberation across F_A and F_B. This stable STM reverberation is not achieved with a lateral inhibition or competitive[12,23] connection topology within the F_A and F_B fields, as it is in the adaptive resonance model[4], since there are no connections within F_A and F_B. The idea behind an adaptive BAM is to gradually let some of this stable STM reverberation seep into the LTM connections M. Since the BAM rapidly converges and since the STM variables a_i and b_j change faster than the LTM variables m_{ij} change in learning, it seems reasonable that some type of convergence should occur if the m_{ij} change gradually relative to a_i and b_j. Such convergence depends on the choice of learning law for m_{ij}.

In this section we show that, if m_{ij} adapts according to a generalized Hebbian learning law, every BAM adaptively resonates in the sense that all nodes (STM traces) and edges (LTM traces) quickly equilibrate. This real-time learning result extends the Lyapunov approach to the product space $I^n \times I^p \times R^{n \times p}$. The LTM traces m_{ij} tend to learn the associations (A_i, B_i) in unsupervised fashion simply by presenting A_i to the bottom-up field of nodes F_A and simultaneously presenting B_i to the top-down field of nodes F_B. Input patterns sculpt their own attractor basins in which to reverberate. In addition to simple heteroassociative storage and recall, simulation results show that a pure bivalent association (A_i, B_i) can be quickly learned, or abstracted from, noisy gray-scale samples of (A_i, B_i). Many continuous mappings, such as rotation mappings, can also be learned by sampling instantiations of the mappings, often more instantiations than permitted by the storage capacity constraint $m < \min(n, p)$ for simple heteroassociative storage.

How should a BAM learn? How should synapse m_{ij} change with time given successive experience? In the simplest case no learning occurs, so m_{ij} should decay to 0. Passive decay is most simply a model with a first-order decay law:

$$\dot{m}_{ij} = -m_{ij}, \tag{20}$$

so that $m_{ij}(t) = m_{ij}(0)e^{-t} \to 0$ as time increases. This simple model contains two ubiquitous features of unsupervised real-time learning models: exponentiation and locality. The mechanism of real-time behavior is exponential modulation. Learning only depends on locally available information, in this case m_{ij}. These two properties facilitate hardware instantiation and increase biological plausibility.

What other information is locally available to the synapse m_{ij}? Only information about a_i and b_j. What is the simplest way to additively include information about a_i and b_j into equation (20)? Multiply or add a_i and $b_j - a_i b_j$ or $a_i + b_j$. Multiplicative combination is conjunctive; learning requires signals from both neurons. Additive combination is disjunctive; learning only requires signals from one neuron. Hence associative learning favors the product $a_i b_j$. This choice is also an approximation of the correlation coding scheme (9) and produces a naive Hebbian learning law:

$$\dot{m}_{ij} = -m_{ij} + a_i b_j. \tag{21}$$

Again scale constants can be added as desired. Integration of equation (21) shows that, in principle, m_{ij} can be unbounded since a_i and b_j can, in principle, just grow and grow. This possibility is sure to occur in feedback networks. So equation (21) is unacceptable. Moreover, on closer examination of m_{ij}, which symmetrically connects the ith neuron in F_A with the jth neuron in F_B, we see that the activations a_i and b_j are not locally available to m_{ij}.

Only the signals $S(a_i)$ and $S(b_j)$ are locally available to m_{ij}. In equation (8) the bipolar vectors can be interpreted as vectors of threshold signals. So the simplest way to include the locally available information to m_{ij} is to add the bounded signal correlation term $S(a_i)S(b_j)$ to equation (20). We call this a signal Hebb law:

$$\dot{m}_{ij} = -m_{ij} + S(a_i)S(b_j). \tag{22}$$

Clark Guest (personal communication) notes that (22) is equivalent to the dynamic beam coupling equation in adaptive volume holography. The dynamic system of equations (16), (17), and (22) defines an adaptive BAM. Suppose all nodes and edges have equilibrated. Then the equilibrium value of m_{ij} is found by setting the right-hand side of equation (22) equal to 0:

$$m_{ij} = S_e(a_i)S_e(b_j). \tag{23}$$

The signal Hebb law is bounded since the signals are bounded. Suppose for definiteness that S is a bipolar signal function. Then

$$-1 \le S(a_i)S(b_j) \le 1. \tag{24}$$

The signal product is $+1$ if both signals are $+1$ or both are -1. The product is -1 if one signal is $+1$ and the other is -1. Thus the signal product behaves as a biconditional or equivalence operator in a fuzzy or continuous-valued logic. This biconditionality underlies the interpretation of the association (A_i, B_i) as the conjunction IF A_i THEN B_i, and IF B_i THEN A_i. Moreover, the bipolar endpoints -1 and $+1$ can be expected to abound with a steep bounded S.

Suppose m_{ij} is maximally increasing due to $S(a_i)S(b_j) = 1$. Then equation (22) reduces to the simple first-order equation

$$\dot{m}_{ij} + m_{ij} = 1, \tag{25}$$

which integrates to

$$\begin{aligned} m_{ij}(t) &= e^{-t}m_{ij}(0) + \int_0^t e^{(s-t)}ds \\ &= e^{-t}m_{ij}(0) + (1 - e^{-t}) \\ &\to 1 \text{ as } t \text{ increases for any initial } m_{ij}(0). \end{aligned} \tag{26}$$

Similarly, if m_{ij} is maximally decreasing, the right-hand side of equation (24) is -1 and m_{ij} approaches $+1$ exponentially fast independent of initial conditions. This agrees with equation (23). The signal Hebb law (22) asymptotically approaches the bipolar correlation learning scheme (8) for a single data pair. So the learning BAM for simple heteroassociative storage can still be expected to be capacity constrained by $m < \min(n, p)$.

The BAM memory medium produced by equation (22) is almost perfectly plastic. Scaling constants in equation (22) must be carefully chosen. In particular, the forget term $-m_{ij}$ in equation (22) must be scaled with a constant less than unity. Otherwise present learning washes away past learning $m_{ij}(0)$. In practice this means that a training list of associations $(A_1, B_1), \ldots, (A_m, B_m)$ should be presented to the adaptive BAM system more than once if each pair (A_i, B_i) is presented for the same length of time. Alternatively, the training list can be presented once if the first pair (A_1, B_1) is presented longer than (A_2, B_2) is presented, (A_2, B_2) longer than (A_3, B_3), (A_3, B_3) longer than (A_4, B_4), and so on. This holds because the general integral solution to equation (22) is an exponentially weighted average of sampled patterns.

In what sense does the adaptive BAM converge? We prove below that it always converges in the sense that nodes and edges rapidly equilibrate or resonate when environmentally perturbed. Recall and learning can simultaneously occur in a type of adaptive resonance[4-9].

At this point it is instructive to distinguish simple adaptive BAM behavior from standard adaptive resonance theory (ART) behavior. The high-level processing behavior of the Carpenter-Grossberg[4] ART model can be sketched as follows. Only one node in F_B fires at a time, the instar[8] node b_j that won the competition for bottom-up activation when a binary input pattern was presented to F_A. The winner b_j then fans out its spatial pattern or outstar[8] to the nodes in F_A. If this fan-out pattern sufficiently matches the input pattern presented to F_A, a stable pattern of STM reverberation is set up between F_A and F_B, learning can occur (but need not), and instar b_j has recognized or categorized the input pattern. Otherwise b_j is shut off and another instar winner b_k fans out its spatial pattern, etc., until a match occurs or, if no match occurs, until the binary input pattern trains some uncommitted node b_u to be its instar. Hence each instar node b_j in the ART model recognizes or categorizes a single input pattern or set of input patterns, depending on how high a degree of match is desired. Match degree can be deliberately controlled. Direct access to a trained instar is assured only if the input matches exactly, or nearly, the pattern learned by the instar. The more novel the pattern presented to F_A, and the higher the desired degree of match, the longer the ART system tends to search its instars to classify it.

In the adaptive BAM every F_B node b_j in parallel fans out its outstar across F_A when an STM pattern is active across F_A. The signal Hebb law (22) distributes recognition capability across all the edges of all the b_j nodes so that most bivalent associations are unaffected by removing a particular node. The closest analog to a specifiable degree of match in a BAM is the storage-capacity relationship between pattern number and pattern dimensionality, $m < \min(n, p)$. The closer m is to the maximum reliable capacity, the greater the match between an input pattern and a stored association (A_i, B_i) required to evoke (A_i, B_i) into a stable STM reverberation. When m is small relative to the maximum capacity, there tend to be few basins of attraction in the state space $I^n \times I^p$, the basins tend to have wide diameters, and they tend to correspond to the stored associations (A_i, B_i). Each stored association tends to recognize or categorize a large set of input stimuli. When m is large, there tend to be several basins, with small diameters. When m is large enough, only the exact patterns A_i or B_i will evoke (A_i, B_i). Within capacity constraints, all inputs tend to fall into the basin of the nearest stored association and thus have direct access to nearest stored associations. Novel patterns are classified or misclassified as rapidly as more familiar patterns.

Learning can also occur in an adaptive BAM during the rapid recall process. Familiar patterns tend to strengthen or restrengthen the reverberating associations they elicit. Novel patterns tend to misclassify to spurious energy wells (attractor basins), which in effect recognize them, or by equation (22) they tend to dig their own energy wells, which thereafter recognize them. As the simulation results discussed below show, many more patterns can be stably presented to the BAM than $\min(n, p)$ if they resemble stored associations. Otherwise the forgetting effects of equation (22) prevail and at any moment the adaptive BAM tends to remember no more than the most recent $\min(n,p)$-many distinct inputs (elicited associations).

We now prove that the adaptive BAM converges to local energy minima. Denote the bounded energy function in equation (18) by F. Then the appropriate energy or Lyapunov function for the adaptive BAM dynamic system of equations (16), (17), and (22) is simply

$$E(A,B,M) = F + 1/2 \sum_i \sum_j m_{ij}^2, \tag{27}$$

since the time derivative of $1/2m_{ij}^2$ is $m_{ij}\dot{m}_{ij}$. This new energy function is bounded since each m_{ij} is bounded. When the product rule of differentiation is applied to the time-varying triple product in the quadratic form component of F [equation (18)], we get the triple sum

$$\dot{m}_{ij}S(a_i)S(b_j) + S'(a_i)\dot{a}_i m_{ij}S(b_j) + S'(b_j)\dot{b}_j m_{ij}S(a_i).$$

In the nonlearning continuous BAM the first term of this triple sum was zero and the new sum of squares in equation (27) was constant and hence made no contribution to equation (19). Now the time derivative of E in equation (27) gives, on rearrangement,

$$\dot{E} = -\sum_i \sum_j \dot{m}_{ij}[S(a_i)S(b_j) - m_{ij}] - \sum_i S'\dot{a}_i^2 - \sum_j S'\dot{b}_j^2$$

$$= -\sum_i \sum_j \dot{m}_{ij}^2 - \sum_i S'(a_i)\dot{a}_i^2 - \sum_j S'(b_j)\dot{b}_j^2 \tag{28}$$

$$\leq 0,$$

on substituting the signal Hebb learning law (22) for the term in brackets in equation (28). Hence an adaptive BAM is a dissipative dynamic system that generalizes the nonlearning continuous BAM dissipative system. When energy stability is reached, when $\dot{E} = 0$, equation (28) and $S' > 0$ imply that both edges and nodes have stabilized: $\dot{m}_{ij} = \dot{a}_i = \dot{b}_j = 0$ for all i and j. Hence every signal Hebb BAM adaptively resonates. This result further generalizes in a straightforward way to any number of layered BAM fields that are interconnected, not necessarily contiguously, by equation (22).

Can an adaptive BAM learn and recall simultaneously? In the ART model[4] a mechanism of attentional gain control [inhibition due to the sum of F_B signals $S(b_j)$] is introduced to enable neurons a_i in F_A to distinguish environmental inputs I from top-down feedback patterns B. In principle, an attentional gain control mechanism can also be added to an adaptive BAM. Short of this new mechanism, how can neuron a_i distinguish external input I_i and internal feedback input from F_B? In equation (14) these terms both additively affect the time change of a_i. So external and internal feedback to a_i can only differ in their patterns of magnitude and duration over some short time interval. If the magnitude and duration of inputs are indistinguishable, the inputs are indistinguishable to a_i. When they differ, a_i can in principle learn and recall simultaneously.

Suppose a randomly fluctuating, uninformative environment confronts the adaptive BAM. The I_i tends to have zero mean in short time intervals. This allows a_i to be driven by internal feedback from F_B. If learning is permitted, familiar STM reverberations, evoked perhaps by other a_k (or b_j), can be strengthened. When I_i

Figure 4. Sampling adaptive BAM noisy training set. Forty-eight randomly generated gray-scale noise patterns are presented to the system. Unlike in simple heteroassociative storage, no sample is presented long enough for learning to fully or nearly
converge. Twenty-four of the samples are noisy versions of the bipolar association
(Y, W); twenty-four are noisy versions of (B, Z). Three samples are displayed from
each training set. Samples are presented four at a time—from the (Y, W) training
set, then four from the (B, Z) training set, then the next four from the (Y, W) training set, etc. Both fields F_A and F_B contain forty-nine samples, violate the storage
capacity $m \ll \min(n, p)$ for simple heteroassociative storage.

remains relatively constant over an interval, a new pattern can be learned, and can
be learned while F_A and F_B reverberate, eventually dominating those reverberations.
If the reverberations are spurious, learning is enhanced by appropriately weighting
I_i. In simulations, scaling I_i by p, the number of neurons in F_B, has proved effective
presumably because it balances the magnitude of I_i against the magnitude of the
internal F_B feedback sum in equation (14).

An extension of these ideas is the sampling adaptive BAM. There is a tradeoff between learning time and learning samples. The standard learning model is to
present relatively few samples for long lengths of learning time, typically until learning
converges or is otherwise terminated, as in simple heteroassociative storage, or to

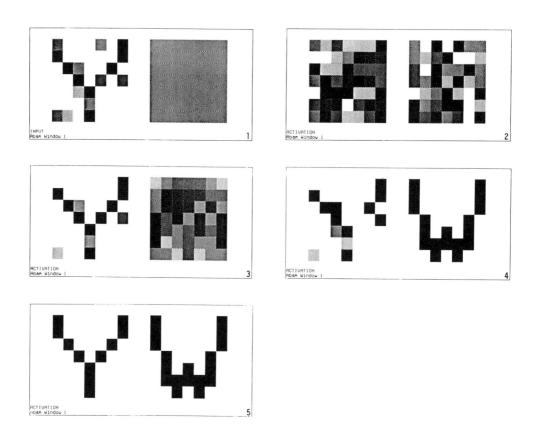

Figure 5. Sampling adaptive BAM associative recall and abstraction. A new noisy version of Y is presented to field F_A. Initial BAM STM activation across F_A and F_B is random. The BAM converges to the pure bipolar association (Y, W) it has never experienced but has abstracted from the noisy training samples in Figure 4.

present few samples over and over, as in backpropagation[17-20]. In what we shall call sampling learning several samples are presented briefly—typically many more patterns than neuron dimensionality—and the underlying patterns, associations, or mappings are better learned as sample size increases. Learning is not allowed to converge. Only a brief pulse of learning occurs for each sample. When the sampling learning technique is applied to the adaptive BAM, a sampling adaptive BAM results. For example, an adaptive BAM can rapidly learn a rotation mapping, if $n = p$, by simply presenting a few spatial patterns at F_A and concurrently presenting the same pattern rotated some fixed degree at F_B. Thereafter any pattern presented at F_A produces the stable STM reverberation with the input pattern at F_A and its rotated version at F_B.

We note that Hecht-Nielsen[24] has developed his feedforward counterpropagation sampling learning technique for learning continuous mappings, and probability density functions that generate mappings, by applying Grossberg's outstar learning theorem[8,9] and by applying the sampling learning technique to Grossberg's unsuper-

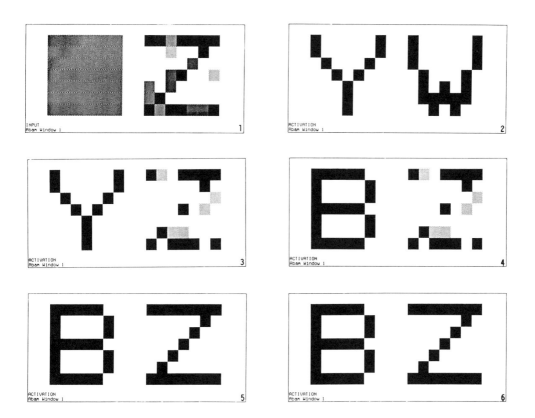

Figure 6. Sampling adaptive BAM STM superimposition and associative recall. A new noisy version of Z is presented to field F_B. This time the bipolar association (Y, W) recalled in Figure 5 is reverberating in STM. This thought is soon crowded out of STM by the environmental stimulus Z. Again the BAM converges to the unobserved pure bipolar association, this time (B, Z), it abstracted from the noisy training samples.

vised competitive learning[2,23]:

$$\dot{m}_{ij} = (i_i - m_{ij})b_j, \tag{29}$$

which is also used in the ART model[4], where $(i_1, \ldots, i_n)$ is a normalized input pattern or probability distribution presented to F_A and b_j provides competitive modulation, e.g., $b_j = 1$ if b_j wins the F_B instar competition for activation and $b_j = 0$ otherwise. For simple autoassociative storage the competitive instar learning law (29) is also dimension bounded for non-sampling learning. No more distibutions at F_A can be recognized at F_B than, obviously, the number p of instar nodes at F_B. Yet Hecht-Nielsen[24] has demonstrated that sampling learning with equation (29) can learn a sine wave, which has minimal dimensionality, well with thirty neurons and a few hundred random samples, almost perfectly with a few thousand random samples.

Figures 4–6 display the results of a sampling BAM experiment. F_A and F_B each contain forty-nine gray-scale neurons arranged in a 7×7 pixel tray. The output of the bipolar logistic signal function $S(x)$ is discretized to six gray-scale levels, where $S(x) = -1$ is white and $S(x) = 1$ is black. $S(x) = -1$ if activation $x < -51$, $S(x) = 1$ if $x > 51$. Forty-eight randomly generated gray-scale noise patterns are presented to the adaptive BAM. The forty-eight samples violate the storage capacity $m \ll \min(n,p)$ for simple heteroassociative storage. Figure 4 displays six of these random samples. Twenty-four of the samples are noisy versions of the bipolar association (Y, W); twenty-four are noisy versions of (B, Z). Noise was created by picking numbers in $[-60, 60]$ according to a uniform distribution, then adding them to the activation values, -52 or 52, underlying the bivalent signal values making up (Y, W) and (B, Z). Unlike in simple heteroassociative storage, no sample is presented long enough for learning to fully or nearly converge. Samples are briefly presented four at a time—four from the (Y, W) training set, then four from the (B, Z) training set, and so on to exploit the exponentially weighted averaging effects of the signal Hebb learning law (22).

Figure 5 demonstrates recall and abstraction with the sampling adaptive BAM. A new noisy version of Y is presented to field F_A. The initial STM activation across F_A and F_B is random. The BAM converges to the pure bipolar association (Y, W) it has never experienced but has abstracted from the noisy training samples. As in Plato's theory of ideals—and unlike the naive empiricist denial of abstraction of Locke, Berkeley, and Hume—it is as if the BAM learns redness from red things, smoothness from smooth things, trangularity from triangles, etc., and thereafter associates new red things with redness, not with most-similar old red things.

In Figure 6 the BAM is thinking about the STM reverberation (Y, W). A new noisy version of Z is presented to field F_B, superimposing it on the (Y, W) reverberation. The reverberating thought is soon crowded out of STM by the environmental stimulus Z. The BAM again converges to the unobserved pure bipolar association, this time (B, Z), it abstracted from the noisy training samples.

REFERENCES

1. Kohonen, T. (1972). Correlation matrix memories. *IEEE Transactions on Computers*, **C-21**, 353.

2. Kohonen, T. (1984). **Self-organization and associative memory**. New York: Springer-Verlag.

3. Anderson, J.A., Silverstein, J.W., Ritz, S.A., and Jones, R.S. (1977). Distinctive features, categorical perception, and probability learning: Some applications of a neural model. *Psychological Review*, **84**, 413.

4. Carpenter, G.A. and Grossberg, S. (1987). A massively parallel architecture for a self-organizing neural pattern recognition machine. *Computer Vision, Graphics, and Image Processing*, **37**, 54.

5. Grossberg, S. (1976). Adaptive pattern classification and universal recoding, II: Feedback, expectation, olfaction, and illusions. *Biological Cybernetics*, **23**, 187.

6. Grossberg, S. (1978). A theory of human memory: Self-organization and performance of sensory-motor codes, maps, and plans. In R. Rosen and F. Snell (Eds.), **Progress in theoretical biology, Volume 5**. New York: Academic Press, 233–374.

7. Grossberg, S. (1980). How does a brain build a cognitive code? *Psychological Review*, **87**, 1.

8. Grossberg, S. (1982). **Studies of mind and brain: Neural principles of learning, perception, development, cognition, and motor control**. Boston: Reidel Press.

9. Grossberg, S. (Ed.) (1987). **The adaptive brain, Volumes I and II**. Amsterdam: North-Holland.

10. Kosko, B. (1987). Bidirectional associative memories. *IEEE Transactions on Systems, Man, and Cybernetics*.

11. Kosko, B. (1987). Fuzzy associative memories. In A. Kandel (Ed.), **Fuzzy expert systems**. Reading, MA: Addison-Wesley.

12. Grossberg, S. (1973). Contour enhancement, short term memory, and constancies in reverberating neural networks. *Studies in Applied Mathematics*, **52**, 217.

13. McCulloch, W.S. and Pitts, W. (1943). A logical calculus of the ideas immanent in nervous activity. *Bulletin of Mathematical Biophysics*, **5**, 115.

14. Kosko, B. (1986). Fuzzy entropy and conditioning. *Information Science*, **40**, 165.

15. Hopfield, J.J. (1982). Neural networks and physical systems with emergent collective computational abilities. *Proceedings of the National Academy of Sciences USA*, **79**, 2554.

16. Cohen, M.A. and Grossberg, S. (1983). Absolute stability of global pattern formation and parallel memory storage by competitive neural networks. *IEEE Transactions on Systems, Man, and Cybernetics*, **SMC-13**, 815.

17. Parker, D.B. (1982). Learning logic. Invention Report S81-64, File 1, Office of Technology Licensing, Stanford University.

18. Parker, D.B. (1985). Learning logic. Report TR-47, MIT Center for Computational Research in Economics and Management Science.

19. Rumelhart, D.E., Hinton, G.E., and Williams, R.J. (1985). Learning internal representations by error propagation. ICS Report 8506, Institute for Cognitive Science, University of California at San Diego.

20. Werbos, P.J. (1974). Beyond regression: New tools for prediction and analysis in the behavioral sciences. PhD Dissertation, Harvard University.

21. Kosko, B. and Guest, C. (1987). Optical bidirectional associative memories. *Proceedings of the Society for Photo-Optical Instrumentation Engineering*, **758**.

22. Hopfield, J.J. (1983). Neurons with graded responses have collective computaitonal properties like those of two-state neurons. *Proceedings of the National Academy of Sciences USA*, **81**, 3088.

23. Grossberg, S. (1976). Adaptive pattern classification and universal recoding, I: Parallel development and coding of neural feature detectors. *Biological Cybernetics*, **23**, 121.

24. Hecht-Nielsen, R. (1987). Counterpropagation networks. In M. Caudill and C. Butler (Eds.), **Proceedings of the first international conference on neural networks**. New York: IEEE.

CHAPTER 14

ART 3: HIERARCHICAL SEARCH USING CHEMICAL TRANSMITTERS IN SELF-ORGANIZING PATTERN RECOGNITION ARCHITECTURES

by

Gail A. Carpenter and Stephen Grossberg

Preface

Both ART 1 and ART 2 use winner-take-all, or maximally compressed, recognition codes. In some circumstances, partially compressed recognition codes may be needed. A considerable amount is known concerning how on-center off-surround networks can be designed to accomplish partial compression (see Chapter 2 as well as Cohen and Grossberg, 1987; Ellias and Grossberg, 1975; Grossberg, 1973; Grossberg and Levine, 1975; and Levine and Grossberg, 1976). Arbitrary partially compressed, or distributed, codes cannot be used in an ART system until it is understood how distributed codes can efficiently be searched when a mismatch occurs between bottom-up and top-down patterns. The ART 3 architecture introduced in this 1990 article embodies a distributed search procedure that works well in a neural network hierarchy with either fast learning or slow learning in response to sequences of asynchronous input patterns in real time.

As in the 1976 article of Chapter 6, the search process uses a Medium Term Memory (MTM) that is defined in terms of a habituating chemical transmitter. In Chapter 6, the habituating chemical transmitter was embedded within a feedback gated dipole. In such a network, habituation is driven by STM signals that are carried along intercellular feedback pathways. The imbalance between the habituation in the on-channel and the off-channel of the dipole set the stage for STM memory reset and search in response to an unexpected event.

In the present 1990 article, it is shown how distributed search can be achieved by an activity-dependent feedback signal that acts *directly* between a postsynaptic cell and the abutting presynaptic synapses containing the transmitter, without intervention of an intercellular feedback pathway or a gated dipole. This mechanism could thus be embedded in ART 1 or ART 2 modules, as well as in other competitive learning systems, without requiring any change in network configuration. The ART 3 MTM mechanism is compared with data concerning synergetic interactions among ions, such as Na^+ and Ca^{++}, in the control of transmitter release.

Simulations in this article show how the spatial pattern of presynaptic MTM transmitter can be made to model the spatial pattern of postsynaptic STM activity that represents the pattern recognition code, and how this MTM model can be used to control a distributed search in response to input changes, top-down mediated mismatch, or reinforcement feedback.

References

Cohen, M.A. and Grossberg, S. (1987). Masking fields: A massively parallel neural architecture for learning, recognizing, and predicting multiple groupings of patterned data. *Applied Optics*, **26**, 1866–1891.

Ellias, S.A. and Grossberg, S. (1975). Pattern formation, contrast control, and oscillations in the short term memory of shunting on-center off-surround networks. *Biological Cybernetics*, **20**, 69–98.

Grossberg, S. (1973). Contour enhancement, short term memory, and constancies in reverberating neural networks. *Studies in Applied Mathematics*, **52**, 217–257.

Grossberg, S. and Levine, D. (1975). Some developmental and attentional biases in the contrast enhancement and short term memory of recurrent neural networks. *Journal of Theoretical Biology*, **53**, 341–380.

Levine, D. and Grossberg, S. (1976). On visual illusions in neural networks: Line neutralization, tilt aftereffect, and angle expansion. *Journal of Theoretical Biology*, **61**, 477–504.

Neural Networks
1990, **3**, 129–152
©1990 Pergamon Press Inc.

ART 3: HIERARCHICAL SEARCH USING CHEMICAL TRANSMITTERS IN SELF-ORGANIZING PATTERN RECOGNITION ARCHITECTURES

Gail A. Carpenter and Stephen Grossberg

Abstract

A model to implement parallel search of compressed or distributed pattern recognition codes in a neural network hierarchy is introduced. The search process functions well with either fast learning or slow learning, and can robustly cope with sequences of asynchronous input patterns in real-time. The search process emerges when computational properties of the chemical synapse, such as transmitter accumulation, release, inactivation, and modulation, are embedded within an Adaptive Resonance Theory architecture called ART 3. Formal analogs of ions such as Na^+ and Ca^{2+} control nonlinear feedback interactions that enable presynaptic transmitter dynamics to model the postsynaptic short term memory representation of a pattern recognition code. Reinforcement feedback can modulate the search process by altering the ART 3 vigilance parameter or directly engaging the search mechanism. The search process is a form of hypothesis testing capable of discovering appropriate representations of a nonstationary input environment.

1. Introduction: Distributed Search of ART Network Hierarchies

This paper incorporates a model of the chemical synapse into a new Adaptive Resonance Theory neural network architecture called ART 3. ART 3 system dynamics model a simple, robust mechanism for parallel search of a learned pattern recognition code. This search mechanism was designed to implement the computational needs of ART systems embedded in network hierarchies, where there can, in general, be either fast or slow learning and distributed or compressed code representations. The search mechanism incorporates a code reset property that serves at least three distinct functions: to correct erroneous category choices, to learn from reinforcement feedback, and to respond to changing input patterns. The three types of reset are illustrated, by computer simulation, for both maximally compressed and partially compressed pattern recognition codes (Sections 20–26).

Acknowledgements: This research was supported in part by the Air Force Office of Scientific Research (AFOSR F49620-86-C-0037 and AFOSR F49620-87-C-0018), the Army Research Office (ARO DAAL03-88-K-0088), and the National Science Foundation (NSF DMS-86-11959 and IRI-87-16960). We wish to thank Diana Meyers, Cynthia Suchta, and Carol Yanakakis for their valuable assistance in the preparation of the manuscript.

Let us first review the main elements of Adaptive Resonance Theory. ART architectures are neural networks that carry out stable self-organization of recognition codes for arbitrary sequences of input patterns. Adaptive Resonance Theory first emerged from an analysis of the instabilities inherent in feedforward adaptive coding structures (Grossberg, 1976a). More recent work has led to the development of two classes of ART neural network architectures, specified as systems of differential equations. The first class, ART 1, self-organizes recognition categories for arbitrary sequences of binary input patterns (Carpenter and Grossberg, 1987a). A second class, ART 2, does the same for either binary or analog inputs (Carpenter and Grossberg, 1987b).

Both ART 1 and ART 2 use a maximally compressed, or choice, pattern recognition code. Such a code is a limiting case of the partially compressed recognition codes that are typically used in explanations by ART of biological data (Grossberg, 1982a, 1987a, 1987b). Partially compressed recognition codes have been mathematically analysed in models for competitive learning, also called self-organizing feature maps, which are incorporated into ART models as part of their bottom-up dynamics (Grossberg, 1976a, 1982a; Kohonen, 1984). Maximally compressed codes were used in ART 1 and ART 2 to enable a rigorous analysis to be made of how the bottom-up and top-down dynamics of ART systems can be joined together in a real-time self-organizing system capable of learning a stable pattern recognition code in response to an arbitrary sequence of input patterns. These results provide a computational foundation for designing ART systems capable of stably learning partially compressed recognition codes. The present results contribute to such a design.

The main elements of a typical ART 1 module are illustrated in Figure 1. F_1 and F_2 are fields of network nodes. An input is initially represented as a pattern of activity across the nodes, or feature detectors, of field F_1. The pattern of activity across F_2 corresponds to the category representation. Because patterns of activity in both fields may persist after input offset yet may also be quickly inhibited, these patterns are called short term memory, or STM, representations. The two fields, linked both bottom-up and top-down by adaptive filters, constitute the Attentional Subsystem. Because the connection weights defining the adaptive filters may be modified by inputs and may persist for very long times after input offset, these connection weights are called long term memory, or LTM, variables.

An auxiliary Orienting Subsystem becomes active during search. This search process is the subject of the present article.

2. An ART Search Cycle

Figure 2 illustrates a typical ART search cycle. An input pattern **I** registers itself as a pattern **X** of activity across F_1 (Figure 2a). The F_1 output signal vector **S** is then transmitted through the multiple converging and diverging weighted adaptive filter pathways emanating from F_1, sending a net input signal vector **T** to F_2. The internal competitive dynamics of F_2 contrast-enhance **T**. The F_2 activity vector **Y** therefore registers a compressed representation of the filtered $F_1 \rightarrow F_2$ input and corresponds to a category representation for the input active at F_1. Vector **Y** generates a signal vector **U** that is sent top-down through the second adaptive filter, giving rise to a net top-down signal vector **V** to F_1 (Figure 2b). F_1 now receives two input vectors, **I** and **V**. An ART system is designed to carry out a matching process

ART 1   MODULE

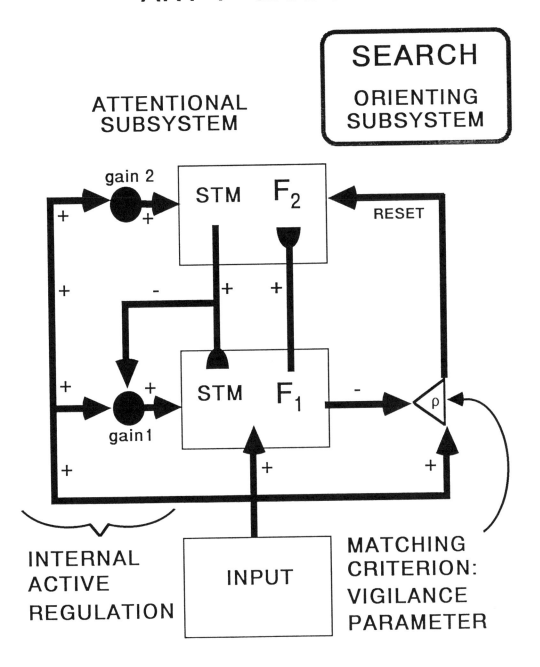

Figure 1. Typical ART 1 neural network module (Carpenter and Grossberg, 1987a).

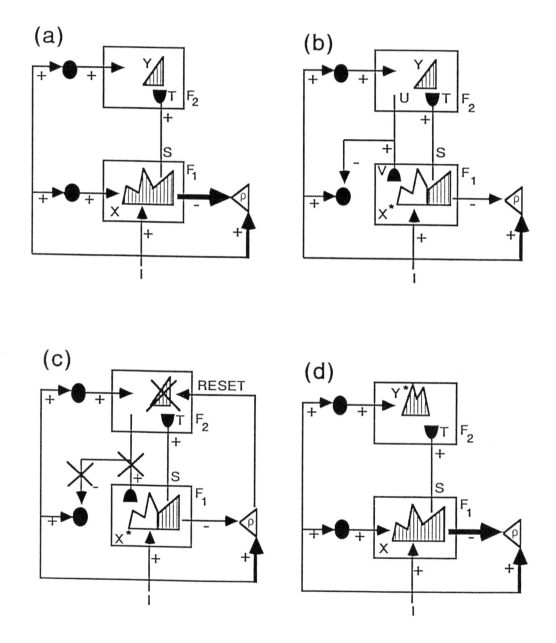

Figure 2. ART search cycle (Carpenter and Grossberg, 1987a).

ART 2 MODULE

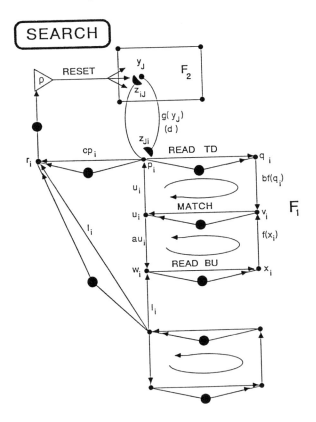

Figure 3. Typical ART 2 neural network module, with three-layer F_1 field (Carpenter and Grossberg, 1987b). Large filled circles are gain control nuclei that nonspecifically inhibit target nodes in proportion to the Euclidean norm of activity in their source fields, as in equation (33).

whereby the original activity pattern **X** due to input pattern **I** may be modified by the *template pattern* **V** that is associated with the current active category. If **I** and **V** are not sufficiently similar according to a matching criterion established by a dimensionless *vigilance parameter* ρ, a reset signal quickly and enduringly shuts off the active category representation (Figure 2c), allowing a new category to become active. Search ensues (Figure 2d) until either an adequate match is made or a new category is established.

In earlier treatments (e.g., Carpenter and Grossberg, 1987a), we proposed that the enduring shut-off of erroneous category representations by a nonspecific reset signal could occur at F_2 if F_2 were organized as a gated dipole field, whose dynamics depend on depletable transmitter gates. Though the new search process does not here use a gated dipole field, it does retain and extend the core idea that transmitter dynamics can enable a robust search process when appropriately embedded in an ART system.

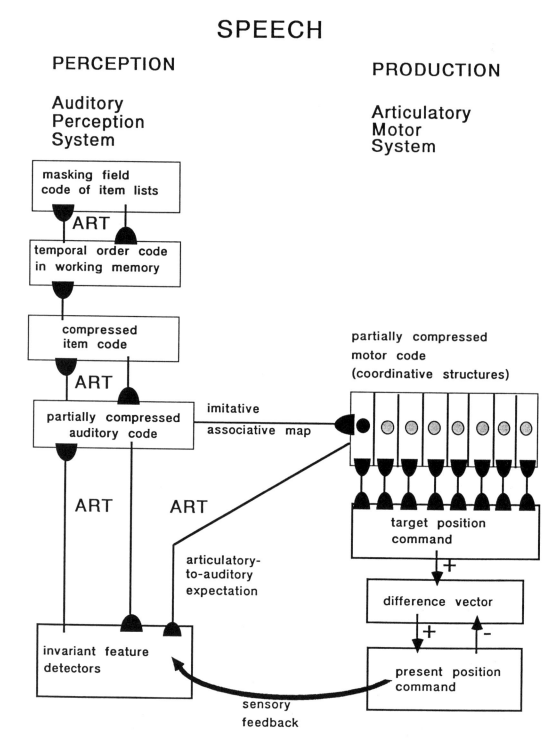

Figure 4. Neural network model of speech production and perception (Cohen, Grossberg, and Stork, 1988).

3. ART 2: Three-Layer Competitive Fields

Figure 3 shows the principal elements of a typical ART 2 module. It shares many characteristics of the ART 1 module, having both an input representation field F_1 and a category representation field F_2, as well as Attentional and Orienting Subsystems. Figure 3 also illustrates one of the main differences between the examples of ART 1 and ART 2 modules so far explicitly developed; namely, the ART 2 examples all have three processing layers within the F_1 field. These three processing layers allow the ART 2 system to stably categorize sequences of analog input patterns that can, in general, be arbitrarily close to one another. Unlike in models such as back propagation, this category learning process is stable even in the fast learning situation, in which the LTM variables are allowed to go to equilibrium on each learning trial. In Figure 3, one F_1 layer reads in the bottom-up input, one layer reads in the top-down filtered input from F_2, and a middle layer matches patterns from the top and bottom layers before sending a composite pattern back through the F_1 feedback loop. Both F_1 and F_2 are shunting competitive networks that contrast-enhance and normalize their activation patterns (Grossberg, 1982a).

4. ART Bidirectional Hierarchies and Homology of Fields

In applications, ART modules are often embedded in larger architectures that are hierarchically organized. Figure 4 shows an example of one such hierarchy, a self-organizing model of the perception and production of speech (Cohen, Grossberg, and Stork, 1988). In Figure 4, several copies of an ART module are cascaded upward, with partially compressed codes at each level. Top-down ART filters both within the perception system and from the production system to the perception system serve to stabilize the evolving codes as they are learned. We will now consider how an ART 2 module can be adapted for use in such a hierarchy.

When an ART module is embedded in a network hierarchy, it is no longer possible to make a sharp distinction between the characteristics of the input representation field F_1 and the category representation field F_2. For example, within the auditory perception system of Figure 4, the partially compressed auditory code acts both as the category representation field for the invariant feature field, and as the input field for the compressed item code field. In order for them to serve both functions, the basic structures of all the network fields in a hierarchical ART system should be homologous, in so far as possible (Figure 5). This constraint is satisfied if all fields of the hierarchy are endowed with the F_1 structure of an ART 2 module (Figure 3). Such a design is sufficient for the F_2 field as well as the F_1 field because the principal property required of a category representation field, namely that input patterns be contrast-enhanced and normalized, is a property of the three-layer F_1 structure. The system shown in Figure 5 is called an *ART bidirectional hierarchy*, with each field homologous to all other fields and linked to contiguous fields by both bottom-up and top-down adaptive filters.

5. ART Cascade

For the ART hierarchy shown in Figure 5, activity changes at any level can ramify throughout all lower and higher levels. It is sometimes desirable to buffer activity patterns at lower levels against changes at higher levels. This can be accomplished by inserting a bottom-up pathway between each two-field ART module. Figure 6

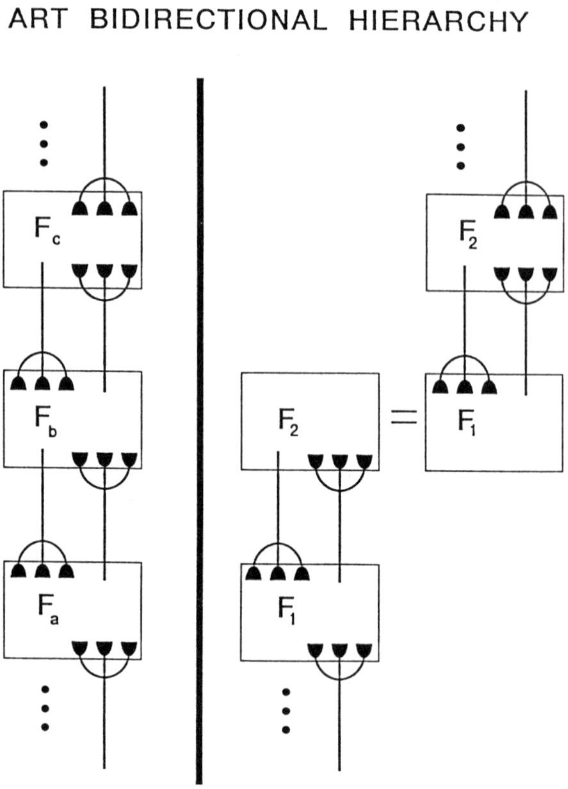

ART BIDIRECTIONAL HIERARCHY

Figure 5. Homology of fields $F_a, F_b, F_c \ldots$ in an ART bidirectional hierarchy.

illustrates a sequence of modules $A, B, C \ldots$ forming an *ART cascade*. The "category representation" field F_{2A} acts as the input field for the next field F_{1B}. As in an ART 2 module (Figure 3), connections from the input field F_{2A} to the first field F_{1B} of the next module are nonadaptive and unidirectional. Connections between F_{1B} and F_{2B} are adaptive and bidirectional. This scheme repeats itself throughout the hierarchy. Activity changes due to a reset event at a lower level can be felt at higher levels via an ascending cascade of reset events. In particular, reset at the lowest input level can lead to a cascade of input reset events up the entire hierarchy.

6. Search in an ART Hierarchy

We now consider the problem of implementing parallel search among the distributed codes of a hierarchical ART system. Assume that a top-down/bottom-up mismatch has occurred somewhere in the system. How can a reset signal search the hierarchy in such a way that an appropriate new category is selected? The search scheme for ART 1 and ART 2 modules incorporates an asymmetry in the design of levels F_1 and F_2 that is inappropriate for ART hierarchies whose fields are homologous. The ART 3 search mechanism described below eliminates that asymmetry.

A key observation is that a reset signal can act upon an ART hierarchy *between* its fields $F_a, F_b, F_c \ldots$ (Figure 7). Locating the site of action of the reset signal between the fields allows each individual field to carry out its pattern processing function

ART CASCADE

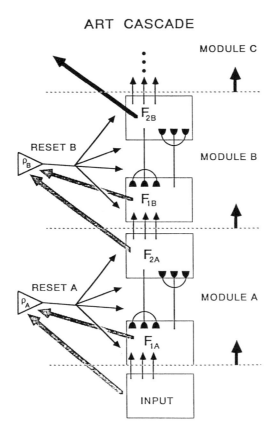

Figure 6. An ART cascade. Nonadaptive connections terminate in arrowheads. Adaptive connections terminate in semicircles.

without introducing processing biases directly into a field's internal feedback loops.

The new ART search mechanism has a number of useful properties. It: (a) works well for mismatch, reinforcement, or input reset; (b) is simple; (c) is homologous to physiological processes; (d) fits naturally into network hierarchies with distributed codes and slow or fast learning; (e) is robust in that it does not require precise parameter choices, timing, or analysis of classes of inputs; (f) requires no new anatomy, such as new wiring or nodes, beyond what is already present in the ART 2 architecture; (g) brings new computational power to the ART systems; and (h) although derived for the ART system, can be used to search other neural network architectures as well.

7. A New Role for Chemical Transmitters in ART Search

The computational requirements of the ART search process can be fulfilled by formal properties of neurotransmitters (Figure 8), if these properties are appropriately embedded in the total architecture model. The main properties used are illustrated in Figure 9, which is taken from Ito (1984). In particular, the ART 3 search equations incorporate the dynamics of production and release of a chemical transmitter substance;

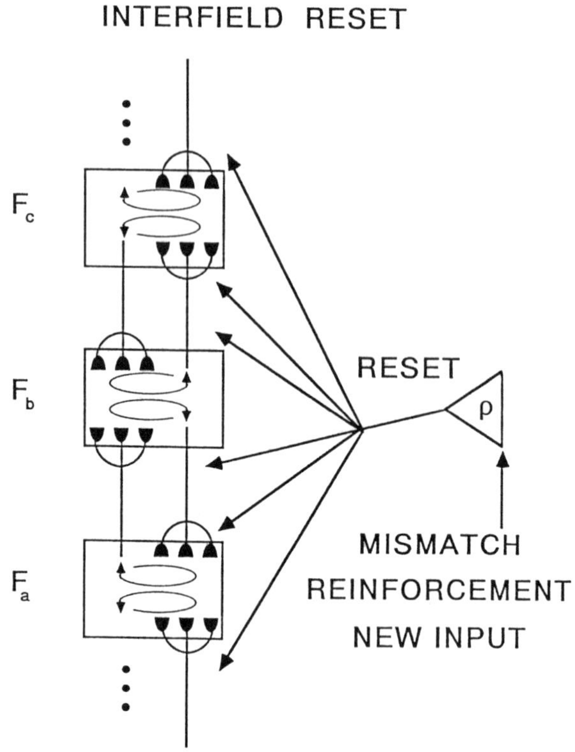

INTERFIELD RESET

Figure 7. Interfield reset in an ART bidirectional hierarchy.

the inactivation of transmitter at postsynaptic binding sites; and the modulation of these processes via a nonspecific control signal. The net effect of these transmitter processes is to alter the ionic permeability at the postsynaptic membrane site, thus effecting excitation or inhibition of the postsynaptic cell.

The notation to describe these transmitter properties is summarized in Figure 10, for a synapse between the ith presynaptic node and the jth postsynaptic node. The presynaptic signal, or action potential, S_i arrives at a synapse whose adaptive weight, or long term memory trace, is denoted z_{ij}. The variable z_{ij} is identified with the maximum amount of available transmitter. When the transmitter at this synapse is fully accumulated, the amount of transmitter u_{ij} available for release is equal to z_{ij}. When a signal S_i arrives, transmitter is typically released. The variable v_{ij} denotes the amount of transmitter released into the extracellular space, a fraction of which is assumed to be bound at the postsynaptic cell surface and the remainder rendered ineffective in the extracellular space. Finally, x_j denotes the activity, or membrane potential, of the postsynaptic cell.

8. Equations for Transmitter Production, Release, and Inactivation

The search mechanism works well if it possesses a few basic properties. These properties can be realized using one of several closely related sets of equations, with corresponding differences in biophysical interpretation. An illustrative system of

ART 3 SEARCH MODEL

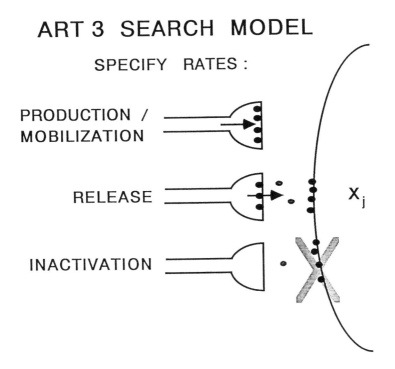

Figure 8. The ART search model specifies rate equations for transmitter production, release, and inactivation.

equations is described below.

Equations (1)–(3) govern the dynamics of the variables z_{ij}, u_{ij}, v_{ij}, and x_j at the ij^{th} pathway and j^{th} node of an ART 3 system.

Presynaptic Transmitter

$$\frac{du_{ij}}{dt} = (z_{ij} - u_{ij}) - u_{ij}[\text{release rate}] \tag{1}$$

Bound Transmitter

$$\frac{dv_{ij}}{dt} = -v_{ij} + u_{ij}[\text{release rate}] - v_{ij}[\text{inactivation rate}]$$
$$= -v_{ij} + u_{ij}[\text{release rate}] - v_{ij}[\text{reset signal}] \tag{2}$$

Postsynaptic Activation

$$\epsilon\frac{dx_j}{dt} = -x_j + (A - x_j)[\text{excitatory inputs}] - (B + x_j)[\text{inhibitory inputs}]$$
$$= -x_j + (A - x_j)\Big[\sum_i v_{ij} + \{\text{intrafield feedback}\}\Big] - (B + x_j)[\text{reset signal}] \tag{3}$$

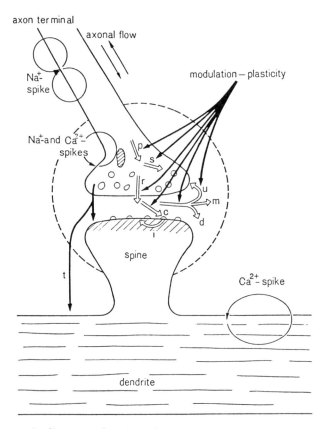

Figure 9. Schematic diagram showing electrical, ionic, and chemical events in a dendritic spine synapse. Open arrows indicate steps from production of neurotransmitter substance (p) to storage (s) or release (r) to reaction with subsynaptic receptors (c), leading to change of ionic permeability of subsynaptic membrane (i) or to removal to extracellular space (m), enzymatic destruction (d), or uptake by presynaptic terminal (u).t, action of trophic substance. (Ito, 1984, p. 52. Reprinted with permission.)

Equation (1) says that presynaptic transmitter is produced and/or mobilized until the amount u_{ij} of transmitter available for release reaches the maximum level z_{ij}. The adaptive weight z_{ij} itself changes on the slower time scale of learning, but remains essentially constant on the time scale of a single reset event. Available presynaptic transmitter u_{ij} is released at a rate that is specified below.

A fraction of presynaptic transmitter becomes postsynaptic bound transmitter after being released. For simplicity, we ignore the fraction of released transmitter that is inactivated in the extracellular space. Equation (2) says that the bound transmitter is inactivated by the reset signal.

Equation (3) for the postsynaptic activity x_j is a shunting membrane equation such that excitatory inputs drive x_j up toward a maximum depolarized level equal to A; inhibitory inputs drive x_j down toward a minimum hyperpolarized level equal to $-B$; and activity passively decays to a resting level equal to 0 in the absence of inputs. The net effect of bound transmitter at all synapses converging on the jth

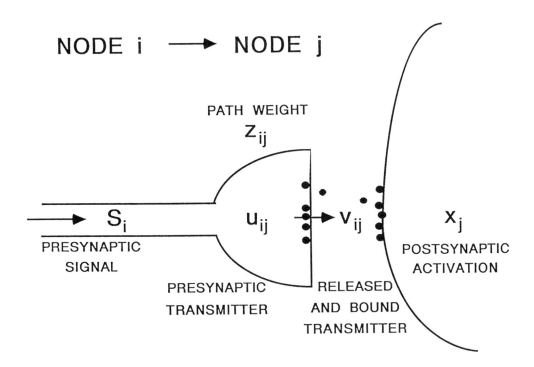

Figure 10. Notation for the ART chemical synapse.

node is assumed to be excitatory, via the term

$$\sum_{i} v_{ij}. \tag{4}$$

Internal feedback from within the target field (Figure 3) is excitatory, while the non-specific reset signal is inhibitory. Parameter ϵ is small, corresponding to the assumption that activation dynamics are fast relative to the transmitter accumulation rate, equal to 1 in equation (1).

The ART 3 system can be simplified for purposes of simulation. Suppose that $\varepsilon \ll 1$ in (3); the reset signals in (2) and (3) are either 0 or $\gg 1$; and net intrafield feedback is excitatory. Then equations (1), (5), and (6) below approximate the main properties of ART 3 system dynamics.

Simplified ART 3 Equations

$$\frac{du_{ij}}{dt} = (z_{ij} - u_{ij}) - u_{ij}[\text{release rate}] \tag{1}$$

$$\begin{cases} \frac{dv_{ij}}{dt} = -v_{ij} + u_{ij} \ [\text{release rate}] & \text{if reset} = 0 \\ v_{ij}(t) = 0 & \text{if reset} \gg 1 \end{cases} \tag{5}$$

$$x_j(t) = \begin{cases} \sum_i v_{ij} + [\text{intrafield feedback}] & \text{if reset} = 0 \\ 0 & \text{if reset} \gg 1. \end{cases} \tag{6}$$

9. Alternative ART 3 Systems

In equations (2) and (3), the reset signal acts in two ways, by inactivating bound transmitter and directly inhibiting the postsynaptic membrane. Alternatively, the reset signal may accomplish both these goals in a single process if all excitatory inputs in (3) are realized using chemical transmitters. Letting w_j denote the net excitatory transmitter reaching the jth target cell via intrafield feedback, an illustrative system of this type is given by equations (1), (2), (7), and (8) below.

Presynaptic Transmitter

$$\frac{du_{ij}}{dt} = (z_{ij} - u_{ij}) - u_{ij}[\text{release rate}] \tag{1}$$

Bound Transmitter

$$\frac{dv_{ij}}{dt} = -v_{ij} + u_{ij}[\text{release rate}] - v_{ij}[\text{reset signal}] \tag{2}$$

$$\frac{dw_j}{dt} = -w_j + \left[\text{intrafield feedback}\right] - w_j[\text{reset signal}] \tag{7}$$

Postsynaptic Activation

$$\epsilon\frac{dx_j}{dt} = -x_j + (A - x_j)(\sum_i v_{ij} + w_j). \tag{8}$$

The reset signal now acts as a chemical modulator that inactivates the membrane channels at which transmitter is bound. It thus appears in equations (2) and (7), but not in equation (8) for postsynaptic activation.

When the reset signal can be only 0 or $>> 1$, the simplified system in Section 8 approximates both versions of the ART 3 system. However, if the reset signal can vary continuously in size, equations (2), (7), and (8) can preserve relative transmitter quantities from all input sources. Thus this system is a better model for the intermediate cases than equations (2) and (3).

An additional inhibitory term in the postsynaptic activation equation (8) helps to suppress transmitter release, as illustrated in Section 25.

10. Transmitter Release Rate

To further specify the ART search model, we now characterize the transmitter release and inactivation rates in equations (1) and (2). Then we trace the dynamics of the system at key time intervals during the presentation of a fixed input pattern (Figure 11). We first observe system dynamics during a brief time interval after the input turns on ($t = 0^+$), when the signal S_i first arrives at the synapse. We next consider the effect of subsequent internal feedback signals from within the target field, following contrast-enhancement of the inputs. We observe how the ART 3 model responds to a reset signal by implementing a rapid and enduring inhibition of erroneously selected pattern features. Then we analyse how the ART 3 model responds if the input pattern changes.

We will begin with the

SYSTEM DYNAMICS

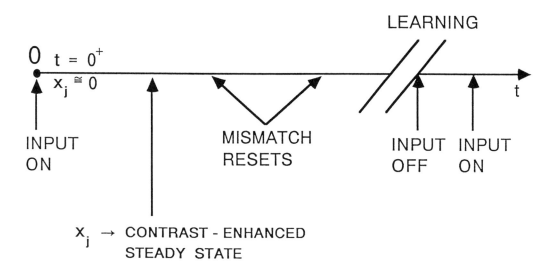

Figure 11. The system is designed to carry out necessary computations at critical junctures of the search process.

ART Search Hypothesis 1:
Presynaptic transmitter u_{ij} is released at a rate jointly proportional to the presynaptic signal S_i and a function $f(x_j)$ of the postsynaptic activity. That is, in equations (1), (2), and (5),

$$\text{release rate} = S_i f(x_j). \tag{9}$$

The function $f(x_j)$ in equation (9) has the qualitative properties illustrated in Figure 12. In particular $f(x_j)$ is assumed to have a positive value when x_j is at its 0 resting level, so that transmitter u_{ij} can be released when the signal S_i arrives at the synapse. If $f(0)$ were equal to 0, no excitatory signal could reach a postsynaptic node at rest, even if a large presynaptic signal S_i were sent to that node. The function $f(x_j)$ is also assumed to equal 0 when x_j is significantly hyperpolarized, but to rise steeply when x_j is near 0. In the simulations, $f(x_j)$ is linear above a small negative threshold.

The form factor $S_i f(x_j)$ is a familiar one in the neuroscience and neural network literatures. In particular, such a product is often used to model associative learning, where it links the rate of learning in the ijth pathway to the presynaptic signal S_i and the postsynaptic activity x_j. Associative learning occurs, however, on a time scale that is much slower than the time scale of transmitter release. On the fast time scale of transmitter relase, the form factor $S_i f(x_j)$ may be compared to interactions between voltages and ions. In Figure 9, for example, note the dependence of the presynaptic signal on the Na$^+$ ion; the postsynaptic signal on the Ca^{2+} ion; and transmitter release

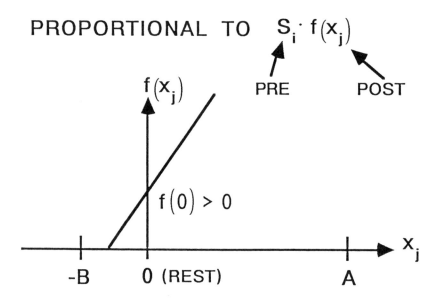

Figure 12. The ART Search Hypothesis 1 specifies the transmitter release rate.

on the *joint* fluxes of these two ions. The ART Search Hypothesis 1 thus formalizes a known type of synergetic relationship between presynaptic and postsynaptic processes in effecting transmitter release. Moreover, the rate of transmitter release is typically a function of the concentration of Ca^{2+} in the extracellular space, and this function has qualitative properties similar to the function $f(x_j)$ shown in Figure 12 (Kandel and Schwartz, 1981, p.84; Kuffler, Nicholls, and Martin, 1984, p.244).

11. System Dynamics at Input Onset: An Approximately Linear Filter

Some implications of the ART Search Hypothesis 1 will now be summarized. Assume that at time $t = 0$ transmitter u_{ij} has accumulated to its maximal level z_{ij} and that activity x_j and bound transmitter v_{ij} equal 0. Consider a time interval $t = 0^+$ immediately after a signal S_i arrives at the synapse. During this brief initial interval, the ART equations approximate the linear filter dynamics typical of many neural network models. In particular, equations (2) and (9) imply that the amount of bound transmitter is determined by equation

$$\frac{dv_{ij}}{dt} = -v_{ij} + u_{ij}S_i f(x_j) - v_{ij}[\text{inactivation rate}]. \tag{10}$$

Thus at times $t = 0^+$,

$$\frac{dv_{ij}}{dt} \approx z_{ij}S_i f(0) \tag{11}$$

and so

$$v_{ij}(t) \approx K(t)S_i z_{ij} \quad \text{for times } t = 0^+. \tag{12}$$

(a) $x_j \approx K(t) \, S \cdot z_j \quad (t = 0^+)$

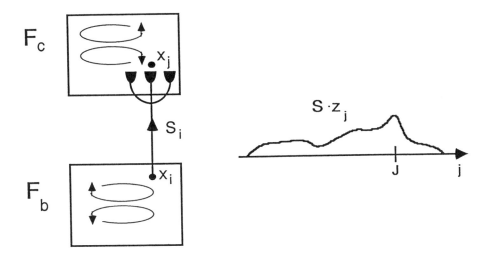

(b) FEEDBACK CONTRAST-ENHANCES x_j

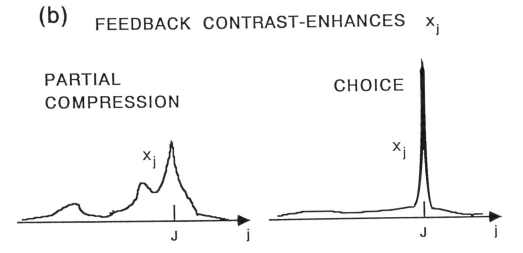

PARTIAL
COMPRESSION

CHOICE

Figure 13. (a) If transmitter is fully accumulated at $t = 0$, low-amplitude post-synaptic STM activity x_j is initially proportional to the dot product of the signal vector **S** and the weight vector z_j. Fields are labeled F_b and F_c for consistency with the ART 3 system in Figure 21. (b) Intrafield feedback rapidly contrast-enhances the initial STM activity pattern. Large-amplitude activity is then concentrated at one or more nodes.

Because equation (12) holds at all the synapses adjacent to cell j, equation (6) implies that

$$x_j(t) \approx \sum_i K(t)S_i z_{ij} = K(t)\mathbf{S} \cdot \mathbf{z}_j \quad \text{for times } t = 0^+. \tag{13}$$

Here $\mathbf{S}$ denotes the vector $(S_1 \ldots S_n)$, $\mathbf{z}_j$ denotes the vector $(z_{1j} \ldots z_{nj})$, and $i = 1 \ldots n$. Thus in the initial moments after a signal arrives at the synapse, the small amplitude activity x_j at the postsynaptic cell grows in proportion to the dot product of the incoming signal vector $\mathbf{S}$ times the adaptive weight vector $\mathbf{z}_j$.

12. System Dynamics after Intrafield Feedback: Amplification of Transmitter Release by Postsynaptic Potential

In the next time interval, the intrafield feedback signal contrast-enhances the initial signal pattern (13) via equation (6) and amplifies the total activity across field F_c in Figure 13a. Figure 13b shows typical contrast-enhanced activity profiles: partial compression of the initial signal pattern; or maximal compression, or choice, where only one postsynaptic node remains active due to the strong competition within the field F_c.

In all, the model behaves initially like a linear filter. The resulting pattern of activity across postsynaptic cells is contrast-enhanced, as required in the ART 2 model as well as in the many other neural network models that incorporate competitive learning (Grossberg, 1988). For many neural network systems, this combination of computational properties is all that is needed. These models implicitly assume that intracellular transmitter u_{ij} is always accumulated up to its target level z_{ij} and that postsynaptic activity x_j does not alter the rate of transmitter release:

$$u_{ij} \approx z_{ij} \quad \text{and} \quad v_{ij} \approx z_{ij}S_i. \tag{14}$$

If the linear filtering properties implied by (14) work well for many purposes, why complicate the system by adding additional hypotheses? Even a new hypothesis that makes a neural network more realistic physiologically needs to be justified functionally, or it will obscure essential system dynamics. Why, then, add two additional nonlinearities to the portion of a neural network system responsible for transmitting signals from one location to another? The following discussion suggests how nonlinearities of synaptic transmission and neuromodulation can, when embedded in an ART circuit, help to correct coding errors by triggering a parallel search, allow the system to respond adaptively to reinforcement, and rapidly reset itself to changing input patterns.

In equation (10), term

$$u_{ij}S_i f(x_j) \tag{15}$$

for the amount of transmitter released per unit time implies that the original incoming weighted signal $z_{ij}S_i$ is distorted both by depletion of the presynaptic transmitter u_{ij} and by the activity level x_j of the postsynaptic cell. If these two nonlinearities are significant, the net signal in the ijth pathway depends jointly on the maximal weighted signal $z_{ij}S_i$; the prior activity in the pathway, as reflected in the amount of depletion of the transmitter u_{ij}; and the immediate context in which the signal

TOTAL POSTSYNAPTICALLY
BOUND TRANSMITTER

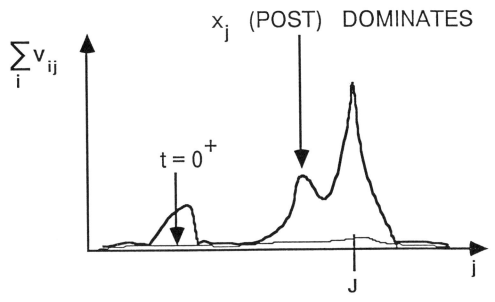

Figure 14. The ART Search Hypothesis 1 implies that large amounts of transmitter (v_{ij}) are released only adjacent to postsynaptic nodes with large-amplitude activity (x_j). Competition within the postsynaptic field therefore transforms the initial low-amplitude distributed pattern of released and bound transmitter into a large-amplitude contrast-enhanced pattern.

is sent, as reflected in the target cell activity x_j. In particular, once activity in a postsynaptic cell becomes large, this activity dominates the transmitter release rate, via the term $f(x_j)$ in (15). In other words, although linear filtering properties initially determine the small-amplitude activity pattern of the target field F_c, once intrafield feedback amplifies and contrast-enhances the postsynaptic activity x_j (Figure 13b), it plays a major role in determining the amount of released transmitter v_{ij} (Figure 14). In particular, the postsynaptic activity pattern across the field F_c that represents the recognition code (Figure 13b) is imparted to the pattern of released transmitter (Figure 14), which then also represents the recognition code, rather than the initial filtered pattern $\mathbf{S} \cdot \mathbf{z}_j$.

13. System Dynamics during Reset: Inactivation of Bound Transmitter Channels

The dynamics of transmitter release implied by the ART Search Hypothesis 1 can be used to implement the reset process, by postulating the

ART Search Hypothesis 2:

The nonspecific reset signal quickly inactivates postsynaptic membrane channels at which transmitter is bound (Figure 15).

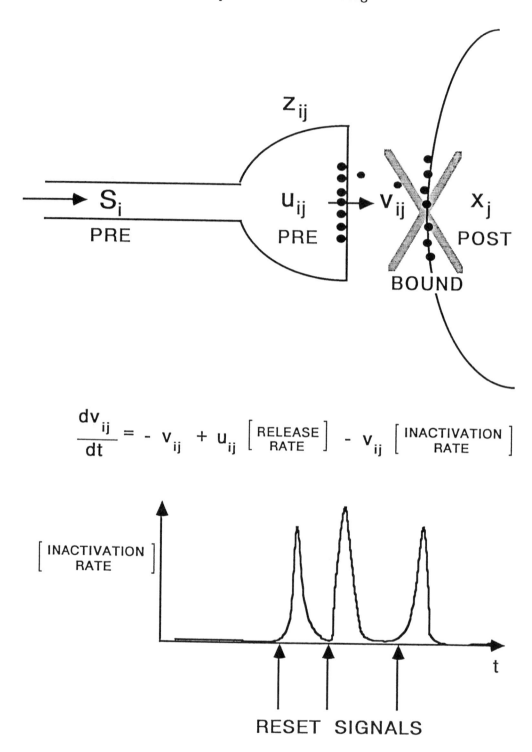

Figure 15. The ART Search Hypothesis 2 specifies a high rate of inactivation of bound transmitter following a reset signal. Postsynaptic action of the nonspecific reset signal is similar to that of a neuromodulator.

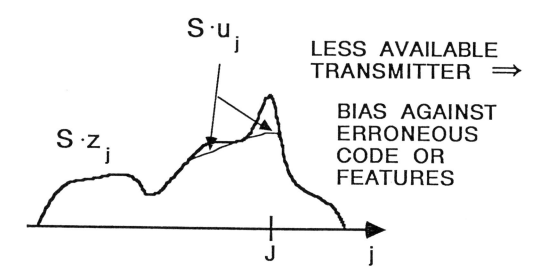

Figure 16. Following reset, the system is selectively biased against pathways that had previously released large quantities of transmitter. After a mismatch reset, therefore, the adaptive filter delivers a smaller signal to the previous category representation, the one that generated the reset signal.

The reset signal in equations (5) and (6) may be interpreted as assignment of a large value to the inactivation rate in a manner analogous to the action of a neuromodulator (Figure 9). Inhibition of postsynaptic nodes breaks the strong intrafield feedback loops that implement ART 2 and ART 3 matching and contrast-enhancement (equation (3) or (6)).

Let us now examine system dynamics following transmitter inactivation. The pattern of released transmitter can be viewed as a representation of the postsynaptic recognition code. The arrival of a reset signal implies that some part of the system has judged this code to be erroneous, according to some criterion. The ART Search Hypothesis 1 implies that the largest concentrations of bound extracellular transmitter are adjacent to the nodes which most actively represent this erroneous code. The ART Search Hypothesis 2 therefore implies that the reset process selectively removes transmitter from pathways leading to the erroneous representation.

After the reset wave has acted, the system is biased against activation of the same nodes, or features, in the next time interval: Whereas the transmitter signal pattern $\mathbf{S} \cdot \mathbf{u}_j$ originally sent to target nodes at times $t = 0^+$ was proportional to $\mathbf{S} \cdot \mathbf{z}_j$, as in equation (12), the transmitter signal pattern $\mathbf{S} \cdot \mathbf{u}_j$ after the reset event is no longer proportional to $\mathbf{S} \cdot \mathbf{z}_j$. Instead, it is selectively biased against those features that were previously active (Figure 16). The new signal pattern $\mathbf{S} \cdot \mathbf{u}_j$ will lead to selection of another contrast-enhanced representation, which may or may not then be reset. This search process continues until an acceptable match is found, possibly through the selection of a previously inactive representation.

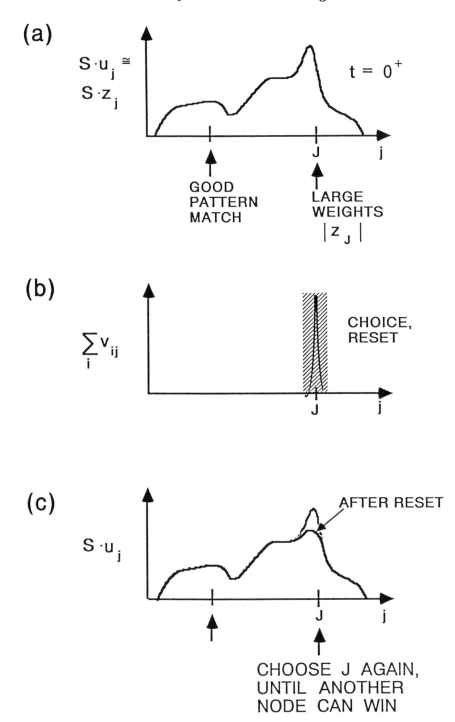

Figure 17. An erroneous category representation with large weights (z_{iJ}) may become active before another representation that makes a good pattern match with the input but which has small weights. One or more mismatch reset events can decrease the functional value (u_{iJ}) of the larger weights, allowing the "correct" category to become active.

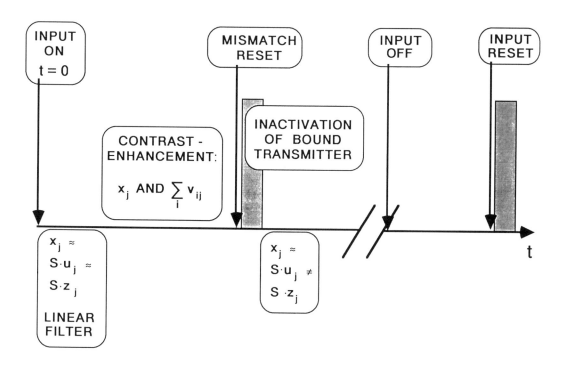

Figure 18. ART Search Hypotheses 1 and 2 implement computations to carry out search in an ART system. Input reset employs the same mechanisms as mismatch reset, initiating search when the input pattern changes significantly.

14. Parametric Robustness of the Search Process

This search process is relatively easy to implement, requiring no new nodes or pathways beyond those already present in ART 2 modules. It is also robust, since it does not require tricky timing or calibration. How the process copes with a typical slow learning situation is illustrated in Figure 17. With slow learning, an input can select and begin to train a new category, so that the adaptive weights correspond to a perfect pattern match during learning. However, the input may not be on long enough for the adaptive weights to become very large. That input may later activate a different category node whose weights are large but whose vector of adaptive weights forms a poorer match than the original, smaller weights.

Figure 17a shows such a typical filtered signal pattern $\mathbf{S} \cdot \mathbf{z}_j$. During the initial processing interval $(t = 0^+)$ the transmitted signal $\mathbf{S} \cdot \mathbf{u}_j$ and the postsynaptic activity x_j are proportional to $\mathbf{S} \cdot \mathbf{z}_j$. Suppose that the weights z_{iJ} in pathways leading to the Jth node are large, but that the vector pattern $\mathbf{z}_J$ is not an adequate match for the signal pattern $\mathbf{S}$ according to the vigilance criterion. Also suppose that dynamics in the target field F_c lead to a "choice" following competitive contrast-enhancement (Figure 17b), and that the chosen node J represents a category. Large amounts of transmitter will thus be released from synapses adjacent to node J, but not from synapses adjacent to other nodes. The reset signal will then selectively inactivate transmitter at postsynaptic sites adjacent to the Jth node. Following such a reset wave, the new signal pattern $\mathbf{S} \cdot \mathbf{u}_j$ will be biased against the Jth node relative to the original signal pattern. However, it could happen that the time interval prior to the reset signal is so brief that only a small fraction of available transmitter is released. Then $\mathbf{S} \cdot \mathbf{u}_J$ could still be large relative to a "correct" $\mathbf{S} \cdot \mathbf{u}_j$ after reset occurs (Figure 17c). If this were to occur, the Jth node would simply be chosen again, then reset again, leading to an accumulating bias against that choice in the next time interval. This process could continue until enough transmitter v_{ij} is inactivated to allow another node, with smaller weights z_{ij} but a better pattern match, to win the competition. Simulations of such a reset sequence are illustrated in Figures 23-26.

15. Summary of System Dynamics during a Mismatch-Reset Cycle

Figure 18 summarizes system dynamics of the ART search model during a single input presentation. Initially the transmitted signal pattern $\mathbf{S} \cdot \mathbf{u}_j$, as well as the postsynaptic activity x_j, are proportional to the weighted signal pattern $\mathbf{S} \cdot \mathbf{z}_j$ of the linear filter. The postsynaptic activity pattern is then contrast-enhanced, due to the internal competitive dynamics of the target field. The ART Search Hypothesis 1 implies that the transmitter release rate is greatly amplified in proportion to the level of postsynaptic activity. A subsequent reset signal selectively inactivates transmitter in those pathways that caused an error. Following the reset wave, the new signal $\mathbf{S} \cdot \mathbf{u}_j$ is no longer proportional to $\mathbf{S} \cdot \mathbf{z}_j$ but is, rather, biased against the previously active representation. A series of reset events ensue, until an adequate match or a new category is found. Learning occurs on a time scale that is long relative to that of the search process.

16. Automatic STM Reset by Real-Time Input Sequences

The ART 3 architecture serves other functions as well as implementing the mismatch-reset-search cycle. In particular it allows an ART system to dispense with additional processes to reset STM at onset or offset of an input pattern. The representation of input patterns as a sequence, $\mathbf{I}_1, \mathbf{I}_2, \mathbf{I}_3, \ldots$, corresponds to the assumption that each input is constant for a fixed time interval. In practice, an input vector $\mathbf{I}(t)$ may vary continuously through time. The input need never be constant over an interval, and there may be no temporal marker to signal offset or onset of "an input pattern" per se. Furthermore, feedback loops within a field or between two fields can maintain large amplitude activity even when $\mathbf{I}(t) = 0$. Adaptive resonance develops only when activity patterns across fields are amplified by such feedback loops and remain stable for a sufficiently long time to enable adaptive weight changes to occur (Grossberg, 1976b, 1982a). In particular, no reset waves are triggered during a resonant event.

The ART reset system functionally defines the onset of a "new" input as a time when the orienting subsystem emits a reset wave. This occurs, for example, in the ART 2 module (Figure 3) when the angle between the vectors $\mathbf{I}(t)$ and $\mathbf{p}(t)$ becomes so large that the norm of $\mathbf{r}(t)$ falls below the vigilance level $\rho(t)$, thereby triggering a search for a new category representation. This is called an *input reset* event, to distinguish it from a *mismatch reset* event, which occurs while the bottom-up input remains nearly constant over a time interval but mismatches the top-down expectation that it has elicited from level F_2 (Figure 2).

REINFORCEMENT RESET CAN OVERRIDE PATH WEIGHT BIAS

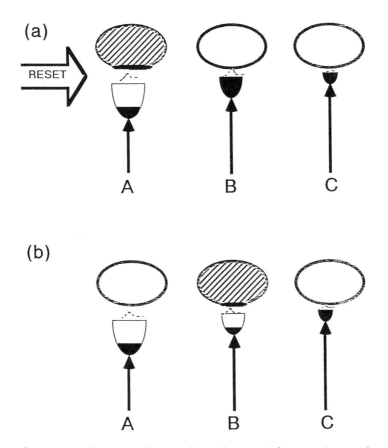

Figure 19. A system whose weights are biased toward feature A over feature B over feature C. (a) Competition amplifies the weight bias in STM, leading to enhanced transmitter release of the selected feature A. (b) Transmitter inactivation following reinforcement reset allows feature B to become active in STM.

This property obviates the need to mechanistically define the processing of input onset or offset. The ART Search Hypothesis 3, which postulates restoration of a resting state between successive inputs (Carpenter and Grossberg, 1989), is thus not needed. Presynaptic transmitter may not be fully accumulated following an input reset event, just as it is not fully accumulated following a mismatch reset event. For both types of reset, the orienting subsystem judges the active code to be incorrect, at the present level of vigilance, and the system continues to search until it finds an acceptable representation.

17. Reinforcement Feedback

The mechanisms described thusfar for STM reset are part of the recognition learning circuit of ART 3. Recognition learning is, however, only one of several processes whereby an intelligent system can learn a correct solution to a problem. We have called Recognition, Reinforcement, and Recall the "3 R's" of neural network

REINFORCEMENT RESET CAN OVERRIDE INPUT BIAS

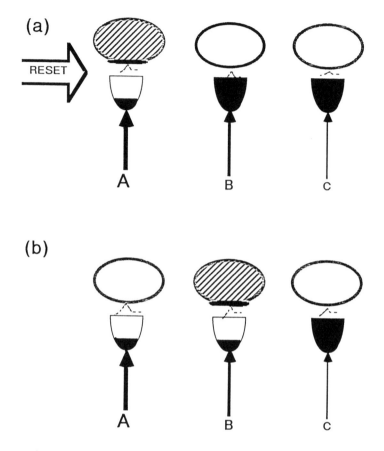

Figure 20. A system whose input signals are biased towards A over B over C. (a) Competition amplifies the input bias in STM, leading to enhanced transmitter release of the selected feature A. (b) Transmitter inactivation following reinforcement reset allows feature B to become active in STM.

learning (Carpenter and Grossberg, 1988).

Reinforcement, notably reward and punishment, provides additional information in the form of environmental feedback based on the success or failure of actions triggered by a recognition event. Reward and punishment calibrate whether the action has or has not satisfied internal needs, which in the biological case include hunger, thirst, sex, and pain reduction, but may in machine applications include a wide variety of internal cost functions.

Reinforcement can shift attention to focus upon those recognition codes whose activation promises to satisfy internal needs based on past experience. A model to describe this aspect of reinforcement learning was described in Grossberg, (1982a, 1982b, 1984; reprinted in Grossberg, 1987a) and was supported by computer simulations in Grossberg and Levine (1987; reprinted in Grossberg, 1988). An attention shift due to reinforcement can also alter the structure and learning of recognition codes by amplifying (or suppressing) the STM activations, and hence the adjacent adaptive weights, of feature detectors that are active during positive (or negative) reinforcement.

A reset wave may also be used to modify the pattern of STM activation in response to reinforcement. For example, both green and yellow bananas may be recognized as part of a single recognition category until reinforcement signals, contingent upon eating the bananas, differentiate them into separate categories. Within ART 3, such a reinforcement signal can alter the course of recognition learning by causing a reset event. The reset event may override a bias in either the learned path weights (Figure 19) or in the input strengths (Figure 20) that could otherwise prevent a correct classification from being learned. For example, both green and yellow bananas may initially be coded in the same recognition category because features that code object shape (e.g., pathway A in Figures 19 and 20) prevent features that code object color (e.g., pathway B in Figures 19 and 20) from being processed in STM. Reset waves triggered by reinforcement feedback can progressively weaken the STM activities of these shape features until both shape and color features can simultaneously be processed, and thereby incorporated into different recognition codes for green bananas and yellow bananas.

In technological applications, such a reset wave can be implemented as a direct signal from an internal representation of a punishing event. The effect of the reset wave is to modify the spatial pattern of STM activation whose read-out into an overt action led to the punishing event. The adaptive weights, or LTM traces, that input to these STM activations are then indirectly altered by an amount that reflects the new STM activation pattern. Such a reinforcement scheme differs from the competitive learning scheme described by Kohonen (1984, p. 200), in which reinforcement acts directly, and by an equal amount, on all adaptive weights that lead to an incorrect classification.

Reinforcement may also act by changing the level of vigilance (Carpenter and Grossberg, 1987a, 1987b). For example, if a punishing event increases the vigilance parameter, then mismatches that were tolerated before will lead to a search for another recognition code. Such a code can help to distinguish pattern differences that were previously considered too small to be significant. Such a role for reinforcement is illustrated by computer simulations in Figures 25-28.

All three types of reaction to reinforcement feedback may be useful in applications. The change in vigilance alters the overall sensitivity of the system to pattern differences. The shift in attention and the reset of active features can help to overcome prior coding biases that may be maladaptive in novel contexts.

18. Notation for Hierarchies

Table 1 and Figure 21 illustrate notation suitable for an ART hierarchy with any number of fields $F_a, F_b, F_c \ldots$ This notation can also be adapted for related neural networks and algorithmic computer simulation.

Each STM variable is indexed by its field, layer, and node number. Within a layer, x denotes the activity of a node receiving inputs from other layers, while y denotes the (normalized) activity of a node that sends signals to other layers. For example, x_i^{a2} denotes activity at the ith input node in layer 2 of field $F_a (i = 1 \ldots n_a)$; and y_i^{a2} denotes activity of the corresponding output node. Parameters are also indexed by

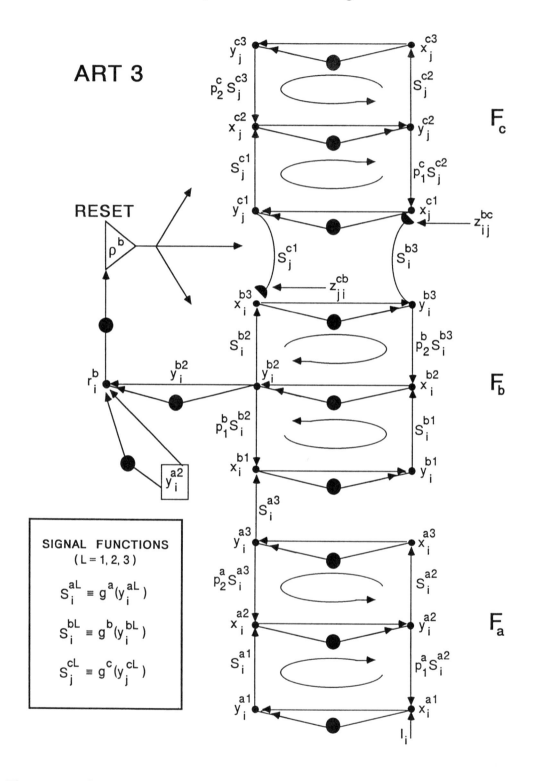

Figure 21. ART 3 simulation neural network. Indices $i = 1 \ldots n_a = n_b$ and $j = 1 \ldots n_c$. The reset signal acts at all layers 1 and 3 (Section 8).

NOTATION FOR ART 3 HIERARCHY

$F_{field} = F_a$	STM field a
$i = i_a = 1...n_a$	node index, field a
$L = 1,2,3$	index, 3 layers of an STM field
x_i^{aL}	STM activity, input node i, layer L, field a
y_i^{aL}	STM activity, output node i, layer L, field a
$g^a(y_i^{aL}) = S_i^{aL}$	signal function, field a
p_k^a	parameter, field a, $k = 1, 2, ...$
r_i^b	STM activity, reset node i, field b
ρ^b	vigilance parameter, field b
z_{ij}^{bc}	LTM trace, pathway from node i (field b) to node j (field c)
u_{ij}^{bc}	intracellular transmitter, pathway from node i (field b) to node j (field c)
v_{ij}^{bc}	released transmitter, pathway from node i (field b) to node j (field c)

Table 1. Notation for ART 3 hierarchy.

field $(p_1^a, p_2^a, \ldots)$, as are signal functions (g^a). Variable r_i^b denotes activity of the ith reset node of field F_b, and ρ^b is the corresponding vigilance parameter.

Variable z denotes an adaptive weight or LTM trace. For example, z_{ij}^{bc} is the weight in the bottom-up pathway from the ith node of field F_b to the jth node of field F_c. Variables u_{ij}^{bc} and v_{ij}^{bc} denote the corresponding presynaptic and bound transmitter quantities, respectively. Variables for the top-down pathways are z_{ji}^{cb}, u_{ji}^{cb}, and v_{ji}^{cb}.

Complete simulation equations are specified in Section 26.

19. Trade-Off between Weight Size and Pattern Match

The simulations in Sections 20–24 illustrate the dynamics of search in the ART 3 system shown in Figure 21. The simulation time scale is assumed to be short relative to the time scale of learning, so all adaptive weights z_{ij}^{bc} and z_{ji}^{cb} are held constant. The weights are chosen, however, to illustrate a problem that can arise with slow learning or in any other situation in which weight vectors are not normalized at all times. Namely, a category whose weight vector only partially matches the input vector may become active because its weights are large. This can prevent initial selection of another category whose weight vector matches the input vector but whose weight magnitudes are small due, say, to a brief prior learning interval.

The search process allows the ART 3 system to reject an initial selection with large weights and partial pattern match, and then to activate a category with smaller

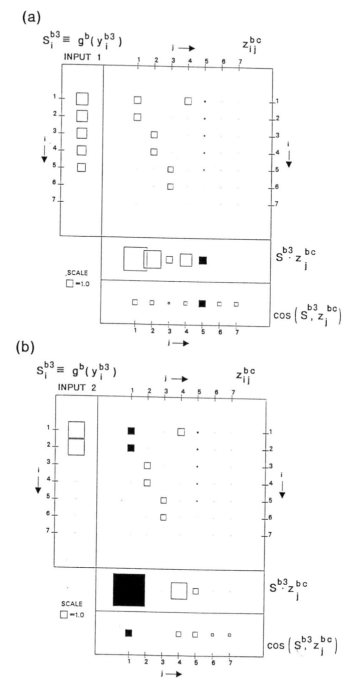

Figure 22. The length of a side of the square centered at position i or j or (i,j) gives the value of a variable with the corresponding index. Shown are quantities S_i^{b3}, z_{ij}^{bc}, $\mathbf{S}^{b3} \cdot \mathbf{z}_j^{bc}$, and $\cos(\mathbf{S}^{b3}, \mathbf{z}_j^{bc})$. (a) Vector $\mathbf{S}^{b3}$ is the signal response to Input 1 in the simulations. Vector $\mathbf{z}_5^{bc}$ (filled squares) is parallel to $\mathbf{S}^{b3}$, but $\|\mathbf{z}_5^{bc}\|$ is small. Thus $\mathbf{S}^{b3} \cdot \mathbf{z}_5^{bc}$ is smaller than $\mathbf{S}^{b3} \cdot \mathbf{z}_j^{bc}$ for $j = 1, 2,$ and 4, despite the fact that $\cos(\mathbf{S}^{b3}, \mathbf{z}_5^{bc})$ is maximal. (b) Vector $\mathbf{S}^{b3}$ is the signal response to Input 2 in the simulations. Vector $\mathbf{z}_1^{bc}$ (filled squares) is parallel to $\mathbf{S}^{b3}$.

weights and a better pattern match. As in ART 2, when weights are very small (nodes $j = 6, 7, \ldots$, Figure 22) the ART system tolerates poor pattern matches in order to allow new categories to become established. During learning, the weights can become larger. The larger the weights, the more sensitive the ART system is to pattern mismatch (Carpenter and Grossberg, 1987b).

Figure 22 illustrates the trade-off between weight size and pattern match in the system used in the simulations. In Figures 22a and 22b, vector $\mathbf{S}$ illustrates the STM pattern stored in F_a and sent from F_a to F_b when an input vector $\mathbf{I}$ is held constant. The S_i values were obtained by presenting to F_a an input function $\mathbf{I}$ with I_i a linearly decreasing function of i. Vector $\mathbf{S}$ is also stored in F_b, as long as F_c remains inactive. Initially $\mathbf{S}$ is the signal vector in the bottom-up pathways from F_b to F_c. In Figure 22a, $S_1 > S_2 > \ldots > S_5$; for $i = 6, 7 \ldots 15 (= n_a = n_b), S_i$ is small. Each vector $\mathbf{z}_1, \mathbf{z}_2, \mathbf{z}_3$, and $\mathbf{z}_4$, plotted in columns within the square region of Figure 22a, partially matches the signal vector $\mathbf{S}$. These weights are significantly larger than the weights of vector $\mathbf{z}_5$. However $\mathbf{z}_5$ is a perfect match to $\mathbf{S}$ in the sense that the angle between the two vectors is 0:

$$\cos(\mathbf{S}, \mathbf{z}_5) = 1. \tag{16}$$

The relationship

$$\mathbf{S} \cdot \mathbf{z}_j = \|\mathbf{S}\| \|\mathbf{z}_j\| \cos(\mathbf{S}, \mathbf{z}_j) \tag{17}$$

implies a trade-off between weight size, as measured by the length $\|\mathbf{z}_j\|$ of $\mathbf{z}_j$, and pattern match, as measured by the angle between $\mathbf{S}$ and $\mathbf{z}_j$. If the initial signal from F_b to F_c is proportional to $\mathbf{S} \cdot \mathbf{z}_j$, as in (13), then the matched node ($j = 5$) may receive a net signal that is smaller than signals to other nodes. In fact, in Figure 22a,

$$\mathbf{S} \cdot \mathbf{z}_1 > \mathbf{S} \cdot \mathbf{z}_2 > \mathbf{S} \cdot \mathbf{z}_4 > \mathbf{S} \cdot \mathbf{z}_5 > \ldots. \tag{18}$$

Figure 22b shows a signal vector $\mathbf{S}$ that is parallel to the weight vector $\mathbf{z}_1$.

20. ART 3 Simulations: Mismatch Reset and Input Reset of STM Choices

The computer simulations summarized in Figures 23-26 use the inputs described in Figure 22 to illustrate the search process in an ART 3 system. In these simulations, the F_c competition parameters were chosen to make a choice; hence, only the node receiving the largest filtered input from F_b is stored in STM. The signal function of F_c caused the STM field to make a choice. In Figures 27 a different signal function at F_c, similar to the one used in F_a and F_b, illustrates how the search process reorganizes a distributed recognition code. The simulations show how, with high vigilance, the ART search process rapidly causes a series of mismatch resets that alter the transmitter vectors $\mathbf{u}_1, \mathbf{u}_2, \ldots$ until $\mathbf{S} \cdot \mathbf{u}_5$ becomes maximal. Once node $j = 5$ becomes active in STM it amplifies transmitter release. Since the pattern match is perfect, no further reset occurs while Input 1 (Figure 22a) remains on. Input reset is illustrated following an abrupt or gradual switch to Input 2 (Figure 22b).

Each simulation figure illustrates three system variables as they evolve through time. The time axis (t) runs from the top to the bottom of the square. A vector pattern, indexed by i or j, is plotted horizontally at each fixed time. Within each square, the value of a variable at each time is represented by the length of a side of a square centered at that point. In each figure, part (a) plots y_j^{c1}, the normalized STM

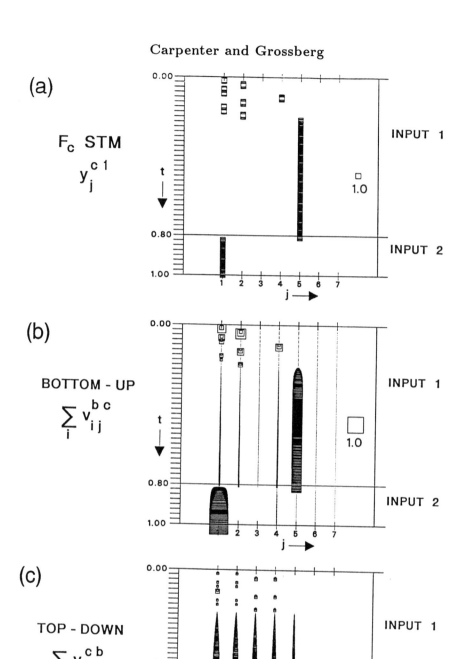

Figure 23. ART 3 simulation with $\rho \equiv .98$. A series of 9 mismatch resets lead to activation of the matched category $(j = 5)$ at $t = .215$. Input 1 switches to Input 2 at $t = .8$ causing an input reset and activation of a new category representation $(j = 1)$.

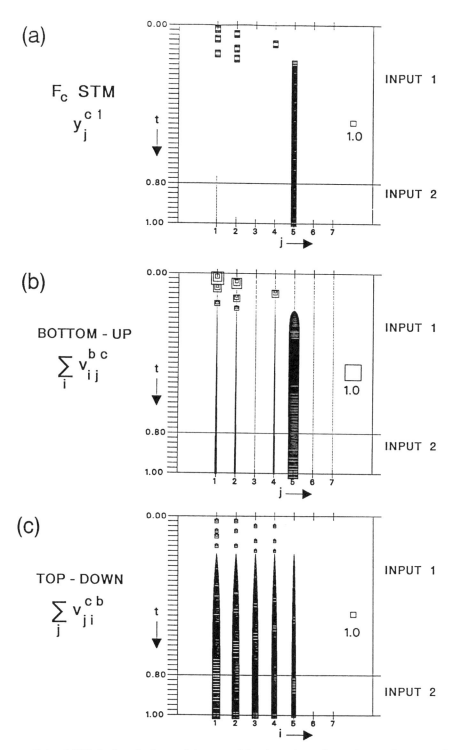

Figure 24. ART 3 simulation with $\rho = .94$. A series of 7 mismatch resets lead to activation of the matched category ($j = 5$) at $t = .19$ Input 1 switches to Input 2 at $t = .8$, but no input reset occurs, and node $j = 5$ remains active, due to the lower vigilance level than in Figure 23.

variables at layer 1 of field F_c. Part (b) plots $\sum_i v_{ij}^{bc}$, the total amount of transmitter released, bottom-up, in paths from all F_b nodes to the jth F_c node. Part (c) plots $\sum_j v_{ji}^{cb}$, the total amount of transmitter released, top-down, in paths from all F_c nodes to the ith F_b node. The ART Search Hypothesis 1 implies that the net bottom-up transmitter pattern in part (b) reflects the STM pattern of F_c in part (a); and that the net top-down transmitter pattern in part (c) reflects the STM pattern of F_b.

In Figure 23, the vigilance parameter is high and fixed at the value

$$\rho \equiv .98. \tag{19}$$

For $0 \le t < .8$, the input (Figure 22a) is constant. The high vigilance level induces a sequence of mismatch resets, alternating among the category nodes $j = 1, 2$, and 4 (Figure 23a), each of which receives an initial input larger than the input to node $j = 5$ (Figure 22a). At $t = .215$, the F_c node $j = 5$ is selected by the search process (Figure 23a). It remains active until $t = .8$. Then, the input from F_a is changed to a new pattern (Figure 22b). The mismatch between the new STM pattern at F_a and the old reverberating STM pattern at F_b leads to an input reset (Figures 18 and 23). The ART Search Hypothesis 2 implies that bound transmitter is inactivated and the STM feedback loops in F_b and F_c are thereby inhibited. The new input pattern immediately activates its category node $j = 1$, despite some previous depletion at that node (Figure 23a).

Large quantities of transmitter are released and bound only after STM resonance is established. In Figure 23b, large quantities of bottom-up transmitter are released at the F_c node $j = 5$ in the time interval $.215 < t < .8$, and at node $j = 1$ in the time interval $.8 < t < 1$. In Figure 23c, the pattern of top-down bound transmitter reflects the resonating matched STM pattern at F_b due to Input 1 at times $.215 < t < .8$ and due to Input 2 at times $.8 < t < 1$.

21. Search Time Invariance at Different Vigilance Values

Figure 24 shows the dynamics of the same system as in Figure 23 but at the lower vigilance value

$$\rho \equiv .94. \tag{20}$$

The F_c node $j = 5$ becomes active slightly sooner ($t = .19$, Figure 24a) than it does in Figure 23a, where $\rho = .98$. At a lower vigilance, more transmitter needs to be released before the system reacts to a mismatch so that each "erroneous" category node is active for a longer time interval than at higher vigilance. When $\rho = .98$ (Figure 23b), node $j = 1$ is searched 5 times. When $\rho = .94$ (Figure 24b), node $j = 1$ is searched only 3 times, but more transmitter is released during each activation/reset cycle than at comparable points in Figure 23b. Inactivation of this extra released transmitter approximately balances the longer times to reset. Hence the *total* search time remains approximately constant over a wide range of vigilance parameters. In the present instance, the nonlinearities of transmitter release terminate the search slightly sooner at lower vigilance.

Figure 24a illustrates another effect of lower vigilance: the system's ability to tolerate larger mismatches without causing a reset. When the input changes at $t = .8$, the mismatch between the input pattern at F_a and the resonating pattern at F_b is

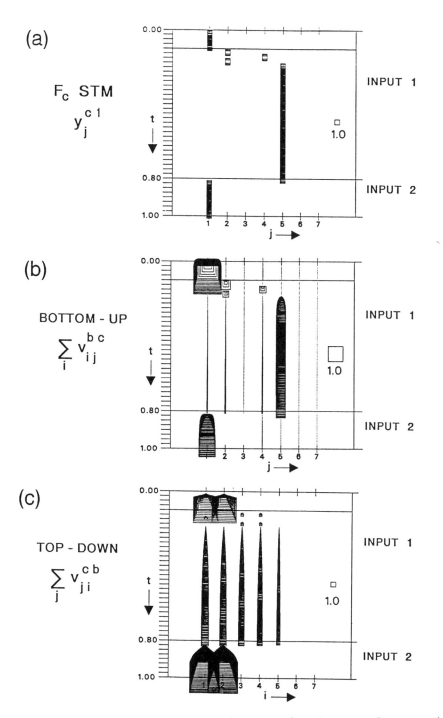

Figure 25. ART 3 simulation with $\rho = .9$ $(0 \le t < .1)$ and $\rho = .98$ $(.1 < t \le 1)$. At low vigilance, activation of node $j = 1$ leads to resonance. When vigilance is suddenly increased due, say, to reinforcement feedback, a series of 4 mismatch resets lead to activation of the matched category $(j = 5)$ at $t = .19$. As in Figure 23, switching to Input 2 at $t = .8$ causes an input reset and activation of a new category representation $(j = 1)$.

not great enough to cause an input reset. Despite bottom-up input only to nodes $i = 1, 2$, the strong resonating pattern at nodes $i = 1 \ldots 4$ maintains itself in STM at F_b (Figure 24c).

22. Reinforcement Reset

In Figure 25 vigilance is initially set at value

$$\rho = .9, \tag{21}$$

in the time interval $0 < t < .1$. At this low vigilance level, the STM pattern of F_b does not experience a mismatch reset series. Node $j = 1$ is chosen and resonance immediately ensues (Figure 25a), as is also reflected in the amplification of transmitter release (Figure 25b). The simulation illustrates a case where this choice of category leads to external consequences, including reinforcement (Section 17), that feed back to the ART 3 module. This reinforcement teaching signal is assumed to cause vigilance to increase to the value

$$\rho = .98 \tag{22}$$

for times $t \geq .1$. This change triggers a search that ends at node $j = 5$, at time $t = .19$. Note that, as in Figure 24, enhanced depletion of transmitter at $j = 1$ shortens the total search time. In Figure 23, where ρ also equals .98, the search interval has length .215; in Figure 25, the search interval has length .09, and the system never again activates node $j = 1$ during search.

23. Input Hysteresis Simulation

The simulation illustrated in Figure 26 is nearly the same as in Figure 25, with $\rho = .9$ for $0 \leq t < .1$ and $\rho = .98$ for $t > .1$. However, at $t = .8$, Input 1 starts to be slowly deformed into Input 2, rather than being suddenly switched, as in Figure 25. The $F_a \rightarrow F_b$ input vector becomes a convex combination of Input 1 and Input 2 that starts as Input 1 ($t \leq .8$) and is linearly shifted to Input 2 ($t \geq 1.7$). Despite the gradually shifting input, node $j = 5$ remains active until $t = 1.28$. Then an input reset immediately leads to activation of node $j = 1$, whose weight vector matches Input 2. Competition in the category representation field F_c causes a history-dependent choice of one category or the other, not a convex combination of the two.

24. Distributed Code Simulation

Issues of learning and code interpretation are subtle and complex when a code is distributed. However, the ART 3 search mechanism translates immediately into this context. The simulation in Figure 27 illustrates how search operates on a distributed code. The only difference between the ART 3 system used for these simulations and the one used for Figures 23-26 is in the signal function at F_c. In Figures 23-26, a choice is always made at field F_c. The signal function for Figure 26 is, like that at F_a and F_b, piecewise linear: 0 below a threshold, linear above. With its fairly high threshold, this signal function compresses the input pattern; but the compression is not so extreme as to lead inevitably to choice in STM.

Distributed code STM activity is shown in Figure 27a. At a given time more than one active node may represent a category ($2.6 < t < 7$), or one node may be chosen ($7.7 < t \leq 9$).

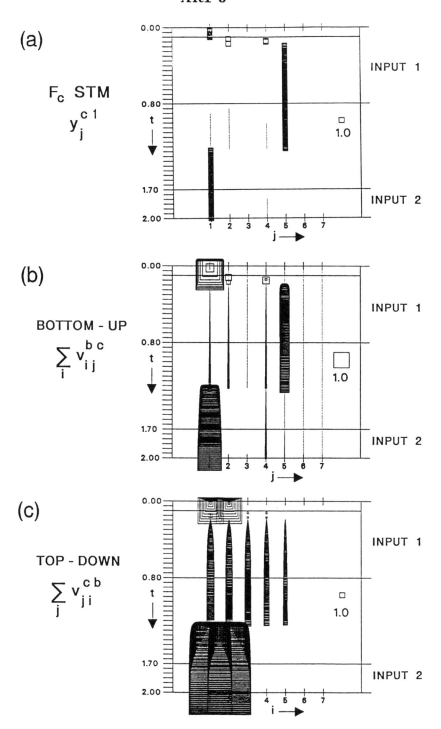

Figure 26. ART 3 simulation with $\rho = .9$ $(0 \leq t < .1)$ and $\rho = .98$ $(1 < t \leq 2)$. Input 1 is presented for $0 \leq t < .8$. For $.8 < t < 1.7$ the input to F_b is a convex combination of Input 1 and Input 2. Then Input 2 is presented for $1.7 < t \leq 2$. At $t = 1.28$ an input reset causes the STM choice to switch from node $j = 5$, which matches Input 1, to node $j = 1$, which matches Input 2.

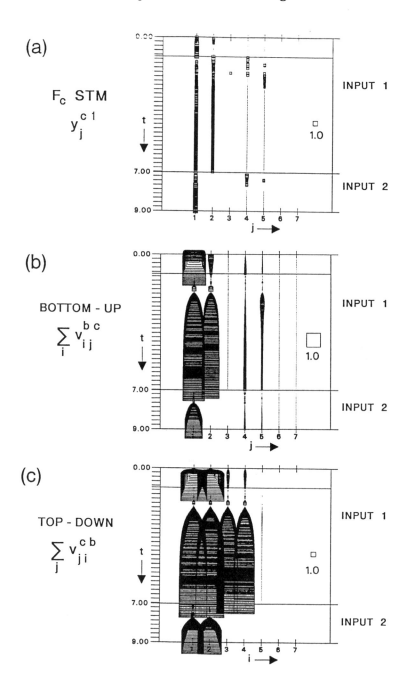

Figure 27. ART 3 simulation of a distributed code. Parameter $\rho = .9$ for $0 \leq t < 1$, and $\rho = .98$ for $1 < t \leq 9$. Input 1 is presented for $0 \leq t < 7$ and Input 2 is presented for $7 < t \leq 9$. At resonance, the single node $j = 1$ is active for $t < 1$ and $t > 7.7$. For $2.6 < t < 7$, simultaneous activity at two nodes ($j = 1$ and $j = 2$) represents the category. Top-down weights z_{ji}^{cb} are large for $j = 1$ and $i = 1$ and 2; and for $j = 2$ and $i = 3$ and 4. Together the top-down signals (c) match enough of the bottom-up input pattern to satisfy the vigilance criterion.

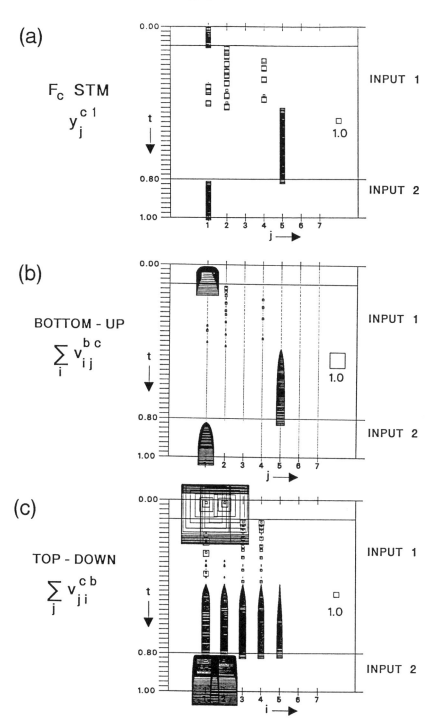

Figure 28. An alternative ART 3 model, which allows hyperpolarization of x_j^{c1}, gives results similar to those illustrated in Figure 25. As in Figure 25, $\rho = .9$ for $0 \le t < .1$, $\rho = .98$ for $t > .1$, and Input 1 switches to Input 2 at $t = .8$. Category node $j = 5$ becomes active at $t = .44$, but immediately switches to node $j = 5$ at $t = .8$, when Input 2 is presented.

25. Alternative ART 3 Model Simulation

ART 3 systems satisfy the small number of design constraints described above. In addition ART 3 satisfies the ART 2 stability constraints (Carpenter and Grossberg, 1987b). For example, top-down signals need to be an order of magnitude larger than bottom-up signals, all other things being equal, as illustrated below by equation (24) and parameters p_1 and p_2 in Table 4 and equations (31) and (34). At least some of the STM fields need to be competitive networks. However, many versions of the ART systems exist within these boundaries. A simulation of one such system is illustrated in Figure 28, which duplicates the conditions on ρ and input patterns of Figure 25. However, the system that generated Figure 28 uses a different version of the ART 3 STM field F_c than the one described in Section 26. In particular, in the STM equation (3), $B > 0$. STM nodes can thus be hyperpolarized, so that $x_j < 0$, by intrafield inhibitory inputs. The transmitter release function $f(x_j)$ (equation (9)) equals 0 when x_j is sufficiently hyperpolarized. The system of Figure 28 thus has the property that transmitter release can be terminated at nodes that become inactive during the STM competition. Since $f(0)$ needs to be positive in order to allow transmitter release to begin (Figure 12), low-level transmitter release by nodes without significant STM activity is unavoidable if nodes cannot be hyperpolarized. Figure 28 shows that a competitive STM field with hyperpolarization gives search and resonance results similar to those of the other simulations.

Similarly, considerable variations in parameters also give similar results.

26. Simulation Equations

Simulation equations are described in an algorithmic form to indicate the steps followed in the computer program that generated Figures 23-27.

TIME SCALE

The simulation time scale is fixed by setting the rate of transmitter accumulation equal to 1. The intrafield STM rate is assumed to be significantly faster, and the LTM rate significantly slower. Accordingly, STM equations are iterated several times each time step; and LTM weights are held constant. The simulation time step is

$$\Delta t = .005. \tag{23}$$

INTEGRATION METHOD

Transmitter variables u and v are integrated by first order approximation (Euler's method). The IMSL Gear package gives essentially identical solutions but requires more computer time.

LTM WEIGHTS

The bottom-up LTM weights z_{ij}^{bc} illustrated in Figure 22 are specified in Table 2. At "uncommitted" nodes $(j \geq 6)$ $z_{ij}^{bc} \equiv 0.001$. Top-down LTM weights z_{ji}^{cb} are constant multiples of corresponding z_{ij}^{bc} weights:

$$z_{ji}^{cb} = 10 \cdot z_{ij}^{bc}. \tag{24}$$

This choice of LTM weights approximates a typical state of an ART system undergoing slow learning. Weights do not necessarily reach equilibrium on each presentation, but while the Jth F_c node is active,

$$z_{Ji}^{cb} \rightarrow x_i^{b3} \tag{25}$$

LTM WEIGHTS z_{ij}^{bc}

$j \longrightarrow$

1	2	3	4	5	6	
1.0	0.0	0.0	1.0	0.176	0.0001	1
1.0	0.0	0.0	0.0	0.162	0.0001	2
0.0	0.9	0.0	0.0	0.148	0.0001	3
0.0	0.9	0.0	0.0	0.134	0.0001	4
0.0	0.0	0.8	0.0	0.120	0.0001	5
0.0	0.0	0.8	0.0	0.0	0.0001	6
0.0	0.0	0.0	0.0	0.0	0.0001	7
.	.	.	.	.	.	.

$i = 1 \ldots n_a = n_b = 15$

$j = 1 \ldots n_c = 20$

Table 2. LTM weights z_{ij}^{bc}.

and

$$z_{iJ}^{bc} \rightarrow S_i^{b3}. \tag{26}$$

Given the parameters specified below, as STM and LTM variables approach equilibrium,

$$x_i^{b3} \cong 10 \cdot S_i^{b3}. \tag{27}$$

Equations (25)-(27) imply that equation (24) is a good approximation of a typical weight distribution.

INITIAL VALUES

Initially,

$$u_{ij}^{bc}(0) = z_{ij}^{bc} \tag{28}$$

and

$$u_{ji}^{cb}(0) = z_{ji}^{cb}. \tag{29}$$

All other initial values are 0.

INPUT VALUES

The F_b input values (S_i^{a3}) are specified in Table 3. All simulations start with Input 1. Several of the simulations switch to Input 2 either with a jump or gradually.

$$F_a \rightarrow F_b \text{ INPUT VALUES } \left(S_i^{a3}\right)$$

i	INPUT 1	INPUT 2
1	1.76	2.36
2	1.62	2.36
3	1.48	0.0
4	1.34	0.0
5	1.20	0.0
6	0.0	0.0
7	0.0	0.0
.	.	.
.	.	.
.	.	.

Table 3. $F_a \rightarrow F_b$ input values (S_i^{a3}).

Input 1 values are obtained by presenting a linear, decreasing function I_i to F_a. Input 2 values are obtained by setting $I_1 = I_2 = 1$ and $I_i = 0$ ($i \geq 3$).

Implicit in this formulation is the assumption that a changing input vector $\mathbf{I}$ can register itself at F_a. This requires that STM at F_a be frequently "reset." Otherwise new values of I_i may go unnoticed, due to strong feedback within F_a. Feedback within F_b allows the STM to maintain resonance even with fluctuating amplitudes at F_a.

STM EQUATIONS

Except during reset, equations used to generate the STM values for Figures 23-27 are similar to the ART 2 equations (Carpenter and Grossberg, 1987b). Dynamics of the fields F_a, F_b, and F_c are homologous, as shown in Figure 21. Steady-state variables for the field F_b, when the reset signal equals 0, are given by equations (31)-(36). Similar equations hold for fields F_a and F_c.

Layer 1, input variable

$$\varepsilon \frac{dx_i^{b1}}{dt} = -x_i^{b1} + S_i^{a3} + p_1^b S_i^{b2}. \tag{30}$$

In steady state,

$$x_i^{b1} \cong S_i^{a3} + p_1^b S_i^{b2}. \tag{31}$$

PARAMETERS

$$p_1^a = p_1^b = p_1^c = 10.0$$

$$p_2^a = p_2^b = p_2^c = 10.0$$

$$p_3^a = p_3^b = p_3^c = 0.0001$$

$$p_4^c = 0.9$$

$$p_5^b = p_5^c = 0.1$$

$$p_6^b = p_6^c = 1.0$$

SIGNAL FUNCTIONS g^a, g^b, g^c

F_a, F_b DISTRIBUTED	F_c CHOICE	F_c DISTRIBUTED
$p_7^a = p_7^b = 0.0$	$p_7^c = 1/\sqrt{n_c}$	$p_7^c = 0.0$
$p_8^a = p_8^b = 0.3$	$p_8^c = 0.2$	$p_8^c = 0.4$

DISTRIBUTED

$$g(w) = \begin{cases} 0 & \text{if } w \le p_7 + p_8 \\ \left(\dfrac{w - p_7}{p_8}\right) & \text{if } w > p_7 + p_8 \end{cases}$$

CHOICE

$$g(w) = \begin{cases} 0 & \text{if } w \le p_7 \\ \left(\dfrac{w - p_7}{p_8}\right)^2 & \text{if } w > p_7 \end{cases}$$

Table 4. Simulation parameters and signal functions.

Table 4 specifies parameter $p_1^b, p_2^b, \ldots$ values and the signal function

$$g^b(y_i^{bL}) \equiv S_i^{bL} \tag{32}$$

for layers $L = 1, 2, 3$. Equation (31) is similar to the simplified STM equation (6), with x_i^{b1} equal to the sum of an interfield input (S_i^{a3}) and an intrafield input ($p_1^b S_i^{b2}$).

Layer 1, output variable

$$y_i^{b1} \cong \frac{x_i^{b1}}{p_3^b + \|\mathbf{x}^{b1}\|}. \tag{33}$$

Layer 2, input variable

$$x_i^{b2} \cong S_i^{b1} + p_2^b S_i^{b3} \tag{34}$$

Layer 2, output variable

$$y_i^{b2} \cong \frac{x_i^{b2}}{p_3^b + \|\mathbf{x}^{b2}\|} \tag{35}$$

Layer 3, input variable

$$x_i^{b3} \cong S_i^{b2} + p_4^c \sum_j v_{ji}^{cb} \tag{36}$$

Layer 3, output variable

$$y_i^{b3} \cong \frac{x_i^{b3}}{p_3^b + \|\mathbf{x}^{b3}\|} \tag{37}$$

Normalization of the output variables in equations (33), (35), and (37) accomplishes two goals. First, since the nonlinear signal function g^b in equation (32) has a fixed threshold, normalization is needed to achieve orderly pattern transformations under variable processing loads. This goal could have been reached with other norms, such as the L^1 norm ($|\mathbf{x}| \equiv \sum_i x_i$). The second goal of normalization is to allow the patterns to have direct access to category representations, without search, after the code has stabilized (Carpenter and Grossberg, 1987a, 1987b). Equations (13) and (17) together tie the Euclidean norm to direct access in the present model. If direct access is not needed, or if another measure of similarity of vectors is used, the Euclidean norm may be replaced by L^1 or another norm.

TRANSMITTER EQUATIONS

When the reset signal equals 0, levels of presynaptic and bound transmitter are governed by equations of the form (1) and (5), as follows.

Presynaptic transmitter, $\mathbf{F_b} \rightarrow \mathbf{F_c}$

$$\frac{du_{ij}^{bc}}{dt} = (z_{ij}^{bc} - u_{ij}^{bc}) - u_{ij}^{bc} p_5^c (x_j^{c1} + p_6^c) S_i^{b3} \tag{38}$$

Bound transmitter, $\mathbf{F_b} \rightarrow \mathbf{F_c}$

$$\frac{dv_{ij}^{bc}}{dt} = -v_{ij}^{bc} + u_{ij}^{bc} p_5^c (x_j^{c1} + p_6^c) S_i^{b3} \tag{39}$$

Presynaptic transmitter, $\mathbf{F_c} \rightarrow \mathbf{F_b}$

$$\frac{du_{ji}^{cb}}{dt} = (z_{ji}^{cb} - u_{ji}^{cb}) - u_{ji}^{cb} p_5^b (x_i^{b3} + p_6^b) S_j^{c1} \tag{40}$$

Bound transmitter, $\mathbf{F_c} \rightarrow \mathbf{F_b}$

$$\frac{dv_{ji}^{cb}}{dt} = -v_{ji}^{cb} + u_{ji}^{cb} p_5^b (x_i^{b3} + p_6^b) S_j^{c1} \tag{41}$$

Note that equations (38) and (39) imply that

$$u_{ij}^{bc} + v_{ij}^{bc} \rightarrow z_{ij}^{bc} \tag{42}$$

and equations (40) and (41) imply that

$$u_{ji}^{cb} + v_{ji}^{cb} \to z_{ji}^{cb}. \tag{43}$$

RESET EQUATIONS

Reset occurs when patterns active at F_a and F_b fail to match according to the criterion set by the vigilance parameter. In Figure 21,

$$r_i^b \cong \frac{y_i^{a2} + y_i^{b2}}{p_3^a + \|\mathbf{y}^{a2}\| + \|\mathbf{y}^{b2}\|}. \tag{44}$$

Reset occurs if

$$\|\mathbf{r}^b\| < \rho^b, \tag{45}$$

where

$$0 < \rho^b < 1. \tag{46}$$

As in equations (5) and (6), the effect of a large reset signal is approximated by setting input variables $x_i^{b1}, x_i^{b3}, x_j^{c1}, x_j^{c3}$ and bound transmitter variables v_{ij}^{bc}, v_{ji}^{cb} equal to 0.

ITERATION STEPS

Steps 1-7 outline the iteration scheme in the computer program used to generate the simulations.

Step 1. $t \to t + \Delta t$.

Step 2. Set ρ and S_i^{a3} values.

Step 3. Compute r_i^b and check for reset.

Step 4. Iterate STM equations F_b, F_c five times, setting variables to 0 at reset.

Step 5. Iterate transmitter equations (38)-(41).

Step 6. Compute sums $\sum_i v_{ij}^{bc}$ and $\sum_j v_{ji}^{cb}$.

Step 7. Return to Step 1.

27. Conclusion

In conclusion, we have seen that a functional analysis of parallel search within a hierarchical ART architecture can exploit processes taking place at the chemical synapse as a rich source of robust designs with natural realizations. Conversely, such a neural network analysis embeds model synapses into a processing context that can help to give functional and behavioral meaning to mechanisms defined at the intracellular, biophysical, and biochemical levels.

REFERENCES

Carpenter, G.A. and Grossberg, S. (1987a). A massively parallel architecture for a self-organizing neural pattern recognition machine. *Computer Vision, Graphics, and Image Processing,* **37**, 54–115.

Carpenter, G.A. and Grossberg, S. (1987b). ART 2: Self-organization of stable category recognition codes for analog input patterns. *Applied Optics,* **26**, 4919–4930.

Carpenter, G.A. and Grossberg, S. (1988). The ART of adaptive pattern recognition by a self-organizing neural network. *IEEE Computer*: Special issue on Artificial Neural Systems, **21**, 77–88.

Carpenter, G.A. and Grossberg, S. (1989). Search mechanisms for Adaptive Resonance Theory (ART) architectures. *Proceedings of the International Joint Conference on Neural Networks,* June 18–22, Washington, DC, pp. I 201–205.

Cohen, M.A., Grossberg, S., and Stork, D. (1988). Speech perception and production by a self-organizing neural network. In Y. C. Lee (Ed.), **Evolution, learning, cognition, and advanced architectures.** Hong Kong: World Scientific Publishers, 217–231.

Grossberg, S. (1976a). Adaptive pattern classification and universal recoding, I: Parallel development and coding of neural feature detectors. *Biological Cybernetics,* **23**, 121–134.

Grossberg, S. (1976b). Adaptive pattern classification and universal recoding, II: Feedback, expectation, olfaction, and illusions. *Biological Cybernetics,* **23**, 187–202.

Grossberg, S. (1982a). **Studies of mind and brain: Neural principles of learning, perception, development, cognition, and motor control.** Boston: Reidel Press.

Grossberg, S. (1982b). Processing of expected and unexpected events during conditioning and attention: A psychophysiological theory. *Psychological Review,* **89**, 529–572.

Grossberg, S. (1984). Some psychophysiological and pharmacological correlates of a developmental, cognitive, and motivational theory. In R. Karrer, J. Cohen, and P. Tueting (Eds.), **Brain and information: Event related potentials.** New York: New York Academy of Sciences, 58–151.

Grossberg, S. (Ed.) (1987a). **The Adaptive Brain, I: Cognition, learning, reinforcement, and rhythm.** Amsterdam: North-Holland.

Grossberg, S. (Ed.) (1987b). **The Adaptive Brain, II: Vision, speech, language, and motor control.** Amsterdam: North-Holland.

Grossberg, S. (Ed.) (1988). **Neural networks and natural intelligence.** Cambridge, MA: MIT Press.

Grossberg, S. and Levine, D.S. (1987). Neural dynamics of attentionally modulated Pavlovian conditioning: Blocking, inter-simulus interval, and secondary reinforcement. *Applied Optics,* **26**, 5015–5030.

Ito, M. (1984). **The cerebellum and neural control.** New York: Raven Press.

Kandel, E.R. and Schwartz, J.H. (1981). **Principles of neural science.** New York: Elsevier/North-Holland.

Kohonen, T. (1984). **Self-organization and associative memory.** New York: Springer-Verlag.

Kuffler, S.W., Nicholls, J.G., and Martin, A.R. (1984). **From neuron to brain, 2nd edition.** Sunderland, MA: Sinauer Associates.

ARTMAP:
SUPERVISED REAL-TIME LEARNING AND CLASSIFICATION OF NONSTATIONARY DATA BY A SELF-ORGANIZING NEURAL NETWORK

by
Gail Carpenter, Stephen Grossberg, and John Reynolds

Preface

This 1991 article introduces ARTMAP, an ART architecture for supervised learning. The ART 1, ART 2, and ART 3 networks were designed to learn and perform pattern recognition tasks in an unsupervised way. Recognition learning is, however, not the only type of neural network learning. We like to call Recognition, Reinforcement, and Recall the 3 R's of neural network learning.

The 3-level instar-outstar maps that were described in Chapters 3–9 combine the processes of recognition and recall. These mapping architectures introduce the simplest type of "supervision" into the learning process by associatively linking recognition categories, that are learned in an unsupervised way, with output vectors, predictions, or names that are supplied by the environment. In this way, different recognition categories for script, capital, and lower case versions of a letter can all be associated with the same letter name.

A stronger type of supervision can, however, occur during learning. The success or failure of predictions or actions based upon a recognition event can reorganize the recognition categories themselves. For example, the color of green bananas can be selectively attended and learned after the unripe taste of these bananas is experienced. Likewise, an object such as a loveseat, which has previously been identified by the single name "sofa," can be separately recognized by visually attending to finer features of its design after its new name is experienced, even if the distinguishing features are not explicitly pointed out.

Biological architectures which combine recognition learning and recall learning with reinforcement learning illustrate how predictive success or failure can influence the recognition learning process. A recent contribution to developing a biological theory of reinforcement is described in Chapter 20. Other recent contributions are summarized in Grossberg (1987, 1988) and Buonomano, Baxter, and Byrne (1990). The Buonomano *et al.* article discusses the remarkable fact that the invertebrate *Aplysia* seems to use neural circuits that are similar to model circuits that were previously derived from an analysis of vertebrate reinforcement learning data.

The ARTMAP architecture described in this chapter is an ART mapping system that combines self-organizing modules for recognition and recall with an associative learning module for linking recognition of $\Re^n$ vectors with recall of $\Re^m$ vectors. In addition, the control structure of the architecture autonomously reorganizes the recognition categories that are learned in response to the predictive success or failure of their recall vectors; hence the alternative name "Predictive ART" for this class of architectures. Although ARTMAP is a self-organizing architecture, and is capable of "unsupervised" learning, its ability to reorganize its recognition categories based upon predictive feedback incorporates "supervision" into the learning process.

The ARTMAP architecture is designed to conjointly *maximize* predictive success and *minimize* predictive error by linking predictive success to learned category size on a *trial-by-trial* basis using only *local* operations. This enables ARTMAP to quickly learn to distinguish rare but important events from frequent events that are perceptually similar but that predict different consequences. Back propagation, in contrast, operates in a slow learning mode that tends to average across all similar events.

We call the new learning constraint that is realized by ARTMAP systems the ART Minimax Learning Principle. Minimax learning can be realized in ARTMAP by exploiting properties of the ART orienting subsystem that regulates the search for new categories. A vigilance parameter determines the criterion of search, and thus how fine the learned categories will be. Since the advent of ART 1 (see Chapter 10), it has been known that predictive success should be used to control the vigilance parameter and thus the size of learned categories. ARTMAP systems provide a computationally effective procedure for realizing this design goal. This procedure, called *match tracking*, responds to a predictive failure by increasing the vigilance parameter of the recognition learning system by the minimal amount needed to search for a new recognition category.

ARTMAP networks build upon the basic ART designs that link recognition learning to knowledge discovery and hypothesis testing by further linking the course of hypothesis testing to predictive feedback. ARTMAP systems hereby carry the ART research program one step closer to the design of self-organizing expert systems that can stably continue to learn about one or more nonstationary databases until their full memory capacity, which can be chosen arbitrarily large, is utilized.

References

Albus, J.S. (1971). A theory of cerebellar function. *Mathematical Biosciences*, **10**, 25–61.

Buonomano, D.V., Baxter, D.A., and Byrne, J.H. (1990). Small networks of empirically derived adaptive elements simulate some higher-order features of classical conditioning. *Neural Networks*, **3**, 507–524.

Grossberg, S. (Editor) (1987). **The adaptive brain, I: Cognition, learning, reinforcement, and rhythm.** Amsterdam: Elsevier/North-Holland.

Grossberg, S. (Editor) (1988). **Neural networks and natural intelligence.** Cambridge, MA: MIT Press.

Neural Networks
1991, **4**
©1991 Pergamon Press, Inc.

ARTMAP:
SUPERVISED REAL-TIME LEARNING AND CLASSIFICATION
OF NONSTATIONARY DATA BY A SELF-ORGANIZING
NEURAL NETWORK

Gail A. Carpenter†, Stephen Grossberg‡, and John H. Reynolds§

Abstract

This article introduces a new neural network architecture, called ARTMAP, that autonomously learns to classify arbitrarily many, arbitrarily ordered vectors into recognition categories based on predictive success. This supervised learning system is built up from a pair of Adaptive Resonance Theory modules (ART_a and ART_b) that are capable of self-organizing stable recognition categories in response to arbitrary sequences of input patterns. During training trials, the ART_a module receives a stream $\{a^{(p)}\}$ of input patterns, and ART_b receives a stream $\{b^{(p)}\}$ of input patterns, where $b^{(p)}$ is the correct prediction given $a^{(p)}$. These ART modules are linked by an associative learning network and an internal controller that ensures autonomous system operation in real time. During test trials, the remaining patterns $a^{(p)}$ are presented without $b^{(p)}$, and their predictions at ART_b are compared with $b^{(p)}$. Tested on a benchmark machine learning database in both on-line and off-line simulations, the ARTMAP system learns orders of magnitude more quickly, efficiently, and accurately than alternative algorithms, and achieves 100% accuracy after training on less than half the input patterns in the database. It achieves these properties by using an internal controller that conjointly maximizes predictive generalization and minimizes predictive error by linking predictive success to category size on a trial-by-trial basis, using only local operations. This computation increases the vigilance parameter ρ_a of ART_a by the minimal amount needed to correct a predictive error at ART_b. Parameter ρ_a calibrates the minimum confidence that ART_a must have in a category, or hypothesis, activated by an input $a^{(p)}$ in order for ART_a to accept that category, rather than search for a better one through an automatically controlled process of hypothesis testing. Parameter ρ_a is compared with the degree of match between $a^{(p)}$ and the top-down learned expectation, or prototype, that is read-out subsequent to activation of an ART_a category. Search occurs if the degree of match is less than ρ_a.

----

† Supported in part by BP (98-A-1204), DARPA (AFOSR 90-0083), and the National Science Foundation (NSF IRI-90-00539).

‡ Supported in part by the Air Force Office of Scientific Research (AFOSR 90-0175 and AFOSR 90-0128), the Army Research Office (ARO DAAL-03-88-K0088), and DARPA (AFOSR 90-0083).

§ Supported in part by DARPA (AFOSR 90-0083). The authors wish to thank Cynthia E. Bradford for her valuable assistance in the preparation of the manuscript.

ARTMAP is hereby a type of self-organizing expert system that calibrates the selectivity of its hypotheses based upon predictive success. As a result, rare but important events can be quickly and sharply distinguished even if they are similar to frequent events with different consequences. Between input trials ρ_a relaxes to a baseline vigilance $\overline{\rho_a}$. When $\overline{\rho_a}$ is large, the system runs in a conservative mode, wherein predictions are made only if the system is confident of the outcome. Very few false-alarm errors then occur at any stage of learning, yet the system reaches asymptote with no loss of speed. Because ARTMAP learning is self-stabilizing, it can continue learning one or more databases, without degrading its corpus of memories, until its full memory capacity is utilized.

Introduction

Predictive ART. As we move freely through the world, we can attend to both familiar and novel objects, and can rapidly learn to recognize, test hypotheses about, and learn to name novel objects without unselectively disrupting our memories of familiar objects. This article describes a new self-organizing neural network architecture—called a Predictive ART or ARTMAP architecture—that is capable of fast, yet stable, on-line recognition learning, hypothesis testing, and adaptive naming in response to an arbitrary stream of input patterns.

The possibility of stable learning in response to an arbitrary stream of inputs is required by an autonomous learning agent that needs to cope with unexpected events in an uncontrolled environment. One cannot *restrict* the agent's ability to process input sequences if one cannot *predict* the environment in which the agent must successfully function. The ability of humans to vividly remember exciting adventure movies is a familiar example of fast learning in an unfamiliar environment.

Fast learning about rare events. A successful autonomous agent must be able to learn about rare events that have important consequences, even if these rare events are similar to frequent events with very different consequences. Survival may hereby depend on fast learning in a *nonstationary* environment. Many learning schemes are, in contrast, slow learning models that average over individual event occurrences and are degraded by learning instabilities in a nonstationary environment[1,2].

Many-to-one and one-to-many learning. An efficient recognition system needs to be capable of many-to-one learning. For example, each of the different exemplars of the font for a prescribed letter may generate a single compressed representation that serves as a visual recognition category. This exemplar-to-category transformation is a case of many-to-one learning. In addition, many different fonts—including lower case and upper case printed fonts and scripts of various kinds—can all lead to the same verbal name for the letter. This is a second sense in which learning may be many-to-one.

Learning may also be one-to-many, so that a single object can generate many different predictions or names. For example, upon looking at a banana, one may classify it as an oblong object, a fruit, a banana, a yellow banana, and so on. A flexible knowledge system may thus need to represent in its memory many predictions for each object, and to make the best prediction for each different context in which the object is embedded.

Control of hypothesis testing, attention, and learning by predictive success. Why does not an autonomous recognition system get trapped into learning only that interpretation of an object which is most salient given the system's initial biases? One factor is the ability of that system to reorganize its recognition, hypothesis testing, and naming operations based upon its predictive success or failure. For example, a person may learn a visual recognition category based upon seeing bananas of various colors and associate that category with a certain taste. Due to the variability of color features compared with those of visual form, this learned recognition category may incorporate form features more strongly than color features. However, the color green may suddenly, and unexpectedly, become an important differential predictor of a banana's taste.

The different taste of a green banana triggers hypothesis testing that shifts the focus of visual attention to give greater weight, or salience, to the banana's color features without negating the importance of the other features that define a banana's form. A new visual recognition category can hereby form for green bananas, and this category can be used to accurately predict the different taste of green bananas. The new, finer category can form, moreover, without recoding either the previously learned generic representation of bananas or their taste association.

Future representations may also form that incorporate new knowledge about bananas, without disrupting the representations that are used to predict their different tastes. In this way, predictive feedback provides one means whereby one-to-many recognition and prediction codes can form through time, by using hypothesis testing and attention shifts that support new recognition learning without forcing unselective forgetting of previous knowledge.

Adaptive Resonance Theory. The architecture described herein forms part of Adaptive Resonance Theory, or ART, which was introduced in 1976[3,4] in order to analyse how brain networks can autonomously learn in real time about a changing world in a rapid but stable fashion. Since that time, ART has steadily developed as a physical theory to explain and predict ever larger data bases about cognitive information processing and its neural substrates[5-8]. A parallel development has described a series of rigorously characterized neural architectures—called ART 1, ART 2, and ART 3—with increasingly powerful learning, pattern recognition, and hypothesis testing capabilities[1,9-11].

Self-organizing predictive maps. The present class of architectures are called Predictive ART architectures because they incorporate ART modules into systems that can learn to predict a prescribed m-dimensional output vector $\mathbf{b}$ given a prescribed n-dimensional input vector $\mathbf{a}$ (Figure 1). The present example of Predictive ART is called ARTMAP because its transformation from vectors in $\Re^n$ to vectors in $\Re^m$ defines a *map* that is learned by example from the correlated pairs $\{\mathbf{a}^{(p)}, \mathbf{b}^{(p)}\}$ of sequentially presented vectors, $p = 1, 2, \ldots$ [12]. For example, the vectors $\mathbf{a}^{(p)}$ may encode visual representations of objects, and the vectors $\mathbf{b}^{(p)}$ may encode their predictive consequences, such as different tastes in the banana example above. The degree of code compression in memory is an index of the system's ability to *generalize* from examples.

Figure 1 compares properties of the ARTMAP network with those of the Back Propagation network[13-16]. Both ARTMAP and Back Propagation are supervised

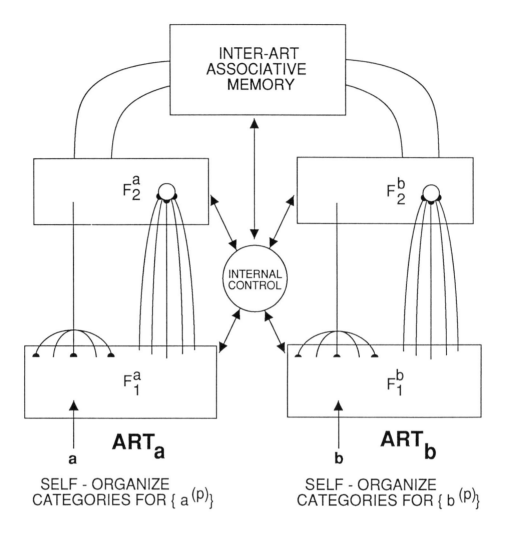

	Predictive ART	Back Propagation
supervised	yes	yes
self-organizing	yes	no
real-time	yes	no
self-stabilizing	yes	no
learning:	fast or slow match	slow mismatch

Figure 1. A Predictive ART, or ARTMAP, system includes two ART modules linked by an inter-ART associative memory. Internal control structures actively regulate learning and information flow. Back Propagation and Predictive ART both carry out supervised learning, but the two systems differ in many respects, as indicated.

learning systems. With supervised learning, an input vector $\mathbf{a}^{(p)}$ is associated with another input vector $\mathbf{b}^{(p)}$ on each training trial. On a test trial, a new input $\mathbf{a}$ is presented that has never been experienced before. This input predicts an output vector $\mathbf{b}$. System performance is evaluated by comparing $\mathbf{b}$ with the correct answer. This property of *generalization* is the system's ability to correctly predict correct answers to a test set of novel inputs $\mathbf{a}$.

• **Conjointly maximizing generalization and minimizing predictive error**—The ARTMAP system is designed to conjointly *maximize* generalization and *minimize* predictive error under *fast learning* conditions in *real time* in response to an *arbitrary ordering* of input patterns. Remarkably, the network can achieve 100% test set accuracy on the machine learning benchmark database described below. Each ARTMAP system learns to make accurate predictions quickly, in the sense of using relatively little computer time; efficiently, in the sense of using relatively few training trials; and flexibly, in the sense that its stable learning permits continuous new learning, on one or more databases, without eroding prior knowledge, until the full memory capacity of the network is exhausted. In an ARTMAP network, the memory capacity is chosen arbitrarily large without sacrificing the stability of fast learning or accurate generalization.

• **Match tracking of predictive confidence by attentive vigilance**—An essential feature of the ARTMAP design is its ability to conjointly maximize generalization and minimize predictive error on a *trial-by-trial* basis using *only local operations*. It is this property which enables the system to learn rapidly about rare events that have important consequences even if they are very similar to frequent events with different consequences. This property builds upon a key design feature of all ART systems; namely, the existence of an *orienting subsystem* that responds to the unexpectedness, or novelty, of an input exemplar $\mathbf{a}$ by driving a hypothesis testing cycle, or parallel memory search, for a better, or totally new, recognition category for $\mathbf{a}$. Hypothesis testing is triggered by the orienting subsystem if $\mathbf{a}$ activates a recognition category that reads out a learned expectation, or prototype, which does not match $\mathbf{a}$ well enough. The degree of match provides an analog measure of the predictive *confidence* that the chosen recognition category represents $\mathbf{a}$, or of the *novelty* of $\mathbf{a}$ with respect to the hypothesis that is symbolically represented by the recognition category. This analog match value is computed at the orienting subsystem where it is compared with a dimensionless parameter that is called *vigilance*[9,10]. A cycle of hypothesis testing is triggered if the degree of match is less than vigilance. Conjoint maximization of generalization and minimization of predictive error is achieved on a trial-by-trial basis by increasing the vigilance parameter in response to a predictive error on a training trial[9]. The minimum change is made that is consistent with correction of the error. In fact, the predictive error causes the vigilance to increase rapidly until it just exceeds the analog match value, in a process called *match tracking*.

Before each new input arrives, vigilance relaxes to a baseline vigilance value. Setting baseline vigilance to 0 maximizes code compression. The system accomplishes this by allowing an "educated guess" on every trial, even if the match between input and learned code is poor. Search ensues, and a new category is established, only if the prediction made in this forced-choice situation proves wrong. When predictive error carries a cost, however, baseline vigilance can be set at some higher value, thereby decreasing the "false alarm" rate. With positive baseline vigilance, the system responds "I don't know" to an input that fails to meet the minimum matching criterion. Predictive error rate can hereby be made very small, but with a reduction in code compression. Search ends when the internal control system (Figure 1) determines that a global consensus has been reached.

• **Self-organizing expert system**—ARTMAP achieves its combination of desirable properties by acting as a type of self-organizing expert system. It incorporates the basic properties of all ART systems[1] to carry out autonomous hypothesis testing and parallel memory search for appropriate recognition codes. Hypothesis testing terminates in a sustained state of resonance that persists as long as an input remains approximately constant. The resonance generates a focus of attention that selects the bundle of critical features common to the bottom-up input and the top-down expectation, or prototype, that is read-out by the resonating recognition category. Learning of the critical feature pattern occurs in this resonant and attentive state, hence the term *adaptive resonance*.

• **2/3 Rule matching, priming, intentionality, and logic**—The resonant focus of attention is a consequence of a matching rule called the 2/3 Rule[9]. This rule clarifies how a bottom-up input pattern can *supraliminally* activate its feature detectors at the level F_1 of an ART network, yet a top-down expectation can only *subliminally* sensitize, or *prime*, the level F_1. Supraliminal activation means that F_1 can automatically generate output signals that initiate further processing of the input. Subliminal activation means that F_1 cannot generate output signals, but its primed cells can more easily be activated by bottom-up inputs. For example, the verbal command "Look for the yellow banana" can prime visual feature detectors to respond more sensitively to visual inputs that represent a yellow banana, without forcing these cells to be fully activated, which would have caused a visual hallucination.

Carpenter and Grossberg[6] have shown that the 2/3 Rule is realized by a kind of analog spatial logic. This logical operation computes the spatial intersection of bottom-up and top-down information. The spatial intersection is the focus of attention. It is of interest that subliminal top-down priming, which instantiates a type of "intentionality" in an ART system, implies a type of matching law, which instantiates a type of "logic." Searle[17] and others have criticized some AI models because they sacrifice intentionality for logic. In ART, intentionality implies logic.

The ARTMAP system

The main elements of an ARTMAP system are shown in Figure 2. Two modules, ART_a and ART_b, read vector inputs **a** and **b**. If ART_a and ART_b were disconnected, each module would self-organize category groupings for the separate input sets. In the application described below, ART_a and ART_b are fast-learn ART 1 modules coding binary input vectors. ART_a and ART_b are here connected by an inter-ART module that in many ways resembles ART 1. This inter-ART module includes a *Map Field* that controls the learning of an associative map from ART_a recognition categories to ART_b recognition categories. This map does not directly associate exemplars **a** and **b**, but rather associates the compressed and symbolic representations of families of exemplars **a** and **b**. The Map Field also controls match tracking of the ART_a vigilance parameter. A mismatch at the Map Field between the ART_a category activated by an input **a** and the ART_b category activated by the input **b** increases ART_a vigilance by the minimum amount needed for the system to search for and, if necessary, learn

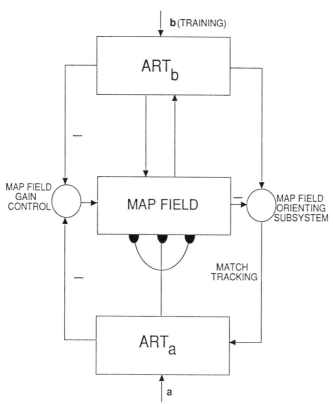

Figure 2. Block diagram of an ARTMAP system. Modules ART_a and ART_b self-organize categories for vector sets **a** and **b**. ART_a and ART_b are connected by an inter-ART module that consists of the Map Field and the control nodes called Map Field gain control and Map Field orienting subsystem. Inhibitory paths are denoted by a minus sign; other paths are excitatory.

a new ART_a category whose prediction matches the ART_b category.

This inter-ART vigilance resetting signal is a form of "back propagation" of information, but one that differs from the back propagation that occurs in the Back Propagation network. For example, the search initiated by inter-ART reset can shift attention to a novel cluster of visual features that can be incorporated through learning into a new ART_a recognition category. This process is analogous to learning a category for "green bananas" based on "taste" feedback. However, these events do not "back propagate" taste features into the visual representation of the bananas, as can occur using the Back Propagation network. Rather, match tracking reorganizes the way in which visual features are grouped, attended, learned, and recognized for purposes of predicting an expected taste.

The following sections describe ARTMAP simulations using a machine learning benchmark database. The ARTMAP system is then described mathematically. The Appendix summarizes ART 1 and ARTMAP system equations for purposes of simulation, and outlines system responses to various input protocols.

ARTMAP simulations: Distinguishing edible and poisonous mushrooms

The ARTMAP system was tested on a benchmark machine learning database that partitions a set of vectors **a** into two classes. Each vector **a** characterizes observable features of a mushroom as a binary vector, and each mushroom is classified as edible or poisonous[18]. The database represents the 11 species of genus *Agaricus* and the 12 species of the genus *Lepiota* described in **The Audubon Society Field Guide to North American Mushrooms**[19]. These two genera constitute most of the mushrooms described in the **Field Guide** from the familiy *Agaricaceae* (order *Agaricales*, class *Hymenomycetes*, subdivision *Basidiomycetes*, division *Eumycota*). All the mushrooms represented in the database are similar to one another: "These mushrooms are placed in a single family on the basis of a correlation of characteristics that include microscopic and and chemical features..." [19] (p. 500). The **Field Guide** warns that poisonous and edible species can be difficult to distinguish on the basis of their observable features. For example, the poisonous species *Agaricus californicus* is described as a "dead ringer" (p. 504) for the Meadow Mushroom, *Agaricus campestris*, that "may be known better and gathered more than any other wild mushroom in North America" (p. 505). This database thus provides a test of how ARTMAP and other machine learning systems distinguish rare but important events from frequently occurring collections of similar events that lead to different consequences.

The database of 8124 exemplars describes each of 22 observable features of a mushroom, along with its classification as poisonous (48.2%) or edible (51.8%). The 8124 "hypothetical examples" represent ranges of characteristics within each species; for example, both *Agaricus californicus* and *Agaricus campestris* are described as having a "white to brownish cap," so in the database each species has corresponding sets of exemplar vectors representing their range of cap colors. There are 126 different values of the 22 different observable features. A list of the observable features and their possible values is given in Table 1. For example, the observable feature of "cap-shape" has six possible values. Consequently, the vector inputs to ART_a are 126-element binary vectors, each vector having 22 1's and 104 0's, to denote the values of an exemplar's 22 observable features. The ART_b input vectors are (1,0) for poisonous exemplars and (0,1) for edible exemplars.

Performance. The ARTMAP system learned to classify test vectors rapidly and accurately, and system performance compares favorably with results of other machine learning algorithms applied to the same database. The STAGGER algorithm reached its maximum performance level of 95% accuracy after exposure to 1000 training inputs[20]. The HILLARY algorithm achieved similar results[21]. The ARTMAP system consistently achieved over 99% accuracy with 1000 exemplars, even counting "I don't know" responses as errors. Accuracy of 95% was usually achieved with on-line training on 300–400 exemplars and with off-line training on 100–200 exemplars. In this sense, ARTMAP was an order of magnitude more efficient than the alternative systems. In addition, with continued training, ARTMAP predictive accuracy always improved to 100%. These results are elaborated below.

Almost every ARTMAP simulation was completed in under 2 minutes on an IRIS 4D computer, with total time ranging from about 1 minute for small training sets to 2 minutes for large training sets. This is comparable to 2–5 minutes on a SUN 4 computer. Each timed simulation included a total of 8124 training and test samples, run on a time-sharing system with non-optimized code. Each 1–2 minute computation included data read-in and read-out, training, testing, and calculation of

TABLE 1: 22 Observable Features and their 126 Values

Number	Feature	Possible Values
1	cap-shape	bell, conical, convex, flat, knobbed, sunken
2	cap-surface	fibrous, grooves, scaly, smooth
3	cap-color	brown, buff, gray, green, pink, purple, red, white, yellow, cinnamon
4	bruises	bruises, no bruises
5	odor	none, almond, anise, creosote, fishy, foul, musty, pungent, spicy
6	gill-attachment	attached, descending, free, notched
7	gill-spacing	close, crowded, distant
8	gill-size	broad, narrow
9	gill-color	brown, buff, orange, gray, green, pink, purple, red, white, yellow, chocolate, black
10	stalk-shape	enlarging, tapering
11	stalk-root	bulbous, club, cup, equal, rhizomorphs, rooted, missing
12	stalk-surface-above-ring	fibrous, silky, scaly, smooth
13	stalk-surface-below-ring	fibrous, silky, scaly, smooth
14	stalk-color-above-ring	brown, buff, orange, gray, pink, red, white, yellow, cinnamon
15	stalk-color-below-ring	brown, buff, orange, gray, pink, red, white, yellow, cinnamon
16	veil-type	partial, universal
17	veil-color	brown, orange, white, yellow
18	ring-number	none, one, two
19	ring-type	none, cobwebby, evanescent, flaring, large, pendant, sheathing, zone
20	spore-print-color	brown, buff, orange, green, purple, white, yellow, chocolate, black
21	population	abundant, clustered, numerous, scattered, several, solitary
22	habitat	grasses, leaves, meadows, paths, urban, waste, woods

Table 1: 126 values of 22 observable features represented in ART_a input vectors.

multiple simulation indices.

On-line learning. On-line learning imitates the conditions of a human or machine operating in a natural environment. An input **a** arrives, possibly leading to a prediction. If made, the prediction may or may not be confirmed. Learning ensues, depending on the accuracy of the prediction. Information about past inputs is available only through the present state of the system. Simulations of on-line learning by the ARTMAP system use each sample pair (**a**, **b**) as both a test item and a training item. Input **a** first makes a prediction that is compared with **b**. Learning follows as dictated by the internal rules of the ARTMAP architecture.

Four types of on-line simulations were carried out, using two different baseline settings of the ART_a vigilance parameter ρ_a: $\overline{\rho_a} = 0$ (forced choice condition) and $\overline{\rho_a} = 0.7$ (conservative condition); and using sample replacement or no sample replacement. With sample replacement, any one of the 8124 input samples was selected at random for each input presentation. A given sample might thus be repeatedly encountered while others were still unused. With no sample replacement, a sample was removed from the input pool after it was first encountered. The replacement condition had the advantage that repeated encounters tended to boost predictive accuracy. The no-replacement condition had the advantage of having learned from a somewhat larger set of inputs at each point in the simulation. The replacement and no-replacement conditions had similar performance indices, all other things being equal. Each of the 4 conditions was run on 10 independent simulations. With $\overline{\rho_a} = 0$, the system made a prediction in response to every input. Setting $\overline{\rho_a} = 0.7$ increased the number of "I don't know" responses, increased the number of ART_a categories, and decreased the rate of incorrect predictions to nearly 0%, even early in training. The $\overline{\rho_a} = 0.7$ condition generally outperformed the $\overline{\rho_a} = 0$ condition, even when incorrect predictions and "I don't know" responses were both counted as errors. The primary exception occurred very early in training, when a conservative system gives the large majority of its no-prediction responses.

Results are summarized in Table 2. Each entry gives the number of correct predictions over the previous 100 trials (input presentations), averaged over 10 simulations. For example, with $\overline{\rho_a} = 0$ in the no-replacement condition, the system made, on the average, 94.9 correct predictions and 5.1 incorrect predictions on trials 201–300. In all cases a 95% correct-prediction rate was achieved before trial 400. With $\overline{\rho_a} = 0$, a consistent correct-prediction rate of over 99% was achieved by trial 1400, while with $\overline{\rho_a} = 0.7$ the 99% consistent correct-prediction rate was achieved earlier, by trial 800. Each simulation was continued for 8100 trials. In all four cases, the minimum correct-prediction rate always exceeeded 99.5% by trial 1800 and always exceeded 99.8% by trial 2800. In all cases, across the total of 40 simulations summarized in Table 2, 100% correct prediction was achieved on the last 1300 trials of each run.

Note the relatively low correct-prediction rate for $\overline{\rho_a} = 0.7$ on the first 100 trials. In the conservative mode, a large number of inputs initially make no prediction. With $\overline{\rho_a} = 0.7$ an average total of only 2 *incorrect* predictions were made on each run of 8100 trials. Note too that Table 2 underestimates prediction accuracy at any given time, since performance almost always improves during the 100 trials over which errors are tabulated.

Off-line learning. In off-line learning, a fixed training set is repeatedly presented

TABLE 2: On-Line Learning

Average number of correct predictions on previous 100 trials

Trial	$\overline{\rho_a} = 0$ no replace	$\overline{\rho_a} = 0$ replace	$\overline{\rho_a} = 0.7$ no replace	$\overline{\rho_a} = 0.7$ replace
100	82.9	81.9	66.4	67.3
200	89.8	89.6	87.8	87.4
300	94.9	92.6	94.1	93.2
400	95.7	95.9	96.8	95.8
500	97.8	97.1	97.5	97.8
600	98.4	98.2	98.1	98.2
700	97.7	97.9	98.1	99.0
800	98.1	97.7	99.0	99.0
900	98.3	98.6	99.2	99.0
1000	98.9	98.5	99.4	99.0
1100	98.7	98.9	99.2	99.7
1200	99.6	99.1	99.5	99.5
1300	99.3	98.8	99.8	99.8
1400	99.7	99.4	99.5	99.8
1500	99.5	99.0	99.7	99.6
1600	99.4	99.6	99.7	99.8
1700	98.9	99.3	99.8	99.8
1800	99.5	99.2	99.8	99.9
1900	99.8	99.9	99.9	99.9
2000	99.8	99.8	99.8	99.8

Table 2: On-line learning and performance in forced choice ($\overline{\rho_a} = 0$) or conservative ($\overline{\rho_a} = 0.7$) cases, with replacement or no replacement of samples after training.

to the system until 100% accuracy is achieved on that set. For training sets ranging in size from 1 to 4000 samples, 100% accuracy was almost always achieved after one or two presentations of each training set. System performance was then measured on the test set, which consisted of all 8124 samples not included in the training set. During testing no further learning occurred.

The role of repeated training set presentations was examined by comparing simulations that used the 100% training set accuracy criterion with simulations that used only a single presentation of each input during training. With only a few exceptions, performance was similar. In fact for $\overline{\rho_a} = 0.7$, and for small training sets with $\overline{\rho_a} = 0$, 100% training-set accuracy was achieved with single input presentations, so results were identical. Performance differences were greatest for $\overline{\rho_a} = 0$ simulations with mid-sized training sets (60–500 samples), when 2–3 training set presentations tended to add a few more ART_a learned category nodes. Thus, even a single presentation of training-then-testing inputs, carried out on-line, can be made to work almost as well as off-line training that uses repeated presentations of the training set. This is an important benefit of fast learning controlled by a match tracked search.

Under all training conditions, each of the 8124 ART_a input vectors is a 126-dimensional binary vector with 22 positive entries. Simulation dynamics are illustrated by projecting these vectors onto the first two principal components of the data set[22]. These two components represent 31% of the total variance of the data set.

Figure 3a shows the projections of all 3916 exemplars representing poisonous mushrooms, and Figure 3b shows the 4208 exemplars representing edible mushrooms. These figures show that, in these two dimensions, certain clusters are readily distinguishable, such as the clusters of poisonous samples on the top and left portions of Figure 3a. However, poisonous and edible samples are densely mixed near the positive x-axis.

• **Off-line forced-choice learning**—The simulations summarized in Figure 4 and Table 3 illustrate off-line learning with $\overline{\rho_a} = 0$. In this forced choice case, each ART_a input led to a prediction of poisonous or edible. The number of test set errors with small training sets was relatively large, due to the forced choice.

Figure 4 shows the evolution of test set errors as the training set is increased in size from 5 to 500. In Figure 4a, a set of 5 randomly chosen exemplars (3 poisonous, 2 edible) established 2 ART_a categories (1 poisonous, 1 edible) during training. For each of the 8119 test set exemplars, the system was forced to choose between poisonous and edible, even if no category representation was a close match. The system made 73.0% correct predictions. Many of the errors were in the dense cluster of poisonous exemplars in the upper quarter of the graph (Figure 3a). By chance, this cluster was not represented in the 5-sample training set.

Table 3 summarizes the average results over 10 simulations at each size training set. For example, with very small, 5-sample training sets, the system established between 1 and 5 ART_a categories, and averaged 73.1% correct responses on the remaining 8119 test patterns. Success rates ranged from chance (51.8%, 1 category) in one instance where all 5 training set exemplars happened to be edible, to surprisingly good (94.2%, 2 categories). The range of success rates for fast-learn training on very small training sets illustrates the statistical nature of the learning process. Intelligent sampling of the training set or, as here, good luck in the selection of representative

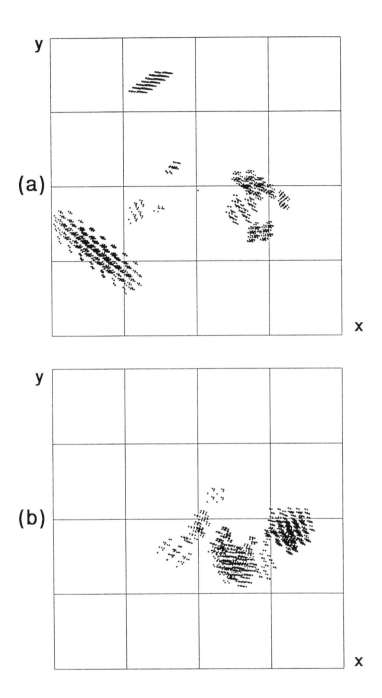

Figure 3. Mushroom observable feature data projected onto first 2 principal compo
nents. Each point represents a 126-dimensional ART$_a$ input vector. Axes are scaled
to run from −1 to +1. (a) 3916 exemplars representing poisonous mushrooms (48.2%).
(b) 4208 exemplars representing edible mushrooms (51.8%).

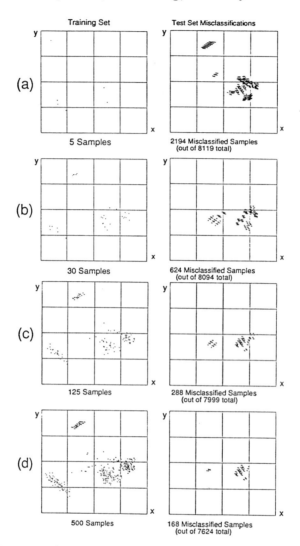

Figure 4. Training sets of increasing size (left column) and test set exemplars that were incorrectly classified (right column), projected onto first two principal components. Baseline vigilance $\overline{\rho_a}$ equals 0. (a) With a 5-sample training set that established 2 ART_a categories, the test set of 8119 inputs made 2194 errors (27.0%). On 10 other 5-sample runs, the number of ART_a categories ranged from 1 to 5 and the error rate ranged from 5.8% to 48.2%, averaging 26.9%. (b) With a 30-sample training set that established 3 ART_a categories, the test set of 8094 inputs made 624 errors (7.7%). On 10 other 30-training sample runs, the number of ART_a categories ranged from 4 to 6; and the error rate ranged from 6.7% to 25.1%, averaging 12.4%. (c) With a 125-sample training set that established 9 ART_a categories, the test set of 7999 inputs made 288 errors (3.6%). On 10 other 125-training sample runs, the number of ART_a categories ranged from 5 to 14, and the error rate ranged from 1.2% to 8.5%, averaging 4.4%. (d) With a 500-sample training set that established 15 ART_a categories, the test set of 7624 inputs made 168 errors (2.2%). On 10 other 500-training sample runs, the number of ART_a categories ranged from 9 to 22; and the error rate ranged from 0.7% to 3.1%, averaging 1.6%.

TABLE 3: Off-Line Forced-Choice Learning

Training Set Size	Average % Correct (Test Set)	Average % Incorrect (Test Set)	Number of ART_a Categories
3	65.8	34.2	1–3
5	73.1	26.9	1–5
15	81.6	18.4	2–4
30	87.6	12.4	4–6
60	89.4	10.6	4–10
125	95.6	4.4	5–14
250	97.8	2.2	8–14
500	98.4	1.6	9–22
1000	99.8	0.2	7–18
2000	99.96	0.04	10–16
4000	100	0	11–22

Table 3: Off-line forced choice ($\overline{\rho_a} = 0$) ARTMAP system performance after training on input sets ranging in size from 3 to 4000 exemplars. Each line shows average correct and incorrect test set predictions over 10 independent simulations, plus the range of learned ART_a category numbers.

samples, can dramatically alter early success rates. In addition, the evolution of internal category memory structure, represented by a set of ART_a category nodes and their top-down learned expectations, is influenced by the selection of early exemplars. Nevertheless, despite the individual nature of learning rates and internal representations, all the systems eventually converge to 100% accuracy on test set exemplars using only (approximately) 1/600 as many ART_a categories as there are inputs to classify.

Figure 4 and Table 3 summarize the rate at which learning converges to 100% accuracy. In Figure 4b, 25 exemplars were added to the 5 used for Figure 4a, and the resulting 30-sample training set was presented to a new ARTMAP system. The 25 additional training exemplars increased the number of ART_a categories to 3 and improved the test set correct-prediction rate to 92.3%. The addition of poisonous training exemplars in the upper quarter of the graph eliminated all errors there. However, errors persisted for exemplars near the positive x-axis. On 10 other simulations with 30-sample training sets, the correct prediction rate averaged 87.6% and ranged from 74.9% (4 categories) to 93.3% (6 categories).

The simulation that generated Figure 4c added 95 training samples to the 30 used for Figure 4b. The number of ART_a categories increased to 9 and the correct prediction rate increased to 96.4%. On 10 other simulations with 125 randomly chosen training exemplars, the correct-prediction rate averaged 95.6%, ranging from 91.5% (10 categories) to 98.8% (9 categories).

The simulation of Figure 4d added 375 samples to the set used in Figure 4c. This 500-sample training set increased the correct prediction rate to 97.8% on the test set, establishing 15 categories. On 10 other runs, each with 500 randomly chosen training exemplars, the correct-prediction rate averaged 98.4%, ranging from 96.9% (14 categories) to 99.3% (9 categories). The low error rate of this latter 9-category simulation appears to reflect success of early sampling. On other runs, additional categories were added as errors in early category structures were detected.

With 1000-sample training sets, 3 out of 10 simulations achieved 100% prediction accuracy on the 7124-sample test set. With 2000-sample training sets, 8 out of 10 simulations achieved 100% accuracy on the 6124-sample test sets. With 4000-sample training sets, all simulations achieved 100% accuracy on the 4124-sample test sets. In all, 21 of the 30 simulations with training sets of 1000, 2000, and 4000 samples achieved 100% accuracy on test sets. The number of categories established during these 21 simulations ranged from 10 to 22, again indicating the variety of paths leading to 100% correct prediction rate.

• **Off-line conservative learning**—As in the case of poisonous mushroom identification, it may be important for a system to be able to respond "I don't know" to a novel input, even if the total number of correct classifications thereby decreases early in learning. For higher values of the baseline vigilance $\overline{\rho_a}$, the ARTMAP system creates more ART_a categories during learning and becomes less able to generalize from prior experience than when $\overline{\rho_a}$ equals 0. During testing, a conservative coding system with $\overline{\rho_a} = 0.7$ makes no prediction in response to inputs that are too novel, and thus initially has a lower proportion of correct responses. However, the number of incorrect responses is always low with $\overline{\rho_a} = 0.7$, even with very few training samples, and the 99% correct-response rate is achieved for both forced choice ($\overline{\rho_a} = 0$) and conservative ($\overline{\rho_a} = 0.7$) systems with training sets smaller than 1000 exemplars.

Table 4 summarizes simulation results that repeat the conditions of Table 3 except that $\overline{\rho_a} = 0.7$. Here, a test input that does not make a 70% match with any learned expectation makes an "I don't know" prediction. Compared with the $\overline{\rho_a} = 0$ case of Table 3, Table 4 shows that larger training sets are required to achieve a correct prediction rate of over 95%. However, because of the option to make no prediction, the average test set error rate is almost always less than 1%, even when the training set is very small, and is less than .1% after only 500 training trials. Moreover, 100% accuracy is achieved using only (approximately) 1/130 as many ART_a categories as there are inputs to classify.

Category structure. Each ARTMAP category code can be described as a set of ART_a feature values on 1 to 22 observable features, chosen from 126 feature values, that are associated with the ART_b identification as poisonous or edible. During learning, the number of feature values that characterize a given category is monotone decreasing, so that generalization within a given category tends to increase. The total number of classes can, however, also increase, which tends to decrease generalization. Increasing the number of training patterns hereby tends to increase the number of categories and decrease the number of critical feature values of each established category. The balance between these opposing tendencies leads to the final net level of generalization.

Table 5 illustrates the long term memory structure underlying the 125-sample forced-choice simulation shown in Figure 4c. Of the 9 categories established at the end of the training phase, 4 are identified as poisonous (P) and 5 are identified as edible (E). Each ART_a category assigns a feature value to a subset of the 22 observable features. For example, Category 1 (poisonous) specifies values for 5 features, and leaves the remaining 17 features unspecified. The corresponding ART_a weight vector has 5 ones and 121 zeros. Note that the features that characterize category 5 (poisonous) form a subset of the features that characterize category 6 (edible). Recall that this category structure gave 96.4% correct responses on the 7999 test set samples, which are partitioned as shown in the last line of Table 5. When 100% accuracy is achieved, a few categories with a small number of specified features typically code large clusters, while a few categories with many specified features code small clusters of rare samples.

Table 6 illustrates the statistical nature of the coding process, which leads to a variety of category structures when fast learning is used. Test set prediction accuracy of the simulation that generated Table 6 was similar to that of Table 5, and each simulation had a 125-sample training set. However, the simulation of Table 6 produced only 4 ART_a categories, only one of which (category 1) has the same long term memory representation as category 2 in Table 5. Note that, at this stage of coding, certain features are uninformative. For example, no values are specified for features 1, 2, 3, or 22 in Table 5 or Table 6; and feature 16 (veil-type) always has the value "partial." However, performance is still only around 96%. As rare instances form small categories later in the coding process, some of these features may become critical in identifying exemplars of small categories.

We will now turn to a description of the components of the ARTMAP system.

TABLE 4: Off-Line Conservative Learning

Training Set Size	Average % Correct (Test Set)	Average % Incorrect (Test Set)	Average % No-Response (Test Set)	Number of ART_a Categories
3	25.6	0.6	73.8	2–3
5	41.1	0.4	58.5	3–5
15	57.6	1.1	41.3	8–10
30	62.3	0.9	36.8	14–18
60	78.5	0.8	20.8	21–27
125	83.1	0.7	16.1	33–37
250	92.7	0.3	7.0	42–51
500	97.7	0.1	2.1	48–64
1000	99.4	0.04	0.5	53–66
2000	100.0	0.00	0.05	54–69
4000	100.0	0.00	0.02	61–73

Table 4: Off-line conservative ($\overline{\rho_a} = 0.7$) ARTMAP system performance after training on input sets ranging in size from 3 to 4000 exemplars. Each line shows average correct, incorrect, and no-response test set predictions over 10 independent simulations, plus the range of learned ART_a category numbers.

TABLE 5

#	Feature	1=P	2=E	3=E	4=E	5=P	6=E	7=P	8=P	9=E
1	cap-shape									
2	cap-surface									
3	cap-color									
4	bruises?							yes	no	yes
5	odor		none				none			
6	gill-attachment	free	free		free	free	free	free	free	free
7	gill-spacing	close			close	close	close	close	close	close
8	gill-size		broad						narrow	broad
9	gill-color								buff	
10	stalk-shape								tapering	enlarged
11	stalk-root								missing	club
12	stalk-surface-above-ring			smooth	smooth	smooth	smooth	smooth	smooth	smooth
13	stalk-surface-below-ring			smooth						smooth
14	stalk-color-above-ring					white	white	white	pink	white
15	stalk-color-below-ring							white		white
16	veil-type	partial	partial	partial	partial	partial	partial	partial	partial	partial
17	veil-color	white	white		white	white	white	white	white	white
18	ring-number	one		one	one		one	one	one	one
19	ring-type			pendant				pendant	evanescent	pendant
20	spore-print-color								white	
21	population					several	several	scattered	several	scattered
22	habitat									
	# coded/category:	2367	1257	387	1889	756	373	292	427	251

Table 5: Critical feature values of the 9 category prototypes learned in the 125-sample simulation illustrated in Figure 4c ($\overline{\rho_a} = 0$). Categories 1, 5, 7 and 8 are identified as poisonous (P) and categories 2, 3, 4, 6, and 9 are identified as edible (E). These prototypes yield 96.4% accuracy on test set inputs.

TABLE 6

#	Feature	1=E	2=P	3=P	4=E
1	cap-shape				
2	cap-surface				
3	cap-color				
4	bruises?			no	
5	odor	none			
6	gill-attachment	free	free		
7	gill-spacing			close	close
8	gill-size	broad			broad
9	gill-color				
10	stalk-shape				enlarging
11	stalk-root				
12	stalk-surface-above-ring				smooth
13	stalk-surface-below-ring				
14	stalk-color-above-ring				
15	stalk-color-below-ring		white		
16	veil-type	partial	partial	partial	partial
17	veil-color	white	white	white	
18	ring-number		one		one
19	ring-type				pendant
20	spore-print-color				
21	population				
22	habitat				
	# coded/category:	3099	1820	2197	883

Table 6: Critical feature values of the 4 prototypes learned in a 125-sample simulation with a training set different from the one in Table 6. Prediction accuracy is similar (96.0%), but the ART_a category boundaries are different.

ART modules ART_a and ART_b

Each ART module in Figures 1 and 2 establishes compressed recognition codes in response to sequences of input patterns **a** and **b**. Associative learning at the Map Field links pairs of pattern classes via these compressed codes. One type of generalization follows immediately from this learning strategy: If one vector **a** is associated with a vector **b**, then any other input that activates **a**'s category node will predict the category of pattern **b**. Any ART module can be used to self-organize the ART_a and ART_b categories. In the application above, **a** and **b** are binary vectors, so ART_a and ART_b can be ART 1 modules. The main computations of an ART 1 module will here be outlined. A full definition of ART 1 modules, as systems of differential equations, along with an analysis of their network dynamics, can be found in Carpenter and Grossberg[9].

In an ART 1 module, an input pattern **I** is represented in field F_1 and the recognition category for **I** is represented in field F_2. We consider the case where the competitive field F_2 makes a choice and where the system is operating in a fast-learn mode, as defined below. An algorithm for simulations is given in the Appendix.

F_1 **activation.** Figure 5 illustrates the main components of an ART 1 module. A field of M nodes F_1 with output vector $\mathbf{x} \equiv (x_1, \ldots, x_M)$ registers the $F_0 \to F_1$ input vector $\mathbf{I} \equiv (I_1, \ldots, I_M)$. Each F_1 node can receive input from 3 sources: the $F_0 \to F_1$ bottom-up input; nonspecific gain control signals; and top-down signals from the N nodes of F_2, via an $F_2 \to F_1$ adaptive filter. A node is said to be *active*, if it generates an output signal equal to 1. Output from inactive nodes equals 0. In ART 1 an F_1 node is active iff at least 2 of the 3 input signals are large. This rule for F_1 activation is called the *2/3 Rule*. The 2/3 Rule is realized in its simplest, dimensionless form as follows.

• **2/3 Rule matching**—The ith F_1 node is active iff its net input exceeds a fixed threshold. Specifically,

$$x_i = \begin{cases} 1 & \text{if } I_i + g_1 + \sum_{j=1}^{N} y_j z_{ji} > 1 + \bar{z} \\ 0 & \text{otherwise,} \end{cases} \tag{1}$$

where term I_i is the binary $F_0 \to F_1$ input, term g_1 is the binary nonspecific F_1 gain control signal, term $\sum y_j z_{ji}$ is the sum of $F_2 \to F_1$ signals y_j via pathways with adaptive weights z_{ji}, and $\bar{z}$ is a constant such that

$$0 < \bar{z} < 1. \tag{2}$$

• F_1 **gain control**—The F_1 gain control signal g_1 is defined by

$$g_1 = \begin{cases} 1 & \text{if } F_0 \text{ is active and } F_2 \text{ is inactive} \\ 0 & \text{otherwise.} \end{cases} \tag{3}$$

Note that F_2 activity inhibits F_1 gain, as shown in Figure 5. These laws for F_1 activation imply that, if F_2 is inactive,

$$x_i = \begin{cases} 1 & \text{if } I_i = 1 \\ 0 & \text{otherwise.} \end{cases} \tag{4}$$

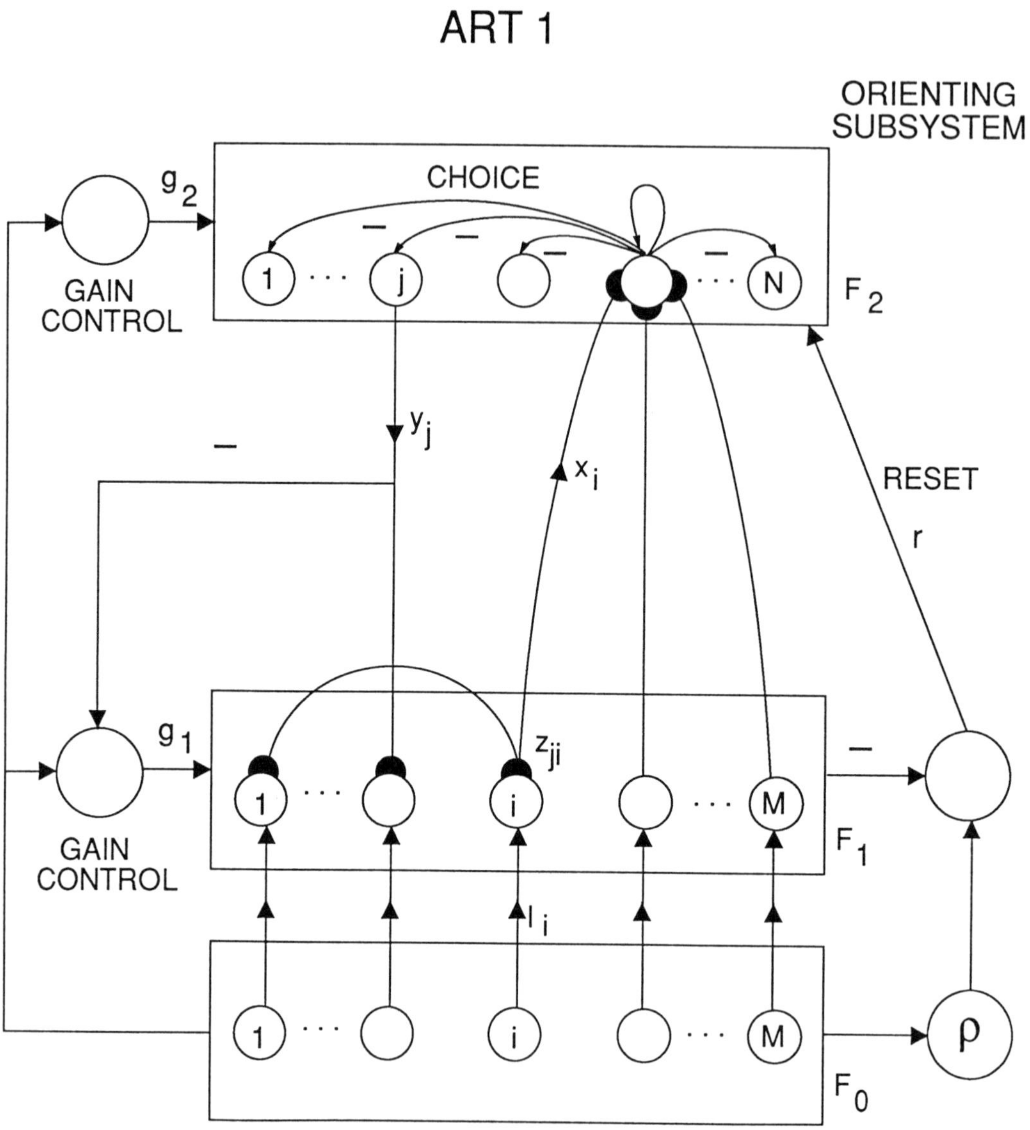

ART 1

Figure 5. ART 1 schematic diagram[9]. The binary vector **I** forms the bottom-up input to the field F_1 whose activity vector is denoted **x**. The competitive field F_2 is designed to make a choice. Adaptive pathways lead from each F_1 node to all F_2 nodes, and from each F_2 node to all F_1 nodes. Reset occurs when the match between **x** and **I** fails to meet the criterion established by the vigilance parameter ρ. All paths are excitatory unless marked with a minus sign.

If exactly one F_2 node J is active, the sum $\sum y_j z_{ji}$ in (1) reduces to the single term z_{Ji}, so

$$x_i = \begin{cases} 1 & \text{if } I_i = 1 \text{ and } z_{Ji} > \bar{z} \\ 0 & \text{otherwise.} \end{cases} \tag{5}$$

F_2 **choice.** Let T_j denote the total input from F_1 to the jth F_2 node, given by

$$T_j = \sum_{i=1}^{M} x_i Z_{ij}, \tag{6}$$

where the Z_{ij} denote the $F_1 \to F_2$ adaptive weights. If some $T_j > 0$, define the F_2 choice index J by

$$T_J = \max\{T_j : j = 1 \ldots N\}. \tag{7}$$

In the typical case, J is uniquely defined. Then the F_2 output vector $\mathbf{y} = (y_1, \ldots, y_N)$ obeys

$$y_j = \begin{cases} 1 & \text{if } j = J \\ 0 & \text{if } j \neq J. \end{cases} \tag{8}$$

If two or more indices j share maximal input, then they equally share the total activity. This case is not considered here.

Learning laws. In fast-learn ART 1, adaptive weights reach their new asymptote on each input presentation. The learning laws, as well as the rules for choice and search, are conveniently described using the following notation. If $\mathbf{a}$ is a binary M-vector, define the norm of $\mathbf{a}$ by

$$|\mathbf{a}| \equiv \sum_{i=1}^{M} a_i. \tag{9}$$

If $\mathbf{a}$ and $\mathbf{b}$ are two binary vectors, define a third binary vector $\mathbf{a} \cap \mathbf{b}$ by

$$(\mathbf{a} \cap \mathbf{b})_i = 1 \iff a_i = 1 \text{ and } b_i = 1. \tag{10}$$

Finally, let $\mathbf{a}$ be a *subset* of $\mathbf{b}$ ($\mathbf{a} \subseteq \mathbf{b}$) iff $\mathbf{a} \cap \mathbf{b} = \mathbf{a}$.

All ART 1 learning is gated by F_2 activity; that is, the adaptive weights z_{Ji} and Z_{iJ} can change only when the Jth F_2 node is active. Then both $F_2 \to F_1$ and $F_1 \to F_2$ weights are functions of the F_1 vector $\mathbf{x}$, as follows.

• **Top-down learning**—Top-down $F_2 \to F_1$ weights in active paths learn $\mathbf{x}$; that is, when the Jth F_2 node is active

$$z_{Ji} \to x_i. \tag{11}$$

All other z_{ji} remain unchanged. Stated as a differential equation, this learning rule is

$$\frac{d}{dt} z_{ji} = y_j (x_i - z_{ji}). \tag{12}$$

In (12), learning by z_{ji} is *gated* by y_j. When the y_j gate opens—that is, when $y_j > 0$—then learning begins and z_{ji} is attracted to x_i. In vector terms, if $y_j > 0$, then $\mathbf{z}_j \equiv (z_{j1}, z_{j2}, \ldots, z_{jM})$ approaches $\mathbf{x}$. Such a law is therefore sometimes called learning by *gated steepest descent*. It is also called the *outstar learning* rule, and was introduced into the neural modelling literature in 1969[23].

Initially all z_{ji} are maximal:

$$z_{ji}(0) = 1. \tag{13}$$

Thus with fast learning, the top-down weight vector $\mathbf{z}_J$ is a binary vector at the start and end of each input presentation. By (4), (5), (10), (11), and (13), the F_1 activity vector can be described as

$$\mathbf{x} = \begin{cases} \mathbf{I} & \text{if } F_2 \text{ is inactive} \\ \mathbf{I} \cap \mathbf{z}_J & \text{if the Jth } F_2 \text{ node is active.} \end{cases} \tag{14}$$

By (5) and (12), when node J is active, learning causes

$$\mathbf{z}_J \to \mathbf{I} \cap \mathbf{z}_J^{(\text{old})}, \tag{15}$$

where $\mathbf{z}_J^{(\text{old})}$ denotes $\mathbf{z}_J$ at the start of the input presentation. By (11) and (14), $\mathbf{x}$ remains constant during learning, even though $|\mathbf{z}_J|$ may decrease.

The first time an F_2 node J becomes active, it is said to be *uncommitted*. Then, by (13)–(15),

$$\mathbf{z}_J \to \mathbf{I} \tag{16}$$

during learning. Thereafter node J is said to be *committed*.

• **Bottom-up learning**—In simulations it is convenient to assign initial values to the bottom-up $F_1 \to F_2$ adaptive weights Z_{ij} in such a way that F_2 nodes first become active in the order $j = 1, 2, \ldots$. This can be accomplished by letting

$$Z_{ij}(0) = \alpha_j \tag{17}$$

where

$$\alpha_1 > \alpha_2 > \ldots > \alpha_N. \tag{18}$$

Like the top-down weight vector $\mathbf{z}_J$, the bottom-up $F_1 \to F_2$ weight vector $\mathbf{Z}_J \equiv (Z_{1J} \ldots Z_{iJ} \ldots Z_{MJ})$ also becomes proportional to the F_1 output vector $\mathbf{x}$ when the F_2 node J is active. In addition, however, the bottom-up weights are scaled inversely to $|\mathbf{x}|$, so that

$$Z_{iJ} \to \frac{x_i}{\beta + |\mathbf{x}|}, \tag{19}$$

where $\beta > 0$. This $F_1 \to F_2$ learning law, called the Weber Law Rule[9], realizes a type of competition among the weights $\mathbf{z}_J$ adjacent to a given F_2 node J. This competitive computation could alternatively be transferred to the F_1 field, as it is in ART 2[10]. By (14), (15), and (19), during learning

$$\mathbf{Z}_J \to \frac{\mathbf{I} \cap \mathbf{z}_J^{(\text{old})}}{\beta + |\mathbf{I} \cap \mathbf{z}_J^{(\text{old})}|}. \tag{20}$$

The Z_{ij} initial values are required to be small enough so that an input $\mathbf{I}$ that perfectly matches a previously learned vector $\mathbf{Z}_J$ will select the F_2 node J rather than an uncommitted node. This is accomplished by assuming that

$$0 < \alpha_j = Z_{ij}(0) < \frac{1}{\beta + |\mathbf{I}|} \tag{21}$$

for all $F_0 \rightarrow F_1$ inputs $\mathbf{I}$. When $\mathbf{I}$ is first presented, $\mathbf{x} = \mathbf{I}$, so by (6), (15), (17), and (20), the $F_1 \rightarrow F_2$ input vector $\mathbf{T} \equiv (T_1, T_2, \ldots, T_N)$ is given by

$$T_j = \sum_{i=1}^{M} I_i Z_{ij} = \begin{cases} |\mathbf{I}|\alpha_j & \text{if } j \text{ is an uncommitted node} \\ |\mathbf{I} \cap \mathbf{z}_j|/(\beta + |\mathbf{z}_j|) & \text{if } j \text{ is a committed node.} \end{cases} \tag{22}$$

In the simulations above, β is taken to be so small that, among committed nodes, T_j is determined by the size of $|\mathbf{I} \cap \mathbf{z}_j|$ relative to $|\mathbf{z}_j|$. If β were large, T_j would depend primarily on $|\mathbf{I} \cap \mathbf{z}_j|$. In addition, α_j values are taken to be so small that an uncommitted node will generate the maximum T_j value in (22) only if $|\mathbf{I} \cap \mathbf{z}_j| = 0$ for all committed nodes. Larger values of α_j and β bias the system toward earlier selection of uncommitted nodes when only poor matches are to be found among the committed nodes. A more complete discussion of this aspect of ART 1 system design is given by Carpenter and Grossberg[9].

Hypothesis testing, confidence, novelty, and search. By (7), (21), and (22), a committed F_2 node J may be chosen even if the match between $\mathbf{I}$ and $\mathbf{z}_J$ is poor; the match need only be the best one available. If the match is too poor, then the ART 1 system can autonomously carry out hypothesis testing, or search, for a better F_2 recognition code. This search process is mediated by the orienting subsystem, which can reset F_2 nodes in response to poor matches at F_1 (Figure 5). The orienting subsystem is a type of novelty detector that measures system confidence. If the degree of match between bottom-up input $\mathbf{I}$ and top-down weight vector $\mathbf{z}_J$ is too poor, the system's confidence in the recognition code labelled by J is inadequate. Otherwise expressed, the input $\mathbf{I}$ is too unexpected relative to the top-down vector $\mathbf{z}_J$, which plays the role of a learned top-down expectation.

An unexpected input triggers a novelty burst at the orienting subsystem, which sends a nonspecific reset wave r from the orienting subsystem to F_2. The reset wave enduringly shuts off node J so long as input $\mathbf{I}$ remains on. With J off and its top-down $F_2 \rightarrow F_1$ signals silent, F_1 can again instate vector $\mathbf{x} = \mathbf{I}$, which leads to selection of another F_2 node through the bottom-up $F_1 \rightarrow F_2$ adaptive filter. This hypothesis testing process leads to activation of a sequence of F_2 nodes until one is chosen whose vector of adaptive weights forms an adequate match with $\mathbf{I}$, or until an uncommitted node is selected. The search takes place so rapidly that essentially no learning occurs on that time scale. Learned weights are hereby buffered against recoding by poorly matched inputs that activate unacceptable F_2 recognition codes. Thus, during search, previously learned weights actively control the search for a better recognition code without being changed by the signals that they process.

Vigilant search and resonant learning. As noted above, the degree of match between bottom-up input $\mathbf{I}$ and top-down expectation $\mathbf{z}_J$ is evaluated at the orienting subsystem, which measures system confidence that category J adequately represents input $\mathbf{I}$. A reset wave is triggered only if this confidence measure falls below a dimensionless parameter ρ that is called the *vigilance parameter*. The vigilance parameter calibrates the system's sensitivity to disconfirmed expectations.

One of the main reasons for the successful classification of nonstationary data sequences by ARTMAP is its ability to recalibrate the vigilance parameter based on predictive success. How this works will be described below. For now, we characterize the ART 1 search process given a constant level of vigilance.

In fast-learn ART 1 with choice at F_2, the search process occurs as follows:

- **Step 1**—Select one F_2 node J that maximizes T_j in (22), and read-out its top-down weight vector $\mathbf{z}_J$.

- **Step 2**—With J active, compare the F_1 output vector $\mathbf{x} = \mathbf{I} \cap \mathbf{z}_J$ with the $F_0 \to F_1$ input vector $\mathbf{I}$ at the orienting subsystem (Figure 5).

- **Step 3A**—Suppose that $\mathbf{I} \cap \mathbf{z}_J$ fails to match $\mathbf{I}$ at the level required by the vigilance criterion, i.e., that

$$|\mathbf{x}| = |\mathbf{I} \cap \mathbf{z}_J| < \rho |\mathbf{I}|. \tag{23}$$

Then F_2 reset occurs: node J is shut off for the duration of the input interval during which $\mathbf{I}$ remains on. The index of the chosen F_2 node is reset to the value corresponding to the next highest $F_1 \to F_2$ input T_j. With the new node active, Steps 2 and 3A are repeated until the chosen node satisfies the resonance criterion in Step 3B. Note that reset never occurs if

$$\rho \le 0. \tag{24}$$

When (24) holds, an ART system acts as if there were no orienting subsystem.

- **Step 3B**—Suppose that $\mathbf{I} \cap \mathbf{z}_J$ meets the criterion for resonance; i.e., that

$$|\mathbf{x}| = |\mathbf{I} \cap \mathbf{z}_J| \ge \rho |\mathbf{I}|. \tag{25}$$

Then the search ceases and the last chosen F_2 node J remains active until input $\mathbf{I}$ shuts off (or until ρ increases). In this state, called *resonance*, both the $F_1 \to F_2$ and the $F_2 \to F_1$ adaptive weights approach new values if $\mathbf{I} \cap \mathbf{z}_J^{(\text{old})} \ne \mathbf{z}_J^{(\text{old})}$. Note that resonance cannot occur if $\rho > 1$.

If $\rho \le 1$, search ceases whenever $\mathbf{I} \subseteq \mathbf{z}_J$, as is the case if an uncommitted node J is chosen. If vigilance is close to 1, then reset occurs if $F_2 \to F_1$ input alters the F_1 activity pattern at all; resonance requires that $\mathbf{I}$ be a subset of $\mathbf{z}_J$. If vigilance is near 0, reset never occurs. The top-down expectation $\mathbf{z}_J$ of the first chosen F_2 node J is then recoded from $\mathbf{z}_J^{(\text{old})}$ to $\mathbf{I} \cap \mathbf{z}_J^{(\text{old})}$, even if $\mathbf{I}$ and $\mathbf{z}_J^{(\text{old})}$ are very different vectors.

F_2 **gain control.** For simplicity, ART 1 is exposed to discrete presentation intervals during which an input is constant and after which F_1 and F_2 activities are set to zero. Discrete presentation intervals are implemented in ART 1 by means of the F_1 and F_2 gain control signals g_1 and g_2 (Figure 5). The F_2 gain signal g_2 is assumed, like g_1 in (3), to be 0 if F_0 is inactive. Then, when F_0 becomes active, g_2 and F_2 signal thresholds are assumed to lie in a range where the F_2 node that receives the largest input signal can become active. When an ART 1 system is embedded in a hierarchy, F_2 may receive signals from sources other than F_1. This occurs in the ARTMAP system described below. In such a system, F_2 still makes a choice and gain signals from F_0 are still required to generate both F_1 and F_2 output signals. In the simulations, F_2 nodes that are reset during search remain off until the input shuts off. A real-time ART search mechanism that can cope with continuously fluctuating analog or binary inputs of variable duration, fast or slow learning, and compressed or distributed F_2 codes is described by Carpenter and Grossberg[11].

The Map Field

A Map Field module links the F_2 fields of the ART_a and ART_b modules. Figure 6 illustrates the main components of the Map Field. We will describe one such system

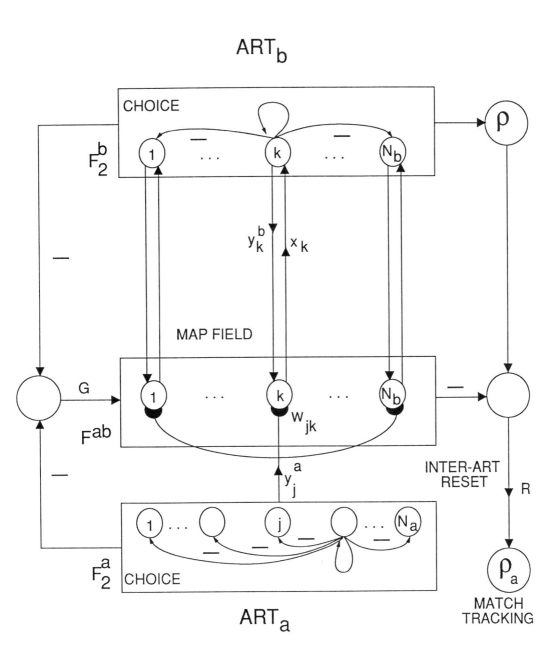

Figure 6. The Map Field is connected to F_2^b with one-to-one, non-adaptive pathways in both directions. Each F_2^a node is connected to all Map Field nodes via adaptive pathways. A mismatch between the category predicted by **a** and the actual category of **b** activates the Map Field orienting subsystem. This leads to F_2^a reset and increased vigilance (ρ_a) via match tracking.

in the fast-learn mode with choice at the fields F_2^a and F_2^b. As with the ART 1 and ART 2 architectures themselves[9,10], many variations of the network architecture lead to similar computations. In the ARTMAP hierarchy, ART_a, ART_b, and Map Field modules are all described in terms of ART 1 variables and parameters. Indices a and b identify terms in the ART_a and ART_b modules, while Map Field variables and parameters have no such index. Thus, for example, ρ_a, ρ_b, and ρ denote the ART_a, ART_b, and Map Field vigilance parameters, respectively.

ART_a, ART_b, and complement coding. Both ART_a and ART_b are fast-learn ART 1 modules. With one optional addition, they duplicate the design described above. That addition, called *complement coding*, represents both the on-response to an input vector and the off-response to that vector. This ART coding strategy has been shown to play a useful role in searching for appropriate recognition codes in response to predictive feedback[24,25]. To represent such a code in its simplest form, let the input vector **a** itself represent the on-response, and the complement of **a**, denoted by $\mathbf{a}^c$, represent the off-response, for each ART_a input vector **a**. If **a** is the binary vector $(a_1, \ldots, a_{Ma})$, the input to ART_a is the $2M_a$-dimensional binary vector

$$(\mathbf{a}, \mathbf{a}^c) \equiv (a_1, \ldots, a_{Ma}, a_1^c, \ldots, a_{Ma}^c) \tag{26}$$

where

$$a_i^c = 1 - a_i. \tag{27}$$

The utility of complement coding for searching an ARTMAP system will be described below. Conditions will also be given where complement coding is not needed. In fact, complement coding was not needed for any of the simulations described above, and the ART_a input was simply the vector **a**.

In the discussion of the Map Field module below, F_2^a nodes, indexed by $j = 1 \ldots N_a$, have binary output signals y_j^a; and F_2^b nodes, indexed by $k = 1 \ldots N_b$, have binary output signals y_k^b. Correspondingly, the index of the active F_2^a node is denoted by J, and the index of the active F_2^b node is denoted by K. Because the Map Field is the interface where signals from F_2^a and F_2^b interact, it is denoted by F^{ab}. The nodes of F^{ab} have the same index k, $k = 1, 2, \ldots, N_b$, as the nodes of F_2^b because there is a one-to-one correspondence between these sets of nodes. The output signals of F^{ab} nodes are denoted by x_k.

2/3 Rule Map Field matching. Each node of F^{ab} can receive input from three sources: F_2^a, F_2^b, and a Map Field gain control G. The F^{ab} output vector **x** obeys the 2/3 Rule of ART 1; namely,

$$x_k = \begin{cases} 1 & \text{if } y_k^b + G + \sum_{j=1}^{N_a} y_j^a w_{jk} > 1 + \overline{w} \\ 0 & \text{otherwise} \end{cases} \tag{28}$$

where term y_k^b is the F_2^b output signal, term G is a binary gain control signal, term $\sum y_j^a w_{jk}$ is the sum of $F_2^a \to F^{ab}$ signals y_j^a via pathways with adaptive weights w_{jk}, and $\overline{w}$ is a constant such that

$$0 < \overline{w} < 1. \tag{29}$$

Values of the gain control signal G and the $F_2^a \to F^{ab}$ weight vectors $\mathbf{w}_j \equiv (w_{j1}, \ldots, w_{jN_b})$, $j = 1 \ldots N_a$, are specified below.

F^{ab} **gain control.** Comparison of (1) and (28) indicates an analogy between fields F_2^b, F^{ab}, and F_2^a in a Map Field module and fields F_0, F_1, and F_2, respectively, in an ART 1 module. Differences between these modules include the bidirectional non-adaptive connections between F_2^b and F^{ab} in the Map Field module (Figure 6) compared to the bidirectional adaptive connections between fields F_1 and F_2 in the ART 1 module (Figure 5). These different connectivity schemes require different rules for the gain control signals G and g_1.

The Map Field gain control signal G obeys the equation

$$G = \begin{cases} 0 & \text{if } F_2^a \text{ and } F_2^b \text{ are both active} \\ 1 & \text{otherwise.} \end{cases} \qquad (30)$$

Note that G is a persistently active, or tonic, signal that is turned off only when both ART_a and ART_b are active.

$F_2^a \to F^{ab}$ **initial values.** If an active F_2^a node J has not yet learned a prediction, the ARTMAP system is designed so that J can learn to predict any ART_b pattern if one is active or becomes active while J is active. This design constraint is satisfied using the assumption, analogous to (13), that

$$w_{jk}(0) = 1 \qquad (31)$$

for $j = 1 \ldots N_a$ and $k = 1 \ldots N_b$.

Map Field activation. Rules governing G and $\mathbf{w}_j(0)$ enable the following Map Field properties to obtain. If both ART_a and ART_b are active, then learning of $\text{ART}_a \to \text{ART}_b$ associations can take place at F^{ab}. If ART_a is active but ART_b is not, then any previously learned $\text{ART}_a \to \text{ART}_b$ prediction is read out at F^{ab}. If ART_b is active but ART_a is not, then the selected ART_b category is represented at F^{ab}. If neither ART_a nor ART_b is active, then F^{ab} is not active. By (28)–(31), the 2/3 Rule realizes these properties in the following four cases.

- F_2^a **active and** F_2^b **active**—If both the F_2^a category node J and the F_2^b category node K are active, then $G = 0$ by (30). Thus by (28),

$$x_k = \begin{cases} 1 & \text{if } k = K \text{ and } w_{JK} > \overline{w} \\ 0 & \text{otherwise.} \end{cases} \qquad (32)$$

All $x_k = 0$ for $k \neq K$. Moreover $x_K = 1$ only if an association has previously been learned in the pathway from node J to node K, or if J has not yet learned to predict any ART_b category. If J predicts any category other than K, then all $x_k = 0$.

- F_2^a **active and** F_2^b **inactive**—If the F_2^a node J is active and F_2^b is inactive, then $G = 1$. Thus

$$x_k = \begin{cases} 1 & \text{if } w_{Jk} > \overline{w} \\ 0 & \text{otherwise.} \end{cases} \qquad (33)$$

By (31) and (33), if an input $\mathbf{a}$ has activated node J in F_2^a but F_2^b is not yet active, J activates all nodes k in F^{ab} if J has learned no predictions. If prior learning has occurred, all nodes k are activated whose adaptive weights w_{Jk} are still large.

- F_2^b **active and** F_2^a **inactive**—If the F_2^b node K is active and F_2^a is inactive, then $G = 1$. Thus

$$x_k = \begin{cases} 1 & \text{if } k = K \\ 0 & \text{otherwise.} \end{cases} \qquad (34)$$

In this case, the F^{ab} output vector $\mathbf{x}$ is the same as the F_2^b output vector $\mathbf{y}^b$.

• F_2^a **inactive and** F_2^b **inactive**—If neither F_2^a nor F_2^b is active, the total input to each F^{ab} node is $G = 1$, so all $x_k = 0$ by (28).

F_2^b **choice and priming.** If ART_b receives an input $\mathbf{b}$ while ART_a has no input, then F_2^b chooses the node K with the largest $F_1^b \to F_2^b$ input. Field F_2^b then activates the Kth F^{ab} node, and $F^{ab} \to F_2^b$ feedback signals support the original $F_1^b \to F_2^b$ choice. If ART_a receives an input $\mathbf{a}$ while ART_b has no input, F_2^a chooses a node J. If, due to prior learning, some $w_{JK} = 1$ while all other $w_{Jk} = 0$, we say that $\mathbf{a}$ *predicts* the ART_b category K, as F^{ab} sends its signal vector $\mathbf{x}$ to F_2^b. Field F_2^b is hereby *attentionally primed*, or sensitized, but the field remains inactive so long as ART_b has no input from F_0^b. If then an $F_0^b \to F_1^b$ input $\mathbf{b}$ arrives, the F_2^b choice depends upon network parameters and timing. It is natural to assume, however, that $\mathbf{b}$ simultaneously activates the F_1^b and F_2^b gain control signals g_1^b and g_2^b (Figure 5). Then F_2^b processes the F^{ab} prime $\mathbf{x}$ as soon as F_1^b processes the input $\mathbf{b}$, and F_2^b chooses the primed node K. Field F_1^b then receives $F_2^b \to F_1^b$ expectation input $\mathbf{z}_K^b$ as well as $F_0^b \to F_1^b$ input $\mathbf{b}$, leading either to match or reset.

$F_2^a \to F^{ab}$ **learning laws.** The $F_2^a \to F^{ab}$ adaptive weights w_{jk} obey an outstar learning law similar to that governing the $F_2 \to F_1$ weights z_{ji} in (12); namely,

$$\frac{d}{dt} w_{jk} = y_j^a (x_k - w_{jk}). \tag{35}$$

According to (35), the $F_2^a \to F^{ab}$ weight vector $\mathbf{w}_J$ approaches the F^{ab} activity vector $\mathbf{x}$ if the Jth F_2^a node is active. Otherwise $\mathbf{w}_J$ remains constant. If node J has not yet learned to make a prediction, all weights w_{Jk} equal 1, by (31). In this case, if ART_b receives no input $\mathbf{b}$, then all x_k values equal 1 by (33). Thus, by (35), all w_{jk} values remain equal to 1. As a result, category choices in F_2^a do not alter the adaptive weights w_{jk} until these choices are associated with category choices in F_2^b.

Map Field reset and match tracking. The Map Field provides the control that allows the ARTMAP system to establish different categories for very similar ART_a inputs that make different predictions, while also allowing very different ART_a inputs to form categories that make the same prediction. In particular, the Map Field orienting subsystem becomes active only when ART_a makes a prediction that is incompatible with the actual ART_b input. This mismatch event activates the control strategy, called *match tracking*, that modulates the ART_a vigilance parameter ρ_a in such a way as to keep the system from making repeated errors. As illustrated in Figure 6, a mismatch at F^{ab} while F_2^b is active triggers an inter-ART reset signal R to the ART_a orienting subsystem. This occurs whenever

$$|\mathbf{x}| < \rho |\mathbf{y}^b|, \tag{36}$$

where ρ denotes the Map Field vigilance parameter. The entire cycle of ρ_a adjustment proceeds as follows through time. At the start of each input presentation, ρ_a equals a fixed baseline vigilance $\overline{\rho_a}$. When an input $\mathbf{a}$ activates an F_2^a category node J and resonance is established,

$$|\mathbf{x}^a| = |\mathbf{a} \cap \mathbf{z}_J^a| \geq \rho_a |\mathbf{a}|, \tag{37}$$

as in (25). An inter-ART reset signal is sent to ART_a if the ART_b category predicted by $\mathbf{a}$ fails to match the active ART_b category, by (36). The inter-ART reset signal R

raises ρ_a to a value that is just high enough to cause (37) to fail, so that

$$\rho_a > \frac{|\mathbf{a} \cap \mathbf{z}_J^a|}{|\mathbf{a}|}. \tag{38}$$

Node J is therefore reset and an ART_a search ensues. Match tracking continues until an active ART_a category satisfies both the ART_a matching criterion (37) and the analogous Map Field matching criterion. Match tracking increases the ART_a vigilance by the minimum amount needed to abort an incorrect $\text{ART}_a \rightarrow \text{ART}_b$ prediction and to drive a search for a new ART_a category that can establish a correct prediction. As shown by example below, match tracking allows $\mathbf{a}$ to make a correct prediction on subsequent trials, without repeating the initial sequence of errors. Match tracking hereby conjointly maximizes predictive generalization and minimizes predictive error on a trial-by-trial basis, using only local computations.

• **Match tracking using VITE dynamics**—The operation of match tracking can be implemented in several different ways. One way is to use a variation on the Vector Integration to Endpoint, or VITE, circuit[26] as follows. Let an ART_a binary *reset signal* r_a (Figure 7) obeys the equation

$$r_a = \begin{cases} 1 & \text{if } \rho_a|\mathbf{a}| - |\mathbf{x}^a| > 0 \\ 0 & \text{otherwise,} \end{cases} \tag{39}$$

as in (23). The complementary ART_a *resonance signal* $r_a^c = 1 - r_a$. Signal R equals 1 during inter-ART reset; that is, when inequality (36) holds. The size of the ART_a vigilance parameter ρ_a is determined by the *match tracking equation*

$$\frac{d}{dt}\rho_a = (\overline{\rho_a} - \rho_a) + \gamma R r_a^c, \tag{40}$$

where $\gamma \gg 1$. During inter-ART reset, $R = r_a^c = 1$, causing ρ_a to increase until $r_a^c = 0$. Then $\rho_a|\mathbf{a}| > |\mathbf{x}^a|$, as required for match tracking (38). When $r_a^c = 0$, ρ_a relaxes to $\overline{\rho_a}$. This is assumed to occur at a rate slower than node activation, also called short term memory (STM), and faster than learning, also called long term memory (LTM). Such an intermediate rate is called medium term memory (MTM)[11].

Comparing the match tracking circuit in Figure 7 to a VITE circuit, the inter-ART reset signal R is analogous to the VITE GO signal; total F_1^a output $|\mathbf{x}^a|$ is analogous to the Target Position Code (TPC); total F_0^a output, gated by ρ_a, is analogous to the Present Position Command (PPC); and the quantity $(\rho_a|\mathbf{a}| - |\mathbf{x}^a|)$ in (39) is analogous to the Difference Vector (DV). (See Bullock and Grossberg[26], Figure 17.)

An ART_a search that is triggered by increasing ρ_a according to (40) ceases if some active F_2^a node J satisfies

$$|\mathbf{a} \cap \mathbf{z}_J^a| \geq \rho_a|\mathbf{a}|. \tag{41}$$

If no such node exists, F_2^a shuts down for the rest of the input presentation. In particular, if $\mathbf{a} \subseteq \mathbf{z}_J^a$, match tracking makes $\rho_a > 1$, so $\mathbf{a}$ cannot activate another category in order to learn the new prediction. The following anomalous case can thus arise. Suppose that $\mathbf{a} = \mathbf{z}_J^a$ but the ART_b input $\mathbf{b}$ mismatches the ART_b expectation $\mathbf{z}_K^b$ previously associated with J. Then match tracking will prevent the recoding that would have associated $\mathbf{a}$ with $\mathbf{b}$. That is, the ARTMAP system with fast learning

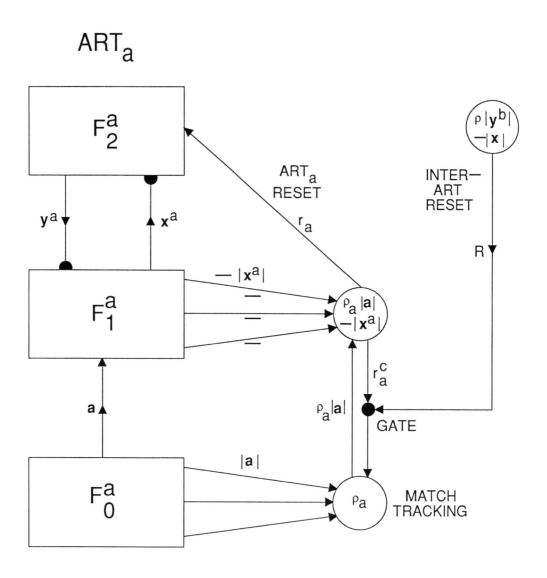

Figure 7. Match tracking by a scalar VITE circuit. When $r_a^c = R = 1$, ρ_a rapidly increases until $\rho_a|\mathbf{a}| > |\mathbf{x}^a|$. Once this occurs, $r_a^c = 0$ and $r_a = 1$, causing ART$_a$ reset. The inter-ART reset signal R plays a role analogous to the VITE model GO signal.

and choice will not learn the prediction of an exemplar that *exactly* matches a learned prototype when the new prediction contradicts the previous predictions of the exemplars that created the prototype. This situation does not arise when all ART_a inputs **a** have the same number of 1's, as follows.

- **Equal-norm inputs and search**—Consider the case in which all ART_a inputs have the same norm:

$$|\mathbf{a}| \equiv \text{constant.} \tag{42}$$

When an ART_a category node J becomes committed to input **a**, then $|\mathbf{z}_J^a| = |\mathbf{a}|$. Thereafter, by the 2/3 Rule (15), $\mathbf{z}_J^a$ can be recoded only by decreasing its number of 1 entries, and thus its norm. Once this occurs, no input **a** can ever be a subset of $\mathbf{z}_J^a$, by (42). In particular, the situation described in the previous section cannot arise.

In the simulations reported in this article, all ART_a inputs have norm 22. Equation (42) can also be satisfied by using complement coding, since $|(\mathbf{a}, \mathbf{a}^c)| = M_a$. Preprocessing ART_a inputs by complement coding thus ensures that the system will avoid the case where some input **a** is a proper subset of the active ART_a prototype $\mathbf{z}_J^a$ and the learned prediction of category J mismatches the correct ART_b pattern.

Finally, note that with ARTMAP fast learning and choice, an ART_a category node J is permanently committed to the first ART_b category node K to which it is associated. However, the set of input exemplars that access either category may change through time, as in the banana example described in the introduction.

- **Match tracking example**—The role of match tracking is illustrated by the following example. The input pairs shown in Table 7 are presented in order $(\mathbf{a}^{(1)}, \mathbf{b}^{(1)})$, $(\mathbf{a}^{(2)}, \mathbf{b}^{(2)})$, $(\mathbf{a}^{(3)}, \mathbf{b}^{(3)})$. The problem solved by match tracking is created by vector $\mathbf{a}^{(2)}$ lying "between" $\mathbf{a}^{(1)}$ and $\mathbf{a}^{(3)}$, with $\mathbf{a}^{(1)} \subset \mathbf{a}^{(2)} \subset \mathbf{a}^{(3)}$, while $\mathbf{a}^{(1)}$ and $\mathbf{a}^{(3)}$ are mapped to the same ART_b vector. Suppose that, instead of match tracking, the Map Field orienting subsystem merely activated the ART_a reset system. Coding would then proceed as follows.

Choose $\overline{\rho_a} \leq 0.6$ and $\rho_b > 0$. Vectors $\mathbf{a}^{(1)}$ then $\mathbf{b}^{(1)}$ are presented, activate ART_a and ART_b categories $J = 1$ and $K = 1$, and the category $J = 1$ learns to predict category $K = 1$, thus associating $\mathbf{a}^{(1)}$ with $\mathbf{b}^{(1)}$. Next $\mathbf{a}^{(2)}$ then $\mathbf{b}^{(2)}$ are presented. Vector $\mathbf{a}^{(2)}$ first activates $J = 1$ without reset, since

$$\frac{|\mathbf{a}^{(2)} \cap \mathbf{z}_1^a|}{|\mathbf{a}^{(2)}|} = \frac{3}{4} \geq \rho_a = \overline{\rho_a}. \tag{43}$$

However, node $J = 1$ predicts node $K = 1$. Since

$$\frac{|\mathbf{b}^{(2)} \cap \mathbf{z}_1^b|}{|\mathbf{b}^{(2)}|} = 0 < \rho_b, \tag{44}$$

ART_b search leads to activation of a different F_2^b node, $K = 2$. Because of the conflict between the prediction ($K = 1$) made by the active F_2^a node and the currently active F_2^b node ($K = 2$), the Map Field orienting subsystem resets F_2^a, but without match tracking. Thereafter a new F_2^a node ($J = 2$) learns to predict the correct F_2^b node ($K = 2$), associating $\mathbf{a}^{(2)}$ with $\mathbf{b}^{(2)}$.

Vector $\mathbf{a}^{(3)}$ first activates $J = 2$ without ART_a reset, thus predicting $K = 2$, with $\mathbf{z}_2^b = \mathbf{b}^{(2)}$. However, $\mathbf{b}^{(3)}$ mismatches $\mathbf{z}_2^b$, leading to activation of the F_2^b node $K = 1$,

TABLE 7

$\mathbf{ART}_a$ inputs	$\mathbf{ART}_b$ inputs
$\mathbf{a}^{(1)}$ (111000)	$\mathbf{b}^{(1)}$ (1010)
$\mathbf{a}^{(2)}$ (111100)	$\mathbf{b}^{(2)}$ (0101)
$\mathbf{a}^{(3)}$ (111110)	$\mathbf{b}^{(3)}$ (1010)

Table 7: Nested ART_a inputs and their associated ART_b inputs.

since $\mathbf{b}^{(3)} = \mathbf{b}^{(1)}$. Since the predicted node ($K = 2$) then differs from the active node ($K = 1$), the Map Field orienting subsystem again resets F_2^a. At this point, still without match tracking, the F_2^a node $J = 1$ would become active, without subsequent ART_a reset, since $\mathbf{z}_1^a = \mathbf{a}^{(1)}$ and

$$\frac{|\mathbf{a}^{(3)} \cap \mathbf{a}^{(1)}|}{|\mathbf{a}^{(3)}|} = \frac{3}{5} \geq \rho_a = \overline{\rho_a}. \tag{45}$$

Since node $J = 1$ correctly predicts the active node $K = 1$, no further reset or new learning would occur. On subsequent prediction trials, vector $\mathbf{a}^{(3)}$ would once again activate $J = 2$ and then $K = 2$. When vector $\mathbf{b}^{(3)}$ is not presented, on a test trial, vector $\mathbf{a}^{(3)}$ would not have learned its correct prediction.

With match tracking, when $\mathbf{a}^{(3)}$ is presented, the Map Field orienting subsystem causes ρ_a to increase to a value slightly greater than $|\mathbf{a}^{(3)} \cap \mathbf{a}^{(2)}||\mathbf{a}^{(3)}|^{-1} = 0.8$ while node $J = 2$ is active. Thus after node $J = 2$ is reset, node $J = 1$ will also be reset because

$$\frac{|\mathbf{a}^{(3)} \cap \mathbf{a}^{(1)}|}{|\mathbf{a}^{(3)}|} = 0.6 < 0.8 < \rho_a. \tag{46}$$

The reset of node $J = 1$ permits $\mathbf{a}^{(3)}$ to choose an uncommitted F_2^a node ($J = 3$) that is then associated with the active F_2^b node ($K = 1$). Thereafter each ART_a input predicts the correct ART_b output without search or error.

• **Complement coding example**—The utility of ART_a complement coding is illustrated by the following example. Assume that the nested input pairs in Table 7 are presented to an ARTMAP system in order $(\mathbf{a}^{(3)}, \mathbf{b}^{(3)}), (\mathbf{a}^{(2)}, \mathbf{b}^{(2)}), (\mathbf{a}^{(1)}, \mathbf{b}^{(1)})$, with match tracking but without complement coding. Choose $\overline{\rho_a} < 0.5$ and $\rho_b > 0$.

Vectors $\mathbf{a}^{(3)}$ and $\mathbf{b}^{(3)}$ are presented and activate ART_a and ART_b categories $J = 1$ and $K = 1$. The system learns to predict $\mathbf{b}^{(3)}$ given $\mathbf{a}^{(3)}$ by associating the F_2^a node $J = 1$ with the F_2^b node $K = 1$.

Next $\mathbf{a}^{(2)}$ and $\mathbf{b}^{(2)}$ are presented. Vector $\mathbf{a}^{(2)}$ first activates $J = 1$ without reset, since $|\mathbf{a}^{(2)} \cap \mathbf{z}_1^a||\mathbf{a}^{(2)}|^{-1} = 1 \geq \rho_a = \overline{\rho_a}$. However, node $J = 1$ predicts node $K = 1$. As in the previous example, after $\mathbf{b}^{(2)}$ is presented, the F_2^b node $K = 2$ becomes active and leads to an inter-ART reset. Match tracking makes $\rho_a > 1$, so F_2^a shuts down until the pair $(\mathbf{a}^{(2)}, \mathbf{b}^{(2)})$ shuts off. Pattern $\mathbf{b}^{(2)}$ is coded in ART_b as $\mathbf{z}_2^b$, but no learning occurs in the ART_a and F^{ab} modules.

Next $\mathbf{a}^{(1)}$ activates $J = 1$ without reset, since $|\mathbf{a}^{(1)} \cap \mathbf{z}_1^a||\mathbf{a}^{(1)}|^{-1} = 1 \geq \rho_a = \overline{\rho_a}$. Since node $J = 1$ predicts the correct pattern $\mathbf{b}^{(1)} = \mathbf{z}_1^b$, no reset ensues. Learning does occur, however, since $\mathbf{z}_1^a$ shrinks to $\mathbf{a}^{(1)}$. If each input can be presented only once, $\mathbf{a}^{(2)}$ does not learn to predict $\mathbf{b}^{(2)}$. However if the input pairs are presented repeatedly, match tracking allows ART_a to establish 3 category nodes and an accurate mapping.

With complement coding, the correct map can be learned on-line for any $\overline{\rho_a} > 0$. The critical difference is due to the fact that $|\mathbf{a}^{(2)} \cap \mathbf{z}_1^a||\mathbf{a}^{(2)}|^{-1}$ now equals $5/6$ when $\mathbf{a}^{(2)}$ is first presented, rather than equaling 1 as before. Thus either ART_a reset (if $\overline{\rho_a} > 5/6$) or match tracking (if $\overline{\rho_a} \leq 5/6$) establishes a new ART_a node rather than shutting down on that trial. On the next trial, $\mathbf{a}^{(1)}$ also establishes a new ART_a category that maps to $\mathbf{b}^{(1)}$.

The Appendix outlines ARTMAP system responses to various input situations, namely, combinations of: **a** without **b**, **b** without **a**, **a** then **b**, **b** then **a**, **a** making a prediction or making no prediction, and **a**'s prediction matching or mismatching **b**.

REFERENCES

[1] Carpenter, G.A. and Grossberg, S. (1988). The ART of adaptive pattern recognition by a self-organizing neural network. *Computer*, **21**, 77–88.

[2] Grossberg, S. (1988a). Nonlinear neural networks: Principles, mechanisms, and architectures. *Neural Networks*, **1**, 17–61.

[3] Grossberg, S. (1976a). Adaptive pattern classification and universal recoding, I: Parallel development and coding of neural feature detectors. *Biological Cybernetics*, **23**, 121–134.

[4] Grossberg, S. (1976b). Adaptive pattern classification and universal recoding, II: Feedback, expectation, olfaction, and illusions. *Biological Cybernetics*, **23**, 187-202.

[5] Grossberg, S. (1982). **Studies of mind and brain: Neural principles of learning, perception, development, cognition, and motor control.** Boston: Reidel Press.

[6] Grossberg, S. (Ed.) (1987a). **The adaptive brain, I: Cognition, learning, reinforcement, and rhythm.** Amsterdam: Elsevier/North-Holland.

[7] Grossberg, S. (Ed.) (1987b). **The adaptive brain, II: Vision, speech, language, and motor control.** Amsterdam: Elsevier/North-Holland.

[8] Grossberg, S. (Ed.) (1988b). **Neural networks and natural intelligence.** Cambridge, MA: MIT Press.

[9] Carpenter, G.A. and Grossberg, S. (1987a). A massively parallel architecture for a self-organizing neural pattern recognition machine. *Computer Vision, Graphics, and Image Processing*, **37**, 54–115.

[10] Carpenter, G.A. and Grossberg, S. (1987b). ART 2: Stable self-organization of pattern recognition codes for analog input patterns. *Applied Optics*, **26**, 4919–4930.

[11] Carpenter, G.A., and Grossberg, S. (1990). ART 3: Hierarchical search using chemical transmitters in self-organizing pattern recognition architectures. *Neural Networks*, **3**, 129–152.

[12] Carpenter, G.A. (1989). Neural network models for pattern recognition and associative memory. *Neural Networks*, **2**, 243–257.

[13] Parker. D.B. (1982). Learning-logic. Invention Report S81-64, File 1, Office of Technology Licensing, Stanford University.

[14] Rumelhart, D.E. and McClelland, J.L. (Eds.), (1986). **Parallel distributed processing, Volume 1.** Cambridge, MA: MIT Press.

[15] Werbos, P. (1974). Beyond regression: New tools for prediction and analysis in the behavioral sciences. Cambridge, MA: Harvard University.

[16] Werbos, P. (1982). Applications of advances in nonlinear sensitivity analysis. In A.V. Balakrishnan, M. Thoma, R.F. Drenick, and F. Kozin (Eds.), **Lecture notes in control and information sciences, Volume 38: System modeling and optimization.** New York: Springer-Verlag.

[17] Searle, J.R. (1983). **Intentionality, an essay in the philosophy of mind.** Cambridge: Cambridge University Press.

[18] Schlimmer, J.S. (1987a). Mushroom database. UCI Repository of Machine Learning Databases. (aha@ics.uci.edu)

[19] Lincoff, G.H. (1981). **The Audubon Society field guide to North American mushrooms**. New York: Alfred A. Knopf.

[20] Schlimmer, J.S. (1987b). Concept acquisition through representational adjustment (Technical Report 87–19). Doctoral dissertation, Department of Information and Computer Science, University of California at Irvine.

[21] Iba, W., Wogulis, J., and Langley, P. (1988). Trading off simplicity and coverage in incremental concept learning. In **Proceedings of the 5th international conference on machine learning**. Ann Arbor, MI: Morgan Kaufmann, 73–79.

[22] Kendall, M.G. and Stuart, A. (1966). **The advanced theory of statistics, Volume 3**. New York: Haffner, Chapter 43.

[23] Grossberg, S. (1969). On learning and energy-entropy dependence in recurrent and nonrecurrent signed networks. *Journal of Statistical Physics*, **1**, 319–350.

[24] Grossberg, S. (1982). Processing of expected and unexpected events during conditioning and attention: A psychophysiological theory. *Psychological Review*, **89**, 529–572.

[25] Grossberg, S. (1984). Some psychophysiological and pharmacological correlates of a developmental, cognitive, and motivational theory. In R. Karrer, J. Cohen, and P. Tueting (Eds.), **Brain and information: Event related potentials**. New York: New York Academy of Sciences, 58–151.

[26] Bullock, D. and Grossberg, S. (1988). Neural dynamics of planned arm movements: Emergent invariants and speed-accuracy properties during trajectory formation. *Psychological Review*, **95**, 49–90.

APPENDIX

Simulation Algorithms

ART 1 algorithm. Fast-learn ART 1 with binary $F_0 \rightarrow F_1$ input vector $\mathbf{I}$ and choice at F_2 can be simulated by following the rules below. Fields F_0 and F_1 have M nodes and field F_2 has N nodes.

• **Initial values**—Initially all F_2 nodes are said to be *uncommitted*. Weights Z_{ij} in $F_1 \rightarrow F_2$ paths initially satisfy

$$Z_{ij}(0) = \alpha_j, \tag{A1}$$

where $\mathbf{Z}_j \equiv (Z_{1j}, \ldots, Z_{Mj})$ denotes the bottom-up $F_1 \rightarrow F_2$ weight vector. Parameters α_j are ordered according to

$$\alpha_1 > \alpha_2 > \ldots > \alpha_N, \tag{A2}$$

where

$$0 < \alpha_j < \frac{1}{(\beta + |\mathbf{I}|)} \tag{A3}$$

for $\beta > 0$ and for any admissible $F_0 \rightarrow F_1$ input $\mathbf{I}$. In the simulations in this article, α_j and β are small.

Weights z_{ji} in $F_2 \rightarrow F_1$ paths initially satisfy

$$z_{ji}(0) = 1. \tag{A4}$$

The top-down, $F_2 \rightarrow F_1$ weight vector $(z_{j1}, \ldots, z_{jM})$ is denoted $\mathbf{z}_j$.

• F_1 **activation**—The binary F_1 output vector $\mathbf{x} \equiv (x_1, \ldots, x_M)$ is given by

$$\mathbf{x} = \begin{cases} \mathbf{I} & \text{if } F_2 \text{ is inactive} \\ \mathbf{I} \cap \mathbf{z}_J & \text{if the } J\text{th } F_2 \text{ node is active.} \end{cases} \tag{A5}$$

• $F_1 \rightarrow F_2$ **input**—The input T_j from F_1 to the jth F_2 node obeys

$$T_j = \begin{cases} |\mathbf{I}|\alpha_j & \text{if } j \text{ is an uncommitted node index} \\ |\mathbf{I} \cap \mathbf{z}_j|/(\beta + |\mathbf{z}_j|) & \text{if } j \text{ is a committed node index.} \end{cases} \tag{A6}$$

The set of committed F_2 nodes and update rules for vectors $\mathbf{z}_j$ and $\mathbf{Z}_j$ are defined iteratively below.

• F_2 **choice**—If F_0 is active ($|\mathbf{I}| > 0$), the initial choice at F_2 is one node with index J satisfying

$$T_J = \max_j (T_j). \tag{A7}$$

If more than one node is maximal, one of these is chosen at random. After an input presentation on which node J is chosen, J becomes *committed*. The F_2 output vector is denoted by $\mathbf{y} \equiv (y_1, \ldots, y_N)$.

• **Search and resonance**—ART 1 search ends upon activation of an F_2 category with index $j = J$ that has the largest T_j value and that also satisfies the inequality

$$|\mathbf{I} \cap \mathbf{z}_J| \geq \rho|\mathbf{I}| \tag{A8}$$

where ρ is the ART 1 vigilance parameter. If such a node J exists, that node remains active, or in *resonance*, for the remainder of the input presentation. If no node satisfies (A8), F_2 remains inactive after search, until $\mathbf{I}$ shuts off.

• **Fast learning**—At the end of an input presentation the $F_2 \rightarrow F_1$ weight vector $\mathbf{Z}_J$ satisfies

$$\mathbf{Z}_J = \mathbf{I} \cap \mathbf{z}_J^{(\text{old})} \qquad (A9)$$

where $\mathbf{z}_J^{(\text{old})}$ denotes $\mathbf{z}_J$ at the start of the current input presentation. The $F_1 \rightarrow F_2$ weight vector $\mathbf{Z}_J$ satifies

$$\mathbf{Z}_J = \frac{\mathbf{I} \cap \mathbf{z}_J^{(\text{old})}}{\beta + |\mathbf{I} \cap \mathbf{z}_J^{(\text{old})}|}. \qquad (A10)$$

ARTMAP algorithm. The ARTMAP system incorporates two ART modules and an inter-ART module linked by the following rules.

• **ART$_a$ and ART$_b$**—ART$_a$ and ART$_b$ are fast-learn ART 1 modules. Inputs to ART$_a$ may, optionally, be in the complement code form. Embedded in an ARTMAP system, these modules operate as outlined above, with the following additions. First, the ART$_a$ vigilance parameter ρ_a can increase during inter-ART reset according to the *match tracking* rule. Second, the Map Field F^{ab} can *prime* ART$_b$. That is, if F^{ab} sends nonuniform input to F_2^b in the absence of an $F_0^b \rightarrow F_1^b$ input $\mathbf{b}$, then F_2^b remains inactive. However, as soon as an input $\mathbf{b}$ arrives, F_2^b chooses the node K receiving the largest $F^{ab} \rightarrow F_2^b$ input. Node K, in turn, sends to F_1^b the top-down input $\mathbf{z}_K^b$. Rules for match tracking and complement coding are specified below.

Let $\mathbf{x}^a \equiv (x_1^a \ldots x_{Ma}^a)$ denote the F_1^a output vector; let $\mathbf{y}^a \equiv (y_1^a \ldots y_{Na}^a)$ denote the F_2^a output vector; let $\mathbf{x}^b \equiv (x_1^b \ldots x_{Mb}^b)$ denote the F_1^b output vector; and let $\mathbf{y}^b \equiv (y_1^b \ldots y_{Nb}^b)$ denote the F_2^b output vector. The Map Field F^{ab} has N_b nodes and binary output vector $\mathbf{x}$. Vectors $\mathbf{x}^a, \mathbf{y}^a, \mathbf{x}^b, \mathbf{y}^b$, and $\mathbf{x}$ are set to $\mathbf{0}$ between input presentations.

• **Map Field learning**—Weights w_{jk}, where $j = 1 \ldots N_a$ and $k = 1 \ldots N_b$, in $F_2^a \rightarrow F^{ab}$ paths initially satisfy

$$w_{jk}(0) = 1. \qquad (A11)$$

Each vector $(w_{j1}, \ldots, w_{jNb})$ is denoted $\mathbf{w}_j$. During resonance with the ART$_a$ category J active, $\mathbf{w}_J \rightarrow \mathbf{x}$. In fast learning, once J learns to predict the ART$_b$ category K, that association is permanent; i.e., $w_{JK} = 1$ for all times.

• **Map Field activation**—The F^{ab} output vector $\mathbf{x}$ obeys

$$\mathbf{x} = \begin{cases} \mathbf{y}^b \cap \mathbf{w}_J & \text{if the Jth } F_2^a \text{ node is active and } F_2^b \text{ is active} \\ \mathbf{w}_J & \text{if the Jth } F_2^a \text{ node is active and } F_2^b \text{ is inactive} \\ \mathbf{y}^b & \text{if } F_2^a \text{ is inactive and } F_2^b \text{ is active} \\ \mathbf{0} & \text{if } F_2^a \text{ is inactive and } F_2^b \text{ is inactive.} \end{cases} \qquad (A12)$$

• **Match tracking**—At the start of each input presentation the ART$_a$ vigilance parameter ρ_a equals a baseline vigilance $\overline{\rho_a}$. The Map Field vigilance parameter is ρ. If

$$|\mathbf{x}| < \rho |\mathbf{y}^b|, \qquad (A13)$$

then ρ_a is increased until it is slightly larger than $|\mathbf{a} \cap \mathbf{z}_J^a||\mathbf{a}|^{-1}$. Then

$$|\mathbf{x}^a| = |\mathbf{a} \cap \mathbf{z}_J^a| < \rho_a|\mathbf{a}|, \qquad (A14)$$

where $\mathbf{a}$ is the current ART_a input vector and J is the index of the active F_2^a node. When this occurs, ART_a search leads either to activation of a new F_2^a node J with

$$|\mathbf{x}^a| = |\mathbf{a} \cap \mathbf{z}_J^a| \geq \rho_a|\mathbf{a}| \qquad (A15)$$

and

$$|\mathbf{x}| = |\mathbf{y}^b \cap \mathbf{w}_J| \geq \rho|\mathbf{y}^b|; \qquad (A16)$$

or, if no such node exists, to the shut-down of F_2^a for the remainder of the input presentation.

- **Complement coding**—This optional feature arranges ART_a inputs as vectors

$$(\mathbf{a}, \mathbf{a}^c) \equiv (a_1 \ldots a_{Ma}, a_1^c \ldots a_{Ma}^c), \qquad (A17)$$

where

$$a_i^c \equiv 1 - a_i. \qquad (A18)$$

Complement coding may be useful if the following set of circumstances could arise: an ART_a input vector $\mathbf{a}$ activates an F_2^a node J previously associated with an F_2^b node K; the current ART_b input $\mathbf{b}$ mismatches $\mathbf{z}_K^b$; and $\mathbf{a}$ is a subset of $\mathbf{z}_J^a$. These circumstances never arise if all $|\mathbf{a}| \equiv$ constant. For the simulations in this article, $|\mathbf{a}| \equiv 22$. With complement coding, $|(\mathbf{a}, \mathbf{a}^c)| \equiv M_a$.

ARTMAP processing

The following nine cases summarize fast-learn ARTMAP system processing with choice at F_2^a and F_2^b and with Map Field vigilance $\rho > 0$. Inputs $\mathbf{a}$ and $\mathbf{b}$ could appear alone, or one before the other. Input $\mathbf{a}$ could make a prediction based on prior learning or make no prediction. If $\mathbf{a}$ does make a prediction, that prediction may be confirmed or disconfirmed by $\mathbf{b}$. The system follows the rules outlined in the previous section assuming, as in the simulations, that all $|\mathbf{a}| \equiv$ constant and that complement coding is not used. For each case, changing weight vectors $\mathbf{z}_J^a, \mathbf{z}_K^b$, and $\mathbf{w}_K$ are listed. Weight vectors $\mathbf{Z}_J^a$ and $\mathbf{Z}_K^b$ change accordingly, by (A11). All other weights remain constant.

Case 1: a only, no prediction. Input $\mathbf{a}$ activates a matching F_2^a node J, possibly following ART_a search. All $F_2^a \to F^{ab}$ weights $w_{Jk} = 1$, so all $x_k = 1$. ART_b remains inactive. With learning $\mathbf{z}_J^a \to \mathbf{z}_J^{a(\mathrm{old})} \cap \mathbf{a}$.

Case 2: a only, with prediction. Input $\mathbf{a}$ activates a matching F_2^a node J. Weight $w_{JK} = 1$ while all other $w_{Jk} = 0$, and $\mathbf{x} = \mathbf{w}_J$. F_2^b is primed, but remains inactive. With learning, $\mathbf{z}_J^a \to \mathbf{z}_J^{a(\mathrm{old})} \cap \mathbf{a}$.

Case 3: b only. Input $\mathbf{b}$ activates a matching F_2^b node K, possibly following ART_b search. At the Map Field, $\mathbf{x} = \mathbf{y}^b$. ART_a remains inactive. With learning, $\mathbf{z}_K^b \to \mathbf{z}_K^{b(\mathrm{old})} \cap \mathbf{b}$.

Case 4: a then b, no prediction. Input $\mathbf{a}$ activates a matching F_2^a node J. All x_k become 1 and ART_b is inactive, as in Case 1. Input $\mathbf{b}$ then activates a matching

F_2^b node K, as in Case 3. At the Map Field $\mathbf{x} \to \mathbf{y}^b$; that is, $x_K = 1$ and other $x_k = 0$. With learning $\mathbf{z}_J^a \to \mathbf{z}_J^{a(\text{old})} \cap \mathbf{a}$, $\mathbf{z}_K^b \to \mathbf{z}_K^{b(\text{old})} \cap \mathbf{b}$, and $\mathbf{w}_J \to \mathbf{y}^b$; i.e., J learns to predict K.

Case 5: a then b, with prediction confirmed. Input $\mathbf{a}$ activates a matching F_2^a node J, which in turn activates a single Map Field node K and primes F_2^b, as in Case 2. When input $\mathbf{b}$ arrives, the Kth F_2^b node becomes active and the prediction is confirmed; that is,

$$|\mathbf{b} \cap \mathbf{z}_K^b| \geq \rho_b |\mathbf{b}|. \tag{A19}$$

Note that K may not be the F_2^b node $\mathbf{b}$ would have selected without the $F^{ab} \to F_2^b$ prime. With learning, $\mathbf{z}_J^a \to \mathbf{z}_J^{a(\text{old})} \cap \mathbf{a}$ and $\mathbf{z}_K^b \to \mathbf{z}_K^{b(\text{old})} \cap \mathbf{b}$.

Case 6: a then b, prediction not confirmed. Input $\mathbf{a}$ activates a matching F_2^a node, which in turn activates a single Map Field node and primes F_2^b, as in Case 5. When input $\mathbf{b}$ arrives, (A19) fails, leading to reset of the F_2^b node via ART_b reset. A new F_2^b node K that matches $\mathbf{b}$ becomes active. The mismatch between the $F_2^a \to F^{ab}$ weight vector and the new F_2^b vector $\mathbf{y}^b$ sends Map Field activity $\mathbf{x}$ to $\mathbf{0}$, by (A12), leading to Map Field reset, by (A13). By match tracking, ρ_a grows until (A14) holds. This triggers an ART_a search that will continue until, for an active F_2^a node J, $w_{JK} = 1$, and (A15) holds. If such an F_2^a node does become active, learning will follow, setting $\mathbf{z}_J^a \to \mathbf{z}_J^{a(\text{old})} \cap \mathbf{a}$ and $\mathbf{z}_K^b \to \mathbf{z}_K^{b(\text{old})} \cap \mathbf{b}$. If the F_2^a node J is uncommitted, learning sets $\mathbf{w}_J \to \mathbf{y}^b$. If no F_2^a node J that becomes active satisfies (A15) and (A16), F_2^a shuts down until the inputs go off. In that case, with learning, $\mathbf{z}_K^b \to \mathbf{z}_K^{b(\text{old})} \cap \mathbf{b}$.

Case 7: b then a, no prediction. Input $\mathbf{b}$ activates a matching F_2^b node K, then $\mathbf{x} = \mathbf{y}^b$, as in Case 3. Input $\mathbf{a}$ then activates a matching F_2^a node J with all $w_{Jk} = 1$. At the Map Field, $\mathbf{x}$ remains equal to $\mathbf{y}^b$. With learning, $\mathbf{z}_J^a \to \mathbf{z}_J^{a(\text{old})} \cap \mathbf{a}$, $\mathbf{w}_J \to \mathbf{y}^b$, and $\mathbf{z}_K^b \to \mathbf{z}_K^{b(\text{old})} \cap \mathbf{b}$.

Case 8: b then a, with prediction confirmed. Input $\mathbf{b}$ activates a matching F_2^b node K, then $\mathbf{x} = \mathbf{y}^b$, as in Case 7. Input $\mathbf{a}$ then activates a matching F_2^a node J with $w_{JK} = 1$ and all other $w_{Jk} = 0$. With learning $\mathbf{z}_J^a \to \mathbf{z}_J^{a(\text{old})} \cap \mathbf{a}$ and $\mathbf{z}_K^b \to \mathbf{z}_K^{b(\text{old})} \cap \mathbf{b}$.

Case 9: b then a, prediction not confirmed. Input $\mathbf{b}$ activates a matching F_2^b node K, then $\mathbf{x} = \mathbf{y}^b$ and input $\mathbf{a}$ activates a matching F_2^a node, as in Case 8. However (A16) fails and $\mathbf{x} \to \mathbf{0}$, leading to a Map Field reset. Match tracking resets ρ_a as in Case 6, ART_a search leads to activation of an F_2^a node (J) that either predicts K or makes no prediction, or F_2^a shuts down. With learning $\mathbf{z}_K^b \to \mathbf{z}_K^{b(\text{old})} \cap \mathbf{b}$. If J exists, $\mathbf{z}_J^a \to \mathbf{z}_J^{a(\text{old})} \cap \mathbf{a}$; and if J initially makes no prediction, $\mathbf{w}_J \to \mathbf{y}^b$, i.e., J learns to predict K.

CHAPTER 16

NEURONAL ACTIVITY AS A SHAPING FACTOR
IN THE SELF-ORGANIZATION OF NEURON ASSEMBLIES
by
Wolf Singer

Preface

This 1983 article by Singer is one of the first to review accumulating neurobiological evidence for several of the basic ART predictions. At the beginning of the article,
Singer describes the experiments concerning adaptive tuning of cortical feature detectors that led to the competitive learning models in Chapters 5 and 6. He then relates
more recent experiments about cortical learning which suggest four rules governing
Hebbian learning. These rules, summarized in Table 1, support the 1976 prediction
of Chapter 6 that a gated steepest descent law governs the adaptive tuning of cortical feature detectors. As noted in the Preface to Chapter 5, a classical "Hebbian"
learning law is unable to explain these cortical data, or indeed even to learn in real
time without diverging towards unbounded values. Singer sometimes uses the term
"Hebbian" to mean any associative learning law. Such a usage does not distinguish
differences in associative learning laws, and has thus been abandoned by many investigators. Singer reaffirms the central theme of competitive learning that "sensory
experience as a shaping factor in developmental processes allows to attain a degree of
specificity of neuronal connections that could not be realized by genetic instructions
alone."

Singer next describes data showing that several of the most important 1976 ART
predictions (see Preface of Chapter 9) have also begun to receive experimental support. These include the predictions that norpinephrine (NE) and attention modulate
the cortical code learning process. He also describes evidence for other processes
that are modelled in ART systems, including nonspecific arousal sources to maintain
information processing and learning. The type of attentional gain control that is
used, say, in ART 1 to achieve supraliminal bottom-up activation within a recognition learning network needs to be conceptually distinguished from other nonspecific
arousal sources, such as the incentive motivation that is activated during reinforcement learning (see Chapter 20). Singer's review does not distinguish between these
two types of arousal.

Singer does present evidence that learning may take place on the dendrites of
cortical neurons and may involve an activity-dependent Ca^{++} current. The earliest
neural network predictions about activity-dependent Ca^{++} currents seem to be those
in Grossberg (1968, 1969a). The earliest neural network predictions about neural
network learning on dendrites seem to be those in Brindley (1964) and Grossberg
(1964, 1969b). These predictions interpreted known anatomy. A later prediction
(Grossberg, 1975, Section 21) emphasized the need to functionally separate the
read-out of associative memory (from a previously learned LTM trace) from its read-in
(which changes the values of the LTM trace through new learning). It was noted that,
if read-in automatically learned the total read-out by many converging pathways, then
the learning process could be seriously destabilized by noise contamination. It was

suggested that associative synapses on dendritic spines could read-out old associations without reading-in new associations until an auxiliary feedback event occurred. The problem of how best to dissociate read-out from read-in is still an important topic of neural network research. For example, the ART 3 architecture in Chapter 14 uses an activity-dependent Ca^{++} current at dendritic spines to functionally separate read-out from transmitter inactivation during distributed memory search. A signal may be read-out without triggering a large amount of transmitter inactivation if its target node is not stored in STM by the postsynaptic competition. Grossberg and Schmajuk (1987) have used dendritic learning to dissociate associative read-out from read-in during reinforcement learning. A direct test is needed of whether dendritic learning carries out the type of dissociation between associative read-out and read-in that has been theoretically predicted.

References

Brindley, G.S. (1964). The use made by the cerebellum of the information that it receives from sense organs. *International Brain Research Organizational Bulletin*, **3**, 80.

Grossberg, S. (1964). **The theory of embedding fields with applications to psychology and neurophysiology**. New York: Rockefeller Institute for Medical Research.

Grossberg, S. (1968). Some physiological and biochemical consequences of psychological postulates. *Proceedings of the National Academy of Sciences*, **60**, 758–765.

Grossberg, S. (1969a). On the production and release of chemical transmitters and related topics in cellular control. *Journal of Theoretical Biology*, **22**, 325–364.

Grossberg, S. (1969b). On learning and spatiotemporal patterns by networks with ordered sensory and motor components, I: Excitatory components of the cerebellum. *Studies in Applied Mathematics*, **48**, 105–132.

Grossberg, S. (1975). A neural model of attention, reinforcement, and discrimination learning. *International Review of Neurobiology*, **18**, 263–327.

Grossberg, S. and Schmajuk, N.A. (1987). Neural dynamics of attentionally-modulated Pavlovian conditioning: Conditioned reinforcement, inhibition, and opponent processing. *Psychobiology*, 1987, **15**, 195–240.

Synergetics of the Brain
E. Basar, H. Flohr, H. Haken, and A.J. Mandell (Eds.)
New York: Springer-Verlag, 1983, 89–101
©1983 Springer-Verlag, Inc.

NEURONAL ACTIVITY AS A SHAPING FACTOR
IN THE SELF-ORGANIZATION OF NEURON ASSEMBLIES

Wolf Singer

Abstract

Neuronal activity and hence sensory signals serve as a shaping factor in the development of the structural and functional organization of the mammalian visual cortex. The electrical responses of cortical neurons control the consolidation and repression of interneuronal connections. The algorithms of this activity-dependent selection process closely resemble those proposed by Hebb for adaptive synaptic connections. These local modifications depend in addition on internally generated gating signals. The latter exert a "now print" function by controlling Hebbian modifications as a function of the animal's central state. These permissive gating signals are related to mechanisms which control arousal and visual attention. Evidence is available which suggests that the activation of voltage-dependent Ca^{++} channels in the dendrites of cortical neurons is the trigger signal for a Hebbian modification. The permissive gating signals appear to control the probability of Ca^{++} channel activation. It is concluded that these activity-dependent modifications of neuronal connectivity have an associative function. They are capable of developing assemblies of cooperating neurons by specifying according to functional criteria which neurons should interact with each other.

Introduction

Evidence is increasing that the electrical activity of neurons serves as a shaping factor in the development of neuronal connections. In this review I shall discuss the principles of activity-dependent self-organization as they emerged from our developmental studies in the visual cortex of kittens. In order to provide an adequate background for the evaluation of these experimental data I shall review briefly the phenomenology of the effects that can be obtained by manipulating early visual experience.

By the time kittens or monkeys open their eyes most neurons in the visual cortex respond to stimulation of both eyes (Hubel and Wiesel [13]). With normal visual experience but also with complete deprivation of contour vision this condition is maintained. However, when visual signals are available but not identical in the two eyes, either because one eye is occluded (Wiesel and Hubel [40]) or because the images on the two retinae are not in register—as is the case with strabismus (Hubel and Wiesel [15]), cyclotorsion (Blakemore et al. [6]), or anisometropia (Blakemore and van Sluyters [5])—cortical cells lose their binocular receptive fields. In the first case they stop responding to the deprived eye; in the other cases they segregate into two groups of approximately equal size, one responding exclusively to the ipsilateral and the other exclusively to the contralateral eye. These functional changes in eye preference are associated with distortions of the columnar organization. The territories occupied by afferents from the normal eye and by cells responding preferentially to this eye increase at the expense of territories innervated by the deprived eye (Hubel et al. [17]). These effects are obtainable only during a critical period of early development. During this period, but not thereafter, the effects of monocular deprivation can be fully reversed by closing the open eye and at the same time reopening the previously closed eye. This indicates that the efficacy of connections does not only decrease but can also increase as a function of retinal stimulation (Wiesel and Hubel [41]).

Not only the degree of binocularity but also the selectivity of cortical cells for stimulus orientation can be modified by manipulating visual experience. Normally, nearly all cells in the striate cortex of cats respond selectively to contours with a particular orientation. Cells preferring the same orientation are clustered together, forming a system of fairly regularly spaced iso-orientation columns or bands (Hubel and Wiesel [14]). In this columnar system preferences for all orientations are equally represented. However, when contour vision is prevented by dark rearing or binocular lid suture, only a small fraction of cortical cells develop orientation selectivity, the majority remain or become responsive to contours of all orientations. In addition, the vigor of responses to light decreases and about 30% to 50% of the cells stop responding to retinal stimulation altogether. Throughout the critical period, but not thereafter, these deprivation effects, too, are fully reversible. Eight hours of normal vision suffice to reinstall orientation selectivity (Buisseret et al. [7]). When visual experience is available throughout the critical period but restricted to contours of a single orientation, the majority of cortical cells come to prefer this orientation (Blakemore and Cooper [3]; Hirsch and Spinelli [12]). Cortical territories which contain cells preferring the experienced orientation expand at the expense of territories which normally would have been reserved for cells preferring the other orientations (Singer et al. [36]).

The mechanisms underlying these experience-dependent changes of receptive field properties are still largely unknown. Changes of the gain of synaptic connections, selective stabilization and repression of newly formed connections and activity-dependent growth processes have all been implicated as possible mechanisms mediating experience dependent modifications of cortical functions. Whatever the dominant mechanisms are, it is established, however, that the activation of the postsynaptic neuron is essential for a long-term modification of excitatory transmission (Rauschecker and Singer [26]; Singer et al. [35]). If, e. g., one eye is occluded and the other exposed to contours of only a single orientation, differential gain changes occur only for

Rules for the modification of excitatory transmission

	Rule 1	Rule 2	Rule 3	Rule 4
state of A	+	−	+	−
state of C	+	+	−	−
state of E	↑	↓	↔	↔

A = excitatory afferent

E = efficacy of
    exitatory transmission

C = postsynaptic neuron

+ = active

− = inactive

↑ = increased

↓ = decreased

↔ = no change

Table 1.

pathways connecting to those postsynaptic cells that are capable of responding to the signals conveyed by the open eye (Rauschecker and Singer [26]; Singer [20]). For these cells the efficacy of afferents from the stimulated eye increases while that of afferents from the deprived eye decreases. Cells whose orientation preference does not correspond to the orientations seen by the stimulated eye cannot respond to activity from this eye. These cells do not change their ocular dominance. The afferents from the stimulated eye, even though they are much more active than those from the deprived eye, do not increase their efficacy at the expense of the latter. The results of these and related experiments (Rauschecker and Singer [27]) made it possible to establish a set of rules for the modification of excitatory transmission which have proven sufficient to account for the results of most deprivation experiments published so far. These rules closely resemble those postulated by Hebb (Hebb [11]) for adaptive neuronal connections and can be summarized in the following way: (1) The gain of excitatory transmission increases for afferent pathways if they are active in temporal contiguity with the postsynaptic target. (2) The gain decreases when the postsynaptic target is active while the presynaptic terminal is silent. (3) Irrespective of the amount of activation of presynaptic terminals differential gain changes do not occur when the postsynaptic cell is inactive (Table 1).

A similar selection process is likely to account for the experience-dependent modification of orientation selectivity. Two recent studies, one based on single cell recording (Rauschecker and Singer [27]) and the other on deoxyglucose mapping of orientation columns (Singer et al. [36]), indicate that Hebbian competition between converging excitatory pathways can cause the characteristic distortions in the system of orientation columns and the related change in the distribution of orientation preferences. The reorganization of the orientation column system after orientation deprivation closely resembles the reorganization of the ocular dominance columns after monocular deprivation (Hubel et al. [17]). Only the site of competition is different. In the case of monocular deprivation, competition occurs where afferents from the two eyes converge onto the common cortical target cells which are located mainly in layer IV. In the case of orientation deprivation competition occurs most likely at the level where axons from orientation selective layer IV cells converge onto second-order target cells that are located mainly in non-granular layers.

A Teleological Argument

This evidence of a striking cortical malleability raises the question why nature allows visual experience to interfere with the development of cortical functions, thus exposing the developmental process to the risk that transient and accidental disturbances of the uptake of visual signals entrain severe and irreversible impairments of cortical functions. I propose that nature takes this risk because including sensory experience as a shaping factor in developmental processes allows to attain a degree of specificity of neuronal connections that could not be realized by genetic instructions alone. The following example illustrates this proposition. Animals with binocular vision have the problem to develop neurons which possess two corresponding receptive fields, one in each eye. This implies that the pathways connecting the two eyes with the binocular target cells in visual cortex have to originate from precisely corresponding retinal loci. However, which retinal loci will actually be corresponding in the mature system cannot be anticipated with any great precision. Retinal correspondence depends on parameters such as the size of the eyes, the position of the eyes in the orbit and the interocular distance, parameters which are themselves dependent on epigenetic influences. Clearly, an economical and elegant solution to this problem would be to identify according to functional criteria the pathways which originate from corresponding retinal loci. Per definition, afferents originating from corresponding retinal loci convey identical activity patterns when the animal is fixating a target with both eyes. Since Hebbian modifications have the effect to selectively stabilize connections which convey correlated activity they would be ideally suited to optimize the correspondence of binocular connections. However, if such were indeed the role of the adaptive processes, an important implication follows. Selection according to function can be successful only when the Hebbian processes are gated. Selection should occur only when the kitten is actually fixating a target with both eyes and it must not occur in all the many other instances in which the eyes are not properly aligned. In the latter conditions, Hebbian modifications would lead to competition between the afferents from the two eyes and cause disruption rather than optimization of binocular connectivity.

Evidence for a Central Control of Local Hebbian Modifications

Several recent studies provide evidence that the generation of action potentials in the postsynaptic neuron is only a necessary but not a sufficient condition for the occurrence of Hebbian modifications in the developing visual cortex. Even when contour vision is unrestricted and retinal signals readily elicit responses in the neurons of the visual cortex, vision-dependent modifications of excitatory transmission may fail to occur in a variety of rather different conditions. Thus, neurons of the cat striate cortex remain binocular despite monocular deprivation when cortical norepinephrine (NE) is depleted shortly before the beginning of monocular deprivation (Kasamatsu and Pettigrew [19]). Local microperfusion of the cortical tissue with NE reinstalls plasticity (Kasamatsu et al. [20]). Cortical cells also maintain binocular receptive fields when the open eye of monocularly deprived kittens is surgically rotated within the orbit (Singer *et al.* [37]). In this case contour vision *per se* is unimpaired but the abnormal eye position and motility lead to massive disturbances of the kittens' visuo-motor coordination. Initially the inappropriate retinal signals cause abnormal visuo-motor reactions and are effective in influencing cortical ocular dominance. Subsequently, however, the kittens rely less and less on visual cues and develop a near complete neglect of the visual modality. In this phase, retinal signals no longer modify ocular dominance and they also fail to support the development of orientation-selective receptive fields.

Another manipulation which prevents retinal signals from inducing cortical modifications is the abolition of proprioceptive signals from the extraocular muscles. When this input is disrupted by severing the ophthalmic branch of the IIIrd cranial nerve bilaterally, the animals are deprived of feedback signals from the eye muscles. In this case retinal signals neither stimulate the development of orientation selectivity (Trotter *et al.* [39]) nor do they induce changes of ocular dominance (Buisseret and Singer [8]). As the kittens with the rotated eye, the kittens with the severed proprioceptive afferents developed also a neglect for the visual modality and relied on their other sensory systems for orientation.

These latter results suggested that retinal signals only influence the development of cortical functions when the animal pays attention to these signals and uses them for the control of behavior. This view is compatible with two lines of evidence: Firstly, independent results from three laboratories indicate that retinal signals never lead to changes of cortical functions when the kittens are paralyzed and/or anaesthetized while exposed to light. Even though the light stimuli undoubtedly drive cortical cells vigorously, they fail to bring about changes of ocular dominance (Freeman and Bonds [9]; Singer [31]) or to develop orientation selectivity (Buisseret *et al.* [7]). Secondly, the very same retinal signals may induce changes in the visual cortex of one hemisphere but not in the other when the latter is "paying less attention" to the visual signals than the former (Singer [32]). This evidence comes from experiments in which a sensory hemineglect was induced in dark reared kittens by placing small unilateral lesions in the intralaminar nuclear complex of the thalamus. Simultaneously one eye was sutured closed to instigate ocular dominance changes and to use these changes as an indicator for Hebbian modifications. As adult cats with comparable lesions (Orem *et al.* [25]) the kittens would consistently neglect stimuli in the hemifield contralateral to the lesion. After the kittens had grown up for at least three more months in normally lighted colony rooms the receptive fields of single cells were investigated in the visual cortex of the two hemispheres. In areas 17 and 18 of the normal hemispheres conditions were identical to those obtained with conventional monocular deprivation, i. e., most cortical cells had become monocular and excitable from the normal eye but otherwise they had developed normal receptive field properties. By contrast, in the hemisphere containing the lesion the majority of the cells had remained binocular showing only a slight bias in the ocular dominance distribution towards the open eye. Thus, although both hemispheres had received exactly the same signals from the open eye, these signals induced modifications only in the normal hemisphere and remained ineffective in the hemisphere which—because of the lesion—"attended" less to retinal stimulation. In this hemisphere also other parameters such as responsiveness to light and selectivity for stimulus orientation were abnormal, indicating that retinal signals had not only failed to induce competitive suppression of the deprived afferents but had also failed to support the development or consolidation of normal receptive field properties.

Another significant abnormality of the hemisphere containing the lesion became apparent when during the experiment we tried to raise cortical excitability with electrical stimulation of the mesencephalic reticular formation. In normal animals this stimulus produces a massive facilitation of thalamic and cortical transmission (for review see Singer [30, 31]). In the experimental kittens these effects were greatly attenuated in the hemisphere containing the lesion while they were fully developed in the other. Thus, the thalamic lesion had obviously affected modulatory systems known to control thalamic and cortical excitability as a function of arousal and perhaps also selective attention. This agrees with the behavioral evidence that the lesion had actually produced deficits in attention and supports the notion that modulatory systems might be involved in the control of cortical plasticity and act as a permissive gate.

This conclusion received further support from stimulation experiments. By pairing monocular light stimulation with electrical activation of central core structures it proved to be possible to induce changes of ocular dominance in kittens that were anaesthetized and paralyzed. As expected, monocular light stimulation alone never led to changes in ocular dominance even when it was continued over two to three days. However, in 9 out of 10 kittens in which the light stimulus was paired with brief electrical stimulation of either the reticular formation or medial thalamus, clear changes in ocular dominance towards the open, stimulated eye became apparent after one night of monocular conditioning (Singer and Rauschecker [34]). Moreover, there was an indication from both evoked potential and single unit analyses that the gain of excitatory transmission in the pathways from the conditioned eye had increased and that cortical cells had become more selective for contrast gradients and stimulus orientation. These results are in line with the issue of the lesion experiments and further corroborate the hypothesis that non-specific modulatory systems which increase cortical excitability facilitate experience-dependent modifications.

At present it is difficult to decide whether these different possibilities to modify cortical plasticity reflect the existence of several independent gating systems or whether the various manipulations act through a common final pathway. Recently Schlag and Schlag-Rey [28] described units in the intralaminar thalamic nuclei which discharge vigorously right at the end of saccadic eye movements. This is the moment when new visual signals are expected to arrive and therefore these authors proposed that this activity could serve as an alerting signal and direct attention to visual events. Moreover, since these units are located in the area whose destruction caused the hemineglect and reduced cortical plasticity and whose stimulation enhanced cortical plasticity, the Schlags suggested that these cells might be involved in the postulated gating process. This interpretation is particularly attractive since it provides a link between the gating functions of the ascending arousal system on the one hand and of the proprioceptive signals about eye position and motility on the other. Proprioceptive input from the extraocular muscles to these cells has not yet been studied, but it would be ideally suited to generate corollary activity that is time-locked with eye movements.

The Gating Mechanism

The evidence presented so far indicates that in a variety of conditions, retinal signals fail to induce Hebbian modifications even though they are eliciting responses in cortical cells. Thus, temporal contiguity between pre- and postsynaptic activity appears to be only a necessary but not a sufficient condition for the occurrence of adaptive changes. Additional "now print" signals are required. These can be substituted by electrical stimulation of the mesencephalic reticular formation or of the intralaminar nuclear complex of the thalamus. Those stimulations greatly facilitate the transmission of retinal signals through the lateral geniculate nucleus (for review see Singer [30]). Furthermore, they raise cortical excitability, enhancing dramatically intracortical transmission (for review see Singer [31]). A predictable consequence of both effects is that the depolarization of cortical dendrites increases. Thus, it might be a necessary prerequisite for the occurrence of adaptive changes that cortical dendrites become depolarized above a critical threshold. A dendritic process which is voltage-dependent and does have a high threshold is the activation of dendritic Ca^{++} channels (Llinas [23]). We hypothesized, therefore, that the final trigger signal for the occurrence of an adaptive change in response to retinal stimulation might be the influx of Ca^{++} ions through activated, voltage-dependent Ca^{++} channels. This working hypothesis predicts that the extracellular Ca^{++} concentration should transiently decrease with stimulation conditions which induce adaptive changes.

Measurements of stimulus-induced changes of extracellular Ca^{++} concentrations conform with this expectancy. When light stimuli are coincident with central core stimulation—a condition sufficient to induce Hebbian modifications—the extracellular Ca^{++} concentration decreases. With light or central core stimulation alone— conditions which do not lead to adaptive changes—the extracellular Ca^{++} concentration is not altered. Likewise in adult cats, in which modifications of striate cortex functions can no longer be easily induced, even continguous stimulation of the retina and of the modulatory projections failed to alter extracellular Ca^{++} concentrations (Geiger and Singer [10]). Calculations of the observed Ca^{++} fluxes in the kittens warrant the conclusion that the resulting increase of intracellular Ca^{++} concentration reaches a physiologically significant level. This covariation between the activation of Ca^{++} channels and the occurrence of adaptive modifications is no proof for a causal relation between the two processes, but four aspects render the Ca^{++} hypothesis attractive. Firstly, as summarized in Figure 1, it allows for a heterosynaptic control of adaptive changes and hence can account for the fact that so many different non-retinal projections to striate cortex interfere with the Hebbian modifications. Secondly, the appearance of free Ca^{++} ions in the cytosol is an important trigger signal for a variety of biochemical processes (for review see Kretsinger [22]). Thirdly, the membranes of developing neurons are particularly rich in Ca^{++} channels (Llinas and Sugimori [24]). Fourthly, a heterosynaptic control of long-term changes in excitatory transmission has recently been demonstrated in the cerebellar cortex. Modifications of the gain of parallel fiber synapses require that these are active in temporal contiguity with the climbing fibers (Ito et al. [18]). Activation of the latter produces a strong depolarization of Purkinje cell dendrites which is sufficient to reach the threshold of dendritic Ca^{++} channels.

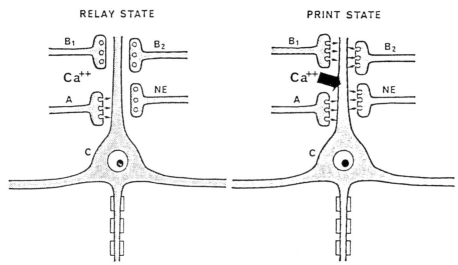

A = specific modifiabel input

NE= norepinephrinergic terminal

C = cortical neuron

B = modulatory inputs (B₁: nonspecific ascending projection; B₂: recurrent feedback pathways)

Figure 1. Schematic representation of the postulated heterosynaptic control of adaptive changes in the kitten striate cortex. The specific pathway (A) is modified only when additional modulatory input systems are active. It is hypothesized that these modulatory inputs facilitate the activation of dendritic Ca^{++} channels. The direction of the modification, increase or decrease of the efficacy of A, depends on the temporal contiguity of the activation of A and C and follows the rules summarized in Table 1.

Functional Implications of Developmental Plasticity

It follows from this brief survey that we are still at the very beginning of understanding the mechanisms which mediate activity dependent modifications of neuronal transmission. The fact, however, that the long-term changes in the developing visual cortex seem to follow the Hebbian rules and are in addition gated by non-retinal projections which exert a state-dependent control renders them sufficiently interesting to warrant a few speculations on their role in normal development.

Hebbian modifications have an associative function in that they selectively stabilize those connections between neurons that have been most often simultaneously active. This has different consequences at different levels of cortical processing. As discussed above, at the level where afferents from the two eyes converge such a selection could assure that only those afferents become consolidated which come from corresponding retinal loci in the two eyes. Likewise, in the domain of orientation selectivity Hebbian modifications could assure that second-order cortical cells receive excitatory input only from those first-order cells that share the same orientation preference. Two considerations suggest that this selection problem is again not a trivial one. Second-order cells with large receptive fields have to receive input from numerous first order cells that may be distributed over several hypercolumns (Albus [1, 2]; Hubel and Wiesel [16]). Because first-order cells which share the same orientation preference are clustered within discrete regularly spaced columns this implies discontinuous sampling from clusters of first-order cells which may be several millimeters apart. Moreover, because of the retinotopic organization of striate cortex, second-order cells with elongated vertical receptive fields must receive input from first-order cells along the longitudinal axis of striate cortex while second-order cells with elongated horizontal fields must integrate input from first-order cells along the mediolateral axis. Because of the continuity of contours in the natural environment this extremely complex specification of connections can again be achieved by selectively consolidating connections which have a high probability of being activated simultaneously. This selection is aided by the strong inhibitory interactions between cells with differing orientation preferences (Blakemore and Tobin [4]) since this inhibition effectively prevents simultaneous firing of cells in columns with different orientation preferences.

Evidence is further available that such activity-dependent association may occur over rather large cortical distances. When young animals are exposed selectively to regularly spaced contours which share the same orientation, about one-third of the cortical neurons develop large, rather unconventional receptive fields with several widely spaced excitatory regions. The spacing of these excitatory regions corresponds to the angular distance between the contrast borders of the periodic patterns which the animals had experienced previously (Singer and Tretter [33]). We ignore the anatomical substrate of these large receptive fields. Candidates are of course the recurrent collaterals of cortical neurons which can mediate horizontal interactions over considerable distances (Szentagothai [38]).

The functional role of Hebbian modifications at the level of these recurrent intracortical connections is still unclear. With normal experience the combinatorial complexity of possible contingencies becomes so exceedingly large that it is impossible to predict the resulting pattern of differentially weighted interactions. Again it can be expected that cells become associated preferentially which have a high probabilty of responding simultaneously in the presence of particular feature combinations. Such preferential coupling would enhance and prolong by reverberation the responses of distinct cell assemblies to particular, frequently occurring patterns. This would distinguish cells of the assembly from other neurons which are not able to join or to form a cooperating ensemble. Hebbian modifications at this level of cortical processing could thus be a crucial step toward the formation of cooperative cell assemblies whose coherent and reverberating responses could represent the neuronal code for particular activation patterns at the sensory surfaces. The fact that these associative processes are not solely dependent on the pattern of activity on the sensory surface but are gated by internally generated "now print" signals provides the developing system with the option to create neuronal assemblies not only as a function of the patterns in afferent sensory pathways but also as a function of the central state of the system itself. This implies that the formation of assemblies is a process of active selection whereby the selection criteria emerge from the genetically determined properties of the system and from the actual dynamic (behavioral) state which the system maintains while it interacts through its sensory surfaces with the "outer" world. Thus, at least at the level of formal descriptions the adaptive processes during early ontogeny closely resemble what is usually termed associative learning. It remains to be seen whether learning in the adult shares only these formal aspects with developmental plasticity or whether both processes actually depend on similar neuronal mechanisms. In the latter case it would obviously become difficult to segregate the being from the becoming state and the continuous activity-dependent changes of the nervous system would have to be considered as an integral property of its function and would no longer figure as a peculiarity which is restricted to early ontogeny.

REFERENCES

[1] K. Albus (1975a). *Experimental Brain Research*, **24**, 159–179.

[2] K. Albus (1975b). *Experimental Brain Research*, **24**, 181–202.

[3] C. Blakemore and G.F. Cooper (1970). *Nature*, **228**, 477–478.

[4] C. Blakemore and E.A. Tobin (1972). *Experimental Brain Research*, **15**, 439–440.

[5] C. Blakemore and R.C. van Sluyters (1974). *British Journal of Ophthalmology*, **58**, 176–182.

[6] C. Blakemore, R.C. van Sluyters, C.K. Peck, and A. Hein (1975). *Nature*, **257**, 584–586.

[7] P. Buisseret, E. Gary-Bobo, and M. Imbert (1978). *Nature*, **272**, 816–817.

[8] P. Buissert and W. Singer (1983). *Experimental Brain Research*, in print.

[9] R.D. Freeman and A.B. Bonds (1979). *Science*, **206**, 1093–1095.

[10] H. Geiger and W. Singer (1982). *Int. I. Develop. Neurosci. Suppl.*, **R328**.

[11] D.O. Hebb (1949). **The organization of behavior**. New York: John Wiley and Sons.

[12] H.V.B. Hirsch and D.N. Spinelli (1970). *Science*, **168**, 869–871.

[13] D.H. Hubel and T.N. Wiesel (1963). *Journal of Neurophysiology*, **26**, 994–1002.

[14] D.H. Hubel and T.N. Wiesel (1963). *Journal of Physiology (London)*, **160**, 106–154.

[15] D.H. Hubel and T.N. Wisel (1965). *Journal of Neurophysiology*, **28**, 1041–1059.

[16] D.H. Hubel and T.N. Wiesel (1974b). *Journal of Comparative Neurology*, **158**, 295–306.

[17] D.H. Hubel, T.N. Wiesel, and S. LeVay (1977). *Philosophical Transactions of the Royal Society of London (B)*, **278**, 377–409.

[18] M. Ito, M. Sakurai, and P. Tongroach (1982). *Journal of Physiology (London)*, **324**, 113–134.

[19] T. Kasamatsu and J.D. Pettigrew (1979) *Journal of Comparative Neurology*, **185**, 139–162.

[20] T. Kasamatsu, J.D. Pettigrew, and M. Ary (1979). *Journal of Comparative Neurology*, **185**, 163–181.

[21] M.J. Keating (1976). *Studies in Developing and Behaving Nervous Systems*, **3**, 59–110.

[22] R.H. Kretsinger (1981). Mechanisms of selective signalling by calcium. **NRP-Bulletin, Volume 19**. Cambridge, MA: MIT Press.

[23] R. Llinas (1979). The role of calcium in neuronal function. In F.O. Schmitt and F.G. Worden (Eds.), **The neurosciences fourth study program**. Cambridge, MA: MIT Press, 555–571.

[24] R. Llinas and M. Sugimori (1979). *Progress in Brain Research*, **51**, 323–334.

[25] J. Orem, M. Schlag-Rey, and J. Schlag (1973). *Experimental Neurology*, **40**, 784–797.

[26] J.P. Rauschecker and W. Singer (1979). *Nature*, **280**, 58–60.

[27] J.P. Rauschecker and W. Singer (1981). *Journal of Physiology (London)*, **310**, 215–239.

[28] J. Schlag and M. Schlag-Rey (1983). *Experimental Brain Research*, in press.

[29] W. Singer (1976). *Brain Research*, **118**, 460–468.

[30] W. Singer (1977). *Physiological Reviews*, **57**, 386–420.

[31] W. Singer (1979). Central-core control of visual cortex functions. In F.O. Schmitt and F.G. Worden (Eds.), **The neurosciences fourth study program**. Cambridge, MA: MIT Press, 1093–1109.

[32] W. Singer (1982). *Experimental Brain Research*, **47**, 209–222.

[33] W. Singer and F. Tretter (1976). *Experimental Brain Research*, **26**, 171–184.

[34] W. Singer and J.P. Rauschecker (1982). *Experimental Brain Research*, **47**, 223–233.

[35] W. Singer, J.P. Rauschecker, and R. Werth (1977). *Brain Research*, **134**, 568–572.

[36] W. Singer, B. Freeman, and J.P. Rauschecker (1981). *Experimental Brain Research*, **41**, 199–215.

[37] W. Singer, F. Tretter, and U. Yinon (1982). *Journal of Physiology*, **324**, 221–237.

[38] J. Szentagothai (1975). *Brain Research*, **95**, 475–496.

[39] Y. Trotter, E. Gary-Bobo, and P. Buisseret (1981). *Developmental Brain Research*, **1**, 450–454.

[40] T.N. Wiesel and D.H. Hubel (1965). *Journal of Neurophysiology*, **28**, 1029–1040.

[41] T.N. Wiesel and D.H. Hubel (1965). *Journal of Neurophysiology*, **28**, 1060–1072.

CHAPTER 17

PROBING COGNITIVE PROCESSES THROUGH THE STRUCTURE OF EVENT-RELATED POTENTIALS: AN EXPERIMENTAL AND THEORETICAL ANALYSIS

by

Jean-Paul Banquet and Stephen Grossberg

Preface

This 1987 article reviews some of the psychophysiological experiments that have been accumulating evidence in support of ART predictions. It also discusses areas where further testing is needed. Such psychophysiological experiments collect data about event-related potentials, or ERPs, by recording from scalp electrodes while humans carry out carefully controlled cognitive tasks. ERP experiments provide information about how ensembles of brain cells work together during behavioral tasks. As such, they probe an intermediate level of brain organization that lies between the levels probed by behavioral experiments and neurophysiological experiments.

The article points out that the introduction of ART mechanisms in 1976–1978 anticipated the discovery of several ERPs whose dynamics have been shown in subsequent experiments to closely mirror formal ART properties. These are the processing negativity (PN) and early positive wave (P120). In addition, the theory rationalizes the existence of other important ERP waves, such as components of the N200, P300, and contingent negative variation (CNV). In particular, the PN behaves like the resonant matching of a learned top-down expectation. The P120 behaves like the suppression of activity due to the 2/3 Rule during a mismatch condition. A component of the N200 behaves like activation of the orienting subsystem. Components of the P300 behave like suppression, or updating, of a compressed STM representation by a reset wave, and activation of the somatic orienting response, respectively. The present article grew out of a successful experimental test by the Banquet lab in Paris of the ART prediction that a correlated sequence of P120–N200–P300 waves should be elicited during a mismatch condition. The article discusses these and related data.

The CNV event-related potential was suggested in Grossberg (1975, Section 7) to reflect incentive motivational feedback to cortical sensory and cognitive representations from the drive representations at which reinforcing and homeostatic signals are processed. A more recent discussion of CNV is provided in Chapter 20.

Reference

Grossberg, S. (1975). A neural model of attention, reinforcement, and discrimination learning. *International Review of Neurobiology*, **18**, 263–327.

Applied Optics
1987, **26**, 4931–4946
©1987 Optical Society of America

PROBING COGNITIVE PROCESSES THROUGH THE STRUCTURE OF EVENT-RELATED POTENTIALS DURING LEARNING: AN EXPERIMENTAL AND THEORETICAL ANALYSIS

Jean-Paul Banquet† and Stephen Grossberg‡

Abstract

Data reporting correlated changes, due to learning, in the amplitudes and chronometry of several event related potentials (ERPs) are compared with neural explanations and predictions of the *adaptive resonance theory*. The ERP components processing negativity (PN), early positive wave (P120), N200, and P300 covary with model processes of attentional priming and top-down expectancy learning, matching of bottom-up input patterns with learned top-down expectations, mismatch-mediated activation of the orienting subsystem, reset by the orienting subsystem of recognition codes in short term memory, and direct activation of recognition codes via a bottom-up adaptive filter. These model mechanisms enable a recognition code to be learned in a self-stabilizing fashion in response to an input environment of arbitrary complexity. Thus spatiotemporal correlations among several ERPs during learning provide important evidence in support of postulated neural mechanisms for self-stabilizing self-organization of cognitive recognition codes.

1. Introduction

This article describes a convergence between theoretical predictions and recent data concerning event-related potentials (ERP). The theory in question is *adaptive resonance theory* (ART), which was introduced in Grossberg (1976a, 1976b) and has since undergone extensive empirical and formal development. This theory arose through an analysis of neural mechanisms that are capable of self-organizing and self-stabilizing the learning of cognitive recognition codes in response to arbitrarily complex input environments. Such mechanisms can buffer their learning against inappropriate recoding by the "blooming buzzing confusion" of a continuous stream of irrelevant experiences, yet can also learn quickly from novel environments which are important to behavioral survival.

---

† Supported in part by INSERM.

‡ Supported in part by the Air Force Office of Scientific Research (AFOSR F49620-87-C-0018) and the National Science Foundation (NSF IRI-84-17756). We wish to thank Cynthia Suchta and Carol Yanakakis for their valuable assistance in the preparation of the manuscript.

This dynamic balance between memory stability and adaptive plasticity is controlled by the action of learned top-down expectations and pattern matching processes. An ideal experimental paradigm for testing such a theory is thus one in which expectations are learned, matching processes are parametrically manipulated, and the experimental measures are sensitive to state-dependent patterning of neuronal activities across large ensembles of cells. Banquet, Renault, and Lesèvre (1981); Banquet Baribeau-Braun, and Lesèvre (1984); Banquet, El Massioui, and Godet (1986); Banquet, Guenther, and Smith (1987); Johnson and Donchin (1982); and Squires, Wickens, Squires, and Donchin (1976) have collected such data from event related potential (ERP) experiments designed to determine the influence of probabilistic contextual information on processing strategies in a choice reaction time (RT) task.

The goal herein is to compare theoretical predictions of the adaptive resonance theory with data concerning the transformations which occur among four ERP components—processing negativity (PN), early positive wave (P120), N200, and P300—as learning proceeds (Table 1). The theory anticipated the discovery of two of these components—processing negativity (Näätänen, Gaillard, and Mäntysalo, 1978) or Nd (Hansen and Hillyard, 1980) and early positive wave (Desmedt et al., 1983; Goodin et al., 1978). The data of Banquet et al. (1981, 1984) and Banquet et al. (1986a, 1986b) provide detailed information which support the theoretically postulated correlations between these waves. These data were selected herein for particular comparison with ART mechanisms because they analyse how the waveforms of several ERP components covary across experimental trials during which recognition learning occurs. Such spatiotemporal correlations provide a much stronger test of theoretical predictions than do ERP data which describe only the existence of an individual ERP component or the behavior of an individual component during performance trials which do not include a learning manipulation. Relevant ERP data from a number of other laboratories will also be discussed.

A brief review is first given of the main operations postulated by the adaptive resonance theory. More detailed recent expositions are given in Grossberg (1984, 1987b) and in Carpenter and Grossberg (1987a, 1987b, 1987c, 1987d). The Carpenter and Grossberg articles describe, moreover, mathematical analyses and computer simulations which characterize the trial-by-trial course of category learning and recognition in a number of specific examples. The theoretical introduction in Sections 2–7 is followed by a summary of the meaning of the different ERPs in Section 8 and a presentation of the experimental data in Section 9. The remainder of the article compares theory with data and calls attention to theoretical predictions which have not yet been supported or disconfirmed by ERP experiments.

2. Attentional Subsystem and Orienting Subsystem

Within the adaptive resonance theory, interactions between two functionally complementary subsystems are often used to process familiar and unfamiliar events. An attentional subsystem learns ever more precise internal representations of familiar events. It also builds up the learned top-down expectations that help to stabilize the learned bottom-up recognition codes of familiar events. By itself, however, the attentional subsystem is unable simultaneously to maintain stable representations of familiar recognition codes and to create new recognition codes for unfamiliar patterns in response to certain input environments. An isolated attentional subsystem may

TABLE 1

ERP	ART Mechanism
PN	Read-out learned top-down expectation from processing level F_2 to processing level F_1 and amplification of total activity at F_1 in a match situation.
P120	Reduction of total activity at F_1 in a mismatch situation.
N200	Disinhibition of the orienting subsystem A in a mismatch situation.
P300	Reset of short term memory at F_2.

be either too rigid to create new categories for unfamiliar patterns, or so unstable that it can ceaselessly recode the categories for familiar patterns as it learns about unfamiliar patterns (Carpenter and Grossberg, 1987a, 1987c; Grossberg, 1976a). The latter difficulty is typical of many learning systems whose plasticity is not switched off through time.

The second subsystem is an orienting subsystem that overcomes the rigidity of the attentional subsystem when unfamiliar events occur and enables the attentional subsystem to learn from these novel experiences without destabilizing its established learning. Interactions between the attentional subsystem and the orienting subsystem are essential for expressing whether a pattern is familiar and well represented by an existing recognition code, or unfamiliar and in need of a new recognition code.

All input events start to be processed by the attentional subsystem. A familiar event can activate a recognition code which reads out a top-down template, or expectation, which is matched against the input within the attentional subsystem (Figure 1). A successful approximate match can deform, amplify, and sustain in short-term memory (STM) the activity pattern that was initially activated by the input within the attentional subsystem. Amplified, or resonant, STM activities throughout the attentional subsystem constitute the fully elaborated recognition event. They inhibit the orienting subsystem and engage the learning, or long-term memory (LTM), process. A familiar event can maintain or modify its prior learning as its recognition takes place.

An unfamiliar event also starts to be processed by the attentional subsystem. Such

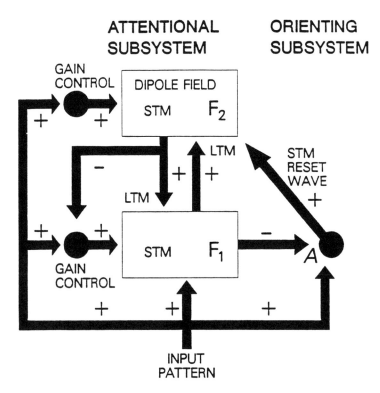

ATTENTIONAL SUBSYSTEM   **ORIENTING SUBSYSTEM**

Figure 1. Anatomy of the attentional-orienting system: Two successive stages, F_1 and F_2, of the attentional subsystem encode patterns of activation in short term memory (STM). Bottom-up and top-down pathways between F_1 and F_2 contain adaptive long term memory (LTM) traces which multiply the signals in these pathways. The remainder of the circuit modulates these STM and LTM processes. Modulation by gain control enables F_1 to distinguish between bottom-up input patterns and top-down priming, or template, patterns, as well as to match these bottom-up and top-down patterns. Gain control signals also enable F_2 to react supraliminally to signals from F_1 while an input pattern is on. The orienting subsystem generates a reset wave to F_2 when sufficiently large mismatches between bottom-up and top-down patterns occur at F_1. This reset wave selectively and enduringly inhibits active F_2 cells until the input is shut off. (Reprinted with permission from Carpenter and Grossberg, 1987c.)

an event may also activate a recognition code which thereupon reads-out a top-down template. If the unfamiliar event can approximately match this template, then it can be recognized as an exemplar of the recognition code on its first presentation. If the unfamiliar event is too different from familiar exemplars of the sampled code, then it cannot approximately match this template. A sufficiently large mismatch within the attentional subsystem activates the orienting subsystem. Activation of the orienting subsystem functionally expresses the novelty, or unexpectedness, of the unfamiliar event. The orienting subsystem, in turn, rapidly resets the active representation within the attentional subsystem as it simultaneously energizes an orienting response.

The reset of the attentional subsystem by the orienting subsystem leads to the selection of a new representation within the attentional subsystem. This new representation may cause yet another mismatch, hence another STM reset event and the selection of yet another representation. In this way, the orienting subsystem mediates a rapid search which continues until a representation is found that does not cause a large mismatch. Then the search ends, an STM resonance develops, and the LTM learning process can encode the active representation to which the search led. The system's recognition codes are hereby altered in either of two ways. If the search leads to an established code, then learning may refine the criteria, namely the LTM bottom-up code and top-down expectation, for accessing that code. If the search leads to uncommitted cells, then learning can add a new learned representation to the total recognition code.

3. Bottom-Up Adaptive Filtering and Contrast-Enhancement in Short Term Memory

The main mechanisms of the theory are now introduced in a qualitative way by considering the typical network reactions to a single input pattern I within a temporal stream of input patterns. Each input pattern may be the output pattern of a preprocessing stage. The input pattern I is received at the stage F_1 of the attentional subsystem. Pattern I is transformed into a pattern X of activation across the nodes of F_1 (Figure 2). The transformed pattern X represents a pattern in short term memory (STM). In F_1 each node whose activity is sufficiently large generates excitatory signals along pathways to target nodes at the next processing stage F_2. A pattern X of STM activities across F_1 hereby elicits a pattern S of output signals from F_1. When a signal from a node in F_1 is carried along a pathway to F_2, the signal is multiplied, or *gated*, by the pathway's long term memory (LTM) trace. The LTM gated signal (i.e., signal times LTM trace), not the signal alone, reaches the target node. Each target node sums up all of its LTM gated signals. In this way, pattern S generates a pattern T of LTM-gated and summed input signals to F_2 (Figure 3a). The transformation from S to T is called an *adaptive filter*.

The input pattern T to F_2 is quickly transformed by interactions among the nodes of F_2. These interactions contrast-enhance the input pattern T. The resulting pattern of activation across F_2 is a new pattern Y. The contrast-enhanced pattern Y, rather than the input pattern T, begins to be stored in STM by F_2.

Only those nodes of F_2 which maintain stored activity in STM can elicit new learning at contiguous LTM traces. Whereas all the LTM traces in the adaptive filter, and thus all learned past experiences of the network, are used to determine recognition via the transformation I→X→S→T→Y, only those LTM traces in the pathways $S \to T$ whose STM activities Y in F_2 survive the contrast-enhancement process can learn in response to the activity pattern X.

4. Top-Down Template Matching and Stabilization of Code Learning

We now summarize how top-down template matching can stabilize code learning. In order to do so, top-down template matching at F_1 must be able to prevent learning at bottom-up LTM traces whose contiguous F_2 nodes are only momentarily activated in STM. This ability depends upon the different rates at which STM activities and LTM traces can change. The STM transformation I→X→ S→T→Y takes place very quickly; that is, much more quickly than the rate at which the LTM traces in the

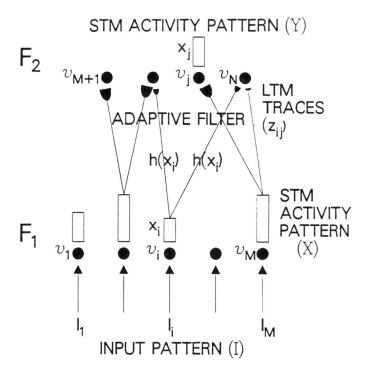

Figure 2. Stages of bottom-up activation: The input pattern I generates a pattern of STM activation $X = (x_1, x_2, \ldots, x_m)$ across the nodes v_i of F_1. Sufficiently active F_1 nodes emit bottom-up signals $h(x_i)$ to F_2. This signal pattern, which is denoted by S in Figure 3, is multiplied, or gated, by long term memory (LTM) traces z_{ij} within the $F_1 \to F_2$ pathways. The LTM-gated signals are summed before activating their target nodes in F_2. This LTM-gated and summed signal pattern, which is denoted by T in Figure 3, generates a pattern of activation $Y = (x_{M+1}, x_{M+2}, \ldots, x_N)$ across the nodes v_j of F_2. (Reprinted with permission from Carpenter and Grossberg, 1987c.)

adaptive filter S→T can change. As soon as the bottom-up STM transformation X→Y takes place, the STM activities Y in F_2 elicit a top-down excitatory signal pattern U back to F_1. Only sufficiently large STM activities in Y elicit signals in U along the feedback pathways $F_2 \to F_1$.

As in the bottom-up adaptive filter, the top-down signals U are also gated by LTM traces before the LTM-gated signals are summed at F_1 nodes. The pattern U of output signals from F_2 hereby generates a pattern V of LTM-gated and summed input signals to F_1. The transformation from U to V is thus also an adaptive filter. The pattern V is called a *top-down template*, or *learned expectation*.

Two sources of input now perturb F_1: the bottom-up input pattern I which gave rise to the original activity pattern X, and the top-down template pattern V that resulted from activating X. The activity pattern X* across F_1 that is induced by I and V taken together is typically different from the activity pattern X that was previously induced by I alone. In particular, F_1 acts to match V against I. The result of this matching process determines the future course of learning and recognition by the network.

The entire activation sequence

$$I \to X \to S \to T \to Y \to U \to V \to X^* \tag{1}$$

takes place very quickly relative to the rate with which the LTM traces in either the bottom-up adaptive filter S→T or the top-down adaptive filter U→V can change. Even though none of the LTM traces changes during such a short time, their prior learning strongly influences the STM patterns Y and X^* that evolve within the network. We now review how a match or mismatch of I and V at F_1 regulates the course of learning in response to the pattern I.

5. STM Reset and Search

Level F_1 can compute a match or mismatch between a bottom-up input pattern I and a top-down template pattern V, but it cannot compute which STM pattern Y across F_2 generated the template pattern V. Thus the outcome of matching at F_1 must have a *nonspecific* effect upon F_2 that can potentially influence all of the F_2 nodes, any one of which may have read-out V. The internal organization of F_2 must be the agent whereby this nonspecific event, which is called an *arousal burst* or a *reset wave*, selectively alters the stored STM activity pattern Y. A mismatch of I and V within F_1 generates a nonspecific arousal burst that inhibits the active populations in F_2 which read-out V. In this way, an erroneous STM representation Y at F_2 is quickly eliminated before any LTM traces can encode this error.

The attentional subsystem and the orienting subsystem work together to carry out these interactions. All learning takes place within the attentional subsystem. All matches and mismatches are computed within the attentional subsystem. The orienting subsystem is the source of the nonspecific arousal bursts that reset STM within level F_2 of the attentional subsystem. The outcome of matching within F_1 determines whether or not such an arousal burst will be generated by the orienting subsystem. Thus the orienting system mediates reset of F_2 due to mismatches within F_1.

Figure 3 depicts a typical interaction between the attentional subsystem and the orienting subsystem. In Figure 3a, an input pattern I instates an STM activity pattern X across F_1. The input pattern I also excites the orienting population A, but pattern X at F_1 inhibits A before it can generate an output signal.

Activity pattern X also generates an output pattern S which, via the bottom-up adaptive filter, instates an STM activity pattern Y across F_2. In Figure 3b, pattern Y reads a top-down template pattern V into F_1. Template V mismatches input I, thereby significantly inhibiting STM activity across F_1. The amount by which activity in X is attenuated to generate X^* depends upon how much of the input pattern I is encoded within the template pattern V.

When a mismatch causes a sufficient attenuation of STM activity across F_1, this activity no longer prevents the arousal source A from firing. Typically, if the total activity in X^* is less than a fixed fraction of the total activity in X, then A is activated. This fraction is called the *vigilance parameter* of the network (Capenter and Grossberg, 1987a, 1987b). The vigilance parameter can be altered by environmental feedback, notably punishment. Higher vigilance enables the network to make finer

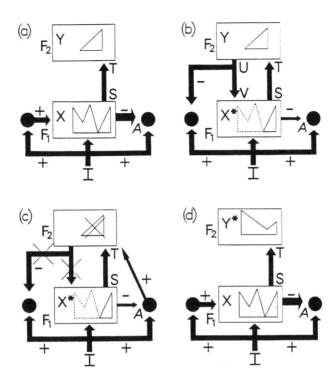

Figure 3. Search for a correct F_2 code: (a) The input pattern I generates the specific STM activity pattern X at F_1 as it nonspecifically activates A. Pattern X both inhibits A and generates the output signal pattern S. Signal pattern S is transformed into the input pattern T, which activates the STM pattern Y across F_2. (b) Pattern Y generates the top-down signal pattern U which is transformed into the template pattern V. If V mismatches I at F_1, then a new STM activity pattern X* is generated at F_1. The reduction in total STM activity which occurs when X is transformed into X* causes a decrease in the total inhibition from F_1 to A. (c) Then the input-driven activation of A can release a nonspecific arousal wave to F_2, which resets the STM pattern Y at F_2. (d) After Y is inhibited, its top-down template is eliminated, and X can be reinstated at F_1. Now X once again generates input pattern T to F_2, but since Y remains inhibited, T can activate a different STM pattern Y* at F_2. If the top-down template due to Y* also mismatches I at F_1, then the rapid search for an appropriate F_2 code continues. (Reprinted with permission from Carpenter and Grossberg, 1987c.)

discriminations between pattern exemplars and to learn more selective recognition codes. Lower vigilance has the opposite effect.

Net activation of the orienting subsystem A is due to reduction in the total inhibition from F_1 to A when the total activity X* decreases due to a pattern mismatch. Thus A is activated due to a disinhibitory process. Figure 3c depicts how disinhibition of A releases a nonspecific arousal burst to F_2. This arousal burst, in turn, selectively inhibits the most active populations in F_2. This inhibition is long-lasting. One physiological design for F_2 processing which has these reset properties is a *gated* *dipole field* (Grossberg, 1980, 1982a, 1984). A gated dipole field consists of opponent processing channels whose signals are multiplied, or gated, by habituating chemical transmitters. A nonspecific arousal burst induces selective and enduring inhibition within a gated dipole field.

In Figure 3c, inhibition of Y leads to inhibition of the top-down template V, and thereby terminates the mismatch between I and V. Input pattern I can thus reinstate the activity pattern X across F_1, which again generates the output pattern S from F_1 and the input pattern T to F_2. Due to the enduring, arousal-initiated, selective inhibition at F_2, the input pattern T can no longer activate the same pattern Y at F_2. A new pattern Y^* is thus generated at F_2 by I (Figure 3d). Despite the fact that some F_2 nodes may remain inhibited by the STM reset property, the new pattern Y^* may encode large STM activities. This is because level F_2 is designed so that its total suprathreshold activity remains approximately constant, or normalized, despite the fact that some of its nodes may remain inhibited by the STM reset mechanism. This property is related to the limited capacity of STM. A physiological process capable of achieving the STM normalization property, based upon recurrent on-center off-surround interactions among cells obeying membrane equations, is described in Grossberg (1980, 1982a, 1987b).

The new activity pattern Y^* reads-out a new top-down template pattern V^*. If a mismatch again occurs at F_1, the orienting subsystem is again engaged, thereby leading to another arousal-mediated reset of STM at F_2. In this way, a rapid series of STM matching and reset events may occur. Such an STM matching and reset series controls a search of LTM that sequentially engages the novelty-sensitive orienting subsystem. The mismatch-mediated search of LTM ends when an STM pattern across F_2 reads-out a top-down template which either matches I, to the degree of accuracy tolerated by the orienting subsystem due to the setting of the vigilance parameter, or which has not yet undergone any prior learning. In the former case, the bottom-up code and top-down template of the selected representation may be refined by learning any new information that is in the input exemplar I. In the latter case, a new recognition code is established as a bottom-up code and top-down template are learned for the first time by the selected rerpresentation in response to I.

The mismatch-mediated search of STM at F_2 may profitably be thought of as a sequential test of hypotheses. Each reset wave from A to F_2 inhibits an "incorrect hypothesis". The next input wave from F_1 to F_2 is evaluated conditional on the hypothesis that the previous interpretations by F_2 of the input at F_1 were incorrect. Thus an adaptive resonance theory architecture is a cognitive system capable of discovering, testing, and learning hypotheses in a stable fashion in response to input environments whose statistical properties may change unpredictably or may be arbitrarily complex.

6. Attentional Gain Control and Attentional Priming

The same top-down template matching process which stabilizes learning is also a mechanism of attentional priming. Consider, for example, a situation in which F_2 is activated by a level other than F_1 before F_1 is itself activated. In such a situation, F_2 can generate a top-down template V to F_1. The level F_1 is then primed, or ready, to receive a bottom-up input that may or may not match the active expectancy. Level F_1 can be primed to receive a bottom-up input without necessarily eliciting suprathreshold output signals in response to the priming expectancy. If this were not possible, then every priming event would lead to suprathreshold consequences. Such a property would prevent subliminal anticipation of a future event.

On the other hand, an input pattern I must be able to generate a suprathreshold activity pattern X even if no top-down expectancy is active across F_1 (Figure 3). How does F_1 know that it should generate a suprathreshold reaction to a bottom-up input pattern but not to a top-down input pattern? In both cases, an input pattern stimulates F_1 cells. Some auxiliary mechanism must exist to distinguish between bottom-up and top-down inputs. Such considerations led Grossberg (1986, 1987b) to distinguish this auxiliary mechanism, called *attentional gain control*, from *attentional priming* by the top-down template itself. Carpenter and Grossberg (1987a, 1987c) have developed this qualitative distinction into a quantitative computational mechanism, and Grossberg and Stone (1986a) have used the distinction to help explain data from word recognition experiments.

In particular, the attentional priming mechanism delivers *specific* template patterns to F_1. The attentional gain control mechanism has a *nonspecific* effect on the sensitivity with which F_1 responds to the template pattern, as well as to other patterns received by F_1. With the addition of attentional gain control, a qualitative explanation can be given of how F_1 can tell the difference between bottom-up and top-down signal patterns.

The need to dissociate attentional priming from attentional gain control can also be seen from the fact that top-down priming events do not lead necessarily to subliminal reactions at F_1. Under certain circumstances, top-down expectancies can lead to suprathreshold consequences. Internal conversations or images can, for example, be experienced at will. Thus there exists a difference between the read-out of a top-down template, which is a mechanism of attentional priming, and the translation of this operation into suprathreshold signals due to attentional gain control. An "act of will" can amplify attentional gain control signals to elicit a suprathreshold reaction at F_1 in response to an attentional priming pattern from F_2.

Figures 4a–4c depict a scheme whereby subliminal reactions to top-down signals, supraliminal reactions to bottom-up signals, and supraliminal reactions to matched bottom-up and top-down signals can be achieved. Figure 4d shows how competitive interactions between the attentional gain control mechanisms of different modalities can prevent F_1 from automatically generating a supraliminal reaction to bottom-up signals when attention shifts from that modality to another.

7. Matching via the 2/3 Rule

A rule for matching bottom-up input patterns with top-down templates, called the 2/3 Rule (Carpenter and Grossberg, 1987a, 1987c), follows naturally from the distinction between attentional gain control and attentional priming. It says that two out of three signal sources must activate an F_1 node in order for that node to generate suprathreshold output signals. In Figure 4a, for example, during bottom-up processing, a suprathreshold node in F_1 is one which receives a specific input from the input pattern I and a nonspecific attentional gain control signal. All other nodes in F_1 receive only the nonspecific gain control signal. Since these cells receive inputs from only one pathway, they do not fire.

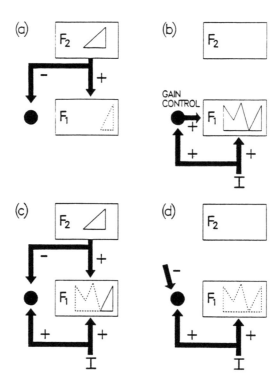

Figure 4. Matching by 2/3 Rule: (a) A top-down template from F_2 inhibits the attentional gain control source as it subliminally primes target F_1 cells. (b) A bottom-up input activates both the (nonspecific) attentional gain control channel and certain F_1 cells. Only F_1 cells that receive bottom-up inputs and gain control signals can become supraliminally active. (c) When a bottom-up input pattern and a top-down template are simultaneously active, only those F_1 cells that receive inputs from both sources can become supraliminally active, since the gain control source is inhibited. (d) Intermodal competition can shut off the attentional gain control source and thereby prevent a bottom-up input from supraliminally activating F_1 when attention is directed to a different modality.

In Figure 4b, during top-down processing, or priming, some nodes in F_1 receive a template signal from F_2, whereas other nodes receive no signal whatsoever. All the nodes of F_1 receive inputs from at most one of their three possible input sources. Hence no cells in F_1 are supraliminally activated by a top-down template.

During simultaneous bottom-up and top-down signalling, the attentional gain control signal is inhibited by the top-down channel (Figure 4c). Despite this fact, some nodes of F_1 may receive sufficiently large inputs from both the bottom-up and the top-down signal patterns to generate suprathreshold outputs. Other nodes may receive inputs from the top-down template pattern or the bottom-up input pattern, but not both. These nodes receive signals from only one of their possible sources, hence do not fire. Cells which receive no inputs do not fire either. Thus only cells that are conjointly activated by the bottom-up input and the top-down template can fire when a top-down template is active. The 2/3 Rule clarifies the apparent paradox that the addition of top-down excitatory inputs to F_1 can lead to an overall decrease, or collapse, in F_1's STM activity (Figures 3a and 3b). Carpenter and Grossberg (1987c) have shown that learning may become unstable if the 2/3 Rule is violated, but is absolutely stable when the 2/3 Rule is reinstated.

8. ERP Components

The understanding of the experimental results and of the discussion requires a brief presentation of the main ERP components. The term "wave" or "deflection" refers to the different possible morphologies of an ERP. The term "component" is attributed to an independent source of variability or a generator of the ERP waveform.

An early component (100 msec) labelled Nd (negative displacement) was first demonstrated by Hillyard et al. (1973) in a dichotic listening experiment with short (100–800 msec) random interstimulus intervals (ISI). The attended stimuli elicited an enhanced negativity at about 100 msec from stimulus onset (N1), compared to the N1 elicited by an identical but unattended stimulus to the other ear. The authors interpreted this effect as a selective increase of the activity in the N1 generators and related it to the "stimulus set" mechanism of early stimulus filtering on the basis of physical features, which was proposed by Broadbent (1970).

With a longer and constant ISI (800 msec), Näätänen et al. (1978) observed a selective attention effect going beyond the time window of the N1 component and extending for several hundred milliseconds. These authors proposed that this negative shift expresses a different ERP component of endogenous origin (the N1 being exogenous) which they labelled the processing negativity (PN). PN can be taken as an early sign of selective attention in a dichotic listening paradigm. Our paradigm, however, is not a situation of dichotic listening; two identical stimuli in the two ears have to be attended. Nevertheless, a selection has to be made between what is a stimulus and what is not, and also between target and non-target. Since the experimental situation and the method of subtraction by which our negativity has been revealed differs from the previous ones, the first endogenous negative component will be called "Early Negativity" (EN).

An early centroparietal positivity was first described as a P165 by Goodin et al. (1978) and as a P100 by Desmedt et al. (1983) in response to auditory and somesthesic stimuli, respectively. In both cases, the Early Positivity (EP) was elicited by attending rare relevant target stimuli. A P165–N200–P300 complex was observed in attended sequences of deviant tones as compared to standard tones (Näätänen and Picton, 1986). The early positivity was interpreted either as an early manifestation of decision processes related to the later N200–P300 potentials (Goodin et al., 1978) or as an expression of the process of sorting out and identifying input signals against target templates (Desmedt et al., 1983).

The N200 wave of the ERPs has been one of the less easy to interpret, largely because it reflects the existence of multiple components. We will mention here only the two most widely accepted components of the N200 deflection. The N2a was named Mismatch Negativity (MMN) by Näätänen et al. (1978) because of its occurrence in response to stimuli physically deviant from those in the immediate past, be they attended or unattended. This is in contrast to the PN which can be elicited only by attended stimuli. MMN is sensitive to dynamic changes in the stimuli presented, such as pitch or intensity, and to the magnitude of the change. In an attention condition, it precedes or overlaps the P165–N200–P300 complex, which is more centrally located. MMN seems therefore to represent an automatic process which is not influenced by selective attention. It could reflect short-duration memory processes such as sensory registers or preattentive storage taking place in the sensory cortex (Näätänen and Picton, 1986).

N2b (Renault and Lesevre, 1978; Näätänen et al., 1982) is a negative component which precedes P300. The topography of N2b is distributed across modalities. It is elicited by temporally unexpected or rare stimuli. Its occurrence depends not only on the degree of stimulus change, but also on the orientation of focal attention to the stimulus source. N2b could also reflect transient activation of the subcortical centers releasing the orienting reflex (Näätänen and Gaillard, 1983).

P300 has been one of the most explored ERP deflections since its discovery by Sutton et al. (1965). First explained in terms of different psychological constructs (task relevance, expectancy, equivocation) or theories (information theory, signal detection theory), it was later explored for its specific functional role, as a scalp manifestation of information transactions in the brain (Donchin, 1979). P300 soon also appeared to be a non-unitary phenomenon. Squires et al. (1975), examining P300s in response to occasional shifts in ongoing trains of tones under conditions of attention and non-attention, found components of different latency and topography during the non-attended (P3a) and the attended (P3b) conditions. Courchesne et al. (1975, 1978) further investigated various ERP components in situations of "novelty".

The P3a wave, ever since its discovery, (Squires et al., 1975), appeared to reflect events distinct from the P3b complex. In some experiments, a P3a was elicited by an unpredictable shift in an ongoing repetitive series of auditory stimuli even though the sounds were task irrelevant or not attended (Ritter et al., 1968; Roth, 1973; Roth et al., 1973). Conversely, in dichotic listening tasks (Näätänen et al., 1978) or in distraction situations with slightly deviant auditory stimuli (Näätänen et al., 1982, 1983), no P3a was elicited. Only a N200 mismatch negativity could be recorded. These apparently contradictory results may be explained by the fact that at present there is no reliable measure of the degree of subjects' awareness of the stimulus shift in the ignore condition. It could well turn out that the dichotic listening paradigm is a better guarantee of a true unattended situation than a simple ignore instruction. In any case, the N200-P3a complex has been interpreted by most authors as a reflection of a mismatch detector (Squires et al., 1975; Snyder and Hillyard, 1976). Courchesne (1978) has shown that the P300 amplitude response to novel events shifts from a frontal to a parietal maximum with repeated presentations. More recently, it has been shown that this component is less sensitive to the prior probability of events than P3b (Banquet et al., 1981, 1984). Munson et al. (1984) have also described a similar component, P300E, which does not react to prior probability. Therefore, the individuality of P3a from P3b seems clear.

The frontocentral P3a thus occurs, not only for attended task-relevant events, but also for unattended, task-irrelevant intermittent stimuli, its amplitude being related to the degree of physical contrast with the background and to immediately preceding probability rather than prior probability *per se* (Banquet et al., 1984). The similarity of these eliciting conditions with those of N200 led several authors to regard N2b and P3a as aspects of the same process and, in particular, to relate it to the orienting reaction.

On the contrary, P3b is a later component elicited by attended task-relevant target stimuli. Subjective probability, stimulus meaning, and information transmission are the three dimensions used in the model of Johnson (1986) to explain variations in P3b amplitude. Since P3b covaries with so many different variables, it has also been suggested that it represents a general subroutine invoked in different cognitive operations, such as updating of the context or of models of the environment (Donchin, 1979; Donchin et al., 1978). Grossberg (1975, 1978, 1984) postulated the existence of two parallel output pathways from the orienting subsystem A whose effects on their target networks may be compared with data about the P3a and P3b, as in Section 11. One branch, from A to the attentional subsystem (Section 2), causes reset of STM. The other branch of A activates processes associated with the orienting response, including processes which gate the release of orienting movements. Recent relation of P3b amplitude to the quality of subsequent recall seems to confirm the association of P3b to short-term memory processes (Karis et al., 1984; Johnson, 1986).

9. Experimental Paradigm

Hypotheses. The original purpose of the experimental research was to determine the influence of probabilistic contextual information (Donchin and Heffley, 1978; Donchin and Isreal, 1980) on processing strategies in a choice RT task (Banquet et al., 1981, 1984; Banquet et al., 1986a, 1986b). This influence of contextual probability processing on single trial processing, for events delivered in Bernoulli sequences, was suggested by previous results (Banquet and Lesèvre, 1980). These results showed how chronometry and amplitude evolution of P300 during practice were correlated with performance. Subjects were divided into high performance and low performance groups.

In the high performance group, the P300 peak occurred after the reaction time (RT) and increased in amplitude with practice. Conversely, in the low performance group, P300 peaked before RT, and its amplitude decreased with practice. Such variable timing of RT and P300 was first demonstrated by Ritter et al. (1979). A possible interpretation of these data was that more thorough processing and/or use of the probability information (indexed by P300 amplitude) was carried out by the better performing group.

Experimental Procedure. One of the simplest ways to manipulate the degree of contextual processing is a passive learning procedure in an odd-ball paradigm with a choice RT task. In an odd-ball paradigm, the subject receives Bernoulli series of two types of stimuli of complementary probability. One of the stimuli is frequent or "standard"; the other is rare and usually serves as the target. The subject has to perform a task such as counting target stimuli or releasing a motor response in response to each target stimulus.

In this experiment, Bernoulli series of high-pitched (2000 Hz) and low-pitched (500 Hz) tones of equal intensity and duration (10 msec) were delivered through headphones at fixed ISI (1500 msec). Target probability was also manipulated: Five consecutive runs of unequally probable (.2/.8 or .8/.2) stimuli were followed by two runs of equally probable (.5/.5) stimuli and then by five runs of the unequal complementary probability (.8/.2 or .2/.8). Each unequal probability run ended after a total of 15 rare stimuli had been delivered. One session consisted of these three consecutive probability conditions.

Subjects performed a Go/No Go task with a lever-press response to a single type of sound in both high and low probability conditions. They were not asked to monitor the probability changes. A second session was a replication of the first session one week later. Since perceptual discrimination and motor response tasks were easy to perform and identical in the different probability conditions, it was assumed that RT and ERP differences over consecutive runs and sessions would reflect learning.

Learning effects could be detected within this paradigm in two different ways. A *within-condition* analysis was performed of the unequal probability data for each session. RTs and ERPs averaged separately during the first two runs and the last two runs of each unequal probability condition (.2/.8 and .8/.2) were compared. A *between-session* analysis compared the grand averages across the five runs of the unequal probability conditions.

The shift from unequal to equal probabilities after a block of five runs served two functions. It created a mismatch condition in which prior probability learning in one condition became unappropriate due to the unsignalled change in probability. In addition, the block of equal probability runs was chosen sufficiently long to damp previous learning effects due to unequal probability, and thereby to prepare the subject for the reversed unequal probability condition.

In summary, three experimental factors were explored by the paradigm: 1) a prior probability factor due to the different probability conditions; 2) a practice factor resulting from the five-run blocks and two sessions for each condition; 3) a mismatch factor by the unwarned shift in probability.

Data Recording and Analysis. EEG was recorded from six electrodes referred to linked ears, spaced at intervals of 10 percent of the nasion-inion distance, starting from F_z and including C_z and P_z. Supraorbital and suborbital electrodes around the right eye monitored ocular potentials. RTs and ERPs were averaged separately for the different experimental situations. An analysis of these averaged waveforms was described by Banquet, Renault, and Lesèvre (1981). In the present article ERPs were measured both by subtracting ERPs to the frequent stimuli from ERPs to the infrequent stimuli (Simson *et al.*, 1977; Ritter *et al.*, 1982) and by subtracting the auditory evoked potentials obtained in a passive situation with purely random stimuli (no task) from ERPs to both rare and frequent stimuli in a task situation (Banquet *et al.*, 1981). This last procedure was proposed by Näätänen (1982) as a better way to compute processing negativity (PN). The main pupose of both subtraction techniques is to neutralize the overlapping of N100 and P200 exogenous evoked potentials on the early endogenous ERPs. The results were tested by a two way repeated measures analysis of variance. Only results at $p < .01$ were considered significant (Banquet, Guenther, and Smith, 1987b). Factorial analysis (Donchin and Heffley, 1978; Curry *et al.*, 1983; Rösler and Manzey, 1981) was also performed on these ERP data.

In a Go/No Go paradigm, a motor response is made only to the target stimulus. However, in order to selectively perform this response, both target and non-target stimuli are relevant and thus must be actively attended and processed. This is confirmed by the approximately equal amplitudes of the ERP components to targets and non-targets of equal probability, thereby showing an absence of task effect (Banquet *et al.*, 1981).

The absence of task effect on the amplitude of the ERPs in this experiment (Go and No Go ERP profiles are similar) indicates: (1) The pre-eminence of probability over other factors in determining the amplitude of N200 and P300; (2) The efficacy of the random "washout" session (.5/.5) between the two learning sequences of complementary probability (.8/.2 and .2/.8), even if it cannot be excluded that the learning in the second sequence of runs was faster than in the first one. The absence of task effect enables the comparison of No Go ERPs with RTs in the same probability condition, since Go and No Go ERP amplitudes are similar. These non-target data provide ERP measures of cognitive processing that are relatively uncontaminated by motor components and are therefore the primary focus of the experimental analysis.

The analysis of the first experimental session was broken up into four cases, two of which generate almost identical ERP profiles: (1) Frequent stimuli in the early runs (Fe); (2) Rare stimuli in the early runs (Re); (3) Frequent stimuli in the late runs (Fl); (4) Rare stimuli in the late runs (Rl). According to the law of the stimulus probability effect, faster reaction times were expected to frequent target stimuli than to rare target stimuli. In view of previous ERP results, larger ERP components were expected to rare stimuli than to frequent stimuli.

10. Experimental Results: ERP Profiles

The results will be reported in greater detail elsewhere (Banquet et al., 1987b). There was good agreement between behavioral (RT) and ERP data. At both levels, the four cases combined to form three patterns or profiles of response (Figure 5).

(1.) and (2.) Cases Fe and Re: During the early runs of the first session, whether with low or high probability non-targets (Figure 5, dotted lines), there was practically no difference between the ERP profiles in response to rare or frequent stimuli. The only significant amplitude difference occurred for the P300 component at P_z, which is called P3b. In addition, RT to frequent and rare stimuli were not significantly different.

(3.) Case Fl: In contrast, during the late runs of the first session, a high probability non-target caused a widespread flattening of both negative and positive components with only one alternation between negativity and then positivity (full-line square in Figure 5). Simultaneously, RT decreased dramatically.

(4.) Case Rl: Greater amplitude peaks appeared at three points of the time axes: early positivity P120, N200 mismatch, and P300. In parallel, RT increased as compared to cases Fe and Re. These trends were even more striking when the data are replotted as in Figure 6, where the peaks of the ERP components are positioned at their mean latency.

A comparison of ERP amplitudes in cases (3.) and (4.) with cases (1.) and (2.) in light of the functional significance of the ERP components is consistent with the following conclusions. A high-frequency event leads to learning of an expectancy which tends to be matched during condition Fl and tends to be mismatched during condition Rl. This possibility is supported by a component-by-component parametric analysis of the chronometry and amplitude of the ERP profiles as a function of probability and learning. We now summarize the main features of this analysis.

A comparison of the square and circle curves in Figure 5 showed that the P3b was the first component to monitor the prior probability of the stimuli according to the classical law of the inverse relation between P3b amplitude and stimulus probabil-

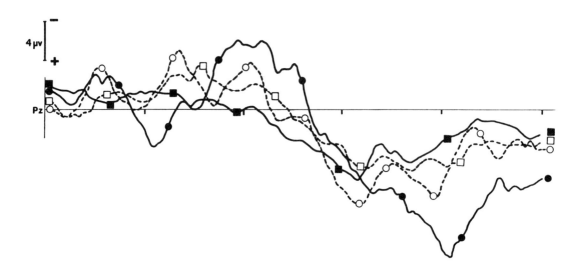

Figure 5. Grand average chronograms of the ERPs recorded at P_z, obtained after subtraction of the auditory evoked potentials for each subject in a passive situation (no task) from the No Go condition of the task situation. The ERP amplitudes (in microvolts) are displayed as a function of time (a unit scale: 100 msec), stimulus probability (squares: high probability; circles: low probability), and runs (dotted lines: first two runs; full lines: last two runs). Cases Fe and Re (dotted lines with squares and circles, respectively) and cases Fl and Rl (full lines with squares and circles, respectively) are superimposed.

ity. This result confirmed a multitude of experiments on the P300 probability effect (Donchin *et al.*, 1978; Duncan-Johnson and Donchin, 1977; Tueting *et al.*, 1971; Pritchard, 1981 for a review). In particular, the inverse relation held both for cases Fe and Re, which correspond to the first practice runs of the unequal probability condition (dotted curves of Figure 5) where little expectancy or random expectancy obtain. These relationships become more obvious when replotted as in Figure 7a. The inverse relation persisted during the two runs of the equal probability condition which create a condition of erroneous expectancy, as illustrated in Figure 7b.

These results show that P3b monitors quite closely the actual probability of the stimuli and is relatively independent of prior expectancies. Independence is supported by the observation that the relationship of P3b amplitude to prior probability (Ritter *et al.*, 1968) or probability shifts (Johnson and Donchin, 1982) has been shown to adapt after only a few trials. In the present experiment, the P3b relationship to probability adapts during the first runs of practice and continues even after an erroneous expectancy is generated by a shift from the unequal probability condition to the equal probability condition. Yet, such independence of P3b from expectancy is only relative because the inverse relationship between P3b amplitude and probability is amplified by practice—that is, after the build-up of an expectancy—as can be seen

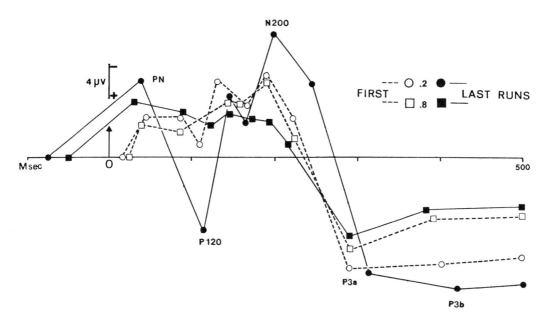

Figure 6. Mean amplitudes of the ERP components over all subjects displayed with the same code as in Figure 5. The peaks were measured on interpolated maps at their maximum amplitude value, in different locations. Therefore the diagram does not represent a unique electrode site. Cases He, Le, Hl, and Ll are superimposed as in the previous figure. The main advantage of this representation is to suppress the smoothing of the peaks due to inter-subject latency jitter for the different components.

by the comparison of the dotted and solid lines in Figures 5 and 6.

By contrast with the P3b component, the N200 was not an early index of stimulus probability. Indeed, during the first practice runs (cases Fe and Re), there was no amplitude difference in the N200 responses to rare and frequent stimuli at times where P3b amplitude was already well differentiated (Figure 7a). Nonetheless, the N200 amplitude difference for high probability and low probability non-targets became as large, and in the same direction, as the P3b difference by the last runs of the unequal probability conditions (cases Fl and Rl). Furthermore, N200 amplitude adapted slowly to stimulus probabilities, whether during the first runs of the unequal probability conditions or after the shift from unequal probabilities to equal probabilities. This lag of N200 suggests that this component may reflect a learning process, which develops slowly compared to the rate of P3b adaptation to stimulus probabilities.

At an earlier stage of processing, a positivity (P120 msec) abruptly interrupts the early negativity (EN), but only in case Rl (Figures 5 and 6). This result suggests that the P120 component reflects the mismatch of a learned expectancy with a rare (low probability) non-target. A similar type of component has already been described by Desmedt *et al.* (1983) and Goodin *et al.* (1978) under analogous conditions.

Finally, a negative potential arises about 100 msec prior to stimulus delivery in cases Fl and Rl, but only 50 msec after stimulus delivery in cases Fe and Re (Figure

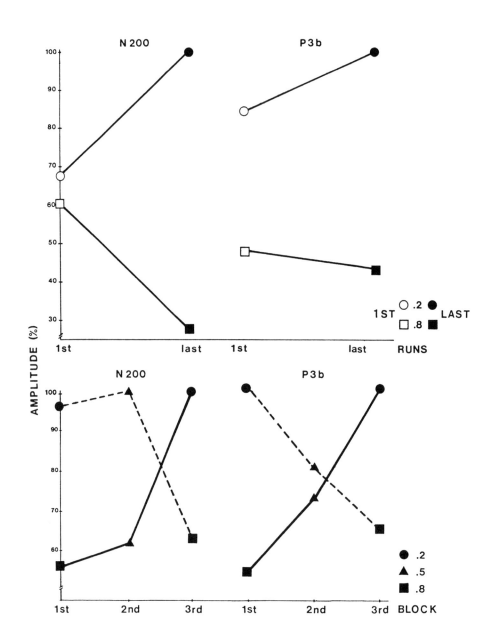

Figure 7. Relative amplitudes of the N200 and P3b components are plotted as a function of stimulus probability and practice. (a) 1st runs, no practice; last runs, end of the session. (b) Relative amplitude of the N200 and P3b components are plotted as a function of stimulus probability and the relative ordering of the probability condition blocks. The transition from unequal to equal probability is accurately reflected by the P3b amplitude. The response of N200 to equal probability continues to reflect the previous unequal probability condition.

6). We suggest that the learning of the expectancy which leads to the P120 in a mismatch situation (case Rl) is reflected by the shift in onset of this negative component with respect to the stimulus. Thus relationships among changes in components across conditions Fe, Re, Fl, and Rl provide additional constraints upon the possible interpretations of each component.

11. Comparison of ERP Profiles with Adaptive Resonance Theory Mechanisms

Adaptive resonance theory models how neural information is processed in a cyclic fashion in both the bottom-up and the top-down directions. Top-down expectancy read-out and consequent priming of an expected event can be induced in at least two ways: by instruction, as in a dichotic listening paradigm wherein the subject is asked to selectively pay attention to only one channel, and in this channel to a single target stimulus; or if there is no pre-selected channel and all stimuli must be attended, by practice of Bernoulli series in unequal probability conditions wherein the subject learns to expect the most frequent stimulus. Both cases result in a priming of the expected stimulus. In the latter condition, prior to any practice there is no clearly defined expectancy about the forthcoming inputs. Thus top-down expectancy read-out can at first be triggered only by the initiation of bottom-up filtering and coding. As practice proceeds, however, top-down expectancies become progressively better learned, and hence stronger and more precise. In addition, internal representations which control these top-down expectancies may perseverate in short-term memory if they are frequently reactivated by their target stimuli. Thus, as learning proceeds, the balance between bottom-up and top-down processing may shift, such that top-down processes may become more dominant in the information processing chain. Then specific expectancies about the nature of the future events may be read-out without prior bottom-up processing. Subliminal priming of F_1 by such a top-down template generates a faster supraliminal activation to a matched bottom-up input, but delays the response to a mismatched event which attenuates F_1 activation and drives the search for a better hypothesis unless the gain of F_2 is set too high to prevent easy reset. A more detailed correspondence between observed ERP components and adaptive resonance theory mechanisms will now be articulated.

We first consider the negativity which arises during cases Fl and Rl. In these cases, the negativity arises prior to the delivery of the stimulus (Figure 6). Right after the stimulus delivery, the electrical activity profiles diverge according to whether an expectancy is either matched or mismatched. In the Fl case of *expectancy match*, the electrical profile exhibits only one alternation between negative and then positive activity. We suggest that the enduring post-stimulus negativity includes Processing Negativity, PN (Näätänen *et al.*, 1978) or Nd (Hillyard *et al.*, 1973), which is typically recorded in a dichotic listening paradigm. Indeed, the plateau of activity occurs just before 100 msec when there is no P120 to interrupt it, and two peaks, prior to and after 100 msec, can be located when a P120 is generated. This early negativity (EN) therefore occurs in the time-window of the PN. The PN component has properties of the match process between the subliminal template and the input code. In particular, the negativity is greater in the Fl case. According to the theory, this match process induces a supraliminal reverberant STM activity between the F_1 and F_2 levels. The subliminal priming of F_1 by a top-down template before a stimulus occurs enables F_1

to respond more rapidly to input patterns that match the primed template (Grossberg and Stone, 1986a). This property of F_1 matching is sufficient to explain the ~ 50 msec difference in RT between case Fl and case Rl in the target condition. It can also account for part of the smaller size of the early negative components in the no expectancy (Fe and Re) situation.

Although processing negativity of maximal amplitude is elicited by relevant target stimuli, recent results (Alho *et al.*, 1986) also indicate that the more irrelevant stimuli resemble the relevant ones, the larger the PN they elicit, which is consistent with the 2/3 Rule (Section 7). Also consistent with the 2/3 Rule is the striking reversal in the amplitude relations between the components EN and N200 across the experimental conditions Fl and Rl. After 150 msec, Rl shows a greater negativity than Fl. Indeed, 150–250 msec is the time window of the N200, which arises in a mismatch condition.

The long duration early negativity is followed by a minimal amplitude N200–P300 (Figures 5 and 6). This is also expected from the theory. The rapid emergence of vigorous supraliminal activation at F_1 during expectancy-match prevents activation of the orienting subsystem A (Section 5) and thereby prevents STM reset of F_2. Because the N200 is interpreted to reflect the arousal burst, there is only a small N200 in this match situation. Since the P300 is interpreted to reflect the reset of STM at F_2, there is only a small P300 in the match situation.

The alternative case Rl is initiated by occurrence of a rare stimulus which leads to an expectancy mismatch. Here the prestimulus negativity and its poststimulus continuation are abruptly interrupted by an early (less than 50 msec onset) polarity reversal which peaks at about 120 msec. A possible interpretation for this pattern of positive activity (the P120) is the collapse of activity at F_1 due to input-template mismatch (Section 5). Such an interpretation would provide strong support for the theory, because it would confirm that a mismatch between two input patterns, each of which is generated by excitatory signals, can cause less activation than the bottom-up input pattern alone due to the 2/3 Rule.

This interpretation must, however, be tested further before it is accepted without reservation. The positive polarity of P120 does not necessarily imply an inhibitory process. The scalp polarity of the evoked potentials depends not only on the nature of the underlying process (activation or inhibition), but also on the depth of the concerned neuronal populations. An alternative explanation is consistent with factorial analysis results which locate P120 and P300 on the same (unrotated) factor and therefore indicate a correlation between the two components: It may be that P120 conveys a similar function to that of P300. This issue is complicated further by the theory's suggestion that a causal link exists between P120, N200, and P300 in the situation of expectancy mismatch, as the following discussion indicates.

If the interpretation of P120 as a measure of mismatch at F_1 is confirmed, then the next property provides even stronger support for the theory because it mirrors the theory's postulated causal link between mismatch within the attentional subsystem at F_1 and activation of the orienting subsystem at A. In the theory, mismatch causes a collapse of F_1 activation (interpret: P120), which thereby disinhibits the activation of A (interpret: N200). Thus within the situation of expectancy mismatch, one expects to find a maximal N200. Moreover, one expects to find that the two electrical indices P120 and N200 should covary in amplitude across experimental trials even though they are of opposite polarity. This relation is verified in Figure 5. Therefore, the experimental results provide striking support for the hypothesis of a mismatch-mediated burst of arousal. Further experimental tests of this correlation in other experimental paradigms which include a learning manipulation and a mismatch condition are much to be desired.

The N200 has a major modality-specific component N2a or MMN (Näätänen *et al.*, 1978, 1982) whose location depends on the nature of the stimulus (Simpson *et al.*, 1977). A nonspecific component, N2b, peaking in the fronto-central region is added when attention is directed to the stimulus (Renault and Lesèvre, 1979; Näätänen *et al.*, 1982). Both are largely overlapping in time and space. Further experimentation is needed to determine which one of the two represents the arousal burst. In order for the orienting subsystem to work well, each F_1–F_2 processing channel must be able to calibrate its own internal mismatches by evaluating the collapse in STM activity at F_1 against the total excitatory input to its orienting subsystem A (Figure 3b). After this comparison is carried out at A to determine whether an arousal burst should be released, A can, in principle, broadcast this arousal burst to a single F_2 level or to several F_2 levels in different modalities. This is possible because the STM reset signal is *nonspecific*; it need not encode detailed featural properties of any code or modality. The actual distribution field of each orienting subsystem A to its target modalities also requires further experimental study.

It remains to consider how the data compare to the theoretical concept that activation of A causes a reset of STM at F_2. We compare activation of A with data about N200 and reset of STM at F_2 with data about P300. In the model, such an STM reset can initiate a rapid series of mismatch-mediated STM reset events, which constitute a search for an appropriate F_2 code (Figure 3). This hypothesis testing scheme of the theory utilizes both the attentional and the orienting subsystems disposed in parallel, even though the search which they generate operates sequentially in time. It is well known since Sternberg's seminal experiments that each single hypothesis testing cycle is very fast, not exceeding 40 msec (Sternberg, 1966). Each rapid reset of the F_2 level causes an enduring inhibition of the previously most active F_2 cells in order to allow for the sequential testing of new hypotheses, as well as to avoid error perseveration. It is hereby suggested that, in a task requiring iterative hypothesis testing, the search process could be reflected by a rapid succession of N200 negative components which may merge with an incremental build up of P300 positivity resulting from enduring reset-contingent inhibition.

In support of this conception, it is found in many complex tasks that the reaction time (RT) may occur hundreds of milliseconds after the positivity onset. Thus several search cycles may be needed before a code capable of meeting a behavioral criterion is accessed. The masking of individual search cycles by an enduring and cumulative inhibition may partially explain this delay. Kramer, Schneider, Fisk, and Donchin (1986) have reported further data which are consistent with this analysis. They have shown in a varied mapping paradigm that a larger N200 merges with a late frontal negativity when the memory set size is increased from 1 to 4 items. It was concluded that the prolonged negativity may reflect the need for additional controlled processing of the stimuli in the mismatch situation. In the present experiments, one expects a brief search since the memory set has only two elements.

The final event to occur, the maximal *late positive complex* of P300, has two components: P3a and P3b. Adaptive resonance theory links two functionally different types of processes to the P300 complex: STM reset and orienting processes. Because the theory admits multiple coding levels in addition to the simplified two-level scheme summarized herein (Cohen and Grossberg, 1986; Grossberg, 1978, 1982a; Grossberg and Stone, 1986a), one can envisage within the theory STM reset processes going on at different levels of perceptual and cognitive organization. In addition, the STM reset wave elicited by a nonspecific arousal burst from an orienting generator A may be distributed either within a sensory modality or across a wide range of intermodality processing levels. Thus one cannot infer from differences in P300 topography alone qualitative differences in underlying mechanism or function. Finally, Grossberg (1975, 1978, 1984) pointed out that an orienting generator A may give rise to two parallel output branches. One branch, such as the one posited from A to F_2, causes reset of STM. The other branch activates processes associated with the orienting response, including gain control signals which gate the release of orienting movements. The co-ordinated parallel action of these two branches can activate rapid movements oriented towards an unexpected source of information as they simultaneously prepare STM to efficiently process the unexpected data. Because the interplay of these orienting and STM reset factors across all relevant processing levels may *in vivo* be complex, we content ourselves herein with qualitative comparisons between theory and data and summarize some hypotheses which are in need of further experimental tests.

Donchin *et al.* (1984) have related P3a to a brain equivalent of the somatic orienting response, which is also related to attention shifts. Our primary attention will be focussed upon the theoretical conception of how STM reset at F_2 (and possibly higher levels) is triggered by an arousal burst from A that is contingent upon a pattern mismatch at F_1.

The major effect of the arousal burst is to inhibit the most active F_2 cells. Limited capacity STM resources are hereby freed for reallocation to less active F_2 representations. Due to this inhibition of the most active sources of top-down template signals, the mismatch at F_1 is eliminated (Figure 3c). The F_1 reaction to the bottom-up input pattern is hereby unmasked and begins once again to activate the $F_1 \to F_2$ adaptive filter (Figure 3d).

As this is happening, a complementary effect of the arousal burst begins to take effect. This effect is the STM enhancement (dishabituation, unblocking) of F_2 representations which previously were only weakly activated. This unblocking effect may be intuitively understood as follows. The previously attenuated STM representations may have been encoding important information which was erroneously unattended, thereby leading to activation of the wrong hypothesis and read-out of the wrong expectation. Unblocking rectifies this error by endowing these STM representations with large activation levels. Unblocking begins to occur as the unmasked inputs from F_1 begin to influence F_2. The combination of unblocking at F_2 and inputs from F_1 generates a new pattern of activity across F_2; that is, a new code, or hypothesis, is instated in STM at F_2. Thus reset of STM includes two types of operations, those which are modulated by learned top-down expectancies and those which are directly induced by bottom-up processing of the input. These functional properties are consistent with the amplitude response of the P3a and P3b components (Figure 7a), which shows a significant increase in response to rare events across learning trials (top-down effect), as well as baseline differences between responses to frequent and rare events before learning develops (bottom-up effect).

As noted above, the inhibitory effect of the arousal burst at F_2 is enduring, so that when F_1 input again activates F_2, perseveration of the old erroneous hypothesis is prevented. This enduring inhibition persists and accumulates when a series of mismatch-mediated arousal bursts develops in a task that triggers several hypothesis testing cycles. Such hypothesis testing cycles may generate a sustained F_2 inhibition, or positivity, superimposed on more momentary activations, or negativities, thereby generating longer late positive complexes. A different but possibly related situation is created by increasing the difficulty of a discrimination task. In this case Ruchkin, Munson, and Sutton (1982), Ruchkin and Sutton (1983), Ruchkin, Sutton, Kietzman, and Silver (1980), and Ruchkin, Sutton, and Stega (1980) have shown an increased amplitude of the slow wave component. This last component is made of simultaneous positive and negative activity, each predominant at different locations. In summary, the STM reset properties within a cortical F_2 field, including its activity-dependent sustained inhibition mechanism, suggest a physiological model of how properties of P3b may reflect contextual updating.

According to recent ERP results relating P300 and memory, during certain strategies of memorization the amplitude of the P300 component at the moment of the stimulus delivery is related to the strength of the consecutive LTM trace (Karis *et al.*, 1984). Such a result does not, however, imply that P300 is a direct reflection of the long term memorization process. Grossberg (1982b, 1984) has, for example, noted that an unexpected event can be stored in STM with amplified activity by inheriting limited capacity STM resources from the F_2 representations which it has just reset. These larger STM values can generate larger learning signals. Larger learning signals support faster encoding into LTM. Thus the relationship between P300 amplitude and subsequent LTM strength may be mediated by properties of the STM reset process which is hypothesized to be a major cause of the P300 components.

Adaptive resonance theory has suggested several detailed neural network models which contain candidates for P3a and/or P3b generators. The theory admits several processes that are candidates for P3a generators. Further experiments are needed to decide between them. One possibility is that a P300 (possibly a P3a) occurs when the orienting subsystem activates orienting responses, as it inhibits the midbrain reinforcement circuits which motivate consummatory motor commands (Grossberg, 1975, 1978). A second possibility is that a P300 is generated when STM reset at F_2 indirectly causes an STM reset at midbrain reinforcement circuits (Grossberg, 1982b, 1984). Such a secondary reset can disconfirm the motivational bias that had been set by the erroneous cognitive representation. This type of STM reset was predicted to involve circuits which include the hippocampus (Grossberg, 1975, 1980). In partial support of this prediction, P300 activity has been recorded in the hippocampus (Halgren *et al.*, 1980; Squires *et al.*, 1983; Wood *et al.*, 1984) or indirectly located in this structure (Okada *et al.*, 1983). In order to further clarify this situation, learning experiments capable of dissociating cortical and hippocampal generators have been suggested (Grossberg, 1982b, 1987b).

It is also worth emphasizing why, even in the absence of an experimentally trained expectancy, P300 amplitude reflects in "real time" the difference in stimulus probability and N200 does not. One explanation of this derives from the nature of the direct activation of higher processing levels by lower processing levels in the theory.

Bottom-up STM encoding in the theory is sensitive to the frequency and temporal ordering of individual events (Cohen and Grossberg, 1986; Grossberg, 1982a, 1987c; Grossberg and Stone, 1986a, 1986b). Therefore, even if a top-down template does not yet differentiate individual events, STM reset due to direct bottom-up activation can reflect the prior probability of events. In particular, less reset of a frequent event may be expected due to the stronger STM perseveration of that event as a result of its many previous occurrences.

Although bottom-up activation of certain processing levels is sensitive to event frequency and even to temporal order, both bottom-up code learning and top-down template learning can influence the form of ERPs through time as events become more familiar. In particular, results reported elsewhere (Banquet *et al.*, 1984) demonstrate the influence of long term memorization on the P3b amplitude response. The amplitude of this component increases after long term (1 week interval) learning, reflecting the learning of new top-down templates. Simultaneously, the N200 amplitudes to rare and frequent stimuli become less different (Banquet *et al.*, 1987b). These results illustrate that a classification of ERPs in terms of their different topographies alone provides an insufficient measure of their functional independence, since direct bottom-up activation of STM and top-down read-out from LTM into STM can converge upon the same cell targets and can vary in different ways through time as a function of the experimental task.

The learning-dependent N200 changes discovered by Banquet *et al* (1984) and Banquet *et al.* (1985) can be explained using the following concepts. The top-down template of the frequent stimulus may be learned relatively rapidly, whereas the template corresponding to the rare stimulus may be learned at a slower rate. When the frequent stimulus template alone is active, sharp matches or mismatches would be expected with the frequent and rare events, respectively. As the template of the rare stimulus is progressively but more slowly learned, the total top-down template becomes a composite of frequent and rare event templates. In this later phase of learning, pure matches or mismatches are replaced by partial matches or mismatches, due to the presence of both template components. This analysis is consistent with the existence of two learning phases, and with the fact that after long term learning, the N200 to rare and frequent stimuli becomes less different in amplitude. In addition, the hypothesized difference in the rate of template learning in response to frequent and rare stimuli is supported by the behavioral results which show no significant difference in RT at the beginning of the first session, while a large difference occurs by the end of the first session. This difference results from a decreased RT to frequent events *and* an increased RT to rare events which is consistent with theoretical properties of matching both frequent and rare events against a learned template for the frequent event. Thus, at least during the first session, most of the learning occurs in response to the frequent event.

12. Conclusion: The Relationship of Learning to ERPs

The concepts and mechanisms of adaptive resonance theory which are most important for the analysis of ERPs—learning of top-down templates, matching of bottom-up input patterns with learned top-down templates, frequency-sensitive bottom-up encoding of events in STM, activation of the orienting subsystem, and reset of event codes in STM—were all derived from an analysis of how a cognitive system can learn recognition codes in a self-stabilizing and globally self-consistent fashion. This theoretical framework has, by now, been useful for analysing and predicting data in a number of fields, such as visual perception (Grossberg, 1976b, 1987a, 1987c; Grossberg and Mingolla, 1985), classical and instrumental conditioning (Cohen and Grossberg, 1987b; Grossberg, 1982, 1987b; Grossberg and Levine, 1987; Grossberg and Schmajuk, 1987), speech processing (Cohen and Grossberg, 1986, 1987a; Grossberg, 1982a, 1986, 1987c; Grossberg and Stone, 1986b), word recognition and recall (Grossberg, 1982a, 1986, 1987c; Grossberg and Stone, 1986a), decision making under risk (Grossberg and Gutowski, 1987), and self-organization of cognitive recognition codes (Carpenter and Grossberg, 1987a, 1987b, 1987c, 1987d; Grossberg, 1982a, 1987b), and has suggested neural principles and mechanisms for interpreting and sharpening many concepts within the ERP literature. In particular, the relationship of adaptive resonance theory concepts to the concepts of Donchin about P300 are reviewed in Grossberg (1984; reprinted in Grossberg, 1987b) and to those of Näätänen about PN and N200 are reviewed in Carpenter and Grossberg (1987b).

Despite the critical role of learning constraints on the design of cognitive mechanisms, much of the ERP literature has utilized performance paradigms to analyse individual ERPs. It seems to us that an informative way to understand the role of learning constraints upon the cognitive designs probed by ERPs is to investigate paradigms in which correlated changes in amplitudes and chrometric relationships among several ERP components as a function of learning are the units of the experimental and theoretical analysis. The present article contributes to this enterprise.

Due to the fact that only a small number of ERP experiments have explicitly tested how multiple ERPs covary as a function of learning manipulations, many more experimental studies of such correlations will be needed before ART mechanisms are unequivocably supported in many behavioral situations. It is also to be expected that such data will provide useful guidelines for further theoretical development and refinement. On the other hand, the facts that known ART mechanisms have predicted both the existence of key ERPs and their main correlations in available data provide a hopeful beginning for such a systematic analysis, as well as a serious challenge to alternative cognitive theories in which these ERP data have no natural interpretation.

REFERENCES

Alho, K., Sams, M., Paavilainen, P., and Näätänen, R. (1986). Small pitch separation and the selective-attention effect on the ERP. *Psychophysiology*, **23**, 189–197.

Banquet, J.-P., Baribeau-Braun, J., and Lesèvre, N. (1984). Learning of "single trial" and "contextual" information processing in an odd-ball paradigm. In R. Karrer, J. Cohen, and P. Tueting (Eds.), **Brain and information: Event related potentials**. New York: New York Academy of Sciences, pp. 162–165.

Banquet, J.-P., El Massioui, F., and Godet, J.L. (1986). ERP–RT chronometry and learning in normal and depressed subjects. In W.C. McCallum, R. Zappoli, and F. Denoth (Eds.), **Cerebral psychophysiology: Studies in event-related potentials**. Amsterdam: Elsevier.

Banquet, J.-P. and Guenther, W. (1985). Intuitive statistics and related memory models. In Cesta-Afcet (Ed.), **Cognitiva 85, Volume 1**. Paris, pp. 49–56.

Banquet, J.-P., Guenther, W., and Smith, M. (1987a). Probability processing in depressed patients. Supplement to *Electroencephalography and Clinical Neurophysiology*, in press.

Banquet, J.-P., Guenther, W., and Smith, M. (1987b). Probability mapping, task performance and learning: An ERP model. Submitted for publication.

Banquet, J.-P. and Lesèvre, N. (1980). Event-related potentials in altered states of consciousness. In H.H. Kornhuber and L. Deecke (Eds.), **Motivation, motor, and sensory processes of the brain: Progress in brain research**. Amsterdam: Elsevier, pp. 447–453.

Banquet, J.-P., Renault, B., and Lesèvre, N. (1981). Effect of task and stimulus probability on evoked potentials. *Biological Psychology*, **13**, 203–214.

Broadbent, D.E. (1970). Stimulus set and response set: Two kinds of selective attention. In D. Mostofsky (Ed.), **Attention: Contemporary theory and analysis**. New York: Appleton-Century-Crofts, pp. 51–60.

Carpenter, G.A. and Grossberg, S. (1987a). Neural dynamics of category learning and recognition: Attention, memory consolidation, and amnesia. In J. Davis, R. Newburgh, and E. Wegman (Eds.), **Brain structure, learning, and memory**. AAAS Symposium Series, in press.

Carpenter, G.A. and Grossberg, S. (1987b). Neural dynamics of category learning and recognition: Structural invariants, reinforcement, and evoked potentials. In M.L. Commons, S.M. Kosslyn, and R.J. Herrnstein (Eds.), **Pattern recognition and concepts in animals, people, and machines**. Hillsdale, NJ: Erlbaum.

Carpenter, G.A. and Grossberg, S. (1987c). A massively parallel architecture for a self-organizing neural pattern recognition machine. *Computer Vision, Graphics, and Image Processing*, **37**, 54–115.

Carpenter, G.A. and Grossberg, S. (1987d). ART 2: Stable self-organization of pattern recognition codes for analog input patterns. *Applied Optics*, **26**, 4919–4930.

Cohen, M.A. and Grossberg, S. (1986). Neural dynamics of speech and language coding: Developmental programs, perceptual grouping, and competition for short term memory. *Human Neurobiology*, **5**, 1–22.

Cohen, M.A. and Grossberg, S. (1987a). Masking fields: A massively parallel neural architecture for discovering, learning, and recognizing multiple groupings of patterned data. *Applied Optics*, **26**, 1866–1891.

Cohen, M.A. and Grossberg, S. (1987b). Unitized recognition codes for parts and wholes: The unique cue in configural discriminations. In M.L. Commons, S.M. Kosslyn, and R.J. Herrnstein (Eds.), **Pattern recognition and concepts in animals, people, and machines**. Hillsdale, NJ: Erlbaum.

Courchesne, E. (1978). Changes in P3 waves with event repetition: Long-term effects on scalp distribution and amplitude. *Electroencephalography and Clinical Neurophysiology*, **45**, 754–766.

Courchesne, E., Hillyard, S.A., and Galambos, R. (1975). Stimulus novelty, task relevance, and the visual evoked potential in man. *Electroencephalography and Clinical Neurophysiology*, **39**, 131–143.

Curry, S.H., Cooper, R., McCallum, W.C., Popock, P.V., Papakostopoulos, D., Skidmore, S., and Newton, P. (1983). The principal components of auditory target detection. In A.W.K. Gaillard and W. Ritter (Eds.), **Tutorials in event-related potential research: Endogenous components**. Amsterdam: North-Holland, pp. 79–117.

Desmedt, J.E., Tran Huy, N., and Bourguet, M. (1983). The cognitive P40, N60, and P100 components of somato-sensory evoked potentials and the earliest electrical signs of sensory processing in man. *Electroencephalography and Clinical Neurophysiology*, **56**, 272–282.

Donald, M.W. (1983). Neural selectivity in auditory attention: Sketch of a theory. In A.W.K. Gaillard and W. Ritter (Eds.), **Tutorials in event related potential research: Endogenous components**. Amsterdam: North-Holland, pp. 37–77.

Donchin, E. (1981). Surprise!...Surprise? *Psychophysiology*, **18**, 493–513.

Donchin, E. and Heffley, E. (1978). Multivariate analysis of event-related potential data: A tutorial review. In D.A. Otto (Ed.), **Multidisciplinary perspectives in event-related potential research**. Washington, DC: USGPO, pp. 552–572.

Donchin, E., Heffley, E., Hillyard, S., Loveless, N., Maltzman, I., Öhman, A., Rösler, F., Ruchkin, D., and Siddle, D. (1984). The orienting reflex and P300. In R. Karrer, J. Cohen, and P. Tueting (Eds.), **Brain and information: Event-related potentials**. New York: New York Academy of Sciences.

Donchin, E. and Isreal, J.B. (1980). Event related brain potentials and psychological theory. In H.H. Kornhuber and L. Deecke (Eds.), **Motivation, motor, and sensory processes of the brain: Progress in brain research**. Amsterdam: Elsevier, pp. 697–715.

Donchin, E., Ritter, W., and McCallum, W.C. (1978). Cognitive psychophysiology: The endogenous components of the ERP. In E. Callaway, P. Tueting, and S. Koslov (Eds.), **Brain event-related potentials in man**. New York: Academic Press, pp. 349–441.

Duncan-Johnson, C.C. and Donchin, E. (1977). On quantifying surprise: The variation in event-related potentials with subjective probability. *Psychophysiology*, **14**, 456–467.

Gaillard, A.W.K. (1976). Effects of warning-signal modality on the Contingent Negative Variation (CNV). *Biological Psychology*, **4**, 139–154.

Goodin, D.S., Squires, K.C., Henderson, B.H., and Starr, A. (1978). An early event-related cortical potential. *Psychophysiology*, **15**, 360–365.

Grossberg, S. (1975). A neural model of attention, reinforcement, and discrimination learning. *International Review of Neurobiology*, **18**, 263–327.

Grossberg, S. (1976a). Adaptive pattern classification and universal recoding, I: Parallel development and coding of neural feature detectors. *Biological Cybernetics*, **23**, 121–134.

Grossberg, S. (1976b). Adaptive pattern classification and universal recoding, II: Feedback, expectation, olfaction, and illusions. *Biological Cybernetics*, **23**, 187–202.

Grossberg, S. (1978). A theory of human memory: Self-organization and performance of sensory-motor codes, maps, and plans. In R. Rosen and F. Snell (Eds.), **Progress in theoretical biology**, Vol. 5. New York: Academic Press, pp. 233–374.

Grossberg, S. (1980). How does a brain build a cognitive code? *Psychological Review*, **87**, 1–51.

Grossberg, S. (1981). Adaptive resonance in development, perception, and cognition. In S. Grossberg (Ed.), **Mathematical psychology and psychophysiology**. Providence, RI: American Mathematical Society.

Grossberg, S. (1982a). **Studies of mind and brain: Neural principles of learning, perception, development, cognition, and motor control.** Dordrecht, Boston, London: Reidel Press.

Grossberg, S. (1982b). Processing of expected and unexpected events during conditioning and attention: A psychophysiological theory. *Psychological Review*, **89**, 529–572.

Grossberg, S. (1984). Some psychophysiological and pharmacological correlates of a developmental, cognitive, and motivational theory. In R. Karrer, J. Cohen, and P. Tueting (Eds.), **Brain and information: Event related potentials.** New York: New York Academy of Sciences, pp. 58–151.

Grossberg, S. (1986). The adaptive self-organization of serial order in behavior: Speech, language, and motor control. In E.C. Schwab and H.C. Nusbaum (Eds.), **Pattern recognition by humans and machines, Volume 1: Speech perception.** New York: Academic Press, pp. 187–294.

Grossberg, S. (1987a). Cortical dynamics of three-dimensional form, color, and brightness perception: I. Monocular theory. *Perception and Psychophysics*, **41**, 87–116.

Grossberg, S. (Ed.) (1987b). **The adaptive brain, I: Cognition, learning, reinforcement, and rhythm.** Amsterdam: Elsevier/North-Holland.

Grossberg, S. (Ed.) (1987c). **The adaptive brain, II: Vision, speech, language, and motor control.** Amsterdam: Elsevier/North Holland.

Grossberg, S. and Gutowski, W. (1987). Neural dynamics of decision making under risk: Affective balance and cognitive-emotional interactions. *Psychological*

Review, **94**, 300–318.

Grossberg, S. and Levine, D.S. (1987). Neural dynamics of attentionally modulated Pavlovian conditioning: Blocking, inter-stimulus interval, and secondary reinforcement. *Applied Optics*, **26**, 5015–5030.

Grossberg, S. and Marshall, J. (1987). A computational model of how cortical complex cells multiplex information about position, contrast, orientation, spatial frequency, and disparity. In M. Caudill and C. Butler (Eds.), **Proceedings of the IEEE international conference on neural networks, IV**, 203–214.

Grossberg, S. and Mingolla, E. (1985). Neural dynamics of perceptual grouping: Textures, boundaries, and emergent segmentations. *Perception and Psychophysics*, **38**, 141–171.

Grossberg, S. and Schmajuk, N. (1987). Neural dynamics of attentionally-modulated Pavlovian conditioning: Conditioned reinforcement, inhibition, and opponent processing. *Psychobiology*, **15**, 195–240.

Grossberg, S. and Stone, G.O. (1986a). Neural dynamics of word recognition and recall: Attentional priming, learning, and resonance. *Psychological Review*, **93**, 46–74.

Grossberg, S., and Stone, G.O. (1986b). Neural dynamics of attention switching and temporal order information in short term memory. *Memory and Cognition*, **14**, 451–468.

Halgren, E., Squires, N.K., Wilson, C.L., Rohrbaugh, J.W., Babb, T.L., and Crandall, P.H. (1980). Endogenous potentials generated in the human hippocampal formation and amygdala by infrequent events. *Science*, **210**, 803–805.

Hansen, J.C. and Hillyard, S.A. (1980). Endogenous brain potentials associated with selective auditory attention. *Electroencephalography and Clinical Neurophysiology*, **49**, 277–290.

Hillyard, S.A., Hink, R.F., Schwent, V.L., and Picton, T.W. (1973). Electrical signs of selective attention in the human brain. *Science*, **182**, 177–179.

Johnson, R. Jr. (1986). Triarchic model of P300 amplitude. *Psychophysiology*, **23**, 367–384.

Johnson, R. Jr. and Donchin, E. (1982). Sequential expectancies and decision making in a changing environment: An electrophysiological approach. *Psychophysiology*, **19**, 183–199.

Karis, D., Fabiani, M., and Donchin, E. (1984). P300 and memory: Individual differences in the von Restorff effect. *Cognitive Psychology*, **16**, 177-216.

Kok, A. (1978). The effect of warning stimulus novelty on the P300 and components of the contingent negative variation. *Biological Psychology*, **6**, 219–233.

Kramer, A., Schneider, W., Fisk, A., and Donchin, E. (1986). The effects of practice and task structure on components of the event-related brain potential. *Psychophysiology*, **23**, 33–47.

Luria, A.R. (1973). **The working brain**. New York: Basic Books.

McCallum, W.C. and Unott, J. (1981). Late slow components of auditory evoked potentials: Their cognitive significance and interaction. *Electroencephalography and Clinical Neurophysiology*, **51**, 123–137.

Munson, R., Ruchkin, D.S., Ritter, W., Sutton, S., and Squires, N.K. (1984). The relation of P3b to prior events and future behavior. *Biological Psychology*, **19**, 1–29.

Näätänen, R. (1982). Processing negativity: An evoked-potential reflection of selective attention. *Psychological Bulletin*, **92**, 605–640.

Näätänen, R. and Gaillard, A.W. (1983). The orienting reflex and the N2 deflection of the ERPs. In A.W.K. Gaillard and W. Ritter (Eds.), **Tutorials in event-related potential research: Endogenous components**. Amsterdam: North-Holland, pp. 119–142.

Näätänen, R., Gaillard, A.W., and Mäntysalo, S. (1978). Early selective attention effect on evoked potential reinterpreted. *Acta Psychologica*, **42**, 313–329.

Näätänen, R. and Michie, P.T. (1979). Early selective attention effects on the evoked potential: A critical review and reinterpretation. *Biological Psychology*, **8**, 81–136.

Näätänen, R. and Picton, T.W. (1986). N2 and automatic versus controlled processes. In W.C. McCallum, R. Zappoli, and F. Denoth (Eds.), **Cerebral psychophysiology: Studies in event-related potentials**. Amsterdam: Elsevier.

Näätänen, R., Simpson, M. and Loveless, N.E. (1982). Stimulus deviance and evoked potentials. *Biological Psychiatry*, **14**, 53–98.

Okada, Y.C., Kaufman, L., and Williamson, S.J. (1983). The hippocampal formation as a source of the slow endogenous potentials. *Electroencephalography and Clinical Neurophysiology*, **55**, 417–426.

Pribram, K.H. and McGuiness, D. (1975). Arousal, activation, and effort in the control of attention. *Psychological Review*, **82**, 116–149.

Pritchard, W.S. (1981). Psychophysiology of P300. *Psychological Bulletin*, **89**, 506–540.

Renault, B. and Lesèvre, N. (1978). Topographical study of the emitted potential obtained after the omission of an expected visual stimulus. In D. Otto (Ed.), **Multidisciplinary perspectives in event-related brain potential research**. Washington, DC: U.S. Government Printing Office, pp. 202–208.

Ritter, W., Simson, R., Herbert, G., Vaughan, H.G. Jr., and Friedman, D. (1979). A brain event related to making a sensory discrimination. *Science*, **203**, 1358–1361.

Ritter, W., Simson, R., and Vaughan, H.G. Jr. (1983). Event-related potential correlates of two stages of information processing in physical and semantic discrimination tasks. *Psychophysiology*, **20**, 168–179.

Ritter, W., Simson, R., Vaughan, H.G. Jr., and Macht, M. (1982). Manipulation of event-related potentials manifestation of information processing stages. *Science*, **218**, 909–911.

Ritter, W., Vaughan, H.G. Jr., and Costa, L.D. (1968). Orienting and habituation to auditory stimuli: A study of short term changes in average evoked responses. *Electroencephalography and Clinical Neurophysiology*, **25**, 550–556.

Rohrbaugh, J. and Gaillard, A.W.K. (1983). Sensory and motor aspects of contingent negative variations. In A.W.K. Gaillard and W. Ritter (Eds.), **Tutorials in** event-related potential research: Endogenous components. Amsterdam: North-Holland.

Rösler, F. and Manzey, D. (1981). Principal components and varimax-rotated components in event-related potentials research: Some remarks on their interpretation. *Biological Psychology*, **13**, 3–26.

Roth, W.T. (1973). Auditory evoked responses to unpredictable stimuli. *Psychophysiology*, **10**, 125–138.

Roth, W.T. and Kopell, B.S. (1973). P300—An orienting reaction in the human auditory evoked response. *Perceptual and Motor Skills*, **36**, 219–225.

Ruchkin, D.S., Munson, R., and Sutton, S. (1982). P300 and slow wave in a message consisting of two events. *Psychophysiology*, **19**, 629–642.

Ruchkin, D.S. and Sutton, S. (1983). Positive slow wave and P300: Association and dissociation. In A.W.K. Gaillard and W. Ritter (Eds.), **Tutorials in event-related potential research: Endogenous components**. Amsterdam: North-Holland, pp. 233–250.

Ruchkin, D.S, Sutton, S., Kietzman, M.L., and Silver, K. (1980). Slow wave and P300 in signal detection. *Electroencephalography and Clinical Neurophysiology*, **50**, 35–47.

Ruchkin, D.S., Sutton, S., and Stega, M. (1980). Emitted P300 and slow wave event-related potentials in guessing and detection tasks. *Electroencephalography and Clinical Neurophysiology*, **49**, 1–14.

Sams, M., Alho, K., and Näätänen, R. (1984). Short-term habituation and dishabituation of the mismatch negativity of the ERP. *Psychophysiology*, **21**, 434–441.

Simson, R., Vaughan, H.G., and Ritter, W. (1977). Scalp topography of potentials in auditory and visual discrimination tasks. *Electroencephalography and Clinical Neurophysiology*, **42**, 528–535.

Snyder, E. and Hillyard, S.A. (1976). Long-latency evoked potentials to irrelevant, deviant stimuli. *Behavioral Biology*, **16**, 319–331.

Squires, N.K., Halgren, E., Wilson, C., and Crandall, P. (1983). Human endogenous limbic potentials: Cross-modality and depth-durface comparison in epileptic subjects. In A.W.K. Gaillard and W. Ritter (Eds.), **Tutorials in event-related potential research: Endogenous components**. Amsterdam: North-Holland, pp. 217–232.

Squires, N.K., Squires, K.C., and Hillyard, S.A. (1976). Two varieties of long-latency positive waves evoked by unpredictable auditory stimuli in man. *Electroencephalography and Clinical Neurophysiology*, **38**, 387–407.

Squires, K.C., Wickens, C., Squires, N.K., and Donchin, E. (1975). The effect of stimulus sequence on the waveform of the cortical event-related potentials. *Science*, **193**, 1142–1146.

Sternberg, S. (1966). High speed scanning in human memory. *Science*, **153**, 652–654.

Sutton, S., Braren, M., Zubin, J., and John, E.R. (1965). Evoked potential correlates of uncertainty. *Science*, **150**, 1187–1188.

Theios, F., Smith, P., Haviland, S.E., Traupmann, J., and Moy, M.C. (1973). Memory scanning in a serial self-terminating process. *Journal of Experimental Psychology*, **97**, 323–336.

Timsit-Berthier, M. (1984). Variation contingente négative et composantes endogènes du potentiel evoqué. *Rev. EEG Neurophysiol.*, **14**, 77–96.

Tueting, P., Sutton, S., and Zubin, J. (1971). Quantitative evoked potential correlates of the probability of events. *Psychophysiology*, **7**, 385–394.

Wood, M., McCarthy, G., Squires, N.K., Vaughan, H.G., Woods, D.L., and McCallum, W.C. (1984). Anatomical and physiological substrates of event-related potentials. In R. Karrer, J. Cohen, and P. Tueting (Eds.), **Brain and information: Event-related potentials**. New York: New York Academy of Sciences.

UNITIZATION, AUTOMATICITY, TEMPORAL ORDER, AND WORD RECOGNITION

by

Stephen Grossberg

Preface

This 1984 article critiqued several core ideas of cognitive science and suggested how they could be overcome by ART principles and mechanisms. The time seemed ripe for such a critique because recent cognitive data had challenged traditional cognitive concepts while providing encouraging support for several ART predictions. All of these data concerned aspects of the learning and recognition of temporally ordered sequences of events.

One set of ART predictions grew out of a solution of the Temporal Chunking Problem. This is a fundamental problem for an autonomous agent that is learning about temporally ordered events in an unsupervised way. It asks how new recognition codes for novel sequences of familiar events can be learned despite competition from the recognition codes of the already familiar events. A solution to this problem involves introducing new processing levels that code abstract properties of an input stream.

One level is a *working memory* that encodes temporal order information of item sequences. "Items" are compressed representations of feature patterns that are processed together during a unit time interval. Such a working memory is designed to obey an LTM Invariance Principle. This principle says that new events are encoded in STM by working memory in a way that leaves invariant the LTM codes of event sequences that are already coded in working memory. In other words, temporal STM is designed to preserve stable learning and memory of temporal LTM. Remarkably, this stability principle implies that the temporal order encoded in STM is not always veridical, and its breakdown mirrors similar breakdowns that occur during free recall experiments on human subjects.

A second level is a multiple-scale chunking, unitization, or code compression network, called a *masking field* (see Chapters 2 and 19), whose self-similar design enables it to solve the Temporal Chunking Problem. The abstract chunks coded by a masking field may, in the case of language, encode phonemic fragments, syllables, letters, words, or other units that can survive the network's context-sensitive competition.

These levels and their dynamics suggested that the functional units of language are more abstract than had previously been realized. An analysis of these units was used to clarify why such models as the McClelland-Rumelhart interactive activation model, the Shiffrin-Schneider controlled and automatic human information processing model, and the Atkinson-Shiffrin serial buffer model were not able to explain various basic data. At bottom, the design principles of these models are inconsistent with basic principles of behavioral self-organization.

All of the results in the article apply competitive learning and ART design principles to the realm of temporal processing. That is why the key networks, such as masking fields, are relevant to a broad range of temporal processing competences, including speech perception, word recognition, and adaptive sensory-motor planning and control.

Cognition and Brain Theory
1984, **7**, 263–283
©1984 Erlbaum Associates, Inc.

UNITIZATION, AUTOMATICITY, TEMPORAL ORDER, AND WORD RECOGNITION

Stephen Grossberg†

Abstract

Samuel, van Santen, and Johnston (1982, 1983) reported a word length effect in a word superiority paradigm. A word length effect was predicted in Grossberg (1978a). This article describes the main concepts about the unitization process that led to this prediction. The article also discusses recent data and models of word and letter perception, controlled and automatic information processing, temporal order information in short term memory and in long term memory, spreading activation, and limited capacity due to inhibitory interactions in terms of the unitization process. It is shown that several popular models have been based upon an inadequate definition of the functional units of cognitive processing, and of the principles subserving the unitization process. The dichotomy between automatic processing and limited capacity processing is, for example, based on a fundamental misunderstanding of the unitization process. These problems have caused internal paradoxes and predictive limitations of the models, which have prevented them from being unified into a single processing theory. A "self-organization critique" is applied to some recent models to illustrate their internal difficulties. It is also shown how principles of self-organization can be used to generate a theory wherein these data domains and their empirical models can begin to be unified.

1. The Word Length Effect

The recent experiments of Samuel, van Santen, and Johnston (1982, 1983) discovered a word length effect in word superiority studies. That is, a letter is better recognized as it is embedded in longer words of lengths from 1 to 4. A word length effect was predicted in Grossberg (1978a, p. 329; reprinted in 1982a, p. 595). This prediction arose from an analysis of how unitization of new internal representations takes place in real time. The same design principle is needed to unitize new internal representations in response to sound streams, visual letter arrays, or sequences of motor commands. Thus although the Samuel *et al.* experiments seem to study a narrowly defined information processing issue, my theory suggests that this type of experiment probes a general principle governing the learning of serial order in behavior, and thus should be generally known.

† Supported in part by the Office of Naval Research (ONR N00014-83-K0037). The author wishes to thank Cynthia Suchta for her valuable assistance in the preparation of the manuscript.

2. Unitization and Psychological Progress

Samuel, van Santen, and Johnston also wrote that "lexical ... theories ... have difficulty explaining the length effect in a principled manner" (1982, p. 104) and that "lexical theories had not previously included mechanisms that were explicitly length dependent" (1983, p. 322). These assertions are true of lexical theories that are concerned entirely with information processing issues, such as letter and word recognition. By contrast, the lexical theory that led to the word length prediction was derived from an analysis of how behaving individuals adapt in real-tine to environments whose properties can unpredictably change. Such an analysis leads to design principles and mechanisms that cannot easily be inferred from processing data. Other lexical processing theories did not predict the word length effect because they overlooked fundamental constraints upon the design of behavioral mechanisms.

These design constraints concern the evolutionary process—variously called chunking, unitization, automation, or coding—whereby behavioral fragments are grouped into new control units that become the fragments of still higher behavioral units in a continuing process of hierarchical organization and command synthesis. It is perhaps surprising that lexical theories have been so unconcerned with unitization, since pseudowords can acquire many of the recognition properties of words after just five or six presentations (Salasoo, Shiffrin, and Feustel, 1984).

In the remainder of this article, I will outline the main concepts needed to understand the word length prediction. I will also note some of the internal problems that beset several types of popular information processing models because they do not deal with the unitization issue. These models have arisen independently from one another and contain no principles whereby they can be unified. I will indicate how an analysis of unitization leads to a different theory that is free from these internal problems and also unifies the main insights of the disparate models.

3. The Temporal Chunking Problem

The critical design problem that leads to the word length prediction is called the *temporal chunking problem*. Suppose that an unfamiliar list of familiar items is sequentially presented; e.g., a novel word composed of familiar letters. In terms of frequency and familiarity, the most familiar units in the list are the items themselves. In order to even know what the novel list is, all of its individual items must first be presented. All of these items are more familiar than the list itself. What prevents item familiarity from forcing the list to always be processed as a sequence of individual items, rather than eventually as a list as a whole? How does a not-yet-established word representation overcome the salience of well-established letter representations? How does unitization of unfamiliar lists of familiar items ever get off the ground?

Another version of the temporal chunking problem becomes evident by noticing that every sublist of a list is a perfectly good list in its own right. Letters and words are special sublists that have achieved a privileged status due to experience. In order to understand how this privileged status emerges, we need to analyse the processing substrate upon which all possible sublists struggle to be represented even before learning occurs. The design of this processing framework must also enable learning to unfold through time in a stable and self-consistent way. In particular, what design constraints prevent the presentation of new list items from destabilizing the encoding of all past item sublists? What design constraints enable the totality of represented sublists to define a more global and predictive representation of the environment than any individual list chunk could?

The subtlety of this unitization process is reflected even by the trivial fact that novel words composed of familiar letters can be learned. This fact shows that not all sublists have equal prewired weights in the competitive struggle to be represented. Such prewired weights include the number of coding sites in a sublist representation and the strength of the competitive signals that are emitted from each sublists's representation. Somehow a word as a whole can use such prewired processing biases to overcome, or to mask, the learned potency of its constituent items. This is the primary reason in my theory for the existence of a word length effect in word superiority studies.

This conclusion seems, however, to be self-contradictory upon further reflection. If prewired word biases can *inhibit* learned letter biases, then how is perception of letters *facilitated* by a word context, which is the main result of word superiority studies? This paradox can also be resolved through an analysis of the unitization process.

4. All Letters are Sublists

Some insight into this paradox can be gleaned by further considering what it means to say that every sublist of a list is also a list. In order for sublists of a list to struggle for representational status, sets of individual items of the list need first to be simultaneously represented in STM at some level of processing. For definiteness, call this level F_i, where the index i does not equal 1 because, in the full theory, this level of processing is not the first one. The theory shows how item representations that are simultaneously active in STM across F_i can be grouped, or chunked, into representations of sublists at the next level of processing F_{i+1}. The sublist representations can then compete with each other for STM activation within F_{i+1}. Once the two levels F_i and F_{i+1} are clearly distinguished, it becomes obvious that individual items, being sublists, can be represented at F_{i+1} as well as at F_i. In the special case of letters and words, this means that letters are represented at the item level, as well as at the list level. Prewired word biases can inhibit learned letter biases at the level F_{i+1}, but not at the level F_i. That is why I call level F_{i+1} a *masking field*.

To clearly understand how the item representations at F_i differ from the sublist representations at F_{i+1}, one must study the theory's processes in some detail. Even without such a study, one can conclude that "all letters are sublists." Indeed, all events capable of being represented at F_{i+1} exist on an equal dynamical footing. In the full theory, the implications of this conclusion clarify how changes in the context of a verbal item can significantly alter the processing of that item, and why the problem of identifying the functional units of language has proved to be so perplexing (Darwin, 1976; Studdert-Kennedy, 1980; Young, 1968). In F_{i+1}, no simple verbal description of the functional unit, such as phoneme or syllable, has a privileged status. Only the STM patterns that survive a context-sensitive interaction between associative and competitive rules have a concrete existence.

The dictum that "all letters are sublists" helps to explain the data of Wheeler (1970) that were a starting point for the Samuel *et al.* (1982, 1983) experiments. One might intuitively believe that, since a word context can improve the recognition of its constituent letters, letters such as I and A that are also words would be better recognized than other letters. Wheeler (1970) showed that this is not the case. In my theory, this is due to the property that *all* familiar letters have a unitized sublist representation at F_{i+1}, not only letters that are also used as words. The Wheeler (1970) data thus demonstrate how perilous it is to directly translate the distinctions of lay language into the definition of an underlying psychological process. The lay concept of a word is a misleading guidepost for understanding the process whereby all familiar sublists can achieve a unitized status. In fact, letters such as I and A may be reported slightly worse than other letters. The same masking mechanism also helps to explain why word superiority effects do not occur in Chastain's paradigm (Chastain, 1982; Grossberg, 1986, Section 44), although the experimental manipulations that engage the masking mechanism differ in the two paradigms. The masking mechanism thus explains how opposite effects can be generated within closely related performance paradigms as an expression of the unitization process.

5. Expectancy Learning and Priming

To avoid possible misunderstanding, I should promptly say what the dictum "all letters are sublists" does not imply. It is well known that a human subject can be differentially primed to preferentially respond to letters rather than words, or to numbers rather than letters, and so on. Such a capability involves the activation of learned top-down templates, or expectancies, that selectively sensitize some internal representations more than others. Top-down excitatory feedback, or priming, from F_{i+1} to F_i is also used to explain how the word length bias in F_i can differentially excite item representations in F_i to generate the word length effect. This is because the prewired biases of a masking field enable the sublist representations of longer sublists to generate larger top-down excitatory signals, other things being equal. The phrase "all letters are sublists" is thus a conclusion about the local processing laws that letters and words share, not about the global contextual effects that can flexibly modulate the STM and LTM processes that these laws define.

The existence in my theory of learned top-down templates, or expectancies, does not arise from a desire to fit data about word superiority, object superiority, attentional priming, phonemic restoration, and the like. The need for such templates, and the laws that govern their properties, were derived from an analysis of how the unitization process stabilizes itself against adventitious recoding by behaviorally irrelevant environmental events. This analysis led to many unexpected conclusions that have begun to unify a large data base. In Grossberg (1980), for example, these templates were used to analyse how STM is reset by unexpected events in a way that preserves the stability of unitized representations. This analysis led to the prediction (p. 25) that a hippocampal generator of the P300 evoked potential exists. A hippocampal P300 generator has been experimentally reported by Halgren *et al.* (1980). The validity of this prediction can be further tested by performing discrimination learning experiments that should be able to dissociate possible cortical and hippocampal generators of the P300 (Grossberg, 1982b, Section 48).

6. The McClelland and Rumelhart Model

Before continuing my theoretical discussion, I should note that the conclusions which have already been drawn have major implications for popular models of letter and word recognition, such as the McClelland and Rumelhart model (McClelland

and Rumelhart, 1981; Rumelhart and McClelland, 1982), for which I now sketch a self-organization critique.

By a "self-organization critique" I mean an internal analysis of a model from the viewpoint of whether its information processing mechanisms could, in principle, develop or be learned. A model which cannot, in principle, self-organize must be using certain mechanisms that are physically incorrect. Both the nodal units and the internodal interactions that McClelland and Rumelhart postulate are seriously challenged by a self-organization critique.

For example, McClelland and Rumelhart identify a stage of letter nodes that precedes a stage of word nodes. They use these stages to discuss the processing of letters in 4-letter words. The hypothesis of separate stages for letter and word processing implies that letters are not also represented on the level of words of length four.

In order to be of general applicability, these concepts should certainly be generalizable to words of length less than four, notably to 1-letter words such as A and I. A consistent extension of the McClelland and Rumelhart stages would require that those letters which are also words, such as A and I, are represented on both the letter level and the word level, whereas those letters which are not words, such as E and F, are represented only on the letter level. How this distinction can be learned without using a homunculus is unclear.

This problem of processing units is symptomatic of a more general difficulty. The letter and word levels contain only nodes that represent letters and words. What did these nodes represent before their respective letters and words were learned? Where will the nodes come from to represent the letters and words that the model individual has not yet learned? Are these nodes to be created *de novo*? Are they created *de novo* within the five or six trials that enable a pseudoword to acquire many of the recognition characteristics of a word (Salasoo, Shiffrin, and Feustel, 1984)?

These concerns clarify the need to define, once and for all, a processing substrate that can represent the learned units of a subject's internal lexicon before, during, or after they are learned. Such a substrate cannot be defined in terms of letters and words without forcing the untenable conclusion that all letters and words from all possible languages past, present, and future, and *only* these units, have prelabelled nodes awaiting their use in every human brain. The assumption of separate letter and word levels also requires special assumptions to deal with various data, such as the data of Wheeler (1970) and Samuel, van Santen, and Johnston (1982, 1983) concerning word superiority effects. If separate letter and word levels exist, then letters such as A and I which are also words should, as words, be able to prime their letter representations. By contrast, letters such as D and E which are not words should receive no significant priming from the word level. One might therefore expect easier recognition of A and I than of D and E. This is not the case.

The assumption of separate letter and word levels could escape this contradiction by assuming that *all* letters can be recognized so much more quickly than words of length at least two that no priming whatsoever can be received from the word level before letter recognition is complete. This assumption would, however, appear to be incompatible with the word length data of Samuel, van Santen, and Johnston (1982, 1983). These authors showed that recognition improves if a letter is embedded in words of greater length. Thus a letter that is presented alone for a fixed time before a mask appears is recognized less well than a letter presented for the same amount of time in a word of length 2, 3, or 4. These data cast doubt on any explanation based on speed of processing alone.

A related problem arises due to the manner in which McClelland and Rumelhart have interconnected their letter level and their word level. "Each letter node is assumed to activate all of those word nodes consistent with it and inhibit all other word nodes. Each active word node competes with all other word nodes... (Rumelhart and McClelland, 1982, p. 61). Knowledge of which letters and words are consistent can only be achieved by learning a particular language. However, when learning mechanisms are superimposed upon these hypotheses, it can be shown that either the learning process whereby the letter-to-word connections are formed cannot get started, so that no word representations are ever learned, or that after learning gets started, a forced oscillation between learning and forgetting is triggered. Thus the model is unstable in a learning mode. This instability problem is one reason why all learned inter-level interactions within the lexical theory of Grossberg (1978a) were chosen to be excitatory.

The instability of learning in the McClelland and Rumelhart (1981) model can be understood by considering combinations of two possible cases: (a) Before learning occurs, strong inhibitory interactions exist from the letter level to the word level. Excitatory connections are learned until net excitatory connections exist from letters to compatible words. (b) Before learning occurs, strong excitatory interactions exist from the letter level to the word level. Inhibitory connections are learned until net inhibitory connections exist from letters to incompatible words. In case (a), the excitatory connections can be learned only if the word nodes to be conditioned can first be activated. They can be activated only by their letter nodes. Since all the strong connections from letter nodes to word nodes are initially inhibitory, the word nodes cannot receive a net excitatory signal, hence conditioning can never get started. In case (b), the inhibitory connections can be learned only if the word nodes to be conditioned can first be activated, since strong excitatory connections exist initially. Suppose, therefore, that conjoint activation of a letter node and a word node strengthens the inhibitory connection from a letter node to a word node. As the inhibitory connection becomes increasingly strong, activating the letter node progressively inhibits its target word node. As the connection strength tracks the size of this progressively decreasing word node activation, it too becomes smaller. As the connection strength becomes smaller, the word node activation can begin to recover. Then the connection strength can also grow larger once more. A cycle of forced learning and forgetting is hereby perpetuated.

In response to these observations, one might say: why not make all the learned inter-level connections excitatory, and let pre-wired intra-level connections be both excitatory and inhibitory. The conditionable inter-level connections can adjust themselves to the pre-wired intra-level connections to achieve the designed consistency and inconsistency relationships as a function of experience. This is, in fact, what the Grossberg (1978a) theory postulates.

Another conceptual difficulty of the McClelland and Rumelhart (1981) model is that it does not contain any principles suggesting how parameter choices that vary with list length, prior learning, or serial order can influence the coding of *individual* lists. Instead, the model assigns the same parameters to all word nodes, and derives all processing differences between words, pseudo-words, and non-words from differences in the *number* of activated words in the network hierarchy. Such an approach also leads to unstable learning, in addition to providing no ready explanations of data such as the word length effect of Samuel, van Santen, and Johnston (1982, 1983). To see why learning in such a network can become unstable, note that a word node corresponding to a word of length 4 can learn a subword of length 2 as quickly as a node corresponding to the subword itself, even in verbal contexts where the entire word is not presented. This property can cause unselective activation and coding of long word nodes by all of its subwords. The noise level in such unselective codes rapidly becomes unmanageable as the complexity of the word set that is to be encoded increases. All of these conceptual problems are overcome in a masking field (Grossberg, 1978a, Sections 36–43; 1984, Sections 37–44).

7. The Schneider and Shiffrin Model

The seminal articles of Schneider and Shiffrin (1977) and Shiffrin and Schneider (1977) have organized a large and complex data base in terms of the dichotomy between automatic and controlled processing. Concepts of unitization capable of explaining these data, as well as the word length effect, are fundamentally different from those espoused by Schneider and Shiffrin (Grossberg, 1978a). Experimental support for these concepts have accumulated at an accelerating rate during the last few years (Francolini and Egeth, 1980; Hoffman, Nelson, and Houck, 1983; Kahneman and Chajczyk, 1983; Kahneman and Treisman, 1983; Schneider and Fisk, 1984). Although the experimental models that have arisen from these data are also closer to the unitization theory, they have not yet incorporated some of this theory's most important insights.

Schneider and Shiffrin posited two complementary types of information processing to explain a larger data base. *Automatic* processing is said to be a simultaneous parallel, relatively independent detection process. *Controlled* processing is said to be a serial terminating search process. The authors showed that the two types of processing can be experimentally probed using different experimental manipulations. Automatic processing occurs when the subject has practiced at giving a consistent detection response to memory set items that are never distractors, as in detecting digits among letter distractors. This is called a *consistent mapping* (CM) condition. Controlled processing occurs when memory set items and distractors are mixed from trial to trial, as in detecting digits among digit distractors. This is called a *varied mapping* (VM) condition. CM performance is usually better than VM performance. During CM performance, there is little effect of varying the number of distractors in a frame or of memory set size. By contrast, VM performance is monotonically related to each of these variables. Also during CM performance, false alarms (detections when no target is present) increase significantly at fast frame speeds, but this does not occur during VM performance.

The distinction between controlled and automatic processing may be viewed as a contribution to the unitization literature. Roughly speaking, controlled processing is used before an item or task is unitized, whereas automatic processing is used after unitization has occurred. The use of distinct VM and CM paradigms to experimentally probe these different situations provided a static view of unitization by looking at "before" and "after" unitization conditions, but not at the process of unitization itself.

When one considers Schneider and Shiffrin's conception of controlled versus automatic processing during the unitization process, it is seen to be fraught with difficulties. Consider, for example, the learning of any new list of familiar items, as in the temporal chunking problem of Section 2. According to Schneider and Shiffrin, each familiar item is assumed to be processed by a parallel process, while each unfamiliar inter-item contingency is processed by a serial process. Thus their theory claims that the brain rapidly alternates between parallel and serial processing in this situation. Moreover, as the whole list becomes unitized, their theory suggests that this hybrid of serial and parallel processing somehow switches to exclusively parallel processing.

A similar conceptual difficulty occurs when one considers visual information processing. When a subject views a picture whose left half contains a familiar face and whose right half contains a collection of unfamiliar features, the Schneider and Shiffrin theory would claim that the visual process somehow splits itself into a parallel half and a serial half. As unitization occurs, the visual process then somehow reintegrates itself into a parallel process as the unfamiliar features are unitized.

The conceptually paradoxical nature of these conclusions is matched by unexplained data. Why is it that the "time for automatic search is at least as long as that for an easy controlled search" (Schneider and Shiffrin, 1976)? Do not such data violate the intuitive understanding of the concept "automatic"?

I claim that these problems arise from associating a serial *process* to the serial *properties* of controlled search, and a parallel *process* to the parallel *properties* of automatic search. By contrast, the unitization theory in Grossberg (1978a) suggests that both types of properties are generated by parallel mechanisms. As unitization proceeds, the distribution of learned bottom-up codes and top-down templates changes in an experimentally dependent fashion. The parallel mechanisms of the unitization theory do not change, but the learning that they control can make the difference between controlled and automatic performance properties.

Below I quote from Grossberg (1978a, Section 61) as a point of departure for further discussion of how concepts about controlled and automatic processing can be modified and thereby integrated into this theory of unitization. The most critical points in the quote occur at its beginning and end. The middle section alludes to mechanisms that have recently been incorporated into some empirical models. I have included bracketed terms to help the reader make the bridge between concepts of the unitization theory and concepts that are being used to explain more recent information processing experiments.

"Below it is argued that both types of processing utilize common parallel operations, and that their apparent differences are due to shifts in the relative balance of these operations that are caused by experimental conditions. In particular, serial *properties* do not necessarily imply serial *operations* ... Consider CM [consistent mapping] search. Repeated use of the same memory set gradually generates a higher-order auditory code [category] that can sample the visual codes for all the items over successive trials. When the higher-order code is activated, the visual codes of *all* memory set items can be subliminally activated. Matching with any one of these codes generates a resonant burst [recognition event]. The process therefore seems to be more parallel than VM [varied mapping] search. I claim, however, that this is primarily because the higher-order code must be established before the visual codes of all memory set items can be sampled by a single internal representation ... the ... *codes* [filters] and *templates* [sets] that are activated in VM and CM conditions are different, but the two conditions otherwise share common mechanisms ... Attention enters the search process in several ways. The simplest attentional reaction is amplification of network response to expected items [priming by gain control] ... The 'time for automatic search is at least as long as that for a very easy controlled search'. This is paradoxical if CM search is a more efficient processing scheme. Is partial normalization [limited capacity] of the visual template one reason for this? If more cues are subliminally active [subthreshold] during CM than during VM search, then each cue will have less subliminal activity. The reaction time for supraliminal [superthreshold] signals to be generated during a match will then be greater during CM than during VM ... Also of interest are the data concerning performance accuracy when a memory set item occurs 0, 1, 2, or 3 frames away from an identical, or different, memory set item ... Matching one item does not require reset to match a different item. However, if two identical items occur simultaneously, then the first match can interfere with the registration of the second match ... By explaining the Schneider and Shiffrin data in a unified way, we avoid several serious problems of their theory. They claim, and I agree, that automatic processing is used to rapidly code familiar behavioral units so that controlled processing can then build these units into new unitized elements. I disagree that the 'automatic attention response' in the CM condition is a mechanism that is qualitatively different from mechanisms operating in the VM condition. If the two types of conditions use serial versus parallel *operations*, as Shiffrin and Schneider claim, then how does the brain tirelessly alternate between serial and parallel mechanisms as it practices any new list of unitized elements? How do the serial and parallel processes compete when a visual scene contains both unitized and unfamiliar but relevant objects? How does the switchover from serial to parallel processing take place as an item is unitized? These problems evaporate in the present theoretical framework."

Just as the McClelland and Rumelhart model assigns a letter level and a word level to verbal items that are so labelled by lay language, the Schneider and Shiffrin model assigns a serial process to ostensibly serial behavioral properties and a parallel process to ostensibly parallel behavioral properties. Consideration of how we unitize as novel list of familiar items reveals the paradoxical nature of these conclusions in both the McClelland and Rumelhart model and the Schneider and Shiffrin model, and provides a way to unify the two types of models.

Recent data have led several authors to reconsider the validity of the dichotomy between automatic and controlled processing. Some authors have attempted to save the binary nature of this distinction in a weakened form by introducing epicyclic concepts like *strongly automatic* and *partly automatic* (Kahneman and Chajczyk, 1983). Such epicycles often precede the final breakdown of a conceptual framework.

8. Parallel Processing and Unlimited Capacity

Schneider and Shiffrin's dichotomy between controlled processing as a serial process and automatic processing as a parallel process has led to other assumptions that are challenged by a self-organization critique. For example, Hoffman, Nelson, and

Houck (1983, p. 380) write: "Stage 1 is characterized as a large interconnected set of nodes or logogens ... which are automatically 'activated' by presentation of their corresponding sensory inputs ... Processing in this stage is assumed to be parallel and unlimited in capacity." The assumption that "parallel processing" and "unlimited capacity processing" co-exist has been broadly accepted in the literature, and is one reason why it seems natural to identify controlled processing with a serial (that is, non-parallel) mechanism. A self-organization critique seriously challenges whether automatic activation and limited capacity processing form a creditable processing dichotomy, in even an approximate sense. The fundamental inadequacy of this dichotomy becomes clear using a microscopic analysis of the unitization process. Such an analysis shows that the activation of a *single* unitized representation *seems* to be automatic *because* of the action of a limited capacity competitive process. The process that is usually identified as the *antithesis* of automatic activation is *responsible for* the consensual impression of automatic activation. I claim that on the level of microscopic processing, the dichotomy between automatic activation and limited capacity processing is invalid.

To see why this is so, let us again consider the STM level F_{i+1} that regulates the LTM chunking of sublists. My analysis of this process suggests that sublists of a list competitively struggle for representational status within F_{i+1}. When a familiar word is processed, the sublist representation corresponding to the word rapidly wins the competition *because* the word is familiar. The associative LTM changes that subserve word familiarity have altered the balance of competitive processing in favor of the word representation, but they have not eliminated the existence of the competitive process that *could have* chosen a different winning representation in response to different learning conditions. The apparent automaticity of the word interpretation derives from the network's ability to rapidly suppress these alternative sublist parsings using a limited capacity competitive masking process.

This conclusion does not undermine the claim (Grossberg, 1978a, Section 61), that apparent capacity changes can be due to learning of new chunks (or filters) and expectancies (or sets), as well as to several types of attentional mechanisms. These processes enable the network to reorganize its reactions to the same input patterns. A different learned top-down set can, for example, match an input pattern that a previous set mismatched. A different learned bottom-up filter can, for example, match a top-down set that a previous filter mismatched. Attentional gain control can, for example, focus network sensitivity at a subfield where an approximate match occurs, or at a different subfield where a serious mismatch occurs.

9. The Functional Unit of Cognitive Processing: Not Spreading Activation

The above example illustrates my claim that the traditional discussion of unlimited capacity suffers from an inadequate choice of the functional unit of cognitive processing. I suggest that the functional unit is not activation of a single node, or a "spreading activation" among individual nodes. The functional unit is a spatial pattern of activity that is coherently processed across a field of nodes. Once one accepts that the functional unit of processing is a spatially distributed activity pattern, rather than individual nodal activations, then "a large interconnected set of nodes" may simply transform one spatial pattern into another spatial pattern. The popular processing metaphor that directly relates the number of nodes or pathways to processing capacity then collapses.

This processing metaphor has often been used to explain how unitized representations can be automatically activated without capacity limitations. One imagines
an appealing picture in which content addressable nodes are automatically activated
by signals along labelled pathways. If many nodes exist, then they can process their
labelled signals with less interference, other things being equal. Given this metaphor,
the antithesis of automatic activation seems to be a limited capacity process in which
many nodes compete for a limited activation resource. An analysis of unitization
undermines the internal logic behind this assumption. Along the way, it also vitiates
the assumption that the computer is a viable model of human information processing.

10. Capacity versus Matching

If the metaphor that many people use to discuss limited capacity is question-
able, then the notion of capacity itself needs reinvestigation. Various experiments
have demonstrated, for example, that recognition accuracy and reaction time do not
depend on processing load *per se*, but rather on factors like the goodness of match
between priming and test cues (Fisher and Craik, 1980; Myers and Lorch, 1980;
Schvaneveldt and McDonald, 1981). An increased reaction time is thus not due just
to competition for a limited activation resource among many mutually inhibitory
nodes. Mutual inhibition can subserve a match (which can speed up reaction time)
or a mismatch (which can slow down reaction time) over the same set of activated
nodes.

An analysis of the unitization process leads to mechanisms which also have these
properties (Grossberg, 1976b, 1980). These mechanisms describe competitive and
cooperative internodal interactions that occur at every level of network processing.
Such interactions enable each level to sensitively process its patterned functional units
without major contamination by internal noise or saturation effects. The masking
geometry of the sublist level F_{i+1} is, in fact, a special case of these interactions.
One can view the masking geometry as a competitive-cooperative interaction scheme
that developmentally equilibrates to input patterns which vary in spatial scale and
processing load (Grossberg, 1984, Sections 42–43).

Satisfying the general need for sensitive registration of patterned functional units
at each network level *automatically* leads to properties that are compatible with
the aforementioned reaction time data. This is true because an approximate match
between a pair of bottom-up and top-down input patterns at a level can enhance its
activation, thereby reducing its reaction time. By contrast, a mismatch between a
pair of bottom-up and top-down input patterns at a level can suppress its activation,
thereby increasing its reaction time. In both the match and the mismatch situations,
the same number of nodes can receive inputs, the total input size can be the same,
and thus the same network capacity is utilized.

This relationship between matching, activity amplification, and reaction time
plays a fundamental role in the theory's explanation of how the stability-plasticity
dilemma is solved, and about how a mismatch can trigger a search of associative memory (Grossberg, 1980). The relationship also shows that certain types of matching
are more appropriate as cognitive mechanisms than others. In particular, it argues
against the use of Euclidean matching algorithms (Grossberg, 1983, Section 22).

These remarks illustrate how a seemingly elementary problem about real-time processing, such as the noise-saturation problem, if carefully posed and quantitatively solved, can have unsuspected implications that ramify into and thereby help to unify a large and difficult experimental literature.

11. Adaptive Filter: The Processing Bridge between Sublist Masking and Temporal Order Information over Item Representations

A still broader unification of data and models emerges when one considers how signals are relayed from level F_i to the next level F_{i+1}, and conversely. When a signal from a node in F_i is carried along a pathway to F_{i+1}, the signal is multiplied, or *gated*, by the pathway's LTM trace. The LTM gated signal then reaches the target node. Each target node sums up all of its LTM gated signals. In this way, a pattern of output signals from F_i generates a pattern of input signals to F_{i+1}. This transformation is said to define an *adaptive filter*.

The input pattern to F_{i+1} is itself quickly transformed further by the competitive-cooperative interactions within F_{i+1}. In the simplest example of this process, these interactions choose the node which received the largest input. The choice transformation executes a particularly severe type of contrast enhancement. In a masking geometry such as F_{i+1}, the contrast enhancing transformation is considerably more subtle than a simple choice. The transformed pattern, not the input pattern itself, is then stored in STM. Only nodes which are active in STM across F_{i+1} can elicit new learning at their contiguous LTM traces.

This type of interaction between associative LTM mechanisms and competitive-cooperative STM mechanisms has many desirable properties. It generalizes the Bayesian tendency to minimize risk in a noisy environment. It spontaneously tends to form learned categories. Its categories are stable under several types of perturbations. Its STM patterns are context-sensitive. Its learning at each LTM trace is sensitive at each time to the entire STM pattern that is active at that time, as well as to all prior learning that ever occurred at *all* the LTM traces. The learning capabilities of the choice model are mathematically characterized in Grossberg (1976a). The properties of the masking field model are described in Grossberg (1978a, 1986).

In the special case where the levels are the item level F_i and the sublist level F_{i+1}, the activity pattern across F_i encodes temporal order information (TOI) in STM across the item representations of F_i, and the LTM traces in the pathways between F_i and F_{i+1} encode temporal order information (TOI) in LTM. The similarity between the patterns of LTM TOI in certain pathways and the pattern of STM TOI that is stored at any moment across the item representations of F_i helps to determine which unitized sublist representations will be activated across F_{i+1} by the bottom-up filter.

Unless a model explicitly defines how TOI in LTM is encoded, the model cannot determine how to compute TOI in STM so that a reasonable comparison process between STM and LTM can take place. The reverse conclusion is also true. If one does understand how TOI in LTM is computed, then one can use this information to *derive* laws for the temporal unfolding of TOI in STM. This was done in Grossberg (1978a, 1978b).

These STM laws have many implications for data and models about STM. For example, these STM laws suggest an alternative to serial buffer models such as the

Atkinson and Shiffrin (1968, 1971) model of free recall by showing how to encode TOI in STM without using a serial buffer, and by explaining data that are at variance with the classical buffer model, such as data of Lee and Estes (1977), Ratcliff (1981), Reeves and Sperling (1983), and Sperling and Reeves (1980). The model also provides a principled derivation of mechanisms similar to those in the empirically derived Reeves and Sperling (1983) Generalized Attention Gating Model (GAGM), and raises processing issues that have not yet been addressed by experiments. The fact of greatest importance is that this approach shows how temporal order information of items in STM, temporal order information of sublist chunks and templates in LTM (filters and sets), and competitive masking of sublist chunks in STM are designed together as parts of the unified processing module that regulates unitization. The next sections indicate how this unified processing module is designed, and discusses some related experimental issues.

12. The LTM Invariance Principle: Temporal Order Information without a Serial Buffer

I now summarize how the adaptive filter is used to constrain the law of STM TOI. To do this, I again consider how we learn a novel list of familiar items. Suppose that list items $r_1, r_2, \ldots, r_j$ have already been presented. Suppose that these items have generated a spatial pattern of STM activation across the item representations of F_i. This STM pattern represents "past" order information. I assume that a new list item r_{j+1} can alter the total pattern of STM across F_i, but that this new STM pattern does not cause LTM recoding of that part of the pattern which represents past order information. For example, learning a novel word does not force unlearning of its constituent letters. New events are permitted to weaken the influence of LTM codes representing past order information on STM decision-making within F_{i+1}, but not to deny the fact that the past events occurred. This hypothesis prevents the LTM record of past order information from being destroyed by every future event that happens to occur.

To translate this intuitive discussion into a precise computation, let us again recognize that every sublist of the list $r_1, r_2, \ldots, r_j$ is a perfectly good list in its own right. Every such sublist can, in principle, be encoded by LTM patterns in the adaptive filter from F_i to F_{i+1}. To prevent a future event r_{j+1} from destroying these past list encodings, I assume that the following principle holds (Grossberg, 1978a, 1978b):

LTM Invariance Principle: The spatial patterns of STM TOI across F_i are generated by a sequentially presented list in such a way as to leave the LTM codes of past events invariant.

The LTM Invariance Principle is instantiated by choosing STM activities across F_i so that the *relative* activities of *all possible filterings* of a past event sequence $r_1, r_2, \ldots, r_j$ are left invariant by a future event r_{j+1}. It turns out that this property is also generated by a suitably designed competitive-cooperative interactions across F_i, in keeping with general requirements that pattern processing across F_i be free from massive noise or saturation. Some of the most important properties of the STM TOI patterns that can arise in F_i are the following ones.

Primacy gradients, recency gradients, and bowed gradients in STM can occur. Primacy gradients can be generated by sufficiently short lists. Direct read-out of

TOI from STM can then be accomplished by the combination of a reaction time rule that reads-out the largest activities first, and a self-inhibitory reset rule that prevents read-out of a single item from perseverating for all time. Several recent empirical models have used variants of these rules (Reeves and Sperling, 1984; Rumelhart and Norman, 1982). The STM gradients, and thus the TOI, that develop through time are sensitive to the amount of attention that an item receives when it enters STM and to the subsequent transformation of these STM activities by lateral inhibition. The GAGM model of Reeves and Sperling (1984) also makes this point.

The existence of a primacy gradient in STM raises an issue that has not yet been addressed by experimentalists. Interference experiments (Rundus, 1971) suggest that a primacy gradient in STM does not exist in the free recall paradigm. Such data have been used to support models of free recall in which the only primacy gradient in free recall is due to LTM (Atkinson and Shiffrin, 1968, 1971). The possibility of recalling a short list correctly out of STM suggests, by contrast, that a primacy gradient in STM can sometimes exist during free recall. Free recall data of Korsakoff amnesics (Baddeley and Warrington, 1970) and of normals (Hogan and Hogan, 1975) also support this conclusion. In Grossberg (1978b, Section 7), I showed how this apparent contradiction can be theoretically explained. My explanation suggests that a limited capacity competitive process prevents a primacy gradient in STM from being measured in an interference experiment, even in cases where it exists. Moreover, this limited capacity process is a parallel process, not a serial process. This explanation has not yet been experimentally tested. It illustrates that, even though the words "limited capacity process" and "parallel process" are freely used in the experimental literature, their implications are not widely understood.

Another important issue is raised by this STM TOI model. The model is capable of generating STM TOI without the use of a serial buffer. The TOI evolves through time as it does across item representations due to the network's competitive rules. The GAGM model of Reeves and Sperling (1984) also works without a serial buffer using mechanisms similar to those introduced in my theory. Classical serial buffers, by contrast, such as those of Atkinson and Shiffrin (1968, 1971) and Raaijmakers and Shiffrin (1981), do not fare well when they are analysed from the viewpoint of the unitization process (Grossberg, 1978b). The interplay of factors relating to attention, competition, serial buffers, and primacy gradients in STM require much more experimental study.

A related set of remarks can be made about ideas concerning TOI in LTM, notably the LTM TOI that evolves within the top-down conditionable pathways from F_{i+1} to F_i during serial verbal learning and paired associate learning. The bowed and skewed serial position effect and related verbal learning data were analysed using such a buffer-free interaction between STM and LTM in Grossberg (1969) and Grossberg and Pepe (1970, 1971). These LTM TOI rules turned out to have the right properties to build up a theory of how goal-oriented cognitive plans are self-organized (Grossberg, 1978a). A number of predictions concerning how the bowed serial position curve should change with state variables like arousal were made in 1970–71, but still have not been experimentally tested, despite their importance for understanding verbal learning, cognitive planning, and the transition to abnormal overaroused-attentive states such as those found in schizophrenia (Maher, 1977). A nontechnical review of these serial learning concepts is found in Grossberg (1982c). Murdock (1979) has been using related ideas about cross-correlation to analyse verbal learning data, but his model's computations have not yet enabled him to explain the bowed and skewed serial position curve.

13. Spatial Frequency Analysis of Temporal Order Information

The discussion of STM TOI at F_i and of sublist masking at F_{i+1} shows that both levels F_i and F_{i+1} are designed as competitive networks, even though they accomplish different functional tasks. The fact that both F_i and F_{i+1} possess a "limited capacity" provides little insight into how they work, or how they work so differently; notably how F_{i+1}, but not F_i, is capable of computing a "magic number seven" (Miller, 1957). One of the important tasks of cognitive science is, I believe, to classify specialized competitive networks according to the functional transformations that these networks can compute. A great deal is now known about these transformations (Grossberg, 1982a).

To end this discussion, I will now indicate how an analysis of unitization leads to the conclusion that the competitive masking process in F_{i+1} does a type of spatial frequency analysis of the LTM-filtered STM TOI that it receives from F_i. This observation shows that mechanisms which are more familiar in visual, or more generally spatial, processing are also important in language or, more generally temporal, processing. The interactions between experimentalists in these two areas should thus be stronger than they are at present.

The last section indicated how the LTM Invariance Principle can be used to generate STM TOI across item representations in F_i. A spatial pattern of STM activity over a set of item representations encodes this information. As more items are presented, new spatial patterns are registered that include larger regions of the item field, up to some maximal list length. Thus the *temporal* processing of items is converted into a succession of expanding *spatial* patterns.

Given this insight, the temporal chunking problem can be rephrased as follows. How do sublist chunks in F_{i+1} that encode broader regions of the item field mask sublist chunks that encode narrower regions of the item field? When I asked this question about language processing in 1974, I already knew the answer due to work on visual masking that my colleague Dan Levine and I were just finishing (Grossberg and Levine, 1975; Levine and Grossberg, 1976). We had shown how to define competitive networks that are composed of masking subfields. Each masking subfield was characterized by a different choice of numerical parameters. At the risk of oversimplifying the analysis, we found that subfields whose cell populations have broader spatial frequencies and more coding sites can mask STM activation of subfields with narrower spatial frequencies and fewer coding sites. The temporal chunking problem then suggested how to put together results about STM TOI and competitive masking by suggesting the following design principle, whose relevance to the word length effect of Samuel *et al.* (1982, 1983) should now be obvious.

Sequence Masking Principle: Broader regions of the item field F_i are filtered in such a way that they selectively excite nodes in F_{i+1} with larger masking parameters.

The sequence masking principle is capable of organizing a series of simple design rules for the integrated construction of the network module consisting of F_i, F_{i+1}, and their mutual interactions. Many predictions about cognitive processing, neural development, neuroanatomy, and neurophysiology are consequences of this construction. See Grossberg (1986) for a recent description of these and related properties.

14. Conclusion

This article has avoided most of the technical considerations that are needed to precisely characterize the dynamics of unitization. Instead it has focused on a few of the intuitive ideas that motivate a larger theory. These ideas illustrate how models can be strengthened and unified by analysing their internal structure from the viewpoint of the unitization process, and indicate that this process of unification is already well underway.

REFERENCES

Anderson, J.R. and Bower, G.H. (1973). **Human associative memory**. Washington, DC: V.H. Winston and Sons.

Atkinson, R.C. and Shiffrin, R.M. (1968). Human memory: A proposed system and its control processes. In K.W. Spence and J.T. Spence (Eds.), **Advances in the psychology of learning and motivation research and theory** (Volume 2). New York: Academic Press.

Atkinson, R.C. and Shiffrin, R.M. (1971). The control of short term memory. *Scientific American*, August.

Baddeley, A.D. and Warrington, E.K. (1970). Amnesia and the distinction between long- and short-term memory. *Journal of Verbal Learning and Verbal Behavior*, **9**, 176–189.

Chastain, G. (1982). Scanning, holistic encoding, and the word-superiority effect. *Memory and Cognition*, **10**, 232–236.

Cole, R.A. and Rudnicky, A.I. (1983). What's new in speech perception? The research and ideas of William Chandler Bagley, 1874–1946. *Psychological Review*, **90**, 94–101.

Darwin, C.J. (1976). The perception of speech. In E.C. Carterette and M.P. Friedman (Eds.), **Handbook of perception, Volume VII: Language and speech**. New York: Academic Press.

Fisher, R.P. and Craik, F.I.M. (1980). The effects of elaboration on recognition memory. *Memory and Cognition*, **8**, 400–404.

Francolini, C.M. and Egeth, H. (1980). On the non-automaticity of "automatic" activation: Evidence of selective seeing. *Perception and Psychophysics*, **27**, 331–342.

Grossberg, S. (1969). On the serial learning of lists. *Mathematical Biosciences*, **4**, 201–253.

Grossberg, S. (1976a). Adaptive pattern classification and universal recoding, I: Parallel development and coding of neural feature detectors. *Biological Cybernetics*, **23**, 121–134.

Grossberg, S. (1976b). Adaptive pattern classification and universal recoding, II: Feedback, expectation, olfaction, and illusions. *Biological Cybernetics*, **23**, 187–202.

Grossberg, S. (1978a). A theory of human memory: Self-organization and performance of sensory-motor codes, maps, and plans. In R. Rosen and F. Snell (Eds.), **Progress in theoretical biology**, Vol. 5. New York: Academic Press, 223–374.

Grossberg, S. (1978b). Behavioral contrast in short term memory: Serial binary memory models or parallel continuous memory models? *Journal of Mathematical Psychology*, **3**, 199–219.

Grossberg, S. (1980). How does a brain build a cognitive code? *Psychological Review*, **1**, 1–51.

Grossberg, S. (1982a). **Studies of mind and brain: Neural principles of learning, perception, development, cognition, and motor control**. Boston: Reidel Press.

Grossberg, S. (1982b). Processing of expected and unexpected events during conditioning and attention: A psychophysiological theory. *Psychological Review*, **89**, 529–572.

Grossberg, S. (1982c). Associative and competitive principles of learning and development: The temporal unfolding and stability of STM and LTM patterns. In S.I. Amari and M. Arbib (Eds.), **Competition and cooperation in neural networks**. New York: Springer-Verlag.

Grossberg, S. (1983). The quantized geometry of visual space: The coherent computation of depth, form, and lightness. *Behavioral and Brain Sciences*, **6**, 625–692.

Grossberg, S. (1986). The adaptive self-organization of serial order in behavior: Speech, language, and motor control. In E.C. Schwab and H.C. Nusbaum (Eds.), **Pattern recognition by humans and machines, Vol. 1: Speech perception**. New York: Academic Press, 187–294.

Grossberg, S. and Levine, D. (1975). Some developmental and attentional biases in the contrast enhancement and short term memory of recurrent neural networks. *Journal of Theoretical Biology*, **53**, 341–380.

Grossberg, S. and Pepe, J. (1970). Schizophrenia: Possible dependence of associational span, bowing, and primacy versus recency on spiking threshold. *Behavioral Science*, **15**, 359–362.

Grossberg, S. and Pepe, J. (1971). Spiking threshold and overarousal effects in serial learning *Journal of Statistical Physics*, **3**, 95–125.

Halgren, E., Squires, N.K., Wilson, C.L., Rohrbaugh, J.W., Babb, T.L., and Crandall, P.H. (1980). Endogenous potentials generated in the human hippocampal formation and amygdala by infrequent events. *Science*, **210**, 803–805.

Hoffman, J.E., Nelson, B., and Houck, M.R. (1983). The role of attentional resources in automatic detection. *Cognitive Psychology*, **51**, 379–410.

Hogan, R.M. and Hogan, M.M. (1975). Structural and transient components of memory. *Memory and Cognition*, **3**, 210–215.

Kahneman, D. and Chajczyk, D. (1983). Tests of the automaticity of reading: Dilution of Stroop effects by color-irrelevant stimuli. *Journal of Experimental Psychology: Human Perception and Performance*, **9**, 497–509.

Kahneman, D. and Treisman, A. (1983). Changing views of attention and automaticity. In R. Parasuramen, R. Davies, and J. Beatty (Eds.), **Varieties of attention**. New York: Academic Press.

Lee, C. and Estes, W.K. (1977). Order and position in primary memory for letter strings. *Journal of Verbal Learning and Verbal Behavior*, **16**, 395–418.

Levine, D.S. and Grossberg, S. (1976). Visual illusion in neural networks: Line neutralization, tilt aftereffect, and angle expansion. *Journal of Theoretical Biology*, **61**, 477–504.

Macchi, G. and Rinvik, E. (1976). Thalamo-telencephalic circuits: A neuroanatomical survey. In A. Remond (Ed.), **Handbook of electroencephalography and clinical neurophysiology** (Volume 2, Part A). Amsterdam: Elsevier/North-Holland.

Maher, B.A. (1977). **Contributions to the psychopathology of schizophrenia.** New York: Academic Press.

McClelland, J.L. and Rumelhart, D.E. (1981). An interactive activation model of context effects in letter perception, Part 1: An account of basic findings. *Psychological Review*, **88**, 375–407.

Miller, G.A. (1956). The magic number seven plus or minus two. *Psychological Review*, **63**, 81.

Murdock, B.B. (1979). Convolution and correlation in perception and memory. In L.G. Nilsson (Ed.), **Perspectives in memory research.** Hillsdale, NJ: Erlbaum Associates.

Myers, J.L. and Lorch, R.F. Jr. (1980). Interference and faciliation effects of primes upon verification processes. *Memory and Cognition*, **8**, 405–414.

Neisser, U. (1967). **Cognitive psychology.** New York: Appleton Century Crofts.

Posner, M.I. (1978). **Chronometric explorations of mind.** Hillsdale, NJ: Erlbaum Associates.

Raaijmakers, J.G.W. and Shiffrin, R.M. (1981). Search of associative memory. *Psychological Review*, **88**, 93–134.

Ratcliff, R. (1981). A theory of order relations in perceptual matching. *Psychological Review*, **88**, 552–572.

Reeves, A. and Sperling, G. (1984). Attentional theory of order information in short-term visual memory. Preprint.

Rumelhart, D.E. and McClelland, J.L. (1982). An interactive activation model of context effects in letter perception, Part 2: The contextual enhancement effect and some tests and extensions of the model. *Psychological Review*, **89**, 60–94.

Rumelhart, D.E. and Norman, D.A. (1982). Simulating a skilled typist: A study of skilled cognitive-motor performance. *Cognitive Science*, **6**, 1–36.

Rundus, D. (1971). Analysis of rehearsal processes in free recall. *Journal of Experimental Psychology*, **89**, 63–77.

Salasoo, A., Shiffrin, R.M., and Feustel, T.C. (1984). Building permanent memory codes: Codification and repetition effects in word identification. Preprint.

Samuel, A.G., van Santen, J.P.H., and Johnston, J.C. (1982). Length effects in word perception: We is better than I but worse than you or them. *Journal of Experimental Psychology: Human Perception and Performance*, **8**, 91–105.

Samuel, A.G., van Santen, J.P.H., and Johnston, J.C. (1983). Reply to Matthei: We really is worse than you or them, and so are ma and pa. *Journal of Experimental Psychology: Human Perception and Performance*, **9**, 321–322.

Schneider, W. and Fisk, A.D. (1984). Automatic category search and its transfer. *Journal of Experimental Psychology: Learning, Memory, and Cognition*, **10**, 1–15.

Schneider, W. and Shiffrin, R.M. (1976). Automatic and controlled information processing in vision. In D. LaBarge amd S.J. Samuels (Eds.), **Basic processes in reading: Perception and comprehension.** Hillsdale, NJ: Erlbaum Associates.

Schneider, W. and Shiffrin, R.M. (1977). Controlled and automatic information processing, I: Detection, search, and attention. *Psychological Review*, **84**, 1–66.

Schvaneveldt, R.W. and McDonald, J.E. (1981). Semantic context and the encoding of words: Evidence for two modes of stimulus analysis. *Journal of Experimental Psychology: Human Perception and Performance*, **3**, 673–687.

Shiffrin, R.M. and Schneider, W. (1977). Controlled and automatic information processing, II: Perceptual learning, automatic attending, and a general theory. *Psychological Review*, **84**, 127–190.

Sperling, G. and Reeves, A. (1980). Measuring the reaction time of a shift of visual attention. In R. Nickerson (Ed.), **Attention and performance VIII**. Hillsdale, NJ: Erlbaum Associates.

Studdert-Kennedy, M. (1980). Speech perception. *Language and Speech*, **23**, 45–65.

Tsumoto, T., Creutzfeldt, O.D., and Legéndy, C.R. (1978). Functional organization of the corticofugal system from visual cortex to lateral geniculate body of the cat. *Experimental Brain Research*, **25**, 291–306.

Wheeler, D.D. (1970). Processes in word recognition. *Cognitive Psychology*, **1**, 59–85.

Young, R.K. (1968). Serial learning. In T.R. Dixon and D.L. Horton (Eds.), **Verbal behavior and general behavior theory**. Englewood Cliffs, NJ: Prentice-Hall.

SPEECH PERCEPTION AND PRODUCTION BY A SELF-ORGANIZING NEURAL NETWORK

by

Michael Cohen, Stephen Grossberg, and David Stork

Preface

This 1988 article outlines a neural network architecture for self-organization of speech perception and production. It hereby embeds the working memory and masking field levels thst were described in Chapter 18 into a larger processing framework. The article uses this framework to suggest resolutions of some basic problems in speech perception. It does so by suggesting new organizational principles, processing levels, and interactions whereby a speech communication system can self-organize in real time.

One such problem concerns the role of articulatory constraints on the speech perception code. This is a much-debated problem that is usually identified with the motor theory of speech perception. Motor theory claims that sounds are heard the way they would be uttered, even during passive listening. The present theory suggests that this property reflects the process whereby an auditory-to-articulatory *imitative map* self-organizes so that infants can begin to imitate novel adult utterances. In order to be learnable, the imitative map needs to join dimensionally consistent auditory and articulatory representations. A learned top-down articulatory-to-auditory expectation is predicted to select the articulatorily-consistent auditory patterns via 2/3 Rule matching. The auditory patterns are thereby rendered dimensionally consistent with articulatory commands, and thus an imitative map can be learned. The paradox of motor theory is hereby reduced to the computational problem of how ART mechanisms can self-organize a self-stabilizing imitative map.

Another perplexing problem concerns phonemic restoration. Here, the meaning of events that occur in the future can affect the way noisy sounds that occurred in the past are heard. Such data place strong demands on the processing levels of a speech system, as well as upon its dynamics. How can *meaning* influence *phonetics*? How can a *future* event reorganize the way a *past* sound is heard? Why does the process whereby a sound reaches consciousness proceed so slowly that such a reorganization can occur?

It turns out that the way in which noisy sounds are reorganized by top-down events is consistent with 2/3 Rule matching. Conscious perception is identified with a resonant wave due to nonlinear feedback between a working memory and a multiple-scale chunking network, such as a masking field. This resonant wave emerges on a slower time scale than the purely bottom-up activation of working memory. The working memory activates the masking field, which in turn emits learned top-down expectations that reorganize and bind the working memory patterns into a coherent speech code as the resonance develops.

These results illustrate the need for interdisciplinary research on mind and brain. The proposed resolution of speech paradoxes became possible through a synthesis of results about self-organizing pattern recognition, adaptive sensory-motor control, temporal order information in working memory, and speech preprocessing. The traditionally defined boundaries of speech research exclude most of these studies. An analysis of language self-organization provides enough new constraints to guide such a synthesis, which is now under active development.

Evolution, Learning, Cognition,
and Advanced Architectures
Y.C. Lee (Editor)
Singapore: World Scientific, 1988, 217–231

SPEECH PERCEPTION AND PRODUCTION
BY A SELF-ORGANIZING NEURAL NETWORK

Michael A. Cohen*, Stephen Grossberg*, and David G. Stork*+

Abstract

Considerations of the real-time self-organization of neural networks for speech recognition and production have lead to a new understanding of several key issues in such networks, most notably a definition of new processing units and functions of hierarchical levels in the auditory system. An important function of a particular neural level in the auditory system is to provide a partially-compressed code, mapped to the articulatory system, to permit imitation of novel sounds. Furthermore, top-down priming signals from the articulatory system to the auditory system help to stabilize the emerging auditory code. These structures help explain results from the motor theory, which states that speech is analyzed by how it would be produced. Higher stages of processing require chunking or unitization of the emerging language code, an example of a classical grouping problem. The partially compressed auditory codes are further compressed into item codes (e.g., phonemic segments), which are stored in a working memory representation whose short-term memory pattern is its code. A masking field level receives input from this working memory and encodes this input into list chunks, whose top-down signals organize the items in working memory into coherent groupings with invariant properties. This total architecture sheds new light on key speech issues such as coarticulation, analysis-by-synthesis, motor theory, categorical perception, invariant speech perception, word superiority, and phonemic restoration.

Acknowledgements: M.A.C. was supported in part by the Air Force Office of Scientific Research (AFOSR F49620-86-C0037) and the National Science Foundation (NSF IRI-84-17756), S.G. was supported in part by the Air Force Office of Scientific Research (AFOSR F49620-86-C0037 and AFOSR F49620-87-C0018), and D.G.S. was supported in part by the Air Force Office of Scientific Research (AFOSR F49620-86-C0037). The authors wish to thank Cynthia Suchta and Carol Yanakakis for their valuable assistance in the preparation of the manuscript.

1. The Learning of Language Units

During a human's early years, an exquisitely subtle and sensitive speech recognition and production system develops. These two systems develop to be well-matched to each other, enabling rapid and reliable broadcast and reception of linguistic information. The development of these systems can be viewed as resulting from two fundamental processes: self-organization through *circular reaction* and through *chunking* or *unitization*. This chapter sketches some issues concerning these processes in speech and provides a summary of its key neural components, developed to address more general cognitive problems.

2. Low Stages of Processing: Circular Reactions and the Emerging Auditory and Motor Codes

The concept of circular reaction (Piaget, 1963) is illustrated in Figure 1. For our purposes, the reaction links the *motor* or *articulatory* system (mouth, tongue, velum, etc., and the neural structures controlling them) with the *auditory* system (ear and its neural perceptual mechanisms). In a developing infant, endogenously generated babbling signals in the motor system lead to auditory feedback, thereby allowing the auditory system to tune its evolving recognition codes. Moreover, the auditory system can compare the self-generated sounds to those from external speakers.

Figure 2 shows in slightly greater detail relevant neural interconnections in the auditory model. After processing by low-level auditory feature detectors (detecting energy in various frequency wavebands, "sweeping" frequency signals, broad-band or burst energy distributions) the auditory information is partially compressed and passed to a subsequent level, where it is represented by significant activity in a smaller number of neurons.

There is a learned auditory-to-articulatory associative map at this level, important for the following purposes. First, it permits the motor system to *interpolate* novel heard sounds. That is, if a novel sound leads to an auditory code "between" those for other, previously coded sounds, then this novel sound will be mapped to a motor code "between" those for the sounds previously heard. Second, the associative map permits the motor system to *imitate* such sounds. In this manner, a novel sound will lead to a novel, interpolated motor code. When accessed, this new motor code will lead to an utterance closer to the novel one heard. This (imitated) utterance then accesses an auditory code very similar to the interpolated one.

The auditory code at the level for this interpolation and imitation must be only *partially* compressed; a fully compressed (or *unitized*) code would map to a previously organized motor code, precluding interpolation of novel sounds. Furthermore, the auditory level for interpolation must be above stages of invariant preprocessing—only in this way can effects such as vocal tract normalization be explained (Lieberman, 1984, pp.219–223). It has been argued (Lieberman, 1984, p.222) that such normalization is due to the existence of innate mechanisms, and hence is not modifiable in the manner of the auditory-to-motor map.

3. The Vector Integration to Endpoint Model

The motor code in our network is based on the recent Vector Integration To Endpoint (VITE) model of arm movement control (Bullock and Grossberg, 1987), due

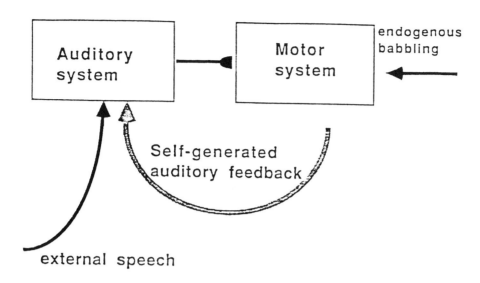

Figure 1. Circular reaction linking the motor system to the auditory system. Such a loop permits imitation of novel sounds from an external speaker.

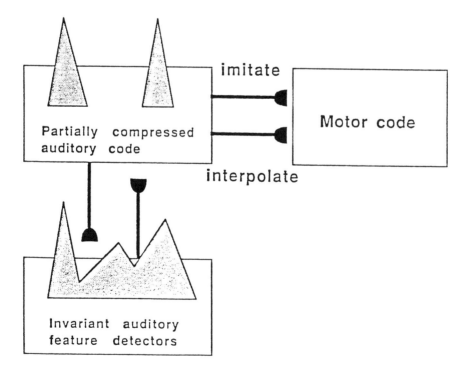

Figure 2. Neural interactions between a partially-compressed auditory code and a motor code permits the imitation of novel heard sounds.

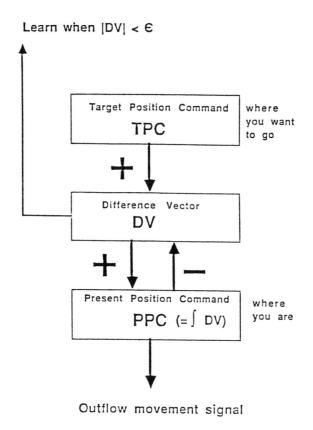

Figure 3. Basic VITE module and its learning gate, for use in encoding the TPC codes.

to functional similarities between speech articulation and arm movement problems. Moreover, we agree with Lieberman (1984) that phylogenetically the speech system appropriated the speech articulators and their neural controlling structures from their original tasks of swallowing, chewing, and so forth—tasks more typical of standard motor control concerns. The VITE model posits three interacting neural levels: (1) a Target Position Command (TPC) level, whose spatial distribution of activity codes where the limb "wants to go," (2) a Present Position Command (PPC) level, which generates an outflow movement command, and (3) a Difference Vector (DV) level, which compares the TPC and PPC codes. Such a structure has been used to explain a range of motor control psychophysics and physiology results, in particular (for our speech system) the simultaneous contraction of several muscle groups in a synergy, even at different overall rates. The learning of a motor task, in this scheme, involves the printing (i.e., modification of synapses for long-term memory) of the motor code when the limb is at or near the target position. Put another way, learning occurs when the present position and the target position form a near match (i.e., when $DV < \epsilon$). Hence in our speech system the Difference Vector layer can act as a learning *gate*, regulating the formation of the auditory-to-articulatory map during the near match condition, as shown in Figure 3.

Speech articulators, however, do not all function as a single, unitized system;

rather, there are several muscle synergies or *coordinative structures* (Fowler, 1980) working quasi-independently. For instance, one coordinative structure might link the jaw and front of the tongue for bringing the top of the tongue to the hard palate in order to utter [t], while a different coordinative structure is controlling the back of the tongue to utter a (coarticulated) [a]. Each of the coordinative structures must have its own TPC, PPC, and DV layers, to preserve such quasi-independence. Figure 4 shows how the TPC's of different coordinative structures are chunked into distinct motor control commands. Thus the imitative map can associate different aspects of the partially compressed auditory code with different coordinative structures. Figure 4 also shows the basic structure of the circular reaction loop linking the auditory system and the motor system, incorporating the VITE circuit and its learning gate.

4. Self-Stabilization of Imitation via Motor-to-Auditory Priming

In a self-organized system, a key issue concerns the ability of the system to *self-stabilize* its learning under natural conditions (Carpenter and Grossberg, 1987a, 1987b). During speech the auditory code varies (in general) *continuously* due to its representation of a stream of varying sounds, whereas the controlling motor code varies more *discretely* due to the fact that new target position commands (TPCs) are printed by the imitative associative map only when the motor system achieves an approximate match (Figure 3), either at an initial TPC or a final TPC of a simple utterance (Figure 5). This raises the issue of insuring that the emerging auditory code is *consistent* with the motor code so that the imitative map can self-stabilize. Such consistency can be achieved through top-down motor priming which associates the compressed motor codes that represent the coordinative structures with activation patterns across the auditory feature detectors, as shown in Figure 6—an example of active internal regulation by top-down resonant feedback.

The top-down motor expectations (or priming signals) reorganize the auditory code to make it consistent with the evolving motor code. Such priming occurs during the activity of any given motor code, and hence reinforces the activity patterns across auditory feature detectors that are heard contemporaneous and consistent with such motor codes. These motorically-modified feature activity patterns are encoded in long-term memory within the auditory-to-auditory pathways to the partially compressed auditory code. Even during passive listening, these motorically-influenced auditory codes are activated. Heard speech is thereby analyzed by "how it would have been phonated." This is in agreement with the motor theory of speech perception (c.f., Studdert-Kennedy, 1984) and finds support from physiology (Ojemann, 1983). These results and the architecture of Figure 6 clarify why the concerted attempts to find purely auditory correlates of speech segments have not met with greater success (c.f., Zue, 1976; Cooper, 1980, 1983), and suggests how an artificial system capable of recognizing natural speech can incorporate motor information that human listeners employ.

5. Higher Stages of Processing: Context-Sensitive Chunking and Unitization of the Emerging Auditory Speech Code

Stages of the auditory system higher than the ones described above rely on processes other than circular reactions for stabilizing the emerging language code. Such processes *unitize*, *chunk*, or *group* the emerging discrete linguistic units in a context-

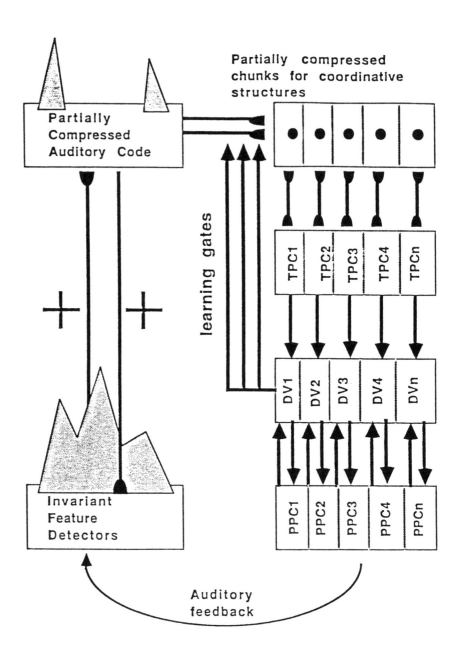

Figure 4. Circular reaction loop linking the motor system (right) with auditory system (left). Parallel motor channels for coordinative structures are shown, each with its associated learning gate, which prints (modifies the synapses for long-term memory) the imitative map between the partially-compressed auditory code and the motor code.

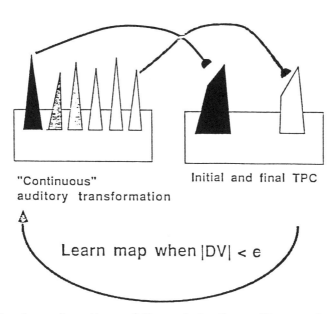

Figure 5. The dynamic pattern of the code in the auditory system is more continuous, while that in the control structure for the motor system is more discrete. When activated, such a motor code initiates a unitized, stereotyped synergetic action of articulators.

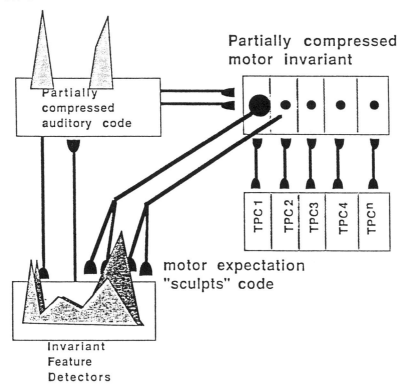

Figure 6. Top-down priming from the motor to the auditory system reorganizes the emerging auditory code to be consistent with the motor commands. This motorically-influenced auditory code is further compressed at higher stages of the auditory system.

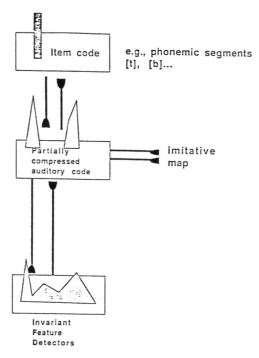

Figure 7. Unitization is achieved by compressing the partially compressed auditory code to yield an item code, which includes such units as phonemic segments.

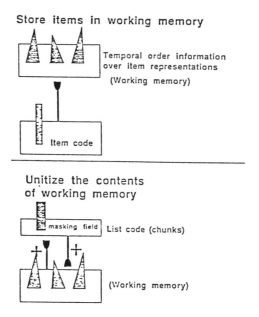

Figure 8. Context-sensitive list codes are formed via a two-level process: (top) Items are placed in *working memory*, which encodes temporal order information. Then (bottom) a masking field uses bottom-up flow and top-down priming to yield context-sensitive list codes.

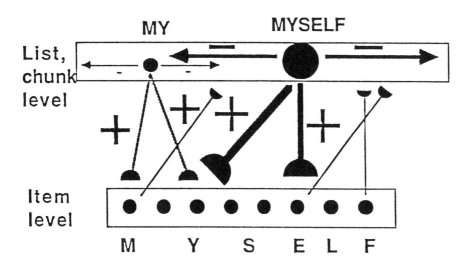

Figure 9. A masking field architecture creates context-sensitive list codes by using both bottom-up filtering signals and top-down priming signals from the list level. There is competition between units in the list level. "Larger" nodes—ones that pool information from a larger number of items—inhibit "smaller" nodes more effectively than vice versa. For instance, if list nodes for MY, SELF, ELF, and MYSELF are encoded, the presentation of the letters M-Y-S-E-L-F at the item level will lead to a resonance between the MYSELF node and the six items, while nodes representing smaller, less predictive, groupings are quickly suppressed.

sensitive manner. Such context-sensitivity is crucial if the network is to be able to classify any given phonemic segment (say) in all its coarticulated forms.

An early stage of unitization is achieved by compressing the partially compressed auditory code to yield an *item code*, as shown in Figure 7. Grouping such items into context-sensitive chunks requires two stages, as shown in Figure 8. First, sequentially occurring items are stored in a *working memory* level to encode temporal order information over the items. Next, these items are grouped by a *masking field* (Cohen and Grossberg, 1986, 1987) into context-sensitive list chunks.

6. Masking Fields

In brief, a masking field neural structure possesses both bottom-up and top-down interconnections with the item level (Figure 9). Nodes at the list level compete through mutual inhibition. List nodes that are best predictive of *longer* patterns of items will inhibit the less predictive nodes for shorter lists. Recognition of a unitized grouping of items occurs when a bottom-up top-down context-sensitive *resonance* develops. In speech networks, such a masking field can thus unitize the evolving auditory code into predictive chunks, representing, say, phonemic segments.

Figure 10 schematizes the anatomy of a masking field. Figure 11 schematizes

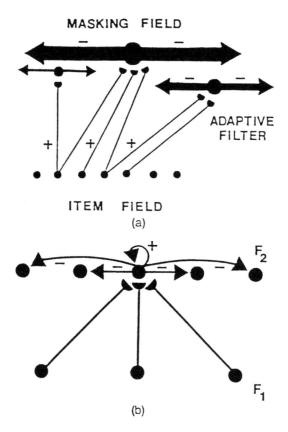

Figure 10. Masking field interactions: (a) Cells from an item field F_1 grow randomly to a masking field F_2 along positionally sensitive gradients. The nodes in the masking field grow so that larger item groupings, up to some optimal size, can activate nodes with broader and stronger inhibitory interactions. Thus the $F_1 \rightarrow F_2$ connections and the $F_2 \leftrightarrow F_2$ interactions exhibit properties of self-similarity. (b) The interactions within a masking field F_2 include positive feedback from a node to itself and negative feedback from a node to its neighbors. Long term memory (LTM) traces at the ends of $F_1 \rightarrow F_2$ pathways (designated by hemidisks) adaptively tune the filter defined by these pathways to amplify the F_2 reaction to item groupings which have previously succeeded in activating their target F_2 nodes.

the two primary types of coding sensitivity of which a masking field is capable in response to bottom-up inputs from an item field. Figures 12 and 13 summarize computer simulations which demonstrate this coding competence.

The interactions between these levels can explain many speech properties, including properties of temporal invariance and phonemic restoration. When designed to incorporate a "long-term memory invariance principle" (Grossberg, 1986, 1987; Grossberg and Stone, 1986a, 1986b), the spatial pattern of activation across working memory defines an invariant code, and an attentional gain control signal to the working memory stage preserves this spatial code under changes in overall speaking rate.

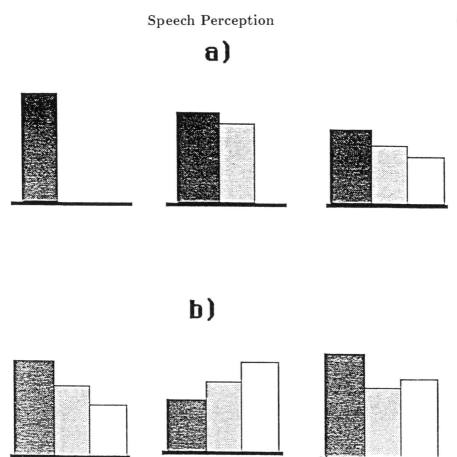

Figure 11. Two types of masking field sensitivity: (a) A masking field F_2 can automatically rescale its sensitivity to differentially react as the F_1 activity pattern expands through time to activate more F_1 cells. It hereby acts like a "multiple spatial frequency filter." (b) A masking field can differentially react to different F_1 activity patterns which activate the same set of F_1 cells. By (a) and (b), F_2 acts like a spatial pattern discriminator which can compensate for changes in overall spatial scale without losing its sensitivity to pattern changes at the finest spatial scale.

Phonemic restoration occurs when an ambiguous or missing sound is clearly heard when presented in the proper context. The top-down priming of a masking field can complete ambiguous elements of the item code, so long as these items can be reorganized by the 2/3 Rule properties of the prime (Carpenter and Grossberg, 1987a, 1987b). The speech code results from a resonant wave which is controlled by feedback interactions between the working memory and masking field levels. Although the list chunks which reorganize the form and grouping of item codes utilize "future" information, this resonant wave can emerge from "past" to "future" because the internal masking of unpredictive list codes within the masking field occurs much faster than the time scale for unfolding the resonant wave (Figure 14.)

The overall neural architecture employing the elements described above is shown in Figure 15.

Additional network designs are being developed for dealing with additional prob-

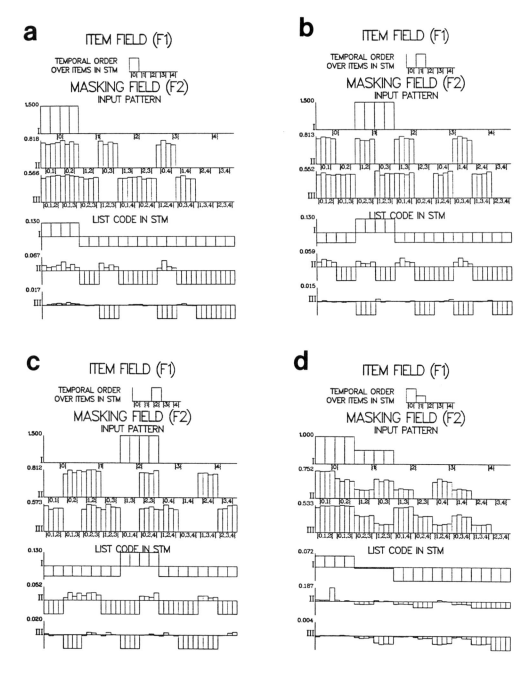

Figure 12. (a) The correct list code {0} is preferred in STM, but predictive list codes which include {0} as a part are also activated with lesser STM weights. The prediction gets less activation if {0} forms a smaller part of it. (b) The correct list code {1} is preferred in STM, but the predictive list codes which include {1} as a part are also activated with lesser STM weights. (c) The list code in response to item {2} also generates an appropriate reaction. (d) A list code of type {0,1} is maximally activated, but part codes {0} and predictive codes which include {0,1} as a part are also activated with lesser STM weights.

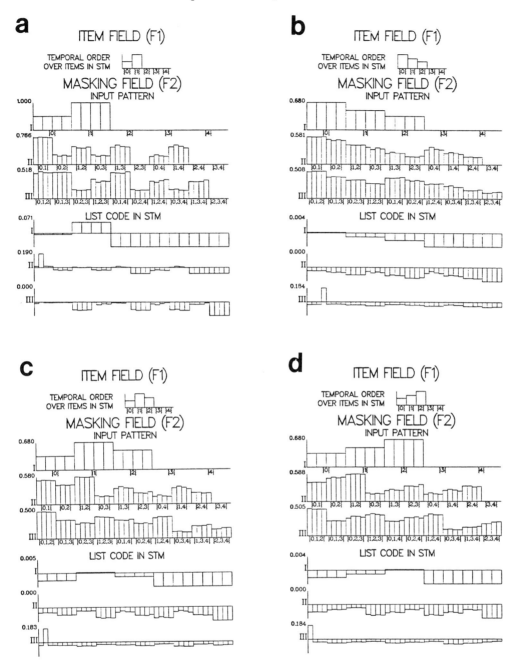

Figure 13. (a) A different list code of type {0,1} is maximally activated, but part codes {1} are also activated with lesser STM weight. Due to the random growth of $F_1 \to F_2$ pathways, no predictive list codes are activated (to 3 significant digits). (b)–(d) When the STM pattern across F_1 includes three items, the list code in STM strongly activates an appropriate list code. Part groupings are suppressed due to the high level of predictiveness of this list code. Comparison of Figures 12a, 12d, and 13b shows that as the item code across F_1 becomes more constraining, the list code representation becomes less distributed across F_2.

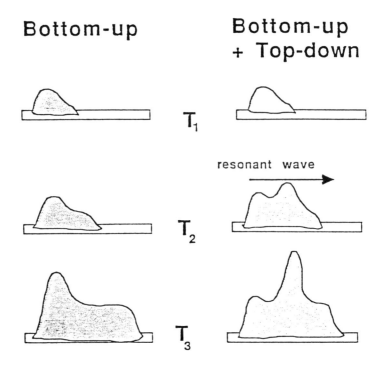

Figure 14. (Left): The activity pattern in working memory as new items enter the system, if the architecture had purely bottom-up connections. (Right): If the system has top-down priming, on the other hand, crucial features in the working memory that fit into a coherent pattern are reinforced, leading to a different distribution of neural activity. This resonant wave constitutes the speech code.

lems such as factoring rhythm information from linguistic information and the coding of repetitive patterns. Even as it stands, however, the architecture and design considerations described above provide a new processing architecture for understanding such issues as analysis-by-synthesis, the motor theory of speech perception, categorical perception, invariant speech perception, and phonemic restoration.

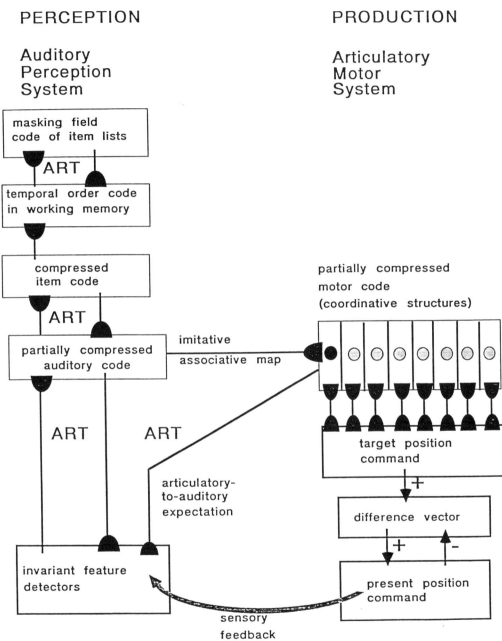

Figure 15. Global architecture for a speech recognition and synthesis system, employing the processing described above. See text for details.

REFERENCES

Bullock, D. and Grossberg, S. (1987). Neural dynamics of planned arm movements: Emergent invariants and speed-accuracy properties during trajectory formation. *Psychological Review*, in press.

Carpenter, G.A. and Grossberg, S. (1987a). A massively parallel architecture for a self-organizing neural pattern recognition machine. *Computer Vision, Graphics, and Image Processing*, **37**, 54–115.

Carpenter, G.A. and Grossberg, S. (1987b). ART 2: Self-organization of stable category recognition codes for analog input patterns. *Applied Optics*, **26**, 4919–4930.

Cohen, M.A. and Grossberg, S. (1986). Neural dynamics of speech and language coding: Developmental programs, perceptual grouping, and competition for short term memory. *Human Neurobiology*, **5**, 1–22.

Cohen, M.A. and Grossberg, S. (1987). Masking fields: A massively parallel neural architecture for learning, recognizing, and predicting multiple groupings of patterned data. *Applied Optics*, **26**, 1866–1891.

Cooper, F.S. (1980). Acoustics in human communication: Evolving ideas about the nature of speech. *Journal of the Acoustical Society of America*, **68**, 18–21.

Cooper, F.S. (1983). Some reflections on speech research. In P.F. MacNeilage (Ed.), **The production of speech**. New York: Springer-Verlag.

Fowler, C. (1980). Coarticulation and theories of extrinsic timing. *Journal of Phonetics*, **8**, 113–133.

Grossberg, S. (1986). The adaptive self-organization of serial order in behavior: Speech, language, and motor control. In E.C. Schwab and H.C. Nusbaum (Eds.), **Pattern recognition by humans and machines, Vol. 1: Speech perception**. New York: Academic Press, 187–294.

Grossberg, S. (Ed.) (1987). **The adaptive brain, II: Vision, speech, language, and motor control**. Amsterdam: Elsevier/North-Holland.

Grossberg, S. and Stone, G.O. (1986a). Neural dynamics of attention switching and temporal order information in short-term memory. *Memory and Cognition*, **14**, 451–468.

Grossberg, S. and Stone, G.O. (1986b). Neural dynamics of word recognition and recall: Attentional priming, learning, and resonance. *Psychological Review*, **93**, 46–74.

Lieberman, P. (1984). **The biology and evolution of language**. Cambridge, MA: Harvard University Press.

Ojemann, G. (1983). Brain organization for language from the perspective of electrical stimulation mapping. *Behavioral and Brain Sciences*, **2**, 189–230.

Piaget, J. (1963). **The origins of intelligence in children**. New York: Norton.

Studdert-Kennedy, M. (1984). Perceptual processing links to the motor system. In M. Studdert-Kennedy (Ed.), **Psychobiology of language**. Cambridge, MA: MIT Press, 29–39.

Zue, V.W. (1976). Acoustic characteristics of stop consonants: A controlled study. Ph.D. Dissertation, Massachusetts Institute of Technology, Electrical Engineering and Computer Science Department.

NEURAL DYNAMICS OF ADAPTIVE TIMING
AND TEMPORAL DISCRIMINATION DURING
ASSOCIATIVE LEARNING
by
Stephen Grossberg and Nestor A. Schmajuk

Preface

Chapters 18 and 19 describe the type of temporally organized processing of event sequences that occurs during speech, language, and goal-oriented actions. The present chapter is a 1989 article that describes a type of process that helps to control the timing of individual events.

This sort of timing is needed to control interactions between brain recognition and reinforcement systems. In particular, humans and animals need to distinguish between *expected nonoccurrences* and *unexpected nonoccurrences* of a goal object. An expected nonoccurrence refers to the nonoccurrence of a reinforcing event earlier than its expected arrival time, based upon prior learning. Such a nonoccurrence should not be treated as a predictive failure. An unexpected nonoccurrence of a goal is the nonappearance of the goal during a time frame when previous experience has taught that it should occur. Such an event should trigger a range of adaptive reactions, such as selective forgetting, emotional frustration, and exploratory behaviors, that are aimed at overcoming the predictive failure.

The main thrust of the article is that ART recognition and reinforcement mechanisms include processes that enable a natural solution of this problem to be developed. Once again, the existence of an orienting subsystem plays a key role. Also needed are feedback interactions between cognitive representations and drive representations. The latter representations, first described in Grossberg (1971), are predicted to be the midbrain sites, including but not restricted to hypothalamus, at which reinforcing and homeostatic events are represented. The ART model of these interactions was further developed in Grossberg (1982, 1984) and Grossberg and Levine (1987). Buonomano, Baxter, and Byrne (1990) have used this model to explain their data on conditioning in *Aplysia*. This convergence of theory and experiment represents a striking confirmation of an early neural network prediction, and suggests that some conditioning circuits, laid down early in evolution, have been preserved in subsequent evolutionary variations.

The article proposes a new type of timing model, called Spectral Timing, to explain how expected nonoccurrences are discounted while unexpected nonoccurrences are not. The model suggests that habituative chemical transmitters may play a key role in spectral timing. This role for transmitters may be compared to the one proposed in Chapter 14 to realize a Medium Term Memory for distributed memory search in ART 3. The spectral timing model is tested by using it to quantitatively fit data about adaptively timed conditioning of the rabbit nictitating membrane, and to discuss data about timed hippocampal conditioning and CNV event-related potentials.

References

Buonomano, D.V., Baxter, D.A., and Byrne, J.H. (1990). Small networks of empirically derived adaptive elements simulate some higher-order features of classical conditioning. *Neural Networks*, **3**, 507–524.

Grossberg, S. (1971). On the dynamics of operant conditioning. *Journal of Theoretical Biology*, **33**, 225–255.

Grossberg, S. (1982). Processing of expected and unexpected events during conditioning and attention: A psychophysiological theory. *Psychological Review*, **89**, 529–572.

Grossberg, S. (1984). Some psychophysiological and pharmacological correlates of a developmental, cognitive, and motivational theory. In R. Karrer, J. Cohen, and P. Tueting (Eds.), **Brain and information: Event related potentials**. New York: New York Academy of Sciences, 58–151.

Grossberg, S. and Levine, D.S. (1987). Neural dynamics of attentionally-modulated Pavlovian conditioning: Blocking, inter-stimulus interval, and secondary reinforcement. *Applied Optics*, **26**, 5015–5030.

Neural Networks
1989, **2**, 79–102
©1989 Pergamon Press, Inc.

NEURAL DYNAMICS OF ADAPTIVE TIMING AND TEMPORAL DISCRIMINATION DURING ASSOCIATIVE LEARNING

Stephen Grossberg† and Nestor A. Schmajuk‡

Abstract

A neural network model that controls behavioral timing is described and simulated. This model, called the Spectral Timing Model, controls a type of timing whereby an animal or robot can learn to wait for an expected goal by discounting expected nonoccurrences of a goal object until the expected time of arrival of the goal. If the goal object does not then materialize, the animal can respond to unexpected nonoccurrences of the goal with appropriate changes in information processing and exploratory behavior. The model is a variant of the gated dipole model of opponent processing. When the gated dipole model is generalized to include a spectrum of cellular response rates within a large population of cells, the model's total output signal generates accurate learned timing properties that collectively provide a good quantitative fit to animal learning data. In particular, the Spectral Timing Model utilizes the habituative transmitter gates and adaptive long term memory traces that are characteristic of gated dipole models. The Spectral Timing Model is embedded into an Adaptive Resonance Theory (ART) neural architecture for the learning of correlations between internal representations of recognition codes and reinforcement codes. This type of learning is called conditioned reinforcer learning. The two types of internal representations are called sensory representations (S) and drive representations (D). Activation of a drive representation D by the Spectral Timing Model inhibits output signals from the orienting subsystem (A) of the ART architecture and activates a motor response. The inhibitory pathway helps to prevent spurious resets of short term memory, forgetting, and orienting responses from being caused by events other than the goal object prior to the expected arrival time of the goal. Simulated data properties include the inverted U in learning as a function of the interstimulus interval (ISI) that occurs between onset of the conditioned stimulus (CS) and the unconditioned stimulus (US); correlations of peak time, standard deviation, Weber fraction, and peak amplitude of the conditioned response as a function of the

---

† Supported in part by the Air Force Office of Scientific Research (AFOSR F49620-86-C-0037 and AFOSR F49620-87-C-0018) and the National Science Foundation (NSF IRI-84-17756).

‡ Supported in part by the National Science Foundation (NSF IRI-84-17756). The authors thank Carol Yanakakis and Cynthia Suchta for their valuable assistance in the preparation of the manuscript and illustrations.

ISI; increase of conditioned response amplitude, but not its timing, with US intensity; speed-up of the timing circuit by an increase in CS intensity or by drugs that increase concentrations of brain dopamine or acetylcholine; multiple timing peaks in response to learning conditions using multiple ISI's; and conditioned timing of cell activation within the hippocampus and of the contingent negative variation (CNV) event-related potential. The results on speed-up by drugs that increase brain concentrations of dopamine and acetylcholine support a 1972 prediction that the gated dipole habituative transmitter is a catecholamine and its long term memory trace transmitter is acetylcholine. It is noted that the timing circuit described herein is only one of several functionally distinct neural circuits for governing different types of timed behavior competence.

1. Introduction: Timing the Expected Delay of a Goal Object in a Spatially Distributed and Nonstationary World

This article presents a model of a neural circuit that controls behavioral timing. There are several different types of brain processes that organize the temporal unfolding of serial order in behavior. The present article describes in detail a model of one type of timing circuit, and outlines how this circuit may be embedded in larger neural systems that regulate several different types of temporal organization. It seems to us that such timing circuits are just as important for the survival of animals as they are for the design of robots that are capable of freely moving in a spatially distributed world that is characterized by unexpected events and nonstationary statistics.

Many goal objects in such a world may be delayed subsequent to the actions that elicit them, or the environmental events that signal their subsequent arrival. Were all causes followed immediately by their consequences, the world would be a much simpler place to live. In the world as it is, humans and many animal species can learn to wait for the anticipated arrival of a delayed goal object. In part, this capability enhances the efficiency of the consummatory behavior that is triggered by the arrival of the goal object, such as eating when the goal object is food, because the animal can time the preparations to eat so that they are synchronized with the arrival of the food.

The need for behavioral timing becomes even more important in the lives of animals that are capable of exploring their environments for novel sources of gratification. Although the evolution of efficient locomotion greatly enhanced the range of alternative goals that an animal could sample, it also created the danger that the animal may never be able to consummate at all. For example, if an animal could not inhibit its exploratory behavior, then it could easily starve to death by restlessly moving from place to place, unable to remain in one place long enough to carry out the consummatory behaviors needed to acquire food there. On the other hand, if an animal inhibited its exploratory behavior for too long, and remained in one place waiting for an expected source of food to materialize, then it could starve to death if food was not, after all, forthcoming.

2. Timing the Balance between Exploration for Novel Rewards and Consummation of Expected Rewards

Thus the animal's task is to accurately time the *expected* delay of a goal object based upon its previous experiences in a given situation. It needs to regulate the balance between its exploratory behavior aimed at searching for novel sources of reward, and its consummatory behavior aimed at acquiring expected sources of reward. To effectively control this balance, the animal needs to be able to suppress its exploratory behavior and focus its attention upon an expected source of reward at around the time that the expected delay transpires for acquiring the reward.

3. Distinguishing Expected Nonoccurrences from Unexpected Nonoccurrences: Inhibiting the Negative Consequences of Expected Nonoccurrences

The type of timed behavior described above is restricted to calibrating the delay of a single behavioral act, rather than organizing a correctly timed and speed-controlled sequence of acts. The key problem that needs to be mechanistically understood is illustrated by the following example. Suppose that, after pushing a lever, an animal typically receives a food pellet from a food magazine two seconds later. Suppose that the animal orients to the food magazine right after pushing the lever. When the animal inspects the food magazine, it perceives the nonoccurrence of food during the subsequent two seconds. These nonoccurrences disconfirm the sensory expectation that food will appear in the magazine. Moreover, the perceptual processing cycle that processes this sensory information occurs at a much faster rate than two seconds, so that it can compute this sensory disconfirmation many times before the two second delay has elapsed.

The key issue is: What spares the animal from erroneously reacting to these *expected nonoccurrences* of food during the first two seconds as predictive failures? Why does not the animal immediately become frustrated by the nonoccurrence of food and release exploratory behavior aimed at searching for food in another place? On the other hand, if food does not appear after two seconds have elapsed, why does the animal then react to the *unexpected nonoccurrence* of food by becoming frustrated and releasing exploratory behavior?

We assert that a primary role of the timing mechanism is to inhibit, or *gate*, the process whereby sensory mismatches trigger the orienting and reinforcing mechanisms that would otherwise reset the animal's attentional focus, negatively reinforce its previous consummatory behavior, and release its exploratory behavior. The process of *registering* these sensory mismatches or matches, as the case might be, is not inhibited. Indeed, if the food happened to appear earlier than expected, the animal could certainly perceive its occurrence and begin to respond accordingly. The sensory matching process, as such, is thus not inhibited by the timing mechanism. Rather, the effects of sensory mismatches upon processes of sensory reset and reinforcement are inhibited.

This inhibitory action is assumed to be part of a more general competition that occurs between the motivational, or arousal, sources that energize different types of behavior. Exploratory behaviors enable the animal to come into contact with novel goal objects. Such behaviors are assumed to be energized by endogenously active motivational sources. Hence, unless they are actively inhibited, these endogenously active arousal sources could remove the animal from all sources of delayed reward.

Consummatory behaviors, such as eating, enable the animal to complete behavioral cycles involving familiar and accessible goal objects. The inhibitory action posited above is from the motivational sources of consummatory behaviors to the motivational sources of orienting and exploratory behaviors.

It is also assumed that the consummatory arousal sources are in mutual competition, enabling only the strongest combinations of sensory, reinforcing, and homeostatic signals to control observable behaviors (Grossberg, 1982, Chapter 6; Staddon, 1983). Thus the posited competition is a special case of the general hypothesis that the output signals from all motivational sources compete for the control of observable behaviors.

To explain how this process works, the present article is organized into two parts:

Part I describes a model of the timing circuit and shows that it can be used to quantitatively explain data from a number of classical and instrumental conditioning experiments about how timed behavior is learned.

Part II shows how this timing circuit can be embedded in a larger neural system to carry out the gating function described above. This larger system is a specialized Adaptive Resonance Theory, or ART, circuit that has been progressively developed in a number of articles since its first appearances in Grossberg (1975, 1978). These and relevant subsequent articles are brought together in several books (Grossberg, 1982, 1987, 1988). The present article provides a summary of the major circuit concepts.

PART I
SPECTRAL TIMING MODEL

4. Spectral Timing Model: An Application of Gated Dipole Theory

The timing model presented herein grew out of, and forms part of, a larger theory of cognitive-emotional interactions (Grossberg, 1982, 1987, 1988; Grossberg and Levine, 1987; Grossberg and Schmajuk, 1987). These are the interactions whereby reinforcing events influence the course of conditioning or associative learning through time and thereby regulate the salience of the events to which an animal will subsequently attend. The model is evaluated by demonstrating its competence in explaining data about how animals time their responses during conditioning experiments.

The two major experimentally controlled events during a conditioning experiment are the conditioned stimulus (CS) and the unconditioned stimulus (US). The CS is a sensory stimulus which does not initially possess the reinforcing properties of the US, but gains (some of) these properties by being paired with the US during learning trials. We denote by $I_{CS}(t)$ the internal input generated by the CS to the timing circuit, and by $I_{US}(t)$ the internal input generated by the US to the timing circuit.

The timing model specializes a design for an opponent processing network, called a *gated dipole*, that was introduced in Grossberg (1972a, 1972b). One version of the model is described. It is called the Spectral Timing Model for reasons described below. The model developed herein uses only feedforward anatomical pathways. On the other hand, as is often the case, the learning is controlled by feedback signals within these pathways.

The circuit diagram of the Spectral Timing model is schematized in Figure 1. A key property of the model is that the CS activates a population of cells whose members react at different rates, according to a spectrum of rates α_i. Neural populations whose elements are distributed along a temporal or spatial parameter are familiar throughout the nervous system. Two examples are the *size principle*, which governs variable rates of responding in spinal motor centers (Henneman, 1957, 1985), and the spatial frequency-tuned cells of the visual cortex, which also react at different rates (Jones and Keck, 1978; Musselwhite and Jeffreys, 1985; Parker and Salzen, 1977a, 1977b; Parker *et al.*, 1982a, 1982b; Plant *et al.*, 1983; Skrandies, 1984; Vassilev and Strashimirov, 1979; Vassilev *et al.*, 1983; Williamson *et al.*, 1978).

SPECTRAL TIMING EQUATIONS

Spectral Activation

$$\frac{d}{dt}x_i = \alpha_i[-Ax_i + (1 - Bx_i)I_{CS}(t)]; \tag{1}$$

Transmitter Gate

$$\frac{d}{dt}y_i = C(1 - y_i) - Df(x_i)y_i, \tag{2}$$

where $f(x_i)$ is a sigmoid signal function of the form

$$f(x_i) = \frac{x_i^n}{\beta^n + x_i^n}; \tag{3}$$

Associative Learning (LTM Trace)

$$\frac{d}{dt}z_i = Ef(x_i)y_i[-z_i + I_{US}(t)]; \tag{4}$$

Output Signal

$$R = [\sum_i f(x_i)y_i z_i - F]^+; \tag{5}$$

where

$$[w]^+ = \begin{cases} w & \text{if } w > 0 \\ 0 & \text{if } w \leq 0. \end{cases} \tag{6}$$

A. The Activation Spectrum

The function $I_{CS}(t)$ is assumed to be a step function whose amplitude is proportional to the CS intensity, and which stays on for a fixed time after CS offset because it is internally stored in short term memory (STM). Figure 2 depicts a typical relationship between CS, $I_{CS}(t)$, and the US input $I_{US}(t)$. Input $I_{CS}(t)$ activates all potentials x_i in (1) of the cells in its target population. The potentials x_i respond at rates proportional to α_i, $i = 1, 2, \ldots, n$.

Each potential x_i generates the output signal $f(x_i)$. Figure 3a depicts the results of a computer simulation in which $f(x_i(t))$ is plotted as a function of time t for values of α_i ranging from .2 ("fast cells") to .0025 ("slow cells").

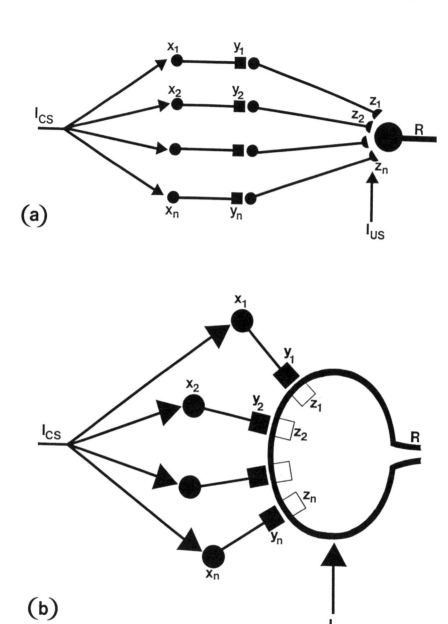

Figure 1. Circuit diagram of the Spectral Timing Model. The function $I_{CS}(t)$ denotes a step function input that is proportional to the CS intensity and stays on after the CS offset; x_i denote cell activities with different growth rates α_i; z_i denote adaptive long term memory traces; and $R(t)$ denotes the total circuit output. In version (a) of the model, the z_i are computed in terminals of the presynaptic pathways converging upon the output neuron, and the I_{US} activates them presynaptically. In (b), the z_i are computed as part of the postsynaptic membrane of the output neuron, and the I_{US} activates them via a postsynaptic route.

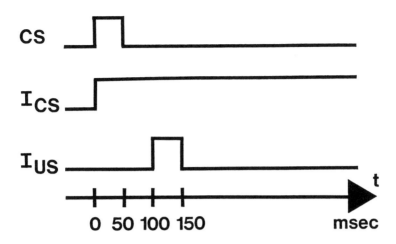

Figure 2. Temporal arrangement of a 50-msec CS and a 50-msec US separated by a 100-msec ISI. I_{CS} is the step function activated by the CS that inputs to the Spectral Timing Model.

B. The Habituation Spectrum

Each output signal $f(x_i)$ activates a neurotransmitter y_i. According to equation (2), process y_i accumulates to a constant target level 1, via term $C(1 - y_i)$, and is inactivated, or *habituates*, due to a mass action interaction with signal $f(x_i)$, via term $-Df(x_i)y_i$. Although the rate parameters C and D that govern each process y_i are independent of i, the different rates α_i at which each x_i is activated causes the corresponding y_i to become habituated at a different rate. A habituation spectrum is thereby generated at which the y_i processes are successively inactivated. The signal functions $f(x_i(t))$ in Figure 3a generate the habituation spectrum of $y_i(t)$ curves shown in Figure 3b.

C. The Gated Signal Spectrum

Each signal $f(x_i)$ interacts with y_i via mass action. This process is also called the *gating* of $f(x_i)$ by y_i to yield a net signal g_i proportional to $f(x_i)y_i$. Each of these gated signals, as a function of time $g_i(t) \equiv f(x_i(t))y_i(t)$, has a different rate of growth and decay. The set of all these curves thereby generates a gated signal spectrum, which is shown in Figure 3c. The curves in Figure 3c exhibit the following properties:

a) Each function $g_i(t)$ is a unimodal function of time, where function $g_i(t)$ achieves its maximum value M_i at time T_i;

b) T_i is an increasing function of i; and

c) M_i is a decreasing function of i.

D. Temporally Selective Associative Learning

Each *long term memory (LTM) trace* z_i in (4) is activated by its own temporally selective sampling signal g_i. The sampling signal g_i turns on the learning process, and causes z_i to approach I_{US} during the sampling interval at a rate proportional to

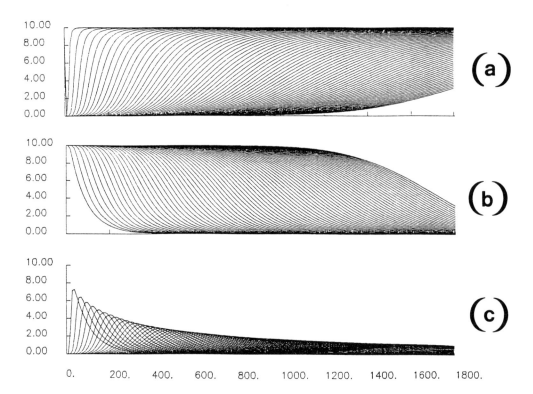

Figure 3. The spectrum of reactions to a step input I_{CS}: (a) Eighty signal functions $f(x_i(t)), i = 1, 2, \ldots, 80$, are plotted as a function of t. (b) The corresponding eighty habituative transmitter gates $y_i(t)$ are plotted as a function of t. (c) The corresponding gated signals $g_i(t) = f(x_i(t))y_i(t)$ are plotted as a function of t. Parameters are: $\alpha_i = .2i^{-1}$ for $i = 1, 2, \ldots, 80$; A=1; B=1; C=.0001; D=.125; $\beta = .8$; n=8; $I_{CS}(t) = 1$ for $t > 0$. In all simulations, one time step represents 1 msec and all $f(x_i(0)) = 0$ and $y_i(0) = 1$.

g_i. Each z_i thus grows by an amount that reflects the degree to which the curves $g_i(t)$ and $I_{US}(t)$ have simultaneously large values through time.

The time interval between CS onset and US onset is called the *interstimulus interval*, or ISI. The individual LTM traces differ in their ability to learn at different values of the ISI. This is the basis of the network's timing properties.

Figure 4 illustrates how six different LTM traces z_i, $i = 1, \ldots, 6$, learn during a simulated learning experiment. The CS and US are paired during 4 learning trials, after which the CS is presented alone on a single performance trial.

E. The Doubly Gated Signal Spectrum

The CS input $I_{CS}(t)$ remains on and constant throughout the duration of each learning trial. The US input $I_{US}(t)$ is presented after an ISI of 500 msec. unit and remains on for 50 msec. The upper panel in each part of the figure depicts the gated signal function $g_i(t)$ with α_i chosen at progressively slower rates. The middle panel plots the corresponding LTM trace $z_i(t)$, and the lower panel plots the doubly gated signal $h_i(t) = f(x_i(t))y_i(t)z_i(t)$. Each doubly gated signal function $h_i(t)$ registers how well the timing of CS and US is registered by the ith processing channel. Note that in

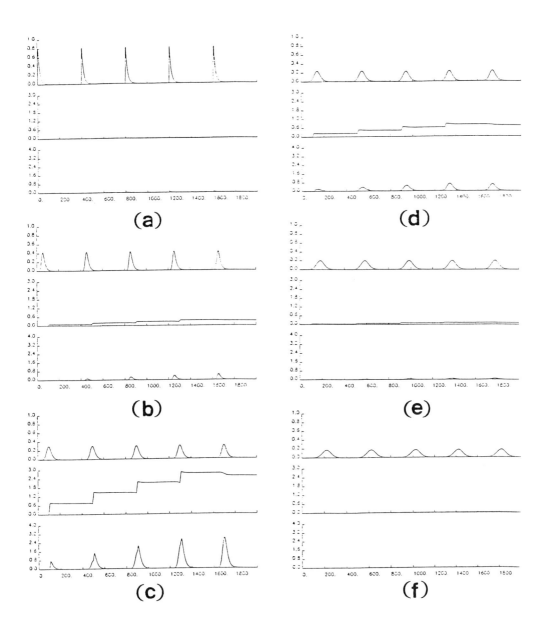

Figure 4. Selective learning within different spectral populations at a fixed ISI = 500 msec. Each three-image panel from (a) to (f) represents the gated signal $g_i(t)$ [top], long term memory trace $z_i(t)$ [middle], and doubly gated signal $h_i(t) = g_i(t)z_i(t)$ [bottom], at a different value of i. In (a), $i = 1$; in (b), $i = 10$; in (c), $i = 20$; in (d), $i = 30$; in (e), $i = 40$; in (f), $i = 50$. The same parameters as in Figure 3 were used. In addition, E=.01 and $I_{US}(t) = 10$ for $t \in (500, 550)$ and $= 0$ otherwise.

Figure 4c, whose gated signal $g_i(t)$ peaks at approximately 500 msec. the LTM trace $z_i(t)$ exhibits maximum learning. The doubly gated signal $h_i(t)$ also shows a maximal exhancement due to learning, and exhibits peaks of activation at approximately 500 msec. after onset of the CS on each trial. This behavior is also generated on the fifth trial, during which only the CS is presented.

F. The Output Signal

The output signal $R(t)$ defined in equation (5) is the sum of all the doubly gated signal functions $h_i(t)$ minus a threshold F. The output signal computes the cumulative learned reaction of all the cells to the input pattern.

Figure 5a plots the output signal generated in a computer experiment through time across all five trials, using an ISI of 400 msec. In Figure 5b, successive responses in Figure 5a are superimposed to show how they are aligned with respect to the ISI and increase due to learning on successive trials. Figure 5c plots all of the doubly gated signal functions $h_i(t)$ that are summated to form $R(t)$ on the fifth trial. Figure 5d plots all the gated signal functions $g_i(t)$ whose multiplication by $z_i(t)$ generates the $h_i(t)$ curves. Together these Figures illustrate how function $R(t)$ generates an accurately timed response from the cumulative partial learning of all cells in the population spectrum.

5. Effect of Increasing ISI and US Intensity

Figures 6a–6c plot the curves that are generated by ISI's of 0, 500, and 1000 msec. In every case, the learned cumulative response $R(t)$ is accurately centered at the correct ISI.

Figure 7 plots the functions $R(t)$ that are generated by different ISI's in a series of learning experiments. These are the $R(t)$ functions generated on the fifth trial of each experiment in response to a CS alone, after four trials of prior learning, with all time axes synchronized with CS onset. In Figure 7a, the $I_{US}(t)$ was chosen twice as large as in Figure 7b. Halving $I_{US}(t)$ amplitude reduces the $R(t)$ amplitudes without changing their timing or overall shape. Note that the envelope of the $R(t)$ functions increases and then decreases through time, and that the individual $R(t)$ functions corresponding to larger ISI's are broader.

6. Comparison with Nictitating Membrane Conditioning Data

The computer simulations summarized in Figure 7 are strikingly similar to the data of Smith (1968) summarized in Figure 8. Smith (1968) studied the effect of manipulating the CS-US interval and the US intensity on the acquisition of the classically conditioned nictitating membrane response. The CS was a 50 msec tone and the US was a 50 msec electric shock. The ISI values were 125, 250, 500, and 1000 msec. The fact that conditioning occurred at ISI's much larger than CS duration implies that an internal trace of the CS, which we have called I_{CS}, is stored in short-term memory subsequent to CS offset, as in Figure 2. The US intensities were 1, 2, and 4 mA.

Smith (1968) found that the conditioned response, measured as percentage of responses and response amplitude, was determined by both ISI and US intensity, whereas response onset rate and peak time were determined by the ISI essentially independently of US intensity. In addition, an increase in the mean of the peak

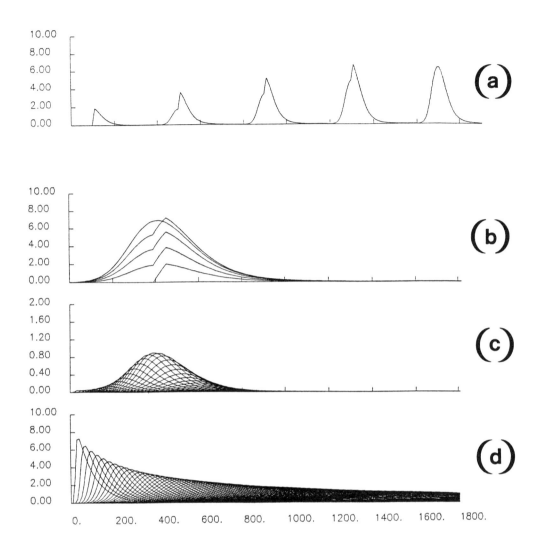

Figure 5. Generation of the response function $R(t)$. The CS was presented at the beginning of each learning trial. The US was prsented 400 msec later (thus the ISI=400) and kept on for 50 msec during 4 learning trials, which were followed by one test trial during which only the CS was presented. (a) Graph of the output signal $R(t)$ through time on all five trials. (b) After each trial, the time scale was reset to $t = 0$ to superimpose the output signal with a common initial time. The sudden jump in four of the five curves is due to the I_{US}. All the output curves are centered at the ISI because the output threshold $F = 0$ in (5). If F is chosen positive, the successive output curves move progressively backwards in time and become progressively better centered at the ISI as learning proceeds. (c) All the doubly gated signals $h_i(t) = f_i(x_i(t))y_i(t)z_i(t), i = 1, 2, \ldots, 80$, are plotted through time on the fifth trial. (d) All the gated signals $g_i(t) = f_i(x_i(t))y_i(t), i = 1, 2, \ldots, 80$, are plotted through time on the fifth trial. Parameters are chosen as in Figure 4.

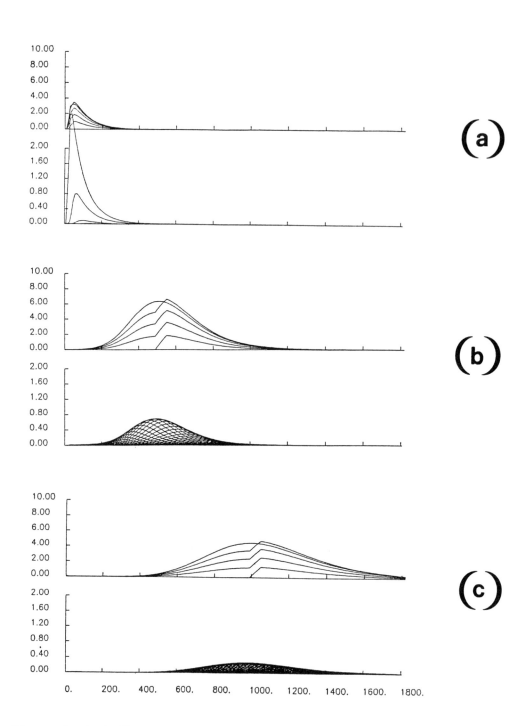

Figure 6. As in Figure 5b, superimposed plots of the output signal $R(t)$ on four successive learning trials and one performance trial are shown, along with plots of all the doubly gated signals $h_i(t), i = 1, 2, \ldots, 80$, on the fifth trial. Each panel displays the results at a different ISI: (a) ISI = 0 msec; (b) ISI = 500 msec; and (c) ISI = 1000 msec.

$$\sum_i f(x_i)y_i z_i$$

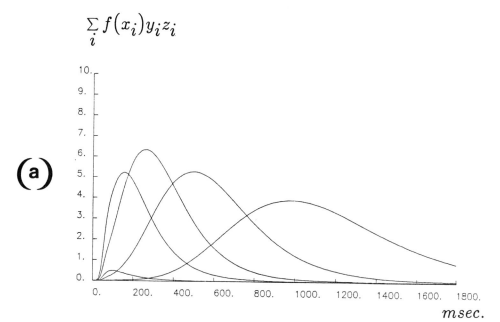

(a)

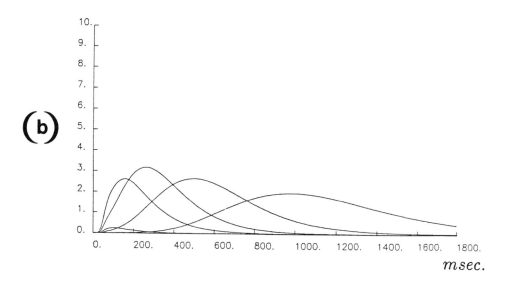

(b)

Figure 7. Inverted U in learning as a function of ISI. The output signal functions $R(t)$ are plotted on a test trial, in response to the CS alone, subsequent to 10 prior learning trials with CS–US separated by different ISI's. Successive curves from left to right were generated by ISI's of 0 (the lowest amplitude curve), 125, 250, 500, and 1000 msec using a US duration of 50 msec. Two different I_{US} intensities were used in (a) and (b), respectively. In (a), $I_{US} = 10$. In (b), $I_{US} = 5$. All other parameters were chosen as in previous figures.

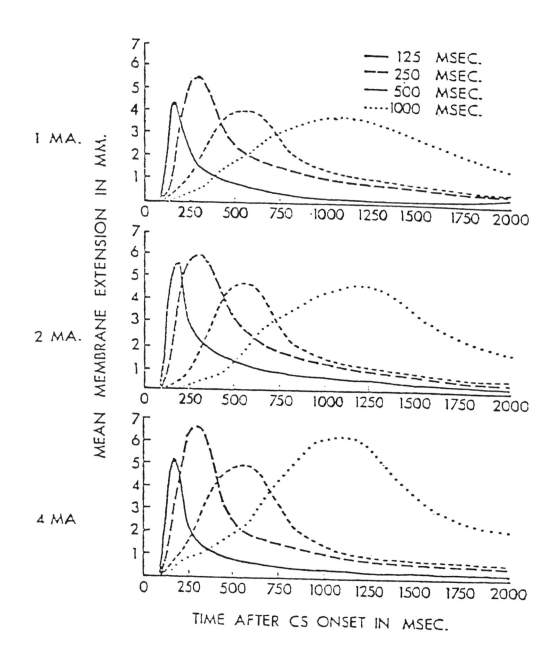

Figure 8. Conditioning data from a nictitating membrane learning paradigm. Mean topography of nictitating membrane response after learning trial 10 with a 50 msec CS, ISI's of 125, 250, 500, and 1000 msec, and different (1, 2, 4 MAmp) intensities of the shock US in each subsequent panel. Reprinted from Smith (1968) with permission.

$$\sum_i f\left(x_i\right) y_i z_i$$

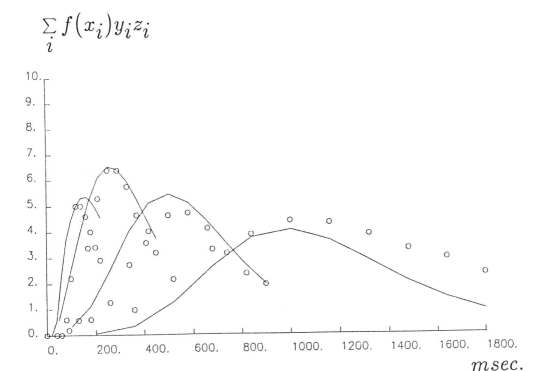

Figure 9. Comparison of experimental data from Figure 8 (US intensity equal 1 MAmp) with computer simulation from Figure 7a (I_{US} intensity equal 10). Simulated values are computed as curves interpolated through 10 values around the time of US presentation separated by .16 × ISI. Open circles represent experimental data computed at the same times corrected to make the peak values of the experimental and simulated 250 msec ISI curves coincide. The correlation between simulated and experimental points equals $r = .835$.

response time correlated with an increase in the variance of the response curve, for each ISI.

All of these properties are evident in the computer simulation of Figure 7. The absolute sizes of the empirically measured responses increase slower-than-linearly in Figure 8 as a function of shock intensity, rather than linearly as in the computer simulations in Figure 7. This fact suggests that shock intensity is transformed by a slower-than-linear signal function *in vivo*, rather than the linear signal function that we used to engage the activation spectrum of the model. Such a slower-than-linear transformation can easily be generated by a preprocessing step at which the CS is averaged by a shunting on-center off-surround feedback network at which the CS is stored in short term memory (Grossberg, 1982, 1988). The output from this short term memory representation to the timing circuit is I_{CS}.

The qualitative similarities between the data in the top panel of Figure 8 and the computer simulation in Figure 7a are quantified in Figures 9 and 10. Figure 9 plots data points and computer simulations together. Figure 10 plots four measures of data and simulation at ISI values of 0, 125, 250, 500, and 1000 msec. The four measures are

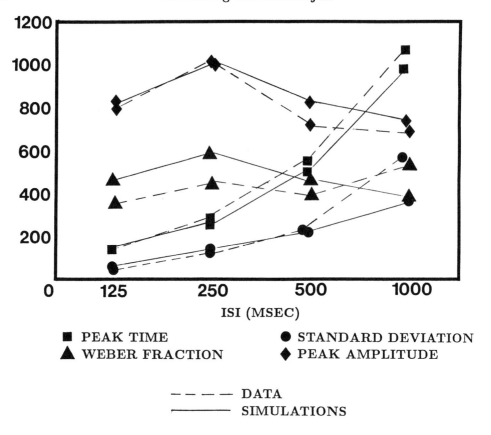

ISI (MSEC)

■ PEAK TIME   ● STANDARD DEVIATION
▲ WEBER FRACTION   ◆ PEAK AMPLITUDE

– – – – DATA
———— SIMULATIONS

Figure 10. Comparison between experimental and simulated peak time (μ), standard deviation (τ), Weber fraction (W), and peak amplitude (A). See text for details. The correlation between simulated and experimental points for μ is $r = .9996(p < .001)$, for σ is $r = .9761(p < .005)$, and for A is $r = .9666(p < .01)$.

peak time (μ), standard deviation (σ), Weber fraction (W), and peak amplitude (A). Peak time (μ) was defined at the time at which the response amplitude reached its maximum value at each ISI. Standard deviation (σ) was estimated by approximating each response curve by a normal distribution and determining the times at which the amplitude was equal to .61 of the curve's peak value. This criterion was chosen because the interval between the times at which response amplitude equals .61 of its peak value is approximately 2σ in length. To see this, consider a normal distribution $\frac{1}{\sqrt{2\pi}\sigma}\exp[-\frac{(t-\mu)^2}{2\sigma^2}]$. Its amplitude when $|t-\mu| = \sigma$ is $\frac{1}{\sqrt{2\pi}\sigma}\exp(-\frac{1}{2})$. Its amplitude when $t = \mu$ is $\frac{1}{\sqrt{2\pi}\sigma}$. The ratio of these amplitudes is $\exp(-\frac{1}{2}) \cong .61$. The Weber fraction W was defined as $W = \frac{\sigma}{\mu}$.

Despite the coarse nature of these approximations, Figure 10 reveals a remarkably good fit between experimental and simulated values of all the parameters μ, σ, W, and A at all the reported ISI's. Of particular interest is the approximately constant value of the Weber fraction W as a function of ISI, in particular its tendency to approach a positive asymptote with increasing values of the ISI (Killeen and Weiss, 1987).

Although the Spectral Timing Model provides a good quantitative fit to conditioning data acquired over a relatively small number of trials, say 1–20, the associative learning equation (4) needs to be made slightly more complex to work well over very large numbers of trials. This is true because all z_i for which $f(x_i)y_i > 0$ during times when $I_{US} > 0$ can approach I_{US}, albeit at different rates, as $t \to \infty$. Adding a very slow passive decay term $-\epsilon z_i$ to equation (4) can overcome this potential difficulty.

7. Inverted U in Learning as a Function of ISI

A basic property of both the simulated response functions $R(t)$ in Figure 7 and the data summarized in Figure 8 is an inverted U in learning as a function of the ISI. In other words, there exists a positive ISI that is optimal for learning. In Figure 7, this optimal ISI is approximately 250 msec. Learning is weaker at both smaller and larger values of the ISI.

A number of experimental conditions have been developed to better understand this fundamental property. In simultaneous conditioning (zero ISI), CS and US begin together. In delay conditioning, the CS precedes the US, and the US overlaps the CS. In trace conditioning, the CS precedes the US, and the US is presented after the CS offset. Conditioning is typically more efficacious when the CS precedes the US than when the two are presented together (Gormenzano *et al.*, 1983).

It has been found that different response systems in a given species present different optimal ISI's. As illustrated above, the nictitating membrane conditioned response in rabbits has an optimal ISI of around 250 msec (Smith, 1968). Heart rate conditioning in rabbits is optimal with a 7-second ISI (Schneiderman, 1972). Conditioned leg flexion in cats is optimal with a 500-msec ISI (McAdam *et al.*, 1965). Salivary conditioning in dogs is optimal with a 20-second ISI (Konorski, 1948). Conditioned licking in rats is optimal with a 3-second ISI (Boice and Denny, 1965). Heart rate conditioning in rats is optimal with a 5-second ISI (Black and Black, 1967).

Although the Spectral Timing Model successfully generates such a positive optimal ISI, it seems clear that this circuit is not the only one subserving the optimal ISI that is behaviorally observed.

This can be seen by considering the phenomenon of secondary excitatory conditioning. In secondary excitatory conditioning, two CS's are employed; call them CS_1 and CS_2. Let CS_1 be conditioned with a US until CS_1 can elicit some of the reinforcing properties of the US. Then present the two CS's simultaneously as a compound stimulus $CS_1 + CS_2$. The conditioning of CS_2 to the new reinforcer CS_1 is much attenuated relative to the conditioning that would have occurred if CS_1 was presented before CS_2.

On the other hand, consider an experiment in which CS_1 and CS_2 are equally salient to the organism and the compound cue $CS_1 + CS_2$ is presented before a US on conditioning trials. Then both CS_1 and CS_2 can be effectively conditioned to the US.

Thus the attenuation in the conditioning of CS_2 to CS_1 when CS_1 and CS_2 are simultaneously presented and CS_2 has previously been conditioned to US cannot be due merely to the *simultaneity* of CS_1 and CS_2 in their capacity as sensory events. Rather it must be due to the effects of reading-out within the network the *reinforcing properties* of CS_2 by the sensory representation of CS_2.

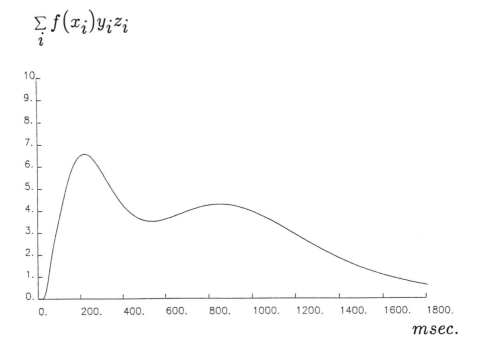

Figure 11. Multiple timing peaks due to learning with more than one ISI. The output signal function $R(t)$ is plotted on a test trial after 20 learning trials during which a US of intensity 10 was presented alternately at an ISI of 200 msec and 800 msec.

A model capable of explaining how such attentional blocking of CS_2 by a simultaneous conditioned reinforcer CS_1 is outlined in Part II. Computer simulations of attentional blocking within this model are found in Grossberg and Levine (1987; reprinted in Grossberg, 1988).

8. Multiple Timing Peaks

Another functionally useful model property that matches experimental conditioning data concerns the ability of a single CS to read out responses at a series of learned delays. This multiple timing property provides strong indirect evidence that each CS sends signals to a complete activation spectrum, rather than to a single tunable delay.

Figure 11 depicts the outcome of a computer simulation in which a CS is paired with a US whose ISI is chosen on alternate trials at two different values. When the CS is subsequently activated on a recall trial, the response function $R(t)$ generates two peaks, with each peak centered at one of the ISI's.

The parameters used in the simulation of Figure 11 are the same as those used to fit the data in Figure 10 concerning response time, amplitude, standard deviation, and Weber fraction. It is therefore of particular interest that the model simulations in Figure 11 strikingly resemble the multiple timing data of Millenson, Kehoe, and Gormenzano (1977) that are summarized in Figure 12.

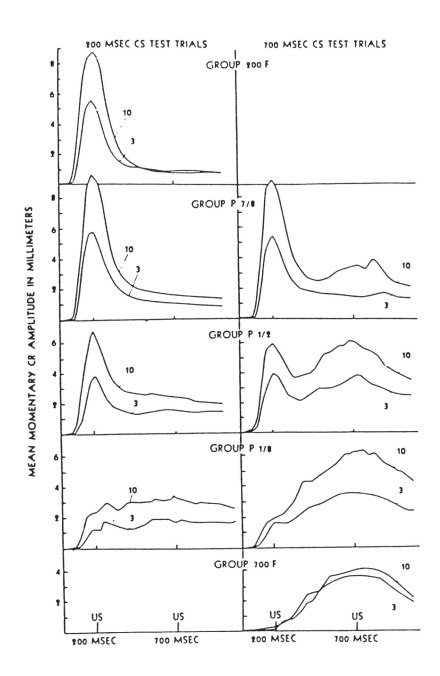

Figure 12. Conditioning data from the nictitating membrane learning paradigm of Millenson, Kehoe, and Gormenzano (1977). Data shown after learning trials 3 and 10 using a tone CS of duration 200 msec and 700 msec, ISI's of 200 msec and 700 msec, and a shock US of 50 msec duration. See text for details. Reprinted with permission.

Millenson, Kehoe, and Gormenzano (1977) presented rabbits in a nictitating membrane paradigm with a tone CS followed by a shock US at two randomly alternating ISI's of 200 and 700 msec. The CS terminated at US onset, and the US had a 50 msec duration. Each row in Figure 12 corresponds to a different experimental condition. The experiment summarized in row 1 used a 200 msec ISI throughout. The experiment in row 5 used a 700 msec ISI throughout. Compare these relative peak times, amplitudes, and Weber fractions with the model simulation in Figure 11.

Experiments summarized in the middle three rows used varying fractions of the two ISI delays during learning trials. In the second row, the ISI equaled 200 msec on 7/8 of the learning trials and 700 msec on 1/8 of the learning trials. In the third row, the ISI equaled each of these values on 1/2 of the learning trials. In row four, the ISI equaled 200 msec on 1/8 of the trials and 700 msec on 7/8 of the trials.

Each column in Figure 12 corresponds to a different test condition subsequent to a set of learning trials. During such a test, a CS, but no US, was presented. In column 1, the CS duration was 200 msec. In column 2, the CS duration was 700 msec. In each panel, a test curve is displayed after 3 days and after 10 days of prior learning.

The data curves of greatest interest are in row 3, column 2. These curves are strikingly similar to the model simulation in Figure 11. Row 3, column 1 is also of interest, because it shows that termination of a CS of 200 msec duration under these conditions prevents strong perseveration of its I_{CS} curve for the additional 500 msec needed to read out a large response at 700 msec.

The parameters used to fit the data in Figures 9, 10, and 12 generate broadly tuned timing peaks. Finer peaks can, however, be generated, should technological applications so require, without disturbing other useful qualitative properties. For example, using a different set of parameters, the simulation reported in Figure 13 generates the same qualitative series of peaks as in Figure 7, but a sharper multiple timing curve (Figure 13b) than in Figure 11.

9. Effect of Increasing US Duration

Figure 14 depicts the results of a simulation that illustrates the effects of increasing US duration upon the response $R(t)$. The I_{US} intensity was twice as large in Figure 14a than in Figure 14b. A zero ISI was employed throughout. Two effects are generated: a shift of peak time to a value towards the midpoint of the US, and an overall increase in conditioned response.

Burkhardt and Ayres (1978) have collected analogous data (Figure 15) in a paradigm wherein rats were presented with an auditory CS and a simultaneous (zero ISI) shock US. When the CS was later presented while the rats were drinking water, the CS presentation elicited a suppression of licking whose relative magnitude before and after CS onset (the suppression ratio) was used to measure the strength of the conditioned fear elicited by the CS. During conditioning, a grid-shock US of 2, 4, or 8 seconds duration began simultaneously with a noise CS of 2, 4, or 8 seconds duration in the combinations 2-2, 2-4, 4-4, 4-8, and 8-8. As in Figure 14, Burkhardt and Ayres (1978) found that conditioning increased as a function of US duration, as well as of CS-US overlap, another property easily explained by the model.

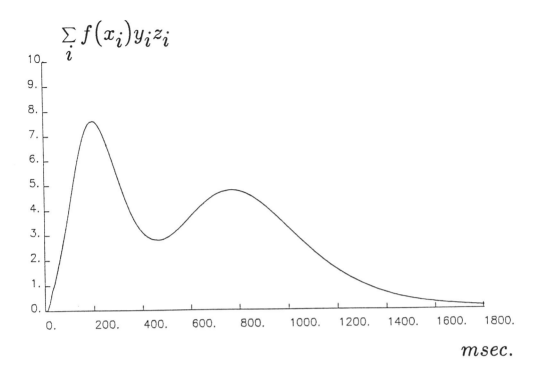

$$\sum_i f(x_i) y_i z_i$$

msec.

Figure 13. Multiple timing peaks due to learning with more than one ISI. The parameters were chosen as in Figure 4, with the exception of $\beta = .4$.

10. Effect of Increasing CS Intensity

Figure 7 showed that an increase of US intensity alters the amplitude of the response functions $R(t)$, but not their timing, and Figure 8 showed that the conditioning data of Smith (1968) conform to these properties. A different pattern of results obtains if the CS intensity is altered. Figure 16 illustrates a computer simulation in which the system was trained with a CS and US of constant intensity and an ISI of 800 msec across learning trials. The Figure shows that a test trial using the same CS intensity generates a response function $R(t)$ that peaks at 800 msec, but a test trial using a CS of twice that intensity generates a response function $R(t)$ that peaks at 400 msec. Thus, increasing CS intensity "speeds up the clock" that calibrates the response reaction time. Such a speed-up is a straightforward consequence of equation (1).

Section 17 below describes experimental data which are consistent with these properties. In order to analyse these data, we first need to explain how the timing circuit is embedded within a larger architecture that controls the stable self-organization of cognitive-emotional representations.

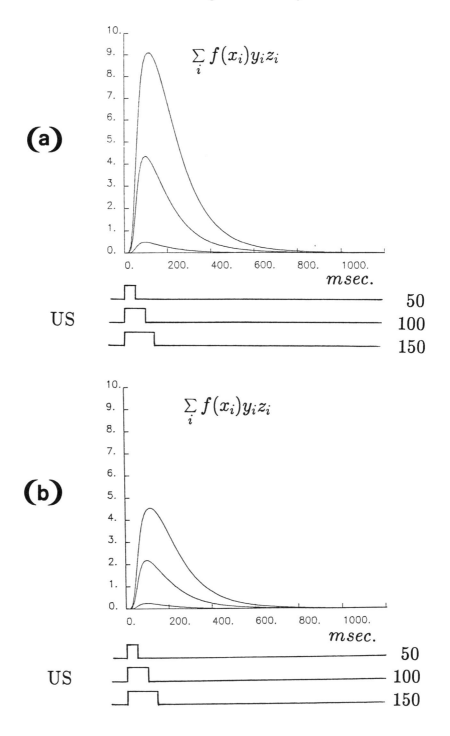

Figure 14. Effect of increasing US duration and intensity on learning. In both (a) and (b), ISI = 0. The output signal $R(t)$ is plotted on a test trial after 4 learning trials using I_{US} functions of duration 50, 100, and 150 msec. In (a), US intensity equals 10. In (b), US intensity equals 5.

MEDIAN CS TIMES IN SECONDS
FOR EACH GROUP IN EXPERIMENTS 1, 2, AND 3

Group	Baseline-Lick Last Training	Test 1	Test 2
	Experiment 1		
0	1.6	5.2	3.2
1	1.6	3.4	3.4
4	1.9	37.8	6.2
64	1.4	2.7	4.8
128	1.6	8.8	7.8
	Experiment 2		
0	1.8	3.2	1.9
1	1.7	15.1	4.8
2	1.9	12.9	3.8
4	1.7	94.4	6.4
8	1.6	64.5	8.3
	Experiment 3		
2-2	1.5	4.9	4.7
2-4	1.5	15.6	8.9
4-4	1.4	30.6	5.4
4-8	1.5	58.2	9.9
8-8	1.4	107.8	7.0

Figure 15. Data of Burkhardt and Ayres (1978) on conditioning an auditory CS and a simultaneous (zero ISI) shock US. See the text for details. Reprinted with permission.

PART II
TIMED GATING OF READ-OUT
FROM THE ORIENTING SUBSYSTEM

11. Locating the Timing Circuit within a Self-Organizing Sensory-Cognitive and Cognitive-Reinforcement ART Network

The timing circuit is hypothesized to form part of interacting sensory-cognitive and cognitive-reinforcement circuits which have been progressively developed since the late 1960's to explain behavioral and neural data about recognition, reinforcement, and recall.

Sensory-cognitive interactions in the theory are carried out by an Adaptive Resonance Theory (ART) circuit (Carpenter and Grossberg, 1987a, 1987b, 1988; Cohen and Grossberg, 1986, 1987; Grossberg, 1976, 1982, 1987; Grossberg and Stone, 1986). Such ART architectures are designed to explain how internal representations of sensory events, including conditioned stimuli (CS) and unconditioned stimuli (US), are learned in real-time in a stable fashion in response to noisy, nonstationary environments.

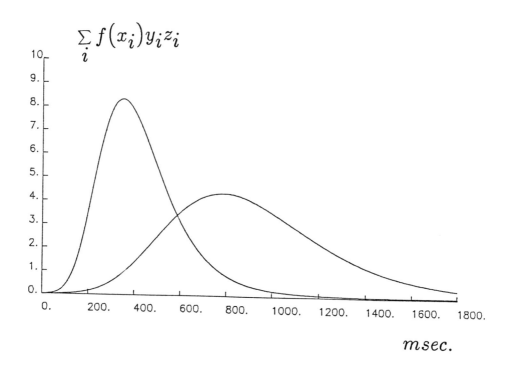

$$\sum_i f(x_i) y_i z_i$$

Figure 16. Effect of CS intensity on "clock speed." After 10 learning trials were carried out with an ISI $= 800$ msec, 2 test trials were carried out, one with the CS intensity of 1 used in training, whose output $R(t)$ peaked at 800 msec, and one with a CS intensity of 2 that caused the output $R(t)$ to peak at 400 msec.

As in Figure 17, a sensory-cognitive ART circuit is broken up into an attentional subsystem and an orienting subsystem. The attentional subsystem learns ever more precise internal representations of and responses to events as they become more familiar. The attentional subsystem also learns the top-down expectations that help to stabilize memory of the learned bottom-up codes of familiar events. The orienting subsystem resets the internal representation that is active in short term memory (STM) in the attentional subsystem when an unfamiliar or unexpected event occurs. The orienting subsystem also energizes the orienting response, including the movements triggered by novel events that enable such events to be more efficiently processed.

The orienting subsystem is activated when a sufficiently large mismatch occurs within the attentional subsystem between bottom-up sensory input signals and learned top-down expectations. In Figure 17a, the learned top-down expectations are read-out from level F_2 to level F_1, and matching of expectations with bottom-up input patterns occurs at level F_1. When a mismatch occurs, the orienting subsystem A is activated and causes an STM reset wave to be delivered to level F_2. This STM reset wave resets the sensory representations of cues that are currently being stored in STM at F_2.

As noted in Section 3, one function of the timing circuit is to prevent spurious

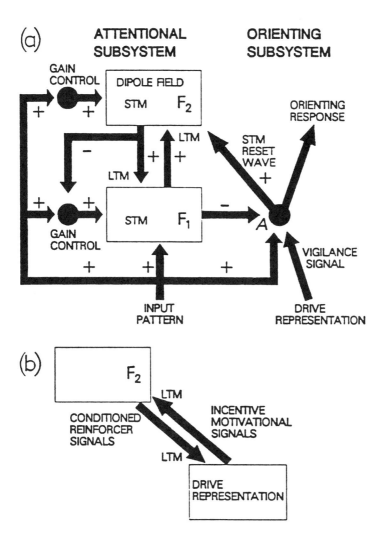

Figure 17. Anatomy of an adaptive resonance theory (ART) circuit: (a) Interactions between the attentional and orienting subsystems: Learning of recognition codes takes place at the long term memory (LTM) traces within the bottom-up and top-down pathways between levels F_1 and F_2. The top-down pathways can read-out learned expectations, or templates, that are matched against bottom-up input patterns at F_1. Mismatches activate the orienting subsystem A, thereby resetting short term memory (STM) at F_2 and initiating search for another recognition code. Output from subsystem A can also trigger an orienting response. Sensitivity to mismatch at F_1 is modulated by vigilance signals from the drive representations. (b) Trainable pathways exist between level F_2 and the drive representations. Learning from F_2 to a drive representation endows a recognition category with conditioned reinforcer properties. Learning from a drive representation to F_2 associates the drive representation with a set of motivationally compatible categories.

resets of active internal representations in response to mismatches due to *expected nonoccurrences* of sensory events. In addition, the timing circuit should not prevent registration of bottom-up input patterns and their matching with active top-down expectations. Thus the timing circuit does not interfere with processing within the attentional subsystem.

Instead, we hypothesize that the timing circuit inhibits read-out of the STM reset wave from the orienting subsystem A (Figure 17a). Thus when the timing circuit is active, both STM reset within the attentional subsystem and the orienting response are inhibited. When the timing circuit is inactive, an *unexpected nonoccurrence* of an event is able to trigger the STM reset and orienting response needed to cope with the unexpected event.

To analyse how the timing circuit works, we summarize some basic properties of another part of the attentional subsystem. This is the network which controls the learned interactions between recognition and reinforcement mechanisms that focus attention upon motivationally salient events. We assume, in particular, that the timing circuit forms part of the interaction from cognitive to reinforcement representations whereby sensory cues learn to become conditioned reinforcers (Figure 17b).

12. Cognitive-Reinforcement Circuit

Recognition is only one of several processes whereby an intelligent system can learn a correct solution to a problem. Reinforcement and recall are no less important in designing an autonomous intelligent system.

Reinforcement, notably reward and punishment, provides additional information in the form of environmental feedback based on the success or failure of actions triggered by a recognition event. Reward and punishment calibrate whether the action has or has not satisfied internal needs, which in the biological case include hunger, thirst, sex, and pain reduction, but may in machine applications include a wide variety of internal cost functions. Reinforcement can modify the formation of recognition codes and can shift attention to focus upon those codes whose activation promises to satisfy internal needs based upon past experience. For example, both green and yellow bananas may be recognized as part of a single recognition category until reinforcement signals, contingent upon eating these bananas, differentiates them into separate categories.

Recall can generate equivalent responses or actions to input events that are classified by different recognition codes. For example, printed and script letters may generate distinct recognition codes, yet can also elicit identical learned naming responses.

The type of ART circuit depicted in Figure 17a is devoted entirely to the stable self-organization of sensory and cognitive recognition codes. Feedback interactions among recognition and reinforcement circuits, as in Figure 17b, are also posited by the theory, and in fact were the first type of ART circuit to be defined (Grossberg, 1975, 1982). In these applications, the circuit at which recognition codes are processed is called a *sensory representation S*, and the circuit at which reinforcement and homeostatic, or drive, signals are processed is called a *drive representation D* (Grossberg, 1971, 1972b, 1987), as in Figure 17b. Thus a reinforcing event, such as a reward or punishment, possesses both a sensory representation in its capacity as a sensory event, and a drive representation in its capacity as a motivationally significant reinforcer.

During classical conditioning, a familiar conditioned stimulus (CS) may initially have a sensory representation S, but no drive represenation D. Pairing a CS with an unconditioned stimulus (US) that does have reinforcing properties causes several types of learning to occur. In particular, repeated pairing of a CS sensory representation, S_{CS}, with activation of a drive representation, D, by a US reinforcer causes the modifiable synapses connecting S_{CS} with D to become strengthened. This conditioning process converts the CS into a *conditioned reinforcer* (Figures 17b and 18). Incentive motivation pathways from the drive representations to the sensory representations are also assumed to be conditionable. These conditioned $S \to D \to S$ feedback pathways shift attention to focus upon the subset of active sensory representations which have been previously reinforced and are motivationally compatible. This shift of attention occurs because the sensory representations which emit conditioned reinforcer signals $S \to D$ and receive conditioned incentive motivation signals $D \to S$ compete among themselves for a limited capacity short-term memory (STM) via on-center off-surround interactions (Figure 18). When incentive motivational feedback signals are received at the sensory representational field, these signals can bias the competition for STM activity towards motivationally salient cues. More generally, such feedback interactions between S and D can reorganize the STM pattern across S to be compatible with reinforcement constraints. This STM pattern can then be incorporated through learning into the sensory-cognitive recognition code via an ART circuit of the type shown in Figure 17.

In order to explain the moment-by-moment dynamics of conditioning, an additional microcircuit needs to be embedded in the drive representations of the macro-circuit depicted in Figure 18. This microcircuit, called a *gated dipole* (Grossberg, 1972a, 1972b), instantiates a neurophysiological theory of opponent processing. The need for a certain type of opponent processing for conditioning circuits can be seen from the following considerations.

13. The Gated Dipole Opponent Process

In the cognitive-reinforcement circuit, CS's can become conditioned reinforcers by being associated with either the onset or the offset of a reinforcer. For example, a CS that is conditioned to the onset of a shock can become a source of conditioned fear (excitor). A CS that is conditioned to the offset of a shock can become a source of conditioned relief (inhibitor). A gated dipole opponent process explains how the offset of a reinforcer can generate an off-response, or antagonistic rebound, to which a simultaneous CS can be conditioned. A gated dipole is a minimal neural network opponent process which is capable of generating a sustained, but habituative, on-response (e.g., a fear reaction) to onset of a cue (e.g., a shock), as well as a transient off-response (e.g., a relief reaction), or antagonistic rebound, to offset of the cue. The on-responses are processed through the on-channel D^+ of the gated dipole, whereas the off-responses are processed through the off-channel D^- of the gated dipole. In addition, such a gated dipole must be joined to a mechanism of associative learning, whereby CS's learn to become conditioned excitors via $S \to D^+$ learning and conditioned inhibitors via $S \to D^-$ learning.

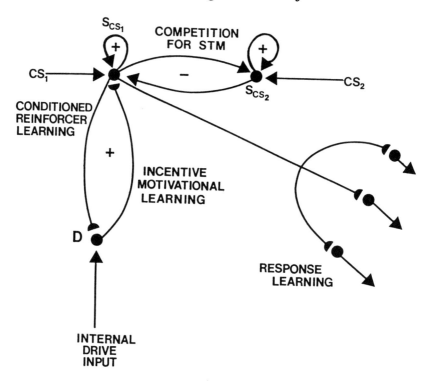

Figure 18. Schematic conditioning circuit: Conditioned stimuli (CS_i) activate sensory representations (S_{CS_i}) which compete among themselves for limited capacity short term memory activation and storage. The activated S_{CS_i} elicit conditionable signals to drive representations and motor command representations. Learning from a S_{CS_i} to a drive representation $\mathcal{D}$ is called conditioned reinforcer learning. Learning from $\mathcal{D}$ to a S_{CS_i} is called incentive motivational learning. Signals from $\mathcal{D}$ to S_{CS_i} are elicited when the combination of external sensory plus internal drive inputs is sufficiently large.

14. Adaptive Timing as Spectral Conditioned Reinforcer Learning

The feedforward adaptive timing circuit is assumed to be a variant of $S \to D+$ conditioned reinforcer learning. The main new idea is that the on-channel's population of neurons $D+$ is broken up into neuron subpopulations whose membrane properties enable them to respond to inputs at different rates α_i, as in equation (1). In other words, by selecting a sloppy parametric specification of cell reaction rates, nature can discover an adaptive timing mechanism—*if* such sloppiness is permitted at the proper processing stage of a gated dipole circuit!

Once this is achieved, standard gated dipole mechanisms respond to the activation spectrum α_i in the manner described in Part I. In particular, equation (2) for the transmitter gate is the standard gating equation that gave a gated dipole its name; equation (3) is a variant of the dipole's standard associative learning law; and equation (4) simply computes the total output from all subpopulations of the dipole's on-channel. We summarize this fact by saying that adaptive timing is a type of *spectral conditioned reinforcer learning*.

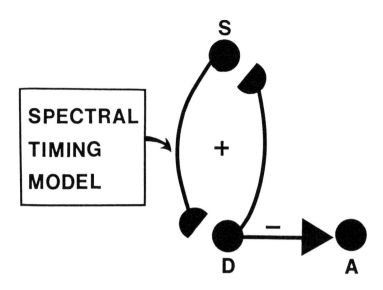

Figure 19. Inhibition of the orienting subsystem A by the output from a drive representation D. The Spectral Timing Model is assumed to be part of the network whereby conditioning of a sensory representation S to a drive representation D endows S with conditioned reinforcer properties. As S reads-out spectrally timed conditioned signals to D, D inhibits output signals from A and thereby prevents expected nonoccurrences of the US from resetting STM and triggering orienting responses.

15. Timed Inhibition of the Orienting Subsystem by Drive Representations

It remains to explain how a timing circuit embedded within the on-channels of gated dipole drive representations achieves the functional properties described in Section 3. These properties follow if we assume, in addition, that the drive representations D inhibit the orienting subsystem A, as in Figure 19. In Figure 17a, level F_1 also inhibits A. Thus several processing levels within the attentional subsystem are assumed to inhibit the orienting subsystem. The hypothesis of competition from D to A representations was first made within the context of ART-type models in Grossberg (1975; reprinted in Grossberg, 1982, pp. 284-286). Given $D \rightarrow A$ inhibition, spectral conditioned reinforcer learning generates the desired adaptive timing properties as follows.

After CS–US conditioning at a fixed ISI, presentation of the CS activates its sensory representation S_{CS}, which activates its conditioned drive representation D with a response curve $R(t)$ of the form depicted in Figure 7. Each of these response curves $R(t)$ begins to grow right after I_{CS} read-out; remains positive throughout an interval whose total width covaries with the ISI, due to the approximate constancy of the Weber fraction W (Figure 10); and peaks at the ISI. Inhibition of A by D thus prevents STM reset by expected nonoccurrences of the US throughout a time interval that is centered at the expected delay of the US whose width covaries with this delay.

16. Timed Activation of the Hippocampus and the Contingent Negative Variation

Because it is activated by the drive representations D, positive feedback from D to S along the $D \rightarrow S$ incentive motivational pathways is also timed to provide peak motivational support for release of a conditioned response (Figure 18) at the expected delay of the US.

In Grossberg (1975, Section VII, and 1978, Section 16; reprinted in 1982), such $D \rightarrow S$ feedback was first interpreted to be a formal analog of the contingent negative variation, or CNV, event-related potential. The CNV had earlier been experimentally shown to be sensitive to an animal's expectancy, decision (Walter, 1964), motivation (Cant and Bickford, 1967; Irwin, Rebert, McAdam, and Knott, 1966), preparatory set (Low, Borda, Frost, and Kellaway, 1966), and arousal (McAdam, 1969). It is also a conditionable wave whose timing tends to match the ISI. Until the present work, development of our conditioning theory, as summarized in Grossberg (1987, Chapter 1, Sections 23 and 25, and Chapter 2, Sections 30, 43, 53, 57, and 60), suggested how the CNV is conditioned and how it is related to expectancy, decision, motivation, preparatory set, and arousal. The theory had not, however, heretofore explained how the learning process enables CNV timing to mimic the ISI. The present extension of the theory provides an explanation through the hypothesis of spectral conditioned reinforcer learning. The interpretation of drive representations in terms of hypothalamo-hippocampal interactions (Grossberg, 1971, 1982, 1987) provides an anatomical marker for directly testing the existence of spectral activation.

The hypotheses that drive representations include hippocampus and that the hippocampus is involved in conditioned timing have also received support from neurophysiological experiments (Berger and Thompson, 1978; Delacour and Houcine, 1980; Hoechler and Thompson, 1980; Rawlins, 1985; Rawlins, Feldon, and Gray, 1982; Solomon, 1979, 1980; Solomon, van der Schaaf, Thompson, and Weisz, 1986).

17. Effect of CS Intensity on Timed Motor Behavior

We are now ready to use the model property illustrated in Figure 16 to suggest how changes in CS intensity and various drug manipulations may cause observed changes in certain timed motor behaviors of animals.

For example, changes in CS intensity alter the conditioned key pecking behavior of pige ons (Wilkie, 1987). In these experiments, each pigeon was pre-trained to discriminate between short (2 second) and long (10 second) houselight presentations. In one set of 30 sessions, a bright houselight was used. In another, a dim houselight was used. In all learning sessions, the 20-second intertrial interval was spent in complete darkness. In each of the 80 trials in a session, the probability was .5 that the houselight presentation was short.

Immediately after the short or long houselight presentation was completed, two pecking keys were lit, one with red light and the other with green light. The right-left locations of the red and green keys was varied randomly over trials. For some pigeons, red was designated as the correct key to peck after a short stimulus, and green was the correct key to peck after a long stimulus. For other pigeons, the colors were reversed. Pecking of the correct key produced 5-second access to mixed grain on a partial 75% reinforcement schedule.

During the experiment proper, all pigeons received approximately 35 sessions, each comprising 80 trials. On one-half of the trials (randomly determined), the house-light was bright. On the other trials, it was dim. On a quarter of all trials (randomly determined), the light presentation was 2 seconds in duration. On another quarter, it was 10 seconds. On the remaining trials, it was equally probable that the light would be 4, 6, or 8 seconds in duration. Thus there were 10 types of trials in total: 2, 4, 6, 8, and 10 second bright lights, and 2, 4, 6, 8, and 10 second dim lights, presented in randomized order. Correct choices on 2 and 10 second trials of both dim and bright lights always produced 5-second access to grain. Choices on 4, 6, and 8 second trials were never rewarded.

In each session, a record was kept of the number of times the "short" choice key was selected when 2, 4, 6, 8, and 10 second lights were presented. These values were accumulated over sessions and used to calculate the percentage of trials on which pigeons chose the "short" alternative after durations of 2, 4, 6, 8, and 10 second lights. These measures were calculated separately for bright and dim light trials.

It was found that the pigeons chose the "short" key more frequently in response to longer durations of the dim light. In other words, a dim light slowed down the time scale, as in Figure 16. Wilkie (1987, p.38) noted that "it is not intuitively obvious how intensity would affect something like a counter or how any such effect would be manifested in dim signals' being perceived as being shorter."

In order to provide a more detailed explanation of these data based upon the model property illustrated in Figure 16, several properties of the experiment need to be kept in mind. In particular, the presentation of the red and green keys immediately followed the short or long houselight stimulus, and reward or non-reward immediately followed a correct key peck. Suppose that an internal representation of a dim or bright houselight activated a full activation spectrum, and that food reward caused conditioning of those spectral populations that were active when the reward occurred, as in Figure 4. In response to a short CS, only rapidly reacting spectral populations could become conditioned. In response to a long stimulus, only those spectral populations which became active after a longer CS duration could become conditioned. Thus the basic properties of the timing model explain how, in response to a CS of any fixed intensity, only a properly timed subset of spectral populations could become conditioned. In addition, the model property depicted in Figure 16 shows how dimming of the CS can, other things being equal, slow down the read-out of the clock.

Further discussion is needed, however, to explain how dim and bright houselights are discriminated in the first place, and how differential reward of both dim and bright short lights and of dim and bright long lights generated the main effect that pigeons peck the "short" key in response to longer durations of dim light. Indeed, *both* the dim light and the bright light are conditioned to different key pecks based on their *duration*, not their *intensity*. Why should longer dim lights tend to generate the key peck that was associated with a short duration light independent of its intensity?

The computer simulations reported in Figure 16 would imply this result if some of the spectral cells that are activated by a *short bright* light are also activated by a *long dim* light. On those learning trials when these cells are activated by a short bright light, they would be conditioned, via incentive motivational feedback signals (Figure

18), to the internal representation of the key that signifies a short stimulus. On those learning trials when these cells are activated by a long dim light, they would amplify these internal representations and thereby favor this key in the STM competition for which key the pigeon will attend and thereupon peck.

18. Spatial Coding of Stimulus Intensity by a PTS Shift Map

We trace this property to the manner in which different intensities of the same stimulus are discriminated by the animal. Suppose that a particular stimulus input, such as a white light, is coded by a population of cells. Grossberg and Kuperstein (1986, pp.160–167) have developed a model of such a coding population in which different input intensities maximally activate different subsets of the total population. Thus input *intensity* is recoded into the maximally activated *spatial location* within the population. Since distinct subsets of the population can activate different output pathways, different input intensities can control their own spectral populations, and can be conditioned to activate the drive representations at different times.

The Grossberg and Kuperstein (1986) model is called a Position-Threshold-Slope (PTS) Shift Map. To generate this spatial map of input intensity, the cells within the population are assumed to possess different output thresholds and different sensitivities to input increments. Cells with higher thresholds are assumed to be more sensitive. Thus, essentially all input intensities (e.g., dim and bright lights) can generate output signals from cells with low output thresholds, whereas only high input intensities (e.g., bright lights) can generate output signal from cells with high thresholds. Due to the greater sensitivity of the high-threshold cells, the spatial locus of maximal activation changes as with input intensity.

Populations of cells whose output thresholds and input sensitivities covary have been found in the abducens and oculomotor nuclei (Luschei and Fuchs, 1972; Robinson, 1970; Schiller, 1970). The present analysis suggests that such populations may also exist in thalamocortical sensory processing areas.

19. Effect of Drugs on Timed Motor Behavior

Wilkie (1987, p.38) has speculated, based on earlier results of Maricq, Roberts, and Church (1981), that "drug and light-intensity effects might both be mediated by a state of arousal that affects the pacemaker rate." Meck and Church (1987) have reviewed a number of experiments, including the Maricq *et al.* (1981) and Meck (1983) experiments, and have collected additional data on the effects of drugs on timed motor behavior. The major properties of these drug manipulations are consistent with Spectral Timing Model.

Meck and Church (1987) noted that an increase in the effective level of brain dopamine at the synapse increases clock speed and that a decrease in the effective level of brain dopamine decreases clock speed. Methamphetamine and L-dopa increase dopamine at the synapse and change timing functions in a manner that can be interpreted as an increase in clock speed. Neuroleptics, such as haloperidol, which block dopamine receptors change timing functions in a manner that can be interpreted as a decrease in clock speed.

Likewise, experimental evidence suggests that an increase in the effective level of brain acetylcholine at the synapse reduces the remembered time of reinforcement in long term memory, and thus speeds up the clock in short term memory. A decrease in the effective level of brain reinforcement increases the remembered time of reinforcement in long term memory, and thus slows down the clock in short term memory. For example, both physostigmine and phosphatidylcholine change timing in a manner interpretable as a decrease in remembered time of reinforcement, whereas atropine and aging cause an increase.

Since the introduction of gated dipole theory in 1972 (Grossberg, 1972b; reprinted in Grossberg, 1982), it has been predicted that the habituative transmitter gates, as defined in equation (2), are chemically realized in the brain by a catecholamine, such as dopamine or norepinephrine, and that the long term memory traces, as defined in equation (4), are realized in the brain by acetylcholine. Thus the present model is consistent with the recent dopamine and acetylcholine data if a gated dipole circuit exists that processes the CS input before it generates I_{CS} in equation (1). In this way, the aforementioned drug manipulations would alter the intensity of the CS, and thereby speed up or slow down the clock in the manner indicated in Figure 16.

Such habituative and LTM transmitter systems are, in fact, postulated as part of the adaptive coding circuitry that self-organizes an internal representation of the CS in an ART circuit such as that depicted in Figure 17 (Grossberg, 1982, 1987).

These drug data also raise the question whether the habituative transmitter and the LTM transmitter *within* the Spectral Timing Model itself can influence clock speed. This would be the case if the timing circuit included internal feedback loops whereby the two types of transmitters feed back their influence to the spectral activities defined in equation (1). Such feedback pathways have previously been postulated to exist in the gated dipole circuits that regulate the learning of conditioned reinforcers (Grossberg, 1982; Grossberg and Schmajuk, 1987), of which the Spectral Timing Model is herein assumed to be a specialization. It remains for future research to determine how a Spectral Timing Model with internal feedback pathways may be designed.

20. Concluding Remarks: Timing Paradox and Multiple Types of Timing Circuits

There exist multiple types of timing mechanisms in the brain. The present article considers only the type of timing that enables an organism to time and differentially respond to an expected nonoccurrence, an expected occurrence, and an unexpected nonoccurrence of a sensory event subsequent to a prior sensory event or action.

In so doing, the article clarifies a Timing Paradox that becomes apparent upon closer inspection of this type of timing problem. On the one hand, in response to *any* fixed choice of conditionable ISI, it is desired that the learned *optimal* response delay approximate the ISI. Thus the model must be capable of an accurate discrimination of individual temporal delays. On the other hand, it is also desired that spurious orienting responses be inhibited in response to expected nonoccurrences that may occur *throughout* the ISI interval subsequent to a CS onset. Thus the inhibitory signal must be temporally distributed throughout the ISI interval.

The Spectral Timing Model reconciles the two requirements of accurate optimal temporal delay and temporally distributed activation via the Weber law property (Section 6). According to this property, the standard deviation of the model response scales with its peak time. Consequently the model begins to immediately generate an output signal that may be used to inhibit the orienting subsystem, even though its peak output is accurately located at the ISI.

This key property distinguishes the Spectral Timing Model from a model that uses conditionable pathways with brief sampling signals and variable delay lines to learn to time the ISI delay. In such a model, use of a single ISI during training would lead to a zero learned output in response to the CS until the ISI had elapsed. The output from such a model could not be used to inhibit orienting responses in response to expected nonoccurrences.

The Spectral Timing Model is also not mechanistically the same as model circuits which have been identified to self-organize the learning and long term memory of serially ordered behaviors, or the encoding of event sequences in short term memory, or the encoding of sequential rhythmic properties in short term memory, or the clock-like oscillatory timing of circadian rhythms. In particular, the type of timing controlled by the Spectral Timing Model occurs within hundreds of milliseconds or a few seconds at most of a single behavioral response. It is not the type of timing that may be spread over many seconds or minutes whereby sequences of behavioral acts are regulated. Neural network models for these alternative timing capabilities have been described in the books Grossberg (1982, 1987) and Grossberg and Kuperstein (1986).

For example, the Spectral Timing Model, at least in its present form, cannot explain how an animal can learn to interrupt a timed behavioral sequence during a signalled time-out period and continue the timed behavioral sequence where it left off after the time-out period is over (Meck and Church, 1984; Meck, Church, Wenk, and Olton, 1987). On the other hand, a self-organizing avalanche circuit does have this competence (Grossberg, 1982, pp.519–531; Grossberg and Kuperstein, 1986, Chapter 9). Moreover, each sensory representation in the avalanche can activate its own spectrally timed read-out to a drive representation.

This example illustrates the manner in which the totality of known temporally-discriminative neural networks have begun to delineate a global neural network architecture in which several distinct types of behavioral timing circuits cooperate to regulate the accurately timed autonomous unfolding of complex behaviors.

REFERENCES

Berger, T.W. and Thompson, R.F. (1978). Neuronal plasticity in the limbic system during classical conditioning of the rabbit nictitating membrane response, I: The hippocampus. *Brain Research*, **145**, 323–346.

Black, R.W. and Black, P.E. (1967). Heart rate conditioning as a function of inter-stimulus interval in rats. *Psychonomic Science*, **8**, 219–220.

Boice, R. and Denny, M.R. (1965). The conditioned licking response in rats as a function of the CS-US interval. *Psychonomic Science*, **3**, 93–94.

Burkhardt, P.E. and Ayres, J.J.B. (1978). CS and US duration effects in one-trial simultaneous fear conditioning as assessed by conditioned suppression of licking rats. *Animal Learning and Behavior*, **6**, 225–230.

Cant, B.R. and Bickford, R.G. (1967). The effect of motivation on the contingent negative variation (CNV). *Electroencephalography and Clinical Neurophysiology*, **23**, 594.

Carpenter, G.A. and Grossberg, S. (1987a). A massively parallel architecture for a self-organizing neural pattern recognition machine. *Computer Vision, Graphics, and Image Processing*, **37**, 54–115.

Carpenter, G.A. and Grossberg, S. (1987b). ART 2: Stable self-organization of pattern recognition codes for analog input patterns. *Applied Optics*, **26**, 4919–4930.

Carpenter, G.A. and Grossberg, S. (1988). The ART of adaptive pattern recognition by a self-organizing neural network. *Computer*, **21**, 77–88.

Cohen, M.A. and Grossberg, S. (1986). Neural dynamics of speech and language coding: Developmental programs, perceptual grouping, and competition for short term memory. *Human Neurobiology*, **5**, 1–22.

Cohen, M.A. and Grossberg, S. (1987). Masking fields: A massively parallel architecture for learning, recognizing, and predicting multiple groupings of patterned data. *Applied Optics*, **26**, 1866–1891.

Delacour, J. and Houcine, O. (1980). Conditioning to time: Evidence for a role of hippocampus from unit recording. *Neuroscience*, **23**, 87–94.

Gormenzano, I., Kehoe, E.J., and Marshall, B.S. (1983). Twenty years of classical conditioning research with the rabbit. *Progress in Psychobiology and Physiological Psychology*, **10**, 197–275.

Grossberg, S. (1971). On the dynamics of operant conditioning. *Journal of Theoretical Biology*, **33**, 225–255.

Grossberg, S. (1972a). A neural theory of punishment and avoidance, I: Qualitative theory. *Mathematical Biosciences*, **15**, 39–67.

Grossberg, S. (1972b). A neural theory of punishment and avoidance, II: Quantitative theory. *Mathematical Biosciences*, **15**, 253–285.

Grossberg, S. (1975). A neural model of attention, reinforcement, and discrimination learning. *International Review of Neurobiology*, **18**, 263–327.

Grossberg, S. (1976). Adaptive pattern classification and universal recoding, I: Parallel development and coding of neural feature detectors. *Biological Cybernetics*,

23, 121–134.

Grossberg, S. (1978). A theory of human memory: Self-organization and performance of sensory-motor codes, maps, and plans. In R. Rosen and F. Snell (Eds.), **Progress in theoretical biology**, Vol. 5. New York: Academic Press.

Grossberg, S. (1982). **Studies of mind and brain: Neural principles of learning, perception, development, cognition, and motor control.** Boston: Reidel Press.

Grossberg, S. (Ed.) (1987). **The adaptive brain, Volumes I and II.** Amsterdam: Elsevier/North-Holland.

Grossberg, S. (Ed.) (1988). **Neural networks and natural intelligence.** Cambridge, MA: MIT Press.

Grossberg, S. and Kuperstein, M. (1986). **Neural dynamics of adaptive sensory-motor control: Ballistic eye movements.** Amsterdam: Elsevier/North-Holland.

Grossberg, S. and Levine, D.S. (1987). Neural dynamics of attentionally-modulated Pavlovian conditioning: Blocking, inter-stimulus interval, and secondary reinforcement. *Applied Optics*, **26**, 5015–5030.

Grossberg, S. and Schmajuk, N.A. (1987). Neural dynamics of attentionally-modulated Pavlovian conditioning: Conditioned reinforcement, inhibition, and opponent processing. *Psychobiology*, **15**, 195–240.

Grossberg, S. and Stone, G.O. (1986). Neural dynamics of word recognition and recall: Attentional priming, learning, and resonance. *Psychological Review*, **93**, 46–74.

Henneman, E. (1957). Relation between size of neurons and their susceptibility to discharge. *Science*, **26**, 1345–1347.

Henneman, E. (1985). The size-principle: A deterministic output emerges from a set of probabilistic connections. *Journal of Experimental Biology*, **115**, 105–112.

Hoechler, F.K. and Thompson, R.F. (1980). Effect of the interstimulus (CS-UCS) interval on hippocampal unit activity during classical conditioning of the nictitating membrane response of the rabbit (*Oryctolagus cuniculus*). *Journal of Comparative and Physiological Psychology*, **94**, 201–215.

Irwin, D.A., Rebert, C.S., McAdam, D.W., and Knott, J.R. (1966). Slow potential change (CNV) in the human EEG as a function of motivational variables. *Electroencephalography and Clinical Neurophysiology*, **21**, 412–413.

Jones, R. and Keck, M.J. (1978). Visual evoked response as a function of grating spatial frequency. *Investigative Ophthalmology and Visual Science*, **17**, 652–659.

Killeen, P.R. and Weiss, N.A. (1987). Optimal timing and the Weber function. *Psychological Review*, **94**, 455–468.

Konorski, J. (1948). **Conditioned reflexes and neuron organization.** London: Cambridge University Press.

Low, M.D., Borda, R.P., Frost, J.D., and Kellaway, P. (1966). Surface negative slow potential shift associated with conditioning in man. *Neurology*, **16**, 711–782.

Luchei, E.S. and Fuchs, A.F. (1972). Activity of brain stem neurons during eye movements of alert monkeys. *Journal of Neurophysiology*, **35**, 445–461.

Maricq, A.V., Roberts, S., and Church, R.M. (1981). Methamphetamine and time estimation. *Journal of Experimental Psychology: Animal Behavior Processes*, **7**, 18–30.

McAdam, D.W. (1969). Increases in CNS excitability during negative cortical slow potentials in man. *Electroencephalography and Clinical Neurophysiology*, **26**, 216–219.

McAdam, D., Knott, J.R., and Chiorini, J. (1965). Classical conditioning in the cat as a function of the CS-US interval. *Psychonomic Science*, **3**, 89–90.

Meck, W.H. (1983). Selective adjustment of the speed of internal clock and memory processes. *Journal of Experimental Psychology: Animal Behavior Processes*, **9**, 171–201.

Meck, W.H. and Church, R.M. (1984). Simultaneous temporal processing. *Journal of Experimental Psychology (Animal Behavior)*, **10**, 1–29.

Meck, W.H. and Church, R.M. (1987). Cholinergic modulation of the content of temporal memory. *Behavioral Neuroscience*, **101**, 457–464.

Meck, W.H., Church, R.M., Wenk, G.L., and Olton, D.S. (1987). Nucleus basalis and magnocellularis and medial septal area lesions differentially impair temporal memory. *Journal of Neuroscience*, **7**, 3505–3511.

Millenson, J.R., Kehoe, E.J., and Gormenzano, I. (1977). Classical conditioning of the rabbit's nictitating membrane response under fixed and mixed CS-US intervals. *Learning and Motivation*, **8**, 351–366.

Musselwhite, M.J. and Jeffreys, D.A. (1985). The influence of spatial frequency on the reaction times and evoked potentials recorded to grating pattern stimuli. *Vision Research*, **25**, 1545–1555.

Plant, G.T., Zimmern, R.L., and Durden, K. (1983). Transient visually evoked potentials to the pattern reversal and onset of sinusoidal gratings. *Electroencephalography and Clinical Neurophysiology*, **56**, 147–158.

Parker, D.M. and Salzen, E.A. (1977a). Latency changes in the human visual evoked response to sinusoidal gratings. *Vision Research*, **17**, 1201–1204.

Parker, D.M. and Salzen, E.A. (1977b). The spatial selectivity of early and late waves within the human visual evoked response. *Perception*, **6**, 85–95.

Parker, D.M., Salzen, E.A., and Lishman, J.R. (1982a). Visual-evoked responses elicited by the onset and offset of sinusoidal gratings: Latency, waveform, and topographic characteristics. *Investigative Ophthalmology and Visual Sciencs*, **22**, 675–680.

Parker, D.M., Salzen, E.A., and Lishman, J.R. (1982b). The early waves of the visual evoked potential to sinusoidal gratings: Responses to quadrant stimulation as a function of spatial frequency. *Electroencephalography and Clinical Neurophysiology*, **53**, 427–435.

Rawlins, J.N.P. (1985). Associations across time: The hippocampus as a temporary memory store. *The Behavioral and Brain Sciences*, **8**, 479–496.

Rawlins, J.N.P., Feldon, J., and Gray, J.A. (1982). Behavioral effects of hippocampectomy depend on inter-event intervals. *Society for Neuroscience Abstracts*, **8**, 22.

Robinson, D.A. (1970). Oculomotor unit behavior in the monkey. *Journal of Neurophysiology*, **35**, 393–404.

Schiller, P.H. (1970). The discharge characteristics of single units in the oculomotor and abducens nuclei of the unanesthetized monkey. *Experimental Brain Research*, **10**, 347–362.

Schneiderman, N. (1972). Response system divergencies in aversive classical conditioning. In A.H. Black and W.F. Prokasy (Eds.), **Classical conditioning, II: Current research and theory**. New York: Appleton Century Crofts.

Skrandies, W. (1984). Scalp potential fields evoked by grating stimuli: Effects of spatial frequency and orientation. *Electroencephalography and Clinical Neurophysiology*, **58**, 325–332.

Smith, M.C. (1968). CS-US interval and US intensity in classical conditioning of the rabbit's nictitating membrane response. *Journal of Comparative and Physiological Psychology*, **3**, 679–687.

Solomon, P.R. (1979). Temporal versus spatial information processing views of hippocampal functions. *Psychological Bulletin*, **86**, 1272–1279.

Solomon, P.R. (1980). A time and a place for everything? Temporal processing views of hippocampal function with special reference to attention. *Physiological Psychology*, **8**, 254–261.

Solomon, P.R., van der Schaaf, E.R., Thompson, R.F., and Weisz, D.J. (1986). Hippocampus and trace conditioning of the rabbit's classically conditioned nictitating membrane response. *Behavioral Neuroscience*, **100**, 729–744.

Staddon, J.E.R. (1983). Static and dynamic competition. Handout at Tutorial Conference on Neural Modelling, Scottsdale, Arizona.

Vassilev, A., Manahilov, V., and Mitov, D. (1983). Spatial frequency and pattern onset-offset response. *Vision Research*, **23**, 1417–1422.

Vassilev, A. and Strashimirov, D. (1979). On the latency of human visually evoked response to sinusoidal gratings. *Vision Research*, **19**, 843–846.

Walter, W.G. (1964). Slow potential waves in the human brain associated with expectancy, attention, and decision. *Arch. Psychiat. Nervenkr.*, **206**, 309–322.

Wilkie, D.M. (1987). Stimulus intensity affects pigeons' timing behavior: Implications for an internal clock model. *Animal Learning and Behavior*, **15**, 35–39.

Williamson, S.J., Kaufman, I., and Brenner, D. (1978). Latency of the neuromagnetic response of the human visual cortex. *Vision Research*, **18**, 107–110.

AUTHOR INDEX